A DICTIONARY OF
EPITHETS
AND
TERMS OF
ADDRESS

Leslie Dunkling

London and New York

First pubilshed 1990
by Routledge
11 New Fetter Lane, London EC4P 4EE

Simultaneously published in the USA and Canada
by Routledge
a division of Routledge, Chapman and Hall, Inc.
29 West 35th Street, New York, NY 10001

© 1990 Leslie Dunkling

Phototypesetting by Input Typesetting Ltd, London
Printed in Great Britain by Richard Clay Ltd, Bungay

British Library Cataloguing in Publication Data
Dunkling, Leslie, 1935–
A dictionary of epithets and terms of address.
1. English language usage—Dictionaries
I. Title
423

Library of Congress Cataloging in Publication Data

ISBN 0–415–007615

Contents

Introduction

This dictionary deals as comprehensively as possible with the terms of address – names, words, and phrases such as 'John', 'darling', 'you stupid fool' – used by English-speaking people. It adopts a descriptive approach and is, I believe, the first dictionary of its kind for any language. It is, of course, quite unlike the prescriptive and highly limited guides to the use of titles which have previously appeared, though some guidance on vocative usage is given in passing. I have no doubt that it was time for a dictionary like this to be compiled, and it is right that it should be concerned with English.

Reasons for this dictionary

As I shall argue later, terms of address have been especially important in English since the breakdown of the 'thou/you' pronoun system in the sixteenth and seventeenth centuries. Since that time they have had a greater grammatical importance in English than in languages which retain two or more 'you' words. This aspect of grammatical integration has been relatively little discussed, and is one reason why a full-scale study of terms of address is justified.

A second reason is that since the seventeenth century (earlier for specialist readers) a considerable body of English literature has come into being which is studied by each new generation. Modern readers soon become aware that terms of address are used rather differently in, say, the eighteenth- or nineteenth-century novels they happen to be reading, compared with their use today. The entries in this dictionary discuss where appropriate the use of terms in the past, and the changes in usage that have taken place. These changes are fascinating in themselves, reflecting as they do changing attitudes to the social hierarchy, to women, to the importance of the family, and so on. The student of literature, then, and the historical sociologist, will find a good deal to interest them in the main body of this book.

However, with the English language spread as it is throughout the world, a synchronic approach to it is as necessary, and as interesting, as a diachronic one. British, American, Australian, Canadian, New Zealand, South African, and other native-speakers of English use varieties of the language that differ from one another to a greater or lesser extent. Some of those differences extend to the use of terms of address, and that provides a third major reason for a book of this kind. I have commented on national, and in some cases, regional differences in the entries concerned. I hope, therefore, that an American who is reading British literature, or an Englishman who watches American films, will now have a reference source which will help to explain certain dialogue mysteries.

But much as I want this dictionary to be of interest and use to native speakers of English, I have very firmly in mind the fact that English is studied as a foreign language by vast numbers of students throughout the world. They, I believe, need special help with terms of address, which their dictionaries, grammars and text-books mention only in a cursory way. This is not to criticize those works, which have much else to deal with, but there are now teachers and advanced students of English in nearly every country who are interested in the fine details of how the English language functions. If they are to understand acts of communication between native-speakers, in literature or life – if they are *truly* to understand them, in all their subtlety, then they must know what part the terms of address are playing in the interchanges that take place. This is an aspect of English usage that needs separate consideration, especially since the vocative systems in their own languages are likely to be very different. This world-wide interest in English as a foreign language provides a fourth major reason for a dictionary of this kind.

These, then, are specific justifications for the present work, though I believe that the average reader, not a student of English as such, who happens to glance through its pages, will require no special pleading for its existence. Words and names, used vocatively or not, are intriguing in their own right, and most have some kind of story to tell. I have been concerned with discovering those stories, and relating them, for most of my professional life. I know that there are many others who enjoy them. Then again, a perusal of the entries in this book will perhaps bring to that average reader's conscious attention much that was previously at sub-conscious level. Such awareness may lead to a rather startling conclusion; namely, that whereas this dictionary merely defines vocative expressions, it is the terms of address we use to others, and those used to us in return, which *define us*, placing us firmly at a social and professional level, indicating our emotional impact on those around us.

To sum up, terms of address provide material of interest to the linguist, psychologist, and sociologist, to the lexicographer, grammarian, and language-student, to the student of literature and the student of life.

Terms of address: towards a definition

In this dictionary 'term of address' and 'vocative' are synonymous umbrella terms which cover a number of sub-categories. The most important of these is 'name'. For the layman, in fact, all terms of address are likely to be referred to as 'names'. A child in a playground who has just been taunted with cries of 'Teacher's pet' or 'Cry-baby' may well retort: 'Sticks and stones may break my bones, but names will never hurt me.' By 'names' he means those terms of address which also happen to be terms of abuse, or insults. When Clive Newcome, in William Thackeray's *The Newcomes*, calls his aunt's servant 'you old Cheshire cat' and 'you old goose', the author tells us that 'by these playful names Clive had been wont to designate Hannah these twenty years past'.

The 'playful names' are again terms of address, slightly insulting in form but turned into covert endearments because they are spoken with affection.

Mistress Millamant in William Congreve's *Way of the World* tells her husband-to-be that she 'won't be called names after I'm married'. She goes on to specify that she will not allow him to call her 'my dear', 'sweetheart', and such-like terms, part of 'that nauseous cant, in which men and their wives are so fulsomely familiar'. Mistress Millamant's 'names' are endearments, which are again terms of address. In his novel *Gideon Planish*, Sinclair Lewis says of his hero that his 'first name' was 'Doctor', 'and as such, along with every Colonel, every Reverend Doctor, every M.D., every Monsignor, every Rabbi, every Herr Geheimrat, every Judge, every Governor, he was so highly exalted that he was not merely a man, but a title'. These professional titles, 'names' to Sinclair Lewis, are another kind of term of address.

One can understand why terms of address are referred to loosely as 'names'. They often appear to function as name-substitutes, so that instead of saying 'Happy birthday, John,' a speaker says 'Happy birthday, darling'; instead of 'Will you come this way, Mr Planish?' we get 'Will you come this way, doctor?' Just as often they are used *with* proper names: 'Happy birthday, John darling'; 'Will you come this way, Dr Planish?'

Describing all terms of address as 'names', however, does not take us very far, and causes some confusion. We know that 'John' is a name, and that 'darling' is a word. They remain a name and word when they are used in direct address, or used vocatively as we can also express it. In 'Happy birthday, John,' 'John' simply becomes a nominal vocative. 'Happy birthday, darling' gives us a verbal vocative. 'Happy birthday, John darling,' which combines the two, we could describe as a complex vocative. What I now propose to do is to look more closely at the two general categories, nominal and verbal vocatives, as I seek a precise definition for 'term of address'.

First, middle, and last names

There are many types of names which can be used as terms of address. Everyone in the English-speaking world has what are called in this dictionary a *first name* and a *last name*. First names are otherwise known as Christian names, fore-names, given names, and, occasionally in dialect, as front names. Last names are commonly referred to as surnames or family names. The majority of English-speaking people also have one *middle name*. Middle names tend to be drawn from the first name stock but can be other family names.

Thus, if Mary Johnson marries Alexander Brown, their son may be named James Brown, James William Brown (perhaps because Mary's father is called William), James Johnson Brown, James William Johnson Brown, and so on. The first name and middle name need have no immediate family connection of any kind. The Browns can, if they wish, name their son George Washington Brown, or for that matter, Washington George Brown. Their daughter might likewise become Elizabeth Brown, Elizabeth Mary Brown, Elizabeth Johnson Brown, Elizabeth Mary Johnson Brown, etc.

This dictionary is only concerned with how such names are used in direct address. Those interested in the individual first names and last names used in the English-speaking world should consult specialized works. The origins and usage of some ten thousand first names, for example, are discussed fully in *Everyman's Dictionary of First Names*, by Leslie Dunkling and William Gosling. Last names are dealt with in *The Penguin Dictionary of Surnames*, by Basil Cottle, and *A Dictionary of Surnames* by Patrick Hanks and Flavia Hodges. There are also several chapters devoted to both topics in *The Guinness Book of Names*, by Leslie Dunkling.

As far as vocative usage is concerned, the first name, middle name, and last name which constitute the average personal name in English-speaking countries allow a number of permutations to be used:

(a) First name: James, Elizabeth. Some people prefer to be known to family and friends by their middle name instead of their first name. This merely means that the circumstances that would normally cause the person's first name to be used now apply to the middle name. The middle name *becomes* the first name.

(b) First name diminutive: Jim, Jimmy, Jimbo; Liz, Liza, Beth, Betty.

(c) First name and middle name: this is unusual but occurs e.g. in some rural areas of the USA.

(d) Last name: Brown. It is more likely to be a man who is addressed in this way.

(e) First name and last name: James Brown. Often in remonstrance: 'That's the last time I'll tell you, James Brown.'

(f) First name, middle name, and last name: e.g. 'Elizabeth Mary Brown, you are brought before this court . . .'

(g) Initials of first and middle names or first and last names: more likely to be a man addressed in this way, perhaps in a business environment.

It is clearly not enough, then, to say that a person is 'addressed by name'. If our putative James Brown meets three people one morning who say 'Good morning, James', 'Hi there, Jimbo', and 'James Brown?' (asking him to confirm his identity), then the three speakers have chosen different terms of address which reveal something of their relationship to him.

Nicknames

'Nickname' refers to 'an eke name', an extra name, normally unofficial and not used for legal purposes or in formal situations, which can serve to identify a person. We are concerned here only with vocative nicknames, used in direct address to the person concerned. Some nicknames are purely referential. Mrs Thatcher, for example, might be referred to by some people as 'the Iron Lady', but that does not mean that they would say to her: 'How are you today, Iron Lady?'

Those nicknames which *are* used vocatively are of different types. There is a private nickname, sometimes called a love-name because it is typically used between lovers. James Brown is 'Snookums' or whatever to his wife, but she calls him that only when they are alone. Then there is a group nickname, by which he is known to a number of people. Let us imagine that to his colleagues he is 'Cap', because he happens to be a landscape gardener. Some wag may have compared him one day to Capability Brown, a famous landscape gardener of the eighteenth century who earned his nickname because he always saw great capabilities in everything. 'Capability' would be too cumbersome for modern use, and a shortening to 'Cap' could easily occur.

People can acquire a number of different group nicknames at various stages of their lives, at school, while doing military service, at work. Others acquire a fairly permanent nickname which they carry with them everywhere. These are public nicknames, which can sometimes virtually replace a person's first name. Many people who admired Bing Crosby, for example, must have thought that 'Bing' was the name on his birth certificate, given to him by his parents.

The nicknames described above are all personal; there is also a generic nickname which can be instantly applied to any person who belongs to a particular category. If James Brown happens to be Irish, he can be addressed as Paddy. If he is particularly tall, a stranger may address him as 'Lofty', or jokingly as 'Shorty'. If he is a carpenter by trade he is likely to be addressed as 'Chips'.

These generic nicknames are part of a general vocative stock in English, and as such are accorded individual entries in this dictionary. The personal nicknames are like individual names, and do not fall within the scope of this work. All that matters when they are selected by a speaker is that the category 'nickname' has been chosen rather than first name, last name, etc. (Further comments on this subject are made at NICKNAME in the main body of this book.)

Transferred, substitute, and nonce names

If we overhear someone saying to a friend: 'I saw you at the cinema last night, Romeo,' we do not assume that 'Romeo' is the first name or nickname of the man being addressed. We know that he is momentarily being compared to Shakespeare's tragic young lover, whose name is used allusively to mean 'a man who is very much in love' or 'a young Don Juan'. We can be fairly sure that the man seen at the cinema was with a girl friend to whom he was paying amorous attention. 'Romeo' is a well-known example of a transferred name. It is used in the way that 'Einstein', for example, is used to someone who is showing signs of great intelligence (or ironically to someone who is being very stupid). 'Tarzan', or 'Superman', might likewise be used to a man displaying great physical strength. If someone is being congratulated on his logical thinking, he may well reply: 'Elementary, my dear Watson,' transferring to the hearer the name of Sherlock Holmes's friend and colleague who was always expressing admiration for the detective's deductive powers.

Transferred names are easy to understand when they are so well known. It is rather more puzzling, say, when Jane Eyre suddenly addresses Mr Rochester as 'King Ahasuerus'. Nor will everyone immediately see the point of 'Massa Legree' used to a love-partner, or 'Dogberry' used to a policeman, though these were amongst the many transferred names which occurred in the corpus used for this book. Those that did occur have separate entries, but of more importance is the underlying principle that brings them into use. At any time a speaker may transfer to the person being addressed the name of a real or fictional person, alluding to qualities of that named person which seem to apply to the hearer. Such a transfer normally occurs in passing, once only. If a speaker continues to use the transferred name throughout a conversation, then it might be described as a temporary nickname. It could also become a more permanent nickname, as with a friend of mine who is known as 'Biggles', but it would remain a transferred name by origin.

A substitute name is slightly different. A man may approach another man in the street and say: 'Got a light, Jack?' 'Jack' might instead be George, Percy, John, or any other standard first name. The name, however, is not an allusion to a particular person, as with Romeo or Tarzan, nor is it a generic nickname, used because the person addressed is thought to belong to a particular category. It is simply a typical first name, used as a temporary substitute for whatever first name the man happens to bear. Probably the most frequently-used substitute name in modern times is the Glaswegian 'Jimmy'.

What I refer to in this dictionary as a nonce name is different again. It is a name brought into temporary existence for use to a particular person, a word being converted to name status for the purpose. The conversion is achieved with the help of a name prefix, such as 'Mr', 'Mrs', or 'Miss'. In earlier times it might have been Madam, Mistress, Goodman. Shakespeare was rather fond of the latter term, creating nonce last names so that his characters could address 'Goodman Rascal', 'Goodman Drivel', 'Goodman Bones' and the like. In *Measure for Measure* (5:i) Lucio says to the Duke, who is in disguise, 'Come hither, Goodman Bald-Pate.'

Modern speakers might also refer to a physical feature, as in 'Miss Pot-Belly', but they are more likely to use a professional description or a more abstract term to create names like: Mr Policeman, Mr Lawyer, Mr Bigshot, Mr Hypocrite, Mr Clever, Mr High-and-Mighty. Once again I have dealt individually with the nonce names that occurred in the corpus, but it is the principle that matters. By using a social or professional title that usually precedes a personal name and following it with a noun or adjective, a term of address which has nominal rather than verbal characteristics can be created at any time, though normally the 'name' has only a very temporary existence.

Some vocative expressions of this type become fossilized as titles. I am thinking here of 'Mr President', 'Mr Speaker', 'Mr Chairman', and the like, which are title forms that have nominal characteristics. I believe it is right to think of such titles as having grown out of a natural tendency to create name-like terms, though since many such fixed expressions now exist, nonce names may sometimes be created by analogy.

Other 'names' used as terms of address

With nonce names we were approaching an area where the distinction between name and word becomes blurred. Such is the case with what I would call 'mock names', another vocative category. A typical example of this relatively small group is 'Buttinsky', a mock last name used by American speakers to someone who intrudes on a conversation. The name is not a normal transfer, since it refers to no real or fictional person. Nor is it a substitute name, which by definition is from the established name stock. It is not created by the speaker for the occasion, but is available, as a kind of name, to any speaker of the language. All this appears to justify a separate category, in which I would include, for example, the archaic 'Rudesby', as well as 'Lady Muck', 'Father Time', 'Mr What's-your name', 'Mr Thingummy'. I do not intend to spend too much time in a theoretical discussion about such terms. They clearly call for individual treatment as entries in this dictionary, and I have dealt with them accordingly.

By contrast, I have not devoted separate entries to what I like to call 'number names'. I discuss this general category in an article at **NUMBER NAME** in the main body of the book. The main point is that for different reasons and in a number of very different circumstances, a number may be used in place of a person's name in direct address. Many people intensely dislike the idea of being identified by a number, though number names can be highly convenient.

Finally, there are other kinds of name – where the name status is not in doubt – which can be used as terms of address. I have dealt with these in articles on **NAMES, COLLECTIVE** and **PLACE NAME**. Collective names are used, for example, to football players taking part in a game, when they are urged on by the name of their club. As for place names, Scottish lairds are addressed by the names of their estates, and while making a long-distance telephone call through an operator, callers may be addressed by the name of the city where they happen to be.

Various types of names, then, can be used as terms of address. I have mentioned first names, middle names, last names, private nicknames, group nicknames, public nicknames, generic nicknames, transferred names, substitute names, nonce names, mock names, number names, collective names, and place names. These constitute our nominal vocatives; we can turn now to those which are verbal.

Family terms of address

The words which indicate family relationship were formerly more frequently used as terms of address than they are today. 'Father' continues to be much used, either in that form or as: da', dad, dada, daddy, pa, pap, papa, pop, poppa, pops. 'Pater' was used at one time, and may still be used within individual families, or occasionally as a joke. In some American families, children still address their father as 'sir'. In Victorian times there were those in Britain and the USA who used 'governor'. Some children are encouraged to use their father's first name; others might have a private nickname for him such as 'popkins'. The term used by a young child, such as 'daddy', is likely to be changed as the child grows older to 'dad' or 'father'.

'Mother' also has many colloquial forms which are well used: ma, mam, mamma, mammy, maw, mom, momma, mum, mumma, mummy. Those who formerly used 'pater' to their fathers were likely to use 'mater' to their mothers, just as those who still use 'sir' to the father will use 'ma'am' to the mother. Personal nicknames such as 'Thingy' may be used, and some mothers are addressed by first name. For useful comments on children changing from one term to another as they get older, see the Margaret Laurence quotation at **Ma** and the Gordon McGill quotation at **Mum**.

Fathers, especially, may use 'son' or 'sonny' to address a son, but 'daughter' is now rarely used by either parent. Twin children may collectively be addressed as 'twins'. Parents are also likely to address their offspring collectively as 'children', 'tribe', 'troops', etc. Individual children will usually be addressed by their first names, nicknames, or by endearments.

Grandparents are usually acknowledged as such when their grandchildren address them as 'grampa', 'grandad', 'gran', 'granny', etc. In some families children have different terms by which they address their paternal and maternal grandparents. The latter normally use first names to address grandchildren, not terms like 'grandson', 'grand-daughter'.

Aunts and uncles are also acknowledged by those terms, which are used alone or followed by the first name of the person concerned. In former times 'aunt' or 'uncle' followed by a last name was also possible, and those so addressed would have answered with 'nephew' and 'niece'. These terms are now never heard as vocatives, other than in period drama.

Some brothers and sisters may remind themselves of their relationship by using those words in direct address. They are more likely, especially at working-class level, to abbreviate them to 'bruv' and 'sis'. Few people today would address a cousin by that term, though it was once very common. Cousins, however, and indeed other family members, may be recognized in some regions by the formula 'our' + first name.

Relationships brought about by marriage can create problem areas in vocative usage. Husbands and wives are now rarely 'husband' and 'wife' in direct address, as they once were, and the middle-class fashion that once prevailed of using 'Mr' and 'Mrs' + last name to one another would now only be resuscitated as a joke. First names and endearments are normal, but it is a matter of individual choice.

That choice can become embarrassing when husbands and wives have to address each other's parents, and when children are confronted with stepparents. 'Father-in-law', 'mother-in-law', 'step-father', and 'step-mother' may accurately describe the relationships, but those terms are seldom, if ever, used vocatively. Perhaps they would be more popular if they followed the brilliantly tactful French example, where both a father-in-law and step-father is a *beau-père*, 'handsome father', while a mother-in-law and step-mother are both *belle-mère*, 'beautiful mother'. We should long ago have borrowed these terms in English, so that *beau* and *belle* could be universally used for parental relationships brought about by marriage.

While it is true that words indicating family relationship are less used than in previous centuries to the relations concerned, some of the kinship terms continue to be well used in other ways. 'Sister', for example, may be used in a friendly way to a woman who is passing a workman in the street. 'Brother' may be used to a trade union colleague. The terms remain basically family terms, but their meanings have been considerably extended.

Endearments and terms of friendship

The kinship terms discussed above form a natural group because of their semantic content. There is another group of words, less clearly identifiable, which express affection or friendliness, subject to certain conditions which I will return to later. Let us for the moment say that words and expressions like 'my darling' and 'mate' are normally endearing and friendly respectively. The boundary between these two vocative categories is difficult to define by the form of the word alone, so I will not try to separate them at this stage. Other words and expressions of the 'my darling' and 'mate' type, however, include: angel, baby, baby doll, boy, boyo, bud, buddy boy, chicken, chum, cock, cocker, comrade, dear, dearest, dear boy, dear girl, dear lady, doll, duck, duckie, ducks, feller, folks, friend, girlie, handsome, hen, hon, honey, honey-bunch, honeylamb, kid, kiddo, lad, laddie, lass, lassie, little man, love, lovely, man, matey; various expressions beginning 'my' and 'my dear': old bean, old boy, old chap, old man, and many more expressions beginning with 'old': pal, pardner, pet, poppet, precious, sausage, son, sonnie, squire, sweet, sweet-heart, sweetie, sweetling, sweets, tosh, wacker.

This is a brief selection of words and phrases which are frequently used as terms of address in English with at least friendly intent. As can be seen at a glance, they have little else in common. Such terms cannot be defined by their meaning alone. Other factors which enable a particular term to be classified accurately will be discussed later.

Polite terms of address

Just as intimacy and friendship can be conveyed by terms of address, so by using a suitable term a speaker can indicate his intention of being polite. If 'endearment' was the word which characterized the former group, 'title' is the word which characterizes this one. A polite speaker accords his hearer the dignity of a social or professional title, or uses a term such as 'sir' or 'madam' which is almost a title in itself. 'Sir' normally becomes 'gentlemen' in the plural; 'madam' becomes 'ladies'. A young woman, one whom the speaker feels to be too young for 'madam', is often addressed as 'miss'.

The normal social titles, of course, are 'Mr', 'Mrs', or 'Miss' followed by the last name of the person being addressed. The British social system distinguishes a number of other categories of person, conventionally addressed by such terms as 'Sir' + first name, 'Lady' + first name, 'Lady' + last name, 'Lord' + first name, 'Lord' + last name, 'Dame' + first name, 'my lord', 'my lady'. Some of these social titles, those most valued, are hereditary; many are bestowed during a person's lifetime.

A far greater number of professional titles are used. Men and women serving in one of the armed services are frequently addressed by their rank. The full form of the word, such as 'Sergeant' or 'Corporal', could be considered to be the polite term. With the lower ranks, especially, there often exists a more friendly abbreviated form – 'Sarge', 'Corp'. Quasi-military organizations such as the police force and fire department also make use of many of these terms.

Ministers of religion are normally addressed by title, such as 'Vicar', 'Rector', 'Dominie', 'Chaplain', though there is a shift towards first name usage in some quarters. A Roman Catholic priest is normally 'Father' or 'Father' + first name, though in Ireland he may be addressed as 'Your reverence'. Members of the medical profession, from the trainee nurse to the eminent surgeon, have titles which place them precisely in the hierarchy, and which are used in polite address. The academic world is another area where professional titles, such as 'Professor', 'Senior Tutor', 'Dean', and the like, abound though some of them are used only on formal occasions. Within the legal profession titles and other polite forms of address are used, as they are to civil dignitaries such as mayors and aldermen.

What is curious about the English-speaking countries, perhaps, is the arbitrary nature of the professional-title system. A medical or academic doctor is identified by that term, but adults, at least, do not address a teacher as 'Teacher', as would be the case in many countries. Nor do we address Architect Smith, Engineer Brown, Company Director Jones in the way that logic would indicate. Most people must fall back on the now humble 'Mr', 'Mrs', or 'Miss'. These have become greatly devalued compared to their past importance, but there are times when the use of one of those words, coupled with our name, is very necessary for the preservation of our dignity.

Neutral terms of address

There are some terms of address associated with particular professions which cannot really be classed as polite titles. If one attracts the attention of a waiter in a restaurant by calling 'Waiter!' or says to a taxi-driver 'Stop here, please, driver', the terms are functional and neutral. A similar vocative is 'bartender', or 'barman' as British speakers would say. These are simply generic terms converted into terms of address. Even words like 'mother' and 'father' can be thought of in that way and used neutrally. A midwife who is assisting at a birth may well address the woman who is about to have the child as 'mother'. In *Kate and Emma*, by Monica Dickens, a magistrate in a juvenile court calls the parents of young offenders 'father' and 'mother' 'because he can't remember their names.' They are simply a father and mother, or *the* father and mother concerned in the case before him.

Many plural terms of address appear to be neutral. Expressions like 'both of you', 'everybody', 'everyone', 'all of you', 'the three of you' put the emphasis on the plurality aspect rather than politeness or friendliness. Such terms become more aggressive, usually, if the 'you' comes first, as in 'you two', 'you lot'. There is another kind of vocative which is used to divide a number of people into sub-groups. The conductor of an orchestra, for example, may address a remark to 'violins' or 'strings'; if a choir is present the tenors, altos or sopranos may be addressed as such. Individual musicians are often spoken to by the name of their instrument. These are again generic terms, which do seem to constitute the main kind of neutral vocative.

There is a small group of indefinite terms of address which by their nature are almost invariably neutral. If a man who is drowning calls out 'Help me, somebody!' he wants all those within earshot, friends or strangers, men or women, to think of identifying themselves with the 'somebody'. Notions of friendliness or politeness are far from his mind, and he cannot be sure who he is addressing.

Many people believe that the surest way of achieving neutrality when addressing someone in English is to avoid using any term of address. Those unable to decide whether to call a mother-in-law by her first name, 'Mrs' + last name or one of the 'mother' terms, may opt for this solution, though it can cause difficulties when it becomes necessary to single out the woman concerned in a group, or attract her attention. The pronoun 'you' is indeed neutral; vocative 'you' is not, and a speaker would have to be careful not to slip from one to the other.

It is also the case that the deliberate avoidance of vocatives, whether friendly or polite, can become noticeable to the hearer, who will interpret the avoidance in one way or another. *The Spy Who Came in From the Cold*, by John le Carré, has a scene in a grocer's shop where a customer says: 'You'd better send me that account.' 'I'm afraid I can't do that,' the shopkeeper replies, and the author remarks that 'the "Sir" was definitely missing.' This is an instance where a zero-vocative becomes in itself an indication of attitude, and is certainly not neutral.

Unfriendly and insulting terms of address

We are still, for the moment, making a tentative classification of vocatives on formal grounds, considering the basic meanings of the words used in direct address and their normal usage. With terms of abuse, whether mild or apparently deeply insulting, we must always remember that they can be turned into covert endearments if said in a particular way in a particular context. However, it is generally true to say that a vocative expression of the type 'you' + adjective + noun is more likely to be unfriendly than friendly.

Typical realizations of the formula would be: you bloody fool, you bloody swine, you cheeky sod, you dirty bastard, you lying bastard, you old cow, you stupid bitch. Often the adjective is omitted, 'you bastard', 'you bitch', 'you fool' being preferred. It also frequently happens that a speaker who is in the grip of strong emotion repeats an expression he has used, expanding it as he does so. Some instances of this phenomenon which occurred in the corpus were: 'you girt fool', 'you girt silly fool', and 'you filthy pig', 'you filthy disgusting pig', both in *A kind of Loving*, by Stan Barstow; 'you bastard', 'you wet futile bastard' in *Within and Without*, by John Harvey; 'you creep', 'you baby-killing creep' in *Rabbit Redux*, by John Updike; 'you skunk', 'you dirty little skunk' in *The Wayward Bus*, by John Steinbeck.

One feature which begins to emerge from the examples of abusive terms so far quoted is that human beings are frequently compared to animals. Abusive comparisons lead to words like: ass, bitch, cat, cow, cur, goat, hog, jackass, louse, pig, rat, runt, shrew, skunk, swine, turkey, and vermin occurring in vocative expressions. Many other animal-related terms, however, are used as endearments: bird, chick, cock, duck, mouse, pigeon, tiger.

There is also a discernible tendency in English to form abusive terms based on ' –head'. The following are not meant as compliments: bighead, blockhead, blunderhead, blunthead, bonehead, dumbhead, fathead, fuckhead, juice-head, lunkhead, meathead, muttonhead, peckerhead, pinhead, puddinghead, sheephead, shithead, stupidhead, turniphead. Again there is no absolute rule that such compounds will be insulting. A mother will address her child as 'sleepyhead' with great affection. Other terms associated with ' –head', incidentally, also occur: funny face, rat face, big mouth, blabbermouth, foulmouth.

However, as I began this section by saying, it is unsafe to rely on the semantic content of words used as terms of address to indicate the category to which they belong, though we obviously have to do so if they occur, say, in a letter. They are more normally spoken, and it is time to pause for a moment to consider the contexts in which terms of address are used, and the ways in which they are uttered.

Vocative contexts

A true assessment of whether a term of address is an endearment, a friendly or unfriendly expression, polite, neutral, or insulting, can only be made when something is known of the overall relationship, if any, between speaker and hearer, and the way in which the vocative is uttered at a given moment. In a long-standing intimate or friendly relationship, terms which appear to be insulting, such as 'you dirty bastard', can easily be converted into friendly, even flattering, expressions. A man using that vocative to a male friend may actually be congratulating him on his sexual prowess, as the tone of voice and facial gesture of the speaker will make clear. The term may even have become one which is habitually used between them, with the man so addressed using something equally insulting in return. Both would know that no offence would be taken as they participated in a kind of private joke.

There may be, nevertheless, an inherent danger in the use of such terms. In *The Philanderer*, Stanley Kauffmann depicts two male friends, one of whom has begun a relationship with the other's wife: 'Every time Perry called him a bastard or stinker or son of a bitch these days – as he had done jokingly thousands of times before – Russell had to pull himself up sharp; he kept imagining that he heard a serious note underneath the joke.'

Conversely, a term which appears to be friendly, such as a first name, may mark a shift to relative unfriendliness. If a wife habitually addresses her husband as 'darling', for instance, or uses a private nickname, the sudden use of the less intimate first name can express coldness. The same shift can be achieved by switching from a diminutive form of the first name to its more correct form.

Almost any word, name or phrase used vocatively can be made to belie its apparent face-value. Since the use of any term of address always says something about the attitude of the speaker to the hearer at the moment of utterance, though it may consciously have been used by the speaker for other reasons, it is meaningful to classify vocatives with attitudinal labels of the kind I have used so far. One can only classify particular occurrences of the terms, however, not the terms themselves. This remark applies equally well, of course, to the nominal vocatives discussed earlier and the terms indicating family relationship. Although those groups have distinctive formal characteristics, they are also attitudinally marked. Each time they are used they can be accommodated within the intimate-friendly-polite-neutral-unfriendly-insulting scale. Thus Monica Dickens, in *Thursday Afternoons*, has a young man addressing the father he heartily dislikes as 'Dad'. Miss Dickens remarks that in saying this he is 'making an insult of the name'.

In real life a person being addressed makes an instinctive assessment of a vocative's current value based on the tone and gestures of the speaker. This dictionary is based on a corpus consisting largely of novels. Novelists frequently indicate how something was said, including any term of address, so that the reader understands exactly what the speaker intended. This is not always necessary, since the general context may make it clear that a friendly discussion or an argument was taking place. In such cases a writer may report the speech using 'said' or a similarly neutral word. When the tone of voice and accompanying facial and bodily gestures become important to an understanding of the communication, the 'said' word is likely to be replaced by a word which gives extra information about those prosodic and paralinguistic features.

In this respect the English language is rich, offering a wide choice of 'said' substitutes. I give below a selection of the words which were noted while collecting vocative examples from the corpus. All occurred immediately after an example of direct speech. The words indicate such things as the degree of intensity with which something was said, or perhaps the facial gesture that accompanied it, the underlying intention of the utterance, and so on. Many of the words refer to a manner of speech which could cause vocative shift, i.e. a shift in category of a term of address away from that which its basic meaning would appear to dictate.

'Said' substitutes

Accepted, accused, acknowledged, admired, admonished, advised, affirmed, allowed, amended, announced, apologized, appealed, applauded, approved, argued, assented, asserted, averred, avowed, babbled, barked, bawled, bayed, beamed, beefed, bellowed, bemoaned, blazed, blurted out, blustered, boasted, boomed, bragged, brayed, breathed, bridled, brooded, bubbled, cackled, cajoled, called out, carolled, cautioned, chaffed, challenged, chanted, chattered, cheered, chimed, chirped, choked, chortled, chuckled, clamoured, coached, coaxed, comforted, commanded, commented, commiserated, complained, confessed, conceded, condescended, confided, confirmed, congratulated, consoled, contradicted, cooed, corrected, coughed, counselled, countered, criticized, crooned, crowed, cried out, cursed, cut in, declaimed, decided, declared, delivered, demanded, demurred, dictated, denied, directed, dissented, doubted, drawled, droned, drooled, echoed, ejaculated, emended, encouraged, enjoined, enquired, entreated, enunciated, essayed, evaded, exclaimed, excused, exhaled, exhorted, explained, exploded, expostulated, exulted, faltered, fenced, flamed, flared, floundered, fluttered, formulated, frowned, fumbled, fumed, gabbled, gagged, gasped, gibbered, giggled, glared, gloated, grated, grieved, grinned, gritted, groaned, groused, growled, grumbled, grunted, guessed, guffawed, gulped, gurgled, gushed, hailed, hallooed, hazarded, hedged, hissed, hollered, hooted, howled, implored, inferred, insinuated, insisted, instructed, intoned, jabbered, jeered, jerked out, joked, lamented, laughed, leered, lisped, maintained, mentioned, mimicked, moaned, mocked, mouthed, mumbled, murmured, mused, muttered, nagged, noted, objected, observed, offered, ordered, panted, parroted, parried, persisted, piped, pleaded, plodded on, plunged on, pointed out, pondered, pounced, pouted, prayed, prattled, predicted, proclaimed, prodded, promised, pronounced, proposed, protested, purred, pursued, quavered, queried, questioned, quoted, rambled on, ranted, rapped out, rasped, raved, read out, reasoned, rebuked, recalled, recited, recollected, reflected, rejoined, remarked, remonstrated, reported, reproached, reproved, requested, resumed, retaliated, retorted, revealed, riposted, roared, ruminated, rushed on, scoffed, scolded, scowled, screamed, seconded, shouted, shrieked, shrilled, sighed, simpered, smiled, smirked, snapped, snarled, sneered, snickered, sniggered, snorted, sobbed, soothed, speculated, spat out, spluttered, squawked, squeaked, squealed, stalled, stammered, stated, stormed, stuttered, suggested, swallowed, swore, taunted, teased, threatened, threw out, thundered, tittered, tutted, urged, uttered, ventured, volunteered, vowed, wailed, warned, wheedled, whimpered, whined, winked, wondered, yawned, yelled.

Adverbial indications of speech

This is not the end of the story. Many novelists prefer to stay with 'said', but they follow it with an adverb which indicates the manner of speech. They will say that something was said abruptly, absently, accusingly, acidly, acrimoniously, admiringly, affably, aggressively, agreeably, angrily, and so on. I was easily able to collect 500 such words while examining the corpus. They can of course be permutated with the 'said' substitutes to give an enormous range of speech styles. In some cases novelists choose to write a sentence or two in order to explain exactly how something was uttered. They know that the message inherent in the words themselves, their basic meaning, is only a part of the total communication.

I have said that one must be aware of that totality before being able to classify vocative occurrences. As a simple illustration of this point, let us imagine that a woman says to a man 'Hello, John.' Where do we place 'John' on the six-point scale? It was an intimacy, perhaps, if said coquettishly or fondly; friendly if said cheerfully or amiably; polite if said respectfully or politely; neutral if said mechanically or matter-of-factly; unfriendly if said testily or grimly; and perhaps insulting if said sneeringly or venomously. The novelist gives us such information, fixing the interpretation of the words. The playwright must rely on an actor to do so. By a slight change in the way he delivers even the simplest line, an actor can modify his underlying attitude to the person being addressed and affect the overall meaning of what he says.

This, then, is what the layman is referring to when he says: 'It wasn't what he said, it was the way he said it.' What we loosely call the 'tone of voice' is mainly concerned with indicating a speaker's attitude both to what he is saying, and the person he is addressing. Since terms of address are also concerned with attitude to the hearer, it is impossible to divorce them from the manner in which they are spoken. No-one has yet catalogued the full range of attitudinal 'meaning' that can be conveyed by the human voice, but the six-term scale I have proposed is obviously highly simplified.

Nevertheless, for working purposes, I believe it is useful to say that a consideration of a vocative's formal characteristics *and* its manner of utterance enable it to be classified as intimate, friendly, polite, neutral, unfriendly, or insulting. When the mode of utterance is at variance with the apparent meaning of the term – so that 'pal' or 'friend' is said aggressively, or 'you bastard' is said admiringly – then the tone of voice is the major factor for classification purposes. This has led to my constantly referring, in the dictionary entries, to 'covert endearments', where an insult becomes an intimacy. I have also quoted throughout the entries many comments by writers on vocative shift, though that is my term, not theirs. See for example the chilling remarks on the use of 'my dear' by Mrs Craik, quoted at **Dear**.

As for the overall context in which a term of address is used, Lois Battle, in her novel *War Brides*, illustrates its importance:

'If I hadn't married him, I wouldn't have met you.'
'I know that, you silly bitch.'
'Don't you dare call me that! Don't you dare!'
'I've called you that before. I've called you that in bed and you even seemed to like it.'

Why are terms of address used?

That last remark raises the interesting question of why speakers use terms of address. The man implied that he used 'you silly bitch' at certain times in order to please his lover. His use of the term was nevertheless optional: many grammarians would say that *any* use of a term of address is optional, but is this the case?

Frequently, terms of address do seem to be unnecessary. It is often obvious to whom a speaker's remarks are being addressed, so designation is not needed. If the emotional atmosphere between speaker and hearer is calm, and the speaker's attitude to the hearer is fairly neutral, that also seems to make the use of vocatives superfluous. In many situations there appears to be no logical need for a term of address to be used, but one is used all the same. One thinks of the passionate lover who whispers the name of his loved one over and over again into her ear. Our literature makes it clear that lovers have been indulging themselves in that habit for centuries; no doubt they will continue to do so.

But it is worth asking whether circumstances ever arise where a term of address *must* be used. To help with the enquiry I list below some possible reasons for vocative usage, noted in the present corpus. These vocative stimuli are in no particular order of importance, and relate to many different situations.

Reasons for vocative usage

(1) To attract the attention of a particular person, especially when other people are present.

(2) To express the speaker's attitude to the hearer, especially if that attitude is highly emotional, of great fondness, or extreme contempt.

(3) To demonstrate to the hearer that he or she has been identified or recognized. This is often a welcoming use of the hearer's name. A head waiter might consider it important to greet regular customers in this way.

(4) To flatter the hearer, perhaps by the use of a title to which the hearer has no right, or by a flattering word such as 'lovely'.

(5) To comment tersely on the behaviour of the hearer and express an opinion of it, using a term like 'bighead'.

(6) To fix the name of a person to whom one has just been introduced in the speaker's mind by immediate repetition and use. This is a standard technique taught in some business schools.

(7) To emphasize that what is being said applies to the hearer, especially if the hearer does not appear to be listening attentively.

(8) To soften, e.g. by the use of an endearment or first name, the speaker's otherwise unpleasant message.

(9) To remind a third party of the hearer's identity, e.g. during a radio interview, though this can also happen when the third party is present.

(10) To remind the hearer, perhaps sarcastically, of his or her professional status, especially if it is lower than that of the speaker. However, the speaker may also remind someone of his or her higher status, especially if he or she feels that the hearer's behaviour does not accord with that high status.

(11) To remind the hearer of the spiritual relationship which exists between speaker and hearer, as when a priest uses 'my daughter' to a parishioner.

(12) To specify the singularity or plurality of 'you' or an imperative verb.

(13) To convey a message to a third party about the state of the relationship between speaker and hearer.

(14) To demonstrate to the hearer, and perhaps to a third party, that the speaker is cultured enough to know the conventionally correct form of address for the occasion.

(15) To identify a sub-group within a larger group, as when a choir-master addresses the tenors.

(16) To win the approval of a third party, e.g. by addressing an infant as 'angel' in the hearing of its mother.

(17) To remind the hearer of fellow-membership of an organization, as when 'brother' is used at a trade union meeting.

(18) To conform to ritualistic requirements, e.g. the use of 'strangers' in the British House of Commons, or 'dearly beloved' in a Christian church.

(19) To draw a parallel between the behaviour of the hearer and a category of person: e.g. someone who is asking searching questions is addressed as 'my lord', because he is acting like a judge in a courtroom.

(20) To display the speaker's linguistic ingenuity or wit, perhaps by using a 'verbal incident' vocative. Examples are given on p. 28.

(21) To respond directly, and perhaps sarcastically, to a vocative used a moment before by the hearer to the speaker: e.g. in *Pamela*, by Samuel Richardson, the use of 'lambkin' to a young girl inspires her immediate use of 'wolfkin' to the woman who used the term.

(22) To inform a third party of the professional or social status of the hearer.

(23) To signal to the hearer that the speaker is ready to be of service, e.g. a shop assistant's use of 'sir' to a male customer.

(24) To include the hearer in a general category, thereby commenting on his behaviour or character. Thus a woman might say 'You men!' or an American 'You British!'

(25) To respond to a particular situation: e.g. a parting leads to the use of 'See you later, alligator.'

(26) To allow one hearer of several to identify himself or herself with a remark, as with 'Coffee, anyone?'

(27) To conceal if possible the fact that the hearer's name has been forgotten. 'Darling' or a similar word is used rather than no vocative at all.

(28) To compare the hearer with a specific real or fictional person by using a transferred name.

(29) To conform to specific rules of vocative usage: e.g. the military use of 'sir', where the term is the verbal equivalent of a salute.

(30) To conceal from the hearer the speaker's actual feelings or attitude.

This is only a preliminary list, and it would make a useful research project for a graduate student to examine the subject in far more detail. Some of the reasons for using terms of address that I have mentioned could easily be divided into sub-categories. For example, the use of a vocative 'to convey a message to a third party about the state of the relationship between speaker and hearer' includes very different situations. One woman's use of 'darling' to a man may be telling another woman that this is *her* man, and that the second woman should stay away from him. Another woman's use of 'darling' to a man may be an attempt to conceal from some new arrivals the fact that she and the man were quarrelling bitterly moments before.

Why vocatives *need* to be used

Even with this brief list, however, some answers about the necessity or not of vocatives begin to emerge. It seems that a term of address might need to be used in certain situations for a number of reasons. We might class these as:

(a) Grammatical: the fact that neither 'you' nor imperative verbs indicate number is occasionally inconvenient. When a number of people are present, the term of address partly functions as a kind of pronominal or verbal inflection, specifying number.

(b) Practical: if it is necessary to attract the attention of one person amongst a group, a term of address becomes necessary as a simple designator. The use of names by radio interviewers is dictated by another kind of practical necessity.

(c) Social: in many situations it is diplomatically important, to the point of necessity, for a speaker to display recognition of someone he has met before by using that person's name and possibly title.

(d) Ceremonial: at a wedding ceremony, for instance, it is necessary for the officiating clergyman to use the traditional 'dearly beloved' opening words. There are many ceremonies where verbal formulae which include terms of address need to be used.

(e) Mandatory: a prisoner is obliged to use 'sir' to a prison governor, a soldier must use 'sir' to an officer. There are other situations where use of a vocative is decreed by a system of rules, and there are penalties for non-compliance with such rules.

We might also allow another classification which we could call

(f) Emotional: the speaker feels an overwhelming desire, or need, to declare his attitude to the hearer.

This final classification would account for many exclamatory uses of vocatives as endearments or insults.

It would seem, then, that the use of a term of address is by no means always as optional as writers on the subject would have us believe. It is difficult to see how speakers of English could function without them.

Some general points about terms of address

One or two other general points about vocatives, revealed by the list of reasons for use, are worth noting. A term of address may be used more for the benefit of the speaker than the hearer. It may also be used because a third person is present, and be meant to convey information to that third person, not the theoretical addressee.

When a term of address is used, for whatever reason, it always (1) carries a certain amount of grammatical information, as indicated in (a) above; (2) designates a hearer or hearers (or allows a hearer or hearers to designate themselves); (3) expresses an attitude to the designated hearer or hearers on the part of the speaker. The attitude displayed may not be the speaker's real attitude, but it is the one he is prepared to reveal at the time. The use of a neutral term, said in a neutral way, is in itself a display of attitude, since the neutral term was chosen, as vocatives always are, from a range of other possible expressions available to the speaker. One of these, or a change in the tone of voice used, could have reflected a different attitude.

The grammar of terms of address

I have mentioned grammatical aspects of vocatives once or twice in passing, and I would now like to pursue that topic in more depth. At one time a speaker of English could indicate formally that he was addressing one person (thou), two people (yit) or more than two people (ye). The number aspect of the second person pronoun was clearly of great importance. The dual form 'yit', however, became redundant in the Middle English period. The oblique form 'you' also replaced 'ye' as the nominative plural form in the fourteenth century. It was about that time, with the gradual development of a more civilized English society and its accompanying social hierarchy, that it became necessary for English-speakers to indicate on occasion that they were being deferential to a hearer. A third person form of address might achieve this, but third person address is clumsy. A form of the second person pronoun was needed that would indicate deference.

The English were by no means the first nation to discover or identify this need to show deference. The Romans had already done so, and had adopted the solution of using the plural form of 'you' to one person. The justification for this practice, which was at first applied to Roman emperors, was that an emperor was both a human being and a god, a plurality contained within a single person. Subsequently, use of plural 'you' in Latin to any one person implied that he was of emperor status, or at least to be greatly respected. As time passed its use spread downwards through society, as is nearly always the case with polite formulae.

The downward shift in English is shown by the history of words like 'mister' and 'sir'. The tendency, however, now appears to have been reversed, both in Britain and throughout Europe. In languages like French and German, where terms equivalent to 'thou' still exist, they are now being used far more frequently, paralleling the freer use of the first name in English. An upward shift of familiarity has replaced the downward shift of politeness.

However, when the need to show deference became felt by English-speakers, they began to imitate the Roman practice, one which had been followed by other Romance languages such as French and Spanish. No doubt plural 'you' in English was at first used to one person only at the highest social levels, but once the downward shift had occurred, there came a time when the *non*-use of plural you to almost anyone became in itself significant. If 'you' was now clearly marked as a polite form, the use of 'thou' could be seen as indicating lack of special respect, to the point of indicating instead condescension or contempt. This made its continued use far more problematic.

In Shakespeare's plays, 'thou' continues to be used alongside 'you' in a way that defies any systematic explanation. The Elizabethans seem to have been thoroughly confused about when to use one term or the other. 'You' was the safer of the two terms, and use of 'thou' diminished rapidly. By the end of the seventeenth century, 'thou' was fast disappearing from standard English, though that did not happen overnight. Even today, at working-class level in the north-east of England, it still fights a rear guard action, 'thou' and its inflected forms being used by dialect speakers.

Nevertheless, it is safe to say that standard English has allowed 'thou' to disappear. It has done so because it can get along without it, even though this would appear to say that:

(a) English-speakers no longer need to specify number in direct address,
(b) that they no longer need to show deference ('you', as the only remaining term, used to everyone, no longer confers any special status on the hearer),
(c) that they no longer need to show condescension to a hearer, as the later use of 'thou' allowed them to do,

(d)   that they no longer need to show particular intimacy to a hearer, as the later use of 'thou' also allowed them to do.

The reality, of course, is that all these needs remain. The functions mentioned above have simply been shifted on to terms of address.

Pronominal and vocative 'you'

It is clear that a term of address is always closely linked with the pronoun 'you', *which in itself has vocative qualities*. One could say, in fact, that whenever pronominal 'you' is used in direct address, vocative 'you' is implicitly present. The two kinds of 'you' are inextricably bound together, though in an utterance like 'You! What do you think you're doing!' the first 'you' is clearly vocative, where the others are pronominal.

Pronominal and vocative 'you' differ in their attitudinal marking. The former is neutral, the latter unfriendly. Pronominal 'you' also conforms to normal rules of syntax; vocative 'you' does not need to do so. Vocative 'you', finally, allows substitution. In 'You! What do you think you're doing!' vocative 'you' could be replaced by 'darling', 'John', 'you stupid fool', and innumerable other terms of address, all of which could be described as vocative-'you' variants. That point is significant, because the corollary of my statement that vocative 'you' is always implicitly present when pronominal 'you' is used in direct address, is that pronominal 'you' is always implicitly present when vocative 'you' is used. It follows that if any term of address is a vocative-'you' variant, then pronominal 'you' is always implicitly present when any term of address is used.

Vocative 'you' is an unusual term of address in that it fails to specify number, but it clearly adds extra information to pronominal 'you', in the way that an inflection adds information to a noun or verb, an auxiliary verb adds information to the main verb, or a particle completes the meaning of a phrasal verb. When a term of address is used, then we can say that pronominal 'you', overtly or implicitly present and in itself neutral, is now more definitely marked as intimate, friendly, polite, neutral, unfriendly, or insulting. When the term of address is not vocative 'you', a number-specifier is also added to each of these six categories.

Phrasal 'you'

We could describe this modification of pronominal 'you' in different ways. Terms of address could be thought of as inflections, and their use could be said to lead to: *youint, youf, youp, youn, youu,* and *youin,* where *youint* = 'you' + intimate term of address, *youf* = 'you' + friendly term of address, etc. There would also be the plural forms *youints, youfs, youps, youns, youus,* and *youins.*

These are not attractive forms. I would prefer to think of a term of address as constituting, together with pronominal 'you', a phrasal 'you', the vocative being the 'particle'. Phrasal 'you', though we may not want to use ugly abstractions such as *youint, youf,* etc., *is* notionally paradigmatic. If we say that pronominal 'you' used alone, without a vocative particle, is the same as 'you' + neutral particle (though in special circumstances, instanced above on p. 11 in the quotation from *The Spy Who Came in From the Cold*, it can also be unfriendly), then the paradigm might read:

I	We
intimate phrasal 'you'	intimate plural phrasal 'you'
friendly phrasal 'you'	friendly plural phrasal 'you'
polite phrasal 'you'	polite plural phrasal 'you'
neutral phrasal 'you'	neutral plural phrasal 'you'
unfriendly phrasal 'you'	unfriendly plural phrasal 'you'
insulting phrasal 'you'	insulting plural phrasal 'you'
he, she, it	they

Realizations of the phrasal 'you' components could be:

'I love you, my darling(s).'
'How are you, my friend(s)?'
'Thank you, sir (gentlemen).'
'Can you help me, please (driver) (all of you)?'
'You! (You two!) What are you doing?'
'I loathe you, you bastard(s)!'

In sentences where pronominal 'you' is not overtly present, such as 'Help me, John!' and 'Come here, you two!' 'John' and 'you two' nevertheless function as friendly and unfriendly examples of phrasal 'you'. The absence of pronominal 'you' makes no difference to the phrasal 'you' theory. It is always known which main component is linking with the vocative particle, after all. Phrasal 'you' is not as vague as 'phrasal verb', where the verb component constantly varies; it is more like 'phrasal look', or 'phrasal run', which might refer respectively to look at, look into, look for, look down on and run into, run down, run up, etc. 'You' also differs from verbs in that it is easily and frequently supported by non-verbal means, such as eye-contact and gesture, or the fact that no-one else is present to whom the speech can be addressed. Given that one component of phrasal 'you' is both invariable and strongly present implicitly, it is not surprising that it is frequently omitted.

To sum up, my contention is that the original 'thou-yit-ye' pronoun system in English, which accurately specified grammatical number, and the later thou-you system, which allowed a speaker to demonstrate a particular attitude to his hearer, has been replaced by a phrasal-'you' system, where 'you' is one invariable component and need not therefore be overtly present, while the particle element is a term of address. The phrasal-'you' system allows a speaker to specify grammatical number (even the original duality of 'yit') and allows a finer display of attitude than was possible with 'thou-you'. Terms of address, of course, were available to a speaker under the 'thou-yit-ye' and 'thou-you' systems. What I am saying is that they were not then integrated into the grammatical system as they are today. The existence of a single 'you' form makes them essential. That is why I began this Introduction by saying that terms of address are now far more important than they once were in English, adding that they are of more importance in English than in languages which retain at least a two-term 'you' system.

Term of address: a definition

Taking into account everything that has so far been said, I would propose the following overall definition of 'term of address'.

A term of address is a numerically and attitudinally-marked designator which:

(a) functions as a particle to pronominal 'you' to form a notionally paradigmatic phrasal 'you',
(b) consists of name(s), word(s), or a combination of both,
(c) is used for the benefit of a speaker, addressee, or third-party hearer either optionally or necessarily for grammatical, practical, social, emotional, ceremonial, or externally-imposed reasons.

Vocative selection factors

I turn now to the question of what causes a speaker in any given situation to choose one term of address rather than another. In many situations, whatever the speaker's attitude to his hearer happens to be, and regardless of whether a term of address is being used optionally or by necessity, a choice must still be made amongst a number of possible terms.

An immediate distinction must be made between situations where prior knowledge of the hearer's name and other personal details, such as his professional and social status, exists and those where it doesn't. Since those terms which can be used to strangers in the street can also be used to people who are known, in what follows it will be assumed that speaker and hearer are already acquainted and are aware of each other's status. The latter point affects in itself the vocative selection process. There is either equality of status between speaker and hearer or inequality. A speaker at a lower *or* a higher level than the addressee may be more polite than he would be to someone at the same level. A number of other factors, relating to both speaker and hearer, then come into play which lead to the selection of a particular vocative.

Nationality

A native-speaker of English can be English, Scottish, Welsh, Irish, American, Canadian, Australian, etc. Each national draws upon a slightly different stock of words, including terms of address. This is not to say that only an Englishman will use 'old boy', for example, as a friendly term of address, and that only an Australian will mildly insult a hearer by calling him 'you drongo' or 'you galah'. Americans and Australians may deliberately imitate what they take to be English vocative usage and use 'old boy' to one another. An Englishman who has visited Australia may take 'you drongo' into his personal vocabulary and use it to other Englishmen. Not that it would do him much good, since few English hearers would understand the term.

One is obliged to make reservations of this kind: nevertheless, if a speaker addresses someone as 'buddy', 'bub', 'you fink', 'you foulball', and the like, he is probably American. A speaker accusing someone of being a 'Swaddler' will probably be Irish, a user of 'you dogan' is likely to be Canadian, and so on. Scottish, Welsh, and Irish speakers may introduce terms from their native languages into an English conversation, but that would be true of any bilingual speaker. Less obvious, perhaps, are so-called calques, or loan-translations. In *Henry's War*, by Jeremy Brooks, one speaker uses the vocative expression 'little pig' on three occasions. He is a Welshman, translating into English a term of address frequently used in colloquial Welsh, *mochyn bach*.

The nationality of the person being addressed can also influence the vocative that is used. Dictionary entries will be found for terms such as **Aussie, Dago, Eyetie, Harp, Limey, Yank**, and the like, where the known or assumed nationality of the hearer is a key factor. It is obviously of equal importance when generic nicknames of the 'Taffy', 'Paddy', and 'Jock' type are used. There would be little point in calling a Scotsman 'Taffy'.

Sometimes a specific reference to nationality is included in a vocative group. In *The Limits of Love*, by Frederic Raphael, occurs 'you bloody Irish scab'; *The Hiding Place*, by Robert Shaw, has 'you poor German idiots'; *The Half Hunter*, by John Sherwood, has an example of 'you horrid old Austrian pig'; *The River of Diamonds*, by Geoffrey Jenkins, has 'you Malay bastard'.

Mere mention of a nationality, however, does not automatically give us accurate information about an addressee. 'You slant-eyed Mongolian pig', in John Braine's *Room at the Top*, is clearly a joke. 'Foolish Greek', addressed to Feste in Shakespeare's *Twelfth Night*, is not meant to tell the audience that Feste is Greek. An Elizabethan audience would have associated 'Greek' with joviality, as they were meant to do.

In *The Heart of the Matter*, by Graham Greene, the transferred name 'Gunga Din' is used to an Indian. Gunga Din in Kipling's poem was certainly Indian, but the name is not normally used in this way. It often refers instead to the courage of the hearer, and his being 'a better man' than the speaker.

Dialect

This is a sub-division of nationality which can influence a speaker's choice of term. Examples of vocatives which occurred in the corpus and which appear to be dialectal include: you-all, youse, honey-child, bonny lad, chiel, feardy gowk, get, hinny, hen, mawther, mazidawk, rodney. Speakers from Tyneside, and in earlier times from other English regions, can also be marked by their late use of 'thou' and its oblique forms.

Sex

A male speaker is likely to use some terms of address far more frequently than a female. In a count of vocative occurrences in fifty sample novels, terms such as 'old boy', 'old man', 'old chap', 'old fellow', and 'old lad' were used 277 times. On only nine occasions was the speaker a woman. Little real research seems to have been done on the differences between male and female use of English. Any research project in this area would do well to include terms of address in the enquiry.

Some terms, because of their meaning, would only normally be used by one sex. 'Husband' and 'wife', used vocatively, are such words, though their use is inspired by the sex of the hearer, not the speaker. Some other family terms, such as 'Daddy' and 'Mummy', possibly become marked as female terms when the age of the speaker is taken into account. After the age of sixteen, for instance, they are probably used far more by women than men, though their use by young children is evenly distributed between boys and girls.

The influence of the speaker's sex as a factor in vocative choice needs more investigation: the sex of the hearer is clearly important. When I looked at well over a thousand vocatives with this point in mind, 32.56 per cent of them contained specific indications of the hearer's sex. There were, in addition, many more of the 'bastard' type, which could theoretically be used to either sex but in practice is always said to a man.

It is curious that this sexual indication seems to be so necessary. Proof that it is comes in the most frequently-used vocatives – first names. The vast majority of first names used in English-speaking countries indicate the sex of the name-bearer. When a name becomes sexually ambiguous, used for a time by both boys and girls, its use for one of the sexes is usually soon abandoned. In this particular battle of the sexes, girls always appear to win. Names such as Shirley, Tracy, Leslie, Hilary, Florence, Beverly, Robin, Jay, once exclusively names for boys, have now become thoroughly female names.

A special situation arises, as Jerome K. Jerome once wittily pointed out, when a speaker is expected to say something to a baby whose sex is not apparent. Jerome recommended using 'angel', which is not only suitable for both sexes but is guaranteed to please the mother.

Age

The speaker's age naturally has a great influence on the terms of address he or she uses, as it does on use of language generally. A speaker under forty, for example, may use first names quite naturally to people of any age that he has just met, whereas a British speaker who was young in the 1920s may still prefer a more formal style. Youth again will be reflected in the slang words which so often occur in aggressive terms of address. No-one over thirty (and for that matter, no-one of any sensitivity under thirty) is likely to use the offensive expression 'you flid', for instance. Older speakers, however, may continue to use words which have gone out of fashion. One cannot imagine a young person naturally saying 'you cad'.

This point hardly needs much emphasis: it is clear that a speaker's personal version of his native language, his idiolect, will tend to become rather fossilized after a certain point. Even if an individual continues to take new words into his active vocabulary, he will not usually abandon the old ones. It is those, unknown to a new generation, which will date his speech.

The age of an addressee can be reflected in vocatives in various ways. I have discussed in separate dictionary articles the use of **old** and **young** as vocative elements (see those entries). 'Little' is also sometimes a reference to youth, though it can express contempt for the hearer's insignificance. It is also often used when men insult women, as in 'you little fool', 'you little whore', 'you little goose'.

'Boy' used vocatively does not necessarily mean that a youth is being addressed, any more than 'old man' means that an old man is the hearer.

Anglo-Saxon Attitudes, by Angus Wilson, has 'my dear boy' being used to a man in his sixties, though the speaker is even older.

'Master' + first name has in fairly recent times been restricted to young male hearers, though 'Miss' is not always addressed to young women. Family terms such as 'Grandad' and 'Granny' logically imply hearers of a certain age, though such terms, like all vocatives, can be jokingly misused.

Social class

This factor probably affects English users of vocatives more than their American, Australian, etc., counterparts. It is also the case that whereas social class differences formerly depended on family background, they now have far more to do with educational and professional level.

The 'old boy' group of vocatives, now far less used, were perceived in Britain as a decidedly middle, and possibly upper-class, marker. At one time there were many speakers who used these terms who consciously or subconsciously wished to emphasize their social level. Inevitably they were frequently used by upwardly mobile speakers who aped what they took to be a feature of middle-class speech. In male society it was indeed the officers who were 'old boy' to one another, not the men. Working-class speakers sometimes parodied the 'old boy' terms, with their 'old cock', 'old fruit', 'old scout', 'old son'. These are still heard in Britain, and may be used especially to someone who is thought to be intent on proving his middle-class status by his accent and other speech habits.

There is a social class differentiation still discernible in family relationship terms. 'Mam', 'maw', 'mum', and the like are working-class. The social climbers need to switch to 'mother' if they are men, to 'mother darling', 'mummykins', and the like if they are women. The corresponding terms for father are 'da', 'dad', 'pop' as opposed to 'father' itself.

'Dear' used on its own crosses social boundaries, but 'dear boy', 'dear girl', 'dear lady', 'my dear chap', 'my dear fellow', 'my dear' + first name are once again middle-class. Working-class speakers express friendship with 'mate', 'ducks', 'love', 'cock', 'tosh', 'wacker', 'hen', 'pet', and the like. These are British examples: it is difficult to get away from England when discussing social class.

Profession

In some professions there are certain terms of address used by insiders that would not be used by others. The courtroom use of 'me lud' by British barristers was one instance of such usage, though I am told that it is now little used. The Royal Navy and other armed services have many professional titles and traditional nicknames which are used by serving men and women. *A Dictionary of Sailors' Slang*, by Wilfred Granville, gives many examples of such terms. Some, such as 'Three-o', occasionally turn up in novels, that one occurring in *Doctor at Sea*, by Richard Gordon.

Clergymen and priests are obliged to be careful with their vocative usage, as with their language generally. They must express sympathy and friendship to many people, while avoiding endearments which could be misunderstood.

As for those addressed, people known to have professional titles are frequently addressed by them when they are in their professional environment. In many cases the generic description of a trade or profession serves as a term of address. Thus a cab-driver is 'cabbie' or 'driver', a waiter is 'waiter'. On a British building site, I am informed by Mr G. Henson, the various tradesmen are usually addressed by fellow workmen by standard professional titles or nicknames, such as 'plumber' or 'plumb', 'brickie' and 'chips'.

Relationship

The fact that speaker and hearer are members of the same family allows the use of certain vocatives. When there are variant forms, such as 'mom', 'mum', 'ma', etc., the selection of one term rather than another will depend on other factors, such as the speaker's nationality, age, and sex.

In more general terms, the relationship that may exist between speaker and hearer, e.g. intimacy, friendship, distance, will have an overall influence on the type of vocative used. Sensitive and polite speakers recognize the boundaries within which their terms of address should remain. Less sensitive speakers may use friendly or intimate terms that the state of the relationship does not actually justify. This almost leads one to a separate selection factor – the speaker's level of social delicacy.

Religion

I have mentioned that ministers of religion have to be restrained with their own use of vocatives. They are also addressed, usually, by professional titles. By 'religion', however, I mean that those who are steeped in the Bible and are obsessed with Christianity may reveal this in the vocatives they use. Evangelical preachers are likely to use terms like 'sinner' and 'blasphemer', and address everyone as 'brother' and 'sister', in a way that marks them out.

The hearer's religious affiliations can become important in places like Northern Ireland. It can lead to words which refer to Protestantism or Roman Catholicism being used as abusive terms of address.

Race

A black American or a West Indian living in Britain may or may not have racially-marked speech, which could include a distinct range of vocatives. The more educated a speaker, the less likely it will be that racial background will be noticeable in the terms of address used. What appear to be racially-marked terms may in fact be shared by white speakers of similar educational and social level. Slang is especially difficult to pin down in racial terms: what is 'black slang' today may be general currency in a month's time.

Jewish speakers, especially if they also speak Yiddish, are likely to introduce Yiddish words such as 'shmuck' and 'boychick' into an English conversation, though many of these terms are now widely known. It can easily happen that a non-Jewish speaker, especially a New Yorker perhaps, will also use them. This is true of calques such as 'clever boy', 'wise guy', which appear to derive from Yiddish. Leo Rosten's *The Joys of Yiddish* is a good source for information about such terms.

The racial origins of the person being addressed can certainly inspire the use of particular vocatives, often insulting in nature. Examples that occurred in the corpus included: boogie, darky, greaseball, gyp, wop, Hebe, honky, paleface, yid, hooknose, kike, sheeny, nigger, nip, white boy, white shit.

Homosexuality

Many male homosexuals appeared as fictional characters in the corpus. Novelists often indicate that such speakers have distinctive speech patterns, which can include a special use of vocatives. Examples of vocatives given to homosexual speakers included 'ducky', 'darling', 'sweety', 'handsome', 'love', 'you mean thing', mostly made unusual by being spoken by a man to a man. Heterosexual men use friendly terms of address to one another, but rarely endearments.

As with the differences between male and female use of English, this subject requires special study before generalizations can be made, if indeed they ever can be made. Homosexual men clearly vary in that some quite deliberately break normal vocative conventions, knowing that this will be remarked upon. Others give no linguistic signals of any kind that would enable a listener to identify them as homosexual.

Terms of address used to homosexual men can vary, if the speaker is male, according to whether he is heterosexual or is himself homosexual. In the former case the term used may comment on the hearer's homosexuality in an insulting way. Fag, faggot, pouff, homo, queer, nelly, punk, poofter, queen, sissy, and fruitcake were terms that occurred vocatively in the corpus. 'Gay' was not used as a term of address.

Individuality

Every native-speaker's use of his language differs at least slightly from that of everyone else. This idiolect, or personal dialect, has mainly come about in a natural, evolutionary way. Occasionally speakers seem consciously to adopt a speech mannerism, which can affect vocative usage in two main ways.

First, there are those who use the same term of address to nearly everyone. I recall being addressed as 'baby' some years ago by a male journalist, the first and only time that such a word has been applied to me during my adult life. I wondered what had inspired the term until I heard the journalist talking to others. They were all, men and women, young and old, 'baby' as far as he was concerned. He used the vocative as a kind of personal trademark, in the way that W. C. Fields identified himself with 'my little chickadee', Arthur Askey with 'playmates', and as Dame Edna Everidge currently does with 'possum'.

Novelists sometimes comment on the vocative trademarks of their characters. In *Bethel Merriday*, for example, Sinclair Lewis tells us that one man's usual term of address is 'my pet', another uses 'darling' and 'kitten', a third uses 'child'. George Eliot, in *Scenes of Clerical Life*, remarks that to Mr Gilfil all boys are 'young shaver', all girls are 'two shoes'. Other novelists make no specific comment on such individual usage, but they demonstrate it. In *Brothers in Law*, by Henry Cecil, it is Grimes who constantly uses 'my dear fellow' (plus the non-vocative phrase 'we shall see'). Cecil ends the novel with 'We shall see, my dear fellow, we shall see,' and no reader would have any problem identifying the speaker. In *The Limits of Love*, by Frederick Raphael, one woman only uses the vocative 'sweets', though in this case it is always to her husband and may qualify as a private nickname.

Second, there is what might be called the 'Sam Weller syndrome'. This is characterized by the use of an exceptionally wide range of vocatives. Sam, who becomes Mr Pickwick's servant in Charles Dickens's *The Pickwick Papers*, uses such terms as 'old 'un', 'governor', 'my patriarch', and 'you portable engine' (all to Job Trotter, a young man); 'my ancient', 'old codger', 'my Prooshan blue', 'corpilence', 'you unnatural wagabone' (to his father); 'young twenty stun' (= stone), 'young dropsy', 'young opium-eater', 'young boa-constructer' (to a fat boy); 'young townskip', 'my infant fernomenon' (to Master Bardell), and various other terms, such as 'young brockiley sprout' and 'old Strike-a-Light' to people encountered on his travels.

Speakers like Sam enjoy creating nonce terms of address, whereas most of us fall back on standard terms. I say 'speakers like Sam' because he is clearly not alone. In *Dandelion Days*, for instance, Henry Williamson gives us a portrait of a schoolmaster whose pupils are variously addressed as: miserable midget, depraved lunatic, bottle-eyed baboon, long-eared ass, snivelling snipe, abandoned wretch. The young hero of *Absolute Beginners*, by Colin MacInnes, uses terms such as: aboriginal, boy Mowgli, clobbo, Cockney boy, half-brother, infant prodigy, Knightsbridge girl, land-lubber, little latch-key kid, Miss Sheba, Sporting Life, Trade Wind, wolverine. I am personally fond, as who can fail to be, of Dane Chandos's *Abbie*, his autocratic aunt who creates an instant vocative for everyone she meets: spectator, haberdasher, apiarist, costermonger, saleswoman, newsurchin, sea-lion keeper.

One might say that all this is suspiciously literary: I personally believe that the novelists are reporting on something they have noticed in real people. It is a kind of linguistic exuberance and playfulness which is mostly enjoyable, though sometimes, as with Henry Williamson's schoolmaster, and the hypocritical Mr Mantalini, in Dickens's *Nicholas Nickleby*, the falsely elaborate terms used by a speaker seem to reveal a rather nasty personality.

The Sam Weller syndrome is mainly a feature of male speech, but in *Gideon Planish* Sinclair Lewis gives us Peony, the hero's wife, who is perhaps inspired by her own unusual first name to use a wide range of terms in vocative address.

Verbal incident

All the selection factors mentioned so far have been non-linguistic. Occasionally a word or words that have just been used prompt the use of a vocative. I am not thinking here of the echo type, where a typical conversational exchange runs: 'You pig!' 'Pig yourself!' Nor did I have in mind the near-echo, where a speaker who has just been addressed by a term he does not like, such as 'pal', 'friend', 'mate', uses the same word or a synonym in return with sarcastic emphasis. By 'verbal incident' I was thinking more of the situation which occurs in *The Limits of Love*, by Frederick Raphael. The dialogue there is as follows:

'The point is, let's go and celebrate.'
'Lovely.'
'All right, lovely, it's a date.'

The same novel has a man who says to a friend: 'There she is! That's the dish I was telling you about.' The speaker then says to the woman concerned: 'Hey, dish, come over here.' Elsewhere in the novel occurs: 'You're a naughty boy.' 'What's your name, naughty girl?'

The Word Child, by Iris Murdoch, has a woman who says at one point: 'Of course I don't know, I'm only the messenger.' 'Well, messenger,' is the reply, 'you'd better go then.'

I mentioned above the near-echo use of a vocative. It can also happen that the use of one vocative will inspire in itself the use of a completely different vocative in return. Sammy Davis Jr describes in his autobiographical *Yes I Can!* how he once addressed a fellow soldier as 'buddy'. The man was highly offended, replying with 'I'm not your buddy, you black bastard.'

Selection factors summary

Perhaps enough examples have been given to show that the process that leads to the selection of one vocative rather than another in a given situation is a fairly complex one. I have isolated certain selection factors: in reality they are inextricably bound together. It is not just a combination of a speaker's nationality, dialect, sex, age, profession, educational level, social class, etc., plus other aspects of his or her personality that cause one term rather than another to be used; the hearer's sex, age, social class, etc., play their part.

My suggested factors in no way complete the list. What should one say about that delicacy of feeling which causes a speaker to use euphemisms, for example? 'Basket' and 'baa-lamb' replace 'bastard', 'beggar' is used for 'bugger', 's.o.b.' for 'son-of-a-bitch', 'shmo' for 'shmuck'. Henry Fielding laughed at such habits in *Tom Jones*: see his comments on 'female dog' under **Bitch**.

Then I wonder whether one should consider the physical appearance of the hearer as an aspect of vocative selection. It is certainly commented on in a great many terms of address, especially the generic nicknames used by children. They have a suitable name for every type of person, tall or short, fat or thin, bespectacled, red-headed, freckle-faced, those with big noses, ears or mouths, those with beards or moustaches. Such terms tend to be jeering, but many friendly expressions such as 'beautiful', 'lovely', 'blondie' are influenced by the appearance of the person being addressed.

There are also temporary factors, which affect speech in general and vocative usage in passing. Illness is one, drunkenness another. In *Whisky Galore*, for example, Compton Mackenzie says of one man that he uses more formal terms of address when he has drunk a great deal. In *The Affair*, by C. P. Snow, a speaker who says 'I'm afraid I'm rather drunk' becomes more prolix than usual, using 'my dear' and 'most admired' + first name as a vocative. There is a similar result of drunkenness in Malcolm Lowry's *Under the Volcano*, where a speaker begins to address a cat as 'my-little-snake-in-the-grass-my-little-anguish-in-herba. . . .'

Speakers sometimes misuse the vocative system accidentally. Shakespeare shows two rustics trying to cope with military titles in *Henry the Fourth Part Two*. In their confusion they use such terms as 'good master corporal captain', 'good my lord captain', 'good master corporate Bardolph'. In *Brothers in Law*, by Henry Cecil, a woman addresses a judge as 'Your Worship' instead of 'Your Honour', which causes a solicitor to murmur to a colleague that 'she's had it'.

This accidental misuse has to be separated from deliberate misuse, as when 'Your Worship' is used to a vicar as a joke or 'Father' is used rather maliciously to an Anabaptist minister in spite of his protests. Accidental misuse may tell the hearer something about the speaker's educational level. Deliberate misuse is a strong indication of the speaker's attitude. Often deliberate misuse of a vocative stems from what is perceived as role-playing by one of the conversational partners. Thus someone who asks questions like a judge in a courtroom is addressed as 'my lord', adults who are behaving childishly are addressed as 'children', someone saying something intelligent is called 'professor'. The wish to comment on such role-playing is often in itself the reason for a vocative being used; inevitably such a situation also affects the kind of vocative that is selected.

In apparently similar circumstances, then, individual speakers will vary greatly in the terms of address they use, unless those circumstances are subject to a specific set of rules, as in military service. In more open situations, it is impossible to predict which term will occur. It would be a little like trying to predict which first name parents will choose for a child. With first names there is a recognized stock from which the parents will probably choose, but there is nothing to stop them inventing a new name. With terms of address there is a stock of words and expressions which are often used vocatively, standing beside personal names, which are always available for vocative use. But a speaker is at liberty to create a term of address which he feels is appropriate at that moment, for use to a particular hearer.

Very few terms of address are exclusively used as such. Even 'sir' can be used referentially in a sentence like 'Sir said I could do that', which might be spoken by a young English schoolboy. What we can say is that personal names and words like 'darling', 'dear', 'mate', etc., have a high degree of vocativeness. Words like 'wall' and 'overcoat' do not, though both have entries in this dictionary because of their vocative use. 'Wall', as it happens, is quite frequently used as a vocative in the context of a football match. 'Overcoat' is simply a nonce conversion.

My intention in the dictionary entries has obviously been to deal thoroughly with the frequently occurring vocative words and expressions. The nonce examples are there to show what *can* happen. A glance at the Shakespearean plays and other seventeenth-century drama will reveal a high proportion of nonce usage. It may be true to say that terms of address subsequently became more formalized.

It is certainly true to say that there are vocative fashions. It is just possible that in the seventeenth century, the creation of nonce vocatives was fashionable *in itself* at a certain level of society, whereas later it was fashionable to display a subtle awareness of the use of a small number of standard terms. The current fashion in the English-speaking countries appears to be an egalitarian simplification centred on first-name usage. This is bound to change, though perhaps not for some considerable time. The last discernible vocative period spanned most of the eighteenth and nineteenth centuries. The present one dates only from about 1930 in Britain, rather earlier in the USA. On that basis some commentator on vocative usage in the mid-twenty-second century will be noting another change of direction.

Reactions to vocative usage

Fictional characters are sometimes made to comment, by the authors who have given them life, on their feelings about having to use particular terms of address to certain people. More often they are made to react as hearers to terms which have been used to them.

In *Lucky Jim*, by Kingsley Amis, the hero comments fully on being obliged to address his head of department as 'professor'. The latter needs to hear his title being used to boost his ego. In *Kingfishers Catch Fire*, Rumer Godden comments on the pomposity of a man who had to be addressed as 'Sir William', even by his niece. Both instances concern a speaker who is on a lower level than the hearer, a situation where in real life, as in literature, true attitudes may have to be concealed.

A common reaction by men, when addressed as 'sir', is one of irritation. Seeing themselves, perhaps, as young and rather interesting individuals, they do not like to be reminded by others that they appear to be elderly and respectable. Equally common, in modern times, is the annoyed reaction of many women when addressed by men in terms which treat them as sexual objects, which make personal allusions, or which appear to be condescending. As an average male I have on occasion committed unwitting offence in recent years, using terms which I considered to be merely friendly to women colleagues, only to be told that I was a male chauvinist. I take comfort, curiously enough, in the fact that they were able to tell me that. More serious are the cases where offence is caused but not voiced, leaving a residue of resentment.

It is tempting to say that in these matters, offence lies in the ears of the individual. Harper Lee illustrates the point in *To Kill a Mockingbird*. A lawyer addresses a rural girl politely as 'Miss Mayella' and 'ma'am', and she is most upset: 'I don't hafta take his sass,' she tells the judge, convinced that the lawyer is making fun of her. The judge is obliged to explain that there is such a thing as courtesy. The general point here is that a speaker's intention should be taken into account before a hearer decides to take offence at the use of a particular term of address.

Reactions by hearers to terms of address that they have not appreciated can be quite violent. Both G. B. Shaw and Thomas Hardy say of 'blockhead' that its use by one man to another is a duelling matter. In Smollett's *Peregrine Pickle*, use of 'impertinent scoundrel' is enough to earn the speaker a punch on the nose. 'Audacious saucy trollop', used by one maid-servant to another in Fielding's *Tom Jones*, leads to a switch from words to fisticuffs. Mr Stiggins, in Dickens's *The Pickwick Papers*, imprudently calls Mr Weller Senior 'miserable sinner'. He is knocked to the floor for his pains.

Name-calling in many a school playground must often end in a physical battle. In 1974 a British workman called a West Indian colleague 'Sambo', and had time to reflect on the wisdom of doing so as he lay in a hospital bed. A judge later ruled that his use of 'Sambo' had not merited such a violent reaction. I was interested to read of another court case concerned with manner of address which occurred in 1976. This was in Germany, where a woman was fined DM 2250 for addressing a policeman as *du*, the equivalent of 'thou'. Her plea that in rural areas the use of a familiar form to everyone was commonplace was evidently ignored.

British policemen are probably more stoical in this matter, though they have been abused since at least the seventeenth century. One thinks of Dogberry, the constable in Shakespeare's *Much Ado About Nothing*. 'This plaintiff here,' he tells Leonato, the governor, 'did call me ass; I beseech you, let it be rememb'red in his punishment.'

The slanging match

The playground name-calling to which I referred a moment ago is in some ways ritualistic, in that the insulting terms of address used by children are fairly traditional. Children are constantly involved in verbal battles, and in order to survive must learn to counter one insult with another. Such skills learnt in childhood may be useful in the adult world, where the slanging, or scolding, matches continue, sometimes taking on special forms. The sixteenth-century Scottish poets versified the whole procedure in the flyting. Many modern black Americans do something similar when they 'play the dozens', as they call it, the insults sometimes taking the form of rhymed couplets.

An important element in the dozens – also called 'sounding' and 'signifying' – is the audience, which evaluates the insults used by the contestants. They encourage with their murmurs of approval whoever demonstrates most wit. Mark Twain describes a primitive and very mild form of such a contest in *Pudd'nhead Wilson*, calling it a friendly duel of 'idle and aimless chatter'. The insults exchanged between Jasper and Roxy include one or two terms of address, Jasper being called 'you black mud cat', Roxy 'you hussy'.

In *The Tenants*, by Bernard Malamud, a black American challenges a white man to play the dozens, 'a game of nothin but naked words', as he describes it. The white man refers to it as 'a contest of imprecation', which is accurate but less vivid. Various obscenities are exchanged which are not worth repeating here, though they gain the approval of those others who are present.

The entertainment value of the slanging match has long been known. Seventeenth-century playwrights regularly provided their audiences with such contests, knowing that they would be well received. There is the well-known exchange in Shakespeare's *Henry the Fourth Part One* (2:iv) between Prince Hal and Falstaff. Hal comments on Falstaff's size and weight, calling him: clay-brain'd guts, thou knotty-pated fool, thou whoreson, obscene, greasy tallow-catch. He also points out that Falstaff is: a bed-presser, a horse-back-breaker, a huge hill of flesh. Falstaff retaliates by remarking on Hal's thinness: you starveling, you eel-skin, you dried neat's tongue, you bull's pizzle, you stockfish, you tailor's yard, you sheath, you bow case, you vile standing tuck. I find it interesting that Falstaff still uses the polite you to address the prince, even when calling him such things as a bull's pizzle, which was a bull's penis, formerly used as a kind of truncheon.

The Elizabethan audience would also have appreciated the verbal duel between Ajax and Thersites in *Troilus and Cressida* (2:i). Ajax uses such terms as: dog, thou bitch-wolf's son, toadstool, porpentine (= porcupine), you whoreson cur, thou stool for a witch. Thersites in turn uses: thou mongrel beefwitted lord, thou sodden-witted lord, you scurvy valiant ass, camel. The groundlings would have been reminded of many similar real-life exchanges, appreciatively overheard in the streets.

I was commenting earlier on the fact that a speaker has the freedom to be innovative with terms of address. In the slanging match two people compare their powers of verbal innovation, and that freedom is exploited to the full. If there is no outside audience, the speakers may well be content to enjoy their own sallies. They may also convert what are formally insults into covert endearments, as a husband and wife do in Mae West's *The Pleasure Man*. For that couple, as perhaps for some couples in real life, every conversation offers an opportunity to play the dozens in a private way.

Terms of address in literature

This dictionary is based on a literary corpus, especially novels, though some plays have been included. If it is necessary to justify using novels as a main source, then I believe it can easily be done. Novelists report on vocative usage in a wide range of specialized situations, usually ones with which they are personally familiar. It would be very difficult indeed to assemble a team of researchers who could report on vocative usage in a senior common room, a hospital, the rehearsal room of a theatre, an officers' mess, the changing room of an American football team, and the thousand and one other professional and social environments in the various English-speaking countries, where terms of address are used. The novelists, usually intelligent and sensitive to the use of their native language, constitute such a research team. In passing they also provide, as we have seen, precise information about the way in which a vocative was said.

When one is also interested in the vocative usage of previous centuries, literary sources clearly become essential. Normally it is possible to check one 'informant' against another, especially in the case of commonly used terms. Those writers whose use of vocatives does not reflect the reality of the time tend to be easily identifiable. They use over-literary expressions, which one cannot believe a real person would have said spontaneously. I have commented on such matters in many individual entries.

Occasionally writers make artistic use of vocatives. C. P. Snow's use of 'Master' in *The Affair* is an outstanding example. In *The Pumpkin Eater*, by Penelope Mortimer, 'duckie' is used to a young girl by a man who behaves very unpleasantly. When the vocative occurs later in the novel, uttered by someone else, it is enough to recall immediately to the heroine's mind the earlier incident. The screenwriter of the English version of Hugo's *Les Miserables*, a film made in the 1930s, had three tiny scenes lasting in all about forty seconds, which showed the development of the relationship between Marius and Cosette over a long period. The couple were saying goodbye to one another and agreeing to meet again. The dialogues ran: 'Tomorrow, mademoiselle?' 'Yes, monsieur'; 'Tomorrow, Cosette?' 'Yes, Marius'; 'Tomorrow, darling?' 'Yes, darling.'

Writers can also make peculiar things happen when it comes to vocative usage. Shakespeare, in *The Taming of the Shrew*, has Petruchio force Kate to accept whatever he says, without argument, no matter how absurd it is. When Vincentio, an old man, appears Petruchio greets him as 'gentle mistress', telling Kate that he is a woman. She obediently addresses Vincentio as 'young budding virgin, fair and fresh and sweet'. A moment later Petruchio decides that Vincentio is a man, who is duly addressed as 'old father' and 'good old grandsire'. Several other characters in the Shakespeare plays undergo vocative sex-changes, usually because they are in disguise. They are not as confused as Vincentio by the terms used to them.

As I have said, allowances must sometimes be made for distortion in reports of vocative usage in literary sources. I have assessed individual instances on the basis of my own experience as a native-speaker, one who has been professionally concerned with the use of English for thirty-five years. I have also added to the dictionary examples of vocative usage based on my own observation, plus examples that have occurred in radio and television plays. Some extra information has come in letters from private individuals, especially in response to broadcasts in which I have discussed terms of address.

Nevertheless, the novelists have been my main sources. There is another advantage to using them in that they sometimes comment very specifically and intelligently on vocative usage. For that reason, this book might also be described as a kind of socio-linguistic anthology, with a large number of distinguished contributors.

Background to this book

In conclusion, I append a few brief notes about the writing of this book, which has been some twenty years in the making. In 1969, when I was a lecturer in English at the University of Stockholm, I submitted a thesis to the Linguistics Department for the degree of Master of Arts. The thesis was entitled 'A Preliminary Survey of English Vocatives', and it was duly accepted by the university authorities.

In that thesis I examined every occurrence of a term of address in fifty novels, 17,240 occurrences in all. Since 1969, during most of which time I have been producing English-teaching radio and television programmes for the BBC, I have continued to collect vocative examples. I have read during that period at least 450 novels, or some 24,000,000 words, which serve as the corpus for this book. Individual sources, incidentally, are mentioned in the entries, rather than in a separate Bibliography with subsequent references by initials or numbers, PhD thesis style.

I have, in fact, tried to distance myself as much as possible from thesis-style writing. The latter acts as a considerable barrier to me when I attempt to read theses, and I believe it would have erected unnecessary barriers in this book.

This dictionary is meant to be accessible to various categories of people, many of whom will not read this Introduction.

Personally I do not think that matters. It is the English language which is important, in all its marvellous complexity, not one person's thoughts about aspects of its usage. As a lifelong lover of that language, I have enjoyed learning a great deal more about it while compiling this dictionary. I can only hope that its readers will both enjoy it and learn from it in a similar way.

Leslie Dunkling

A Dictionary of
Epithets
and
Terms of
Address

Abbot, Father This would be the correct way of addressing the head of an abbey. The original meaning of 'abbot' was 'father', so the expression is tautological. 'Abbot' is sometimes used on its own in direct address. In *Henry the Eighth* Shakespeare has Griffith give an account of Cardinal Wolsey's death:

> the reverend abbot,
> With all his convent, honourably receiv'd him;
> To whom he gave these words: 'O father Abbot,
> An old man, broken with the storms of state,
> Is come to lay his weary bones among ye.'

Ace In American slang this word has many meanings. Applied to a person it implies great skill, great decency of character or close friendship. It is often a permanent nickname, but can be applied in an *ad hoc* way as a vocative. It is so used in *Only a Game*, by Robert Daley, where a woman uses it sarcastically to her husband.

Admiral The title of a naval officer of the highest rank. In Britain the Admiral of the Fleet compares with a Field-marshal in the army; an admiral compares with a general; a vice-admiral with a lieutenant-general; a rear-admiral with a major-general.

The title could easily be jokingly misused to someone as a hotel doorman, dressed in an imposing uniform. In *Persuasion*, by Jane Austen, occurs: ' "I have let my house to Admiral Croft" would sound extremely well; very much better than to any mere *Mr* – ; a *Mr* (save, perhaps, some half dozen in the nation), always needs a note of explanation.'

Ahasuerus, King A transferred name which is used by Jane to Mr Rochester in Charlotte Brontë's *Jane Eyre*. Jane asks him to gratify her curiosity about something, now that they are to be married. Rochester says: 'I wish that instead of a mere inquiry into, perhaps, a secret, it was a wish for half my estate.' Jane replies: 'Now, King Ahasuerus! What do I want with half your estate? Do you think I am a Jew usurer, seeking good investment in land?'

Jane is referring to the *Book of Esther*, in the Old Testament, where Ahasuerus (otherwise Xerxes, the Greek form of his name) marries Esther, a Jewess, after dismissing his wife Vashti. Esther manages to save her people

from the plotting of Haman, because the king says to her: 'What is your petition, Queen Esther? It shall be granted you. And what is your request? Even to the half of my kingdom it shall be fulfilled.' Esther asks instead that her people should be protected.

Nineteenth-century readers were expected to pick up these biblical references, steeped as they were in bible stories and characters. Miss Brontë's reference to this particular incident, however, is somewhat marred by the sentence that follows, with its talk of 'Jew usurer', totally irrelevant in this context. It must have been especially offensive to her Jewish readers, who would all have recognized the name of Ahasuerus and understood the allusion. The victory of Esther and her uncle Mordecai over Haman is celebrated yearly in the feast of Purim.

Alderman An ancient title originally applied to one who was an alder, or elder, the chief of a clan. More recently the title in Britain of a senior member of a local council, elected by the other councillors. In the US an alderman is a member of the governing body of a city.

The term can be used on its own to such a person, or as a prefix followed by his or her family name. An example of the latter usage occurs in *The Fox in the Attic*, by Richard Hughes, where the full vocative expression is 'Alderman' + last name, 'dear lad'.

All Used collectively to a group of people. 'I'm afraid I really must be off', says Jim Dixon in *Lucky Jim*, by Kingsley Amis, 'Goodbye, all.' A customer entering a pub in Britain is likely to greet those present with 'Evening, all.' All may also be added to a plural vocative expression to round it off, though such usage is now rather archaic. 'Take your places, my dear friends all,' says Zenobia, in *The Blithedale Romance*, by Nathaniel Hawthorne.

It is more often used in modern times as a prefix, followed by a noun, as in a call put out by a central radio operator to 'all cars'. 'All stations' is in *Goldfinger*, by Ian Fleming. 'All you flies out there', in *Georgy Girl*, by Margaret Forster, is addressed to a group of children who have been told to come into the room as flies by a dancing teacher. *Lord of the Flies*, by William Golding, has a boy addressing a group of younger boys as 'all you littluns'. A deeply religious man in *The Heart is a Lonely*

Hunter, by Carson McCullers, uses 'all ye disconsolate and sore of heart'.

Alligator This vocative occurs almost exclusively as part of the phrase 'See you later, alligator.' That expression became popular in the 1930s, when an 'alligator' in American slang was a devotee of jive and swing music.

The *New Dictionary of American Slang* says that in black American slang alligator is still used of a flashily dressed, assertive male who prides himself on being up to the minute.

The popular rock and roll number performed by Bill Haley and the Comets, 'See you Later, Alligator' spread the expression to Britain in the 1960s, and the whole phrase is still likely to be heard when two people say goodbye. It is sometimes followed, as in John Updike's *Bech: A Book*, by the response suggested in the song: 'In a while, crocodile.' In *Surfacing*, by Margaret Atwood, 'See you later, alligator' is addressed to a woman by a man. This may well be evidence that many users of the phrase are unaware of the precise slang meaning of alligator but are using a quotation which seems appropriate to the situation.

All of you A collective vocative used to three or more people of either sex and of any age. 'Do, *all* of you, come over for drinks tomorrow' says a woman in *Thursday Afternoons*, by Monica Dickens. There are further examples of its use in *Doctor in the House*, by Richard Gordon; *A Kind of Loving*, by Stan Barstow; *Lord of the Flies*, by William Golding; *The Limits of Love*, by Frederic Raphael; *Under the Volcano*, by Malcolm Lowry. The expression is sometimes expanded to include a specific number, as in *Howard's End*, by E.M. Forster, which has: 'Come in, all three of you!' cried his father.

Altos Addressed to a group of choirboys in *Lord of the Flies*, by William Golding. Male altos have singing voices in the highest range for men; female altos are in the lowest range for women. The term is typically one which would be used by a conductor at a choir practice. 'Tenors' occurs in *Lucky Jim*, by Kingsley Amis, in such a context.

Ambassador An ambassador is formally addressed as 'Your Excellency', but the British ambassador in *Don't Tell Alfred*, by Nancy Mitford, is 'my dear Ambassador' to one of his French colleagues. This expression manages to be both friendly and polite at the same time.

Ambassadress, Mrs This is used to address the wife of the British ambassador to France in *Don't Tell Alfred*, by Nancy Mitford. The speaker is American. He also extends the expression on occasion to 'Mrs Ambassadress, ma'am'. The lady concerned should of course be addressed as 'Mrs' or 'Lady' (as appropriate) + last name, but some speakers do have a tendency to combine a social title with a professional one when addressing the wife of a professional man. She becomes 'Mrs Doctor', 'Mrs Vicar', etc. In some languages this would be a correct form of address.

Americans, you This type of inclusive vocative is discussed in the article on **You + category of person**. An example of 'you Americans' occurs in *The Critic*, by Wilfrid Sheed.

Amigo The Spanish word for 'friend', but frequently used by English-speakers, especially Americans, who assume that even those who do not speak Spanish will at least understand this word. The editors of *Webster's New Collegiate Dictionary* feel that it is English enough to include it, a lead followed by several recent dictionaries published in Britain. It sometimes occurs in the plural form *amigos*.

Anarchists, you *See* **You + category of person**.

Angel A term which likens the person being addressed to a spiritual being who acts as a divine messenger, if one interprets it literally, that is. More usually it reflects the speaker's reaction to the charm and innocence of the other person, who is often a young child or a love-partner.

Romeo calls Juliet his 'bright angel', while Tom Jones, in Henry Fielding's novel of that name, assails his Sophia with 'my charming angel', 'my divine angel', 'my angel'. That was perhaps suitable for an eighteenth-century miss, but her twentieth-century counterpart would perhaps think such terms excessive.

It is noticeable that in a 1988 BBC television series which features a father who hopelessly spoils his daughter, he addresses her as 'my angel' several times each episode. 'Angel' was given full name status by the thirteenth century and is to be found in many Christian countries in forms such as Angelo and Angela.

Neither the name or vocative appealed to Mr Weller Senior, in *The Pickwick Papers*, by Charles Dickens. At one point he says to his son: 'Wot's the good o' callin' a young 'ooman a Wenus or a angel, Sammy?' 'Ah! what, indeed?' replies Sam. 'You might jist as well call her a griffin, or a unicorn, or a king's arms at once, which is wery well known to be a col-lection o' fabulous animals.' British readers would recognize in this an allusion to popular pub names, of which the Angel is one. The Wellers may be right in saying that a woman should not be called 'angel', but Jerome K. Jerome advanced powerful arguments for using the term to a baby in his *Idle Thoughts of an Idle Fellow*.

If you desire to drain to the dregs the fullest cup of scorn and hatred that a fellow human creature can pour out for you, let a young mother hear you call her dear baby 'it'. Your best plan is to address the article as 'little angel'. The noun 'angel' being of common gender suits the case admirably, and the epithet is sure of being favourably received. 'Pet' or 'beauty' are useful for variety's sake, but 'angel' is the term that brings you the greatest credit for sense and good feeling. The word should be preceded by a short giggle, and accompanied by as much smile as possible.

Addressed to adults, angel is used as an intimate term of address in *The Bell*, by Iris Murdoch and *The Half Hunter*, by John Sherwood. The latter novel also has 'my angel' used between lovers. 'My angel' occurs again in *The Pumpkin Eater*, by Penelope Mortimer. 'Darling angel', when it is used in *The Country Girls*, by Edna O'Brien, is merely friendly rather than intimate, the speaker being one who makes little distinction between acquaintances and intimate friends when it comes to vocative usage.

Animal Shakespeare does not use 'animal' as a vocative: had he done so it would have implied stupidity. In *Love's Labour's Lost* (4:ii) Sir Nathaniel describes Dull, the constable by saying: 'He hath never fed of the dainties that are bred in a book; he hath not eat paper, as it were; he hath not drunk ink; his intellect is not replenished; he is only an animal, only sensible in the duller parts.'

In modern times 'animal' seems often to be used between love-partners, as a covert compliment referring to sexual appetite and performance. 'You animal' is thus used by an American woman to a man in *The Late Risers*, by Bernard Wolfe.

'Animal' is used by an American man to a woman in *The Middle Man*, by David Chandler, when the woman invites him to make love to her. Spectators at e.g., a football match who are calling a player 'animal' mean it as an insult. The term is addressed to a player who is committing many fouls and behaving in a brutish way.

Animals Vocatives addressed to animals have not been dealt with separately in this book, but a few general observations may be made. The animals mainly addressed are dogs, cats, and horses, and the most frequent term used to them is the individual name of the animal concerned.

In fifty representative novels, animal names were used vocatively thirty-seven times. Generic and conventional terms also occurred, of the type: doggy, good dog, little cat, my cat, my puss, puss, pussy. In Malcolm Lowry's *Under the Volcano* a speaker plays about with 'puss' to produce vocative expressions such as 'my little Oedipusspusspuss', 'my little Priapuspuss'. Generic terms such as 'boy' and 'girl', 'clever boy', 'clever girl', 'good boy', 'good girl', etc., are regularly used, together with endearments such as 'beautiful', 'darling', 'my little pretty', 'my lovely, pretty girl'.

Some expressions, such as 'clever boy' or 'good boy', have become especially associated with animals, so that a person to whom such terms are addressed may find then odd. Clearly it is not so much the words used that matter when an animal is addressed as the tone in which they are said. Dogs will readily wag their tails when verbally abused, if the tone of voice makes them think they are being verbally caressed.

Animals are sometimes used as intermediaries, as indicated in *An Error of Judgement*, by Pamela Hansford Johnson. A mother-in-law who is in the room with her daughter and son-in-law addresses her cat: 'No, Puss, I am not going to let them turn you off my knee, am I? Because when they've gone to the far-flung Amerikeys, you're going to be all I have in the world.' The cat may not understand much of this, but the speaker knows that the intended hearers will get the message. The quotation also shows the common tendency to lapse into baby-talk when addressing an animal.

One would not normally expect animals to be the speakers of vocatives, but *The Limits of Love*, by Frederic Raphael, has a parrot which says 'Morning, Comrade.'

Ankle-biter A children's word for a very short person, applied as an instant nickname. *See also* **Tich**.

Anybody *See* **Anyone**.

Any of you A collective or indefinite vocative, interchangeable with anybody/anyone when more than two persons other than the speaker are present.

Anyone, Anybody In *The Taste of Too Much*, by Clifford Hanley, a woman says: 'Now there's no need to be nervous, anyone. Mr Garside isn't going to ask why he hasn't seen anyone at church recently.' The anyone in this instance refers to two young people who have just entered the room, the speaker and the vicar being there already. 'Anyone' could have become 'anybody', or for that matter, 'either of you'. Perhaps the latter term was not selected because the speaker was indirectly addressing the vicar as well, warning him not to ask awkward questions.

In *The Half Hunter*, by John Sherwood, a speaker who is approaching a group of friends, seated at a table, says: 'Don't look round, anyone.' In these examples 'anyone' is a collective term of address, in spite of its singular appearance. In each case the reference is clearly to more than one person.

Compare the use of 'anyone' or 'anybody' by the hostess of a party who asks: 'Coffee, anyone?' 'Anyone' is now an indefinite vocative. Whoever hears it can choose to apply it to himself if he wishes. Use of this vocative requires such positive identification. If the speaker said 'Coffee, everybody?' a negative identification would be required from anyone who did not wish to be included in the collective term.

Brothers in Law, by Henry Cecil, shows an expanded form of 'any' being used as an indefinite vocative. In a courtroom scene the judge says: 'Now, does anyone want to mention any of the cases?' A solicitor tries to attract his attention, whereupon the judge continues: 'Any member of the Bar.' *Thursday Afternoons*, by Monica Dickens, has a lecturer who has failed to get an answer from the student he has just addressed. He therefore says: 'Anyone else?'

Anzac Used to an Australian man by his wife in *A Salute to the Great McCarthy*, by Barry Oakley, 'Mr McCarthy here's going to give a demonstration. Show 'em how, you great big Anzac.' Anzac is an acronym formed from the initials of the Australian and New Zealand Army Corps. The word was coined in 1915 for telegraphic use and is well known to every Australian because of Anzac Day, celebrated on 25 April.

Ape In modern American usage 'you big ape' would normally be applied playfully to a muscular, but perhaps clumsy, man. According to *A Dictionary of American Slang*, by Robert Chapman, it can also mean a black person. It has perhaps that meaning in *Gone With The Wind*, by Margaret Mitchell, where one black servant calls another 'you pious black ape'.

Shakespeare uses 'ape' vocatively to mean 'foolish person', as in *Henry the Fourth Part One* (2:iii) where Lady Percy asks her husband 'What is it carries you away?' 'Why, my horse, my love, my horse,' replies Hotspur. 'Out, you mad-headed ape,' says the irritated lady. In *Henry the Fourth Part Two* (2:iv) Doll Tearsheet says to Falstaff: 'Ah, you sweet little rogue, you! Alas, poor ape, how thou sweat'st! Come, let me wipe thy face. Come on, you whoreson chops. Ah, rogue! i' faith, I love thee.'

Doll is adept at using insults, as she shows elsewhere, but here she clearly converts them to covert endearments. *A Salute to the Great McCarthy*, by Barry Oakley, has 'you great ape'

used by an Australian girl to a young man who is of impressive physique, a professional football player.

Arbuckle, Fatty *See* **Harbuckle, Fatty**.

Archbishop An Anglican archbishop is normally addressed in this way: a Roman Catholic archbishop is addressed formally as 'your Grace'.

Archdeacon The title in the Anglican Church of the chief deacon, who serves as an assistant to the bishop. An amusing instance of its use occurs in *The Warden*, by Anthony Trollope. '"As to his vulgarity, archdeacon" (Mrs Grantly had never assumed a more familiar term than this in addressing her husband), "I don't agree with you."' The archdeacon and his wife are in bed at the time.

Aristocrats, you *See* **You + category of person**.

Arsehole, you A coarse reference to the anus, expressing contempt. An example occurs in *Redback*, by Howard Jacobson, where the speaker is an Australian male and is talking to another man. The normal American spelling is 'asshole'.

Artemis The name of a Greek goddess, used by Alec D'Urberville to Tess in Thomas Hardy's *Tess of the D'Urbervilles*. 'He called her Artemis, Demeter, and other fanciful names half teasingly, which she did not like because she did not understand them. "Call me Tess," she would say askance, and he did.' Demeter was another Greek goddess, identified with Ceres, goddess of corn and patroness of agriculture. The name therefore has a certain suitability for Tess, who works for the D'Urberville family as a poultry keeper. It seems likely, however, that Alec's use of these transferred names was inspired by the thought that Tess was goddess-like. Hardy's remark about Tess not liking the names because she did not understand them is interesting, and shows the danger inherent in using transferred names of any kind. The allusion must be meaningful to the listener as well as the speaker. If the allusion is not understood then there will be a tendency, as when a person knows that he is being talked about by others but cannot hear what they are saying, to assume the worst, that one is being made the butt of jokes.

Artist This word never stands alone as a vocative, but is an element in expressions like 'bullshit artist', 'crap artist'. *Portnoy's Complaint*, by Philip Roth, has the hero calling himself 'you jerk-off artist', referring to his skill at masturbation. *St Urbain's Horseman*, by Moredecai Richler, has one man saying to another: 'What's to be done with you? Crap artist. You broke?' 'Crap' here is a synonym for 'bullshit', a reference to pretentious, nonsensical talk.

Ass 'This plaintiff here', says Dogberry the constable, in Shakespeare's *Much Ado About Nothing* (5:i) 'did call me ass; I beseech you, let it be rememb'red in his punishment.' Dogberry is certainly not alone amongst Shakespearean characters in being likened to a donkey. 'Thou whoreson ass' occurs in *The Two Gentlemen of Verona* (2:v), 'preposterous ass' in *Taming of the Shrew* (3:i), 'thou scurvy valiant ass' is in *Troilus and Cressida* (2:i), while in *A Midsummer Night's Dream* an ass is made of Bottom the Weaver in no uncertain terms.

In modern times, 'ass' is a fairly mild insult when it refers to the animal. 'You feeble ass' is said by a boy to a girl in *Mariana*, by Monica Dickens, but it arouses no great passion. There is a similar 'you soppy ass' said by one boy to another in *End of a Summer's Day*, by Adrian Vincent. 'Ass' by itself becomes a covert endearment between lovers in *The Limits of Love*, by Frederic Raphael, *Unconditional Surrender*, by Evelyn Waugh, and *An American Dream*, by Norman Mailer. Fortunately, in the latter, there is a clear indication that the animal is meant. ' "You're rude. In fact . . ." "Yes?" "*Ass*" she said with a Southern bray, and we beamed at each other.' Later, in the same novel, several instances of 'you ass' occur where the buttocks are referred to, as in 'you ass-hole' (British 'arse-hole'). The useful clue given in context is the fact that one speaker uses 'you black-ass ego' as well as 'you ass', while another speaker switches to 'you jackass' when he means the animal, otherwise the spelling 'ass' is decidedly ambiguous when used by an American writer. From an etymological point of view, 'arse' is certainly the correct form to use when referring to the buttocks. 'Ass' for 'arse' had developed as a dialectal pronunciation by the mid-nineteenth century in Britain, but did not replace the normal arse pronunciation as in the USA.

Asshole The normal American spelling of 'arsehole'. The word is used vocatively on its own, and often as 'you asshole'. In the latter form it is said by one American boy to another in *Boulevard Nights*, by Dewey Gram, and by an American woman to her lover in *Oliver's Story*, by Erich Segal. *The Choirboys*, by Joseph Wambaugh, has the following:

If there was one thing Roscoe Rules [a Los Angeles policeman] wished, after having seen all of the world he cared to see, it was that there was a word as dirty as 'nigger' to apply to all mankind. Since he had little

imagination he had to settle for 'asshole.' But he realized that all Los Angeles policemen and most American policemen used that as the best of all possible words.

Ass-licker Said of someone who flatters a superior in order to gain his good favour and win advancement. In American slang 'ass-kisser' or 'ass-sucker' could also occur: 'ass-licker' has the British equivalent 'arse-licker'. In *The Critic*, by Wilfrid Sheed, 'you little ass-licker' is said by one American man to another, and is equated with 'shitface'.

Attendant An attendant in former times would have been a man or woman who attended upon a nobleman. Shakespeare uses the word many times with this meaning, though never in direct address. Today the word is most often used vocatively to the attendant in a parking lot or petrol station.

Auctioneer The original meaning of 'auction' is 'to increase, augment'. The auctioneer is one who raises the sale price of an object in stages. His attention is usually gained by some kind of visual signal, but he may be addressed by his professional title. In *The House with the Green Shutters*, by George Douglas, the vocative is spelt 'owctioner', to indicate the Scottish pronunciation of the speaker. In Sheridan's *The School for Scandal*, where Careless volunteers to act as an auctioneer for Charles Surface, we have: 'But come, get to your pulpit, Mr Auctioneer; here's an old gouty chair of my father's will answer the purpose.' Perhaps the most famous auction scene in literature occurs in *The Mayor of Casterbridge*, by Thomas Hardy, when Michael Henchard offers to sell his wife. A bystander offers to act as auctioneer and is thereafter addressed as such by Henchard. A mocking offer of five shillings begins the sale, but Susan and her daughter Elizabeth Jane are eventually auctioned for five guineas. The rest of the novel examines the consequences of this action.

Aunt The first name of the aunt concerned normally follows this term in direct address, especially when young nephews and nieces are using it. As they become adults they are more likely to use 'aunt' on its own, or to make use of the first name. Both true aunts, sisters of the speaker's father or mother, and aunts-in-law are considered eligible for the title.

In working-class British families it is also often extended to close friends of the parents, though only young children would use the term in such a case. Middle-class speakers might qualify the word and use 'my dear aunt', with or without the first name.

'Good aunt', 'sweet aunt', and the like were possible in Shakespeare's time, according to the evidence of the plays, but this would be most unusual in modern times. It was also possible in the seventeenth century to refer to an aunt and mean a procuress or a prostitute, but such usage is obsolete.

Flora Thompson, in *Lark Rise*, says that her mother was a late-comer, born when her parents were well advanced in years: 'One of her outstanding distinctions in the eyes of her own children was that she had been born an aunt and, as soon as she could talk, had insisted upon her two nieces, both older than herself, addressing her as "Aunt Emma."'

In *Jane Eyre*, by Charlotte Brontë, Mrs Reed is Jane's aunt and guardian, and is normally addressed by her as Aunt Reed. Early in the novel, disgusted by her aunt's ill-treatment of her, Jane says: 'I will never call you aunt again as long as I live,' but years later she again calls her Aunt Reed, saying 'I thought it no sin to forget and break that vow now.' Mrs Reed is by then on her death-bed.

Auntie A diminutive of aunt, used mainly by young children to a real aunt, or to a close female friend of the family. The word is sometimes followed by the first name of the woman concerned. Auntie may also be used by adult speakers, especially by women, but the comment by Raymond Williams in *Border Country* is relevant: ' "We go to the pictures, Auntie," Janie said, breaking into the conversation like a child. She was in her early thirties, but still had a child's intonation and manners.' This is not to say that any adult using 'Auntie' is retarded, of course, but the word does have a childish ring to it.

At one time it became customary in the American South to address older black people as 'Uncle' and 'Auntie'. H.L. Mencken suggested, in *The American Language*, that this custom arose because the whites were reluctant to use 'ordinary American honorifics', by which he meant terms like 'Mr' and 'Mrs', when referring to blacks. The blacks themselves came to detest the contemptuous patronage, as they saw it, of the 'Uncle' and 'Auntie' terms. Their cause, perhaps, was not helped by Harriet Beecher Stowe's well-meaning book, *Uncle Tom's Cabin*. We are never told the family name of Uncle Tom or Aunt Chloe, his wife, and they are certainly never addressed as 'Mr' or 'Mrs'.

A jocular misuse of 'Auntie' occurs in *The Amberstone Exit*, by Elaine Feinstein. A woman is in a railway compartment with some young football supporters who are annoying her. 'The big boy leant forward and looked closely into her face. "How old do you reckon?" he consulted his friends. "I'm twenty-one," she said. At that, they let out hoots of derision, "Give us a kiss, Auntie," someone shouted.'

Aussie Used affectionately by an American speaker to a young Australian woman in *War Brides*, by Lois Battle. The man occasionally uses the term after he has married the woman concerned and moved with her to live in the USA.

Baa-lamb This nursery word for 'lamb' is occasionally used as a euphemism for 'bastard'. e.g. by working-class speakers in London.

Baas The Dutch word for 'master', earlier 'uncle'. It gave rise to 'boss' in normal English, but is retained in its Dutch form in South Africa. Commonly used by black Africans to address white men, as in *Resolve This Day*, by Geoffrey Bainbridge, where 'baas' and 'my baas' are used by a black South African woman to address a white policeman. The term is occasionally used by white speakers to one another in mock humility.

Bab A dialectal form of 'babe' or 'baby'. 'Night-night my beautiful bab' is said by a girl to her sweetheart in *Cider with Rosie*, by Laurie Lee.

Babby, you *See* **Cry-baby**.

Babe This word has been overtaken in general use by its own diminutive form, 'baby'. It was still the more common form in Shakespeare's time, and occurs as a vocative in *The Winter's Tale* (2:iii) where Antigonus says to the infant Perdita: 'Come on, poor babe,/Some powerful spirit instruct the kites and ravens/To be thy nurses.' He has just been instructed to take the infant 'to some remote and desert place' and abandon it. 'Babe' is rarely used in normal modern speech, though a highly literary character in *Laura*, by Vera Caspary, addresses a woman friend as 'my dear babe'. More usually today 'babe' represents an abbreviated form of 'baby'. *The Choirboys*, by Joseph Wambaugh, has a Los Angeles policeman saying to his junior partner: 'Remember one thing, babe, don't never try to overtake a fast car on the outside when you're going in a turn.' This form is extended to 'babes' in *The Philanderer*, by Stanley Kauffmann, where an American greets his wife with 'Lynn, babes, what's the matter?' *The Critic*, by Wilfred Sheed, has a similar 'Nice going, Max babes', said by one American man to another.

Baboon It has been possible to use 'baboon' as a friendly insult since at least the seventeenth century. In Ben Jonson's *The Alchemist* 'my good baboon' occurs, and modern women are likely to refer to clumsy men as 'you big baboon' without too much rancour. In *Resolve This Day*, by Geoffrey Bainbridge, 'you big, ugly baboon' is clearly more genuinely insulting. In Henry Williamson's *Dandelion Days* a schoolmaster calls a boy 'bottle-eyed baboon' equating it with 'long-eared ass' and 'snivelling snipe'. The teacher concerned revels in the inventiveness of his vocative expressions. The more usual modern usage occurs in *Like Any Other Man*, by Patrick Boyle: 'Delia pushed away the pawing hands. "None of that, you big baboon."' The man doing the pawing has been the woman's lover, and there is no real animosity in what she says.

Baby This vocative is occasionally addressed to a real baby, an infant too young to speak. 'We know papa better, don't we, baby?' says the wife of the narrator, in *The Newcomes*, by William Thackeray. He adds: 'Here my wife kisses the infant Pendennis with great effusion.' A young girl similarly addresses a baby in *Jennifer*, by Janet Whitney. To an older child, or an adult, the use of 'baby' can imply childish behaviour. Children, especially, are likely to be very upset if called 'baby', 'cry-baby', or similar terms. In *The Trumpet Major*, by Thomas Hardy, 'you jealous baby' is said scornfully by one woman to another. 'Baby' is also used in a friendly or intimate way to adults, usually to someone of the opposite sex to the speaker. 'Listen, baby', says a man to a woman acquaintance in *World So Wide*, by Sinclair Lewis, 'I hate this formality among us Yanks, even when we're in Europe. I wish you'd call me Lorenzo, or maybe Larry. I'm certainly going to call you Livy.' A possible reaction to such usage is seen in *Thanksgiving*, by Robert Jordan: 'Be reasonable, baby,' 'Don't call me baby. I'm not your baby'; this is a woman reacting to the term. In Malcolm Bradbury's *Eating People Is Wrong* a woman says to a man

'Fasten me up at the back, my baby', causing him to think: 'My baby', there it was again, as always. Treece was the sort of man that people always wanted to mother, or father: indeed, as someone had once said of him in the old bohemian days in London: 'Some men go around leaving illegitimate children; Stuart leaves illegitimate parents,'

Other intimate uses of 'my baby' or 'poor baby' occur in *An Error of Judgement*, by Pamela Hansford Johnson and *The Sophomore*, by

Barry Spacks. These once again occur between the sexes, whereas 'Baby, you got to' is addressed to a man by a man in *An American Dream*, by Norman Mailer. The present author has also been addressed as 'baby' by a man, an English journalist who used the term to address almost everyone. Such usage is friendly rather than intimate, on a par with the working man's use of 'baby' to a passing woman. This could be heard in Britain, but would tend to be an imitation of American usage. There is a special use of 'Baby' in *Tender is the Night*, by F. Scott Fitzgerald. Nicole's sister is named Beth, 'but she's always been called Baby'. *War Brides*, by Lois Battle, has the interesting 'baby' + first name, addressed to a tiny baby: 'He's been a cranky little dickens, haven't oo, baby Joe?'

Baby bunting *See* **Cry-baby**.

Baby-doll, you An expression of the 1920s in the USA, expressing admiration for a young lady on the part of a young man. The expression was not always appreciated by women of the time. In *Main Street*, by Sinclair Lewis, occurs:

> She was sickened by glimpses of the gang of boys from fourteen to twenty who loafed before Dyer's Drug Store, smoking cigarettes, displaying 'fancy' shoes and purple ties and coats of diamond-shaped buttons, whistling the Hoochi-Koochi and catcalling, 'Oh, you baby-doll' at every passing girl.

The expression is apparently not extinct: in *Daughters of Mulberry*, by Roger Longrigg, 'baby doll' is used as a friendly vocative by an English woman to a man who is a stranger to her. *A Woman Called Fancy*, by Frank Yerby, has an American man using it to a young woman, equating it with 'honey-child' and 'baby'. In *My Side of the Matter*, a short story by Truman Capote, it is a young wife who says to her husband, 'Go on, babydoll,' Chapman's *Dictionary of American Slang* mentions that males can occasionally be addressed by the 'baby' terms.

Babykins Used by a mother to her daughter, aged about eight, in *Gideon Planish*, by Sinclair Lewis. *See* **kins**.

Babylonian Used insultingly by one man to another in *The Heart is a Lonely Hunter*, by Carson McCullers. The speaker is a religious fanatic and presumably means that the man he is addressing is devoted to the pursuit of sensual pleasure. Babylon was in ancient times a city with a reputation for materialism and the pursuit of luxury. At one time a Babylonian could also have been a papist, thanks to the identification of Rome with the scarlet woman

mentioned in the New Testament, *Revelations* 17. It seems unlikely that many people would understand what they were being accused of if 'Babylonian' was hurled at them as an insult. The term would only be used by those immersed in biblical language and allusions. The speaker who uses it in the McCullers novel also uses such terms as 'child of Sodom', 'sinner', 'child of adversity'.

Baby-pie This occurs as an endearment in *An American Dream*, by Norman Mailer, used by a woman to a man. In his *Dictionary of American Slang* Robert Chapman lists 'baby-cakes' (or 'honeycakes') as a term of endearment. 'Baby-pie' appears to be a blend of 'baby' and 'honey-pie'.

Bacall, Miss This is used as a kind of type name in *Kimmie*, by John Paddy Carstairs. The reference is to the well-known actress Lauren Bacall (born Betty Joan Perske) and her name is used because it is recognizably that of an actress. The passage in the novel runs as follows: ' "Mornin' Miss Bacall!" she yelled out. That was Priscilla's daily joke. She thought of an actress, usually a most unsuitable comparison, and chi-acked Kimmie with a new name every day.' Kimmie, the heroine of the novel, is an aspiring young actress.

bach The Welsh word for 'little', used by speakers of Welsh, even when speaking English, to form a diminutive by attaching it to, e.g., a first name. Four examples of first name + *bach* occur in *Henry's War*, by Jeremy Brooks. The same novel also has two examples of the common Welsh term of address *mochyn bach*, plus four examples of this term translated into English as 'little pig'. *The Fox in the Attic*, by Richard Hughes, has two examples of Doctor *bach*. *Fares Please*, by Edith Courtney, has *bach* used on its own as a friendly term of address, used by a Welsh woman to another woman.

Bag, you old A contemptuous and insulting term used to a middle-aged or older woman. The earlier term was 'baggage'. This is one of those instances where 'old' is itself used insultingly. In *Festival*, by N.J. Crisp, occurs: 'Oh, shut up, you hypocritical old bag', addressed by one woman to another. There is a rather similar 'Shut up, you horrid old Austrian bag' addressed to an Austrian woman by an Englishman in *The Half Hunter*, by John Sherwood.

Baggage At the beginning of the seventeenth century it was possible to call a man 'a baggage', meaning that he was a worthless fellow, a nuisance. Apart from its luggage sense, the word at that time had also come to mean 'rubbish' or 'refuse'. Applied to women in the early seventeenth century, 'baggage' meant a prostitute or a thoroughly worthless woman. By the latter half of that century, its meaning had considerably softened. A girl could now be called a sly or saucy baggage and would interpret the word as 'wench' or 'rogue'. It is sometimes difficult to know, therefore, the exact force of 'you baggage' in a play like *Romeo and Juliet*, where Capulet uses it to his daughter. When Juliet tells him that she does not want to marry Paris he cries: 'Out, you baggage!' and equates this with 'you tallow-face', 'mistress minion', 'disobedient wretch', 'hilding'. From the early seventeenth century onwards it was only women who were called 'baggages'. The term would only be used now, one suspects, in a jokey way by a fairly literate speaker to a youngish woman. The really insulting use of 'baggage' has been transposed to 'you old bag' or 'bat'.

Bag o' bones *See* Spindleshanks.

Bairn One would expect the user of bairn to be Scottish or from the North of England, though this word for child was once in general use. Shakespeare used it in *The Winter's Tale*, spelling it 'barne'. The *Oxford English Dictionary* makes the interesting point that it stresses relationship rather than age. It is certainly used to an adult daughter in *When the Boat Comes In*, by James Mitchell: 'Come on, me bairn.' A Scottish girl says 'Don't greet so, my poor bairn,' to a young woman in Iris Murdoch's *The Word Child*, but is reproached by another character for using 'affected Scotticisms'. 'Bairn' could, of course, be used to a male child as well as a female. It is used by a man to his son in *The House with the Green Shutters*, by George Douglas, where the characters are Scottish, but there is at least a suggestion in context that the term is meant to be insulting. The son, who has been expelled from university, is considered to be acting like a young child by the speaker. In Charlotte Brontë's *Jane Eyre* an old countrywoman uses 'bairn' to address a young woman who is not related to her.

Baker Used as a term of address to a baker throughout *The House with the Green Shutters*, by George Douglas. The novel is set in a fictional Scottish town at the end of the nineteenth century. Bakers are not normally addressed by their professional title, though no doubt they were in early times, when their role in society was recognized as an important one. It was this, no doubt, which led to the present frequency of Baker as a family name.

Balloon, Barrage Balloon *See* Fatty.

Bandy Used of or to a person whose legs curve outwards at the knees. 'Hi, bandy, throw us a kiss!' is said to a bus-conductress by a cheeky young child in *Fares Please*, by Edith Courtney.

Banker This term is probably used more frequently to someone acting as banker in a game of cards or some other game, than to a person engaged in banking activities as a profession. In *What's Bred in the Bone*, by Robertson Davies, a speaker philosophizes about life in general, the basic thesis being that 'we are all dealt a hand of cards at birth' and that someone dealt a poor hand cannot expect to compete with someone dealt a full flush. The person listening to this replies that he is not a card-player, 'but I am a theologian, consequently I have a different idea of the stakes that are played for than you have, you banker'.

Bantam, young *See* **Cock**.

Barber, Mr Addressed to a barber by Tom in Fielding's *Tom Jones*. He also calls him *tonsor*, which is the Latin word for barber, and later says: 'Mr Barber, or Mr Surgeon, or Mr Barber-Surgeon . . .'. The latter terms are a reminder that in the eighteenth century barbers still practised surgery and dentistry, especially in country areas. Surgery officially separated from the trade of barber in 1745. The red and white poles still used to indicate a barber's shop are a reminder of blood and bandages and the former medical connection.

Bar-fly A slang term in both Britain and the USA for someone who spends a lot of time in bars; a heavy drinker or lush. 'You dirty little bar-fly' is used insultingly by one man to another in *Lucky Jim*, by Kingsley Amis.

Barmy A word which describes a person who is foolish or eccentric, perhaps a little crazy. 'Barm' is the froth that forms on the top of fermenting liquors, so 'barmy' means frothyheaded. The word is used in Britain rather than elsewhere, and is still thought of as slang. It occurs only rarely as a vocative, but there is an instance in *The Pumpkin Eater*, by Penelope Mortimer. A girl is advising a friend to keep boys at a distance, because it 'drives them absolutely wild'. 'Supposing you don't feel snooty?' says her friend. She replies: 'Well, of course you don't, barmy. You just pretend to.'

Baron An English baron would normally be addressed as 'Lord' + family name or 'my Lord'; his wife, a baroness, would be 'Lady' + family name or 'my Lady'. 'Baron' might well be used, however, to address a European holder of the title, as in *The Fox in the Attic*, by Richard Hughes. *Herr Baron* also occurs in the same novel.

Barrel, Barrel-belly   *See* **Fatty**.

Bartender   The American term for a barman, one who serves drinks in a bar. ' "Bartender", shouted Romeo, "five Bromo-Seltzers," ' occurs in *An American Dream*, by Norman Mailer. *Sam*, by Lonnie Coleman, has: ' "Goodnight bartender," he said, leaving his loose change on the bar as a tip.' The British equivalent occurs in *Eating People Is Wrong*, by Malcolm Bradbury: 'Here, serve this man next, barman.'

Basket   *See* **Bastard**

Bass clarinet   *See* **Violins**.

Bastard   When it occurs as a vocative, 'bastard' seldom has its literal meaning of 'a child born out of wedlock'. It is almost a meaningless noise, expressing contempt for the person addressed. The charge of illegitimacy is in any case hardly an insult to the child concerned. It reproaches the parents, or as Dickens points out in *Oliver Twist*, the person who uses the word. It is Mr Brownlow who makes that point, when Monks has referred to Oliver as 'a bastard child'.

Like all insults, 'bastard' can easily be turned into an affectionate term. It needs only to be spoken in the right tone of voice and perhaps with a suitable qualifier. 'You big horny bastard' occurs in *The Exhibitionist*, by Henry Sutton. It is used by a woman to a man and is meant as a compliment, or as the novelist calls it, a 'thrilling vulgarity'. 'You rotten bastard', in *I'll Take Manhattan*, by Judith Krantz, is used by a girl to her brother and equated with the fairly mild 'you beast'.

Other intimate or friendly uses of the term occur as follows: 'you poor old bastard' in *Absolute Beginners*, by Colin MacInnes; 'you lovely bastards', in *The Business of Loving*, by Godfrey Smith; 'you handsome bastard', in *Goldfinger*, by Ian Fleming; 'you bloody bastard', in *The Hiding Place*, by Robert Shaw, (a novel which also has examples of 'you bastard' and 'you old bastard' used in a friendly way); 'you bastard' and 'you old bastard', in *The Limits of Love*, by Frederic Raphael; 'you bastard you', in *The River of Diamonds*, by Geoffrey Jenkins, where 'you stupid bastard' is also friendly; 'you poor bastard', in *The Spy Who Came in From The Cold*, by John le Carré; 'you cocky bastard', in *Saturday Night And Sunday Morning*, by Alan Sillitoe.

In many of these novels insulting uses of 'bastard' also occur. *Saturday Night And Sunday Morning*, for example, has examples of 'you bastard', 'you bastard you', 'you dirty bastard', 'you lying bastard', and 'you sly spine-less bastard' used as seriously intended insults. The instances quoted could easily be multiplied, emphasizing the frequency with which the word is used in one way or another. Occasionally a comment by the novelist accompanies it. Thus, in B.S. Johnson's *Travelling People* we find:

'You bluddy [*sic*] bastard, you ungrateful bluddy bastard.' Henry noticed that, while he had heard these two expletives used severally and in conjunction with others, oh, many, many times, he could not remember ever having heard them coupled before. This he found mildly interesting.

As it happens, there is nothing particularly unusual about this collocation.

Although 'bastard' is, as indicated above, a word that occurs frequently in modern times, there are still those writers and speakers who prefer to side-step it by using a euphemism, such as 'basket' or 'baa-lamb'. 'You old basket' occurs, for instance, in both *Julia*, by H.C. Harwood and *A Season In Love*, by Peter Draper, in a friendly way. *The Half Hunter*, by John Sherwood, has 'you dirty little basket' used as an insult. This euphemistic use of 'basket' appears to have eluded the lexicographers, for it does not appear in a number of dictionaries which have been consulted.

Bat   A reference to the bird-like, nocturnal mammal, usually applied to a woman as 'you old bat', implying that she is repulsive. 'You old bag' would be roughly synonymous. In *A Salute to the Great McCarthy*, by Barry Oakley, 'you vampire bat' is used to a young woman by her husband. The thought here is that she has used him for her own selfish purposes: 'You preyed on me, you vampire bat.'

Battery   One of the collective terms used in military circles, along with 'squad', 'platoon', 'parade', 'party', etc. A battery is a number of big guns assembled together, but the word can be applied to the officers and men who serve them. The order 'Battery, on parade!' is given by a sergeant in *The Magic Army*, by Leslie Thomas.

Bawcock   An English form of French *beau coq*, 'fine cock', used in the sense of 'fine fellow'. Shakespeare used it in two of his plays. 'Good bawcock, bate thy rage!' is in *Henry the Fifth* (3:ii). *Twelfth Night* (3:iv) has: 'Why, how now, my bawcock.' The word appears to have disappeared after the seventeenth century, though speakers who know their Shakespeare well may resuscitate it jokingly.

Bean, old   The *Glasgow Herald*, in 1920, equated the terms 'old bean' and 'old thing' and associated them with the English spoken by Piccadilly toffs. Sinclair Lewis seems to do something rather similar in *Babbitt*, published in 1922. He puts 'old bean' into the mouth of a visiting Englishman, Sir Gerald Doak. The first occurrence of the expression is in *Kipps*, by H. G. Wells, published in 1905, but there it is merely a passing reference to 'this old Bean', Bean being the name of a solicitor. The naming of the character and the use of this phrase may have been a deliberate joke on Wells's part, of course, the expression being already current.

The reason for 'bean' is difficult to guess at. Its slang meaning of 'head' may have helped, a meaning which might still be heard in the sense of beaning someone, i.e. hitting him on the head. Certainly many vocative expressions make use of 'head'. John Galsworthy tells us that 'old bean' was used by women as well as men. In *To Let* (1921) he writes about modern young girls,

> bare-necked, visible up to the knees . . . with their feet, too, screwed around the legs of their chairs while they ate, and their 'So longs' and their 'Old Beans', and their laughter – girls who gave him the shudders whenever he thought of Fleur in contact with them.

'Old Bean' is still occasionally heard in Britain, always humorously and usually in an accent which is supposed to imitate a high-society speaker. There is an example of such usage in *Georgy Girl*, by Margaret Forster, where a girl who bumps into a woman shopping in Knightsbridge, a high-society area, says 'Sorry, old bean' in a very hearty voice.

Bean pole An instant nickname bestowed on a tall, thin person. *See* **Spindleshanks**.

Beardie *See* **Whiskers**.

Beast, you It was at one time an expression of deep disgust to call someone 'you beast'. The speaker was usually a woman, and there would often be the suggestion that the man was being animalistic in his sexual attitudes. As Shakespeare put it, in *The Merry Wives of Windsor:* 'O powerful love, that in some respects makes a beast a man; in some other, a man a beast.' In *Measure for Measure* Isabella exclaims 'O you beast!' to her brother, because he does not opt for his own death before his sister's dishonour. Isabella has just told Claudio that she can only save his life by surrendering herself to Lord Angelo. He replies that 'what sin you do to save a brother's life . . . becomes a virtue,' causing Isabella to call him 'a beast, a faithless coward and dishonest wretch'.

'You beast' could still be used in modern times of a man 'under the sway of animal propensities', as the *Oxford English Dictionary* delightfully puts it. According to Bernard Thompson, in *Love in Quiet Places*, it can be used to a woman similarly swayed. A woman who has stolen another woman's man in that novel is addressed as 'you beast, you dirty filthy beast'. In another context, however 'you beast' has little more than the force of 'you rotter'. In Kipling's *Stalky and Co.* the schoolboys are constantly talking about 'beastly things' and 'beastly people', and calling each other names like 'you unmitigated beast'. 'Hullo, Orrin,' says Stalky at one point, 'you look rather metagrobolized.' 'It was all your fault, you beast!' says Orrin. The use of beast by one man to another in Mary Webb's *Gone to Earth* is made interesting by the dialectal comment that follows: 'Ed'ard! Dunna go for to miscall him!' This useful verb 'miscall', meaning to call someone bad names, to revile them, now appears to be obsolete other than in dialect. In Noel Coward's *Private Lives* the curtain falls at the end of act two as Amanda screams: 'Beast; brute; swine; cad; beast; beast; brute; devil –'

Beatitude, your Used as a title to a primate in the Eastern Church. *The Stork*, by Denison Hatch, has one man telling another that 'You address the Patriarch of Jerusalem as "your Beatitude" '. Beatitude means a state of blessedness. The word is pronounced *bee-attitude*. It is used on its own as an endearment in *Magnus Merriman*, by Eric Linklater, but the speaker who uses it to his lover uses English in rather an inflated way.

Beatnik This term had something of a vogue in the late 1950s and throughout the 1960s. It is said to have been invented by Herb Caen, a San Francisco newspaper columnist. The beat generation was alienated from normal society, advocating the use of drugs, sexually free behaviour, a peripatetic life, and so on. The ' –nik' ending undoubtedly came from the Russian satellite Sputnik I, which was launched on 4 October 1957. The suffix was at least temporarily active, bringing words like 'peacenik' and even 'Bachnik' into being, meaning 'one who is a devotee of'. The 1960s beatniks were distinguishable by their appearance, and may have been addressed by the term as suggested in *The Sophomore*, by Barry Spacks. There a man on a beach says to a young passer-by: 'Hey, Beatnik, watch what you're doing.'

Beautiful 'Hi there, beautiful!' is a typical working man's gambit to a young woman who happens to be passing or with whom he comes into contact for the first time. Women vary greatly in their reactions to it: there are those who greatly object to such personal remarks, others forgive the impertinence. It is interesting that Coverdale, translating the *Song of*

Solomon in the sixteenth century, arrived at: 'My love, my dove, my beautyfull.' The Revised Standard Version of the Bible has the less interesting: 'Arise, my love, my fair one, and come away.' Examples of relatively modern working-class use occur in *Absolute Beginners*, by Colin MacInnes and *Goldfinger*, by Ian Fleming. *The Taste of Too Much*, by Clifford Hanley, has a young lover addressing a girl as 'beautiful', 'beautiful' + first name.

Beauty In Beaumont and Fletcher's *The Wild-Goose Chase*, Lugier enters and says to two young ladies: 'Good day, fair beauties!' 'You have beautified us, we thank you, sir,' replies one of them. Viola, in *Twelfth Night* (1:v) addresses Olivia and Maria as 'good beauties', a moment earlier having called Olivia 'most radiant, exquisite, and unmatchable beauty'. This is presumably a joke, since Olivia is concealed beneath a veil at the time and Viola has no idea whether she is beautiful or not. It is also a hint that young ladies were conventionally called beauties at this time, regardless of their actual appearance. 'My beauty' used in modern times would be a typical form of address to a pet animal, though some speakers would still use it to a woman. In *Dover One*, by Joyce Porter, 'me old beauty' occurs twice as a friendly vocative to a man, the 'me' rather than 'my' indicating the working-class dialect speech of the character who uses it. The latter is a not very convincingly drawn rural 'character'.

Beaver *See* Whiskers.

Bebee This vocative is frequently used in *Lavengro*, by George Borrow. The author adds a glossary of 'gypsy words' as an appendix and explains that this word means grandmother or aunt. 'How old are you, bebee?' 'Sixty-five years, child.'

Beetroot *See* Ginger.

Beggar This is unlikely to have its literal meaning of one who begs when used vocatively. 'Lucky beggar!' said to a friend simply means lucky person. 'You little beggar' addressed to a child is similar to 'you little horror' or 'you little terror'. 'Beggar' in this context could be equated with 'rogue', 'rascal', etc. Some speakers may consciously use it as a euphemism for 'bugger', though there is no evidence to suggest that this was the original reason for its use. 'Beggar' is occasionally used with real disparagement. Shakespeare, for instance, who uses the word only once vocatively, equates it with dog in *Richard the Third* (1:ii):

Unmanner'd dog! Stand thou, when I command,

Advance thy halberd higher than my breast, Or, by St Paul, I'll strike thee to my foot And spurn upon thee, beggar, for thy boldness.'

An American Dream, by Norman Mailer, has: ' "You damned beggar!" I shouted at him. "You shit-face!" '

Beginners As a vocative, heard in the theatre backstage before a performance. 'Beginners, please', the traditional call by the stage-manager for the actors who have to be on stage for the opening scene of a play, is quoted in *Pray for the Wanderer*, by Kate O'Brien. In *Opening Night*, Ngaio Marsh, the call-boy of the theatre tours the dressing-rooms calling: 'Second Act beginners, please.'

Belly, Barrel, Fat belly, Jelly-belly *See* Fatty.

Beloved, dearly The conventional form of address by a priest to his congregation at, e.g. a wedding ceremony. The *Book of Common Prayer* also begins with 'Dearly beloved brethren' in the exhortation for the Morning Prayer. *A Kind of Loving*, by Stan Barstow, has: 'The organ stops and there's dead quiet for a minute. Then the vicar chimes up. "Dearly beloved, we are gathered together to join this man and this woman in holy matrimony . . .".' *The Bell*, by Iris Murdoch, has a man saying to another: 'Since you're in a hurry we'll cut out the hymns and prayers and go straight on to the sermon. In the name of the Father and the Son and the Holy Ghost. Dearly beloved, we are come of a fallen race . . .' 'Beloved' itself would formerly have been used in impassioned declarations of love between men and women, but the word now has a very old-fashioned ring. It is sometimes used sarcastically by a male or female speaker to a love-partner. In Norman Mailer's *An American Dream*, a woman who is telling a male friend about a previous love-affair remarks: 'It was kind of carnal, beloved.'

Benefactor A Dickensian term of address, made well known by its use in *Hard Times* to Mr Bounderby by Mrs Sparsit, his house-keeper. This is the term she uses to his face; behind his back she addresses his portrait as 'you booby'. In *The Pickwick Papers* Mr Winkle is rather more sincere when he calls Mr Pickwick 'my friend, my benefactor, my honoured companion'.

Berk A British slang word, in occasional use, which is now taken to mean fool, though it was originally rather a stronger term of abuse. Its origin lies in Cockney rhyming slang, where 'Berkshire' or 'Berkeley Hunt' was used for 'cunt'. *The Sleepers of Erin*, by Jonathan Gash, has many examples of 'you burke'. 'you stupid burke', 'you thick burke', 'you crass burke', but this spelling is erroneous. There was certainly a slang term in former times, 'to burke someone', which meant to kill someone by strangulation or suffocation, but this was always a verb and at no time indicated foolishness. It derived from a notorious criminal who was executed in 1829. William Burke, an Irish navvy, together with his accomplice William Hare, murdered many victims in order to supply bodies to an Edinburgh surgeon, Dr Robert Knox. In *The Sleepers of Erin* the character who uses 'you burke' and its variants equates the term with 'lunatic', 'cretin', 'goon', 'loon', and 'nerk' at various times.

Best, my This expression is used by Baroness Ingram to her adult daughter in *Jane Eyre*, by Charlotte Brontë. In one instance she equates it with 'my dearest', with which it is entirely analogous. This use of 'best' is, however, rare, and seems to have escaped the observation of the *Oxford English Dictionary* compilers.

Biddy One might in modern English hear a reference to a 'biddy', especially an 'old biddy', meaning a woman, but as a vocative the word is almost never used. What is sometimes heard, especially in Ireland, is 'Biddy' being used as a pet name for a woman who is Bridget. There were at one time so many Irish Bridgets scattered throughout the English-speaking world, all of them familiarly addressed as Biddy, that the name became a slang word for woman, much as 'judy' became 'woman' in Australia for similar reasons. In *Twelfth Night* (3:iv) Sir Toby Belch tells Malvolio: 'Biddy, come with me.' This is a different word, used in some dialects for a chicken. Its use to Malvolio continues Sir Toby's 'fowl' theme, since he has just called him 'my bawcock' and 'chuck'. The word 'chickabiddy', a child's word for a chicken, is not recorded until the eighteenth century but may have been in use earlier.

Big boy This has something of the meaning of 'big shot', but the 'big' often takes on sexual innuendo and is meant to be flattering. Typical usage of this term would be by a prostitute to a prospective client. 'Big Boy, Big Boy, oh give me all you've got', is part of the hero's sexual fantasy in *Portnoy's Complaint*, by Philip Roth. A young Irish woman uses 'big boy' to her lover in *Like Any Other Man*, by Patrick Boyle. The expression is merely friendly when it occurs in *The Limits of Love*, by Frederic Raphael. A woman attracts the attention of a friend by calling to him, 'Big boy! Over here!'

Bighead Used of a self-important, conceited person. ' "I suppose you took Honey Parish home," he muttered. "Bloody bighead," ' says a boy to another in *The Taste of Too Much*, by Clifford Hanley. In *A Kind of Loving*, by Stan Barstow, occurs: ' "Try putting that last equation the other way up." He looks. "Gosh . . . Well fancy me not seeing that." "It's not seeing things like that 'at makes you fail exams." "All right, bighead." ' In both of these examples 'bighead' is said without real rancour.

Big Mans Sinclair Lewis, In *Ann Vickers*, has:

> Privately she had to be a Little Woman – otherwise how, standing beside her, could he be Big Mans? (He had told her of a girl who used to call him 'Big Mans'. But even in her tenderest moments she'd be hanged if she would be as little-womanish as that.)

A similar ' –s' is added in vocatives such as 'Babes', and on the end of a diminutive suffix such as ' –kin'.

Bigmouth Used in American slang to a person who announces his own opinions too readily and too loudly, or to a person who cannot keep a secret. *Only a Game*, by Robert Daley, has a father telling his children a story. 'He's not in this story, Daddy,' says one of the children. 'All right, bigmouth,' says another child, 'you tell it.'

Bigot Used in modern times of a person who has strong views, especially about religion, race, or politics, and believes that those who have differing views are not worth listening to. 'Short-sighted bigot' is the accusation made by one man to another during an argument in *The Heart is a Lonely Hunter*, by Carson McCullers. The origin of 'bigot' is much disputed, but Ernest Weekley makes a good case, in his *Etymological Dictionary of Modern English*, for a derivation from the oath 'by God'.

Big shot An American slang term for an important person, but vocative usage tends to be ironic. In Philip Roth's *Portnoy's Complaint* the hero, as a child, is playing baseball with his father. 'Come on, Big Shot, throw the ball,' his father tells him, and also addresses him as 'Big Shot Ballplayer'. Elsewhere in the novel the father says: 'You're riding for a fall, Mr Big. You're fourteen years old, and believe me, you don't know everything there is to know.' As the conversation continues the father uses 'Mr Big Shot' as the fuller form of the vocative. *St Urbain's Horseman*, by Mordecai Richler, has one man saying to another: 'Whatever happened to that James Bond film you were supposed to direct? Big shot.' Joseph Heller, in *Good as Gold*, has: ' "Hey, bigshot," his father would bellow on the telephone, and Gold would wilt at once.' In Truman Capote's short story *Shut a Final Door* a man who is described as a big shot in a newspaper article is then ironically addressed by an office colleague: 'Whatcha say, bigshot?'

Big spender   Used ironically to a person considered to be mean, or who is ostentatiously spending money. *Lydia*, by E. V. Cunningham, has: 'I asked her if she wanted dessert. "No, big spender," she flung at me. "No, I don't want any dessert. Especially from a louse." '

Big stiff, you   Applied to a large, rough man, often as an endearment rather than an insult. 'Stiff' on its own has a large number of slang meanings in American English, but 'you big stiff' is a fixed expression. It occurs in Sinclair Lewis's *Dodsworth* as a friendly insult between two men.

Billy   A pet form of William used as a substitute name to a stranger in the Liverpool area, according to a letter to the author from Professor W. F. Mainland.

Bimbo   Philip Howard discussed this term at length in *The Times*, saying that 1988 was the year of the 'bimbo' from a linguistic point of view. The word had been much used in newspaper reports of sexist farces involving Ollie North and Gary Hart. It now means a pretty young woman who is considered as a sex-object, though in the early 1900s it meant a man, often a hoodlum. The word derives from Italian *bambino*, 'child', and its modern meaning has been developing since the 1920s. Some male speakers would use it to mean a prostitute, but as Philip Howard says, it can mean 'a young woman content with the role of brainless, pretty-pretty ego-masseuse'. 'You dumb bimbo' is said by a man to a woman in *Last Tango in Paris*, by Robert Alley. A moment later he adds: 'I'm going to get you, bimbo.' The speaker equates the term with 'dummy,' though he uses the latter term in a friendly way.

Bird   This word had been associated with 'girl' since the fourteenth century. Originally it may have been a separate word, 'burd', a poetic word for woman, and there may have been confusion with 'bride', since 'bird' itself was often written as 'brid'. In Beaumont and Fletcher's *The Knight of the Burning Pestle* 'bird' is equated with other seventeenth-century endearments, used by a man to a woman. 'My bonny bird' is used to a young girl in Sir Walter Scott's *Old Morality*, and evidence of this being true nineteenth-century usage, rather than one of Scott's archaisms, comes in *A Tale of Two Cities*, by Charles Dickens. A

woman uses 'my bird' to address a younger woman, equating the term with 'my precious'. It was at one time possible to refer to a young man as a bird, a usage which the *Oxford English Dictionary* considers to be long obsolete. Nevertheless, in *Saturday Night and Sunday Morning*, by Alan Sillitoe, which concerns life in the Nottingham region in the 1950s, a man says to another: 'What's up, Jack, my owd bird?' A little later in the same novel the hero's aunt says to him: 'How are yer, my owd bird?' D. H. Lawrence, another writer from the Nottingham area, has 'old bird' used in a friendly way between young men in *Aaron's Rod*. *A Salute to the Great McCarthy*, by Barry Oakley, has a girl who addresses a young man as 'my husky creature'. He replies: 'You lovely bird. Peck me.' In *Gideon Planish*, by Sinclair Lewis, a mother says to her daughter: 'Now don't interrupt, little mocking bird.'

Bishop   The recommended term of address for an Anglican bishop is 'Bishop'; Roman Catholic bishops are addressed formally as 'my lord'. The latter term was formerly used to Anglican bishops, and may still occasionally be heard. The wife of an Anglican bishop, however , is 'Mrs' + last name, not 'my lady',

Bitch   This word has been applied insultingly to women since at least the fourteenth century. It presumably caused as much offence then as it does now, but it appears to be commonly used, judging by the frequency with which it occurs in novels. Perhaps the fullest commentary on its use comes in *Joseph Andrews*, by Henry Fielding:

'Get out of my house, you whore.' To which she added another name, which we do not care to stain our paper with. It was a monosyllable beginning with a b-, and indeed was the same as if she had pronounced the words 'she-dog.' Which term, we shall, to avoid offence, use on this occasion. 'I can't bear that name,' answered Betty. 'I will go out of your house this moment, for I will never be called "she-dog" by any mistress in England.'

Fielding goes on to say that this word 'is extremely disgustful to females of the lower sort', but it was one which women of the higher sort no doubt never heard applied to themselves.

'You shifty bitch' is used by a father to his daughter when the former is in a rage in *Women In Love*, by D. H. Lawrence. 'You tight-ass bitch' is used by a man to a woman in *Surfacing*, by Margaret Atwood. 'You bloody bitch' occurs in Anthony Powell's *Casanova's Chinese Restaurant*; 'cold bitch' and 'cold little bitch' are in *The Country Girls*, by Edna O'Brien. Examples of insults could easily be multiplied, but intimate uses of the word also occur. In *The Philanderer*, by Stanley Kauffman, an American couple are in bed and chatting amiably. 'We could walk there if we had to', says the wife. 'Bitch', says the husband. She kisses him and says 'Good night, dear' in reply, to which he says 'Good night, dearest'. In *Girl with Green Eyes*, by Edna O'Brien, 'sly bitch' is similarly used as an intimacy. John Wain's *A Travelling Woman* also has three examples of 'you bitch' being used as a disguised endearment. *Fletch*, by Gregory Mcdonald, has: 'Are you all right?' 'Sure.' 'I was afraid of that.' 'I love you, too, bitch.' 'Endearments will get you nowhere.' An interesting comment on how the same expression can be both insulting and a covert endearment occurs in *War Brides*, by Lois Battle. 'If I hadn't married him I wouldn't have met you,' says a young woman to her lover. The conversation continues: 'I know that, you silly bitch.' 'Don't you dare call me that! Don't you dare!' 'I've called you that before. I've called you that in bed and you even seemed to like it.'

Blabbermouth Used of or to a person who talks too much, especially one who reveals things that are meant to remain secret. 'Don't you mention it to Christine, blabbermouth', says one boy to another in *The Taste of Too Much*, by Clifford Hanley.

Blackguard This has become a rarely used word, so much so that some speakers, seeing the word in print, might pronounce it as spelt, instead of as 'blaggard'. When used at all it refers to a villain or criminal, though applied to a child, as 'you young blackguard' in *Funeral in Berlin*, by Len Deighton, it means little more than 'scamp', 'rascal'. It is used as an insult in *Daughters of Mulberry*, by Roger Longrigg, and is said with some vehemence in Smollett's *Peregrine Pickle*, where a girl calls a sailor 'you saucy blackguard'. The original black guards appear to have been the kitchen staff who travelled with the pots and pans on a wagon as a king or nobleman moved about the country. The term also described the camp followers who performed a similar function for an army on the move. There is reason to suppose that 'black guard' was simply an ironic reference to this band of menials, who would no doubt have been dirty enough to be called 'black'.

Blasphemer To blaspheme is literally 'to speak ill, to blame', but blasphemy specifically means to speak ill of God or religion. The word occurs twice as a vocative in *The Heart is a Lonely Hunter*, by Carson McCullers, expanded on one occasion to 'foul blasphemer'. The man addressed is mocking Christianity, while the speaker is a devout believer.

Blatherskite Used in Scotland and in certain American dialects of one who blethers or blathers, that is, talks nonsense in a blustering way. The term was transferred from Scotland to the USA by the song 'Maggie Lauder', where the vocative occurs as 'bletherskate'. The song became a favourite in the American camp during the War of Independence. 'It's a thundering lie, you miserable old blatherskite,' says a young man to a woman in *Pudd'nhead Wilson*, by Mark Twain. He does not like the news she has just given him and hopes that it is nonsense.

Bleeder Originally a euphemism employed in British university circles for 'bloody fool', bleeder seems to have rapidly come into low colloquial use at the end of the nineteenth century, especially in the London region. 'You silly bleeder' would be a typical expression. In *Saturday Night and Sunday Morning*, by Alan Sillitoe, a Nottingham woman shouts at a man: 'Mind what ye'r doin', yer young bleeder.' She equates it with 'you cheeky sod'. *A Kind of Loving*, by Stan Barstow, has an exchange between two men where the older one asks: 'Who mentioned my name?' 'I did', the younger one says, 'I was just saying I'd bought a pig and I didn't know what to call it.' 'You cheeky young bleeder...' is the response, accompanied by a physical attack.

Blighter 'You lucky blighter', addressed by one man to another, and references to 'a poor little blighter', a child, are now becoming rare in British colloquial speech. The word 'blighter' appeared in British slang at the very end of the nineteenth century. Professor Weekley, followed by Eric Partridge, thought that the word may have been suggested by 'blithering', and saw it as a euphemism for 'bugger', or perhaps 'bastard'. The word 'bleeder' was also in use before 'blighter' began to be used, and that too may have needed a euphemism. J. P. Donleavy, in *The Ginger Man*, has a woman saying to her husband: 'So you paid it, did you? Here it is. Exactly where I left it and the money gone. Lies. You blighter. You nasty blighter.' The husband replies: 'Call me a bugger. I can't stand the gentility on top of the yelling.'

Blockhead, you A term used to a person that the speaker thinks is stupid. A blockhead was originally a wooden head on which a wig or hat was kept. The word was applied to a stupid person in the sixteenth century, and is still occasionally used on both sides of the Atlantic. 'You blockhead' is used by Bluntschli in G. B. Shaw's *Arms and the Man* to Sergius, who implies that under normal circumstances that insult would have been a duelling matter: 'I have allowed you to call me a blockhead. You may now call me a coward as well. I refuse to fight you.' Similarly, in Thomas Hardy's *The Trumpet Major*, John Loveday calls Festus Derriman 'you pitiful blockhead', and continues: 'you'll know where to find me, since we can't finish this tonight. Pistols or swords, whichever you like, my boy.' In Sheridan's *The School for Scandal* 'you blockhead, what do you want?' is addressed by a gentleman to his servant.

Bloke, old This occurs in *St Urbain's Horseman*, by Mordecai Richler, when one man says to another: 'Well, pip, pip, old bloke. And up yours with a pineapple.' This is in response to being told: 'I've had enough of your puerile jokes, Uncle Lou.' Both men in this case are Canadian, but the person being addressed as 'old bloke' lives permanently in London. In calling him 'old bloke', the speaker no doubt thinks that he is imitating British vocative usage, though as it happens, he is not. 'Bloke' has certainly been a British slang word for 'man, chap' since the mid-nineteenth century, but 'old bloke' is not normally one of the 'old boy/old man' group of terms used in direct address. 'Blokes' on its own does occur as a friendly term of address, used by one man to a group of men, in *Doctor at Sea*, by Richard Gordon. The same novel has two examples of 'you blokes' used in a similar way.

Blondie This would normally be addressed to a woman with fair hair, a blonde. One would expect the speaker to be a worker, accosting her as she passed in the street. In *Oliver's Story*, by Erich Segal, it is a man who says to another man, very aggressively: 'What's your problem, blondie?' Soon afterwards the same speaker calls the man concerned 'you fruit'. Both vocatives suggest that the speaker considers the other man to be effeminate.

Blood Tub *See* **Fatty**.

bloody A frequent element in unfriendly and insulting vocative expressions of the 'you bloody fool' type. That particular expression occurred ten times in fifty novels chosen at random, though all were by British authors. The word would not be used in polite, formal circles. It has little meaning, but intensifies whatever else is being said. Eric Partridge has a 2000 word essay on the origin of the word, which was not offensive until the late eighteenth century. Swift was able to write to Stella in the *Journal*: 'It was bloody hot walking today.' Samuel Richardson, who would never have allowed a taboo word to soil his pages, says in *Pamela* (1742): 'He is bloody passionate.' 'Bloody drunk' was a frequently used phrase at one time, and probably meant 'as drunk as a blood, i.e. one of the young aristocratic rowdies known as bloods.' These seventeenth-century thugs were of good blood; they were also hot-blooded. The Swift quotation is probably to be interpreted as a reference to the supposed heat of blood, while the Richardson remark reminds one of a hot-blooded lover. We still commonly hear people talking about something which makes their blood boil. It is easy to see how phrases like 'bloody hot', 'bloody passionate', and 'bloody drunk' led to the belief that 'bloody' meant 'very'. But 'blood' to many speakers would have rather disgusting associations, and this seems to have been the sense transposed onto the word when used adjectivally.

Blossom Miss Hilary Pimm writes from Bristol to say that 'blossom' is used vocatively in that area to a woman 'and makes you feel very young and beautiful'. The term was first applied to a human being in the fifteenth century, referring both to loveliness and promise for the future. In Shakespeare's *The Winter's Tale*, Antigonus lays down Hermione's baby, whom he has been instructed to abandon, and says: 'Blossom, speed thee well!' Lord Tennyson, in *The Princess*, has 'My babe, my blossom, ah my child.' Perhaps, then, the term was formerly applied especially to babies, but has been extended locally to adult women. See also **Peach-blossom, Lotus blossom**.

Blubber-face, blubber-bib, blubber-puss (=blubber face) See **Cry-baby**.

Blue meanie, blue meany Explained by Robert Chapman in his *Dictionary of American Slang* as 'a very very cruel and nasty person'. In *The Choirboys*, by Joseph Wambaugh, occurs: 'Pete Zoony pursed his lips and smacked a little kiss and said: "Oh, you're so cute when you're all mad! You blue meanie!" ' The Los Angeles policeman to whom this is addressed objects to the homosexual tone and knocks the speaker to the ground.

Blues, you; Blues, the *See* **COLOURS**.

Bluey, Blue Used by Australians and New Zealanders since 1890 to address a red-headed man. Eric Partridge, a New Zealander himself, is unable to give a reason for such usage in his *Dictionary of Historical Slang*.

Blunderhead Used to a blundering, muddle-headed person, mainly in the eighteenth and nineteenth centuries. It is thought to be an alteration of the earlier term 'dunderhead', which had the same meaning. An example occurs in *Oliver Twist*, by Charles Dickens, where a working-class man uses it to another.

Blunthead Not a standard vocative term, but used aggressively by one American man to another in *The Comeback*, a short story by Dawn Powell. It is not clear in context whether 'blunt' refers to physical appearance or to bluntness of manner.

-bo A diminutive ending used to create a double diminutive in Jimbo, ultimately from James. In a play broadcast on BBC radio in July, 1987, 'Timbo' was used as a double diminutive of Timothy. These examples may have been inspired by 'Sambo', the generic nickname used to a black West Indian or American, for which a Spanish origin is often claimed. Alternatively, the '–bo' ending shows a shortening of boy, since first name + 'boy' occurs fairly frequently as a term of address. 'Sambo' itself could easily have been a corrupt form of 'Sam boy': Sam was a common name amongst black slaves, as a perusal of *Black Names in America*, by Newbell Niles Puckett quickly reveals, and 'boy' was the normal term of address to any black male slave.

Boadicea A transferred name, referring to a famous British warrior queen of the first century. She revolted against the Romans after her husband's death in AD 61. There is a well-known statue of her opposite Big Ben on the Embankment, in London. The name is used to a woman in *Within and Without*, by John Harvey. A woman passenger in an open car acts as if she is Boadicea in her chariot, lashing out with a frond of bracken as she is driven along a country lane. ' "How goes the day, Boadicea?" I said. "Fine," she said. "Lots of dead Romans all about. Heaps of stumps. Piles of heads. Blood." She looked exactly how Boadicea must have looked.' In *The Old Boys*, by William Trevor, 'my beautiful Boadicea' is used to a woman in a friendly way.

Boatswain *See* Bos'n.

Bodach This vocative would only be used by a Scottish speaker acquainted with Gaelic. It means an old man, though it can also mean a goblin or spectre. In Lillian Beckwith's *The Hills is Lonely*, set in the Hebrides, a doctor says to an old man: 'You old bodach, you've never sucked at an empty bottle in your life.' The doctor also calls him 'you old rascal' and 'you devil'.

Bogger *See* Bugger.

Bog-rat This term does not seem to have been recorded by any of the usual dictionaries, but 'you bog-rat', addressed to a man and obviously insulting, occurs in *Within and Without*, by John Harvey. 'Bog' may be used in its slang sense of lavatory.

Bonehead A mainly American term, used to

a person who is thought to be stubborn to the point of stupidity. A typical use occurs in *The River*, by Steven Bauer: ' "Okay, bonehead," Wade said. "You want your eviction notice? You got it." ' This is to a farmer who refuses to give up his land, wanted for industrial development.

Bonny lad, bonny lass Used as friendly terms of address in north-east England, though 'bonny' is now thought of as a Scottish word. It expresses approval in a general way, hinting especially at a pleasant and healthy appearance. 'Bonny lad' is used by one man to another in *When the Boat Comes In*, by James Mitchell.

Boo-baby, boo-hoo *See* Cry-baby.

Booby A word for a fool which was introduced to English from Spanish (*bobo* = fool) at the beginning of the seventeenth century. A booby is the kind of man who would be caught out by a booby-trap, but the term is often used jokingly, to imply mild silliness rather than stupidity. In *The Country Girls*, by Edna O'Brien, 'booby' is used as an endearment rather than an insult. In *Vanity Fair*, by Thackeray, Rebecca calls her husband 'you old booby' in a playful way, but the reader knows that she really does consider Rawdon to be an ignorant fool. In the USA, although expressions like 'booby-trap' and 'booby hatch' (an insane asylum) are used, 'booby' has tended to become 'boob'. It is used as a synonym for sucker, someone who is too trusting. 'You poor boob' is used by a man to his friend in *Tropic of Cancer*, by Henry Miller. There may be some confusion with 'boob' meaning woman's breast, though 'boob' in that sense was earlier 'bub', earlier still 'bubby'. A boob also has the slang meaning of a mistake, perhaps one made by a booby. *See also* Cry-baby.

Booger *See* Bugger.

Boogie Robert Chapman's *Dictionary of American Slang* lists twelve different meanings of boogie, one of which is 'a black person'. It occurs in that meaning in *An American Dream*, by Norman Mailer. A detective who is beating up a prisoner says: 'Goddamn you, you Goddamn stubborn boogie.' H. L. Mencken, in *The American Language*, thinks that the term might be a 'Southern variant of bogey', meaning the devil or a goblin. He also says: 'In the South *boogie man* is still one of the names of the Devil.'

Boots This was the name for the servant in an inn or hotel whose job was to clean the boots of the customers. He was summoned or addressed by his professional title. The term is often found as a vocative in eighteenth- and nineteenth-century literature, e.g. in *The Pickwick Papers* by Charles Dickens and *Vanity Fair*, by William Thackeray. In slang use 'boots' became a synonym for fellow or person in expressions such as 'smooth-boots', 'lazy-boots', 'sly-boots', 'clumsy-boots'.

Bor   Mr. R. N. G. Rowland reports the use of this term in East Anglia and suggests that it derives from neighbour.

Bos'n   The normal modern spelling, representing its usual pronunciation, of 'boatswain'. He is the ship's officer who looks after its equipment, calls the men to work, etc. It is used vocatively four times in *Doctor at Sea*, by Richard Gordon. It occurs more famously, as 'boatswain', as the opening word of Shakespeare's *The Tempest*. The boatswain in that play is also addressed as 'good boatswain' and 'boson'.

Boss   This word was introduced into English only at the beginning of the nineteenth century. It was adapted from Dutch *baas* (master) and may have come from sea-usage, the captain of a Dutch ship being addressed as *baas*. In English the word acknowledges the right of someone to give orders, while avoiding some of the over-servile associations of 'master'. Originally an American term, it was later used jokingly in England by workmen. It is still used jokingly in conversation by, e.g. a husband to his wife, especially if she is being bossy at the time. It is the traditional term by which football managers in Britain are addressed by their players. In *Diamonds are Forever*, Ian Fleming shows another traditional use, when a gang member uses it to his leader. The jokey use between the sexes is shown in *Pray for the Wanderer*, by Kate O'Brien, where a man says to his girl-friend, who is teasing him for not having bothered to open his letters, 'All right, boss – open them for me.' In *My Brother Jonathan*, by Francis Brett Young, it is equated with 'gaffer' and used as a general title of respect to a doctor. Arthur Hailey, in *Hotel*, has it being used by an American cab-driver to his fare. *Like Any Other Man*, by Patrick Boyle, a novel set in Ireland, has it used by one man to another as a friendly term of address.

Both   This can be used on its own to two people in a simple utterance such as 'Thank you, both.' Examples of such usage occur in *The Affair*, by C. P. Snow; *An Error of Judgement*, by Pamela Hansford Johnson; *The Masters*, by C. P. Snow. 'Both of you' is rather more usual.

Both of you   A form of address to two people, including both of them in whatever is being said. 'Good night, both of you', occurs in *Pray for the Wanderer*, by Kate O'Brien. *The Half Hunter*, by John Sherwood, has 'Stop it, both of you' addressed to two men who are fighting. The expression also occurs in *The Affair*, by C. P. Snow, *Anglo-Saxon Attitudes*, by Angus Wilson, *Casanova's Chinese Restaurant*, by Anthony Powell, *A Kind of Loving*, by Stan Barstow, *Lucky Jim*, by Kingsley Amis, *The Old Boys*, by William Trevor, *The River of Diamonds*, by Geoffrey Jenkins, *A Use of Riches*, by J. I. M. Stewart, and so on. It can be friendly, neutral, or unfriendly according to the utterance which accompanies it, or by additional words included in the vocative group. Thus *Doctor at Sea*, by Richard Gordon, has an insulting use of 'both of you bastards'.

Bouncer   *See* **Fatty**.

Boy   A very common term of address throughout the English-speaking world, in modern times as well as in the past. The vocative is extensively used in Shakespeare's plays, for instance, normally to young men, occasionally to older men and sometimes to girls who are temporarily disguised as young men. Schoolboys are especially likely to be called 'boy' by their teachers, though they may not like it. 'I wished to hell he'd stop calling me "boy" all the time,' says the young hero of *The Catcher in the Rye*, by J. D. Salinger, when being interviewed by an elderly schoolmaster. He is sixteen years old at the time, and happens to like the word 'boy' as an exclamation. ' "Boy!" I said. I also say "boy!" quite a lot. Partly because I have a lousy vocabulary and partly because I act quite young for my age sometimes.' This exclamatory use of 'boy' is little more than an almost meaningless noise, expressing surprise, admiration, and similar emotions. There are examples of 'boy' used to schoolboys throughout *Dandelion Days*, by Henry Williamson, a novel in which a father also addresses his son as 'my boy', a more affectionate term.

'Boy' itself is either neutral, or slightly aggressive. Dickens comments on the word in *Nicholas Nickleby*:

> The mutual inspection was at length brought to a close by Ralph withdrawing his eyes, with a great show of disdain, and calling Nicholas 'a boy.' This word is much used as a term of reproach by elderly gentlemen towards their juniors: probably with a view of deluding society into the belief that if they could be young again, they wouldn't on any account.

Between social equals, 'boy' becomes a more flattering term of address as the age of the person to whom it is said increases. A group of men might well be addressed as 'boys' by another adult man or woman, in a club or at a social gathering. Edna O'Brien comments on such usage in *The Country Girls*, when a girl says to two men who are bordering on middle-age, 'Must get a flower, boys.' 'Boys!' says the narrator, another young girl, 'how could she be so false.' In *Howard's End*, by E. M. Forster, a woman in her thirties calls her fiancé, an older man, 'boy' in an affectionate way. This usage resembles the use of 'old boy' (see separate entry).

'Boy' was the normal term for addressing male negro slaves in former times, and was also used to address male servants of other races in many countries where whites were the ruling class. The use of 'boy' to a black American adult would now be considered offensive. This is known to the white speakers who continue to use the term, so that 'boy' in such circumstances must be counted as a positive insult. Carson McCullers in *The Heart is a Lonely Hunter*, has a mild comment on this usage. He is talking of a black doctor:

> The quiet insolence of the white race was one thing he had tried to keep out of his mind for years. In the streets and around white people he would keep the dignity on his face and always be silent. When he was younger it was 'Boy' – but now it was 'Uncle'.

In *Rabbit Redux*, by John Updike, a white man is talking to a black American and says: 'You talk a cool game, but I think you panicked, boy.' 'Don't boy me', is the reply. Updike continues: 'Rabbit is startled; he had meant it neutrally, one athlete calling to another.'

The reaction of this black American to being called 'boy' is as nothing compared to that of Coriolanus, in the closing scene of Shakespeare's play of that name. Aufidius actually calls Coriolanus 'thou boy of tears', but Coriolanus fastens on the word 'boy' and repeats it several times. Almost the last word he utters, before he is cut to pieces by the conspirators, is 'Boy!', still unable to believe that the word has been applied to him.

Boy, clever A vocative that tends to be used by Jewish speakers, suggesting that it might be an alternative to 'wise guy' in translating the Yiddish *chachem*. According to Leo Rosten in *The Joys of Yiddish*, *chachem* (also spelt *haham*, *chaham*) is mainly used sarcastically to one who is being over-clever and is heading for a downfall. *The Limits of Love*, by Frederic Raphael, has six examples of 'clever boy' used by a Jewish speaker. There are two more instances of its use in *Absolute Beginners*, by Colin MacInnes and another in *Within and Without*, by John Harvey. The speakers in the latter novels are British; American speakers in the same circumstances would probably have used 'wise guy', 'wise ass', etc. 'Clever boy' or

'clever girl' is also a typical expression used vocatively to an animal. There are several examples of horses being so addressed in *Daughters of Mulberry*, by Roger Longrigg. It is for this reason that the narrator in *Within and Without*, mentioned above, says after being called 'clever boy' by a woman: 'I wondered if she was going to offer me a lump of sugar.'

Boy, dear This expression is associated by many people in Britain with older actors, who seem to use it rather frequently. It may be the masculine equivalent of the theatrical darling, which is used to disguise the fact that someone's name has been forgotten. Support for this view comes from a non-actor, the journalist Philip Howard, who wrote in *The Times* (20 April 1987):

> The most daunting introduction for those of us who are nominally forgetful is for a complete stranger to come up and say: 'Hullo. You're Philip Howard, aren't you? Do you remember me?' There is no satisfactory answer to that which does not sound rude. Which is why some of us use the vocatives 'dear boy', 'dear girl', and 'old thing' more than seems necessary to those who have good memories for names. The last appellation should be used only to those under 30.

Boy, old Used by British speakers to address a man of any age in a friendly way, whether the man concerned is known to them already or not. The *Oxford English Dictionary*, under 'today', quotes a journalist in 1864 to the effect that ' "Old boy", as a form of familiar address... todayish as it may sound... is at least a century old.' This is certainly true, since examples of 'old boy', used by one man to another, can be found in, e.g., Ben Jonson's *The Alchemist* and Shakespeare's *Twelfth Night*. Nevertheless, 'old boy' does not appear to have been a fixed collocation in the seventeenth century, nor is it all that frequent in eighteenth-century literature. In *Tom Jones*, by Henry Fielding, Tom uses it in a very familiar way to address Square, but a vocative count based on other novels of the period would not place 'old boy' highly, 'sir' being the norm between men.

In modern times 'old boy' has been very frequently used indeed in Britain, though it appears to be waning fast in the late 1980s. It is socially marked, suggesting to most British speakers a decidedly middle-class background, perhaps the public schools and their old boys, i.e. former students. Nina Bawden comments on this aspect in *George Beneath a Paper Moon*: 'He played rugger and put on weight and changed his accent to camouflage his lower middle-class origins... quite soon it became second nature and he would say "old

boy" . . . without twitching an eyelid.' The subtleties of the class system in Britain are such
that one is likely to offend genuinely upper
middle-class and upper-class listeners by
addressing them as 'old boy'. Somerset
Maugham has a short story *Lord Mountdrago*
in which the hero says: 'I wasn't so much
annoyed at his seeing me in that absurd situation as angry that he should address me as
"old boy".' The man who has committed the
offence is a Socialist Member of Parliament.
Even more subtle is the comment in *A Use of
Riches*, by J. I. M. Stewart:

> 'Hullo, old boy,' Jim Voysey said. It was a
> moment before Craine could account for the
> distaste he felt at this encounter. Voysey had
> undoubtedly spoken across a semantic
> chasm, since there existed a highly conven-
> tional Craine who froze at 'old boy' but would
> have taken 'old man' as venial.'

Daphne du Maurier, in *Rebecca*, has a County-
type woman using 'old boy' to a man in a
friendly way, but it is not normally a feminine
term in any sense of the word.

It appears to be still in use between men,
judging by a report in *The Times* newspaper
on 27 January 1984. This concerns a rugby
match in which

> a player of mature years and matching phys-
> ique won the ball at a lineout, to hear the
> opposing captain exclaim: 'Get the fat old
> bastard!' When calm was restored, the victim
> remonstrated with the captain for his unman-
> nerly words. 'I'm awfully sorry, old boy,' was
> the reply, 'but I don't know your Christian
> name'.

In fifty novels by British authors, randomly
selected but all concerned with life since
about 1930, 158 examples of 'old boy' occurred.
A novel such as *Brothers in Law*, by Henry
Cecil, which has many members of the legal
profession featured, has twenty-nine instances
of old boy, plus one 'my dear old boy'. *The
Limits of Love*, by Frederic Raphael, has a
few examples of its normal use, but six more
instances where it is an intimacy between
lovers.

Boychick A term which Leo Rosten, in *The
Joys of Yiddish*, describes as 'pure Yinglish' (a
mixture of Yiddish and English). It is either a
simple diminutive of 'boy' or means a smart
operator. Rosten prefers to spell it 'boychik',
but it is 'boychick' when it occurs in *Portnoy's
Complaint*, by Philip Roth, and in *Shovelling
Trouble*, by Mordecai Richler.

Boyo This is boy with the vocative suffix ' –o',
used as a friendly term of address, usually
between men. Many would expect the user of
this term to be Welsh, but it is given to speak-

ers of other nationalities in e.g. *Goldfinger*,
by Ian Fleming and *The Sleepers of Erin*, by
Jonathan Gash. In *Other Men's Wives*, by Alexander Fullerton, it *is* the expected Welshman
who says: 'Hold on now, Buck boyo.'

Boys and girls Normally used to a group of
young children, as in *The Business of Loving*,
by Godfrey Smith. Occasionally used jokingly
by an adult to a group of adults.

Bozo The origin of this word, which is frequently used in modern American idiom, is
unknown, though it is tempting to link it with
'boy'. It is used mainly by men to other men,
sometimes with the implication that they have
more muscle than brains. The *New Dictionary
of American Slang* says that it has been in use
since 1900. 'Hold on there, bozo, not so fast!'
says one man to another in *The Tropic of
Cancer*, by Henry Miller. 'Whaddya mean, this
is *your* cab? Bark off, bozo!' is a similar usage
in *Glad To Be Here*, by Garrison Keiller. In
The Philanderer, by Stanley Kauffmann, 'Hey,
bozo' is used in a friendly way by an American
to a man who works for him.

Brat A derogatory word for a child, expressing contempt or implying that the child concerned is of little or no significance. The word
has been in use with this meaning since the
beginning of the sixteenth century, and is of
obscure origin. It is probably used far more
often in third person reference than in direct
address, but 'brat' is used with mock severity
to a young niece in *Mariana*, by Monica
Dickens.

Breezy Used to a person who has a breezy
manner, who is 'bright and breezy'. It is
friendly when it occurs in *Absolute Beginners*,
by Colin MacInnes, the complete utterance
being 'Take it easy, breezy.' There are similar
examples of vocatives being suggested by the
need for a rhyme in *The Country Girls*, by
Edna O'Brien: 'Oh, lady divine, will you pass
me the wine?' 'Oh, lady supreme, will you pass
me the cream?' 'You bald-headed scutter, will
you pass me the butter?'

Brethren This was the earliest plural in English of brother. It was still being used in Shakespeare's time, so that both forms – 'brothers'
and 'brethren' – occur in the plays without any
particular distinction being made. But by the
mid-seventeenth century, 'brothers' had
become the normal plural form, while 'brethren' was reserved for spiritual, ecclesiastical,
or professional use. The 'dearly beloved brethren' of the *Book of Common Prayer* is probably
the best-known modern usage. That
expression occurs also in *The Devil on
Lammas Night*, by Susan Howatch, during the

celebration of a black mass. *Babbitt*, by Sinclair Lewis, has: 'My brethren, the real cheap skate is the man who won't lend to the Lord,' spoken by the local Presbyterian pastor to his congregation.

Brickie The normal vocative used to a bricklayer by other men working on a British building site.

Bridegroom, Mr Used as a nonce name in *The Old Bachelor*, by William Congreve.

Broad Used mainly by male American speakers of the working class, usually in third person reference rather than vocatively, of or to a woman. It may derive from the expression 'broad in the beam', but whatever its origin, it is not very flattering. Women are likely to object strongly to being described as or addressed as a broad, other than in the playfully insulting intimacy of a very close relationship. In *The Pleasure Man*, by Mae West, a married couple insult one another continually, as a matter of course, and take no offence. 'What the hell's so funny, ya dumb broad?' is a typical comment by the husband.

Brock 'Hang thee, brock', says Sir Toby Belch to Malvolio, in *Twelfth Night* (2:v). 'Brock' literally means badger, an animal which, in the seventeenth century, was always described as 'stinking'. The word was therefore applied at the time to a man who was especially dirty and smelly, or practised dirty tricks. The modern equivalent of the vocative would be 'you skunk'.

Broomstick *See* Spindleshanks.

Brother This term was formerly used far more frequently than today to a speaker's real brother, a male relation born of the same parents. There are plenty of examples in the Shakespeare plays of such usage, the vocative expression sometimes being extended to 'dear brother', 'gentle brother', etc. Brothers are not always friends, of course, and Prospero says in *The Tempest* (5:i) 'For you, most wicked sir, whom to call brother/Would even infect my mouth, I do forgive the rankest fault.' Oliver, in *As You Like It* (1:i) says 'What, boy!' to Orlando, his younger brother, and strikes him. 'Come, come, elder brother,' replies Orlando, 'you are too young in this.' The use of 'brother' was extended to a brother-in-law, as a comment in *The Comedy of Errors* (5:i) makes clear. Antipholus of Syracuse says of Luciana, his sister-in-law: 'This fair gentlewoman . . . did call me brother.'

This family use of brother continued to be normal until at least the end of the nineteenth century, as the many examples in novels such as *The Pickwick Papers*, by Charles Dickens and *Vanity Fair*, by William Thackeray, make clear. Instances are still found in more recent literature, such as *Absolute Beginners*, by Colin MacInnes, and *The Taste of Too Much*, by Clifford Hanley. The latter novel has examples of both 'brother' and 'wee brother', while the former has both 'brother' and the unusual 'half-brother' used vocatively. *The Kennedys*, by Peter Collier and David Horowitz, remarks that: 'Joe Junior and Jack called each other "Brother", a term neither Bobby nor Teddy ever adopted, as if acknowledging that they were the brothers who counted, the near equals who would struggle for precedence in the future.' It is interesting that two brothers of four should use brother to each other, but not to the others, but the suggested explanation for such usage seems unduly subtle.

When 'brother' continues to be used as a family term of address in modern times it is likely to be in its shortened form 'bruv', which turns the word into a kind of nickname. 'Bruv' is decidedly working-class, English rather than American, and probably regional in usage, being popular in the London area. It matches the short form of 'Sis' used to a sister. Middle-class speakers would expect to use the full form 'brother', but they no longer automatically use the term to a brother or brother-in-law as was the case in former times.

Why the use of family relationship terms in direct address faded considerably at the end of the nineteenth century is something of a mystery, but 'brother', 'sister', and 'cousin' were the terms most affected. Comments on the changing fashion are hard to find in literature of the period, though George Eliot does say of Seth, in *Adam Bede*, that 'he never called Adam "brother" except in solemn moments.' The use of the exclamatory vocative 'good, noble brother' by Becky Sharp to Joseph Sedley, in William Thackeray's *Vanity Fair* is interesting because 'brother' is used to describe Joseph's status as a brother to Amelia. Becky means: you are a good, noble brother to the fortunate woman who is your sister, or that, at least, would be her meaning were she being sincere.

If 'brother' has become less used as a family vocative, its use in other ways continues, especially in religious and trade union contexts. Friars continue to use 'brother' to one another, as they have done since the sixteenth century, and religious congregations are frequently 'brothers and sisters' when addressed by evangelical speakers. 'Brother, have you found Christ?' asks a street-corner preacher, in *The Mackerel Plaza*, by Peter de Vries. 'Is he lost again?' is the irreverent reply. In *Gideon Planish*, by Sinclair Lewis, some young men form a Socialist group and debate whether to address one another as 'Comrade'.

They decide against it. Lewis writes that 'Gil and Hatch were still too close to the horrors of being called "Brother" by loud evangelical pastors.' A typical example of 'dear brothers and sisters', used by a speaker to a religious community, occurs in *The Bell*, by Iris Murdoch, and most members of such congregations would consider this normal usage. The rather archaic form 'brethren' might also occur in such contexts, or when members of a guild or trade-union are being addressed. The use of 'brother' to a fellow member of a society has been common since the fourteenth century, reflecting an obvious extension of the family membership notion.

Earlier still, on the basis that all men are fellow creatures, 'brother' was used to address either a stranger or a man already known in a friendly way. Shakespeare says of Henry V, for example, that 'forth he goes and visits all his host; / Bids them good morrow with a modest smile / And calls them brothers, friends and countrymen' (*Henry the Fifth*, 4:Prologue). This common use of 'brother' as a friendly term of address gave rise to distorted variants of the word such as 'buddy' and 'bub', which have now taken on a life of their own, but 'brother' can still be used in its full form by one man to another as if it were 'mate', 'friend', or a similar term. Roger Longrigg's *Daughters of Mulberry* has an example of such usage. As with most of the 'friend' terms, 'brother' can be used sarcastically or in an obviously unfriendly way. *The Half Hunter*, by John Sherwood, has one man saying to another: 'This is the last warning you get, brother.'

In modern times black Americans or West Indians living in Britain are especially likely to use 'brother' to one another as a marker of racial unity. Such usage probably reflects the most common occurrence of this term, one which is likely to continue. In general terms it reflects the speaker's thought that the man being addressed is linked to him in some way, socially, professionally, racially. It may also be used to remind the listener that there are others with whom those links are not shared. It is a complex term, of some ambivalence, the last point perhaps indicated by the exclamatory use of 'Brother!' or 'Oh brother!' in modern American English. The expression is one of surprise and usually, slight annoyance.

Brother master This is the title assumed by the narrator of J. P. Donleavy's short story *A Fraternal Fraud*. The story begins: 'For the purpose of power or laughs or almost anything, I once made up a fraternity. Had a meeting every week and I was brother master and the rest were brothers.' As the story progresses the narrator is addressed as 'brother master', 'brother', or 'sir'. He addresses the members of the fraternity as 'Pledge', or by a nickname which he bestows on them.

Brown-noser An allusive term used of a flatterer who is servile in order to advance himself with his superiors. The term implies, as *Webster's Dictionary* eloquently puts it, 'that servility is equivalent to kissing the hinder parts of the person from whom advancement is sought'. The brown-noser is an ass-kisser, as American slang might otherwise express it, or an arse-licker as British slang users might say. In Mordecai Richler's *Cocksure* brown-noser is used as if it means a male homosexual.

Brute This becomes a transferred name when a speaker quotes '*Et tu, Brute?*' supposedly the words uttered by Julius Caesar when he saw that Marcus Junius Brutus, 'the noblest Roman of them all', was amongst his assassins. The Latin words simply mean 'you also, Brutus?', and the quotation is used to express regret when a close friend appears to be siding with one's enemies. The speaker is a young husband addressing his wife in *My Side of the Matter*, a short story by Truman Capote: 'I said, "*et tu Brute?*" which is from William Shakespeare.' The full Latin phrase occurs again in *Under the Volcano*, by Malcolm Lowry, where it is thought rather than said aloud. It is applied by one man to another. *The Taste of Too Much*, by Clifford Hanley, has: ' "What is this strange power I have to sicken people with words?" Peter cried. "I've hardly opened my mouth all night, and now you, too, Brute." ' This is strictly speaking a half-translated mis-quotation; *Brute* is an oblique form in Latin of Brutus, and it should take that form in English. It is also a regretful question in the original, not a simple statement. There is a different kind of misuse of the Latin phrase in *A World of Difference*, by Stanley Price. Two men who are house-guests meet each other in the middle of the night, returning to their own rooms after visiting ladies. ' "The midnight conqueror returns on tiptoe." He was mock conspiratorial, pulling the collar of his dressing-gown up. "*Et tu, Brute?*" "Each man conquers what he can." ' It might have been accurate in this context for one man to call the other Brutus, as a 'fellow-conspirator', but there is no question of betrayal to justify the whole quotation.

'Don't talk to me, don't, you brute', says Mrs Raddle to her husband in Dickens's *The Pickwick Papers*. She is not really accusing him of being brutish, but is displeased with him in general terms. She tells him he is a 'creetur' and an 'aggrawatin' thing. In *Oliver Twist*, however, when Mrs Sowerberry calls her husband 'you brute' she means it to be far more of an insult. 'You ignorant brute' occurs between men in *The Mill on the Floss*, by

George Eliot, and again is meant seriously, referring to cruel behaviour. Such vocative usage appears to have begun fairly late. Shakespeare has Gloucester refer to Edgar as a 'brutish villain', but 'brute' itself is not used vocatively in the plays. Modern usage is more likely to be light-hearted than serious. This is certainly the case when a woman calls a young man 'you brute' in *Don't Tell Alfred*, by Nancy Mitford. The same speaker also makes use of the term to a woman, which is unusual: ' "Then the poor little soul will starve," said Northey. "No matter." "Fanny, you brute." ' In *Casanova's Chinese Restaurant*, by Anthony Powell, 'you old brute' is quite clearly friendly in intention. 'Unhand me, you brute,' said by a woman to a man in *Blue Dreams*, by William Hanley, is a joke between intimates.

Bruv A pet form of 'brother', used especially in London at working-class level. Julian Franklyn, in *The Cockney*, thought that the term was 'settling down' in the 1950s. In the late 1980s it occurred regularly in the BBC television series *Only Fools and Horses*, used by an East-ender to his younger brother.

Bub In colloquial American usage 'bub' is usually addressed to a strange man, usually by another man. It is slightly insulting or aggressive. 'What are you bub, crazy or something?' says a man to another in *The Ginger Man*, by J. P. Donleavy. The term appears to be a short form of 'bubba', itself an illiterate transformation of 'brother'. Further examples of usage occur in, e.g., *The Philanderer*, by Stanley Kauffmann, where an American wife uses it to her husband, and *Gone With The Wind*, by Margaret Mitchell. In the latter novel a sergeant addresses one of his men by this term. In *The Adventures of Huckleberry Finn*, by Mark Twain, the watchman of a ferry-boat says to Huck: 'Hello, what's up? Don't cry, bub. What's the trouble?'

Bubba A corruption of 'brother', used in a friendly way, usually by one man to another. The speaker is usually American, and may well be black, as in *North Dallas Forty*, by Peter Gent. 'Hey, Bubba, did you hear Uncle Billy this morning?' is said by a black professional football player to a white team-mate.

Bubbly baby, Bubbly Jock, Mum's big bubbly bairn *See* Cry-baby.

Bubele, Bubeleh, Bobeleh A Yiddish endearment occasionally slipped into an English sentence by those familiar with that language. Leo Rosten, in *The Joys of Yiddish*, says that it rhymes with *hood a la* and is 'widely used for 'darling', 'dear child', 'honey', 'sweetheart', though the original meaning is something like

'little grandmother'. It is used to both sexes, e.g. between husbands and wives and to children. Rosten says that it is also popular amongst show-business people. It occurs relatively rarely in fiction, but there are many examples in, e.g., *St Urbain's Horseman*, by Mordecai Richler. 'Comes his bar mitzvah, he thought, no fountain pens. Instead his first nickel bag. "Today you are a man, bubele. Turn on." '

Buck Technically, a buck is a male deer (or the male of several other species), but the word has been applied to men in various senses since at least the eighteenth century. It can mean a spirited young man, or one who is a dandy. It has the former meaning in *Gone With The Wind*, by Margaret Mitchell, when an old man tells a group of young men, who are eager to go to war: 'You fire-eating young bucks, listen to me. You don't want to fight.'

Bud Normally a short form of 'buddy'. It is used by a male American speaker to another man in *The Philanderer*, by Stanley Kauffmann. There is similar, friendly usage in *Funeral in Berlin*, by Len Deighton; *Goldfinger*, by Ian Fleming. In *Girl with Green Eyes*, by Edna O'Brien, 'bud' is used in its botanical sense, though metaphorically, in the intimate expression 'you poor little lonely bud'.

Buddy A common term of address used mainly by American speakers, though its use in Britain appears to be spreading. The word is thought to be a corrupt form of 'brother', and is similar in use to 'friend'. It is often used positively, as in *The Island*, by Peter Benchley, where a father consistently uses it to his son. In his autobiography *Yes I Can!*, Sammy Davis Junior reports on his attempt to use the term in a friendly way, and the response he obtained from a fellow-soldier: 'Excuse me, buddy, I'm a little lost. Can you tell me where 202 is?' 'Two buildings down. And I'm not your buddy, you black bastard.' The friendliness of the term may be accented by its extension to 'old buddy', as in *Oliver's Story*, by Erich Segal, *The Middle Man*, by David Chandler, etc. It is also frequently extended to 'buddy boy'. This is used by a taxi-driver to his fare in *An American Dream*, by Norman Mailer and by one man to another in *St Urbain's Horseman*, by Mordecai Richler. 'Buddy boy' can easily become rather aggressive, as Peter de Vries indicates in *The Mackerel Plaza*. An American woman tells a man: 'Listen, buddy boy, I'll come and go as I please.' There is friendly usage of 'buddy boy' in *Funeral in Berlin*, by Len Deighton. All forms of this term, 'bud', 'buddy', 'old buddy', 'buddy boy', are mainly used by men to men, especially when the man being addressed is unknown to the speaker. The latter is far more likely to be working class than middle class, unless the two men concerned are genuinely old friends.

Buffalo, you old In *Gone With The Wind*, by Margaret Mitchell, Scarlett O'Hara would like to call Mrs Merriwether 'you old buffalo', but does not have the courage to do so. She merely says it to herself, and thinks 'how heavenly it would be to tell you just what I think of you'. In the USA 'buffalo' is sometimes used for the bison, a hairy cow-like creature. The expression Scarlett has in mind is therefore an alternative form of 'you old cow'.

Bugger Technically this is a reference to a sodomite, but the word is very frequently used in the northern counties of England to mean little more than 'chap, man'. At its most pejorative it is a synonym of 'bastard'. *The Blinder*, by Barry Hines, has a boy saying to another: 'Clever bugger, tha knows what I mean.' 'You stingy bugger' is used in the same book. *When the Boat Comes In*, by James Mitchell, another novel set in the north east of England, has many examples of 'you stupid bugger', 'you daft bugger', etc., used as mild insults by both men and women. *A Cack-Handed War*, by Edmund Blishen, has 'you silly bugger' used by one man to another on a farm. Authors sometimes indicate dialectal pronunciation of the word by variant spellings, such as 'bogger' which occurs in *Saturday Night and Sunday Morning*, by Alan Sillitoe, or the 'booger' which is in Henry Williamson's Devonshire stories. The Sillitoe examples show working-class usage of the term in Nottingham. 'Yer little bogger' is used with affection to a young boy by a male friend of the family. 'Bugger' is also heard in the southern counties of England, but with less frequency and often in the euphemistic form 'beggar'. The term is derived ultimately from Bulgarian, the Bulgars having acquired in former times the reputation of being sexual deviants. All the examples quoted above of 'bugger', 'beggar', etc., refer to British usage, but the term is also used in the USA. In Joseph Wambaugh's *The Choirboys* a Los Angeles policeman says to a man who has attacked him: 'You dirty little bugger!'

Bully 'You bully!' would in modern times be the natural verbal defence of a schoolboy being ill-treated by an older and bigger boy. The school bully is almost an institution, taught his lesson in a thousand and one stories of schoolboy heroism. He is a kind of amateur bully-boy, ignorant and cowardly, but rejoicing in his physical strength and taking advantage of other boys' disinclination to resort to violence. In the eighteenth century the term was applied specifically to a man who protected a prostitute, a pimp. With such unpleasant associations, it is strange to find the word

being used amongst the pitmen in the North of England throughout the nineteenth century as a regular term for 'mate'. Tyneside miners addressed their friends as 'bully Bob', 'bully Jack', and so on. Such usage would not have surprised Shakespeare, who knew the word 'bully' as a term meaning 'good friend'. 'What sayest thou, bully Bottom?' asks Peter Quince, in *A Midsummer Night's Dream*. In *The Merry Wives of Windsor*, which for some reason has far more examples of this word than any other of Shakespeare's plays, the host of the Garter Inn calls to Falstaff: 'Bully knight! Bully Sir John! Speak from thy lungs military.'

The origin of 'bully' is obscure but it is clear that the original meaning in English was something like 'brother', 'friend', or 'kinsman'. Later developments of the sense may have come about by association with the word 'bull', the behaviour of thugs being bullish. The only positive way in which bully is used in modern English is when one congratulates a person on his or her actions by saying 'Bully for you!' It was with something like those positive feelings that people used 'bully' as a term of address in past times. The more modern schoolboy use is illustrated in *Cider with Rosie*, by Laurie Lee: 'I'll give thee a clip in the yer'hole.' 'Gurt great bully.' The term becomes a covert endearment when used by a woman to a man in *Daughters of Mulberry*, by Roger Longrigg.

Bum, you This is far more frequently used by American speakers than by British speakers. In Britain 'bum' is mainly thought of as a slightly rude, childish word for the buttocks. To American speakers it is likely to suggest a tramp, or good-for-nothing hobo, when used in third-person reference. As a vocative it expresses contempt in a fairly general way, but may especially be applied to a poor performer in a sporting or entertainment context. 'If his audience shouted "Scram, bum!",' writes Nathanael West, in *The Day of the Locust*, 'he only smiled humbly and went on with his act.' In *The Late Risers*, by Bernard Wolfe, an American man calls a woman 'you bum'. Soon afterwards he is calling her 'you crazy bitch'. *Doctor at Sea*, by Richard Gordon, has 'you bums' used insultingly. *The Middle Man*, by David Chandler, has: 'Why, you bum! Who do you think you're instructing?' used by an older American man to a younger. 'Thanks fer nuthin', ya bum,' says one man to another in *Waterfront*, by Budd Schulberg, when he fails to receive the money for a cup of coffee that he has asked for, though since he is the one doing the begging, the term applies more to him.

bunch of Used as a plural element, mainly by American working-class speakers. 'Buncha crooks', for example, occurs in Truman Capote's short story *Jug of Silver*.

Bung-hole A bung-hole is literally the hole by which one empties a cask, removing the bung, or stopper, to do so. In American slang 'bung-hole' is the equivalent of 'asshole', though it is used far less frequently. 'Hey, you bung-holes, Merry Christmas!' says a woman to friends in *Mountain of Winter*, by Shirley Schoonover.

Bunny An intimate term of address used by an American wife to her husband in *The Philanderer*, by Stanley Kauffmann. In the seventeenth century it would have been used by the husband to the wife, since 'bunny' was then a term of endearment used for women and children. The allusion is to a bunny rabbit, as a child might call it. The word is connected with a Gaelic *bun*, used to describe a hare's scut, or tail. 'Rabbit' itself is occasionally an endearment, but it can be used insultingly.

Bunter, Billy A character created by Frank Richards, featured in a great many stories of school life which first appeared in 1908. He is a pupil at Greyfriars School and is known to his schoolmates as the Fat Owl of the Remove. He is fat, bespectacled, greedy, cowardly, and foolish, and a huge favourite with a vast number of readers. Modern children transfer his name to any fat child or person, using the name of his sister, Bessie Bunter, for girls and women. The Bunter stories originally appeared in *The Magnet*, but have been reprinted in hardback form many times. *See also* **Fatty**.

Burglar In *One Hundred Dollar Misunderstanding*, by Robert Gover, a young American tells a prostitute that he is a burglar, meaning to impress her. She responds by addressing him as 'burglar', or 'Mister Burglar': 'I ain got nothin fer you t'take jes now, Mister Burglar.'

Burke *See* **Berk**.

Bursar The professional title of a college treasurer and used by formal speakers as a term of address. There are several examples of such usage in *The Affair*, by C. P. Snow. The word derives from Latin *bursa*, a bag or purse, though the original Greek *bursa* was a hide or wine-skin.

Businessman, Mr Used as a nonce name in *North Dallas Forty*, by Peter Gent. This type of name is especially likely to be created when the professional description is not normally used as a title. 'You poor tired businessman' is used vocatively in *Make and Break*, the play by Michael Frayn.

Bussy An unusual vocative, addressed to a bus-driver in *North Dallas Forty*, by Peter Gent.

> The bus crawled into the gray, grimy city amid cries and insults directed at the driver. 'Goddam, bussy!' Jo Bob screamed, 'we got from Dallas to New York faster'n you're gettin' us from the fucking airport into this goddam city.'

Buster This word is thought to be a corruption of 'burster', and was applied in the nineteenth century to a big person, especially a child, who was bursting the seams of his clothes. 'Buster' might still be vaguely complimentary when addressed to a boy, but in normal usage, almost exclusively by American speakers, it is often an aggressive term when used to a man. 'Hiya, buster . . .' says a man to another, in *The Natural*, by Bernard Malamud. 'Roy is the name,' answers the man concerned, but a moment later he is called 'buster' again. 'Roy knew he would never like the guy,' Malamud writes. 'Listen, buster, that's enough,' says a man to someone who is pestering him, in *The Philanderer*, by Stanley Kauffmann, though in the same novel there is a friendly use of the term between two males. Mary McCarthy, in *Birds of America*, has a policeman saying 'Pipe down, buster' to a boy, but the boy's mother says: 'My son asked you a question, and his name is not Buster.' 'That's enough out of you too, lady,' says the policeman. Perhaps American policemen are especially fond of the word. Another one in *An American Dream*, by Norman Mailer, tells the hero: 'Don't piss on me, buster. Just sit down and dictate a little confession.' The mother's remark, quoted above, had some point to it in that 'Buster' can be a nickname, and for that matter, a name given at birth. (Even in England a Buster Smith was named in 1946.) Joseph Francis Keaton became world famous as Buster Keaton, his nickname, according to one legend, having been given him by Harry Houdini when Keaton was only three years old. He may at that time have been plumper than he later became. *Lydia*, by E. V. Cunningham, has: 'Is there an attendant in there?' 'We're not the Waldorf, buster.' 'And don't call me buster and don't crack wise with me.' Arthur Hailey's *Hotel* has a man who says: 'Whoever you are, buster, you're just a hotel slob and I don't take orders from you.' The novel *Like Any Other Man*, by Patrick Boyle, which is set in Ireland, has a woman using 'buster' to her lover in a kind of aggressively intimate way: 'Whipping off her knickers, she would fling them at him, urging: "Come on, buster, you win." '

Busybody Used since the sixteenth century to describe someone who is meddlesome, and takes an unwanted interest in other people's affairs. 'Little busybody' is said to a child aged six by an older boy in *Villette*, by Charlotte Brontë. In *The Pleasure Man*, by Mae West, an American man calls another man 'you damned little busybody'.

Butter-fingers A term used almost exclusively as a vocative, and associated especially with cricket, though it can be applied to anyone who lets a ball or other object slip through his fingers. In *The Pickwick Papers* we learn of Mr Jingle that

> at every bad attempt at a catch, and every failure to stop the ball, he launched his personal displeasure at the head of the devoted individual in such denunciations as – 'Ah, ah!' – 'stupid!' – 'Now, butter-fingers' – 'Muff' – 'Humbug' – and so forth, which seemed to establish him in the opinion of all around, as a most excellent and undeniable judge of the whole art and mystery of the noble game of cricket.

Thackeray, in his *Miscellanies*, has a rather more gruesome example of the word's use: 'When the executioner had come to the last of the heads, he lifted it up but, by some clumsiness, allowed it to drop; at this the crowd yelled out, "Ah, Butter-fingers!" '

Buttinsky A substitute name used by American speakers to someone who is butting in, or intruding, where he is not wanted. The ' –sky' ending is taken from Slavic last names and is added for humorous effect. *The Sophomore*, by Barry Spacks, has: ' "Who are you?" said the third student suspiciously. "Buttinsky!" ' The *New Dictionary of American Slang* says that the term has been in use since 1900.

Buttons From the mid-nineteenth century until the 1930s this was a standard term of address for a bell-boy, or bell-hop, in a hotel. The name derived from the uniform worn by such a person, distinguished by its row of buttons down the front. In modern times the name has become fossilized and is associated in England, at least, with the stock character in the pantomime *Cinderella*, a pageboy. In *The Late Risers*, by Bernard Wolfe, there is an *ad hoc* usage of 'brass buttons', used by an American girl to address a policeman.

Butty, Buttie, But, 'Ole but, Me ole Butty After a BBC radio broadcast in 1975 Mr M. J. Collins wrote to the present author as follows: 'The above terms are in common and frequent use today throughout the Forest of Dean, and are exactly analogous to "cock" and "mate".' 'Butty' was coined by the colliers of the now defunct Forest of Dean pits in the days when they hacked coal from narrow seams by bracing themselves back to back against their mate, their 'butty', derived from 'buttock'. Miss M. J. Levett also wrote about the term ' "ole but", or more commonly said as one word, "olbut". Presumably a contraction of old butty, and sometimes further reduced to "but".' Stephen York, writing from Nottingham, said:

> Butty is not used as a name-substitute here, but was in frequent use among Notts miners to denote the leader of a gang of miners in the old free-enterprise days. He would contract with the mine-owners to work a certain part of the face (a butt?) for a negotiated sum, and split this with his men as he thought fit. D. H. Lawrence's father was a butty, and there is a description in *Sons and Lovers* giving some idea of a butty's work and status.

Eric Partridge, in his *Dictionary of Historical Slang*, says that 'butty' emerged in the 1850s as a word meaning 'mate'. He cites Romany 'booty-pal' as a possible origin, or a Warwickshire dialect word 'butty', which like the Romany word, referred to a fellow-worker. He also queries whether there could be a connection with 'buddy', to which the answer is probably not, since the latter term appeared in Britain only recently. Mr Collins's 'buttock' suggestion is almost too appealing to try to overthrow. In its favour is the common use of 'butt' in slang to refer to the buttocks. The crux of the matter is whether the dialectal word for fellow-worker was in use before the mining term, and with colloquial terms of this kind, exact dating is impossible. First mention of such words in literature is a different matter, and does not necessarily reveal the true history of a word.

Buzzard In Britain this is a name for a hawk; in the USA it describes various large birds of prey, including the vulture. Applied to a person by an American speaker, 'buzzard' describes a rapacious and contemptible individual, though a passing reference to a man as an 'old buzzard' may be humorous. In *Laura*, by Vera Caspary, one man calls another 'my sweet buzzard' because he is metaphorically feeding off the dead, buying the property of a recently deceased person with a view to making a substantial profit. In *A Woman Called Fancy*, by Frank Yerby, occurs: ' "You buzzard," Wyche said. "Now, Wyche," the tall man said, "you ain't got no call to lowrate me like that – 'specially in front of a lady. Haven't taken notice of you letting any suckers off scot-free yourself . . ." '

Cabbage leaf, you squashed One of Professor Higgins's idiosyncratic terms for Eliza Doolittle in Shaw's *Pygmalion*. It conveys the general sense of worthlessness.

Cabby *Oliver's Story*, by Erich Segal, has the following exchange: ' "What are you, buddy," said the cabby, "an amnesiac?" "What are you, cabby," I retorted, "Woody Allen?" ' A British example of 'cabby' used to a taxi-driver occurs in *Thursday Afternoons*, by Monica Dickens. 'Cabby' came into use in the mid-nineteenth century, an abbreviation of cabman. 'Drive to the 'ouse with the yellow door, cabmin,' says a pretentious lady in *The Pickwick Papers*, by Charles Dickens. Dickens also describes the vehicle in which the lady is travelling in all its Victorian splendour as a 'hackney-cabriolet'. It was hardly surprising that the French word *cabriolet* was quickly shortened to 'cab' by the general public. The French had named the carriage concerned, a light two-wheeled vehicle drawn by one horse, and with a leather or wooden hood, because of its bounding motion. *Cabriolet* was a derivative of cabriole or *capriole*, which meant a leap or bound, as that of a goat (Latin *caper*). To return to the subject of modern cabbies, they are in fact more likely to be addressed as 'driver' than 'cabby', though the latter word is used in third-person reference. The vocative usage in J. P. Donleavy's *A Fairy Tale of New York* is unusual. A woman in the story says: 'Go home you crazy cab-driver.'

Cad, you 'Cad' is a short form of 'caddie', in the sense of a lad or man who waited about for chance employment. Such boys and men were to be found in the vicinity of public schools, such as Eton, and universities, especially Oxford. The caddies became popularly known as 'cads' in public school and university slang. Because they were often those who behaved in an ungentlemanly way, caddish behaviour signified low vulgarity. For a public schoolboy or university student to call one of his fellows a cad was therefore to imply that he was no better than one of the townsmen who did odd jobs. Typical public school usage occurs in *Stalky and Co.*, by Rudyard Kipling, and in *Mike*, by P. G. Woodhouse. One aspect of caddish behaviour appears to have been the deceiving of innocent women or behaving dishonourably towards them. There is often this implication in 'you cad' when applied outside school circles, though such applications will be found in literature rather than life. 'Cad' has become a decidedly old-fashioned word, one which would probably arouse amusement rather than dismay in modern times. A reference to it in *Laura*, by Vera Caspary, however, upsets the heroine:

> 'I hate that word.'
> Shelby said, 'It's a good English word.'
> 'It's old-fashioned. It's out of date. People don't talk about cads any more. It's Victorian.'
> 'A cad is a cad, whether the word is obsolete or not.'
> 'Quit being so Southern.'

Caddie The professional title of someone who carries a golf player's clubs. The word is a diminutive form of 'cadet', used in its meaning of a junior who performs menial services while training. A golf caddie is addressed by title in *Goldfinger*, by Ian Fleming. In *The Battle of the Villa Fiorita*, by Rumer Godden, occurs the following conversation between an English girl known as Caddie and a girl of Italian-English parentage called Pia: ' "Caddie?" said Pia. "That is not a name. That is golf, for carrying the clubs." "My name is Candida, after my grandmother." '

Calf 'How now, you wanton calf, Art thou my calf?' says Leontes to his son Mamillius, in Shakespeare's *The Winter's Tale*. Applied to a person, 'calf' seems to have had a wide range of meanings in the seventeenth century. It could imply meekness, harmlessness, immaturity, and sometimes stupidity, perhaps in the last sense being influenced by moon-calf. The human link with 'calf' that has survived into modern times is in 'calf-love', the rather patronizing reference to youthful affections that adults still use. Eric Partridge reports in *A Dictionary of Historical Slang* that 'calf's head' occurred from the end of the sixteenth century to the beginning of the nineteenth century as a term meaning 'a very stupid fellow'. If so it was no doubt used vocatively during that period.

Caller Used by a telephone operator to a person making a call. When the operator has two callers on the line at the same time, the name of the place from which one of them is telephoning may be used as a vocative: 'Go ahead, Paris,' 'Hold the line, London.'

Canary Applied in American slang to a girl or woman, more specifically, to a woman singer of popular songs. In underworld slang there is a reference to 'singing' of a different kind, and a canary is a police-informant. In *Laura*, by Vera Caspary, the following occurs: 'My curiosity was roused by observation of the blossoming of his love for you.' 'For me!' 'Don't sing so high, sweet canary.' It is clear that the words 'For me' were uttered in a tone of great surprise and in a raised voice, hence the choice of phrase and vocative.

Canon The professional title of certain clergymen in the Christian Church. They have particular duties at a cathedral.

Captain This title is met with fairly frequently, since there are both military and civilian captains of various kinds. As an army rank, captain is above lieutenant and below major. Thus the high-ranking brigadier in *The Facemaker*, by Richard Gordon, is able to say: 'Oh, do be quiet, Captain!' to his subordinate officer. In the navy a captain ranks above a commander and below a commodore or rear-admiral. This means that a naval captain is on the same level as an army colonel, while an army captain is on the level of a naval lieutenant. In the USA 'captain' is also an air force and marine corps rank, similar to that of the army. The army, naval, and air force captains referred to above are all commissioned officers; 'captain' is also a title conferred on the master of any ship in the Royal or Merchant navies.

In modern times the senior pilot of a civil aircraft is a captain. The title may also be met with in the fire or police department, where (in the USA) a captain ranks between a lieutenant and a chief. Since 'captain' basically means 'head', Latin *caput* being its etymon, the term is also used of the person who leads a sports team, the captain of a football team, for example. It is also used in restaurants and hotels of the person in charge of waiters or bellboys.

Use of the term is even more widespread because 'captain' has been used since at least the beginning of the seventeenth century as a vaguely complimentary term of address to a male. There are many examples of such usage in the Shakespeare plays. *Timon of Athens* (2:ii) has the page saying to the fool: 'Why, how now, Captain? What do you in this wise company?' In *The Winter's Tale* (1:ii) Leontes says to his son: 'Come, Captain, we must be neat – not neat, but cleanly, Captain.' The plays also have many instances of army and naval captains being addressed by title, sometimes qualified as 'noble captain', 'good captain',

'brave captain'. In *King Henry the Fourth Part Two* (2:iv) the Hostess addresses Pistol, who is Falstaff's ensign, as 'sweet captain', but the term enrages Doll Tearsheet:

Captain! Thou abominable damn'd cheater, art thou not ashamed to be called captain? An captains were of my mind, they would truncheon you out, for taking their names upon you before you have earn'd them. You a captain? You slave, for what? For tearing a poor whore's ruff in a bawdy house? He a captain! hang him, rogue! He lives upon mouldy stew'd prunes and dried cakes. A captain! God's light, these villains will make the word as odious as the word 'occupy'; which was an excellent good word before it was ill sorted. Therefore captains had need look to't.

In Shaw's *Pygmalion* Eliza Doolittle calls Colonel Pickering 'captain' when he is still a stranger to her, pronouncing it, Shaw tells us, as *keptin*. For her the term is equivalent to 'governor', conveying respect, though when she becomes convinced that Higgins is a detective who is about to arrest her, she thinks that this must be 'because I called him Captain'. She pleads: 'Oh, sir, don't let him lay a charge agen me for a word like that.' This kind of usage evidently continues. In his autobiographical *Travels with Charley*, John Steinbeck says that he offered a lift to 'an old Negro' when he was touring the country in 1960. 'How are things going with you?' Steinbeck asked him. 'Fine, just fine, captain, sir.' However, Steinbeck does say that while driving around he usually wore a British naval cap which once belonged to a friend. He was also bearded. *Home*, by Somerset Maugham, has: ' "Well, I'm glad to see you've got here safely, Mr Meadows." "Captain," he corrected,' writes Maugham, the man concerned being a retired sea-captain. Loose pronunciation of the title is sometimes indicated by the spelling 'Cap'n', as in *Doctor at Sea*, by Richard Gordon. It occurs again in *To Kill a Mockingbird*, by Harper Lee, when a lawyer in court asks a witness if his name is Robert Ewell. 'That's m'name, cap'n,' says the witness, at which the lawyer's back 'stiffened a little'. J. B. Priestley, in *The Good Companions*, uses the spelling 'Cap'en' and shows another misuse of the title:

'You be off,' said the policeman to Mr Oakroyd, 'and leave him alone. And you get off home, sir, afore somebody else starts follering you. You've not far to go.' 'Ay, ay, Cap'en.' And George gave another salute and zigzagged down the road.

In very informal use, the abbreviation 'Cap' can occur. 'What happened to your anchor, Cap?' says a speaker in *The Island*, by Peter Benchley. This is also the normal term addressed to the captain of Edna Ferber's *Showboat*. On the one-time fondness for bestowing military titles rather easily, *see also* **Major** and **Colonel**.

Carrots, Carrot top *See* **Ginger**.

Cat This term has a long history, dating back to the thirteenth century, as an insulting description of a spiteful person, especially a back-biting woman. From the fifteenth to the eighteenth century it was also a slang term for a prostitute. In modern slang it can still refer to a black American who dresses in a flashy manner, to a jazz musician, to a hepcat, or – in the language of 'cool' speakers – to any man. Addressed to a woman, 'cat' is usually an insult; addressed to a man it is usually complimentary. In Shaw's *Arms and the Man* occurs:

Sergius: Tiger cat!
Raina: (*running excitedly to Bluntschli*) You hear this man calling me names, Captain Bluntschli?
Bluntschli: What else can he do, dear lady? He must defend himself somehow.

In *Pygmalion*, another of Shaw's plays, Eliza Doolittle tries at one point to scratch Higgins's face. 'Claws in, you cat,' he tells her. *See also* **Cheshire cat, you old**.

Central A term that was formerly used in the USA when addressing a telephone operator. There was a popular American song in 1918 called 'Hello, Central, Give Me No Man's Land'. *Mountain of Winter*, by Shirley Schoonover, has a man in a rural area trying to report a forest fire: ' "Wake up, will you, Central?" Paul muttered as he rang for the central operator.' This scene takes place in the 1940s.

Chairman Used to address the person who is in charge of a formal meeting. When that person is a man, 'Mr Chairman' is commonly used. Some speakers would continue to use 'Chairman', and perhaps even 'Mr Chairman', to a woman who was running a meeting. Other speakers would switch to 'Madame Chairman'. Those uneasy with this formula, which still makes use of the ' –man' element, might employ 'Chairperson', though such 'person' constructions have been derided by many commentators on language use in recent years. A recent fashion is to address the chairman or chairwoman as 'Chair', though in one of her speeches to the Conservative Women's Conference, Mrs Thatcher had this to say: 'Conservative women are above all practical. They do not attempt to advance women's rights by addressing you, Madame Chairman, as Madame Chairperson or Madame Chair, or worse, simply as Chair. With feminists like that who needs male chauvinists?'

Chamberlain At the highest level a chamberlain is an officer of the royal household whose duties include the stage-management of coronations, also overseeing the upkeep of royal buildings. He was originally responsible for the bed-chamber of the monarch. The word was applied at lower levels of society to those whose duties included looking after the bedrooms in an inn, or in the houses of those rich enough to retain a number of servants. In *Joseph Andrews*, by Henry Fielding, Mrs Towwouse, the innkeeper's wife, shouts for her chamberlain to attend on Joseph, who is lying sick in one of the bedrooms: 'Chamberlain, where the devil are you?'

Champ An abbreviation of 'champion', and used in a friendly way as a term of address, usually by one man to another. In boxing circles it might well be used to address the winner of a championship bout; elsewhere it is vaguely complimentary. In *Rabbit is Rich*, by John Updike, it is consistently used by a man to a colleague who was a former professional sportsman.

Chap This term is not used on its own vocatively, other than in the plural. In *Guns at Batasi*, by Robert Holles, an army officer addresses his men as 'chaps'. There is a similar use in *Black Saturday*, by Alexander McKee, where a dying sergeant whispers 'Cheerio, Chaps' to his comrades. *The Affair*, by C. P. Snow, has twenty examples of 'my dear chap' being used between middle-class men who were mostly born at the beginning of the present century. 'Chap' is popular with such speakers in such a collocation, 'my dear fellow' being used even more. 'Chap' derives from 'chapman', a trader, where 'chap' is etymologically related to the word 'cheap'. *See also* **Chap, old**.

Chap, old A fairly popular variant of 'old boy' or 'old man', used in a friendly way to boys or men of any age. In a random selection of fifty British novels, old chap occurred 26 times. This compares with 152 'old boy' examples, 82 'old man' examples. The instances of 'old chap' were spread between at least twenty of the fifty novels, the speakers tending to be middle-class males, and often using a sympathetic tone. They also tended to have been born in the 1920s or 1930s. In *War Brides*, by Lois Battle, a young Australian girl, who addresses her father by his first name, also calls him 'old chap' (and 'mate'). 'Old chappie' is occasionally found. The 'old' is, of course, friendly and not a comment on the age of the person addressed. In *Thursday Afternoons*, by Monica Dickens, a doctor says to a young boy: 'Look here, old chap, supposing you go with

Nurse and play something for a bit while your mother and I have a chat?'

Chap with the red whiskers, thou An interesting example of an *ad hoc* vocative, using a descriptive phrase. The speaker in this case is Captain Peleg, in Herman Melville's *Moby Dick*. He tells another man: 'Spring, thou green pants.'

Chaplain Technically a chaplain is a clergyman in charge of a chapel. In the USA especially the term is used of a clergyman attached to a branch of the military services. It is used in a military context in *Catch 22*, by Joseph Heller, where Corporal Whitcomb tells the Anabaptist minister, who has asked 'Do you mean to say that you actually went over my head to the colonel without asking my permission?' 'That's right, Chaplain.' The chaplain concerned spends much of his time explaining to his fellow officers that it is not necessary for them to call him 'Father'.

Charge Used in the sense of a person who is entrusted to the care of another when Diomedes, in Shakespeare's *Troilus and Cressida* (5:ii) addresses Cressida as 'my charge'. She in turn calls him 'my sweet guardian'. Diomedes has been asked by Troilus to watch over Cressida. A completely different use of the term is explained by a nurse in *An Indecent Obsession*, by Colleen McCullough: 'When I'm put in charge of a ward I understand my title becomes Charge Nurse Langtry – "Charge" for short.'

Charlie A name sometimes transferred to a man whose name is known *not* to be Charles or whose name is unknown. Usage can be friendly or unfriendly. It is the latter in *Doctor at Sea*, by Richard Gordon. The term is extended on occasion to 'Charlie boy'. *See also* the Shaw quotation at **Freddy**.

Charmer A mainly eighteenth- and nineteenth-century vocative, applied to a woman who was fascinating. Usually qualified as 'my charmer', 'sweet charmer', etc., and not always used sincerely. Miss Wardle is 'cruel charmer' to Jingle in *The Pickwick Papers*, by Charles Dickens. Thomas Hardy, in *The Trumpet Major*, has: 'You shall drop your haughty airs, my charmer!' 'Charmer' lives on in modern English, but normally only in third person reference. It could be applied in that way to a man or woman.

Charming, Prince An allusion to the tale of *Cinderella*, by the French writer Charles Perrault. Prince Charming in that tale makes Cinderella's dreams come true, changing her from a household drudge into a princess. One might therefore say that every young woman hopes that a Prince Charming will one day come into her life. When the phrase is used vocatively in *Like Any Other Man*, by Patrick Boyle, it is a sarcastic comment by one man to another, whom he suspects of luring his lover away from him. ' "Up off your seat, Prince Charming,' he said. "You're on your way." '

Chatterbox A term used informally to a person who talks incessantly, especially a child who does so. 'You little chatterbox' is so used in *Villette*, by Charlotte Brontë. The word is recorded from the beginning of the nineteenth century.

Chauvinist pig Often in the phrase 'male chauvinist pig'. Applied to a man, usually by a woman speaker, if she thinks he is displaying an attitude of male superiority over women, or contempt for women who demand equal rights. Such attitudes, of course, are often indicated by the terms of address such men use to women. *The Choirboys*, by Joseph Wambaugh, has the following exchange:

'All these cunts are like that these days. Wanna be truck drivers. I say back em up and give em a load, they wanna be truck drivers.'
'You ain't got a load, Roscoe, you dirty mouthed chauvinist pig!' said Carolina Moon.
'Who asked you? You a libber or something?' Roscoe challenged.

Women's libbers, fighting for the liberation of women, are the arch-enemies of male chauvinist pigs.

Cheapskate A term of reproach in the USA for a miserly person who tries to avoid paying his share of the expenses. It is used in a bar scene in *The Ginger Man*, by J. P. Donleavy. 'Cheapskate' appears to have been formed on the analogy of 'bletherskate', where ' –skate' refers to the fish of that name. *See also* **Blatherskite**.

Cheater A term associated with the 'swaggering rascal', 'the foul-mouth'dst rogue in England', namely Pistol, Sir John Falstaff's ensign in *Henry the Fourth Part Two* (2:iv). Falstaff describes him as 'no swaggerer, hostess; a tame cheater, i' faith'. Doll Tearsheet soon afterwards addresses him as 'thou abominable damn'd cheater'. Falstaff's reference to 'tame cheater' was to a decoy duck or other tame animal used as a decoy in hunting. Doll, of course, was using 'cheater' in its more usual sense of one who cheats. Children are still quick to hurl this accusation at one of their number in the modern playground or classroom, often accompanied by the reminder that

'Cheats never prosper'. Those who cheat during an examination are 'cribbers'.

Cheese-eater 'You stinkin', rotten cheese-eater' is said aggressively by one man to another in *Waterfront*, by Budd Schulberg. There is presumably a reference to the slang meaning of cheese, namely 'vomit'. 'Cheese' also means 'nonsense' in American slang, and as a verb can mean 'to break wind'.

Chef This term is derived from the phrase *chef de cuisine*, French for 'chief, or head, of the kitchen'. It refers in English to a professional cook in a hotel or restaurant, especially to the head chef, or senior chef on duty. Arthur Hailey, in *Hotel*, has: ' "Good evening, Chef; Mr McDermott." Though in hotel precedence Peter [McDermott] outranked the other two, in the kitchen the maître d'hôtel deferred, correctly, to the senior chef.'

Cheshire cat, you old No-one has satisfactorily explained why Cheshire cats are supposed to grin. The saying 'to grin like a Cheshire cat' already existed when Lewis Carroll had his heroine, in *Alice in Wonderland*, ask the Duchess why her cat was grinning, only to be told: 'It's a Cheshire cat, and that's why.' In vocative terms, to call someone 'an old Cheshire cat' is clearly not the same as calling that person an 'old cat'. Thus Clive Newcome, in Thackeray's *The Newcomes*, says to his aunt's servant, Hannah: 'What are you grinning at, you old Cheshire cat?' A moment later he also calls her 'you old goose', but we are told that 'by these playful names [Clive] had been wont to designate Hannah these twenty years past'.

Chick Used as a term of endearment, usually to a young girl. It is used by a father to his daughter in *The Daysman*, by Stanley Middleton, the speaker being British. In both British and American slang, 'chick' is used of a young woman in third person reference. There was an earlier term 'chickabiddy' which was used to young children. It is used in *Dombey and Son*, by Charles Dickens: 'Do you sweet Rob? Do you truly, chickabiddy?' The 'biddy' is possibly from the pet form of Bridget.

Chickadee, my little The chickadee is the black-cap titmouse, a North American bird whose note sounds something like 'chickadee'. 'My little chickadee' as a vocative was almost the exclusive property of the American comedian W. C. Fields (1879–1946), a notable eccentric. So closely associated was he with this expression that it became the title of one of his films, released in 1940. Anyone who uses the term normally tries to imitate Field's characteristic gravel voice while doing so.

Chicken This can be used affectionately, to a girl, or insultingly, normally to a man. 'How would you like that, chicken?' is a mother addressing her daughter in *Mariana*, by Monica Dickens. There is a comparable use in *Resolve This Day*, by Geoffrey Bainbridge. The word is similar in many ways to 'child', and indeed had acquired that meaning by the fifteenth century. This is still acknowledged in modern times when we say that such and such a person is 'no chicken', meaning that he or she is no longer young. When 'chicken' is used vocatively in Iris Murdoch's *The Word Child* as an endearment, one wonders whether the novelist was led to it by her general train of thought. A couple are talking about their future together, and the woman has said that she has always wanted to live in the country. 'There, my chicken, there, my little one,' says the man. 'We'll live in the country, in a country cottage,' says the woman, and adds: 'and we could have animals, couldn't we, some chickens and a dog.' *War Brides*, by Lois Battle, has a young American husband saying to his wife: 'Okay, chicken, let's see if you remember how to cut a rug.' To accuse someone of being a chicken is to say that he is a coward, chicken-hearted. Shakespeare refers to people as 'chickens' in this sense, though he does not use the word vocatively. It occurs in *The Dream Team*, by Joe McGinnis. A woman and a man are taking a shower together. The woman turns on the cold water instead of the hot, causing the man to leap out. ' "*Chicken!*" she said, and made a face. If she had been holding a towel, I believe she would have snapped it at me.'

Chicken-shit A generally insulting term used mainly in the USA. In *Boulevard Nights*, by Dewey Gram, 'you chicken-shit' is applied to the members of a gang by one of its members, and possibly refers to 'chicken' in its cowardly sense. In Mordecai Richler's *Cocksure* it is used by one man to another as an insult, but there is no suggestion of cowardice. *The Choirboys*, by Joseph Wambaugh, has a suspect saying to a policeman in Los Angeles: 'You shot me in the back, you chickenshit!'

Chief In *A Dictionary of Sailor's Slang*, by Wilfred Granville, we are told that '*Chief* is used as a less formal mode of address by an officer to a Chief Petty Officer. *Chiefy* is most used on the lower deck.' 'Chief' might also be used by a British politician to his Chief Whip, as Maurice Edelmann illustrates in his novel *The Minister:* 'Tell me, Chief, have you spoken to Armstrong?' In the USA a chief of police is likely to be addressed by this term. It may also occur more generally, used to someone who is in a senior position, as the boss, but does not necessarily have 'chief' as part of his official title. Thus the new salesman who works for Babbitt in Sinclair Lewis's novel of that name tells him: 'By golly, chief, say, that's great.' 'Chief' is also used in a vaguely flattering way by one man to another, e.g. by a taxidriver to a customer or by a man asking a stranger for money. The speaker in such cases would always be working-class and male. A special use of 'chief' survives in innumerable western films and children's games, as well as on North American Indian reservations, where the leader of an Indian tribe is addressed by this traditional title. An *ad hoc* use of the term is seen in *Moviola*, by Garson Kanin. A woman begins to give her male companion instructions about following another car. He replies: 'Okay, Chief.' In *War Brides*, by Lois Battle, 'Thanks, Chief' is said by an American prostitute to a prospective client. She also addresses him as 'handsome'.

Chief Inspector A British police rank. *See* Inspector.

Chiel 'Why didn't ye speak to me afore, chiel?' says an elderly man to a young woman, in Thomas Hardy's *The Trumpet Major*. The word appears to be a form of 'chield', which the *Oxford English Dictionary* reluctantly accepts as a variant of child. Although the two words look very close, the change of pronunciation does not follow any regular pattern. 'Chield' is normally associated with Scottish speakers, but its use in dialect clearly extended far beyond Scottish borders if Hardy is to be believed. The author seems to have been an accurate reporter of southern dialectal usage in general, and probably heard 'chiel' himself. It is tempting to see it as a backformation from the plural form, children.

Child While this is theoretically a term of address that could be used to a boy or girl, it appears to be used far more often to girls or young women. Every reference in Shakespeare to 'my child' is to a daughter, but that is hardly surprising. In the West Country dialect of Shakespeare's day child did indeed refer to a girl specifically. Thus, in *The Winter's Tale*, when the shepherd finds an abandoned baby, he says: 'What have we here? Mercy on's, a barne! A very pretty barne. A boy or a child, I wonder?' The *Oxford English Dictionary* interestingly speculates that the use of 'child' to girls may have been widespread because girls were more dependent on their parents, over a longer period, than boys. The term, however, is often used to young women by speakers other than their parents. 'But you're ill, child', says Hilda to her younger sister in *Lady Chatterley's Lover*. Connie is also addressed as 'dear child' by the elderly gentleman who is Sir Clifford's god-father. In *Opening Night*, by Ngaio Marsh, a girl of

twenty is 'child' to a considerably older man. In Edna O'Brien's *Girl with Green Eyes* there is a similar use of 'child', 'my child', and 'you poor child' by adults to a young woman. In *The Diviners*, by Margaret Laurence, a husband who is considerably older than his wife makes use of 'child', but has to defend himself.

'I shouldn't have butted in like that, Brooke. I *am* sorry.'

'Hush, child. It's all right.' Morag abruptly pulls away from him.

'Brooke, I am not your child. I am your wife.'

'My God, Morag, can't you see I only used the word as an expression of affection? Remember how you and Ella used to call each other *kid*? What's the difference, except that I meant this a little more tenderly, and in a different kind of relationship?'

Oh God. Quite true. And she had lashed out at him for it.

Nevertheless, in this instance the young wife has perhaps instinctively reacted against a condescending attitude which does not bode well, and the couple eventually divorce.

The generally affectionate use of 'child' and expanded forms of it such as 'honey child' is associated with the American South, where at one time, if we are to believe Mrs Stowe and *Uncle Tom's Cabin*, blacks sometimes referred to themselves as 'this child'. But the word has also been used contemptuously. In *A Midsummer Night's Dream* Puck says to Demetrius: 'Come, recreant, come, thou child; I'll whip thee with a rod.' In Tennyson's *In Memoriam* occurs: 'They called me a fool, they call'd me child.' It would be tempting to say that such contemptuous use normally applies to a man (cf. an expression like 'you old woman' used insultingly to a man) but at one time 'child' was clearly a title of honour, used of youths of noble birth. The modern fashion is to spell the word slightly differently when it has this meaning, as in Byron's *Childe Harold*. Such usage is now purely literary or historical, and the main use of 'child' in modern times is likely to be a girl or young woman. The speaker may be a parent, or more frequently, an older person assuming a kind of parental role, such as a teacher or religious. A teacher's use of it, or of a term such as 'my poor misguided child' (*Lord of the Flies*, by William Golding), will probably be resented if it is a boy who is being addressed. As for the use of 'child' by religion, the following comment in *Joseph Andrews*, by Henry Fielding, is relevant:

The gentleman expressed great delight in the hearty and cheerful behaviour of [Parson] Adams; and particularly in the familiarity with which he conversed with Joseph and Fanny, whom he often called his children, a term he explained to mean no more than his parishioners; saying 'he looked on all those whom God had entrusted to his cure, to stand to him in that relation.'

Fielding then takes the opportunity to comment on the clergymen of the time who adopt no such attitude to their parishioners, but strut around like turkey-cocks. Adams does indeed address Joseph as 'child' throughout the book, sometimes extending it to 'dear child', 'my good child'. It is noticeable that on one occasion, when Joseph says something that he does not like, he switches immediately to 'boy'. Another religious who uses 'child' as a regular term of address is Doctor Primrose, in *The Vicar of Wakefield*, though it is usually his wife, rather than his parishioners, to whom he is speaking. One wonders what Dr Primrose would have made of the remark in D. H. Lawrence's *The Plumed Servant*, about 'calling Kate, in the old Mexican style, *Niña*, which means *child*.' It is the honourable title for a mistress.

Childer A plural form of 'child' used in some northern English dialects, extending down to the Midlands. It is used by a countrywoman to two young women in *Jane Eyre*, by Charlotte Brontë. The same speaker uses 'bairn' when addressing one of them.

Children Used to a group of young children, but occasionally said to adults if they appear to be acting like children. An American speaker in *A World of Difference*, by Stanley Price, says to two men who are quarrelling: 'Now, now, children. No falling out . . .'

China, chiner Used by a London Cockney, this would be the equivalent of 'mate', thanks to the rhyming slang 'china plate'. It is more likely to occur in an expression like 'me old china' than be used alone. Eric Partridge, in his *Dictionary of Historical Slang*, says that 'chiner' is an alternative spelling in this sense. Edward Blishen, in *A Cack-Handed War*, has: 'Accustomed to being called "old 'un" or "'chiner", Jimbo did not respond happily to Pringle's cry of: "Oh *driver* . . . !"' This is in a rural setting, where ' 'chiner' is an abbreviated form of 'machiner'. Jimbo is the operator of a threshing machine.

Chink, Chino Impolite nicknames for a person of Chinese descent, occasionally extended to include those from other oriental countries. *See* **Nip**.

Chippy, Chips A nickname automatically used for a carpenter in the British navy, on a building site, etc. In the navy it is also given to a man whose last name is Carpenter.

Chiseller A person who tries to chisel, i.e. cheat others. *A Kind of Loving*, by Stan Barstow, has: 'Lewis gets his wallet out and opens it. "Ten bob, wasn't it?" "A quid, you chiseller." '

Chisel-pusher, you psalm-singing See **Plumber's mate, you lousy little bastard**.

Chit A chit of a girl is one who is indisciplined and disrespectful. 'You chit' addressed to a girl, as in *The Country Girls*, by Edna O'Brien, is thus a comment on her bad behaviour. The word derives from a dialectal form of 'kitten'.

Chocolate drop, my Used as an endearment and equated with 'my honey' in *Within and Without*, by John Harvey. Both terms are addressed by a man to a woman. A chocolate drop is a small round chocolate sweet, or candy.

Choir Used as a collective term to address a choir in *Lord of the Flies*, by William Golding. Sections of the choir can also be addressed separately as 'Altos', 'Tenors', 'Sopranos', etc.

Chops A reference to the cheeks, as in an expression like 'to lick one's chops'. 'Chaps' is etymologically more accurate in this sense. 'Chops' occurs twice as a vocative in the Shakespearean plays, on both occasions addressed to Sir John Falstaff and drawing attention to his fat chops. It is therefore roughly the equivalent of 'fat-face'. One instance is in *Henry the Fourth Part One* (1:ii). For the other *see also* **Ape**.

Christian name *See* **First name**.

Chubby *See* **Fatty**.

Chuck In modern times, especially in the USA, this is often a nickname of someone whose real first name is Charles. Occasionally it is heard as a survival of a term of endearment well used since the sixteenth century, a variant of 'chick' or 'chicken'. Shakespeare shows it being used to both men and women in *Twelfth Night* (3:iv), *Love's Labour's Lost* (5:i), *Macbeth* (3:ii), *Henry the Fifth* (3:ii), *Antony and Cleopatra* (4:iv), and *Othello* (3:iv). The word occurs alone, or as 'dearest chuck', 'sweet chuck'. 'Chuck' was certainly being used in the nineteenth century, as its occurrence in novels like *Wuthering Heights*, by Emily Brontë shows. In *Edwin Drood*, by Charles Dickens, a woman addresses a man as 'chuckey'. 'Chuckie' is an endearment in *The Sleepers of Erin*, by Jonathan Gash, used by a man to his lover. 'Chuck' itself is used by an English prostitute to an American soldier in *The Magic Army*, by Leslie Thomas. *Rabbit Redux*, by John Updike, has a black American man who consistently calls a white man 'Chuck' in what is usually a friendly tone. He also addresses the man's son as 'Babychuck'. The man addressed is Harry, but 'Chuck' may here be simply a substitute name, the equivalent of Charlie. The reason for the association of 'Chuck' with Charles is not known, unless it be a simple alliteration of the opening sound. There is a traditional English playground rhyme, quoted by the Opies in *The Lore and Language of Schoolchildren*:

Charlie, Charlie, chuck, chuck, chuck,
Went to bed with three young ducks.

Chuckles This term is used by an American man to his secretary in *The Philanderer*, by Stanley Kauffmann. It is not clear whether the word is used in its own right, of someone who habitually chuckles, or whether it is an *ad hoc* extension of 'chuck', used as an endearment. It could also be a watered-down version of 'chucklehead', which in American slang means a stupid person.

Chuff, you This word was once in general use but is perhaps now dialectal. 'Listen to this, you chuff,' says a speaker in *Magnus Merriman*, by Eric Linklater. He equates it with 'you simpleton' and 'you country slab'. 'Chuff' actually means either a clown, or a surly man. The word occurs once in Shakespeare, when Falstaff accosts some travellers in *Henry the Fourth Part One* (2:ii): 'Hang ye, gorbellied knaves, are ye undone? No, ye fat chuffs.' 'Gorbellied' here means 'with fat bellies'. The use of 'you fat little chuff' in Alan Sillitoe's *A Tree on Fire* may be a Shakespearean echo. It is used by a father to his nineteen-year-old daughter.

Chum American soldiers serving in Britain in the late 1940s became accustomed to being accosted by young children who invariably asked: 'Got any gum, chum?' 'Chum' appeared in the late seventeenth century and was originally university slang for a chamber-fellow. It is thought to derive from that expression, so perhaps should be 'cham'. Technically, then, a chum is someone, another male, with whom a young man shares a room. In modern parlance he would be a flat-mate. But the word has been used since the eighteenth century in its more general sense of friend, and is used vocatively rather as that word is used. According to the tone of voice in which it is uttered, it can be either genuinely friendly or rather aggressive. Friendly usage occurs in, e.g., *Doctor in the House*, by Richard Gordon, *The Half Hunter*, by John Sherwood (where there is an example also of unfriendly usage), *Henry's War*, by Jeremy Brooks, *Room at the Top*, by John Braine. 'Old chum' occasionally occurs. The

diminutive 'chummy' is rare, but is to be found in N. J. Crisp's *Festival*: ' "Fuck the Professor," Cramer said. "I've played in more theatres than he's ever set foot in." Or you, chummy, was the unspoken implication.' The British actor Ian Carmichael reportedly addresses everyone as 'chummy'.

Chump This word appeared at the beginning of the eighteenth century, apparently suggested by existing words such as 'chunk', 'clump', and 'stump'. It was at first used of an end piece of wood, then the blunt end of anything, such as a cut of meat. Chump-chops retain this sense of the word. The associations with thickness and bluntness caused 'chump' to be applied humorously to people. It was a fashionable word amongst British schoolboys of the 1920s, parallel to 'idiot' or 'blockhead'. Typical examples of public-school usage occur in *Mike*, by P. G. Wodehouse. The word remains in occasional vocative use as a very mild insult, similar to 'clot'. It is used in a friendly way in *The Limits of Love*, by Frederic Raphael. In **Babbitt**, by Sinclair Lewis, the hero admonishes himself by saying 'Have some sense now, you chump'. *Rabbit is Rich*, by John Updike, has: 'You chump, *that's* not the point.' This occurs in the middle of a friendly conversation, spoken by a man to another man. That the term *can* be used more aggressively is shown in *The Choirboys*, by Joseph Wambaugh: ' "Gimme that wallet," Calvin said suddenly. "Ain't that illegal search and seizure, Officer?" asked the pimp. "Gimme that wallet, chump, or it's gonna be a search and *squeezure* of your fuckin' neck!" '

Chunky See **Fatty**.

Citizen In novels dealing with the French Revolution of 1789, 'citizen' occurs as a translated form of both *citoyen* and *citoyenne*, though 'citizeness' is also used for the latter. These titles were substituted by decree for *Monsieur* and *Madame*, though the latter were subsequently restored. 'Citizen' will thus be found in *A Tale of Two Cities*, by Charles Dickens, when French people are being addressed. In normal English usage 'citizen' is more likely to occur as part of a vocative group such as 'my fellow citizens', when a political speech is being made. That phrase is used by 'Honest Jim' Blausser, in Sinclair Lewis's *Main Street*. He tells the inhabitants of Gopher Prairie that the town will one day be as big as Minneapolis, addressing his audience as 'friends', 'fellow citizens', 'my fellow citizens'. *Jug of Silver*, a short story by Truman Capote, has: ' "Citizens," cried Mayor Mawes, "citizens – I say, this is Christmas." '

Class This is normally used by a teacher

when addressing the entire class of students. 'That's quite enough, class,' says a teacher in *The Diviners*, by Margaret Laurence. Apart from its obvious collective use, 'class' can occasionally occur as an indefinite vocative. An example occurs in *Cocksure*, by Mordecai Richler: 'Now this play we are going to perform for the Christmas concert was written by . . . Class?' One of the students present takes it on himself to reply. This particular usage may only have been possible because a visitor was present in the classroom at the time. The use of 'anyone', 'anybody', or 'one of you' would have been unsatisfactory because it would have theoretically included the visitor.

Clerk This word was originally the same as 'cleric'. The change of meaning to 'one who keeps written records' and the like came about because at one time the members of the clergy tended to be the only literate people in the district. It was they who kept records of births, marriages, deaths, and other parochial happenings. When possible they transferred these duties to lay-clerks. Already by the thirteenth century 'clerk' had come to mean one who could read and write, regardless of his religious status. The word is now generally used in its lay sense, of course, but is not used as a professional title other than in special circumstances, or to special officials such as a clerk of the court. In *Joseph Andrews*, by Henry Fielding, a magistrate addresses his clerk by his title when asking for his advice. Parson Adams tells a story, a page or two later, about the young men who competed for the place of parish clerk and ended by having a near-fatal dispute. The word has its modern sense when it is used vocatively in *A Salute to the Great McCarthy*, by Barry Oakley. A young Australian wife is accusing her husband of being a failure. She sarcastically calls him 'Mr Excitement', then moves on to 'Suburban shit-kicker! Clerk! Nobody! I married a nobody!'

Clever Occasionally used on its own as a term of address, and likely to be sarcastic. An example occurs in *Daughters of Mulberry*, by Roger Longrigg. There is another in *Lord of the Flies*, by William Golding. While the first of these is almost an intimacy, the latter is clearly meant to be insulting. So, too, is the nonce-name form 'Mr Clever' which occurs in *Brothers in Law*, by Henry Cecil. British children have a number of terms for other children who show signs of being too clever by half. Apart from the favourite 'clever dick', a child is likely to be called: cleverguts, cleverpot, cleversides, cleversticks, or know-all.

Clever clogs A 1980s variant of clever dick used by British youngsters. The term possibly has a comic-book origin, 'clogs' being used for purely alliterative reasons.

Clever dick A term frequently used in the slanging matches that take place between British school-children. The speaker is expressing contempt to someone who is trying to display superior knowledge. The second element of the expression is clearly 'Dick', diminutive of Richard, but is no longer associated with that name. Girls are just as likely to use 'clever dick' to one another as boys are. Eric Partridge, in his *Dictionary of Historical Slang*, dates it from the 1880s and links it with London. A typical example of British usage, by an adult rather than a child, occurs in *Saturday Night and Sunday Morning*, by Alan Sillitoe: ' "I'm looking for a friend of mine," she said. "Maybe he's in the Trip," he suggested. "It's a *she*, cleverdick," came the retort.'

For various American expressions comparable to 'clever dick' *see also* **Smarty**.

Clod 'You ignorant clod' is used by Jim Dixon in *Lucky Jim*, by Kingsley Amis. The term of address may be derived from 'clod-hopper', a country lout, one who walks across clods of earth. The '–hopper' is no doubt a humorous allusion to grass-hoppers. In the seventeenth century people also referred derisively to 'clod-pates', men whose heads were as thick as clods of earth. For centuries 'clod' and 'clot' were synonymous, though 'clod' is now used to refer to a mass of earth, while 'clot' refers to coagulated blood. As vocatives, however, 'clod' and 'clot' are still interchangeable, referring to a blockhead. 'Tap the music stand, you clod', says the first violinist to someone who has been asked to conduct the orchestra, in *Brothers' Keepers*, by Frank Smith.

Clodpoll *See* **Dunce**.

Clot This term has been used to refer to a foolish person, or clod, since at least the seventeenth century. In modern use it seems to be restricted to British speakers, who are far more likely to use it as a friendly insult than as a serious one. This may be connected with the comedian Jimmy Edwards, whose cry of 'clumsy clot' became something of a catchphrase in the 1950s. Few people would take real offence at being called 'you clot'. *A Kind of Loving*, by Stan Barstow, has the following exchange: ' "Anyway, she's married," I say. "How d'ye know?" Willy says. "Because she wears a wedding ring, clot, that's how." ' *The Pumpkin Eater*, by Penelope Mortimer, has: ' "Some old General's invaded it or something." "Invaded what?" 'Spain, you clot." ' This is a woman talking to a woman friend. In *The Battle of the Villa Fiorita*, by Rumer Godden, a young

English boy says to his sister: 'You clot! Do you want someone to hear us?'

Clown Normally used of someone who is deliberately acting in a funny way, trying to amuse others, though it can also be applied to someone who has unwittingly done something stupid. 'Bloody clown' as used in *The Country Girls*, by Edna O'Brien, is a good-natured remark, not an insult. *A Kind of Loving*, by Stan Barstow, has a scene between a young man and his mother.

I jump up from the table and throw my arms out and go into my Al Jolson take-off. 'Mammy, how I love yer, how I need yer, my dear old mammy . . .' She can't help smiling, though she does her best. 'Gerraway with yer, you great clown.'

Other Men's Wives, by Alexander Fullerton, has a scene where a wife overhears her husband making an assignation with another woman. When she confronts him she says: 'Any other little service I could render you and your little harem, is there, you stupid-looking clown, you?' There is an authorial comment:

She was rather pleased with herself for having, after all that provocation, limited her epithets to 'stupid-looking clown.' The more obvious terms would have included such words as 'filthy', 'rotten', 'swine', 'bastard', and so on. Whereas her words had downgraded him, she felt, without any indication of pain or damage inflicted on herself. She'd expressed contempt without allowing him to seem to matter to her.

Cluck, you dumb Used mainly in American rather than British speech to refer to a stupid person. 'Cluck' has that meaning on its own, but 'dumb cluck' is very much a standard phrase. The form of the word suggests that it is linked with a clucking hen, but it is more likely to be a corruption of the Yiddish *klutz*, used of an inept blockhead. 'You dumb cluck' occurs insultingly in *Within and Without*, by John Harvey. In *Moviola*, by Garson Kanin, a woman says to a man who is about to close the door of her dressing-room: 'Leave it open, you cluck.'

Clumsy Normally an adjective which means awkward and ungraceful in movement, likely to knock things over or bump into objects and people, but it occurs as a noun in *The Sleepers of Erin*, by Jonathan Gash. A man who is not feeling well says to a male visitor: 'You thundering great *clumsy*, you. You deliberately slammed that door.' 'Clumsy' would more normally occur as a vocative element, as in 'you clumsy sod', used in a friendly way in *Henry's War*, by Jeremy Brooks, and 'you clumsy

moujik', which is insulting in *The Half Hunter*, by John Sherwood.

Coach Used mainly in American sporting contexts, e.g. to the coach of a football or baseball team. It is so used in *Only a Game*, by Robert Daley, where a newspaper reporter says 'We'll take a cab, coach,' when the latter offers some reporters a lift in the team bus. Its use can be extended to anyone who temporarily assumes the role of a coach. In *The Philanderer*, by Stanley Kauffman, one businessman tells another: 'Get in there and pitch, lad.' The metaphor inspires the reply: 'I'll try, coach.' The connection between the horse-drawn carriage kind of coach and the person who gives a sportsman or student help began in British university slang. The human coach was seen as 'a help to progress'. A different kind of thinking has made it possible to refer to a person as a 'slow-coach.'

Coachman The professional title in former times of a stage-coach driver. It occurs regularly as a vocative in eighteenth- and nineteenth-century literature, e.g. 'Dear Coachman, drive on . . .', said by a woman passenger in *Joseph Andrews*, by Henry Fielding; 'Coachman, I get down here,' said by Mr Slurk, editor of the *Eatanswill Independent* in *The Pickwick Papers*, by Charles Dickens. A coachman could also be addressed as 'driver'.

Cobber A common Australian term of friendship, the equivalent of British 'mate', American 'buddy'. Partridge, in his *Dictionary of Historical Slang*, says that the term was in use at race-tracks by 1900. He derives it from Yiddish *chaber*, 'comrade', but other lexicographers are not convinced. Most dictionaries fall back on 'origin unknown'. In *War Brides*, by Lois Battle, an Australian woman who circulates a newsletter to other Australian women living in the USA begins one edition with: 'Greetings Kangaroo Cobbers.'

Cock, old cock Used mainly by British male speakers to other men in a friendly way. The expression dates from the seventeenth century and derives from the slang use of 'cock' to mean a man who fights with great courage. 'He has drawn blood of him yet. Well done, old cock!' (Philip Massinger, *The Unnatural Combat*, 1639). In *The Pickwick Papers* Sam Weller's use of the term causes a special term of address to be used in reply: ' "Do you always smoke arter you goes to bed, old cock?" inquired Mr Weller of his landlord, when they had both retired for the night. "Yes, I does, young bantam," replied the cobbler.' It is perhaps surprising that 'cock', 'old cock', etc., have survived as modern terms of address. The slang meaning that gave rise to the expression is now obsolete, though other slang meanings of a less pleasant nature live on. To describe something as a 'lot of old cock' in British slang is to say that it is rubbish. As a term for penis, a usage which began in the seventeenth century, 'cock' is still a taboo word in polite society. This explains the comment in *Birthstone*, by D. M. Thomas, who describes hearing 'my cock' used as a term of address in Cornwall: 'and it was the barmaid who was "my cock"; as though she wore a dildo under her broad floral dress.' In *The House with the Green Shutters*, by George Douglas, occurs: 'Aha, Deacon, my old cock,' Deacon being the man's professional title. The novel is set in a Scottish town. *A Kind of Loving*, by Stan Barstow, has three examples of 'old cock' and one of 'cock', used by working-class young men to one another in a friendly way. *Aaron's Rod*, by D. H. Lawrence, has 'my young cock' addressed to one young man by another.

Cockatrice The name of a fabulous monster, said to be hatched from a cock's egg, having a fowl's wings, the tail of a dragon, and a cock's head. It was supposedly able to kill at a glance. In the seventeenth and eighteenth centuries cockatrice was used as a term of reproach to a woman, meaning that she was a whore. It is difficult not to link this usage with the slang meaning of 'cock', namely penis, which is recorded from the beginning of the seventeenth century. Use of 'cockatrice' in direct address to a woman occurs in, e.g., *The Alchemist*, by Ben Jonson and *Love for Love*, by William Congreve.

Cock-boat, my little Said by a man to a woman in William Congreve's *Love for Love*, with an obvious reference to the taboo meaning of 'cock'.

Cockchafer Not a term which is habitually used as a vocative, though an interesting example occurs in *Lucky Jim*, by Kingsley Amis. Jim Dixon is careful to address the head of the history department by his professional title to his face, but Amis tells us what he would like to call him:

He'd just say, quite quietly and very slowly and distinctly, to give Welch a good chance of catching his general drift: Look here, you old cockchafer, what makes you think you can run a history department, even at a place like this, eh, you old cockchafer.

The cockchafer is a fairly large insect or beetle which is very destructive to vegetation. Since it emerges from the chrysalis in May it is also known as the Maybug. In slang 'cockchafer' has naturally been re-interpreted in the past to play upon the penis meaning of 'cock', and Amis may have had in mind some such

meaning as masturbator, from 'chafe' in its sense of 'rub'. In his *Dictionary of Historical Slang*, Eric Partridge equates 'cockchafer' with 'cock-teaser', used of a girl or woman 'permitting – and assuming – most of the intimacies but not the greatest'.

Cocker A variant of 'cock' and 'cocky', used as a friendly term of address mainly by London Cockneys. An example of its use between men occurs in *Thirteen Days*, by Ian Jefferies.

Cockroach The name of several beetle-like insects, not normally used vocatively, but 'you filthy cockroach' is said to a youth by a Los Angeles policeman in *Boulevard Nights*, by Dewey Gram. The youth no doubt understood that it implied that he was a pest, certain types of cockroaches being voracious infesters of kitchens during the night.

Cocksucker In *North Dallas Forty*, by Peter Gent, a novel which describes the world of professional American football, 'cocksucker', 'you dumb cocksucker', and the like are regularly used between team-mates. There is no reason to think that the term is meant to be taken literally, accusing the listener of being a homosexual who practises fellatio; the word is simply a synonym for 'bastard'. The equally obscene 'motherfucker' occurs in the novel with equal frequency and is used in a similar way.

Cocky A diminutive of 'cock', used as an endearment or friendly term of address. The *Oxford English Dictionary* cites vocative usage in William Congreve's *The Old Bachelor* (1687): 'Nay, look you now, if she does not weep; 'tis the fondest fool! Nay, cocky, cocky; nay dear cocky, don't cry, I was but in jest.' Partridge thinks such usage is obsolete except amongst London Cockneys and Canadians. It is a Londoner who uses 'cocky' in a friendly way to another man in *Daughters of Mulberry*, by Roger Longrigg.

Codger Etymologically a variant of 'cadger', but 'codger' applied to a man does not imply that he cadges money. 'Codger' is a whimsical term, used with little reverence, of or to an old man. The term is familiar in Britain, and is to some extent kept alive, by the 'Old Codgers' in the national newspaper, *The Daily Mirror*, who theoretically reply to readers' letters. In direct address 'codger' is now decidedly dated. It is found in Dickens's novels, e.g. in *Nicholas Nickleby*, where Mr Squeers says: 'I haven't been drinking your health, my codger.' *The Pickwick Papers* has Sam Weller addressing his father as 'old codger', amongst a number of other terms peculiar to that speaker.

Collop This is a puzzling word which by the sixteenth century had come to mean a slice of meat, especially bacon. It has that sense in Collop Monday, which precedes Shrove Tuesday. Sixteenth- and seventeenth-century writers also referred to parents leaving collops of their own flesh behind them when they died, meaning that their children survived them. In *Henry the Sixth Part One*, the shepherd calls La Pucelle his daughter, 'a collop of my flesh'. In *The Winter's Tale*, therefore, when Leontes calls his page 'my collop', it is to be interpreted as offspring, son. Such a meaning does not seem to have lasted beyond Shakespeare.

Colonel In Britain the title of an army officer of middle rank. In the USA applied also to officers of the air force and marine corps. 'Colonel' is also one of the military titles applied as a civilian honorific in the American South to minor state officials. 'This American fondness for hollow titles', writes H. L. Mencken, in *The American Language*, 'goes back to colonial days.' He adds: '*Colonel* is also often bestowed on American newspaper editors by common consent, especially in the South. Thus the rare journalist who declines a colonelcy on the governor's staff gets it thrust upon him willy-nilly.' The title is sometimes given as a first name. Daniel Defoe seems to make it such in his *Life of Colonel Jack* (1722). In William Faulkner's story *Barn Burning* there is a boy called Colonel Sartoris Snopes. A retired British army officer with whom the writer once discussed the subject remarked that he had always preferred to be called 'Colonel' rather than 'sir', the former being 'more friendly'. Decidedly unfriendly is the use of the term in Compton Mackenzie's *Whisky Galore*, where a minister insists on addressing a Captain of the Home Guard as 'Colonel'.

If there was one thing Captain Waggett disliked it was being called 'Colonel' by Father Macalister. He disliked it so much that he never hesitated to attribute what he considered a breach of good manners to the fact that the priest of Little Todday must have had a drop too much.

COLOURS Colour names are commonly used as collective vocatives in exhortations to sporting teams. Typical shouts at, e.g., a football match in Britain would be 'Come on, the blues!' or 'you blues!' The colour word can be used on its own, though always in the plural form: 'Get stuck in, reds!' In Joyce Cary's short story *A Mysterious Affair* occurs: 'The first one tipped the second one's cap off and shouted, "Forward the reds." The rest at once joined in with shouts of "Up, the Arsenal," "Manchester United", and played football with the cap.'

Commander A professional title used on its own or followed by the last name of the person concerned. In the navy a commander is a commissioned officer who is next in rank to a captain. If he were in command of a ship he would be addressed by the honorary title of 'Captain'. Probably the most famous commander in literature is Commander Bond, otherwise known as 007, the superman created by Ian Fleming. In the police force a commander is a high-ranking officer, his exact status varying slightly in Britain and the USA. In *The Choirboys*, by Joseph Wambaugh, which is a black comedy about the Los Angeles police force, occurs the following:

'Now drink your Pink Lady,' Commander Moss commanded. (It was Hector Moss who had persuaded the chief of police that the traditional police rank of 'inspector' was no longer viable in an era of violence when policemen are called upon to employ counter insurgency tactics. Thanks to Moss all officers formerly of the inspector rank could now call themselves 'commander'.

There is a joking misuse of 'Commander-in-Chief' in *The Limits of Love*, by Frederic Raphael, where an adult son uses it to his father.

Communist 'I'm just on my way to the station house to give them the lowdown on you, you dirty communist,' says a man to a woman in Truman Capote's short story *Master Misery*. The woman so addressed becomes very angry indeed at this insult. 'Fascist' is another political term used as an insult.

Companion The etymological idea behind 'companion' is 'one with whom one shares bread', a mess-mate. In third person reference it usually has positive associations, but by the end of the sixteenth century, in vocative use, it was being used with familiarity bordering upon contempt. 'I scorn you, scurvy companion' occurs in *Henry the Fourth Part Two* (2:iv). *The Oxford English Dictionary* also quotes 'thou jeering companion' and 'insolent companion' from seventeenth- and eighteenth-century sources. But Shakespeare also has 'my spruce companions' used vocatively in *The Taming of the Shrew* (4:i), 'you companion' in *Coriolanus* (5:ii), and 'my companion friends' in *Pericles* (5:i). When we come to *The Pickwick Papers*, by Charles Dickens, it is quite clear that the term is being used positively when Mr Winkle calls Pickwick 'my friend, my benefactor, my honoured companion'. 'Companion' is used on its own in a friendly way in *Absolute Beginners*, by Colin MacInnes, but the speaker is one whose idiolect is marked by the unusual vocatives he uses. The term is normally only used as the head-word in a vocative group, as in the examples given above.

Comrade This word is similar to 'chum' in some respects. Both words originally meant 'chamber-mate' and both came to have the general meaning of 'friend'. 'Comrade', however, was early associated with comrades-in-arms, fellow soldiers who shared one's tent. It was therefore mainly used by men to men, especially if they were serving together. 'Keep your spirits up, old comrade,' says Festus Derriman to his friend Noakes, in Thomas Hardy's *The Trumpet Major*. 'Spur on, comrades,' he adds, to the other fellow soldiers around him. In the 1880s the term 'comrade' was adopted by the communists and socialists as a title that would do away with social and sexual distinctions. This specialized usage, to fellow members of a union or political party, has made the ordinary use of the word, vocatively or otherwise, far less likely. The political use of 'comrade' is marked especially by its being used as a prefix, accompanied by a last name. 'I am with you, Comrade Jackson,' says Psmith to Mike, in P. G. Wodehouse's public school story *Mike*. He continues: 'You won't mind my calling you Comrade, will you? I've just become a Socialist.' In *Gideon Planish*, by Sinclair Lewis, occurs: 'He suggested their calling one another "Comrade" but it didn't go. Gid and Hatch were still too close to the horrors of being called "Brother" by loud evangelical pastors.' This conversation takes place at a meeting of the Adelbert College Socialist League. *St Urbain's Horseman*, by Mordecai Richler, has 'comrade' used in a friendly conversation between two men, who also call each other 'mate'.

Constable Normal use of this term in modern times is to a British policeman of the lowest rank, a member of the constabulary of a particular area. A constable was earlier an officer of the peace, often appointed by a parish or township, whose duties were similar to those of a modern policeman. In *Measure for Measure* (2:i), Shakespeare gives us Elbow, 'a simple constable'. He explains himself to Angelo by saying: 'I am the poor Duke's constable, and my name is Elbow; I do lean upon justice, sir, and do bring in here before your good honour two notorious benefactors.' Angelo points out to him that possibly he means 'malefactors'. After punning allusions to his name, Elbow is addressed as 'constable', 'master constable'. The constable who appears in *Henry the Fifth* is the Constable of France, the principal officer in the household of the French king. He is addressed as 'my lord high constable', 'lord constable', 'my lord constable', etc. There was a similar Lord High Constable of England, a title which was later restored temporarily for special occasions. The Duke of Wellington, for example, was made Lord High Constable at the coronation of Queen Victoria. Certain dig-

nitaries still retain the title of 'Constable', notably the governors of royal castles.

Cony, coney This was at one time the normal word for a rabbit. It was used as a term of endearment for a woman in the sixteenth century, but died away in the seventeenth century. It was at that time pronounced to rhyme with honey, and inevitably took on an indecent sense because of its nearness to 'cunt'. Beaumont and Fletcher no doubt knew that the groundlings would make the connection when they had the citizen, in *The Knight of the Burning Pestle*, address his wife by this term on many occasions.

Cook Used to address a professional cook in domestic service, on merchant ships, in lumberjack camps, etc. In *The Pickwick Papers*, by Charles Dickens, Mr Pickwick is tricked into paying a nocturnal visit to Westgate House, a boarding school for young ladies. Miss Tomkins, ruler of the establishment, orders the cook to go into the garden to see who is prowling about, but the cook is not keen on the idea. '"Do you hear, cook?" said the lady abbess, stamping her foot impatiently. "Don't you hear your missis, cook?" said the three teachers. "What an impudent thing that cook is!" said the thirty boarders.' *Candy*, by Baroness von Hutten, has a domestic cook who is addressed by that term by her employers, though she is often 'cookie' or 'cookums' to the other servants. Older domestic cooks, whether they were married or not, were also addressed as 'Mrs' + last name.

Cookie, cooky Occasionally used by American speakers to an attractive young woman, though the term is more often used in third person reference. This slang meaning of 'cookie' derives from the word (British English 'biscuit'). 'Cookie' is also used of men, in a phrase like 'a smart cookie', where it appears to be a simple synonym of 'guy'. *World So Wide*, by Sinclair Lewis, says of an American man that 'Nowadays he usually called Olivia "Sister", "Cookie", or "Helena Troy".' Olivia in this case is a woman friend of approximately the same age as the speaker. *Lydia*, by E. V. Cunningham, has an American cab-driver addressing a young woman as 'cooky'. 'Cookie/cooky' can also be a diminutive of the professional title 'cook'.

Coot, you old A friendly insult, comparing the person addressed (usually a man) to the water-bird known as a coot, or more accurately, to one of the several birds loosely known by this name. One of them is bald, hence the proverbial 'bald as a coot'. One is reputed to be rather stupid. It is the latter comparison which is usually being made when the vocative is used. 'Glad to see you, you old coot,' says an American to an old friend in *The Mackerel Plaza*, by Peter de Vries.

Cop A short form of 'copper', used in informal speech in both Britain and America to describe a policeman. 'Listen, cop, I don't know *nuthin*',' says a young American in *Waterfront*, by Budd Schulberg. The same speaker also addresses the policeman as 'buster' and 'Shorty', and is told 'Take it easy, kid.' Philip Roth, in *Portnoy's Complaint*, has both forms being used vocatively. 'Blaze, you bastard cop, what do I give a shit' occurs with the equally insulting 'Up society's ass, copper.' *The Late Risers*, by Bernard Wolfe, has 'copper' used aggressively by a prostitute to an American policeman. 'Hey, copper, I want you off this train' occurs in *The Beethoven Conspiracy*, by Thomas Hauser, spoken by a passenger on the New York subway. 'Copper' in this sense derives from the verb 'to cop', meaning to catch or capture.

Copper crust, Coppernob *See* **Ginger**.

Copy-cat An accusation used by children to a child who appears to be imitating their actions. The term is an aggressive one, since imitation, as the Opies point out in *The Lore and Language of Schoolchildren*, 'is not considered the sincerest form of flattery'.

Corporal A corporal is a non-commissioned officer in the army who ranks below a sergeant. He, or she, would correctly be addressed by this professional title and might, if the speaker was a private soldier especially, insist on its use. In *Ginger, You're Barmy*, by David Lodge, a novel about life in the British army, occurs the following: ' "Name?" "Browne." "Browne, *Corporal*." "Browne, Corporal." ' In Thomas Hardy's *The Trumpet Major* the word is corrupted into 'corpel' by a dialect speaker. By those on friendly terms with the man concerned the short form 'Corp' might be used. *When the Boat Comes In*, by James Mitchell, has: ' "What'll you have, corporal?" "Less of your corporal," Headley said. "I'm out now and I've got my discharge to prove it." "All right, *Mr* Headley," said Ford. "What'll you have?" ' While Headley was still serving he could have been addressed either as 'Corporal' or as 'Corporal Headley'. Shakespeare plays with the word in *Henry the Fourth Part Two* (3:ii), where the uneducated country bumpkin Peter Bullcalf uses 'good master corporate Bardolph' as a term of address. The same speaker addresses Falstaff as 'good my lord captain'. Ralph Mouldy also has trouble with military titles. For him Bardolph is 'good master corporal captain'.

Councillor Used to address a member of a municipal council, either alone or as a prefix to the last name of the person concerned. *The Half Hunter*, by John Sherwood, has 'Yes, Councillor Prentice. It's quite true.' In *Life at the Top*, by John Braine, occurs: ' "You're very clever, Councillor Lampton." "Don't call me that," I said. "Please don't call me that. It makes me feel a hundred years old." '

Counselor An American term of address for a lawyer who gives advice to clients in court. *The Middle Man*, by David Chandler, has: ' "I'm going to bring charges against you to the bar association, counselor," he was told. "Or didn't you know it's unethical for an officer of the court to go about hustling business?" '

Count The title of a European nobleman, equivalent to the British earl. The wife of an earl is known as a countess, but 'count' itself has never been a British title. *Dodsworth*, by Sinclair Lewis, has:

'Kindness all yours, Count.'
'Oh, don't call me "Count". I am not a count – there aren't any more counts – the republic has come to stay – I am just a clerk . . . I shall be glad if you call me "Kurt". We Austrians are almost like you Americans in our fondness to call by the first name among people we like.'

Charles Dickens makes fun, in *The Pickwick Papers*, of Count Smorltork: ' "Count, count," screamed Mrs Hunter to a well-whiskered individual in a foreign uniform, who was passing by.' The count then has difficulty with Mr Pickwick's name, which he at first thinks is Pig Vig or Big Vig, finally deciding that it is 'Peek – christian name; Weeks – surname.'

Countess A title used by the wife or widow of a count, the wife or widow of an earl or a woman who, in her own right, has a position equal to that of a count or earl. Charlotte Brontë, in *Villette*, has: 'I am a countess now. Papa, mamma and the girls at home will be delighted to hear that. "My daughter, the Countess! My sister, the Countess!" Bravo! Sounds rather better than Mrs John Bretton, *hein*?'

Country boy This is quite different from 'countryman', as in 'my fellow countryman'. It means a (young) man who comes from a rural background and is perhaps not used to city ways. *The Middle Man*, by David Chandler has: ' "Country boy," she murmured, like an accusal.' The speaker has just been commenting on what she considers to be the man's unsophisticated behaviour.

Countrywoman, my fair *See* **Reader**.

Cousin This is described by Robert Chapman, in his *Dictionary of American Slang*, as 'an amiable form of address', the equivalent of 'friend' in an expression like 'How you doin', cousin?' Like 'friend' itself, 'cousin' in this sense need not necessarily be friendly. In Judith Rossner's *Any Minute I Can Split* its use by a young man to an unrelated young woman is decidedly aggressive. Chester Hines, in *Pinktoes*, remarks that 'black sports from uptown began accosting dignified white ladies on Fifth Avenue with such intimate greetings as "Hello, cuz, how's your fuzz?" ' Those so accosted perhaps consoled themselves by noting the apparent survival from Shakespearean times of 'coz', the familiar abbreviation of 'cousin' found in all seventeenth-century literature. 'Cousin' at that time had a much wider sense than its present meaning – the son or daughter of one's uncle or aunt. It was used for any collateral relative more distant than a brother or sister and was frequently addressed to a nephew or niece. Kings and queens also used it to foreign sovereigns, or to the noblemen of their country. Shakespearean characters are thus constantly addressing one another as 'cousin', 'good cousin', 'valiant cousin', 'my pretty cousin', 'my noble cousin', etc., when they are not using the short form 'coz', 'sweet coz', 'good coz', 'gentle coz', and so on. The word inevitably recalled the verb 'to cozen', which meant to cheat or defraud someone. Shakespeare could be relied upon to exploit the punning opportunities, and Hotspur plays on the two words in *Henry the Fourth Part One* (1:iii):

> Why, what a candy deal of courtesy
> This fawning greyhound then did proffer me!
> Look 'when his infant fortune came to age'
> And 'gentle Harry Percy' and 'kind cousin'
> – O, the devil take such cozeners!

'Cousin' was used alone or with the first name of the person concerned, a usage that continued until the nineteenth century. Mrs Gaskell says in *Cousin Phillis* of Betty, the family servant, that she has adopted the family habit of addressing cousin Paul in that manner, as they do. 'Cousin', with or without the first name, was clearly not confined to first cousins. In *Bleak House*, for instance, Ada is a ward of Mr Jarndyce, but the following conversation occurs: ' "O, cousin –!" Ada hastily began. "Good, my pretty pet. I like cousin. Cousin John, perhaps, is better." "Then, cousin John!" Ada laughingly began again. "Ha ha! Very good indeed!" said Mr Jarndyce, with great enjoyment. "Sounds uncommonly natural." ' In dialectal usage, by this time, especially in Cornwall, 'cousin' was being used as a general term of friendly address, much as in modern American slang. Use of the term by Cornish people to strangers caused 'Cousin Jan' and 'Cousin Jacky' to become nicknames for them, though these no longer appear to be used. 'Cousin' is now very rarely heard as a vocative in Britain, or in any English-speaking country. In middle-class society of the eighteenth and nineteenth centuries it was clearly much used, as the literature of the time reveals. It is difficult to say what caused it to go so completely out of fashion.

Cousins An Englishman addresses some Americans by this term in Ian Fleming's *Goldfinger*. There is a joking allusion to 'our American cousins', a phrase sometimes used by British speakers with reference to a common ancestry.

Covey 'Hallo, my covey' says Jack Dawkins, the Artful Dodger, when he first meets Oliver in Dickens's *Oliver Twist*. 'Covey' is a diminutive form of 'cove', still used in third person reference of a man, or fellow. 'Who's that old cove over there?' The earlier form of 'cove' was 'cofe', a Scottish word meaning a hawker, which would make the sense development of 'cove' similar to that of 'chap' from 'chapman'.

Cow, you This is now a generally contemptuous term for a woman one dislikes. In the nineteenth century it could have been taken to mean 'you prostitute'. That specific meaning probably no longer applies, nor need there be a reference to the large size and slow movement of the woman so addressed, though 'you fat cow' is a fairly frequent collocation. 'Cow' seems to have become more offensive as the centuries have passed; it would not have been so insulting in the seventeenth century. It is, of course, normally used to a woman, but 'Bring the gin, you enormous cow,' in *The Day of the Locust*, by Nathanael West, is spoken by a woman to a man. In *Festival*, by N. J. Crisp, a young woman admonishes herself as 'you silly cow'. She is later addressed by a male colleague as 'you stupid cow'. In *A Kind of Loving*, by Stan Barstow, 'you old cow' is spoken by a young man to his mother-in-law, but only after she has called him 'you little upstart' and 'you filthy pig'. *Up the City Road*, by John Stroud, has a young husband calling his teenage wife 'you great screaming cow'. She is larger than usual because she is in the late stages of pregnancy.

Coward In Act One of Ben Jonson's *The Alchemist*, when Face and Subtle are having a slanging-match, Subtle calls his housekeeper 'Cow-herd!' Perhaps Jonson himself, and his audience, assumed that this was the original form of 'coward', though etymologists tell us that the word has more to do with the hare, especially the tail of the hare, than the cow.

An early form of the word was 'coart', the 'co-' representing Old French *coe*, 'tail'. The hare, after all, is a very timid animal. One is more likely to see its tail as it disappears than any other part of its anatomy. 'Coward!' is a typical playground taunt – *see also* **Custard, cowardy cowardy**. In *An American Dream*, by Norman Mailer, the hero admonishes himself with 'you coward'. Mrs Raddle, in *The Pickwick Papers*, by Charles Dickens, calls her husband 'you coward' 'with supreme contempt'. He has just declined her invitation to knock a number of men down the stairs, which he would do, she tells him, 'if you was a man'. 'Come down from there, you yellow coward' is spoken by a woman to a young man in Truman Capote's short story *My Side of the Matter*.

Coxcomb In the sixteenth century this was a reference to the hat worn by a professional fool. It was like a cock's comb in shape and colour. The word quickly came to refer to the fool himself, then took on the special meaning of a person whose foolishness is shown by his showiness and vanity, or his pretence at knowledge which he does not really possess. Perhaps the meaning of the word that has endured best relates to foppishness in dress, but this is by no means the principal meaning in Shakespeare, where the word is used with slightly different shades of meaning in several of the plays. It means fool when Emilia says to Othello: 'O murderous coxcomb! What should such a fool/Do with so good a wife?' The word is little used in modern times, vocatively or otherwise, though it occurs in Ngaio Marsh's *Opening Night*. The speaker there who addresses another man as 'my young coxcomb' shows throughout the novel that he is steeped in Shakespeare.

Coyote The coyote is a type of small wolf, native to parts of North America and Mexico. The term is not normally used vocatively, but *The Tunnel of Love*, by Peter de Vries, has an American woman telling a man: 'Get out! You – coyote!'

Cracker This is used in the USA to describe a Southern rustic or poor white person. 'You little cracker' is used in that sense in *Trixie*, by Wallace Graves, where it is spoken by a black American man to a black girl. The same vocative used by a British speaker would usually mean 'you beautiful creature', since 'cracker' in modern British slang refers to an attractive woman.

Crapper In American slang this would mean a person who regularly boasts about his own achievements, exaggerating them while doing so. He is something of a bullshit artist, to use another American expression, when it comes to self-advertisement. In Britain 'crapper' would be related to the verb 'to crap', to defecate, and the word would be thought of as a general term of abuse. 'You great blubbermouthed crapper' is addressed by one man to another in *A World of Difference*, by Stanley Price.

Creature In vocative use 'creature' is usually qualified by other words which show whether the term is being used positively or negatively. The word does not necessarily mean an animal, though that is the most obvious modern sense of the word. It has long been applied to human beings, our fellow creatures who like their creature comforts. Originally the word refers to any created being. The term of address was in use long before Shakespeare's time and was used by him as both an admiring and contemptuous expression. 'Teach me, dear creature, how to think and speak' says Antipholus of Syracuse to Luciana in *The Comedy of Errors*. *Julius Caesar* begins with Flavius telling the commoners: 'Hence! home, you idle creatures, get you home.' Many of the vocative instances in Shakespeare, and perhaps elsewhere in literature, are to women rather than men. Shakespeare's ladies are addressed as 'fair creature', 'sweet creature'. In Jane Austen's *Northanger Abbey* the heroine is 'my dearest creature' when addressed by a rather insincere young lady. Tom Jones, in Fielding's novel of that name, calls his Sophia 'divine creature'. *The Bell*, by Iris Murdoch, has 'dearest creature' used between intimates, and there is a similar intimate use in *Funeral in Berlin*, by Len Deighton, of 'you wonderful creature'. In Charlotte Brontë's *Villette* a woman calls another 'scornful, sneering creature', while Liza, in George Bernard Shaw's *Pygmalion*, is 'you infamous creature' according to Professor Higgins. 'Creature' addressed to a man occurs in, e.g., Dickens's *The Pickwick Papers*. Mr Smangle addresses Mr Pickwick as 'my dear creature', and Sam Weller and his father are constantly referring to other men as 'creeturs'. Mrs Raddle also calls her husband 'you perwerse creetur' and 'you creetur'.

Creep A term originally used of someone trying to gain another's favour by being unduly flattering. The term came into American student slang use in the 1930s, with the underlying idea of someone who made your flesh creep. It is probably still more used in the USA than Britain, and has become a general insult for an obnoxious person, its intensity differing according to the accompanying words. 'Don't push me, creep!' says a man to another in *Oliver's Story*, by Erich Segal. A policeman uses it to a male suspect, very aggressively, in *I'll Take Manhattan*, by Judith Krantz. 'You mother-fucking little creep' is not meant to please the man to whom it is addressed in *Getting it Right*, by Elizabeth Jane Howard. In *Rabbit Redux*, by John Updike, a girl calls a man 'you creep', then expands it to 'you baby-killing creep'. 'You creep' used by one Australian man to another occurs in *A Salute to the Great McCarthy*, by Barry Oakley, while 'you miserable creep' is said by an actress to an actor in *Festival*, by N. J. Crisp. *Up the City Road*, by John Stroud, has 'you dirty old creep' addressed to a middle-aged man by a young woman, who also calls him 'you dirty old man'.

Cretin The technical medical sense of cretin is a person whose mental and physical development has been stopped in early childhood because of a weakness in the thyroid. When the word occurs vocatively, however, it is invariably used to mean 'fool', 'idiot', in a far more general sense. Most speakers would be unable to define it technically, and would be unaware of its historical and etymological origins. Cretins were at one time unfortunate creatures who lived mainly in Alpine valleys. 'Cretin' originally meant 'Christian', a word meant to draw attention to the fact that cretins were human beings, not brute animals. Examples of the watered down use of 'you cretin' as a relatively mild insult occur in, e.g., *The Sleepers of Erin*, by Jonathan Gash.

Critic Used as a vocative in *The Critic*, by Wilfred Sheed, but only as a quotation variant. The hero says 'Critic, review thyself' to himself, paraphrasing the better-known 'Physician, heal thyself' of the New Testament.

Crocodile *See* **Alligator**.

Crook, you American slang for a criminal since the 1870s, and used in Britain with a similar meaning since the 1890s, but not frequent as a vocative. 'You dirty crook' occurs in *Daughters of Mulberry*, by Roger Longrigg, used by a woman to a man she is accusing of criminal behaviour. *Moviola*, by Garson Kanin, has : ' "I'm going to ruin you if it costs me a million dollars." "So what?" said Gilbert. "You'll no doubt charge it to the company, you cheap crook." ' 'Buncha crooks!' is addressed to a room full of people in *Jug of Silver*, a short story by Truman Capote.

Cross-examiner, my pretty This term is used by a man to a girl who is asking him questions in *Oliver Twist*, by Charles Dickens. They are not in a courtroom, of course; the situation merely suggests to the speaker a courtroom atmosphere. *See also* **Lord, my** for a similar use of a courtroom vocative used in a situation where questions are being asked.

Cross-patch Applied to an ill-tempered person since the eighteenth century. The word 'patch' had earlier been used of an ill-natured person, especially a child. This use of 'patch' is thought to derive from the nickname of Cardinal Wolsey's domestic fool or jester, not the word for a piece of cloth. The *Oxford English Dictionary* mentions that 'cross-patch' is normally applied to a girl or woman, though Sir Walter Scott used it of a man. It is addressed to a man by a woman speaker when it occurs vocatively in *Like Any Other Man*, by Patrick Boyle.

Crumb, you To an American speaker this expression evokes a thoroughly worthless person, someone who is despised. It has less force to a British speaker, who would use it to imply that someone was insignificant. 'Crumby', as in a vocative expression such as 'you crumby bastard', also varies in meaning according to the speaker. The spelling may also change to 'crummy'. It can mean 'lousy' – literally infested with lice – dirty or insignificant. 'You crumb' occurs in *Daughters of Mulberry*, by Roger Longrigg, but is more friendly than insulting in context. It is also used by one boy to another in *On the Loose*, by John Stroud, where it expresses contempt for the general ignorance of the boy addressed.

Crumb-bun Chapman's *Dictionary of American Slang* gives 'crumb-bun' as the correct form of this vocative, though in *The Catcher in the Rye*, by J. D. Salinger, it is printed as 'crumb-bum'. A prostitute uses it to the young hero as she leaves the room: 'So long, crumb-bum.' In either spelling it is a term of contempt for someone who is a 'crumb' or a 'bum'.

Cry-baby The general term used mainly by children to other children who are thought to cry too easily. Parents might also address a child in this way. As the Opies point out in *The Lore and Language of Schoolchildren*, there are a large number of local variations of 'cry-baby'. According to the district in which the child concerned lives, he is likely to be called: bubbly baby, bubbly Jock, mum's big bubbly bairn (in the north-east of England and parts of Scotland, where 'bubblin' is 'crying'); blubber-face, blubber-bib, blubber-puss (in areas where 'blubber' is used for 'cry'); boo-baby, booby (from 'boo' = 'cry'). The verb 'to grizzle' leads to 'grizzle-guts', 'grizzle-grunt'. Other terms listed by the Opies include: baby bunting, boo-hoo, diddums, howler, leaker, mother's little darling sissy, slobber-baby, sniveller, softy, tap, Tearful Tilly, water-can, water-hog, waterworks, weeping willow, you babby, cry-a-lot, milk sop, squall-ass, wet eyes, drip, drainpipe, lassie boy, Waterworks Willie, and many others. 'Cry-baby' itself is mentioned by

Charles Lamb in his essay on 'All Fools' Day', published in 1821. It is also mentioned in *Deborah*, by Marian Castle, which concerns a school in Dakota. It is normally boys, of course, who have one or more of these names hurled at them; girls normally have more licence when it comes to the shedding of tears. It is a group of young boys in *Lord of the Flies*, by William Golding, who are addressed as 'you useless lot of cry-babies' by an older boy.

Cub, you young An expression which might be used by an irate elderly gentleman to a young man. 'Cub' in this context means more than just 'young person'. There was a widespread belief in the Middle Ages that bear cubs were born in a shapeless mass, and that they had to be licked into shape. Sadistic adults have sometimes interpreted this 'licking into shape' to mean that severe discipline and punishment must be part of a child's education. Shakespeare, as so often, appears to have been one of the first writers to transfer 'cub' to a human being. In *Twelfth Night* (5:i) the Duke addresses Viola, whom he thinks is a young man, as 'O thou dissembling cub!'

Cully 'Old cully' is used by a mortuary attendant when addressing an old man that he is embalming in *What's Bred in the Bone*, by Robertson Davies. 'Old man' is used by the same speaker to the same man, and is synonymous, though the latter expression is of course far more common. 'Old cully' would be a rare term to use even to a living person. Cully derives from a seventeenth-century slang term used by thieves to denote a dupe, one who was easily taken in. The *Oxford English Dictionary* cites evidence of its use to mean 'mate', rather than 'simpleton', in 1676. Partridge, in his *Dictionary of Historical Slang*, says that in the nineteenth and early twentieth centuries it was a Cockney term of address to a man. It was clearly in wider use, however, since the *New York Mercury* quoted 'What's yer hurry, cully?' as an 'Americanism' in 1888. It is now very rare on both sides of the Atlantic.

Cunt A reference to the female pudenda, but this is considered an obscene word in all English-speaking countries, to be strictly avoided in polite society. In the USA used as a term of contempt of or to a woman. 'Look at me, woman. Hey you cunt, look me in the eye,' says a black American male to a white girl in *Rabbit Redux*, by John Updike. 'You queer like your friend?' asks a woman in *Looking for Mr Goodbar*, by Judith Rossner. 'No, cunt, I'm not queer like my friend,' is the reply, with the additional comment: 'God is my witness, I never talked that way to a woman in my life.' In Britain 'you cunt' is frequently addressed to men, as if it were a synonym for 'bastard'. It is not one of those insults that can easily be turned into a friendly term of address when used between intimates. 'Oh shut up, you silly little cunt' is spoken by a young woman to a man in *Festival*, by N. J. Crisp. That 'cunt' *can* be used to a man by an American speaker is shown in *The Choirboys*, by Joseph Wambaugh. 'Wake up, Roscoe, you cunt!' is said by a Los Angeles policeman to a colleague.

Cup-cake In modern American slang 'cup-cake' (a small cake shaped like a cup) can refer either to a person who is thought to be eccentric, or to a girl who is considered attractive. 'Stephen, I want to become a lady,' says a young woman, in Norman Mailer's *An American Dream*. 'Come on, cup-cake' is the reply. The same speaker uses 'honey' to the woman concerned during the same conversation.

Cur, you This is a contemptuous word for a dog, and therefore even more contemptuous when applied to a man. Shakespeare is rather fond of it as a term of abuse. In *The Tempest* Sebastian and Antonio object to the boatswain's cries. 'Hang, cur; hang, you whoreson, insolent noise-maker,' says Antonio, while Sebastian calls him 'you bawling, blasphemous, incharitable dog'. The word is used as a reinforcement for 'dog' in a similar way in *A Midsummer Night's Dream*: 'Out, dog! out, cur! Thou driv'st me past the bounds/Of maiden's patience,' says Hermia to Demetrius. King Lear tells Oswald he is 'a whoreson dog', 'a slave', 'a cur', and 'you whoreson cur' twice occurs in *Troilus and Cressida*, on one occasion expanded to 'you whoreson indistinguishable cur'. 'Cur' lived on into the eighteenth century and beyond as a term of reproach, but it would sound very old-fashioned indeed were it to be used in modern times. It is suspiciously literary, rather than a reflection of real life, when it occurs in *Seven Little Australians*, by Ethel Turner, a children's story first published in 1894. A father there says to his young child: 'You contemptible young cur! I'll thrash this mean spirit of lying and cowardice out of you, or kill you in the attempt.' Mark Twain's *Pudd'nhead Wilson* was published at about the same time, and has a man calling his nephew, whom he considers to have disgraced the family name, 'you cur! you scum! you vermin!'

Curiosity Box, Mr A nonce name used to a man who is trying to elicit information in *Like Any Other Man*, by Patrick Boyle. The speaker is a woman. 'I know what you're after, Mr Curiosity Box, but you'll worm nothing out of me.'

Custard, cowardy cowardy This is the traditional taunt of British children to a child who is considered to be cowardly. Those who use the term would be hard put to it to explain the custard reference, though the fact that custard is yellow, and yellowness is associated with cowardice, might seem significant. 'Custard' in this context is in fact a variant of 'costard'. A costard is a kind of ribbed apple (Latin *costa* 'rib'), and its shape led to its being used as a term for the head. 'Cowardy custard' is therefore equivalent to 'cowardly head'. Until the twentieth century yellow was the colour associated with jealousy, not cowardice. It is highly likely that when the connection between 'costard' and 'custard' had been largely forgotten, 'custard' was thought of purely in its milk pudding sense and its yellowness transferred to cowards. Apart from its survival in mutilated form as a playground taunt, 'costard' survives in the modern 'costermonger', who was originally one who sold apples. *See also* **Scaredy-cat**.

Cutie Used as an endearment to someone who is thought to be 'cute', i.e. attractive and pleasant. 'Let's go, cutie,' says an American prostitute to a client, in *The Choirboys*, by Joseph Wambaugh. The term is sometimes extended to cutie-pie, as in *The Late Risers*, by Bernard Wolfe, where it is said by a man to a woman in a not very friendly way. 'Cutie' is far more likely to be used by an American than a British speaker.

Cut-throat This word occurs mainly in the phrase 'cut-throat competition' in modern times, where ruthlessness is implied, though not to the point where competitors are literally murdered. The cut-throat of the seventeenth and eighteenth centuries was literally a murderer, and Shylock, in *The Merchant of Venice*, who complained of being called a cut-throat dog (see quotation under **Dog**) knew that this was a vile insult. As a vocative 'cut-throat' occurs mainly in pirate literature. There is an instance in *Moby Dick*, by Herman Melville, where a captain addresses would-be mutineers as 'ye cut-throats'.

D

Da A dialectal form of 'Dad', normally used to the speaker's father. In *The Taste of Too Much*, by Clifford Hanley, it is written 'Da'. *When the Boat Comes In*, by James Mitchell, has it as 'da' and shows its use in north-east England. In *War Brides*, by Lois Battle, a young Australian girl addresses her parents as 'Da' and 'Mum'.

Dad It cannot be known for certain when this word came into regular use, but it is recorded from the sixteenth century. From that point on, at least, it can be regarded as a piece of fossilized baby-language, used by children of any age to address their father. The word occurs rarely in Shakespeare's plays. In *King John* Philip the Bastard, natural son of Richard I, makes the rather complicated statement: 'I was never so bethump'd with words/Since I first call'd my brother's father dad.' His brother is in fact his half-brother, Robert Faulconbridge. In modern times 'Dad' is generally used, though middle class families will tend to discourage it in favour of 'Father' or, in very traditional American circles, 'sir'. In *Don't Tell Alfred*, by Nancy Mitford, there is the comment: 'I wouldn't mind the boys calling me Dad,' said Alfred (who did mind, however, and had made great efforts, successful with David and Baz, to be called Father), 'if only they wouldn't pronounce it Dud.' The father in this case is decidedly upper middle-class, and the *dud* pronunciation an idiosyncratic one. 'Dad' is sometimes used to the speaker's father-in-law, but there is certainly no general rule about such usage. It may also be extended to step-fathers, although a group of British children interviewed by The *Observer* newspaper in June, 1988, all of whom had step-fathers, made comments such as: 'I couldn't call him Dad' and 'I've almost called my step-dad Dad once . . . then you feel really weird.' In *The Liberty Man*, by Gillian Freeman, a working-class wife calls her husband 'Dad'. 'Father' and 'Mother' are certainly used by wives and husbands who are parents, especially when the children are present. There is a non-family use of 'Dad', typically by young working-class speakers, to an unrelated older man which is often slightly contemptuous or decidedly aggressive. Other father terms used to a stranger, such as 'Pop' or the extended 'Daddy-o', are for some reason more friendly. In *Chuck*, by Carl Sterland, there is

a horribly contrived incident where a young man says to an older one: 'Well, dad, how was it?' The man addressed chokes into his brandy and says: 'You startled me. Why the "dad" by the way?' 'Just an expression,' replies the young man. The point of all this is that the older man really is the father of the young man, though the latter was adopted at birth and does not know that his natural father has come to seek him out.

Dada A young boy uses this baby-talk version of father in *Border Country*, by Raymond Williams, though he switches to 'Dad' when he becomes an adult. The term occasionally survives into adulthood, but would probably only be used in intimate family circles. In the seventeenth century 'da-da' was also baby-talk for 'goodbye', the fore-runner of modern 'ta-ta'.

Daddy A diminutive of 'Dad', used mainly by young children to their father. Women are likely to continue using it rather longer than men, but at some stage there is usually a switch to 'Dad', and later perhaps, to 'Father'. 'Daddy' is used in a friendly way by a young man to an older man in *Absolute Beginners*, by Colin MacInnes. In *An American Dream*, by Norman Mailer, a black American man says to a white policeman who is hitting him: 'That's the way, daddy, you're improving all the time.' It is possible that 'Daddy' is used as an intimacy by a woman to her 'sugar-daddy', though no examples of such usage occurred in the present corpus. *The God-Seeker*, by Sinclair Lewis, has a scene where a pastor is with a father and his son. The son calls his father 'Dad', and at one point the pastor addresses the older man as 'Daddy' + last name. The father interrupts him immediately to say: 'Not *your* daddy, thank God – or don't think so.'

Daddy-o An amiable term of address to a man of the speaker's own age or older. Used to both strangers and friends, both in Britain and the USA, though British speakers are probably imitating American usage. *The Late Risers*, by Bernard Wolfe, has the term being used by one black American to another, after the latter has addressed him as 'Poppa'. In *Comfort me with Apples*, by Peter de Vries, the use of 'daddy-o' between American men is not especially friendly. It has more warmth when used by a young man to an older man in *Absolute Beginners*, by Colin MacInnes, and it is friendly again in *Georgy Girl*, by Margaret Forster.

Daft'un, you *See* 'Un.

Dago A disparaging term now usually applied in the USA to a person of Italian heritage, though originally it was applied to a Spaniard. The word is a corruption of 'Diego', a Spanish form of James (via Santiago, 'St James'). 'Dago' has been used as an insulting vocative since the beginning of the nineteenth century, with Italians taking over as the target for the abuse in the present century. 'What d'ye want, ye Dago?' says an Irishman to an Italian in the O. Henry short story *Transformation of Martin Burney*.

Dame This word is still used as a social title in Britain. Those women who are entitled to use it are properly addressed as 'Dame', followed by their first name. The rank is equivalent to that of knight for a man, so that 'Dame Edith', etc., parallels the use of 'Sir John', etc. Until the eighteenth century 'dame' was frequently used vocatively without the following name when a woman of rank was being addressed. It was roughly the same as 'my lady' or 'madam'. As with 'madam', 'dame' gradually came to be used to women of lower social rank, and by the end of the seventeenth century could occur where 'mistress' might have been expected. 'Shut your mouth, dame!' says Albany to Goneril, in Shakespeare's *King Lear*. The word usually occurs in more polite contexts, and is often qualified as 'gentle dame', 'fair dame', etc. In the USA 'dame' is used in the third person and is considered slangy, on a par with 'broad' or 'doll'. It is not used in direct address. Ten examples of the British usage of 'Dame' + first name occur in *Memento Mori*, by Muriel Spark.

Dahling *See* Darling.

Damsel A damsel was originally a young unmarried lady of noble birth, but soon after the introduction of the word from French it appears to have taken on the general meaning of 'young woman', 'a country lass'. In French the word *demoiselle* was ultimately a diminutive of Latin *domina*, 'lady'. Used vocatively in former times, 'damsel' is either as polite as 'young lady' or as impersonal as 'girl' according to context. In Beaumont and Fletcher's play *The Wild-Goose Chase*, Mirabel's comment to Oriana: 'Are you caught, damsel?' shows the impersonal use. It is far more polite when Joseph, in Fielding's *Tom Jones*, says to a stranger: 'Be of good cheer, damsel.' In modern times the word would only be used

jokingly, perhaps to a young lady who was experiencing difficulties of some kind, a 'damsel in distress', The latter phrase presumably became fossilized because of its convenient alliteration.

Dandiprat, dandyprat In the sixteenth century this word was variously applied to a small coin, to a person who was either physically or morally insignificant, or to a young lad. The origin of the word is not known, though the first element appears to be a form of 'Andrew' – presumably a name chosen at random – while the second element may have been 'sprat'. Used mainly in the sixteenth and seventeenth centuries, contemptuously to a man but probably with simple allusion to smallness to a boy. 'My little dandiprat' occurs as a vocative in *Kenilworth*, by Sir Walter Scott, but allowance must be made for that author's conscious use of obsolete or archaic terms.

Dark horse Used of a person who reveals unexpected talent, a metaphor from the racing world where it is used of a horse which unexpectedly wins a race. The phrase can be extended to someone who reveals anything about himself which is unexpected, as in *A Kind of Loving*, by Stan Barstow, where the following occurs: ' "I'm married." Percy stares at me. "You never are! Well, you old dark horse, you. When did all this take place?" '

Darky, darkey A rare variant, in either spelling form, of 'nigger', and perhaps slightly less offensive, but little used in modern times. An attempt seems to have been made to substitute this term for 'nigger' at one time, and at first it carried no pejorative implications. It soon began to acquire them, however, and was not liked by the black American community. 'Now, darkey, spring,' says a slave auctioneer to a black child in *Uncle Tom's Cabin*, by Harriet Beecher Stowe. In *Absolute Beginners*, by Colin MacInnes, 'darkie-luvver' is used as an insult, with 'luvver' for 'lover' an attempt to indicate sub-standard pronunciation.

Darling This word was in use by the tenth century and is one of the most frequently used endearments in English. It is composed of the word 'dear' and the suffix '–ling', which converts the adjective into a noun meaning 'a person who has the qualities of the adjective', in this case, a person who is dear. Between lovers the term signals a delicious intimacy, perhaps best shown by a caption to a *Punch* cartoon of the 1890s. A young man says to his lady-friend: 'Darling!' 'Yes, Darling?' is the reply. 'Nothing, darling,' says the young man, 'Only *darling*, darling.'
Shakespeare does not use 'darling' as a vocative, and it seems to have come into use

in the eighteenth century in that role. It was previously used as an adjective and to describe a 'darling' person or object in the third person. In *Tom Jones*, by Henry Fielding, we learn that Squire Western frequently calls his daughter his 'little darling'. In *Jane Eyre*, after Mr Rochester has tormented the heroine by telling her that he is going to marry someone else, Charlotte Brontë has him propose to Jane, be accepted by her, and bid her: 'Good night, my darling.' Jane forces him to wait a month to see whether he means what he says.

> He continued to send for me punctually the moment the clock struck seven; though when I appeared before him now, he had no such honeyed terms as 'love' and 'darling' on his lips; the best words at my service were 'provoking puppet', 'malicious elf', 'sprite', 'changeling', etc.

Darling has probably the most meaning when used by a speaker who does not easily use it. Thus Margaret Drabble writes, in *A Summer Bird-Cage*: 'When he said darling to me the word hit me in the stomach: it isn't a word he uses casually, and he said it with real intimacy.' Soames Forsyte is equally surprised when he hears his ex-wife Irene address her son Jon as 'darling'. She had never used the word to him, John Galsworthy says in *To Let*. There are those speakers, however, who use 'darling' very easily as a friendly term to almost any woman, or in the case of female speakers, to almost any man. A London coster-monger is likely to call his female customers 'darling', whatever their age.

At middle-class level, the term is especially associated with the theatre, and with a slightly affected pronunciation often rendered by novelists as *dahling*. Comments on the use of the word in the theatre occur fairly frequently in literary texts. Sinclair Lewis, in *Bethel Merriday*, says of his heroine that her producer 'had never addressed her by any more intimate form than "Oh darling – look here, sweetest," and in the world of the theatre, that constitutes ignoring a person.' John Wain, in *The Contenders*, has:

> I kept telling myself that it didn't matter that Robert and the crone called each other 'darling'. She was on the stage, after all, or somewhere near it, and theatrical people always called each other 'darling'. Besides, for all I knew to the contrary, the word was a usual mode of address in London.

J.B. Priestley, in *Bright Day*, writes:

> 'Darling!' she cried; held the scene for a moment, and then came hurrying in and kissed me. I was surprised. After twenty years in the theatrical and film worlds I am thoroughly acquainted with this *Darling* and

kissing business, even though I don't indulge in it myself. But this was different. Elizabeth's 'Darling!' sounded as if she meant it. The kiss was real too.

A likely reason for the use of this word amongst actors is given by Tallulah Bankhead in her autobiography, *Tallulah*:

> 'Rarely was I able to catch the names of the dowagers and drinkers I met at parties, in dressing rooms, or in Bond Street. Darling has implications of affection, or, at least, friendliness. It cannot disturb the recipient. Did I try to pin the correct caption on every clown I encounter I'd make embarrassing blunders. They're all darlings to me.

'Darling' is rarely used by a man to a man. When it happens in *The Word Child*, by Iris Murdoch, we are told that the speaker is 'totally homosexual'. In *St Urbain's Horseman*, by Mordecai Richler, the hero calls his brother-in-law 'darling' when he is pretending to be homosexual. He is called 'you filthy bastard', 'you little son-of-a-bitch', 'you snake', 'sewer', and 'you filthy thing' in return. Genuine homosexual usage between American men occurs again in *The Front Runner*, by Patricia Nell Warren. In *The Face-Maker*, by Richard Gordon, a young male actor says 'Goodnight, darlings' to a mixed group of colleagues. Gordon continues: 'Clare looked shocked. He himself had come to learn the endearing expression was merely the equivalent of the Communists' "Comrade" in an ever-shifting and commendably classless society.' Yet another reference to theatrical usage occurs in *Opening Night*, by Ngaio Marsh. An actor says: 'In the theatre we be-darling and be-Christian name each other at the drop of a hat.' 'Darlings' can be used as a friendly plural, or an intimate one to children. *Tender is the Night*, by F. Scott Fitzgerald, has a girl saying 'Goodbye, you darlings' to friends who are a married couple.

Other examples of friendly and intimate usage, noticed in a variety of British and American contemporary fiction, include: darling boy, darling+first name, dear darling, first name+darling, my darling, my little darling, my sweet darling girl, poor darling, you poor darling, darl (by a working-class male speaker), darling angel, old darling. In fifty novels by British authors which were subjected to a detailed vocative count, 'darling' on its own occurred 372 times.

Darlingest A superlative formed on the analogy of dearest, sweetest, etc., but not a term in general use. It is used by a hammy actress in *The Actor*, by Horace Annesley Vachell.

Date An affectionate term, roughly the equivalent of you goose, you silly thing, you prune, etc. 'You date' addressed to the author's five-year-old son on one occasion produced the question: 'Which date am I?' The reference is actually to the fruit, though why it should be so is far from clear. British informants in their fifties agree that the term is generally used, especially as 'soppy date'. This seems to hint that it was first used as a catch phrase by someone in the public eye. It has not yet reached the dictionaries in this sense.

Daughter Anita Brookner, in *Family and Friends*, has: ' "Daughter!" cries Sofka, in a loud voice which startles them both, as does the archaic use of the word.' It is the vocative use of the word which is archaic, of course, though it is still to be found. In *The Heart is a Lonely Hunter*, by Carson McCullers, the black middle-class doctor, of rather formal manners, uses it to his daughter. It occurs also in *The Late Risers*, by Bernard Wolfe, when an American father is making a more serious pronouncement than usual to his daughter. There is an interesting comment in *The Moonflower Vine*, by Jetta Carleton, where a father constantly uses 'daughter' to each of his female offspring. 'It was a little more authoritative than the given name, which might not occur to him at that moment anyway.' In real life, however, one suspects that the modern miss would hoot with laughter rather than respect the 'authority' of 'daughter', and would expect her father to remember her name no matter how many sisters she had. The heroine of *The Stone Angel*, by Margaret Laurence, is speaking of vocative usage at the beginning of the twentieth century when she says of her father: 'He called me "miss" when he was displeased, and "daughter" when he felt kindly disposed towards me. Never Hagar'.

The parental use of 'daughter' as a vocative was, as Anita Brookner implies, far more usual at one time. Shakespearean parents use it regularly, often followed by a first name. 'Now, daughter Silvia,' says the Duke of Milan in *The Two Gentlemen of Verona*. 'Now, master Slender! Love him, daughter Anne,' says Page, in *The Merry Wives of Windsor*. Baptista in *The Taming of the Shrew* says: 'Why, how now, daughter Katherine, in your dumps?' 'Call you me daughter?' replies Katherine, but only because she thinks that her father has otherwise forgotten the relationship between them: 'You have show'd a tender fatherly regard/ To wish me wed to one half lunatic.' *War Brides*, by Lois Battle, has a scene where an upperclass American woman greets her daughter-in-law for the first time with 'Welcome dear daughter.' She also remarks: 'I'm so glad you're here, because I've always wanted a daughter, and now I finally have one.' Her use of

'daughter' encourages the younger woman to respond a little later with 'Mother'.

Beyond its use within the family, 'daughter' has long been employed in a religious context. Older priests, who in the Roman church will themselves be addressed as Father by their women parishioners, may well use 'daughter' in reply. The term is professionally convenient, effectively substituting for a name that may be unknown or temporarily forgotten. Its use is also sanctioned by high authority. At *Matthew* (9.20) we find:

And behold, a woman who had suffered from a hemorrhage for twelve years came up behind him and touched the fringe of his garment; for she said to herself, 'If I only touch his garment, I shall be made well.' Jesus turned, and seeing her he said, 'Take heart, daughter; your faith has made you well.'

One problem with 'daughter', for normal usage purposes, is that it has no diminutive form, unlike 'sonny' from 'son'.

Daughter of Paris, you genuine This is used by Mr Rochester to his natural daughter in *Jane Eyre*, by Charlotte Brontë, when the child is displaying, in his view, typically French characteristics. The vocative is suspiciously literary, one of several such that occur in the novel, far more likely to be used by a writer than a speaker.

Dawbake Special terms of address sometimes live on in dialects. There are several examples of ancient Devonshire terms in *Dandelion Days*, by Henry Williamson. An old woman screams at a man: 'Ye girt dawbake. Master grawbey! Thou girt loobey.' Williamson tells us that 'the tirade of this ancient scold included obscene words that had been learnt in childhood from her father and mother.' 'Girt' in these expressions is 'great'. Dawbake is presumably a form of 'dawpate', i.e. (jack)daw head. To call someone a 'daw' in former times was to imply either that he was a simpleton or that he was very lazy. In Scotland the word was applied to a sluttish woman. Williamson uses 'dawbake' again in his *Dream of Fair Women*: ' "Go on, ye old dawbake," he urged. "Wake up, ye mazidawk." ' This is a boy talking to his drunken father.

Dawling A variant of 'darling', used in *The Taste of Too Much*, by Clifford Hanley. The spelling is meant to indicate a distorted upperclass English pronunciation of the word.

Deacon A deacon is an officer of various Christian churches, of lower rank than a priest. It is often his function to deal with the secular affairs of the Church. The deacon in *The House* *with the Green Shutters*, by George Douglas, is addressed by his professional title throughout the novel, which is set in a Scottish town in the nineteenth century.

Dean A title in the Christian Church of a dignitary who is in charge of several priests or church divisions, the main administrator in a cathedral. In some universities the dean is a college teacher who has administrative control over a large area of study, and special responsibility for the welfare of the students. Jonathan Swift, after being made dean of St Patrick's cathedral, recorded in his *Journal to Stella*, 26 April 1713: 'I dined with Lord-Treasurer and his Saturday people as usual; and was so be-deaned!' *The Masters*, by C.P. Snow has:

> Then Mrs Jago received us, with an air of *grande dame* borrowed from Lady Muriel. 'Do sit down, Dean,' she said to Chrystal. 'Do sit down, Tutor,' she said to Brown. But Mrs Jago's imitation of Lady Muriel was not exact. Lady Muriel, stiff as she was, would never have called men by their college titles.

Dear This has been one of the commonest terms of address in English since the thirteenth century. In a count of fifty novels dealing with fairly contemporary life, 'dear' used on its own as a friendly term occurred 243 times. There were a further 138 examples of 'my dear'. Hundreds of further instances occurred where 'dear' was a vocative element, as in: dear boy, dear+first name, my dear fellow, my dear +first name, my dear chap, my dear boy, etc. 'Dear' is occasionally the head-word in a vocative group. One recalls Mr Pickwick's horror when Mrs Bardell suddenly calls him 'you kind, good, playful dear':

> 'Oh, you dear – ' said Mrs Bardell. Mr Pickwick started. 'Oh, you kind, good, playful dear,' said Mrs Bardell; and without more ado, she rose from her chair and flung her arms around Mr Pickwick's neck, with a cataract of tears and a chorus of sobs. 'Bless my soul!' cried the astonished Mr Pickwick.

Mrs Bardell's misunderstanding of Pickwick's intentions leads to the famous breach of promise case in *The Pickwick Papers*, by Charles Dickens. Dickens, who is a superb commentator on vocative usage, as on most other subjects, remarks humorously in one of his *Sketches* that the word 'dear', used by one young lady to another, 'is frequently synonymous with "wretch"'.

It is certain that the word does not always have its face value. In writing, as a conventional beginning to a letter, its degree of friendliness depends upon the word that follows. 'Dear John' may well be positive; 'Dear

Sir' is merely an empty formula. In speech, everything depends on how the word is spoken and in what circumstances. It can also depend on the listener's attitude to the word. Many young people, especially, regard the word as condescending, and would echo the comment in Edna O'Brien's *The Girl with Green Eyes*: 'I hate people who call me "dear".' With this compare the comment by Dr Phillip Gosse in his autobiographical *An Apple a Day*: 'I took to that old lady from the very first, for she always addressed me as "dear", and no man can help liking a lady who does that.' In *Bless me, Father*, by Neil Boyd, a priest says to a penitent: 'What are your sins, dear?' The author adds: 'I was pleased with that. "Dear" was a good indefinite English word with which to address a child whose age and sex were undetermined.'

This 'indefiniteness' probably holds good in the vast majority of cases where 'dear' is used, the listener interpreting it as a friendly noise. Problems arise when it is used conventionally, the speaker's true feelings not matching the apparent meaning of the word. 'Now run away, and don't let me have any more of this nonsense – dear,' says a father to his child in *Seven Little Australians*, by Ethel Turner. The author adds: 'The last word was a terrible effort.' 'Dear' was only added, in fact, because a visitor was present; it is clear from the context that had there been no-one else there the vocative would probably have begun with 'you little . . .', ending not with 'dear' but a harsher word. In *Festival*, by N.J. Crisp, occurs: ' "You think you've conned everybody, but you haven't, not quite, *dear*." The word was not used affectionately. It was loaded with contempt.' Mrs Craik, in *Olive*, pauses in her story-telling to remark:

> Reader, did you ever notice the intense frigidity that can be expressed in a "my dear"! The coldest, cruellest husband we ever knew once impressed this fact on our childish fancy, by our always hearing him call his wife thus. Poor, pale, broken-hearted creature! He 'my-deared' her into her grave.

One wonders just how close to home this experience was for the author. The thumbnail description of a man who 'my-deared' his wife into her grave is certainly a vivid one. A milder kind of insincerity is noted in *Life at the Top*, by John Braine, when the narrator is talking to his wife: ' "Yes, dear. Sorry, dear. Just as you say, dear," I said, parodying meekness.'

Minor references to the social aptness of 'dear' as a term in its own right or as a vocative element are sometimes found. In *The Needle*, by Francis King, an elderly woman who calls two women doctors 'dear' outside the surgery is very careful to return to 'Doctor' when visiting them as a patient. Sinclair Lewis, in *Gideon Planish*, remarks that 'Mrs Bull was the first of many influential women who he was to call "dear lady".' In *Gone With The Wind*, by Margaret Mitchell, Rhett Butler touchingly asks Scarlett O'Hara's permission to call her 'dear', suggesting that the term would be a meaningful one to him, not a conventional noise. In *Catriona*, by R.L. Stevenson, a young woman's objection to being called 'my dear' is precisely because she interprets the words as a real endearment: 'I am not your dear,' she said, 'and I defy you to be calling me the words.' Inevitably there are characters in novels, as there must be in real life, who joke about the 'expensive' meaning of 'dear'. 'Dear old William', says a speaker in *An Error of Judgement*, by Pamela Hansford Johnson. He replies: 'Not dear. Cheap old William.' *The Contenders*, by John Wain, has ' "Dear" seemed a funny thing to call Myra, unless he meant expensive.'

In spite of attendant problems, 'dear', 'my dear', etc., continue to be well used. In Britain it is probably true to say that, whereas 'dear' on its own is used at all social levels, as is 'my dear', longer vocative groups which begin with 'my dear', such as 'my dear fellow', 'my dear chap', are far more likely to be used by the middle classes. Working-class men do not greet one another as 'My dear John', or whatever. Those middle-class speakers who do use this formula leave the listener with a decision to make about its degree of sincerity. It is easy to forget that use of 'dear' could at one time arouse an impassioned response. When the romantic Mr Tupman, in *The Pickwick Papers*, is accidentally shot, Rachael Wardle murmurs 'Dear – dear – Mr Tupman' when he closes his eyes for a moment. Dickens continues:

Mr Tupman jumped up – 'Oh, say those words again!' he exclaimed. The lady started. 'Surely you did not hear them!' she said bashfully. 'Oh, yes, I did!' replied Mr Tupman; 'repeat them. If you would have me recover, repeat them.'

This word 'dear', it would seem, can either send people to their grave or save them from it.

Dear, old Used with genuine affection, as one might expect, in *Anglo-Saxon Attitudes*, by Angus Wilson, where it occurs four times as an intimacy between husband and wife. The term could be used to either sex; in this instance it is the wife who uses it to address her husband. In *Every Day is Ladies' Day*, a short story by Dawn Powell, a man says to a woman in her fifties: 'I didn't tell you even *half* about it, old dear.' 'Old dear yourself!' she snaps at him. *Babbitt*, by Sinclair Lewis, has sarcastic use of the term by a young American man to his employer, an older man, who is dismissing him. 'Babbitt, old dear, you're

crooked in the first place and a damn skinflint in the second.'

Dearest Whereas 'dear' can be used in a friendly way, 'dearest' used alone or as part of a vocative group usually signifies an intimate endearment. In modern usage 'darling' would probably be preferred in both cases. Shakespeare has at least one example of 'my dearest', used by Leontes to his wife in *The Winter's Tale* (1:ii): 'Hermione, my dearest, thou never spok'st/To better purpose.' More frequently he uses the word as an intensifier in expressions like: my dearest father, my dearest love, my dearest madam, my dearest master, my dearest coz, my dearest queen, my dearest sister, my dearest husband, all of which occur in the plays. (By comparison, Shakespeare makes relatively sparing use of 'darling', whether as a vocative or in third person reference.) Use of 'dearest' between lovers and intimate friends continues today, according to the evidence of modern novels such as *The Bell*, by Iris Murdoch, *Brothers In Law*, by Henry Cecil, *The Country Girls*, by Edna O'Brian, *Kate and Emma*, by Monica Dickens, *The Masters*, by C.P. Snow, *Room at the Top*, by John Braine, and many others. By the nineteenth century, however, 'dearest' appears to have been considerably watered down in meaning. Thackeray observes wryly, in *The Newcomes*:

Miss Ethel and my wife were now in daily communication, and "my-dearesting" each other with that female fervour which, cold men of the world as we are – not only chary of warm expressions of friendship, but averse to entertaining warm feelings at all – we surely must admire in persons of the inferior sex, whose loves grow up and reach the skies in a night; who kiss, embrace, console, call each other by Christian names, in that sweet, kindly sisterhood of Misfortune and Compassion, who are always entering into partnership here in life.

Dearie A diminutive of 'dear' which is meant to be friendly but sometimes sounds condescending. It appears to be used especially by older women, as in Edna Ferber's *Showboat* and Margaret Mitchell's *Gone With The Wind*, where younger women are addressed in each case. In *Letting Go*, by Philip Roth, the following occurs: ' "Make a little tea, dearie," he said. What a sloppy man, thought Paul. What an unattractive played-out old lecher. How many dearies over the years had carried him his tea?' Friendly use of 'dearie' occurs in *The Business of Loving*, by Godfrey Smith, *Free Fall*, by William Golding, *The Half Hunter*, by John Sherwood, *The Liberty Man*, by Gillian Freeman, *Nurse is a Neighbour*, by Joanna

Jones, *A Season in Love*, by Peter Draper, *Under the Net*, by Iris Murdoch.

Degenerate Used in modern times of a person who has low moral standards, or who behaves in a way that is shocking to others. *I'll Take Manhattan*, by Judith Krantz, has a girl saying to her brother, in a friendly way: 'Take your hands off me, you degenerate.'

Demeter See **Artemis**.

Demon A variant of 'devil', rarely used as a vocative. *Aaron's Rod*, by D.H. Lawrence, has a woman whose husband has left her addressing him as 'you selfish demon'.

Deputy, Mr Used in the formal circumstances of a meeting, or outside it by speakers who have a formal manner, to someone who has been deputed to act in place of another official, usually on a temporary basis. There are several examples of its use to a Cambridge College official in *The Masters*, by C.P. Snow. 'Mr Deputy-Speaker' also occurs. *See also* **Speaker, Mr**.

Deserter As a vocative this normally refers to someone who has deserted the speaker, not to a deserter from one of the services. Rochester, in Charlotte Brontë's *Jane Eyre*, calls Jane 'cruel deserter' when she returns to him after a long absence. *A Salute to the Great McCarthy*, by Barry Oakley, has one man saying to another: 'You deserter. Wasting yourself on loose women.' The speaker means: 'you have given up my company for them'.

Detective An American police force rank, and used as a term of address by, e.g., lawyers in a court room. Sherlock Holmes is addressed as 'Mr Detective' in *The Missing Three-Quarter* by Sir Arthur Conan Doyle.

Detective-sergeant A policeman in *The Sleepers of Erin*, by Jonathan Gash, tries vainly to get a woman to address him by this professional title. She addresses him instead as 'Corporal', 'Lieutenant', Major', 'Colonel', or so the novelist would have us believe.

Devil, you 'Devil' is seldom used vocatively in modern times to refer to a person who is considered to be truly fiendish, inhumanly cruel, or wicked. Such usage is found in Shakespeare, as when Albany says to Goneril in *King Lear* (4:ii), 'See thyself, devil! Proper deformity shows not in the fiend/So horrid as in a woman.' Similarly, in *Othello* (4:i) the Moor several times calls Desdemona 'devil', convinced that she has been unfaithful to him. 'I have not deserv'd this,' says that poor lady. But already by the seventeenth century 'devil' was being applied to persons in a milder way, to mean little more than 'you rogue'. 'You little devil' would typically be applied in modern times to a child of either sex who had misbehaved quite badly, perhaps to the extent of physically hurting the speaker, but the implication would be that the child concerned was acting devilishly at that moment, not that he or she had a truly diabolical nature. Dickens chooses to make rather a lot of 'you worldly little devil', which the narrator in *George Silverman's Explanation* says was 'my mother's usual name for me', but the expression does not have the ring of authenticity. Dickens goes on to make much of the 'worldly' reference, saying that the child concerned did indeed have a worldly yearning for food and warmth. 'Dirty old devil', spoken to one man by another in *Life at the Top*, by John Braine, is friendly, as is 'you naughty old devil' in *Dover One*, by Joyce Porter. In an expression like 'you poor devil', which hovers between exclamatory and vocative use, 'devil' is reduced almost to the neutrality of a word like 'person', as it is in 'you lucky devil', 'you jammy devil', etc. Collins *Cobuild English Language Dictionary* rather surprisingly equates the word with the British English use of 'bugger' in such circumstances, though 'bugger' and 'devil' would probably be used by different social strata.

Diddums A word from baby-language, used to a very young child at the pre-speech stage. It corrupts the words 'did you then', but these words are not in the mind of a present-day speaker who would use the word as a caressing noise. It is used by a mother to her baby in *Howard's End*, by E. M. Forster. The association with very young babies makes the word an insult when applied to an older child, usually by other children. *See also* **Cry-baby**.

Digger Associated mainly with Australian men, who have been using this term as a friendly form of address since the 1850s. It began on the gold-fields of Australia and New Zealand, where the word had its literal meaning. In *Redback*, by Howard Jacobson, it is used by an Australian man to address an Englishman. The speaker equates it with 'sport'. Mrs Cecily Dynes, a correspondent from Australia, reports that the short form 'Dig' was much used by Australian soldiers during the Second World War.

Dill Used of a stupid and despicable person, especially by American speakers. The word is probably an abbreviation of 'dildo', an object which acts as a substitute for an erect penis. 'Dill' is certainly synonymous with 'prick' or 'jerk' used vocatively, both of which terms have penial association. *An Indecent Obsession*, by Colleen McCullough, has: ' "She's frustrated," said Luce. Matt chuckled. "Well, X is a frustrating place," he said. "Not that way, you blinkered dill! I mean she's a woman, and she's not getting any, is she?" '

Dim-wit *See* Dunce.

Dipstick, dipshit 'Dip' has long meant a pickpocket in criminal slang, but from the 1920s, in American slang, it took on the new meanings of stupid or eccentric person, the equivalent of 'jerk' or 'nut'. To emphasize the contempt of the speaker for the person being addressed as 'dip', the new form 'dipshit' evolved. 'Dipstick' is considered by Chapman, in his *Dictionary of American Slang*, to be a euphemistic form of 'dipshit'. 'Dipstick' has been much used in Britain in the late 1980s, receiving a great deal of exposure in a popular television series *Only Fools and Horses*. Those hearing the term for the first time probably think only of the graduated metal rod used to check the oil level in an automobile engine, something which clearly has no mind of its own. British users of the term would not be thinking of 'dip' in any of its more modern meanings, the pickpocket sense being retained.

Director, Mr Used by an old actor to a theatre director in *Bethel Merriday*, by Sinclair Lewis. Almost any professional title can be converted into a nonce name of this kind.

dirty A frequently used element in vocative expressions of the 'you dirty bastard' type. The allusion may be to actual dirtiness, or to sexual impropriety. 'Filthy' is also used.

Dish Normally used in third person reference to an attractive woman. It occurs as a kind of incidental vocative in *The Limits of Love*, by Frederic Raphael, which has: 'There she is! That's the dish I was telling you about – hey, dish, come over here.'

Dissembler A highly literary word, rather than one which occurs in relaxed conversation. A dissembler is one who hides his true motives or emotions. *She Stoops to Conquer*, by Oliver Goldsmith, has George Hastings calling Constance 'thou dear dissembler'.

District Attorney, Mr This title could correctly be used to the prosecuting officer of a judicial district in the USA. In *Moviola*, by Garson Kanin, it is used by a woman to a man who is questioning her too closely about her private life.

Doc A friendly abbreviation of 'doctor', often used to a medical practitioner by someone who is not a patient. There are 89 examples of

such usage, for instance, in Richard Gordon's *Doctor at Sea*, where the speaker is usually another member of the crew. In *Main Street*, by Sinclair Lewis, Dr Kennicott is often 'Doc' to his friends and neighbours at social gatherings. In *The Philanderer*, by Stanley Kauffmann, a man says 'Maybe you're right, doc' to a friend who has just given him some advice. The vocative is suggested by the conversation, which resembles temporarily a psychiatric interview. In Frank Yerby's *A Woman Called Fancy*, 'Doc' and 'little Doc' are addressed by an acquaintance to a man who tours the country selling patent medicines, but who has no medical qualifications. The fact that 'Doc' was the name of a dwarf in Disney's popular *Snow White and the Seven Dwarfs* (1937) may have had some influence on the use of this vocative.

Doctor This title is mainly addressed in modern times to a medical practitioner, one who has undergone long and rigorous training but does not necessarily hold an academic doctorate. In the USA 'doctor' might also be used to a dentist and a veterinary surgeon. Richard Gordon, in *The Face-Maker*, talks of an American surgeon who 'disclaimed the English surgeon's self-assumed title of "Mister" '. The man concerned is known as Dr Sarasen, though a consulting surgeon in Britain would be addressed as 'Mr' Smith, or whatever, by his colleagues. Patients would continue to call him 'doctor', or perhaps 'doc' (see separate article). It is difficult to believe that a surgeon would be annoyed by a layman's use of 'Doctor', but the narrator in *The Sleepers of Erin*, by Jonathan Gash, says:

It was two weeks to the day when I got clearance from the consultant surgeon. I'd displeased him by calling him "doctor". "Surgeons are addressed as Mister," he told me testily. "Physicians are addressed as Doctor." "Sorry, er, sir." "Never been the same since that Yank hospital series on telly in the 'sixties," he grumbled.

In *Martin Arrowsmith*, the novel in which Sinclair Lewis dealt with medical practice and research, we are told that: 'Ordinarily, Gottlieb called him "Arrowsmith" or "You" or "Uh". When he was furious he called him, or any other student, "Doctor". It was only in high moments that he honoured him with Martin.' Gottlieb here is a professor of medicine, and a doctor in the etymological sense of the word, a teacher. Lewis comments fully on another use of doctor, in academic circles, in *Gideon Planish*. The hero has just given up his job as dean of a college, but though:

he had lost the Christian name Dean, still he was Dr Planish, always Dr Planish – that was his first name: Dr; and as such, along with every Colonel, every Reverend Doctor, every M.D., every Monsignor, every Rabbi, every Herr Geheimrat, every Judge, every Governor, he was so highly exalted that he was not merely a man, but a title.

The academic use of doctor referred to means that the person concerned holds one of the highest degrees given by a university, such as a Ph.D., D. Litt., etc. Those entitled to be addressed as doctor for this reason vary greatly as individuals in their wish, or need, to be so addressed. Those most sure of themselves have the least need for it, perhaps. Lewis himself says that 'he noted that since his time here, [between the 1920s and 1950s], the Doctoring and Professoring of the faculty members had thinned out. Even that stickler Austin Bull preferred to be called just Mister.' Lewis is refering to long-established faculty members; one would expect that more recent graduates would wish to hear their title used. *Jake's Thing*, by Kingsley Amis, has a man in his late fifties who says to a psychiatrist: 'And by the way, I have got a doctorate but I don't normally use the title.' 'So it's *Mr* Richardson', says the other, who has previously been addressing him as Dr Richardson. In *Names, Designations and Appellations*, R. W. Chapman, writing in 1936, says:

At Oxford, retaining something of our ancient arrogant exclusiveness, we tend to ignore (officially, and even conversationally) doctorates not conferred by ourselves. I never heard the Merton Professor of English Literature called 'Dr Nichol Smith', but I see he is doctor of two universities.

In earlier times, British barristers were required to be Doctors of Law. Shakespeare makes Portia such a 'civil doctor' in *The Merchant of Venice*, where she ably defends Antonio against Shylock. When she reveals her identity to Bassanio he says: 'Sweet Doctor, you shall be my bedfellow;/When I am absent, then lie with my wife.' 'Civil doctor' contrasts with 'reverend doctor', one who holds the degree of Doctor of Divinity, or who, in earlier times, was recognized as an authority on religious matters. Shakespeare's main use of 'doctor' as a title occurs in *The Merry Wives of Windsor*, in which there is the French physician, Dr Caius. He is variously addressed as 'doctor', 'bully doctor', 'good master doctor'. 'Doctor' as a vocative also occurs in *The Comedy of Errors, Macbeth*, and *Cymbeline*. In the Merchant Navy, 'Doctor' is a traditional nickname for a cook. In ordinary conversation, 'doctor' may be used to someone who appears to be assuming the role of a doctor or psychiatrist. Thus in Judith Rossner's *Looking for Mr Goodbar*, a man says to a woman that he is taking

her home 'for her own good'. 'Well, doctor,' she says, when they arrive, '*now* what are you going to do for my own good?' In *Oliver's Story*, by Erich Segal, a man and woman are exchanging their life stories. She tells him that she was divorced. 'But then you moved back in with Daddy?' he asks. This clearly suggests the psychiatrist's couch to the woman concerned, who says: 'Sorry, Doctor, I am not *that* freaky. After the divorce my father wisely sent me on a tour of duty.'

Dodo   The dodo was a bird which was once to be found in Mauritius, but it has long been extinct. It had a massive clumsy body and small wings that were useless for flight. Its ridiculous appearance and movements caused the Portuguese to name it *dondo*, 'fool'. It is almost fitting, then, that the English form of the word, 'dodo', lives on as a slang term for a silly person. 'You dumb dodo' is spoken by a man and addressed to a woman in *Last Tango in Paris*, by Robert Alley. In the idiosyncratic spelling of a young black American prostitute it emerges as 'you dum doe doe' in *One Hundred Dollar Misunderstanding*, by Robert Gover.

Dog   'Dog' is used vocatively in two distinct ways. It is either an insulting term of contempt, or it is almost a compliment, implying that the man addressed is a jolly fellow. As an insult, 'dog' has been in use since at least the fourteenth century. It is a common insult in seventeenth-century literature, the best-known example being in Shakespeare's *Merchant of Venice* (1:1). Shylock reminds Antonio, who has come to ask him to lend him some money, that 'you call me misbeliever, cut-throat dog'. He continues:

. . . you come to me, and you say
'Shylock, we would have moneys'. You say
so –
You that did void your rheum upon my
beard
And foot me as you spurn a stranger cur
Over your threshold; moneys is your suit.
What should I say to you? Should I not say
'Hath a dog money? Is it possible
A cur can lend three thousand ducats?' Or
Shall I bend low and, in a bondman's key,
With bated breath and whisp'ring
humbleness,
Say this:
'Fair sir, you spit on me on Wednesday last,
You spurn'd me such a day; another time
You call'd me dog; and for these courtesies
I'll lend you thus much moneys'.

'You dog' is an insult in Smollett's *Peregrine Pickle*, and Robert Louis Stevenson, in *St Ives*, has 'you white-livered dog' addressed to a man who refuses to fight. The more friendly use of 'dog' can be traced back to the seventeenth century, but only became common in the eighteenth and nineteenth centuries. 'You jolly dog' occurs in *Tom Jones*, by Henry Fielding, showing a typical friendly amplification. 'You sly dog' and 'you lucky dog' are other frequently used expressions. In *Hard Times* Dickens has Mr Harthouse say: 'Tom, you are inconsiderate; you expect too much of your sister. You have had money of her, you dog, you know you have.' In *Poet's Pub*, by Eric Linklater, a man who is still in bed greets a friend with 'You're early.' 'You lazy dog,' is the reply. *Doctor in the House*, by Richard Gordon, has 'you dirty dogs' used in a friendly way.

It is likely that most modern uses of 'you dog' would be friendly. This may reflect the changing status of the domestic dog in modern times, the sentimental view having largely prevailed over the dismissive one in western society. Dogs themselves are sometimes addressed as 'dog' – 'Come here, dog' – or more affectionately as 'doggy' or 'doggie', especially by children. 'Dear, dear doggie' occurs in *A God and his Gifts*, by Ivy Compton-Burnett, and 'doggy' is in *The Bell*, by Iris Murdoch. To insult a dog a speaker would probably call it a 'cur' or a 'tyke'.

Sailors are sometimes known as 'old sea-dogs' (the term was applied to pirates in the time of Queen Elizabeth) because they have spent as much time at sea as seals, themselves known as sea-dogs. Mr Stubb, however, second mate on the *Pequod*, is less than pleased when Captain Ahab, in Herman Melville's *Moby Dick*, calls him a dog. 'I will not tamely be called a dog, sir,' he tells Ahab. 'Then be called ten times a donkey, and a mule, and an ass, and begone, or I'll clear the world of thee,' is Ahab's reply. That it is still possible to use 'dog' in an unfriendly, if not contemptuous way, is shown in *Kes*, by Barry Hines. A boy is being forced to stay in a shower by three others. 'Let me out, you rotten dogs!' he tells them. *The Half Hunter*, by John Sherwood, has a woman use the rather extraordinary 'you dirty dog's breakfast' to a man, where 'you dirty dog' might have been expected.

Dogan In *The Stone Angel*, by the Canadian author Margaret Laurence, two old women are talking to one another. The narrator says: 'Her and me are friends. I kid her. I pray, too, I says to her, what, what do you think of that, you old dogan?' 'Dogan', according to the Supplement to the *Oxford English Dictionary*, is Canadian slang for an Irish Roman Catholic. It has been in use since the mid-nineteenth century, and may derive from an Irish last name, though 'Dogan' is not listed in Maclysaght's *The Sur-*names *of Ireland* or in *A Dictionary of Surnames* by Hanks and Hodges.

Dogberry Addressed to a policeman by a Shakespeare-loving character in *Opening Night*, by Ngaio Marsh. One suspects that the normal policeman would be unlikely to see the point of this transferred name, which relates to the constable in Shakespeare's *Much Ado About Nothing*. In the latter Dogberry is often addressed as 'constable' or 'Master constable'. His name is not firmly enough linked with 'policeman' to allow it to be as regularly used as it is in the novel.

Doll Used by mainly American speakers to a woman, who in modern times is very likely to object to the term. This may well be because she would recognize the definition of the slang term given in Chapman's *Dictionary of American Slang* as an apt one: 'a conventionally pretty and shapely young woman, especially a curly, blue-eyed blonde, whose function is to elevate the status of a male and inspire general lust.' The more recent term for such a girl, though it is seldom used in direct address, is 'bimbo'. 'Doll' of course refers to the representation of a baby or child with which little girls act out their parental fantasies. The word derives from the proper name 'Dorothy', the *l* for *r* substitution being evidenced in other pairs such as Mary – Moll (*via* Mall), Harry – Hal. 'Doll' is used as a vocative on its own, as in *The Sophomore*, by Barry Spacks and *Absolute Beginners*, by Colin MacInnes, or in the fuller form 'baby doll'. The latter is used by a middle-class American man to a woman friend in *The Tunnel of Love*, by Peter de Vries. There is another example in *Daughters of Mulberry*, by Roger Longrigg. *St Urbain's Horseman*, by Mordecai Richler, has a Canadian Jewish woman using 'doll' to her daughter-in-law, in what is clearly meant to be a friendly way. 'Doll' used as a vocative in the Shakespeare plays, along with 'mistress Doll', 'good Doll', is always addressed to Doll Tearsheet, who is also called mistress Dorothy on two occasions in *Henry the Fourth Part Two*. In *One Hundred Dollar Misunderstanding*, by Robert Gover, 'doll' is the head-word in the unusual vocative group 'sweet loving baby sugar doll'. It is also unusual in being addressed to a man, the speaker being a prostitute.

Dollbaby Used to a young woman by a male American speaker who also addresses her as 'babydoll', in *A Woman Called Fancy*, by Frank Yerby.

Dolling A spelling of 'darling' which indicates dialectal uneducated pronunciation. It is used by a black servant woman in *Pudd'nhead*

Wilson, by Mark Twain, addressed to her infant son.

Dolt A dolt is a dull person, a blockhead. The word has been in use since at least the sixteenth century, and was thus available to Shakespeare. He has Pandarus, in *Troilus and Cressida*, refer to the 'asses, fools, dolts', meaning the ordinary soldiers who are passing by who cannot compare with Troilus. More tellingly, in *Othello*, Emilia learns that Othello has killed Desdemona and tells him: 'O gull! O dolt! As ignorant as dirt! Thou hast done a deed.' A modern example of 'dolt', used as a disguised endearment, occurs in *The Word Child*, by Iris Murdoch: ' "I want your 'flu. I want you. I love you viruses and all." She kissed me on the lips. "You dolt, Tomkins." ' In Vera Caspary's novel *Laura* a man addresses a shopkeeper he knows well: 'Claudius, you dolt, why in the sacred name of Josiah Wedgwood have you been keeping this [a vase] from me?' Leslie Thomas, in *The Magic Army*, has 'Clear off, you dozy dolts' addressed to a herd of cows blocking the road. Later in the novel a woman says: 'Come on, you old dolt' to her chauffeur.

Dom From Latin *dominus*, 'lord'. A title given to certain Roman Catholic dignitaries and to the members of some monastic orders, such as the Benedictines. In *Thirteen Days*, by Ian Jefferies, 'Dom' on its own is used almost as a friendly term of address to a non-English bearer of the title.

Dominie Used of a schoolmaster in former times, especially in Scotland. The word occurs fairly frequently in the novels of Sir Walter Scott, for instance, either as a title used alone or as the prefix to a family name. In the USA 'dominie', or 'domine', is the title of a pastor of the Dutch Reformed Church. It is sometimes extended from there to ministers of other denominations. Thus in *Babbitt*, by Sinclair Lewis, the hero says to the pastor of his local Presbyterian Church: 'Tell you how it is, dominie: here a while ago I guess I got kind of slack.' The word derives from the Latin for 'master'.

Don + first name 'Don' is a Spanish title of respect which was originally accorded to men of the highest rank, then became more general as a courtesy title. It may be used by Spanish speakers when speaking English, as in John Steinbeck's *To a God Unknown*: 'Señor, is it you, Don Joseph?' It is also sometimes used by native English speakers addressing a Spanish-speaker in English. 'I have to tell you, Don Pedro, that sort of talk always makes me uncomfortable,' says an American to a Mexican who practises medicine in *The Middle Man*,

by David Chandler. 'Don' derives ultimately from Latin *dominus*, 'lord'.

Don Juan, you 'Don't trifle with her affections, you Don Juan!' says a friend to Jos Sedley, in Thackeray's *Vanity Fair*, knowing that the fat and ridiculous Jos will be mightily pleased with the description. The original Don Juan was Juan Tenorio of Seville, a seducer of women whose adventures were dramatized in the seventeenth century by Gabriel Tellez. Many other playwrights and poets, such as Lord Byron, made use of the name, turning it into a synonym for 'ladies' man', 'lover-boy', or 'lady-killer'. In *A Cack-Handed War*, by Edward Blishen, a man who thinks that the man he is talking to has far too much interest in women as sexual objects says to him: 'Don bloody Juan!'

Donkey A variant of ass, and used as a mildly insulting term to someone considered to be silly since the beginning of the nineteenth century. 'You little donkey' occurs in Charlotte Yonge's *Countess Kate*. 'You butter-fingered donkey' is used in Shaw's *Arms and the Man* to a servant who drops something. (*See also* **Butter-fingers**.) In *The Battle of the Villa Fiorita*, by Rumer Godden, a young English boy tells his sister: 'Go on, donkey.' When the word donkey first came into use in the eighteenth century it rhymed with monkey, which has caused speculation that it might derive from the name 'Duncan'. It is more likely to be connected with the word 'dun', 'brown'.

Dope, you This is a relatively mild insult, often used between intimates as a kind of endearment. Nathanael West writes, in *The Day of the Locust*: 'Not knowing what to say, he accented his awkwardness, playing the inoffensive fool. She smiled and became almost friendly. "Give out, you big dope." ' It is used mildly between men in *The Late Risers*, by Bernard Wolfe. The word carries a strong intimation of stupidity, but it causes less offence than an expression like 'you stupid fool'. *See also* **Dopey**.

Dopey This can be used to someone who is acting as if under the influence of dope, or a drug which causes sleepiness. Since such a person is not thinking clearly, the word also implies stupidity. 'Dopey' can be a mild insult, almost an endearment between intimates, very similar in use to 'you dope', but since it can be interpreted as 'you fool' or 'you idiot' it can also cause offence. The following occurs in *Looking for Mr Goodbar*, by Judith Rossner:

'I meant I'd go with you, dopey.' '*Don't call me dopey!*' He raised his hand as though he was going to strike her. 'If I really thought you were dopey,' she said, 'I'd be afraid to say it.' He lowered his hand, slightly mollified. It was a lie, of course. His dumbness was one of his endearing qualities.

Dopey was one of Walt Disney's seven dwarfs, in the 1937 film *Snow White and the Seven Dwarfs*. There was another dwarf, Sleepy, who was 'dopey' in the earlier meaning of the word, always on the verge of sleep. Dopey was marked by his general lack of intelligence.

Dotey This appears to be the invention of Edna O'Brien, who uses the word in *The Country Girls*. It occurs as an intimacy, presumably referring to the doting nature of the person to whom it is applied, one who is foolishly amorous.

Doubting Thomas Normally used in third person reference of a sceptical person, but it occurs as a vocative in *Like Any Other Man*, by Patrick Boyle. A housekeeper says to a man who is in the room where she is working: 'Doubting Thomas. Standing there surveying. You'd think I meant to plunder all around me.' This is a slight misuse of the term for a suspicious person rather than one who does not easily believe what he is told. The allusion is to New Testament, *John* (20:xx), where the story is told of Thomas's doubt:

Now Thomas, one of the twelve, called the Twin, was not with them when Jesus came. So the other disciples told him, 'We have seen the Lord.' But he said to them, 'Unless I see in his hands the print of the nails, and place my finger in the mark of the nails, and place my hand in his side, I will not believe.'

Thomas is later convinced that Jesus is alive.

Dove 'My dove' has been used as an affectionate term of address since the fourteenth century. In Chaucer's *Merchant's Tale* we have: 'Rise up, my wife, my love, my lady free . . . my dove sweet.' This shows normal usage to a woman or child, someone displaying gentleness. In *Getting it Right*, by Elizabeth Jane Howard, a woman uses it to a male friend. Robert Browning, in his poem *Too Late*, interestingly refers to 'loved you and doved you', which presumably refers to calling a loved one 'my dove'. The 'love-dove' theme was extended in the eighteenth century to the expression 'lovey-dovey'.

Dovey, dovie A diminutive of 'dove', used as an affectionate term of address. It seems to have come into use at about the same time as 'lovey', in the eighteenth century. It is difficult to know whether the terms evolved separately and were then coupled together, or whether 'lovey-dovey' came into being and caused the

individual vocatives to be used. The magazine *Punch* asked, in 1884, 'what would Dovey do if Lovey were to die?' There is some suggestion that 'lovey-dovey' was used of a couple where the man was addressed as 'lovey' by the woman, while he used 'dovey' to her.

Drainpipe See **Cry-baby**.

Drawer A term that was much used between the seventeenth and nineteenth centuries, addressed in English taverns to the person who drew the liquor for the customers. He was the tapster, to use another archaic term, or the barman as he is now in Britain, bartender in the USA. In Shakespeare's *Merry Wives of Windsor* Bardolph is taken on at the Garter Inn. 'He shall draw, he shall tap,' says the host, while Falstaff encourages him by saying that 'A tapster is a good trade.' Having taken up his new trade he is duly addressed as 'drawer' when he brings in Ford to see Falstaff. Dickens shows the term still in use in his *Tale of Two Cities*: 'Bring me another pint of this same wine, drawer.'

Dreamer *Ad hoc* vocative usage of this term occurs in *The Philanderer*, by Stanley Kauffmann, where an American man says to a friend and colleague: 'Let's roll, dreamer.'

Drip See **Cry-baby**.

Driver This neutral professional term is used to anyone who is driving a vehicle of some sort. 'Stop at the house with a green door, driver' says a 'heavy gentleman', in Dickens's *The Pickwick Papers*. A lady in the same 'hackney-cabriolet' countermands the order: 'Drive to the 'ouse with the yellow door, cabmin.' 'Look here, driver, I've got a train to catch, you know,' says a fare to a more modern cabby in *Don't Tell Alfred*, by Nancy Mitford. In *The Magic Army*, by Leslie Thomas, 'Hurry along, driver' is said by a high-ranking army officer to his military driver.

Drone A drone is the male of the honey-bee, famous for doing no work. 'Drone' has therefore been applied to an idle person since the early sixteenth century as a vocative. Thus Dromio of Syracuse, in *The Comedy of Errors* (2:ii), is berated by Luciana, who mistakes him for his twin-brother: 'Dromio, thou drone, thou snail, thou slug, thou sot!' This is Shakespeare's only vocative use of 'drone'. It occurs again in *Deborah*, by Marian Castle, used by one girl to another. The speaker has to get up to go to work, and says to her friend: 'You lucky parasite, to be able to sleep all day if you want to – ' She adds: 'Look, drone, I've got a job to hold! When my alarm goes off at seven, you're to get me up if you have to throw cold water on me!'

Drongo An Australian term for a slow-witted, stupid person, or in military circles, a raw recruit. 'Drongo' is actually an Australian bird name, but *Aussie Talk*, edited by Arthur Delbridge, suggests that there was a race-horse called Drongo in the 1920s which became famous for never winning a race. This may have inspired transferred use of its name. There may, however, be a direct reference to the bird itself, as with another Australian term of mild abuse, 'galah'. This is the Aborigine name of a rather lovely pink and grey cockatoo that is especially noisy. An Australian saying has it that a person can be as 'mad as a gum-tree full of galahs'. 'Galah' itself, applied to a person, means either a fool or a show-off. Examples of 'drongo' used as a vocative occur in *An Indecent Obsession*, by Colleen McCullough. An Australian man calls another 'you stupid drongo'. The same speaker uses this expression again to another man later in the book, equating it with 'you barmy fucker'. As for 'galah', it is not clear whether its use in *War Brides*, by Lois Battle, is vocative or not. An Australian woman says to an American man: 'You're a great galah, aren't you? Galah. Galah. It's a bloody parrot from the islands.'

Drudge Used of someone who slaves away at uninteresting and unrewarding work, a hack. Dr Johnson famously defined 'lexicographer' in his *Dictionary* as 'a writer of dictionaries; a harmless drudge that busies himself in tracing the original, and detailing the signification of words'. Writers of dictionaries have wryly repeated that 'harmless drudge' phrase ever since. It is permissible for the present dictionary writer to do so because 'you little drudge' occurs as a vocative in *The Moonflower Vine*, by Jetta Carleton: 'You little drudge – don't you know how to do anything but work?'

Drunk 'You lousy drunk' occurs in Arthur Hailey's *Hotel*, addressed by an American to a man who is pretending to be drunk. 'Drunk' for 'drunkard' has been in use since the end of the nineteenth century. The earlier form occurs in, e.g., *Bon Ton*, the play by David Garrick first produced in 1774, where Sir John Trotley calls Davy 'you drunkard'.

Duchess A polite way of addressing a duchess, who might more formally be called 'your Grace'. Used by some men, especially Londoners, to their wives, since 'my old Dutch' has long been a Cockney way of referring to one's wife. 'Dutch' in this sense probably comes from rhyming slang, via Duchess of Fife, though the music-hall entertainer Albert Chevalier

claimed that 'old Dutch' referred to the resemblance between his wife's face and that of a Dutch clock. 'This cigar bothering you, Duchess?' is addressed to the Duchess of Croydon in Arthur Hailey's *Hotel*. In Edna O'Brien's *Girls in their Married Bliss* a man in a pub is most impressed when he hears the customers calling a woman 'Duchess'. He is introduced to her after he has sent her over a drink and raised his own glass to say 'Cheers, Duchess.' In a subsequent conversation he asks her about her crest. 'Mop and Pail, governor,' she replies.

Duck, Ducks, Ducky Popular terms of endearment since at least the seventeenth century. In *A Midsummer Night's Dream*, Nick Bottom as Pyramus utters his famous 'O dainty duck! O dear!' to Thisbe, otherwise Flute. There is a less well-known Shakespearean use of ducks in *Troilus and Cressida* (4:iv). Pandarus greets Troilus with 'Ah, sweet ducks!'

In modern Britain 'duck' or 'me duck' continues to be well used as a friendly term of address in the Midlands, while 'ducks' is perhaps the more popular London form. *Unconditional Surrender*, by Evelyn Waugh, has: ' "Just off, ducks," she said, using a form of address that had become prevalent during the Blitz.' In the more recent novel *Up the City Road*, by John Stroud, 'ducks' is used by a policeman in London to address a young woman. It occurs also as a friendly vocative in *The Half Hunter*, by John Sherwood; *The Limits of Love*, by Frederic Raphael (where 'ducky' is also used); *Room at the Top*, by John Braine. These scattered instances in no way compare with the forty-nine examples of duck that occur in *Saturday Night and Sunday Morning*, by Alan Sillitoe, which reflects working-class Nottingham life.

Middle-class speakers also make use of 'duck', but tend to make it part of a longer expression. 'But darling duck,' says a very middle-class English woman to an intimate woman friend in *Don't Tell Alfred*, by Nancy Mitford, 'we can't keep them here.' 'Stop crying, Crystal, my duck,' says a middle-class man to a woman in *The Word Child*, by Iris Murdoch. 'You little duck' is used by a boy to his young sister in George Eliot's *The Mill on the Floss*. There seems to be no particular pattern about the use of the diminutive 'ducky', or 'duckie' as it is often spelt. It occurs, e.g., in *Kate and Emma*, by Monica Dickens; *The Country Girls*, by Edna O'Brien, and *Thirteen Days*, by Ian Jefferies, each time as what seems to be an arbitrary variant of 'duck' or 'ducks'. It is more frequently used in *Anglo-Saxon Attitudes*, by Angus Wilson, because it is made a feature of one character's idiolect. In *Gigolo and Gigolette*, a short story by Somerset Maugham, a husband says to his wife: 'Will you stay here, ducky, or would you like to go to your dressing room?' Used by a man to a woman in this way, this term is friendly if not intimate.

There are some who would associate the use of 'ducky' by a male speaker to almost anyone of his acquaintance, male or female, with homosexuality. Whether this is a justifiable assumption or not probably depends on the area the speaker comes from. 'Duck' and its variants are rarely found in novels written by American authors, though *The Philanderer*, by Stanley Kauffmann, has a man greeting his mistress with: 'Hello, duck, how are you?' The *Oxford English Dictionary* reports that 'duckling' was at one time used as an endearment, but this usage appears to have died out.

Dude In American slang 'dude' refers to a dandy, to an Easterner who is visiting the American West, or simply to a man, especially when used by a black American speaker. The origin of the term is not known. In *Boulevard Nights*, by Dewey Gram, it is used by a young American man to a fellow member of the same teenage gang.

Duffer This word has had many slang meanings in the past (though never, at any time, has it meant 'an elderly man', as Chapman suggests in his *Dictionary of American Slang*). The sense that survives is 'a foolish person, especially one who is slow to learn anything new'. The term is not often used vocatively in modern times, but *To Let*, by John Galsworthy, has a young Englishman calling another 'you young duffer' in a friendly way.

Duke A hereditary title of nobility in Britain, ranking immediately below a prince. A duke may be addressed as 'Duke' or more formally as 'your Grace'. 'Duke' is occasionally a given name, a pet form of Marmaduke.

Dullard, Dull-dick *See* Dunce.

Dumb-head 'Dumb' is used here in the American sense of silly, stupid. A young girl addresses a boy by this term in *Mountain of Winter*, by Shirley Schoonover. She is answered by 'you jackass'.

Dumbo This is the word 'dumb' with the vocative '-o' suffix, which causes the 'b' to be pronounced. It is US slang for a stupid person, though it is a British speaker who uses it in *Eating People Is Wrong*, by Malcolm Bradbury.

Dum-dum 'You take it to avoid getting pregnant, dum-dum,' says a young woman to a boy in *Slouching Towards Kalamazoo*, by Peter de Vries. The narrator adds the comment: 'Another new expression not entirely unknown to us in the sticks.' A 'dum-dum' is actually a kind of bullet that expands when it hits an object, but the vocative is clearly inspired by 'dummy', 'Dummkopf', etc. and implies stupidity.

Dummy The word 'dumb' is used far more often by American speakers than British to mean silly, stupid. 'Dummy' is likewise an Americanism for a person thought to be silly. It can be used banteringly as well as seriously. In *Rabbit is Rich*, by John Updike, a man who calls his golf partner 'you dummy' is quickly answered by 'you creep', but it is without rancour. American usage is no doubt influenced by German *Dummkopf*, 'stupid head'. In modern German 'dumb' is *stumm*, but *dumm* and 'dumb' are etymologically related. 'Dummy' can be used to both sexes. Its mildness is shown by a speaker in *Last Tango in Paris*, by Robert Alley. A man says to a woman: 'Anyway, you dummy, I love you, and I want to live with you.'

Dumpling, diddle diddle *See* Fatty.

Dunce This word is now associated with a child who finds it difficult to learn anything new. Other children might call a dunce: a block-head, a clodpoll, dim-wit, dull-dick, dullard, dunderpate, numbskull, chump, pea-brain, or putty-brain, depending on the area they live in. The present meaning of 'dunce' came about in the sixteenth century, having developed from the earlier sense of 'follower of Duns Scotus'. John Duns Scotus, who died in 1308, was a scholastic theologian, born in Dunse, Scotland. When the Dunsers, as they were known, saw that a more modern theology was replacing the ideas of Duns Scotus, they made a great fuss. Others saw them as being opposed to learning and progress, and Dunser therefore began to take on its new meaning. At one time a child who was thought to be a dunce would be made to stand in the corner of the classroom, wearing a conical cap with a D on it. The dunce's cap was still in use in the first half of the nineteenth century. In its general sense of 'blockhead', 'you dunces' occurs vocatively in *She Stoops to Conquer*, by Oliver Goldsmith. Mr Hardcastle uses the term to address his servants.

Dustbin *See* Greedy.

Editor A term of address used in countless letters addressed to 'Dear Editor' sent by readers of newspapers and magazines, but little used in speech. *Fletch*, by Gregory Macdonald, has a reporter saying: 'It came out totally imbalanced, thanks to you, bitch editor.' The woman concerned has made changes to the reporter's story. She has earlier asked whether his attitude to her is governed by the fact that she is a woman. He says he likes women, but 'what I do mind is your being made an editor – my editor – solely because you are going to bed with the editor-in-chief'.

Eejit *See* **Idiot**.

Eggy *See* **Scaredy-cat**.

Einstein Used as a transferred name to someone who is displaying great intelligence, or ironically to a person who is showing signs of stupidity. The allusion is to Albert Einstein (1879–1955), the Nobel Prize winning physicist, most famous for his theory of relativity. In 1939 he was stressing the urgency of investigating the use of atomic energy in bombs. Einstein was born in Germany but became an American citizen. *Waterfront*, by Budd Schulberg, has a young man counting money. He becomes confused and says 'I gotta start over.' 'Skip it, Einstein,' says a man who is present, with friendly contempt. In *A Kind of Loving*, by Stan Barstow, occurs: 'Over in one corner, curled up as peaceful as if he's by himself in the middle of a field, there's young Jim, with his nose in a book, as per. I reach past somebody and touch his knee. C'mon Einstein.' The younger brother addressed here is considered to be studious.

Either of you An indefinite or collective vocative. *See also* **anyone, anybody**.

Elephant Normally what one calls someone who has just stepped on one's toe, either the word on its own or 'you elephant!' There is a passage in *King Solomon's Mines*, by H. Rider Haggard, which gives a different slant on this term, and reflects in passing the attitudes of a by-gone era:

'Is it to that land that thou wouldst journey, Incubu?' (A native word meaning, I believe, an elephant, and the name given to Sir Henry

by the Kafirs.) I asked him sharply what he meant by addressing his master in that familiar way. It is very well for natives to have a name for one among themselves, but it is not decent that they should call one by their heathenish appellations to one's face.

Eminence, your The conventional form of address to a Cardinal in the Roman Catholic Church. ' "One question, son," asked the first Eminence, "do you believe in God?" "Yes, your Eminence" ' (*An American Dream*, Norman Mailer).

Englishman 'You wicked Englishman' is spoken by an Irishman to an Englishman in *The Sleepers of Erin*, by Jonathan Gash. The national description adds little in this case, 'man' on its own would have carried the same meaning. *Dover One*, by Joyce Porter, has a foreigner addressing an Englishman as 'you English'. The implication of this is that English people have a characteristic way of behaving which the person being addressed is exhibiting. Two further examples of 'you English' occur in *Funeral in Berlin*, by Len Deighton, a novel which also contains sixteen examples of 'English' addressed to an Englishman by a German. This is a slightly incorrect form of Englishman, which the speaker no doubt intends, since we are told that on one occasion he uses *Engländer*. A variation of 'you English' occurs in Rumer Godden's *The Battle of the Villa Fiorita* where a man says to a woman: 'Oh, you middle-class English!' He goes on to define middle-class behaviour as 'stuffy, conventional, prejudiced and ignorant'.

Everybody, Everyone A collective term used to three or more people of either sex and of any age. In *The Watch that Ends the Night*, by Hugh MacLennan, a man says to party guests, as he leaves: 'I'm sorry I talked too much, everybody.' Later in the book the same man announces his presence with: 'Well everybody, here I am!' Examples of 'everyone' occur in *Doctor in the House*, by Richard Gordon and *The Business of Loving*, by Godfrey Smith. In *Absolute Beginners*, by Colin MacInnes, occurs 'every one of you', which has a more aggressive tone about it than 'everyone' used on its own. Even more aggressive is the 'every damn one of you' that is used to address a crowd in *The Heart is a Lonely Hunter*, by Carson McCullers.

Excellency, your A title of honour for an ambassador. It was at one time used to royal personages of either sex, but appears to have been restricted to ambassadors since the end of the seventeenth century. 'You can rely on that,' says the Turkish Ambassador to Lord Wheatley, in *Phroso*, by Anthony Hope. 'That is a diplomatic assurance, your Excellency?' replies the noble lord. The word 'Excellency' is sometimes used on its own in direct address to an ambassador.

Excitement, Mr 'So long, Mr Excitement,' says a wife to her husband, with heavy sarcasm, in *A Salute to the Great McCarthy*, by Barry Oakley. *See also* Nonce Names, Introduction, p. 5.

Expert This is normally a word used in third person reference of, e.g., guests on radio or television chat shows whose names are not otherwise known to the audience. In Mordecai Richler's *St Urbain's Horseman* 'big expert' is used as a vocative when one man asks another for his opinion of a literary work: 'So, big expert, what do you think?' This may well be sarcastic, since the same speaker has a moment before called the same man 'shmock' (*see also* **Shmuck**).

Eye balls *See* **Four eyes**.

Eyetie 'Fucking eyetie' is addressed to an Italian by an Englishman in *Shipmaster*, by Gwyn Griffin. 'Eyetie' is used in British slang as an irreverent term for an Italian person. It is derived from the letters *i* and *t*, the first two letters of 'Italian', the *t* being pronounced wrongly as *tie* in order to make it rhyme with *i*.

Fa-fa Used by a young child to its grandfather in *Getting it Right*, by Elizabeth Jane Howard. Reduplication of a syllable in this manner is a typical feature of children's speech.

Fag Since the late eighteenth century the cry of 'Fag!' in a British public-school has been a summons for a junior boy to attend on a senior boy in order to carry out some duty. The word 'fag' here derives from the verb 'to fag', which means to do wearisome work, work that makes you fagged out. Robert L. Chapman, in *The New Dictionary of American Slang* thinks that the reputation of British public schools and the idea of a younger boy being compelled to do his senior's bidding was enough to bring the current American slang meaning of 'fag' – a male homosexual – into being. If this is so, 'fag' was then extended to 'faggot', in the same sense, rather than 'fag' being an abbreviation of 'faggot' as *Webster's Dictionary* suggests. In Mordecai Richler's *Cocksure* 'fag' is equated with several other terms namely 'pouf', 'homo', 'queer', 'brown-noser', 'lady-bird', 'sodomist', though not all of these would normally mean homosexual. *The Choirboys*, by Joseph Wambaugh, has 'you fag' and 'you insolent fucking sissy' addressed to a man who makes homosexual advances to a Los Angeles policeman.

Faggot See **Fag** for a discussion of the meaning and origin. In *Last Tango in Paris* a man calls another man 'faggot' as a general term of abuse, with no apparent reference to homosexuality. The man at whom the abusive term is levelled was about to have an encounter with a female prostitute. The term is used insultingly to a homosexual man in *The Front Runner*, by Patricia Nell Warren.

Faint-Heart, Mr A nonce name used to a man in *Eustace Chisholm and the Works*, by James Purdy. The expression is a rather antiquated synonym for a coward.

Fair A favourite vocative element in the seventeenth century, forming part of many complimentary expressions. Shakespeare's characters are constantly addressing one another as: fair sir, fair lady, fair lord, fair gentlewoman, fair coz, fair one, fair youth, fair queen, fair prince, etc. Often the word prefixes a name, as in 'fair Diomed', 'most fair Katharine', 'my fair Bianca'. There is some justification for thinking that use of the word came almost automatically when a vocative was employed. In *Twelfth Night*, for instance, are examples of 'fair shrew' and 'fair cruelty'. Inevitably Shakespeare plays with the word on occasion:

> *Hermia*: God speed fair Helena! Whither away?
> *Helena*: Call you me fair? That fair again unsay.
> Demetrius loves your fair. O happy fair!
> Your eyes are lode-stars and your tongue's sweet air
> More tuneable than lark to shepherd's ear
> When wheat is green, with hawthorn buds appear (*A Midsummer Night's Dream*, 1:1).

In the same play, Bottom is composing a prologue and begins 'Ladies'. He immediately corrects this to 'Fair ladies'. 'My fair' becomes the complete vocative in *Love's Labour's Lost*, *A Winter's Tale*, *Henry the Fifth* ('Speak, my fair, and fairly, I pray thee') and other plays. 'Fair' occurs on its own in, e.g., *The Knight of the Burning Pestle*, by Beaumont and Fletcher: 'Nay, do not fly me, fair.' In such cases it is always a woman who is being addressed. As an element in vocative expressions, 'fair' could be compared to 'dear' in modern times, but 'dear' has been used independently far more than was 'fair' at the height of its popularity.

Fans This is used by the presenter of a television chat show to his audience in *Cocksure*, by Mordecai Richler. It may occasionally be used in real life in similar circumstances, or to address any group of enthusiastic supporters of a performing artist, sports team, etc. 'Fan' abbreviates 'fanatic', and was first used jokingly in 1682, according to the *Oxford English Dictionary*. Usage did not become general at that time; the word was re-launched in the USA in the 1880s, applied at first to baseball fans. Although it is now widely used, it occurs rarely as a vocative and would be very difficult to use in its singular form. 'Fan' would be interpreted as a diminutive of Fanny, itself a pet form of Frances.

Farmer Used to a farmer on its own or as a prefix followed by the family name of the man concerned, especially in former times. In *The Trumpet Major*, by Thomas Hardy, Anne Garland regularly addresses her neighbour as 'Farmer Derriman'. Unlike the comparable term 'Miller', 'Farmer' does not occur on its own in that novel, though it is to be found in *The River*, by Steven Bauer. 'I gotta get me some air. How about you, farmer?' is said to a man who is normally a farmer, but is temporarily doing industrial work. The speaker is a fellow workman. He later uses 'dumb-ass farmers' as a friendly term of abuse to two of the farmers working with him. *The Blithedale Romance*, by Nathaniel Hawthorne, has Silas Foster saying to a group of men: 'Take my advice, brother farmers. . . .'

Fart This word is avoided in polite circles, though its meaning as a noun or verb referring to the breaking of wind is well-known. Since the mid-nineteenth century it has been applied in slang to contemptible people, especially older men. 'You fart' is unfriendly when it occurs in *A Cack-Handed War*, by Edmund Blishen, used by one man to another. In Garson Kanin's *Moviola* an American speaker uses 'you old fart' to a man in his nineties. 'You twisted little fart' occurs in *St Urbain's Horseman*, by Mordecai Richler, during an unfriendly conversation between two men. This particular collocation shows clearly that 'fart' is no longer being thought of as a bad smell but as a person who is mentally twisted.

Fascist Used as a general insult to anyone who is thought to be acting in an autocratic way, especially if that person represents a state-run organization. The original Fascists governed in Italy from 1922–1943, and were characterized by extreme nationalism, anti-socialism, militarism, and restrictions on individual freedom, with industrial activity controlled by the state. 'Fascist' is used insultingly to a public librarian in *The Sleepers of Erin*, by Jonathan Gash, and is again insulting in *Absolute Beginners*, by Colin MacInnes.

Fat-ass An American expression used insultingly to a fat person. Examples occur in *The Liberation of Lord Byron Jones*, by Jesse Hill Ford, where a black American woman uses it to a black man who has a huge appetite. She goes on to describe him as 'a lardy old bum', recalling the 'Get over, lard-ass' that occurs in *The Day of the Locust*, by Nathanael West, also addressed to a fat person.

Fat boy *See* **Fat man**.

Fathead A friendly insult rather than a serious one. Wilfred Granville remarks in his *Dictionary of Sailors' Slang* that it is a condition induced by the fug between decks when a ship has her hatches and scuttles closed in heavy weather. It also describes a hangover.

As a term of address it implies foolishness of an acceptable kind. *Like Any Other Man*, by Patrick Boyle, has a woman ask a man where he has parked the car. ' "Parked?" Frowning, he sought to recollect. "Yes, fathead. Did you leave your car outside in the street?" '

Father This would seem to be the natural term for a speaker to use to his or her father, but whether it is used or not depends on individual family practice, which may in turn be influenced by the social and educational level of the family concerned. 'Father' is in fact only one of many terms available to an English-speaker – others include: Dad, Daddy, Pop, Pa, Papa, Poppa, Pater, our Da', etc. On 'father' itself, Mrs Craik has this to say in *John Halifax, Gentleman*:

O solemn name, which Deity Himself claims and owns! Happy these children, who in its fullest sense could understand the word 'father!' to whom, from the dawn of their little lives, their father was what all fathers should be – the truest representative here on earth of that Father in heaven . . .

This was the conventional Victorian view, requiring honour and respect to be paid to one's parent as to one's god. Honour was indeed accorded. When Clive Newcome, in Thackeray's *The Newcomes*, writes to his father as 'My dearest Father,' his parent muses: 'the modern and natural style is a great progress upon the old-fashioned manner of my day, when we used to begin to our fathers, "Honoured Father", or even "Honoured Sir". . . .' Such was the verbal fashion in middle-class families, though Newcome Senior goes on to say: 'I suspect parents were no more *honoured* in those days than nowadays.' Dickens has a particularly unpleasant character in *Barnaby Rudge*, who rejects the title of father. The character of Mr Chester – later Sir John Chester – emerges clearly as he responds to being addressed as 'Father' by his son:

'My good fellow,' interposed the parent hastily, as he set down his glass, and raised his eyebrows with a startled and horrified expression, 'for Heaven's sake don't call me by that obsolete and ancient name. Have some regard for decency. Am I gray, or wrinkled, do I go on crutches, have I lost my teeth, that you adopt such a mode of address?'

There are the modern equivalents of Sir John, who refuse to allow their children to call them by one of the 'father' terms, preferring instead to be known by their first names. Some would argue that their motives, like Sir John's, are related to personal vanity; others would say more charitably that they wish their children to be their friends, and to address them as such. The father-parent relationship is, however, unique, and is almost certainly of unique importance to the child. For the parent to try to negate it, or to reduce it to the level of one relationship amongst many, seems grossly unfair to the child, an unforgivably foolish act by the parent.

As with the other 'father' terms, 'father' may in some families be used to address an adoptive father, a step-father, or a father-in-law. Shakespeare's *Much Ado About Nothing* (4:i) has Claudio saying to Leonato: 'Father, by your leave:/Will you with free and unconstrained soul/Give me this maid, your daughter?' Similarly, in *The Taming of the Shrew* (2:i), Petruchio calls Baptista 'father' once it is agreed that Petruchio will marry Katherina: 'Provide the feast, father, and bid the guests; I will be sure my Katherine shall be fine.' This anticipatory use of a vocative is extended to Katherina, who is addressed immediately as 'wife' on expectation of the marriage.

Apart from family relationship, 'father' refers – as Mrs Craik pointed out – to the spiritual relationship between God and his human family. In prayers God is frequently addressed as 'Father'. The title is also extended to some of His representatives on earth. Much is made of that fact in Joseph Heller's *Catch 22*, where the chaplain fights a losing battle as he tries to convince his colleagues that in his case, 'Father' is not an appropriate title:

'Hiya, Father,' he said tonelessly, without looking at the chaplain. Colonel Korn was proceeding up the stairs without slackening his pace, and the chaplain resisted the temptation to remind him again that he was not a Catholic but an Anabaptist, and that it was therefore neither necessary or correct to address him as Father. He was almost certain now that Colonel Korn remembered and that calling him Father with a look of such bland innocence was just another one of Colonel Korn's methods of taunting him because he was only an Anabaptist.

Later in the novel the chaplain says to a major: 'It isn't necessary to call me Father. I'm not a Catholic.' The major replies: 'Neither am I, Father. It's just that I'm a very devout person, and I like to call all men of God Father.' In *The Outsider*, Albert Camus puts the opposite point of view:

Then he tried to change the subject by asking me why I hadn't once addressed him as 'Father', seeing that he was a priest. That irritated me still more, and I told him that he wasn't my father; quite the contrary, he was on the others' side.

Roman Catholic priests can also be addressed as 'Father' + last name or 'Father' + first name, the latter being the modern fashion when par-ishioners are addressing their priest. *Oliver's Story*, by Erich Segal, has an example of the latter usage, though it is addressed to his former father-in-law, who says: ' "I'm here to save your soul and save your ass. And you will heed me. Do you heed?" "Yes, Father Philip." ' With this one may compare the use of 'my lord', 'your lordship', etc., in social situations that come to resemble court-room scenes because someone is acting like a judge or barrister. Another possible reason for usage of 'Father' + first name is demonstrated in *The Choirboys*, by Joseph Wambaugh. A Los Angeles policeman who is a devout Jehovah's Witness is regularly addressed as 'Father Willie' or 'Padre' by his colleagues. In its religious use 'Father' can take a normal plural form. 'Please be seated, Fathers', says a nun to two priests in *Bless Me, Father*, by Neil Boyd. It cannot be used interchangeably with other 'father' terms, however. To address a priest as 'Dad' would be at best humour misplaced, at worst an aggressive insult.

Fatima Actually a popular Arabic name, that of the Prophet Mohammad's daughter, but used by English children as a transferred name for a fat girl. They also use the invented name 'Thinima' for an especially thin girl. *See also* **Fatty**.

Fat man A variant of 'fatty' or 'fatso', used to a large person. 'You're not so funny tonight, fat man,' says an American speaker to a hoodlum in *Waterfront*, by Budd Schulberg. The same man is elsewhere in the novel addressed by a different speaker as 'fat boy'.

Fatmouth 'I really am disgusted with all of you,' says a speaker in *Catch 22*, by Joseph Heller. 'Okay, fatmouth, out of the car,' he is told. 'Fatmouth' is normally a verb in American slang. It can mean to chatter in a general way or to cajole someone by sweet-talking them. In the above example 'fatmouth' appears to mean 'big-mouth', one who talks too much and to the annoyance of others.

Fatso Used as a disparaging term for a fat person, or as a covert endearment to a love-partner. The word presumably represents the final ' –o' seen in vocatives such as 'kiddo', 'boyo', 'daddyo' added to Fats, a nickname for a fat person. The latter was made well-known by the American jazz pianist and composer Thomas (Fats) Waller.

Fatty Used insultingly to an overweight person, or in modern times jokingly to a woman who is constantly worrying about her weight. 'What's the matter, Fatty?' is addressed to a police sergeant by a seventeen-year-old offender in Ed McBain's short story *First*

Offence. The speaker means to demonstrate that he is not intimidated by policemen. *The Middle Man*, by David Chandler, has one man saying to another: 'Get out of the way, fattie.' Use of this term is 'a score that would remain to be settled'.

The most famous 'fatty' in literature, apart from the Billy Bunter of English children's fiction, is probably Shakespeare's Sir John Falstaff. He is never called 'fatty', though there are many references to him as: a fat rogue, a gross fat man, fat knight, fat fool. Prince Hal refers to him in *Henry the Fourth Part One* (2:iv) as a 'bed-presser', a 'horseback-breaker', a 'huge hill of flesh', and calls him to his face 'thou whoreson, obscene, greasy tallow-catch'. Falstaff in turn comments rudely and forcefully on Prince Hal's thinness. The Opies, in *The Lore and Language of Schoolchildren*, mention that Falstaff is used as a transferred name for a fat person in some parts of England, as is Billy Bunter the Second.

Other playground names for a fat child, or street names for a fat adult, include: Balloon, Barrage Balloon, Barrel, Barrel-belly, Blood Tub, Bouncer, Buster, Chubby, Chunky, Crystal Jellybottom, Diddle Diddle Dumpling, Fat belly, Fatty Harbuckle, Flab, Football, Glutton, Grub Tub, Guts, Jelly-belly, Jelly-wobble, Jumbo, Lumpy, Piggy, Podge, Porker, Porky, Steam-roller, Tank, Ten-ton, Tubs, Tubby, Two-ton Tessie. The last of these is used to a fat girl, as is Bessy Bunter, Fatima, and Tubbelina. There are three examples of 'Fatty' used to a boy who is given the nickname 'Piggy' in *Lord of the Flies*, by William Golding. The same boy is also called 'you fat slug'.

Fayther   *See* **Feyther.**

Feardy gowk   A Scottish children's expression for a child who is thought to be cowardly. 'Gowk' literally means 'cuckoo'. *See also* **Scaredy-cat.**

Fella   *See* **Fellow.**

Feller-me-lad, young   Eric Partridge, in his *Dictionary of Historical Slang*, tells us that this expression has been in use in Britain since the mid-nineteenth century. It can still occasionally be heard, used in a slightly ponderous way by middle-aged men to younger men or boys. It is meant to be jocular. A father uses it to his prospective son-in-law in *Theirs was the Kingdom*, by R. F. Delderfield. In *A Kind of Loving*, by Stan Barstow, a father says to his son, who is aged twenty: 'I asked you a civil question, young feller-me-lad.' This is when the son concerned has replied with great sarcasm to a friendly question about football. Exactly when the two separate vocatives, 'young fellow' and

'my lad', became fused into the single expression is not known.

Fellow   The original sense of this word was business-partner, but by the fourteenth century it also had the meaning of companion in a more general sense. It became the usual way of addressing a male servant, and at first would have been thought to be no more condescending than 'my friend'. The habitual association with servants and men of low rank gradually made it impossible to use the word other than insultingly to a man of equal station. 'None of your fellow,' says Partridge, in Fielding's *Tom Jones*, when a woman addresses him in that way.

'Who's to prove to me that you are Mr Ramornie?' says a character in *St Ives*, by R. L. Stevenson. 'Fellow!' says the narrator. ' "O, fellow as much as you please!" said he. "Fellow, with all my heart! That changes nothing. I am fellow, of course – obtrusive fellow, impudent fellow, if you like – but who are you?" ' Sam Weller in *The Pickwick Papers* objects to being described as a fellow, even though not addressed as one. These unpleasant associations with the word disappear immediately when it is qualified vocatively, as in: old fellow, my dear fellow, my good fellow, young fellow, poor fellow, etc.

In *Little Dorrit*, by Charles Dickens, a man talking to his equal, and normally addressing him as 'Mr' + last name, switches to 'my good fellow', 'if you'll excuse the freedom of that form of address . . .'. 'My fine fellow' is used in a friendly way in *Lady Chatterley's Lover* by D. H. Lawrence, the male speaker addressing another man. Here 'fellow' has clearly reverted to its meaning of friend, one with whom one is on hail-fellow-well-met terms. Such usage, especially 'old fellow' and 'my dear fellow', would still be heard in modern Britain amongst middle-class speakers of a certain age.

In the USA 'fellow' is usable on its own in neutral settings, with a meaning that has been reduced to something like 'man'. Its relaxed pronunciation is frequently indicated by the spelling 'fella'. 'Wait a minute, will you, fella?' says a character in *Audition*, a short story by Dawn Powell. 'Whaddya mean, fella?' occurs in Judith Rossner's *Any Minute I can Split*, used to a young man by another, who is called 'man' in return. 'Feller' is also used as a spelling variant, especially by British writers. It is especially likely to occur in the collocation 'young-feller-me-lad', addressed to a young man or boy in a friendly way.

In modern times, whether used alone or as part of a vocative group, 'fellow' no longer carries demeaning or contemptuous undertones. This is especially true when 'fellows' is used to a group of men. In *Babbitt*, by Sinclair Lewis, the chairman at one point says: 'Take your seats, fellows!' varying the usual formula which would have included 'boys' as the vocative.

fellow As an element other than the head-word in a vocative group, 'fellow' means something like 'similar to me, the speaker'. It occurs especially when a group of people are being addressed. Thus a preacher in *George Silverman's Explanation*, by Charles Dickens, uses 'my friends and fellow-sinners' to his audience. 'Fellow townsmen' occurs in a political speech in *Scenes of Clerical Life*, by George Eliot. Political speakers were perhaps especially fond of the word in the nineteenth century, since Dickens chooses to satirize them in *Hard Times*. He has Slackbridge, representative of the United Aggregate Tribunal, address a group of workers using phrases like 'oh my friends and fellow-countrymen, the slaves of an iron-handed and a grinding despotism', 'oh my friends and fellow-sufferers, and fellow-workmen, and fellow-men!' In a later speech occurs: 'Oh my friends and fellow-countrymen, the down-trodden operatives of Coketown; oh, my fellow-brothers, and fellow-workmen, and fellow-citizens, and fellow-men . . .'. All this contrasts greatly with the simple but effective oratory of Stephen Blackpool, who addresses the same group as 'my friends' and 'my brothers'.

Female This word is very rarely used vocatively. It occurs in Boucicault's nineteenth-century comedy *London Assurance*, addressed by Mr Spanker to Lady Gay. It is clearly meant to be a slightly more insulting term than 'woman', and is followed up by a use of that term as well: *'Spanker.* Female! am I to be immolated on the altar of your vanity? *Lady Gay.* If you become pathetic, I shall laugh. *Spanker.* Farewell – base, heartless, unfeeling woman!' *Gone With The Wind*, by Margaret Mitchell, has Rhett Butler saying to Scarlett O'Hara: 'What would you have me say? "Be mine, beautiful female, or I will reveal all?" ' He is teasing her, and we are told that he is giving 'a very creditable imitation of the stage villains who appeared infrequently at the Athenaeum Hall'. 'Beautiful female' is presumably meant to be typical of the bad writing associated with melodrama.

Feyther A spelling of 'father' which indicates dialectal pronunciation. 'Feyther, the me-a-at's come, an' what's me mother to do-o-o w'it?' is in Flora Thompson's *Lark Rise*, set in Oxfordshire. Henry Williamson, in *The Dream of Fair Women*, uses this spelling to represent Devonshire pronunciation when a girl says it to her father. There is a similar 'Fayther' in *Evan Harrington*, by George Meredith, where the speaker is a 'toddling small rustic'.

Fibber, you This is mainly an expression used by children, or by young women who wish to avoid the harshness of 'you liar'. The origin of 'fib', meaning a falsehood, especially a trivial one, is lost in obscurity. The variant 'fibster' has occasionally been used, as in *Vanity Fair*, by William Thackeray, where Lord Steyne says to Becky: 'You silly little fibster! I heard you in the room overhead, where no doubt you were putting a little rouge on.'

Fiend, you The *Oxford English Dictionary*, in its inimitable way, remarks that fiend can be 'applied with jocular hyperbole to a person or agency causing mischief or annoyance'. The reference is to expressions like 'autograph-fiend', 'cyclist-fiend', which were at one time current. But 'jocular hyperbole' seems just right for the modern use of 'you fiend', which instantly conjures up the late-night horror movie. A being of superhuman wickedness stalks innocent victims until confronted by the hero: 'Now I have you, you fiend!' he says, and the audience knows that it will soon be time for bed.

'Fiend' originally meant 'enemy', but quickly came to mean the arch enemy of mankind, the devil. Certain speakers might still use it seriously to someone whose behaviour they considered to be evil. 'White fiend!' says a black doctor to a white man, in *The Heart is a Lonely Hunter*, by Carson McCullers. Shakespeare used it as a vocative with full force in many of his plays, though in *Twelfth Night* he has the Clown address the devil that is supposed to be plaguing Malvolio as 'hyperbolical fiend', a good example of hyperbole in itself.

filthy A more intensive form of dirty, and frequently used in vocative expressions of the 'you filthy pig' type. The reference may be to filth in its sense of actual dirt, to the use of swear words and filthy language, or to something which is considered to be disgusting morally or sexually.

Fink An Americanism which does not seem to have penetrated British English at the end of the 1980s. The word has several meanings in American slang, such as 'police informer', or 'stool-pigeon', and 'strike-breaker', or 'scab'. It can also mean contemptible person, especially in the expression 'rat-fink'. Examples of the latter meaning occur vocatively in *An American Dream*, by Norman Mailer, where 'you upper-class fink' and 'rat-fink' are both used as insults between men.

Fire bucket *See* **Ginger**.

First name In the English-speaking world at the present time, first names are by far the most commonly used term of address. This was by no means always the case. Until the early part of the twentieth century men who had been friends or colleagues for a life-time habitually used one another's last names. Women used first names to one another when their relationship had developed to the friendship stage, though a relationship between middle-class women would never have begun with the use of first names. For a man to address a woman, or a woman a man, by first name it was necessary for their relationship to have reached an advanced stage of friendship, bordering on a proposal of marriage.

In Britain the change from last name to first name usage amongst middle-class men appears to have begun around 1930 or very soon afterwards. C. Northcote Parkinson, in an authoritative article some years ago, argued that Edward VIII had much to do with it. He was a known advocate of informality, and above all, he was thoroughly Americanized. There may well have been pressure on British society to follow the American lead in using first names before Edward VIII came briefly to the throne in 1936, but George V maintained Victorian values and insisted on Victorian standards of etiquette. Support for the dating of the change comes in *The Affair*, by C. P. Snow.

It occurred to me, still thinking of Martin's manners, that while he kept some of the old-style Cambridge, Crawford had, in just one respect, dropped his. Crawford called his contemporaries by their surnames, and that had been common form until the twenties. Even in my time there were not many Fellows who were generally called by their Christian names. But since the young used nothing else, since Martin and Walter Luke and Julian Skeffington had never been known by anything but their Christian names to their own contemporaries, the old men also began to call them so. With the result that Crawford and Winslow, who after fifty years of friendship still used each other's surnames, seemed oddly familiar when they spoke to the younger Fellows.

In spite of this example, there were those who did not easily give way to the new usage. There are certainly British people alive in the late 1980s who still feel uneasy about the liberal use of first names. They are members of an older generation, to be sure, and they are probably of middle-class background rather than working-class, but they certainly exist. The Second World War, however, produced a combination of circumstances which made the victory of first name over last name inevitable. There was a mixing of the social classes as never before, more and more situations where women were working alongside men and more encounters between British and American people. Men from middle-class backgrounds found themselves working alongside Tom, Dick, and Harry instead of being distanced from them. The working men were the majority, and their vocative usage would have become the norm without the additional pressures brought about by working with women, who would not want to address men by their last names. Middle-class boys, however, had earlier been brought up to believe that the use of their first names, outside the family circle, was almost shameful. Max Beerbohm, who would have been at school in the 1870s, once said that at his school the mere possession of a Christian name was thought to be unmanly. Public school traditions tend to live on, and in *Lord of the Flies*, by William Golding, we have the following exchange: ' "I'm Ralph . . ." "Kids' names," said Merridew. "Why should I be Jack? I'm Merridrew." ' *Brothers in Law*, by Henry Cecil, has the central character say: 'He felt a little like he did in his first days at a public school when he was terrified his mother would call him by his Christian name.' David Benedictus, in *The Fourth of June*, a novel about life at Eton, has: ' "May I sit down, Tom?" Tom? Nobody ever called him that.'

Later on, when these boys were far away from the enclosed environments of their schools, exclusively masculine environments, of course, their attitude towards being addressed by first name might change completely if a young lady was the speaker. 'I would have leaped into the valley of the shadow of death,' says the impassioned young lover in *Lorna Doone*, by R. D. Blackmore, 'only to hear her call me John.' This sounds remarkably dated, but even in *Lucky Jim*, by Kingsley Amis, we have: ' "Jim," Christine said. Dixon's scalp pricked at this, the first use of his Christian name.' *A Kind of Loving*, by Stan Barstow, has a similar comment:

'Have you had a nice Christmas, Vic?' Ingrid says, and I'm so tickled to hear her say my name that I can't think what to say for a minute. Nor Mr Brown, like Miss Price. Not Victor, even; but Vic, just like my mates.

Until fairly recently it was by no means automatic for a young man to begin using the first name of a girl or woman. Sometimes the woman concerned would invite the man to use her first name; sometimes he would hesitantly use it and wait to see what reaction he obtained. *The Business of Loving*, by Godfrey Smith, comments on the process:

'Could you tell us, Mrs Weston – ' began Benedict. But she gently interrupted him. 'Please call me Arabella. After all, I'm not very much older than you.' Benedict began again rather shyly: 'Could you tell us, Arabella – ' It was delectable, the unwonted, the previously forbidden pleasure of using her Christian name.

In *Kate and Emma*, by Monica Dickens, a girl's similar offer embarrasses the older man to whom she makes it, possibly because she is of a higher social background: ' "If you care to, Miss Bullock." I said: "Oh, yes, but please call me Emma." His neck got a bit red, and after that he didn't call me anything, not even Miss Bullock.' The tentative essay is reported in *Agnes Grey*, by Anne Brontë, who writes:

Ceremony was quickly dropped between us. He even called me Agnes: the name had been timidly spoken at first, but, finding it gave no offence in any quarter he seemed greatly to prefer that appellation to 'Miss Grey'; and so did I.

Nurse is a Neighbour, by Joanna Jones, has:

'I can't keep calling you Nurse, can I?' 'My name's Jones,' I said. He waited. I added: 'Joanna Jones.' 'Well, then . . .' He hesitated, and then said tentatively: 'Miss Jones.' The name of Joanna seemed to have trembled on his lips, but he was deferential, respectful, slow to advance.

This hesitancy usually occurred in situations where the man, and possibly the woman, hoped that the relationship might develop meaningfully. If it was clear from the beginning that nothing more than friendship would result, a more matter-of-fact attitude usually prevailed. In *Room at the Top*, by John Braine, a landlady greets a new tenant:

'I'll call you Mr Lampton if you like,' she said, 'but I'd rather call you Joe . . . And my name is Joan,' she added. 'That'll be fine, Joan,' I said; though oddly enough, I never thought of her as anything else than Mrs Thompson.

In *The Bell*, by Iris Murdoch, a woman member of a lay religious community uses first names to male newcomers and remarks in passing: 'We all use Christian names here, you know.' The fact that it is a Christian community and that 'Christian name' is used instead of the now more frequent 'first name', recalls a remark by Charles Lamb, in his essay on *Mackery End, In Hertfordshire*: 'In five minutes we were as thoroughly acquainted as if we had been born and bred up together; were familiar, even to the calling each other by our Christian names. So Christians should call one another.'

Lamb was talking about first name usage between men. When men and women have reached the first name stage, use of the name in an intimate relationship can be made very special by the tone in which it is uttered, and by its repetition. Novelists are firmly in agreement on this point, and most manage to make it economically: ' "Julia, my God, Julia, Julia, Julia," Paul said' (*The Limits of Love*, by Frederick Raphael); '. . . whispering his name over and over again, "Alec, Alec" ' (*The Spy Who Came in From the Cold*, by John le Carré); 'She's saying "Vic, oh, Vic," over and over again' (*A Kind of Loving*, by Stan Barstow); 'In tones of frantic endearment she uttered his name over and over again' (*The Bell*, by Iris Murdoch). R. F. Delderfield, in *Theirs was the Kingdom*, makes more of a meal of it:

She pulled him down on her, kissing his cheeks and eyes and mouth, and murmuring his name over and over again. No more than that, just 'Giles . . . Giles . . . Giles . . .' so that she invested it with a sort of glory and he heard it as music more enthralling than anything Herrick or Marvell had written on the subject of love.

Shakespeare has more than one comment on this use of a name by a lover, but Juliet's comment in *Romeo and Juliet* (2:ii) will suffice: 'Bondage is hoarse, and may not speak aloud;/ Else would I tear the cave where Echo lies,/ And make her airy tongue more hoarse than mine/With repetition of my Romeo's name.' Even with the modern exchange of first names at the first meeting and their subsequent casual use, something of this magical quality must remain when lovers says the names of those they love.

There are still some situations where one person uses another's first name, but expects a more formal term to be used in reply. This was formerly often the case in a working environment, where an office manager might use his employees' first names but expect to be called Mr Smith. *Room at the Top*, by John Braine, comments: 'Not that I was taken in by his chumminess. It was all very nice of him to call us Joe and Reggie but, I reflected, he wouldn't have been pleased if we'd called him Fred.' These unbalanced situations are now probably fewer in number, but a schoolmaster, for instance, using first names to his class-members, would still expect a more formal reply.

C. S. Lewis, in *The Voyage of the Dawn Treader*, says: 'He didn't call his Father and Mother "Father" and "Mother", but Harold and Alberta. They were very up-to-date and advanced people.' The Canadian novelist Alice Munro, in *Lives of Girls and Women*, says: 'He called his mother by her first name, which was Greta. How affected, how *unhealthy* I thought that was.' Both novelists are making the same point, although Lewis is more sarcastic. This use of the parental first names does not appear to have spread widely in any of the English-speaking countries. What appears to be such usage often turns out to be the use of a first name to a step-parent, though *The*

Observer newspaper, in an article about the children of divorced parents published in June 1988, gave an example of a young girl who called her father and mother 'John' and 'Marilyn', mainly because she had to address their new partners by their first names.

But while 'father' and 'mother' terms will probably survive, elsewhere the first name, for the moment, reigns supreme. Like many other terms of address, it can be an intimacy or a verbal friendly gesture, but said in a certain tone of voice it can be as unfriendly a term as any other. As a girl says in *Bhowani Junction*, by John Masters: 'I thought of calling him "Mr Taylor", but it sounded silly. I could be just as cold with "Patrick".' One wonders how long the first-name fashion will last. Vocative usage clearly does go in fashions. It may take a century for it to happen, but some future recorder of the vocative scene will no doubt be dating the change from first-name usage to the use of – what? – numbers, perhaps? But first names are never likely to regain the sacredness they once possessed. One cannot imagine a young lover of the future indignantly complaining about the first name of his loved one being bandied about, as does Frank Churchill in Jane Austen's *Emma*:

'Jane' indeed! You will observe that I have not yet indulged myself in calling her by that name, even to you. Think, then, what I must have endured in hearing it bandied between the Eltons, with all the vulgarity of needless repetition, and all the insolence of imagined superiority.

That kind of reverence for a name reflects a reverence for womanhood itself, an attitude which seems decidedly out-dated in these days of equality. It is perhaps not a very meaningful statistic, but in a count of the vocative occurrences in fifty novels, first names on their own were used 5469 times. To this should be added the many more occurrences of first names qualified in some way, so that the complete vocative expression was 'my dear John', 'Mary dear', 'Sarah my love', 'Peter my boy', etc.

First name (diminutive form) When speakers have agreed to use one another's first names, there can still remain the question of which form of the name is to be used. 'I wish to God you wouldn't call me Wilson,' says Edward Wilson to Louise Scobie in *The Heart of the Matter*, by Graham Green. 'Edward. Eddie. Ted. Teddy,' she says, experimentally. She settles on Teddy, but is told: 'I think I'd rather be Edward, Louise.' In English no formal distinction is made between what a person is named and what he is called, though Miss Peecher, in Dickens's *Our Mutual Friend*, would have argued otherwise:

'She is named Lizzie, ma'am.'
'She can hardly be named Lizzie, I think, Mary Anne,' returned Miss Peecher, in a tunefully instructive voice. 'Is Lizzie a Christian name, Mary Anne?'
'No, it is a corruption, Miss Peecher.'
'Speaking correctly, we say, then, that Hexham's sister is called Lizzie; not that she is named so.'

The passage recalls the comments of Mr Gradgrind, in *Hard Times*:

'Sissy is not a name,' said Mr Gradgrind. 'Don't call yourself Sissy. Call yourself Cecilia.'
'It's father as calls me Sissy, sir,' returned the young girl.
'Then he has no business to do it,' said Mr Gradgrind. 'Tell him he mustn't.'

Mr Gradgrind is of course insensitive to the motivation for using diminutive forms of names.

In *The Business of Loving*, by Godfrey Smith, two English army officers meet. 'What do people call you?' says the senior of the two. 'Benny, sir.' 'Benny. That's fine. My name is Rupert. For God's sake call me that and drop this sir crap.'

If people *are* asked for their first name, they are of course likely to respond by giving the form of it which they would like to have used. If a man whose name is Robert introduces himself by saying 'I'm Bob', then he does not expect to be addressed as Robert. With some first names the distinction between the forms would be quite significant. A working-class James who is normally known as Jim might feel that a speaker who used James to him was making fun of him. A middle-class James might well object to being addressed as Jim. The two forms of the name evoke different images in the mind of the average speaker, in Britain at least, and what is appropriate for one bearer of the name will not be so for another.

In his essay *On Nicknames*, William Hazlitt says: 'Diminutives are titles of endearment.' Mary Webb, in *Precious Bane*, remarks: 'You can make most names into little love names, like you can cut down a cloak or gown for children's wearing.' Some might say that these comments apply to the formation of a diminutive by first shortening the actual name, then adding a diminutive ending. One can otherwise not be sure that the use of a shortened form does not merely reflect that economy of speech which uneducated speakers appear to favour more than the educated. There is evidence, however, that abbreviation in itself is thought of as a kind of verbal friendly gesture. We all know what Tom Sawyer means when Becky Thatcher says she knows his name – Thomas Sawyer. 'That's the name they lick me by,' he tells her. 'I'm Tom when I'm good.' In a similar way short forms of vocatives such as 'Sarge' and 'Ref' indicate relaxed attitudes on the part of speakers. The switch back to 'Sergeant' instead of 'Sarge', 'Referee' instead of 'Ref' comes when the situation is more formal or when the listener – in the case of the referee, is being reminded of his inadequacies.

But while the motivation for abbreviation may be friendliness, such usage may well be interpreted by more educated speakers as laziness, or a sloppy use of language. Such critics are especially surprised by the shortening of names which are already short. The latter may well be former pet-forms of names which are now given as names in their own right, such as 'Betty', from 'Elizabeth'. Historically there was good reason for such pet-forms to take on a life of their own. Before the eighteenth century a small number of first names were used with great intensity, so that in even a small community there were many Elizabeths, Margarets and the like. Different pet-forms of those names were no doubt as necessary for purposes of identification as the many nicknames used in Welsh communities where everyone was called Jones. But with 'Betty' having become a name in its own right, it now often becomes 'Bet', as in *War Brides*, by Lois Battle. Will 'Bet' eventually become the name, and if so, what will be its diminutive form? 'Bet' is one of those reductions which looks a little odd when written, as if it is an instruction to risk one's money on some sporting event. The 'Barb' which is used for 'Barbara' in *Blue Dreams*, by William Hanley, also looks unfortunate, almost as much as the 'Die' which occurs in Charlotte Brontë's *Jane Eyre*. Modern writers, of course, would use 'Di' as the short form of 'Diana', an '–i' ending in names having become acceptable.

Novelists remark on the use of first name diminutives in various ways, and perhaps should be allowed to speak for themselves. They are often informative, telling us of vocative usage in particular sections of society. They can also be witty, as Arnold Bennett demonstrates in *The Old Wives' Tale*, where he is talking about a woman called Amy: ' "Shut up, Ame," he replied, smiling. Life being short, he normally called her Ame when they were alone together.' The following comment is from *Persephone*, by L. M. Boston: ' "How did you enjoy your day by the sea, Zephy?" asked little Sister Agnes in the Common Room. Abbreviations were little used at St Hilarion, because saints' names must be treated with respect, but with a pagan name liberties may be taken.' *Resolve This Day*, by Geoffrey Bainbridge, has:

More than twenty years of marriage, and

there still seemed to be something wrong in her calling him 'Andy'. She was almost the only one who had ever done so. It had always been a stern 'Andrew Cunningham' in his strict Scottish boyhood home. And then, when she'd started calling him Andy during their very brief courtship before the war – it had seemed intimate, special.

With this we may compare, from John Galsworthy's *The Forsyte Saga*: ' "I've been frightened, Freddie." The old pet name, disused for years and years, sent a shiver through Winifred.' *A World of Difference*, by Stanley Price, has the curious comment, made by a woman to a man: 'You don't mind me calling you Nicholas, do you? It's so much less devilish than Nicky.' This would have had more point to it if she had compared Nicholas with Nick, a much more immediate link with Old Nick. A deliberate reinterpretation of a pet form occurs in *Sam*, by Lonnie Coleman: ' "Hello, Addie," Richard said. "Hello, Richard," Addie said, not smiling. "Tell me," Richard said, "what does Addie stand for – adversary?" "That's right," she said. "I suppose Richard is short for prick." ' Addie here is actually a woman whose name is Adeline. The last remark is rather convoluted reference to 'dick', in its slang sense of 'penis'. *Of Human Bondage*, by Somerset Maugham, has a proud father introducing his family:

'Now the girls in order: Maria del Sol . . .' 'Pudding-face,' said one of the small boys. 'Your sense of humour is rudimentary, my son. Maria de los Mercedes, Maria del Pilar, Maria de la Concepcion, Maria del Rosario.' 'I call them Sally, Molly, Connie, Rosie and Jane,' said Mrs Athelny.

A correspondent to a women's magazine a few years ago made a similar point. After much deliberation she and her husband had named their daughters Abigail, Rebecca, and Shoshanna. At school they were known by the affectionate diminutives Biggy, Ecky, and Slosh.

The ways in which diminutive names are formed would make a lengthy linguistic study in itself. The '–y' or '–ie' suffix is the most widely used, added to the stem of a first name. *Thursday Afternoons*, by Monica Dickens, has 'Marry' and 'Amby', for instance, used to a Marion and Ambrose. Some names have more individual pet-forms, such as 'Jimbo' from 'James'. This may be a reduced form of 'Jimboy', since the addition of '–boy' is another way of creating a diminutive. The well-known example 'Del-boy', used in Britain to a man called Derek, shows a consonant change which has been normal for centuries, 'Harry' having given rise to 'Hal', 'Sarah' to 'Sal', 'Mary' to 'Mal', later 'Moll'. In Britain in the late 1980s the tendency is to convert 'Barry' to 'Baz', 'Sharon' to 'Shaz'. Cate Poynton, of the University of Sydney, reports on the use in Australia of 'Bazza' for 'Barry', 'Pezza' for 'Perrin', 'Ekka' for 'Eric', 'Mokka' for 'Maurice'. These are by no means as exclusively Australian as the writer suggests.

By a kind of linguistic playfulness, the initial letter of a pet-form may be changed. 'Mag', from 'Margaret', became 'Meg', then 'Peg'. 'Mary' went through the 'Mal', 'Moll' stages before changing to 'Polly'. With forms like 'Ted' for 'Edward' one suspects that the diminutives of two names may have become confused, since 'Ted' would more logically abbreviate 'Theodore'. With several thousand first names in regular use in the English-speaking world, a full-scale study would be required to arrive at all diminutive elements, and even then it would be difficult to obtain information about private forms of names used between couples, say, when they are alone but never in public. 'Leslie', for example, *can* be converted into 'Lezzums' or 'Les-love', but these are intimacies, unlike the friendly – and more public – 'Les'. All this is really to say that the English language is woefully lacking in a word which would adequately translate German *Rufname*, the name by which a person is actually known, or wishes to be known. There may well be a difference, of course, between *those* two categories, so two words may be needed for 'actual call-name(s)' and 'preferred call-name'.

First name, rhyming forms of It is a habit of many adults to play a rhyming game with a baby's name at the pre-speech stage of the infant. This habit is sometimes transferred into adult life, where the rhyming forms become intimate diminutive forms. 'Georgy-porgy' and 'Jimsy-wimsy' occur in *Georgy Girl*, by Margaret Forster; 'Jeannie-Peenie' is in *The Taste of Too Much*, by Clifford Hanley, which also has an example of 'Petesy-Wetesy'. Such infant forms may also be used to annoy the person concerned, implying that he or she is babyish. *Within and Without*, by John Harvey, has a girl addressed as 'Bridget the Fidget', where the second element is inspired by her movements but no doubt seems especially suitable because of the rhyme. *Fox in the Attic*, by Richard Hughes, shows the playfulness that is possible with a name like 'Polly', going well beyond the simply 'Polly-wolly'. This is at first extended to 'Pollywollydoodle', then to 'Pollyollywollyollydoodleoodleoooo'. The syllabic rhyming game in baby talk is extended to words as well as names. The rhyming forms may then be used as vocatives. There is a reference, for example, to a song which had the lyric 'All day long he called her snookyookums' in *The Dream of Fair Women*, by Henry Williamson.

First name, Lady Used socially to the daughter of a duke, marquess, or earl. There are examples of its use in *Casanova's Chinese Restaurant*, by Anthony Powell. In *The Business of Loving*, by Godfrey Smith, occurs: ' "It's thirteen years, I'm afraid, Lady M." The familiar abbreviation came back naturally.' The wife of a younger son of a duke or marquess is addressed as 'Lady' + first name of her husband.

First name, Lord A style of address used to the younger son of a duke or marquess. 'Good night, Lord Michael,' says a speaker in *A Surfeit of Lampreys*, by Ngaio Marsh, after a death in the family has caused the boy to inherit the title. ' "*Daddy!*" he said. "It's not going to be *that!*" "Well," said Lord Charles, "well, yes, I'm afraid – well, yes, Mike it is." "Good Lord! it's a damn sight worse than Potty!" '

First name, Master Until recently this was a way of addressing politely a boy who was too young to be called 'Mister'. In his autobiographical *Goodbye to All That* Robert Graves comments:

> The servants were trained to call us children, even when we were tiny, 'Master Robert', 'Miss Rosaleen', and 'Miss Clarissa', but I had not recognized these as titles of respect. I had thought of 'Master' and 'Miss' merely as vocative prefixes used for addressing other people's children; but now I found that the servants were the lower classes, and that we were ourselves.

It is noticeable that when Bumble the Beadle, in Dickens's *Oliver Twist*, learns of the hero's good fortune, which makes him a young gentleman, he switches to 'Master Oliver' as a term of address. It was certainly the boys from middle and upper-class families who were normally addressed in this way by their social inferiors, but even boys from working-class backgrounds might in modern times be addressed with mock solemnity as 'Master'+ first name by, e.g., a doctor. 'Master' + last name was also sometimes used. The use of 'Master' as a prefixed title to a boy has now almost died out, though some adults may still use this form jokingly. It is not always appreciated by those to whom it is addressed. *A God and His Gifts*, by Ivy Compton-Burnett, has: 'The Nurse appeared. "May Master Henry come now, ma'am?" "Not *Master*," said Henry, with a wail. "Come then, Nurses's little boy." '

First name, Miss The younger daughters of a middle or upper-class family are traditionally addressed in this way, 'Miss' + last name being the style used for the eldest daughter. But in general terms, 'Miss' + first name is used as a more respectful form of address than the first name on its own. It was far more common at a time when first names were not bandied about as they are today. Festus Derriman and other young swains in Thomas Hardy's *The Trumpet Major* all address Anne Garland as 'Miss Anne', whereas today she would have been 'Anne' to them from childhood. In *Vanity Fair*, by William Thackeray, Joseph Sedley addresses Becky Sharp as 'Miss Sharp' at dinner, though by the end of the meal he is using 'Miss Rebecca'. In *Theirs was the Kingdom*, by R. F. Delderfield, a young man uses 'Miss' + first name to a young woman who is slightly younger than himself, because he respects the social position of her family. She asks him to drop the 'Miss', and eventually they marry. In *Kate and Emma*, by Monica Dickens, a working-class man insists on using 'Miss' + first name to a woman who is obviously of middle-class background. *I'll Get By*, by Elizabeth Byrd, has the comment: 'Mother thinks it terrible that he doesn't call me "Miss Julie" because he's a Negro.' The man concerned uses the first name.

First name, Mr Occasionally used as an intermediate form of address between the politeness of 'Mr' + last name and the informality of first name only. In *Getting it Right*, by Elizabeth Jane Howard, a girl assistant uses 'Mr' + first name to a hairdresser when they are in the shop. In some family businesses, the son of the owner who also works there may be addressed as 'Mr' + first name. The same style is often used by servants in domestic employment to the sons of the household. In *Georgy Girl*, by Margaret Forster, 'Mr James' is equated with 'sir' by the man who addresses his employer. Other examples of this usage occur in, e.g., *Memento Mori*, by Muriel Spark, *Goldfinger*, by Ian Fleming, *A Use of Riches*, by J. I. M. Stewart.

First name, Mrs There is a highly amusing scene in Fielding's *Tom Jones* where Sophia Western's chambermaid objects to being addressed as 'Mrs Honour' by the maid of Sophia's aunt. 'Mrs Honour, forsooth! sure, madam, you might call me by my surname; for though my lady calls me Honour, I have a surname as well as other folks.' This leads to the other maid calling her 'creature', 'hussy', and an 'audacious saucy trollop'. Finally, Fielding tells us, 'the two chambermaids being again left alone began a second bout at altercation, which soon produced a combat of a more active kind.' 'Mrs' + first name is not a normal mode of address, but another possible way of bringing it about is suggested by Somerset Maugham in his short story *Home*. A man named George Meadows is married: 'Her mother-in-law was the only Mrs Meadows we knew,' writes Maugham. 'George's wife was only known as Mrs George.'

First name, Sir The polite form of address to a British baronet or a knight. The baronet's title is a hereditary one, the knight's isn't. *Kingfishers Catch Fire*, by Rumer Godden, has: 'I never called him Uncle William, always Sir William, she thought. That shows how pompous he was.'

First name(s) + last name A fuller version of a person's name is used vocatively in a number of different situations. In a court-room, for example, its use constitutes a formal identification. ' "Emma Adeline Salad," read the clerk, "you are charged that on the fifteenth day of March. . . ." ' So runs a scene in *Anglo-Saxon Attitudes*, by Angus Wilson. *Brothers in Law*, by Henry Cecil, has: 'Now, Margaret Grant, I'm not going to send you to prison. . . .'

In a classroom, where there may be several children who bear the same first name, use of the full name may be necessary: 'What do they show us, children? Could you tell us, Philip Arnold?' says a teacher in *Free Fall*, by William Golding.

Even in social encounters, either face to face or on the telephone, the full name may be said to confirm identification, especially if the people concerned have not met for a long time. *Stop at Nothing*, by John Welcome has: ' "Toni!" I exclaimed. "Toni Velletti!" ' In *No Highway*, by Nevil Shute, there is: ' "Monica Teasdale?" "That's right." ' *A Season In Love*, by Peter Draper, has the narrator begin a telephone conversation by saying 'My name's Wilson.' 'Sam Wilson?' says the voice at the other end of the line. This is on the borderline of vocative usage, but is a common enough happening. A special case of confirming identity is instanced by R. F. Delderfield, in *Theirs was the Kingdom*: 'A girl like you could hook just about anyone, anyone at all. . . .' 'I don't want anyone. I want you, Jamie Higson.'

A more common situation where the full form of a name is used is during a radio broadcast, where the presenter of a chat-show wishes to remind the audience of the studio guest's identity. Apart from its use to identify formally, or to confirm an identification, a person's full name may be used with mock formality or severity, or with genuine anger or annoyance, especially when administering a reproof. 'I heard what you said, Gladys Butler. I have never heard anything so impertinent,' says a headmistress, in *The Liberty Man*, by Gillian Freeman. 'You're horrid. I won't have anything more to do with you, Joe Lampton,' says a girl in *Room at the Top*, by John Braine. 'You take your hands off me, Mark Fearon,' says another girl, in *Within and Without*, by John Harvey. The speaker in *The Taste of Too Much*, by Clifford Hanley, who shouts: 'You shut your mouth, Ria Dougan!' is genuinely very angry with the girl he is addressing. So, perhaps, is the mother in Edna Ferber's *Showboat*, who says to her daughter: 'Magnolia Hawks, get into your bed this very minute!' It may have no significance, but the literary evidence suggests that women are more likely to use the first name + last name formula when reproving than men are.

Finally, though it has little to do with the above, *The Limits of Love*, by Frederic Raphael has an old joke that bears repetition, where an *ad hoc* last name is created: 'You really know what you're doing. My name's Susan, by the way.' 'Hello, Susan by-the-way. My name's Ben-in-case-you-don't-know-Simons.'

First name + last name, Miss, Mrs, or Mr This style of address is occasionally used. In *The Limits of Love*, by Frederic Raphael, occurs: 'The voice on the telephone said: "Mr Colin Adler? My name's Cox." ' In *Brothers in Law*, by Henry Cecil, a judge in court addresses a barrister as 'Mistah Andrew Pain', the 'Mistah' reflecting a North Country bias', as the author puts it. The same judge uses 'Mistah Cruft' to a younger barrister who is present in court. He may be using the fuller form of the name to the senior member of the Bar as a personal acknowledgement of that seniority. In *Girl with Green Eyes*, by Edna O'Brien, the heroine is twice addressed in full as 'Miss Caithleen Brady'. Both speakers who use this form are Irish men, in circumstances that are intimate rather than formal. No reason is mentioned in context for the use of this form of address, which may be a feature of Irish speech.

First name (of husband) + last name (of husband), Mrs When writing to the wife of John Smith it is considered to be 'correct' to write to 'Mrs John Smith' rather than to 'Mrs Mary Smith', using her own first name. This style is very rare in speech, but it can occur in special situations. In *A Woman Called Fancy*, by Frank Yerby, a man who is said to be in love with the woman who is now his sister-in-law addresses her both as 'my dear sister-in-law' and as 'Mrs Tyler Brantley'. He is presumably reminding her, and himself, of her married status, especially since her husband is his brother.

First oboe *See* **Violins**.

First pair Addressed to men who are about to make a parachute jump in *Unconditional Surrender*, by Evelyn Waugh. The men concerned are subsequently addressed No. 1, No. 2, etc.

Fish Used of a person in colloquial speech since the eighteenth century, especially in

phrases like 'an odd fish', 'a queer fish'. The word was sometimes specifically applied to a sailor. In modern American slang 'fish' can have many different meanings, ranging from a newly arrived inmate at a prison to a sucker, or one easily 'caught'. Applied to a woman by homosexual speakers, 'fish' means that she is heterosexual. In student slang 'a fish' is a promiscuous woman. The vocative meaning of 'fish' will therefore vary greatly according to the speaker. A typical vocative expression would be 'you poor fish', implying that the hearer was slightly stupid.

Fishfingers This occurs in Mordecai Richler's *St Urbain's Horseman*, in a situation where 'Butterfingers' might have been expected. A man playing baseball ducks out of the way when the ball comes towards him instead of trying to catch it. Fishfingers are pieces of processed fish in small pieces, roughly finger-shaped. Most American speakers would call them 'fishsticks'.

Flab *See* **Fatty**.

Flatfoot A slang reference to a policeman or private detective. An American man uses it to the latter in *Gideon Planish*, by Sinclair Lewis. 'Gumshoe' is a similar term, and *see also* **Shamus**.

Flatterer In Shakespeare this is usually applied to one who uses false flattery, and is to be despised for it. Antony uses 'you flatterers' to Brutus and his men in *Julius Caesar* (5:i), and it is clearly insulting. Modern usage of the term tends to be milder. 'You can't blame me for looking though, can you?' says a man to a woman in *The Blinder*, by Barry Hines. 'Especially at legs like yours.' 'Flatterer,' says the woman. *A Kind of Loving*, by Stan Barstow, has: ' "Why, Mr Miller," Pauline says, "you're not old." "Flatterer," Miller says.'

Flea Used in British playgrounds as a generic nickname for a very small child. *See also* **Tich**. In Shakespeare's *The Taming of the Shrew* (4:iii), Petruchio calls a tailor 'thou flea', referring to his insignificance. He equates the word with 'nit', which is probably the more commonly used term in modern times.

Fleabag Addressed in an unfriendly way to an elderly man by another man in *The Occupation*, by David Caute. This is an unusual extension of the slang use of 'fleabag', which is normally applied to an inferior horse (or to a mattress, sleeping-bag, or cheap hotel).

Flid A modern English slang word for a stupid person. It can only be described as a sick joke, since it derives from the word 'thalidomide' and first began to be used at the time of the thalidomide trials, when mothers who had taken the drug thalidomide sued the drug companies. The drug caused many children to be born badly deformed.

Flight-lieutenant 'Good morning, Flight-lieutenant Jardine,' says a nurse to a patient in *The Face-Maker*, by Richard Gordon. A flight-lieutenant is a commissioned officer in the Royal Air Force. His rank corresponds with that of a naval lieutenant or an army captain.

Flight sergeant The title of a rank in the Royal Air Force. In the Biggles books of Captain W. E. Johns the flight sergeant is always addressed as 'Flight'.

Flirt This has been used since the eighteenth century in its modern sense of one who tries to attract attention from the opposite sex, and shows sexual interest in members of the opposite sex when conversing with them. *Within and Without*, by John Harvey, has: 'He had to go off to his car to change into his red coat. I grabbed Sue, who had been talking steadily to him all the time. "Hullo, you damn flirt," I said.'

Flock Dr Primrose, in *The Vicar of Wakefield*, by Oliver Goldsmith, addresses his congregation at one point as 'my dear deluded flock'. *See also* **Shepherd**.

Floozie, Floozy A word of unknown origin, used in American slang to refer to a prostitute. 'You floozie' is used to such a woman in *The Late Risers*, by Bernard Wolfe, the term being equated by the speaker with 'slut'.

Flower Used in various parts of Britain as a term of address, usually to a woman or child, though a columnist writing in *The Times* newspaper (10 August 1988) commented on his surprise at being addressed as 'my flower' while on a visit to Wales. Mrs Bridget Mackenzie, writing from Langbank, Renfrewshire, says that 'flower' is commonly used to women in Paisley, being the equivalent of the 'hen' used in Glasgow and Edinburgh. 'It makes you feel really pretty,' Mrs Mackenzie comments. She adds that the term used in Paisley to men is 'Mac'.

Flying officer A title indicating a Royal Air Force rank, equivalent to a naval sub-lieutenant and an army lieutenant. It is used vocatively with the last name of the person concerned in *No Highway*, by Nevil Shute.

Folks A collective term of address which implies that the company is included in the speaker's intimate circle of friends, or is part of his family. In the USA in the nineteenth century it could also imply that the people so addressed were eminently respectable, since that was a meaning the word acquired. Its proper use as a vocative is shown in *Babbitt*, by Sinclair Lewis, where Babbitt himself uses it to address his friends and neighbours who are paying a social visit. It is used more generally by speakers who are trying to evoke a friendly response. Thus a radio announcer in *The Day of the Locust*, by Nathanael West, holds out his microphone to pick up the background noise and says: 'Did you hear it? It's a bedlam, folks.' The term would not be used in formal circumstances.

Fondling A term that was used from the seventeenth to the early nineteenth century to refer to one who was much fondled and caressed, especially a young child. In *The Vicar of Wakefield*, by Oliver Goldsmith, 'my fondlings' is used by Dr Primrose to address his children.

Fool, you A common insult since the seventeenth century, perhaps used with more insulting contempt now than then. In Shakespeare's time 'fool', 'poor fool', and the like could be used on occasion as terms of endearment or genuine pity. In modern times 'you fool' can of course be turned into an endearment between intimates by being uttered in a light-hearted way, but it is more likely to be said with genuine anger. It is frequently expanded as 'you bloody fool' (*passim*), 'you stupid fool', as in *Dandelion Days*, by Henry Williamson, where 'you damn fool' also occurs. 'You blabbing fool' occurs in *Dover One*, by Joyce Porter; 'you pale staring fool' is in *Scenes of Clerical Life*, by George Eliot.

The term was originally used of natural simpletons, but was transferred to those who acted foolishly on particular occasions. Shakespeare often features in his plays the professional fools of former times, who were attached to royal and noble households as jesters. Shakespeare portrays the fool in *Lear*, for example, as an intelligent, sensitive, loving, and faithful young man, but in real life the professional fools must often have been of deficient intelligence. 'Fool' is very frequent as a vocative in Shakespeare, used insultingly, professionally, or more gently.

Some indication of its use in modern times in English-speaking countries is given by the occurrences in fifty novels, selected randomly, but all published since 1950 and with contemporary settings. 'You fool' occurred fifteen times, 'you bloody fool' ten times. To these may be added 'fool' (twice), 'stupid fool' (once), 'you couple of old fools' (once), 'you decrepit old fool' (once), 'you fools' (once), 'you girt fool' (once), 'you girt silly fool' (once), 'you little fool' (once), 'you stupid fool' (once).

Football *See* Fatty.

Football-player, you base This curious insult is used by the earl of Kent to Oswald, Goneril's steward, in Shakespeare's *King Lear*. The game did not have a good reputation in the seventeenth century. According to Sir Thomas Elyot, writing in 1531, it was a game 'wherein is nothing but beastly fury and extreme violence'. A football-player was therefore little more than a brawling ruffian. Such ruffians are unfortunately still associated with the game, though in Britain they now tend to be on the terraces or fighting in nearby streets. 'Football-player' occurs again as a vocative in *North Dallas Forty*, by Peter Gent. A man who associates with professional football-players, but is not one himself, says to a man he knows: 'Fucking pro-football player. Big man. Goddam asshole, that's what you are.' The novel, which describes the world of professional American football, appears to prove that Sir Thomas Elyot's view of the game would still be applicable.

FOREIGN VOCATIVES Novels and plays written in English often introduce characters of other nationalities and give conversations in English that supposedly take place in other languages. A favourite way of indicating the latter is to throw in a few vocative expressions in the language concerned, *Monsieur* or *Señor* for 'sir', for example. Foreigners who are speaking English are also assumed to leave certain vocatives untranslated. It is thought that a Frenchman speaking fluent English will nevertheless address a male friend as *mon vieux*, not being able to cope with 'old man'.

Native speakers of English who are addressing foreigners in English seem to feel that they must show willing by using social titles in the language of the hearer, though *Herr* Schmidt would probably prefer to hear himself called 'Mr Schmidt' rather than hear the mispronunciation of *Herr*. Some foreign vocatives have been dealt with separately in this book because they have a definite function in English. *Madame* + last name, for instance, is the accepted way of addressing a woman visitor of some importance from a country like China. *Amigo* may well be thrown into a conversation between two native speakers of English, it being assumed that the hearer will understand the word. It is now used so frequently by speakers who know no other words in Spanish that it might almost be counted as an English word. In some entries comments have been made on calques, or loan translations. When a Welsh speaker uses the vocative 'little pig' in English, for instance, he is clearly influenced by Welsh *mochyn bach*. Other foreign titles and vocative expressions have been ignored, unless special circumstances applied. *Mein Kapitän*, for instance, occurs in a text as an allusion to *The Goon Show*, not merely as a foreign professional title. *Monsieur* + first name, used to a hairdresser, can be classed as a professional title in English.

Foreman This term is used of the spokesman for the jury in a court of law, and for an experienced workman who directs the labours of others. There is a modern feminine form 'forewoman' which may occur vocatively. Main use of the term is probably during jury deliberations, but only then by rather formal speakers. In *A Cack-Handed War*, by Edward Blishen, an educated man who has become a labourer during wartime addresses the man in charge of the working party as 'foreman'. An Australian television drama, broadcast in December 1988, had the judge in the courtroom using 'Mr Foreman' to the juryman.

Foul Ball, you This is used by an American prostitute to a male client who is cheating her in *The Pleasure Man*, by Mae West. The vocative is not a standard one, but an American hearer would immediately understand the reference to a foul ball in baseball. It is a ball hit into foul territory and therefore useless.

Foulmouth A reference to a person who habitually uses obscenities. The word has been in use since at least the seventeenth century. Shakespeare does not use the word as a vocative, but he refers on three occasions to people who are foul-mouthed. In *Henry the Fourth Part One* (3:iii), for instance, Hostess Quickly tells Prince Hal that Falstaff 'speaks most vilely of you, like a foul-mouth'd man as he is, and said he would cudgel you'. In *The Country Girls*, by Edna O'Brien, 'you stinking little foulmouth' is used insultingly.

Four Eyes A term of abuse used by children to someone who wears glasses. 'Aw, shurrup, Four Eyes!' is addressed to a bus-conductress by an urchin in *Fares Please*, by Edith Courtney. Occasional variants of Four Eyes include 'Eye balls', 'Glass eyes', and 'Goggles'. An earlier term was 'Gig lamps', from the lamps carried on the small one-horse carriage.

Fowl 'You poor boiling fowl' is addressed to a woman by a man in *The Half Hunter*, by John Sherwood. The speaker is characterized in part by his use of unusual vocatives, and this is certainly one of them.

Fraud Fraud is an abstract concept, to do with criminal deception, but 'you old fraud', applied to a person, is a fairly mild way of saying that he is putting on an act of some kind. Use of the expression sometimes implies that the person concerned is being deceptive about his own good qualities, and is perhaps more good-natured than he pretends to be. Those wishing to accuse someone of more serious deceit might well use 'you hypocrite', 'you liar', etc. *Gone With The Wind*, by Margaret Mitchell, has Rhett Butler saying to Scarlett O'Hara: 'You little fraud. You dance all night with the soldiers and give them roses and ribbons and tell them how you'd die for the Cause, but when it comes to bandaging a few wounds and picking off a few lice, you decamp hastily.'

Freak, you Used by some speakers, e.g. American jazz musicians, to mean a male homosexual. The word was later applied to hippies, and is probably even more generally applied in modern times to anyone who acts in an unconventional way. Use of the term has been noted in television plays, mostly American.

Freddy Eliza Doolittle speaks of this as a transferred name to be used for a stranger in *Pygmalion*, by G. B. Shaw: 'I called him Freddy or Charlie same as you might yourself if you was talking to a stranger and wished to be pleasant.' This use of a name plucked out of the air as a vocative is normally restricted to men as those addressed, but *see also* **Mary**.

French, you *See* You + category of person.

Friar A friar is a monk, and would therefore normally be addressed as 'brother', but 'friar', used on its own or followed by a name, seems to have been used in former times. Friars were properly members of the mendicant orders of the Roman Catholic Church, Franciscan, Augustine, Dominican, and Carmelite, but other monks were sometimes loosely accorded the title, a form of French *frère*, 'brother'. Well-known literary friars likely to be addressed by title include the fat and cheerful vagabond Friar Tuck in the Robin Hood tales, and two Franciscans in Shakespeare's *Romeo and Juliet*. The latter are addressed variously as 'friar', 'holy friar', 'comfortable friar', and 'brother'. Two more friars appear in *Measure for Measure* and there is another in *Much Ado About Nothing*. All three are frequently addressed by their professional title.

Friend 'Unless there be real affection in his heart', writes Nathaniel Hawthorne, in *The Blithedale Romance*, 'a man cannot more effectually show his contempt for a brother mortal, nor more gallingly assume a position of superiority, than by addressing him as "friend".' Support for this view comes from another American writer. 'Ain't you got any consideration?' asks a character in *An American Dream*, by Norman Mailer. 'Up your ass, friend,' is the reply. A policeman uses the term in a similar way in *The Late Risers*, by Bernard Wolfe. The man addressed is left in no doubt as to the unfriendly feelings of the speaker. 'My fine friend' is used sarcastically by one man to another in *Rebecca*, by Daphne du Maurier.

One might compare the use of 'my honourable friend' used in parliamentary language, and the legal 'my learned friend', though these occur in third person references, not direct address. Some uses of 'friend', thankfully, are genuinely friendly. When the dean of a college calls a student 'my young friend', in Sinclair Lewis's *Gideon Planish*, he means it kindly. The several instances of 'my friend' in Len Deighton's *Funeral in Berlin*, and the similar instances in *Goldfinger*, by Ian Fleming, all show the word being used as one might expect, to someone who is liked by the speaker. But it is perhaps the possible ambiguity of the term that has caused the members of the Society of Friends to be careful about how and when they use it, though it is the normal mode of address to fellow Quakers. Such speakers may also use 'friend' instead of a social title, addressing someone as 'Friend Jones'. Examples of such usage occur in *Except for Me and Thee*, by Jessamyn West. The Society of Friends adopted that title at a time when the word had only positive connotations. It could even be used for a lover, as Juliet demonstrates in *Romeo and Juliet*, when she addresses Romeo as 'love, lord, ay, husband, friend'.

Curiously, 'friend' remains a very positive expression on nearly all occasions when it is used in the plural. The 'Friends, Romans, countrymen' speech from *Julius Caesar* is probably the best-known Shakespearean example, setting a style for public-speakers ever afterwards. 'Ladies and gentlemen,' says Mr Pickwick, then corrects himself, 'No, I won't say ladies and gentlemen, I'll call you friends, my dear friends, if the ladies will allow me to take so great a liberty. . . .' The ladies show by their applause that the liberty is allowable, for which of them could doubt that Mr Pickwick had 'real affection in his heart'. At the other extreme is the nonce name created by a male speaker in *Like Any Other Man*, by Patrick Boyle: 'You're too bloody smart, Mister-my-fucking friend.'

Frowny-head An *ad hoc* term used by a woman to her lover in *The Dream of Fair Women*, by Henry Williamson: 'Well, what worries you now, my dear frowny-head?'

Fruit British and American speakers use 'fruit' in rather different ways as a vocative. 'Old fruit' is the usual British expression, equivalent to 'old boy', 'old man', etc. The Longman *Dictionary of Contemporary English* thinks that it is becoming rare, but literary examples are easily found. There are several examples of friendly use between males in *Henry's War*, by Jeremy Brooks, another in *Thirteen Days*, by Ian Jefferies. *The Business of Loving*, by Godfrey Smith, has an example of a first name followed by 'old fruit'. The *Oxford English Dictionary* dates the expression from the early 1920s and says that it was also heard as 'old tin of fruit'. The latter phrase is pure nonsense: 'fruit' on its own might have been explained as derived from 'fruit of the womb', where 'fruit' could be said to mean a child. American usage tends to be 'you fruit', or more fully, 'you fruitcake'. Here the origin appears to have been the humorous expression 'nutty (= mad) as a fruitcake', so that a fruitcake was at first a crazy person, a nut, or an odd-ball. By the 1930s, according to *A New Dictionary of American Slang*, both 'fruit' and 'fruitcake' had taken on the meaning of male homosexual. The words are often used with one meaning or the other in the mind of the speaker, but at times they seem to represent merely a vague insult. *Oliver's Story*, by Erich Segal, has: ' "If you're anxious to resolve this issue sooner, there's another process." "Yeah, you fruit?" '

Fuck, you Used mainly in North America as a variant of 'you fucker'. The term merely expresses contempt and dislike without specifically referring to sexual activities. It also says something about the speaker, that he or she is prepared to use a word which is known to be taboo. In *Joshua Then and Now*, by Mordecai Richler, occurs the passage: ' "I'll drive you home, if you like." "I don't like. And neither," she shouted, "do I wish to be humiliated, you fuck. You arrogant prick. Just who do you think you are?" ' *The Choirboys*, by Joseph Wambaugh, has a Los Angeles policeman saying to a male colleague: 'Ya fuck, ya! Ya dirty slant-eyed heathen godless little fuck, ya!' The speaker in this case is supposedly a devout Jehovah's Witness, and it is said of the outburst that he was 'swearing for the first time in anyone's memory'. For a speaker who habitually uses obscenities, 'you fuck' may have no more force than 'you idiot', 'you jerk'. 'You look like death warmed over, you fuck! Go home!' says such a speaker to a friend in *Blue Dreams*, by William Hanley.

Fucker Rarely thought of as meaning 'one who fornicates' when used as a vocative: the word merely expresses extreme contempt. It is considered to be extremely coarse and would be avoided in polite society. 'All right, fucker, I'm asking questions and you're allowed no wrong answers,' says an American policeman to a man who a moment ago was

threatening him with a gun in *The Beethoven Conspiracy*, by Thomas Hauser. *An Indecent Obsession*, by Colleen McCullough, has one man saying to another: 'Do you know who I'm talking about, you barmy fucker?'

Fuckhead Used as the equivalent of 'jerk' and similar terms by mainly American male speakers who regularly use obscenities. An example occurs in *North Dallas Forty*, by Peter Gent, where it is spoken by a professional football player to a team-mate. The speaker equates it with 'asshole'.

Fuckwit Used by a man to another in *Redback*, by Howard Jacobson. The speaker has just been addressed as 'Shithead' by the man concerned. 'Fuckwit' appears to be a neologism based on 'nitwit'.

Fuddy-duddy Used in both Britain and the USA to refer to a stick-in-the-mud, an old fogy. The origin of the expression is not known. In *The Groves of Academe*, by Mary McCarthy, an American wife calls her husband 'you old fuddy-duddy' in a teasing way.

Fungus 'Don't touch me, you greasy fungus!' says a young English army officer to an Italian waiter, in *The Dream of Fair Women*, by Henry Williamson. The 'greasy' is a typically insulting word to apply to an Italian, while the 'fungus' refers to the man's 'gargantuan moustache'. 'Face-fungus' is well-established slang for a moustache or beard. *See also* **Whiskers**.

Funk, funk-pot These are terms of abuse used mainly by children to a child who is thought to be a coward. The implication is that he or she is 'in a funk', i.e. in a state of panic. The origin of this slang expression is obscure, though it seems to have begun at Oxford University. One early meaning of 'funk' was 'smoke', and especially 'to blow smoke upon a person while smoking'. This presumably for being in a 'blue' funk. *See also* **Scaredy-cat**.

Fuse-wire *See* **Spindleshanks**.

Fuss-pot, fuss-budget Used to a person who fusses overmuch about trifling matters. With 'fuss-pot' one may compare 'big-pot', 'swank-pot', 'stink-pot', etc., terms mainly used by children. 'You old fuss-pot' is spoken by one woman to another in *Rebecca*, by Daphne du Maurier. 'Fuss-arse' and 'fuss-box' have also been used to describe this kind of person. 'Fuss-budget' is recorded in American dictionaries. In J. P. Donleavy's *It was my Chimes* an American woman addresses a man by the unusual term 'fussy-face'.

G

Gabbie *See* Grandmother.

Gadabout Used of a person who is restless and constantly moves about. The original sense may have been 'one who moved about as if stung by gad-flies'. 'Little gadabout' is addressed to his fiancée by a man in *Jennifer*, by Janet Whitney.

Gaffer In modern times a British worker might say: 'You'd better see the gaffer about that', meaning that it is necessary to consult the boss. He might also, in a public house, ask where the gaffer is tonight, referring to the landlord. Such situations could also lead to vocative usage, but when 'gaffer' occurs in literary texts it usually has an older meaning. It was originally a term applied in rural areas to an elderly man who held a respectable position in society. The word may have been a corruption of 'godfather', though early spellings show that it was thought to derive from 'grandfather'. It could be used as a prefix before a proper name, as could its feminine form, 'gammer'. Thus, in *Joseph Andrews*, by Henry Fielding, we are told that the hero is esteemed to be the only son of Gaffer and Gammer Andrews. This original meaning soon degenerated, and in the seventeenth century it was possible to address a man as 'gaffer' as if one were merely calling him 'my good fellow'.

A late eighteenth-century writer says that in Buckinghamshire it was the custom for wives to call their husbands 'gaffer'. This was probably more the case with older married couples, since 'gaffer' retains an implication of age in most of its senses.

Friendly, but still respectful, usage is shown in *My Brother Jonathan*, by Francis Brett Young. A drayman who is sobering up after being fighting drunk responds to the doctor's comment to a policeman – 'I guess he's had enough to be going on with, constable' – by saying: 'By Gum, you're right, gaffer!' In the same novel another workman addresses the doctor as 'gaffer' in his surgery, and soon afterwards says: 'Look here, boss, I want my rights.' This would seem to equate 'gaffer' with the modern use of 'chief'. There is vaguely similar usage in *The Magic Army*, by Leslie Thomas, where a Devonshire rustic addresses an American army officer as 'gaffer'.

Gaggie *See* Grandmother.

Gal A variant of 'girl', in use since the early nineteenth century, when it was used by London Cockneys. It was later taken up by the upper-classes, sometimes in the form 'gel'. Thackeray was probably typical of many nineteenth-century writers in considering it a vulgarism. Significantly, it is the decidedly vulgar Mr Sherrick, in *The Newcomes*, who says to his wife and daughter: 'Come, gals!' 'Gal' occurs as the natural pronunciation of 'girl' in some North American dialects. It is also used with deliberate humour by speakers who would not normally make use of this form. An instance of humourous usage occurs in *Love in Quiet Places*, by Bernard Thompson. Non-vocative humorous use occurs in the Marx brothers film *Duck Soup*, where Groucho, as Rufus T. Firefly, is told that it is a gala day. He says, 'A gal a day is enough for me. I don't think I can handle any more.'

Galah *See* Drongo.

Gammer A title of respect in rural areas for an elderly woman, used mainly in the seventeenth and eighteenth centuries. It derived from 'godmother' or 'grandmother' and was used as a prefix, followed by the family name of the person concerned. Unlike its male equivalent, 'gaffer', 'gammer' does not seem to have come into general use as a term of address in its own right.

Gang Used jokingly to a group of friends. 'Let's go, gang' says the hero of J. P. Donleavy's story *The Romantic Life of Alphonse A*. There is a slight suggestion that a gang of friends, rather than a group of friends, will be engaged in slightly disreputable activities. *The Critic*, by Wilfred Sheed, has 'Hey, gang, I think Daddy's going crazy' addressed by a young boy to friends.

Gangan *See* Grandmother.

Geek This is probably the word which Shakespeare used as 'geck', meaning a fool. By the nineteenth century, in English dialect usage, it had taken on the variant forms: geek, gowk, gawk, etc. In American slang, where the word survives in modern times, it can refer either to a pervert or degenerate (recalling the word's use in the circus for someone who was a sideshow freak or was willing to bite the heads off of live chickens), or to a drunkard, a lush. It probably has the latter sense when it occurs as a vocative in *The Ginger Man*, by J. P. Donleavy, used by a man to his male drinking companion.

Gel A variant spelling of 'girl', used to indicate a pronunciation of the word which is either socially or regionally marked. 'Old gel' is used by a middle-class aunt to her niece in *The Dream of Fair Women*, by Henry Williamson.

General The professional title of a high-ranking officer in the British army, or in the American army, air force, or marine corps. He ranks above a colonel. Examples of normal professional use occur in, e.g., *Unconditional Surrender*, by Evelyn Waugh and *The Old Boys*, by William Trevor. In the latter the man concerned is also addressed as 'General' followed by his last name. He has long since retired from the army, but exercises his right to be known by the rank he once held. Deliberate misuse of this title is found from time to time. In Ben Jonson's *Alchemist*, for example, it is addressed to Face when he appears in a captain's uniform. In *North Dallas Forty*, by Peter Gent, a uniformed doorman is told 'It's Sunday, general'. The title referred originally to a commissioned officer who was in general charge of an army.

Genius Said to anyone who is displaying exceptional signs of intelligence, or who has just come up with a good idea, or used sarcastically to a person who has just said or done something stupid. The term is used in a friendly way in *Absolute Beginners*, by Colin MacInnes.

Gentle Formerly a vocative in its own right, especially in the plural when it was used to address a group of nobles or gentlemen and gentlewomen. Examples of such usage occur in, e.g., *The Merry Wives of Windsor* (3:ii) and *Henry the Fifth* (1:i). The main use of gentle by Shakespeare and his contemporaries, however, was as a vocative element, meaning either 'of good birth, noble', or 'mild, tender, kind, of a nature to be expected of one who was well-born'. Throughout the Shakespeare plays there are vocative expressions which contain 'gentle' as an element. A few examples will suffice to show the range, with individual plays not being mentioned since most of the terms occur *passim:* gentle + first name, gentle friend, gentle mistress, gentle my lord, gentle lover, gentle sweet, gentle wife, gentle lady, gentle master, gentle sir, gentle madam, gentle husband, gentle maiden, gentle cousin,

etc. There is even an instance, in *Henry the Fourth Part Two* (3:ii), of 'gentle gentlemen' used vocatively. The only modern survivals of such usage are 'gentleman', and to a far lesser extent, 'gentlewoman'. 'Gentle reader', addressed to the reader of a novel by an author, continued in late use, but that has now gone. One suspects that the value of the word, in vocative use at least, was debased by overuse. What had originally been a high compliment about one's family background was to become devalued to the point where 'genteel', a development from 'gentle', came to have a pejorative meaning, suggesting artificially good manners as displayed by social climbers.

Gentleman In modern use this is a polite form of 'man'; in former times it referred or was used vocatively to a man of noble birth. In Shakespeare's plays it occurs in the singular form, as when Juliet says to Romeo: 'Trust me, gentleman, I'll prove more true/Than those who have more cunning to be strange.' It is frequently used with a qualifying word: worthy gentleman, honest gentleman, good gentleman. Such usage would be strange in modern times, though Shaw has Liza, the flower girl in *Pygmalion*, address a customer as 'kind gentleman'. In *The Dream of Fair Women*, by Henry Williamson, there is a gypsy fortune-teller who addresses a male client as 'my gentleman'.

Today's usage would far more frequently be 'gentlemen', addressed to a group of men, used either alone or as part of the formulaic 'ladies and gentlemen'. Ben Jonson, in *Every Man in his Humour*, has a servant greet two men with: 'Gentlemen, God save you.' 'We do not stand much upon our gentility,' replies one of them, though he goes on to prove that he does. In many of its uses, 'gentlemen' functions as the vocative plural of 'sir'. It can be made less polite, or less formal, in ordinary speech by being abbreviated. Thus, in *The Late Risers*, by Bernard Wolfe, an American male uses 'gents' to two male friends. This abbreviated form has been in use since the sixteenth century, though its joking use as a vocative is modern. It is sometimes used by British publicans as a variant in the 'Time, gentlemen, please' formula which signifies that alcohol may no longer be served. In *David Copperfield*, by Charles Dickens, 'young gentlemen' occurs, addressed to a group of schoolboys by a headmaster. A special vocative use of 'gentleman' occurs in Edna O'Brien's novel *The Country Girls*. The word is converted into a nickname and used in direct address with a social title, as 'Mr Gentleman'. Also special, but less individual, is the 'gentlemens' which occurs in *The Liberation of Lord Byron Jones*, by Jesse Hill Ford. This double plural is a feature of uneducated Southern American speech, occurring in 'womens', 'childrens', 'folkses', and the like. The triple plural form 'menses' has also been reported in Southern states. There is also the curious 'you gentleman', used as a kind of insult by Lady Chatterley to her husband in *Lady Chatterley's Lover*, by D. H. Lawrence. This occurs during a tirade against the ruling classes, and their lack of sympathy for working people. 'My father is ten times the human being you are, you gentleman,' says Lady Chatterley, scornfully.

Gentlewoman This word is rarely used in modern English, 'lady' serving as the usual feminine form of 'gentleman'. In former times the word was used of a woman of good birth and breeding, especially when she was an attendant on a lady of rank. 'Call in my gentlewoman,' says Olivia to Malvolio, in *Twelfth Night*. 'Gentlewoman, my lady calls,' says Malvolio. Elsewhere in Shakespeare the vocative is used to greet or address an unknown lady. 'Gentlewoman, good day!' says Julia to the Duke's daughter, in *Two Gentlemen of Verona*. In *Romeo and Juliet* Mercutio greets the Nurse as 'fair gentlewoman', and Romeo uses the same term to her a moment later, but they are being, as the nurse well knows, 'saucy'. Shakespeare puns on the 'gentle' of this word in *The Taming of the Shrew* (4:iii). Katherina says to Petruchio: 'Gentlewomen wear such caps as these.' 'When you are gentle, you shall have one too,' says Petruchio. 'That will not be in haste,' comments Hortensio to himself.

Geordie Used as an instant nickname to a native of Tyneside, in England. The word is ultimately a form of George. It is used by a corporal to a private soldier in *Ginger, you're Barmy*, by David Lodge, with the comment:

One must never let slip an opportunity of teasing the next man about his geographical origins. Geordie, Scouse, Taff, Paddy, Jock. Shakespeare knew what he was doing when he made the comedy in his army play, *Henry V*, a comedy of dialects.

'Scouse' is used of a native of Liverpool, by association of Liverpudlians with 'lobscouse', a sea-dish consisting of a stew or hash with vegetables or biscuit. 'Taff' is for a Welshman, from Welsh pronunciation of 'Dafydd', David, a common Welsh name. 'Paddy', for an Irishman, is similarly from 'Padraig', Patrick. The Scottish 'Jock' is a form of the name Jack.

George Used as a typical first name to a man whose name is not yet known in *Daughters of Mulberry*, by Roger Longrigg and *An Error of Judgement*, by Pamela Hansford Johnson. In the first of these the tone is slightly aggressive; in the second it is friendly. There is a further friendly example in *Lucky Jim*, by Kingsley

Amis. In J. B. Priestley's *The Good Companions* a conversation between two men who do not know each other begins with one saying to the other: 'Nice day, George.' Priestley continues: ' "Ay," said Mr Oakroyd; and then, not to be outdone in this matter of handing out names, he added, dryly: "Nice enough, Herbert." "'Ere," said the man, straightening himself, "now I ask you. Do I look like Herbert?" ' In private correspondence with the author, Professor W. F. Mainland reports that he was addressed as 'George' by Londoners in the 1930s.

Get In Scotland and the north of England this is a dialectal word for a child, but it is always used contemptuously. The word is connected with the verb 'to beget'; the child has been 'get', or 'begotten'. 'You havering slavering get' is used by Jim Dixon, in Kingsley Amis's *Lucky Jim*. He is addressing this, behind his back, to his professor, so that a word meaning 'brat' is not really appropriate, but in context Dixon is indulging in word-play, inventing a string of insulting vocatives to relieve his feelings. The exact meaning of what is being said is unimportant, the words are merely a vocal safety-valve. The variant 'you git' occurs in *Other Men's Wives*, by Alexander Fullerton, addressed by one man to another in what is clearly meant to be a severely insulting way. *Saturday Night and Sunday Morning*, by Alan Sillitoe, has 'you cross-eyed gett' used insultingly. Clifford Hanley's *The Taste of Too Much* has both 'you snivellin' wee get' and 'you wee Orange get' used in an unfriendly way.

Ghoul Technically a ghoul is an evil spirit which robs graves and preys on corpses. The word is used more loosely of someone who shows a morbid interest in unpleasant matters. 'How did he die, sir? Cut his throat? Stab himself? Hang himself, maybe?' asks a character in *An Indecent Obsession*, by Colleen McCullough. 'You would be the one to want to know that, wouldn't you, you little ghoul,' replies the man to whom the questions were put. In *Funeral in Berlin*, by Len Deighton, 'ghoul' is used as a friendly term of address to a man by a girl. The word appears to be part of her idiolect, used without justification as far as its meaning is concerned. She later calls the man 'you ghoul', and eventually 'my darling ghoul'.

Gig lamps *See* **Four Eyes**.

Ginger One of the many instant nicknames that a red-headed person, especially a child, is likely to attract. The title of David Lodge's novel about army life, *Ginger, you're Barmy* alludes both to the vocative and the traditional playground chant that accompanies it: 'Ginger, you're barmy,/You'll never join the army./You'll never make a scout/With your shirt hanging out,/Ginger, you're barmy.' While 'Ginger' is probably the most frequently employed playground term, it has many variants, some based on Ginger itself. These include: Ginge, Ginger conk (='nose'), Ginger mop, Ginger nob, Ginger nut, Ginger Tom, Gingy. Other favourites include: beetroot, carrots, carrot top, copper crust, coppernob, fire bucket, reddy, red mop, red thatch, Rufus, the last named alluding to Rufus the Red, third son of William the Conqueror who became William II of England.

Girl This can be used by parents to their daughter, but it is probably more often used to an adult woman by a man or woman of her own age. Its use perhaps becomes more affectionate as the age of the woman addressed increases. Working-class husbands in Britain are likely to use it as a flattering term to their wives. Women friends defy time by using it to one another. Notable uses in Shakespeare include the Nurse's comment to thirteen-year-old Juliet: 'Go, girl, seek happy nights to happy days,' and Cleopatra's comment to her attendants about Caesar: 'He words me, girls, he words me.' In former times 'girl' was the usual way of addressing a young maid-servant, often with the implication that if the girl concerned had a name, it was of no interest to the speaker.

As a simple generic term, 'girl' can of course be given meaning by other words used in conjunction with it. Julia, in *The Two Gentlemen of Verona*, addresses her waiting woman as 'girl', but also calls her 'gentle girl' and 'gentle Lucetta'. Celia calls her cousin Rosalind 'sweet girl' in *As You Like It*. A comment on the modern flattering use of 'girl' to a grown woman occurs in *Border Country*, by Raymond Williams: ' "Come on, you two girls." "Girls indeed," Ellen laughed, walking up with Eira. "Well, we look it, anyhow, Auntie." ' The youngest of these two women is in her thirties. In the same novel is an example of 'girl' used affectionately by a Welsh husband to his wife, who uses 'Mister' as an endearment in return. *Up the City Road*, by John Stroud, has several examples of a London girl in her late teens being addressed as 'girl' by young men of her own age, always in a friendly way.

Girl, dear *See* **Boy, dear**.

Girl, little Normally used to a very young girl, with the 'little' implying affection. In *Diamonds are Forever*, by Ian Fleming, Tiffany tells James Bond: ' "Don't worry about me, my friend. I can look after myself. And don't 'little girl' me," she said sharply.' As it happens Bond hasn't addressed her as 'little girl', but his tone has suggested that he might say it. In *The*

Wayward Bus, by John Steinbeck occurs the following: 'Mr. Pritchard always called his wife "little girl" when he was playful, and automatically she fell into his mood. "When do iddle girls see pretty present?" "You'll find out, just keep your hair on, little girl." '

Girl, my Use of this term in many ways parallels that of 'girl' on its own. In *The Tempest*, for instance, Prospero uses it to his daughter Miranda in a kindly way. Othello addresses his wife Desdemona as 'my girl' as she lies on her death bed. In modern times, though, 'my girl' has to be used with caution, since it seems to suggest that the girl so addressed is being admonished. 'You'll do as I say, my girl,' would be a typical utterance to a daughter.

Girl, old Used affectionately to a woman of any age. The 'old' refers to friendly familiarity. In *The Dream of Fair Women*, by Henry Williamson, it is used by an English army officer to his young wife. In *The Needle*, by Francis King, a brother uses it to his adult sister, equating it with 'sweetie'. In *Brothers in Law*, by Henry Cecil, it is used as an intimacy on nine occasions. *Doctor at Sea*, by Richard Gordon, has it used in a similar way. In *Georgy Girl*, by Margaret Forster, it is merely friendly, as it is in *The Heart of the Matter*, by Graham Greene and *A Kind of Loving*, by Stan Barstow. In *Henry's War*, by Jeremy Brooks, the context makes it clear that 'old girl' is unfriendly. A woman has just been told: 'I don't know who you are, young woman, nor what you're doing here, but you clearly have no idea what you're talking about.' The girl concerned replies: 'And I don't know who you are, old girl, or what the hell right you've got to come busting in here, but I do know you're the rudest person I've met in ten years.' The conversation demonstrates how both 'old' and 'young' can be used almost as insults.

Girlie A diminutive of 'girl', normally used by a speaker who is considerably older than the girl or young woman being addressed. A father uses it to his daughter in *The Moonflower Vine*, by Jetta Carleton. In *The Day of the Locust*, by Nathanael West, it is used by a young woman to a friend of roughly the same age, though she also calls her 'kid'. A colleague of the author remarked one day that she objected to being called 'girlie' by an older man who worked in the same office. She added that it had taken her a while to realize that he was saying 'girlie'; she had thought he was calling her 'Curly'.

Git *See* **Get**.

Glamour puss Used in both Britain and the USA to refer to or address a person considered to be highly attractive. Used mainly of or to women. It is used in a friendly way in *Absolute Beginners*, by Colin MacInnes.

Glass eyes *See* **Four Eyes.**

Glutton *See* **Fatty.**

Goalie An abbreviation of 'goal-keeper', and one of the terms by which a goal-keeper in football or similar sports may be addressed during the game by, e.g., the referee. Other terms include 'Keep' and 'Keeper'.

Goat Applied to a man who is lecherous, and used especially of an old man who still has lecherous thoughts. 'You ugly old goat' occurs in *Festival*, by N. J. Crisp, said by a woman to a man. Coriolanus says 'Hence, old goat!' to Sicinius in Shakespeare's *Coriolanus* (3:i), but this is probably a simple reference to the age of the man concerned, who is addressed by Cominius as 'ag'd sir'.

Gobble-guts *See* **Greedy.**

God As a vocative, 'God' occurs most frequently in prayers, but it has occasional usage in other contexts. In *Romeo and Juliet* (2:ii) Romeo asks: 'What shall I swear by?' Juliet replies: 'Do not swear at all;/Or, if thou wilt, swear by thy gracious self,/Which is the god of my idolatry.'

The thought that Juliet is here expressing, that Romeo is her god, the object of her adoration, indicates how 'god' can become a vocative addressed to a loved one. In *The Middle Man*, by David Chandler, a modern Juliet says to her lover: 'Desolate me, destroy me, my lover . . . my pitiless young god. . . .'

God- Used as a prefix in a number of relationships arising from adults acting as godparents to a child. The god-parents sponsor the child at baptism and make a profession of Christian faith on behalf of the infant. They are meant to guarantee the child's subsequent religious education. The child may later address his god-parents as 'god-father' and 'god-mother'. The latter occurs vocatively in *Adam Bede*, by George Eliot, where the woman concerned also uses 'god-son' in return. In *I'll Take Manhattan*, by Judith Krantz, a girl who uses 'god-mother' is told by the woman concerned: 'Could you please stop calling me god-mother?' The unusual 'my little god-sister' is used in *Villette*, by Charlotte Brontë. This is used to a girl who has the same god-parents as the speaker. God-parents continue to sponsor babies at baptism in modern times, but the evidence suggests that the relationships are seldom acknowledged vocatively.

Godot Used as a transferred name in allusion to the man who never arrives in Samuel Beckett's play *Waiting for Godot*, 1952. Two tramps, Vladimir and Estragon, spend most of the time on stage anticipating Godot's arrival. *Down*, by Zoe Fairbanks, has 'One of them said, "Hi, Godot." "What?" "We've been waiting for you." '

Goggles *See* **Four Eyes.**

Goil A variant spelling of 'girl', used to indicate sub-standard pronunciation in *Waterfront*, by Budd Schulberg, set in New York.

good Formerly a very frequently used vocative element. Almost everyone in the Shakespearean plays is addressed sooner or later as 'good my lord', 'good uncle', 'good brother', 'good father', 'good cousin', etc. The word originally referred to good birth, and the good qualities associated with nobility, having much in common in that respect with 'gentle'. But as with that word, 'good' seems to have degenerated into a conventional noise, at most an indefinite commendation, as the *Oxford English Dictionary* expresses it. 'Goodman' and 'Goodwife' took on separate identities as conventional terms of address, but the more general expressions 'my good man' and 'my good woman' became offensively condescending to those so addressed. 'Good' still has this condescending note about it, even when it is used in a congratulatory way in exclamatory vocatives such as 'good boy', 'good girl'. Such expressions become more acceptable, perhaps, when the friendly 'old' is included: 'good old' + first name. As usual, a great deal depends on the tone of voice used by the speaker. 'Good man', said with pure enthusiasm, is unlikely to give offence. 'Good' is of course used in many pure exclamations, which gives rise to a joke in *The Fox in the Attic*, by Richard Hughes. A speaker absently addresses a bishop as 'good lad'. He corrects himself hastily and calls him 'good lord', though he does so under his breath.

Goodman This was used as a social title from the fourteenth century, surviving in some rural areas, and especially in Scotland, until at least the nineteenth century. It was used to yeomen farmers, who did not quite attain the rank of gentlemen, but was also used in some areas to any householder, host of an inn, or husband. It is clear that for Shakespeare it was a contemptuous title, applied to Dull in *Love's Labour's Lost*, and often prefixed to a nonce name. 'Goodman baldpate' is used vocatively in *Measure for Measure* (5:i), as is 'goodman boy' in *Romeo and Juliet* (1:v), where Capulet says to Tybalt: 'He shall be endur'd./What, goodman boy, I say he shall. Go to;/Am I the master here or you?'

Shakespeare also has the expressions 'goodman rascal', 'goodman drivel', 'goodman death', and 'goodman bones'. *The House of the Seven Gables*, by Nathaniel Hawthorne, has one man saying to another: 'I take you at your word, Goodman Maule.' The feminine form of this term was 'Goodwife'.

Goodwife The feminine form of 'Goodman', formerly used as a prefix to a married woman's name, or as a respectable form of address in its own right. By the nineteenth century it survived mainly in Scotland. It would not now be heard in standard English in Britain. *The House with the Green Shutters*, by George Douglas, which is set in a Scottish town in the nineteenth century, has the postman crying out: 'Guidwife! Jennet! Don't ye hear?' 'Gude-wife' also occurs, indicating Scottish pronunciation.

Goody A short form of 'goodwife'. At one time 'Goody' + last name was the usual way of referring to the female keepers of taverns in Edinburgh and other Scottish towns.

Goody-goody A term used in both Britain and the USA for a child who makes up to a teacher. It occurs in *Deborah*, by Marian Castle, set in Dakota, and is mentioned by the Opies in *The Lore and Language of School-children*. *See also* **Teacher's pet**.

Goon, you This is roughly the equivalent of 'you dope', 'you sap' when used by an American wife to her husband in *Rabbit is Rich*, by John Updike. Arthur Hailey, in *Hotel*, has a young man call a girl 'you fool, you stupid goon' when she bites him while he is trying to rape her.'You silly goon' is addressed by one man to another in a not particularly aggressive way in *The Sleepers of Erin*, by Jonathan Gash. There was an earlier word 'gony', sometimes written as 'gooney', which in English dialect use meant a simpleton. It was presumably this word which inspired E. C. Segar, creator of the Popeye cartoon strip, to name a character 'Alice the Goon'. This character no doubt influenced American use of 'goon'; British speakers associate the word with *The Goon Show*, a series of radio comedy shows which became immensely popular in the 1960s. The goons in the show included Peter Sellers and Sir Harry Secombe. There is a special sense of 'goon' in American slang, the word being applied to a mindless thug who is paid to behave violently for illegal purposes.

Goose The goose has long had a reputation for being rather stupid. To call a person a goose therefore implies that he or she is silly, but 'goose' is certainly not meant as a serious insult. It has about the same force as 'you silly

thing' in modern times, though it was probably more forceful when it first began to be used as a vocative in the sixteenth century. Lady Percy addresses her husband as 'ye giddy goose' in *Henry the Fourth Part One*. Romeo also uses it to his friend Mercutio, but in this instance it is partly because of Mercutio's reference to their wits running 'a wild-goose chase'. The latter expression, of course, retains the same silly association with the bird. To lead someone a wild goose chase, or to goose them as it was once possible to say, was to fool them. In *Vanity Fair*, by Thackeray, Miss Crawdon calls Rebecca 'you goose' when she thinks she has said something silly. In Pinero's *The Second Mrs Tanqueray* occurs: '*Aubrey:* What on earth will Morse think? *Paula:* Do you trouble yourself about what servants *think? Aubrey:* Of course. *Paula.* Goose! They're only machines made to wait upon people.' Rumer Godden, in *Kingfishers Catch Fire*, has a mother saying to her eight-year-old daughter: 'I'm not going anywhere, you little goose.' The same author, in *The Battle of the Villa Fiorita*, has a man say to his lover: 'My darling goose, you're jealous.'

Goosie, you Mrs Shelby uses this term to address Eliza, her black servant girl, in *Uncle Tom's Cabin*, by Harriet Beecher Stowe. During the same conversation she calls her 'girl', 'child', 'silly child', 'you foolish girl', etc., all of which show that she is basically fond of Eliza, even when she is behaving clumsily.

Gorgeous This word was originally applied to a person or object adorned with brilliant colours, but a gorgeous girl is now a beautiful one, regardless of her clothes. The workman who hails a passing young lady as 'Hello, gorgeous' is simply expressing general admiration. In *The Exhibitionist* an American addresses his step-daughter in this way. An Englishman uses it to a woman in *Love in Quiet Places*, by Bernard Thompson. In *Sandra*, by Pearl Bell, it is used to the heroine by a new acquaintance, described by the author as a 'slangy young American'. The term may have been in vogue when the novel was published, sometime in the late 1920s. It continues in use, often as in *Fares Please*, by Edith Courtney, where a man working in a bus garage enters a room, puts his arm around a bus-conductress, and says: 'Hello, gorgeous, still love me?' Modern women may object to the term on the grounds that it treats them like sexual objects.

Gossip This is no longer used as a term of address, though in Shakespeare's time it would have been quite normal, especially when linked with a surname. Married women who were friends seem to have been the main users of the term: 'What hoa, gossip Ford, what hoa!' says Mistress Page to Mistress Ford, in *The Merry Wives of Windsor*. In *Henry the Fourth Part Two*, Hostess Quickly reminds Falstaff that goodwife Keech, the butcher's wife, had come in while they were talking and called her 'gossip Quickly'. At this time (seventeenth century) the word must have had the sense of female friend, though it had begun centuries previously as 'God's sib', i.e. a God relation, a god-father or god-mother. It was ultimately extended to a woman's female friends who were invited to be present at a birth. The modern meaning of 'gossip', idle talk about other people, arose from the kinds of conversation that occurred while the women were together, secluded from the men-folk.

Governor Probably the most frequent use of this term is in various parts of Britain, where working-class men use it to address another man, usually one who is unknown to them. In his book *The Cockney*, Julian Franklyn writes:

'Guv'ner', generally so written but rarely so pronounced, expresses a measure of respect, but none of servility. Cockneys of equal status will address each other so at times of slight distance, as, for example, during an argument that is not quite an altercation: 'Scuse me, gubner, wasn't I in front o' year?' 'No, gunner – I don't recon you was.' 'Scuse me, gubner – I was, this 'ere laidy c'n tell yeh. . . .'

Franklyn says that 'the pronunciation varies: *gubner, gunner, gumner*, and as often as not, in simple abbreviation, *guv*.' Perhaps the safest thing to say is that the pronunciation varies with the speaker, but most men so addressed are well aware that 'governor' is meant. As for the written form, it is 'guv'nor', for instance, in D. H. Lawrence's *Women in Love*, when a working-class man uses it to a middle-class stranger. In *Pygmalion*, where Doolittle addresses Professor Higgins by this term, the spelling is given in full as 'Governor'. Doolittle at one point uses 'Governors both' when speaking to Higgins and Pickering. Franklyn thinks the term is in no way a servile one, but it is frequently used in what is meant to be a flattering way to someone who will be asked for some spare change. London taxi-drivers are also likely to use 'Guv' to male customers, avoiding the far more obvious servility of 'sir' or some such term.

In *The Pickwick Papers*, by Charles Dickens, Sam Weller calls a strange man 'Governor', equating it with 'old fellow' and 'old 'un'. He also uses the term to address his father, which was common nineteenth-century usage, albeit at a social level above that of the Wellers. This middle-class family usage was also prevalent in the USA until at least the 1920s. *An American Tragedy*, by Thomas Dreiser,

has Gilbert Griffiths addressing his father in this way. 'Governor' is also used on occasion as a synonym for 'boss', or 'chief'. Ngaio Marsh comments on a special theatrical use in *Opening Night*: 'as yet she had found no label for Poole, unless it was the old-fashioned one of "Governor", which pleased her by its vicarious association with the days of the Victorian actor-managers.' British policemen are likely to address their superior officers as 'guv'nor' or 'guv', especially if they regularly work together as a team. In the USA 'Governor' can be a title of considerable status when used, for example, to the governor of a state. There are many examples of such usage in *Face to Face*, by Edward A. Rogers.

Grace, your A formal title used to a duke, duchess, or archbishop. The title has been in use since the sixteenth century and was formerly used when addressing a king or queen as well as those dignitaries mentioned above. The plays of Shakespeare abound in examples of 'your Grace'; there is even a plural form 'your Graces', used when the Lord Chamberlain greets the dukes of Norfolk and Suffolk in *Henry the Eighth* (2:ii). Arthur Hailey has a duchess in *Hotel* who is addressed as both 'your Grace' and the more informal 'Duchess'. There is quite separately a first name 'Grace' which was introduced by the Puritans at the end of the sixteenth century. They no doubt had religious grace in mind, the grace of God.

Grampa A variant of 'grandpa', which would normally be used by a grandchild to a grandfather. *World So Wide*, by Sinclair Lewis, has a woman saying to a man who is little older than herself: 'Oh, don't look so glum, Grampa Hay.' The man's first name is Hayden. The use of 'Grampa' is inspired by his glum looks, which make him appear old. The same woman later refers to him as 'Uncle Hay'. 'Gramps' can occur as a variant of 'Grampa'.

Gran Normally a family vocative, used to address a grandparent, especially the grandmother. In *Border Country*, by Raymond Williams, it is used by a boy to his grandfather. *Memento Mori*, by Muriel Spark, has four examples of its use by doctors and nursing staff to elderly female patients. Village children, in Laurie Lee's *Cider with Rosie*, also use 'Gran' to address Granny Trill and Granny Wallon, two old ladies who are constantly at war with one another. 'You going bald, Gran?' 'I still got me bits.'

Grandad Normally addressed to the grandfather of the speaker, but also used occasionally to old men, not related in any way to the speaker, who look as if they could be grandfathers. Such a one is addressed as 'Grandad' in *Dandelion Days*, by Henry Williamson. His white beard, in particular, suggests the vocative. The reduced form 'Granda' occurs in *Lark Rise*, by Flora Thompson: 'Didn't you miss your fiddle, Granda?' The speaker is young Laura, the grand-daughter. Monica Dickens, in *Thursday Afternoons*, uses the variant spelling 'Granddad'.

Grandfather Used to the father of the speaker's father or mother. The 'grand' is a direct borrowing from French, where *grandpère, grandmère* indicate the relationship once removed. *Grand* is translated into English for relationships such as great-aunt, great-uncle. In *The Exhibitionist*, by Henry Sutton, occurs:

When they did speak, they addressed each other formally, as 'Grandfather' and 'Grandson', being very careful not to blur the definition of the relationship. Or, on rare occasions, they would relax the merest hairbreadth, so that Sam would say 'Thank you, sir,' and Amos would answer 'You're welcome, boy.'

Charles Dickens, in *Master Humphrey's Clock*, has: ' "Samivel Veller, sir," said the old gentleman, "has con-ferred upon me the ancient title o' grand-father vich had long laid dormouse, and was s'posed to be nearly hex-tinct, in our family".'

Grandmamma A rather upper-class colloquial form of grandmother, used in the late eighteenth century and throughout the nineteenth century. Lady Kew, in *The Newcomes*, by William Thackeray, is so addressed by her favourite grandchild, Ethel. The term may still be in use in certain families. 'Grandmama', which is presumably a simple spelling variant, occurs in *The Middle Man*, by David Chandler. It is said to be used in 1970 in an American family of considerable wealth.

Grandmother Used to the speaker's grandmother. This full form is especially likely to be used by middle and upper-class speakers, as in *Anglo-Saxon Attitudes*, by Angus Wilson. At lower social levels it is likely to become 'Gran' or 'Granny'. These and other common variants are dealt with separately: correspondents sometimes mention more individual family practices in addressing grandmothers. Patrick Montague-Smith, for example, called his father's mother 'Gangan' and his mother's mother 'Gabbie'. Other grandchildren in the family used 'Gingy'. Mrs Gillian Callinan also reported on the use of 'Gabbie', though in her family this was used to a grandfather, the grandmother being 'Gaggie'. All forms clearly represent infant attempts to pronounce long words, with the resulting words being affectionately maintained by those concerned.

Grandpa One of the grandfather variants (for ' -pa' *see* the entry on **Pa**). Normally used to the speaker's grandfather, but often in a friendly way to an old man who is a stranger. Examples of the latter usage occur in, e.g., *Daughters of Mulberry*, by Roger Longrigg and *St Urbain's Horseman*, by Mordecai Richler.

Granny A pet form of 'grandmother', used to the speaker's real grandmother or to an old lady who is referred to and sometimes addressed as **Granny + last name** (*see* following entry). R. W. Chapman, in his tract on *Names, Designations and Appellations*, says: 'If I am obliged to name my mother-in-law direct, I call her, by invitation, "Granny"; a solution not wholly satisfactory, but made possible by a nursery atmosphere.'

Granny + last name Elderly women are addressed by doctors and nurses in this way in Muriel Spark's *Memento Mori*. The practice perhaps has a certain convenience in medical circumstances, avoiding the need to distinguish between 'Miss' and 'Mrs'. It is also possible, if the last name is forgotten, to use 'Gran' or 'Granny' on its own, where 'Miss' or 'Mrs' would sound quite inappropriate. In recent years, however, it has been pointed out that patients' feelings with regard to how they wish to be addressed should always be respected. In dialectal use elderly women might also be known as 'Granny' + surname, but only if they were in fairly humble social positions. In Thomas Hardy's *The Trumpet Major*, Anne Garland meets an old woman who is proud of her spectacles. 'What have you seen, Granny Seamore?' she asks her. Laurie Lee, in *Cider with Rosie*, devotes a chapter to 'Grannies in the Wainscot', describing Granny Trill and Granny Walton, two 'traditional ancients of a kind we don't see today, the last of that dignity of grandmothers to whom age was its own embellishment'. They are variously addressed by the villagers as 'Gran', 'Granny', and 'Granny' + last name. 'You at home, Granny Trill? You in there, Gran?'

Greaseball An American slang term for a man or woman who is dark-skinned and dark-haired, of Mediterranean or Latin American ethnic origin. It is used by one man to another in *A Streetcar Named Desire*, by Tennessee Williams, as a friendly insult. In *The Late Risers*, by Bernard Wolfe, it is used insultingly to a man by a woman.

Grease boy, grease rat *See* **Teacher's pet**.

Great-aunt, Great-uncle Terms which indicate a relationship once removed, a great-aunt being the aunt of one's father or mother. The 'great-' translates French *grand*, which is used for similar purposes in words like *grandpère*, *grandmère*, 'grandfather', 'grandmother'. The French usage was in turn imitative of Latin, where 'great-uncle' would have been *avunculus magnus*. Great-aunt is not used frequently as a vocative, aunt itself would usually be the term used, but much is made of the fuller form in the children's story *The Girl without a Name*, by Agnes M. Miall. There an old lady insists on being called 'Great-Aunt', both by her niece and her niece's children. ' "Great Aunt suits me," said the owner of the title. It certainly did. As Cherry once said: "She's great in every sense of the word." ' The woman concerned happens to be very tall.

Greedy Said by one child to another in *The Fox in the Attic*, by Richard Hughes, but not with reference to food. Those children who do eat food in a greedy manner are likely to have that fact pointed out to them in no uncertain manner by their peer group. 'Greedy' is expanded to 'greedy-glutton', 'greedy-devil', 'greedy-grabs', 'greedy-hog', 'greedy-muffin', or 'greedy-pig', the last of these being especially popular. Other names include: dustbin, gobble-guts, guts, guts-ache, gutsy sod, guzzler, guzzle-guts, hungry guts, piggy, pig-hog, pig-bin.

Greek, foolish This is addressed to Feste, Olivia's clown in Shakespeare's *Twelfth Night* (4:i), but would not have implied to an Elizabethan audience that Feste really was Greek. At the time Greeks had a reputation for being especially jovial, a reputation established for them by the Romans. The Latin verb *graecari* meant 'to live in the Greek manner', that is, to lead an easy-going life.

Greenhorn Originally a reference to a young animal with new horns, but applied to a person with the meaning 'simpleton', or in American slang, 'rookie', since the end of the seventeenth century. Vocative use is more frequent in the USA than in Britain. *The Natural*, by Bernard Malamud, has: ' "Pitch it, greenhorn," warned the Whammer.' In *Moviola*, by Garson Kanin, it is supposedly Thomas Edison, discussing a business deal with a young and inexperienced negotiator, who says: 'No, no, you greenhorn. Sixty you, forty us.'

Green pants, thou *See* **Chap with the red whiskers, thou**.

Greyhead An *ad hoc* term used almost as an endearment in *The Philanderer*, by Stanley Kauffmann: 'She reached over and touched his hair. "Greyhead," she said.' The woman and the man she is addressing are lovers. The term recalls 'Greybeard', which was at one time

used in a contemptuous way to address old men, whether they were bearded or not. In Shakespeare's *Taming of the Shrew* (2:i), the elderly Gremio says to the young Tranio: 'Youngling, thou canst not love so dear as I.' Tranio replies: 'Greybeard, thy love doth freeze.' Gremio is by no means abashed, and is contemptuous in his turn, referring to Tranio as 'Skipper', i.e. one who skips, a child. 'Good greybeard' occurs vocatively again in *Henry the Sixth Part One* (3:ii) and is used elsewhere in the plays in third person reference. *The Limits of Love*, by Frederic Raphael, has a wife saying to her husband: 'You're getting on a bit for playing soldiers, old greysides.' This is said affectionately, but his reply is: 'Here, I say, steady on!'

Grizzle-guts, grizzle-grunt *See* **Cry-baby**.

Groom Originally used of a boy, then a man, 'groom' came to mean a male servant, and finally, a servant who looked after horses. Bridegroom simply means brideman. 'Groom', addressed to a servant, mainly occurs as a vocative in the seventeenth century. In *The Taming of the Shrew*, for instance, Petruchio says: 'You logger-headed and unpolish'd grooms! What, no attendance? no regard? no duty?' Ben Jonson, in *The Silent Woman*, has Truewit address the servant Mute as 'groom'.

Group Captain The title of a Royal Air Force officer whose rank corresponds with an army colonel or a naval captain. *No Highway*, by Nevil Shute, has examples of the title used alone and followed by the last name of the person concerned.

Groveller Used figuratively of someone who is eager to please another, and willingly does whatever is suggested of him. 'You groveller' is used in *The Pickwick Papers*, by Charles Dickens, in its literal sense, referring to one who lies prone on the ground. Bob Sawyer says to the boy who works for him: 'Who do you suppose will ever employ a professional man, when they see his boy playing at marbles in the gutter. Have you no feeling for your profession, you groveller?'

Grumpy, old An intimacy used in *Room at the Top*, by John Braine. It represents an *ad hoc* conversion of the word 'grumpy' rather than a use of Disney's dwarf-name.

Guard Addressed to an individual soldier or a group of soldiers standing guard, or to the guard of a stage-coach or train. *See also* **Coachman**.

Guardian Legally a guardian has the responsibility of looking after a child, or an adult incapable of looking after himself, in place of the natural parent. The word is also more loosely used of one who protects another. Thus Diomedes, in Shakespeare's *Troilus and Cressida* (5:ii), has been asked by Troilus to watch over Cressida and Diomedes greets her: 'How now, my charge!' 'Now, my sweet guardian,' she replies, flirtatiously. In Sheridan's *The School for Scandal* Sir Peter Teazle remarks that 'on their father's death, you know, I acted as a kind of guardian to them both,' i.e. Joseph and Charles Surface. Charles later says to Sir Peter: 'What! my old guardian!' In *Bleak House*, by Charles Dickens, Esther calls Mr Jarndyce 'sir'. 'I think you had better call me Guardian, my dear,' he tells her. Mr Jarndyce has become Esther's protector and guardian in an informal way some years previously, improving the quality of her life greatly. She uses 'Guardian' to him after this, almost as if the word were 'Father'.

Gudewife, Guidwife *See* **Goodwife**.

Gumshoe *See* **Flatfoot**.

Gunga Din The name of a loyal Indian water-carrier in Rudyard Kipling's poem 'Gunga Din', included in his *Barrack-Room Ballads* (1892). He is killed while tending a British soldier, who then becomes the supposed narrator of the poem. Few people read the poem today, though many are familiar with 'You're a better man than I am, Gunga Din'. This sentence is sometimes quoted in full in a situation where the speaker is congratulating someone on being better in some way, displaying more courage perhaps, than he himself. In the Ed McBain short story *Hot* a man says to another: 'You can sleep in this heat, you're a better man than I am, Gunga Din.'

Guts Used by English children as a term of abuse for a fat or greedy child. The latter may also be known as 'guts-ache' or 'gutsy-sod'. *See also* **Fatty** and **Greedy**.

Guv, Guv'nor *See* **Governor**.

Guy The most frequent use of this vocative is in the plural, 'guys' or 'you guys' being addressed to a group of men or women, or to a mixture of both sexes. Such usage is rapidly spreading to Britain in the late 1980s, though it was formerly an Americanism. When it is used in the singular, 'guy' still seems to apply only to men, and to be used by American speakers. Examples of such usage occur in *North Dallas Forty*, where a professional football player says to a team-mate: 'Hey, guy, did you see what that Braniff stock did today?' The same speaker addresses various other colleagues in the same way. *The Magic Army*, by Leslie Thomas, has an American soldier say to another: 'Okay, guy, time's up.' Both novels have examples of 'you guys' addressed to groups of men. 'Guy', in its meaning of 'man', is sometimes said to derive from the personal name 'Guy'. It is more likely to be a variant form of Hebrew 'goy', which describes a gentile.

Guzzler, Guzzle-guts Used by English children as a term of abuse to someone who guzzles large quantities of food and drink. *See also* **Greedy**.

Gyp An abbreviation of 'gypsy', but used in American slang to mean a crook, cheat, or swindler. It has this meaning in Truman Capote's short story *Jug of Silver*, where it is addressed to a man who has just guessed exactly how much money a jar contains. 'Gyp! Lousy gyp!' are the terms used to him. He is described as a poor farmer of French Canadian descent. 'Gypsy' itself is used in quite a different way, as a love-name, in George Eliot's *Scenes of Clerical Life*: ' "I've a capital idea, Gypsy!" (That was his name for his dark-eyed wife when he was in an extraordinarily good humour.)'

H

Hack Applied to a writer of poor quality stories and other works. The word compares such a writer with a hackney horse, one whose services are for hire to anyone. It often collocates with Grub Street, a street in London which was later re-named Milton Street. Dr Johnson said of this street that it was 'much inhabited by writers of small histories, dictionaries, and temporary poems, whence any mean production is called *grubstreet*'. It was Johnsonian modesty, or self-deprecation, one hopes, which made him include dictionary writers amongst the grub street hacks. *The Occupation*, by David Caute, has one writer calling another 'you horny headed son of toil, you grub street hack'.

Hag A word which means an ugly old woman, a witch. It is a strong term of abuse in Shakespeare, expressing extreme disgust and contempt. Perhaps his most famous use of the term, apart from the 'secret, black and midnight hags' of *Macbeth*, is in *The Merry Wives of Windsor* (4:ii). Falstaff is trying to make his escape from Mistress Ford's house, dressed as an old woman. He gets a beating anyway, since Ford happens to dislike the old woman, whom he calls 'you witch, you hag, you baggage, you polecat, you ronyon', almost as much as he dislikes Falstaff. 'Hag' does not seem to be used very often in modern times if literary evidence is anything to go by. 'You old cow' or 'you old bag' occur more frequently.

Hairpin *See* **Spindleshanks**.

Half-brother, Half-sister Half-brothers or sisters share only one parent. The relationship is rarely alluded to vocatively, but a young man in *Absolute Beginners*, by Colin MacInnes, makes use of 'half-brother', to his step-brother as it happens. The latter relationship comes about when a man or woman already has a son and marries someone who also has a son or daughter.

Half-pint Used in Britain and the USA as a slang term for a short person. It was regularly used, for example, by Frank Burns to Radar in the television series *M.A.S.H. See also* **Tich**.

Half-wit, you This seems to be used in Britain more than the USA. It is used, often in a friendly way, to someone who is acting as if he has only half his wits about him. The expression has been in use since the seventeenth century. An example occurs in *Moviola*, by Garson Kanin, where a film producer calls an actress 'you half-wit'. She has just been calling him names such as 'you son-of-a-bitch' and 'you bastard', and is not offended by the 'half-wit' remark.

Ham Used to an actor who rants and over-acts, and more generally of someone who does anything badly, in a clumsy, amateurish way. 'You cheap, lousy ham' is addressed to an actor by a woman in *Pleasure Man*, by Mae West. Several theories have been advanced as to why a bad actor should be a 'ham'. Ham fat was at one time used to remove theatrical make-up, and ham-fatter is still used in American slang of a person who fancies himself as an actor. There was also a troupe of actors touring the USA in the early nineteenth century led by Hamish McCullough. The group is said to have been known as 'Ham's actors', though the normal pronunciation of Hamish would have led to 'Hame's actors'. Another popular link is with Hamlet, since in Shakespeare's play Hamlet in his speech to the players describes ham acting, which he wants them to avoid.

Hands, all Used to address all members of a ship's crew, the speaker usually being the captain. An example of such usage occurs in *Doctor at Sea*, by Richard Gordon, but it was probably far more frequent in the seventeenth and eighteenth centuries than it is today. The term is sometimes used jokingly to address any company of people, especially when the speaker is asking them to do a job of some kind: 'Come on, now, all hands to the wheel.'

Handsome Used by a woman to a man as the equivalent of 'beautiful', 'gorgeous', etc. 'Bettina, you are mad,' says a character in *An American Dream*, by Norman Mailer. 'Better believe me, handsome,' is the reply. In Ian Fleming's *Goldfinger*, use of 'handsome' by one man to another is a sign that the speaker is homosexual. 'Handsome' is an especially popular word with Cornish people, and 'my handsome' is used as a general term of address by speakers from that part of the world. A comment on such usage occurs in *Birthstone*, by D. M. Thomas:

I was tremendously impressed by the lurid

erotic imaginations of these Cornish folk. Practically every remark, however innocent, was climaxed with sexual innuendo. 'There's somethin' funny there, my handsome.' 'I'll have the same as you, my lover.' 'Whereabouts in Cornwall did they come from, my sweetheart?' It was the same amongst themselves. 'See 'ee 'gain, my cock.' 'All right, my bird.' The endearments kept dropping luridly in the smoky air.

Sexual innuendo is certainly overtly present when an American prostitute, in *War Brides*, by Lois Battle, says to a prospective client: 'So how's about it, handsome, wanna tell me about the battles you've been in?' The same novel, however, has an example of 'handsome' used in a friendly way by a young American woman to a long-standing male friend: 'Hey, handsome, help me with these shopping bags, will you?' *One Hundred Dollar Misunderstanding*, by Robert Gover, has a black American prostitute addressing a young white client as 'handsome'.

Happy In Ed McBain's short story *A Very Merry Christmas* a man who is feeling especially cheerful and optimistic offers to buy a stranger in a bar a drink. The man to whom the offer is made is highly suspicious, and thinks that a homosexual approach is being made. 'Get lost, Happy,' he tells the cheerful man. This could be the word 'happy' converted into a nonce nickname, or a transferred use of 'Happy', the name of one of the dwarfs in *Snow White and the Seven Dwarfs*, the 1937 Disney film.

Harbourmaster The professional title of an officer in overall charge of a port. An example of vocative use occurs in *Shipmaster*, by Gwyn Griffin.

Harbuckle, Fatty A reference to Roscoe Arkbuckle, known as Fatty Arbuckle, a grown-up fat boy who appeared in many silent films of the 1920s. English children use this form of his name as a taunt for a fat child. The American actor's career came to an end in 1921 when he was involved in a scandal. *See also* **Fatty**.

Hardass An American slang term used to a tough man, one ready to resort to physical violence. 'How about a day off tomorrow, Hardass?' says a Los Angeles policeman to a colleague, in *The Choirboys*, by Joseph Wambaugh. This is described as 'a remarkable familiarity' since it is used to a superior officer.

Hard-on *See* **Prick**.

Harp Occasionally used in American slang for an Irishman, the harp being emblematically associated with Ireland. At one time there were coins called 'harps', short for harp groat and harp shilling, which were in use in Ireland. They had the figure of a harp on the reverse side. In *Waterfront*, by Budd Schulberg, a hoodlum says to an Irish-American: 'You dumb harp, you must like gettin' hit in the head.'

Hayseed A humorous American term for someone who lives in the countryside, far from civilized city life. The word has been in use since at least the late nineteenth century. In the O. Henry short story *At Arms with Morpheus* 'you unmitigated hayseed' is addressed by a young man to his friend because the latter has just foolishly taken a dose of morphine instead of quinine. The word is clearly meant to mean 'fool' or 'idiot' in this instance, since there is no suggestion that the man addressed is a rustic. When an Australian man introduces someone to another man in *A Salute to the Great McCarthy*, by Barry Oakley, he says: 'This is Tommy Thomson, hayseed.' The man being addressed is from a small town in the bush, now living in the city.

Headmaster The professional title of a male teacher in charge of a school. 'Headmistress' is the corresponding term for a woman who fills that role. Both terms are used on formal occasions to address the people concerned, though such vocative usage was once far more frequent than it is today. 'Headmaster' is used in direct address in novels such as *The Limits of Love*, by Frederick Raphael and *The Old Boys*, by William Trevor.

Heart In some contexts, 'heart' is a synonym for 'inmost being, soul', as in a sentence like: 'He poured out his heart to her.' 'My heart', therefore, used as a vocative to a loved one, is the equivalent of 'my soul, my life'. 'Do stop, Crystal, my darling, do stop crying, my heart,' says a man to a woman in Iris Murdoch's *The Word Child*. 'Michael, my heart!' are the final words of E. F. Benson's *Mike*, as a woman declares her love for the hero. In *Mariana*, by Monica Dickens, it is a grandmother who says to her grand-daughter: 'Enjoy yourself, my heart.' Ngaio Marsh, in *A Surfeit of Lampreys*, has a husband who addresses his wife as 'my darling heart'. 'Dear heart' is a frequently-used phrase of friendship or love, occurring in literature since Chaucer. It is used by a husband to his wife in George Eliot's *The Mill on the Floss*. In *The Tempest* Prospero wakens his Miranda by saying: 'Awake, dear heart, awake; thou hast slept well.' Shakespearean characters also address one another as 'good heart', 'my profound heart', 'my little heart', etc., and of course make use of 'sweetheart' (*see also* **Sweetheart**). 'Dear heart' is still in use, though it has now a rather archaic or dialectal ring to it. It certainly seems to be quite natural when uttered by Hazel, the heroine of Mary Webb's *Gone to Earth*, whose speech reflects her rural life in the Welsh marches.

Since early times the heart has also been regarded as the seat of a person's courage and spirit. We still speak of 'not having the heart' to do something or 'putting heart into somebody'. This is the thought behind 'my hearts', addressed to a group of men, often by another man. 'How now, my hearts,' says a speaker in *Twelfth Night* (2:iii), a man addressing two other men. In later use this vocative became 'my hearties' and was especially associated with seafaring use.

Heartsease An unusual vocative used by a young Scottish man to a girl in *Magnus Merriman*, by Eric Linklater. The same speaker calls her 'honeyheart' and 'beatitude', neither of which is a frequently-occurring endearment. 'Heartsease' means tranquility, peace of mind, though it is also a name for the pansy. The young man who uses it in the novel is described as a passionate admirer of Shakespeare, and is presumably recalling the well-known passage in *Romeo and Juliet* (4:v) when Peter says: 'Musicians, O musicians, "Heart's ease, Heart's ease!" O, an you will have me live, play "Heart's ease."' 'Why "heart's ease"?' asks one of the musicians. 'Because my heart itself plays "My heart is full of woe,"' Peter replies. There is nothing particularly Shakespearean about 'honeyheart' and 'beatitude', however.

Hearty, my Used to a man who is hearty, or brave, and now almost exclusively associated with old-time sailors in the plural form 'my (or me) hearties'. The sailors in the opening scene of Shakespeare's *The Tempest* are addressed by the earlier form 'my hearts'.

Heathen Used of a person who is not conventionally religious, i.e. is not a Christian, Jew, or a Muslim. Loosely used of a person whose behaviour is not conformist. In *Bless me, Father*, by Neil Boyd, a priest calls a neighbour 'you heathen' in mock severity when that person misrepresents a biblical story. 'Ye yaller haythen' is used insultingly in O. Henry's short story *The Transformation of Martin Burney*.

Hebe An abbreviated form of Hebrew, used as an offensive term to a Jew. *See also* **Sheeny**.

Hebrew 'Kindhearted Leventhal, you deep Hebrew . . .' says a character in Saul Bellow's *The Victim*. The vocative is unusual in a modern text, though there is some justification in using it as a synonym for 'Jew'. More fre-

quently in modern times it refers to the Hebrew language.

Hell-hound, you old In its occasional use as a vocative, 'hell-hound' means something like 'fiendish person'. When two old friends meet in *Main Street*, by Sinclair Lewis, 'the two men shook hands a dozen times and, in the Western fashion, bumbled, "Well, well, well, well, you old hell-hound, you old devil, how are you anyway? You old horse-thief, maybe it ain't good to see you again."' For a similar exchange of friendly insults in another Sinclair Lewis novel, *see also* **Horse-thief, you old**. For an earlier use of 'hell-hound' used insultingly, *see also* the quotation under **Ragamuffin**.

Hen The word for a female bird, used by mainly working-class Scottish speakers as a friendly term of address to a girl or woman.

Hero One would expect a vocative such as 'my hero' to be used mockingly in modern times by a woman to a man, alluding to the romantic fiction of former times when weak females looked to strong men for protection. 'Hero' is certainly used mockingly in *The Choirboys*, by Joseph Wambaugh, where a wife whose husband models himself on John Wayne fires a gun at him, causing him to run for cover. She leaves a note for him: 'Who's got the biggest balls now, hero?' In *Only a Game*, by Robert Daley, a woman calls her lover 'my hero' after he has played well in a football game. He takes it as a joke. In James Joyce's *Dubliners* there is a friendly use of 'old hero' by one man to another. A wife who uses a wide range of vocative expressions to her husband in *Gideon Planish*, by Sinclair Lewis, includes 'hero' amongst them. 'Hero' is much used as a vocative in Shakespeare's *Much Ado About Nothing*, but only because that is the name of Leonato's daughter, who plays a major role.

Herr The German equivalent of 'Mr', used as a social title and followed by the last name of the person concerned. Many speakers of English feel obliged to address a German man as 'Herr' Schmidt, or whatever, even when the entire conversation is in English. Novelists also use this term to indicate that a conversation given in English actually took place in German. German *mein Herr* is the equivalent of 'sir'.

High-and-mightiness, Your This mock title occurs in Arthur Hailey's *Hotel*. It is used by an American hotel employee to a British duchess, who would normally be entitled to be called 'your Grace'. The speaker is in a position to blackmail the woman concerned and does not need to be polite. The mock title is based on the phrase 'high and mighty'. This has been used of arrogant persons and actions since the beginning of the nineteenth century. The existence of the title 'your Highness' was also presumably an influence; one might otherwise have expected the phrase to have been converted into a nonce name such as 'Madam High-and-Mighty'. 'Mr High-and-Mighty' occurs in *The Taste of Too Much*, by Clifford Hanley, where a woman first of all says: 'This is a good Catholic house an' if we want to sing good Catholic songs we'll bloody well sing good Catholic songs, we don't need your high an' mighty permission.' She continues: 'I know what Mr High and Mighty thinks of me' and a moment later addresses 'Mr High and Mighty Haddow in his High and Mighty Corporation house.' Earlier in the novel a different speaker says: 'Of course, you know everything, high and mighty.' In earlier times, e.g. in the fifteenth and sixteenth centuries, 'most high and mighty prince', or whatever, would have been a genuine title of dignity.

Highness, your royal The formal mode of address used to royal princes and princesses in Britain. Sarcastic use of this title to someone who is acting like a royal personage, or acting as if they are far more important than they are, at least, is fairly common. 'We thought to ourselves that we better ask Amy about this because Amy is the big shot around here, and even Mama better not make up her mind without bowing to Missus Amy and saying, "Can we, your Royal Highness?"' This is a boy addressing his sister in *William*, by Irene Hunt. *The Diviners*, by Margaret Laurence, has: 'Kid not your husband's?' 'That is my affair, I believe.' 'Oh, beg yer pardon, yer highness. Yer *affair* is right, kid.' *The Actor*, by Horace Annesley Vachell, has a man whose name is Alfred Pugsley addressed by someone as 'Puggy'. He replies: 'Damn your impudence! Who gave you leave to call me Puggy?' 'Pardon, your Royal Highness,' says the original speaker, 'it just slipped out.'

Highwayman In *She Stoops to Conquer*, by Oliver Goldsmith, Mrs Hardcastle twice addresses her husband as 'good Mr Highwayman', believing him to be a highway robber. In *The Wind in the Willows*, by Kenneth Grahame, Ratty reinterprets 'highwayman' to mean a robber of the road in a different sense, equating the word with roadhog. *See also* **Scamp**.

Hilding This word is now obsolete, but is found in several Shakespearean plays and other seventeenth-century sources. Its origin is obscure, but it was applied to animals, especially horses, and both men and women to indicate worthlessness. 'Away, away, you naughty hildings' occurs in Dryden's *Troilus*

and Cressida. In *Romeo and Juliet* Capulet refers to his daughter Juliet by this term. The word seems to have survived until the mid-nineteenth century.

Hinny A Scottish or northern English variant of 'honey', used in affectionate or friendly address. It is said by a mother to her infant son in *When the Boat Comes In*, by James Mitchell. Mr. W. Toyn, writing from Newcastle, says that the term is also spelt 'hinney' and is working class, applied to both men and women as well as children. He adds: 'A further use of the word in an exceptionally endearing sense is to use "canny hinney".'

Historians and your periods, you bloody *See* **You + category of person.**

Hog This variant of 'pig' or 'swine' is used especially when someone is being gluttonous or otherwise self-indulgent. The members of St John's College, Cambridge were at one time known as hogs because they were fond of good living. As a vocative, 'hog' occurs once in Shakespeare, when Queen Margaret, in *King Richard the Third*, calls Gloucester 'thou elvish-mark'd, abortive, rooting hog'. This is only one of a number of 'bitter names', as he calls them, which she heaps upon him. He is also, for instance, 'thou slander of thy heavy mother's womb, thou loathed issue of thy father's loins, thou rag of honour'. In Somerset Maugham's short story *Three Fat Women of Antibes*, a woman finds her two friends indulging themselves when they are supposed to be dieting. 'You beasts. You hogs,' she says, and hastily joins them, happy to become a hog herself.

Hog's rump A highly individual vocative which occurs in *Vile Bodies*, by Evelyn Waugh. One man says to another: 'Go away, hog's rump,' assuming a Cockney accent as he does so, though this is not a Cockney expression.

Holiness, your A title normally reserved for the Pope. For its misuse to a black American minister, *see also* the Jesse Hill Ford quotation under **Reverend**.

Holy angel, little innocent *See* **Teacher's pet**.

Homo Used as an abusive term for a male homosexual, and occasionally for a female homosexual. It is actually the Latin word for 'man'. An instance occurs in *Cocksure*, by Mordecai Richler, where other terms such as 'fag' and 'pouf' are used as well.

Hon A short form of 'honey'. 'What are you thinking about, hon?' a mother asks her daughter in *Breaking Up*, by Norma Klein. The speaker uses 'honey' many times during the novel to the same person. 'Hon' is used by both male and female American speakers in *Blue Dreams*, by William Hanley.

honest A frequently used vocative element in the seventeenth century. Shakespeare has e.g.: honest neighbour, honest gentleman, honest master, honest Launcelot, honest friend, mine honest friend, honest nurse, honest soldier, etc. Occasionally the word appears to be patronizing, used by a social superior to an inferior. In many instances it is merely a conventional word of compliment or approval expressing a friendly attitude. In modern times the word would probably only be used in an exclamatory way to someone who has just proved his honesty, e.g. by returning to its owner something he had found, but the word is certainly not used frequently in vocative expressions.

Honey Used as a term of endearment since the fourteenth century, either alone or as a vocative element. In Shakespeare it is mainly used as the latter, in expressions like 'honey nurse', 'sweet honey Greek', 'my good sweet honey lord', but Othello addresses Desdemona as 'honey' on one occasion: 'Honey, you shall be well desir'd in Cyprus.' A moment later he calls her 'my sweet', which could be said to 'translate' the term (*Othello*, 2:i). In *Villette*, by Charlotte Brontë, a stewardess on a cross-channel ferry addresses a girl passenger as 'honey'. Miss Brontë is at pains to point out that the stewardess is 'vulgar', and that she 'had probably been a barmaid'. This seems to indicate that 'honey' was not used by polite society in the nineteenth century, though it was in common use in Miss Brontë's part of the world then, as now, in the form 'hinny'.

At the end of the nineteenth century, when the *Oxford English Dictionary* first published its H section, the editors were of the opinion that 'honey' was 'now mainly Irish'. If that was so, then it was Irish emigrants who took the expression to the USA, where it was to become firmly established, especially in the southern states. In *Gone With The Wind*, by Margaret Mitchell, we have Honey Wilkes, 'so called because she indiscriminately addressed everyone from her father to the field-hands by that endearment'. Mark Twain, in *The Adventures of Huckleberry Finn*, has the term being used by Jim, the black slave, to Huck. In modern times 'honey' is thought by many English-speakers outside America to be an especially American term. In *War Brides*, by Lois Battle, an Australian woman is addressed by an American sailor as honey. 'These Americans!' she says. 'They haven't any respect.' 'Oh, they call everyone honey,' explains a friend. 'It's just their way of being friendly.'

Honeybag Used by one Australian girl to another in a friendly way in *Redback*, by Howard Jacobson. The bee carries its honey in its honeybag, which is actually an enlargement of the alimentary canal.

Honeybun 'Oh, honeybun, you'll probably murder me, but it did look cheap, and so darling. . . .' Thus runs a familiar domestic conversation in *Gideon Planish*, by Sinclair Lewis, the speaker being a wife, 'honeybun' being her husband. This term may be an allusion to a sweet cake, or an abbreviation of 'honeybunch'.

Honeybunch Regularly used as an endearment by American speakers, especially. A husband uses it to his wife in *The Philanderer*, by Stanley Kauffmann. In *I'll Take Manhattan*, by Judith Krantz, a boss uses it to his secretary. Modern dictionaries are not helpful when it comes to explaining the '–bunch' of this expression. It may be an extension of 'honeybun', or simply be meant to suggest a mass of honey. It is used by Edna O'Brien in *The Country Girls*, so may, like 'honey' itself, have been exported to the USA from Ireland.

Honey-child Often written as 'honey-chile' to indicate its pronunciation, and associated especially with the American South. As H. L. Mencken says, in *The American Language*,

> Southern speech has suffered cruelly on the stage and in the movies, where kittenish actresses from the North think they have imitated it sufficiently when they have thrown in a few *you-alls* and *honey-chiles* and converted every *I* into a long a*h*.

Support for Mencken's view comes from E. V. Cunningham, in *Lydia*. A man says to a woman who has been trying to pass herself off as a Texan: ' "Honey child – did you ever really listen to that southern accent of yours?" "It got by." "Come off it, kid. It did not get by." ' *A Woman Called Fancy*, by Frank Yerby, has a white American living in Georgia addressing a young white woman as 'honey-child', equating it with 'babydoll' and 'baby'.

Honeyheart A term used by a user of rather extravagant English in *Magnus Merriman*, by Eric Linklater. The man who uses it to his lover also calls her 'heartsease' and 'beatitude'.

Honeylamb This appears to be a simple combination of two vocative elements, both used as endearments but otherwise unconnected. 'Honeylamb' is used as an intimacy in *The Pumpkin Eater*, by Penelope Mortimer.

Honey-one An extended form of 'honey', used by a wife to her husband, rather sarcastically, in *An American Dream*, by Norman Mailer.

Honeysuckle The name of this plant was used to some extent as a term of endearment in the sixteenth and seventeenth centuries. Examples of its use occur in *The Knight of the Burning Pestle*, by Beaumont and Fletcher. Another is in *The Fancies Chaste and Noble*, by John Ford. It appears to have been used mainly by men to women. The honeysuckle is actually misnamed, since it is useless to the bee. As for the vocative, the speaker who uses it in O. Henry's short story *While the Auto Waits* to a young lady finds that it does him little good. The conversation runs:

'Didn't know somebody was bowled over by those pretty lamps of yours, did you, honeysuckle?'

'Whoever you are,' said the girl, in icy tones, 'you must remember that I am a lady. I asked you to sit down: if the invitation must constitute me your honeysuckle, consider it withdrawn.'

Honeythighs Normally the kind of intimate private nickname reserved for use when no-one else is present, but said by a man to a woman friend in *The Half Hunter*, by John Sherwood, when others are present. The same speaker uses my passion-flower to the woman concerned.

Honky 'Split, honky, you smell,' says a black American to a white male in *The Tenants*, by Bernard Malamud. 'Honky' is said to be a form of 'hunky', or 'bohunk', originally used by both blacks and whites to describe a foreigner, especially one from central Europe. There may be a connection with the word 'Hungarian'. A British television series in the late 1970s featured a West Indian character who regularly addressed his white neighbour by this term. Its use as a subsidiary element in a vocative expression is seen in: 'Don't you nigger me, you honky prick.' This is used by a black American to a white in *Rabbit Redux*, by John Updike.

Honour, your This form of address was used in the sixteenth and seventeenth centuries to any person of rank, but when Dr Johnson came to write his dictionary in the mid-eighteenth century he was of the opinion that such usage was a thing of the past. In polite society use of the expression may by then have died out, but it continued in rustic and dialect speech far longer. In George Eliot's *Scenes of Clerical Life* it is used as 'sir' might be used in modern times, as a general term of respect. The expression mainly survives in modern times as a title associated with certain offices, such as

that of county court judge. Examples abound in *Brothers in Law*, by Henry Cecil, which has many British court-room scenes. It is also used to the mayor of a town or city, though in *Edwin Drood*, by Charles Dickens, occurs: ' "Who's His Honour?" demanded Durdles. "His Honour the Mayor." "I never was brought afore him," said Durdles, "and it'll be time enough for me to Honour him when I am." '

American usage is also confined to the holders of high office in formal situations such as a court-room. In *The Liberation of Lord Byron Jones*, by Jesse Hill Ford, the city attorney opens formal proceedings by saying: 'I believe we are ready, Mr Mayor, your Honour.' There is a joking corruption of the term in *An American Dream*, by Norman Mailer, where a judge who is in a night-club says 'It's raining'. A girl replies: 'Yes, your Honory, but the sun is shining in court.'

Hoodlum A word of unknown origin referring to a mindless criminal thug, or more mildly, to a young man who behaves badly. It has more of the latter meaning in *A Salute to the Great McCarthy*, by Barry Oakley, where it is equated with 'hooligan' and 'larrikin'.

Hooknose, hookynose An insulting name for a Jew, used mainly in the USA. *See also* **Jew**.

Hooligan This word for a person who is a public nuisance, damaging property, fighting, making a lot of noise, is thought to derive from the family name of an Irish clan who at one time lived in London. 'Hooligan' is occasionally used as a vocative, but is far more frequent as a term of third person reference. 'You hooligans' is insulting in Len Deighton's *Funeral in Berlin*. In *A Salute to the Great McCarthy*, by Barry Oakley, 'hooligan' is shouted at a man who is also called 'larrikin', the Australian synonym for 'hooligan'.

Hope, my This expression means 'the person on whom all my hopes for the future are centred'. Hope is recorded in this sense since the thirteenth century, though it is not frequently so used, either in third person reference or vocatively. *Jane Eyre*, by Charlotte Brontë, has the exclamation: 'Oh, Jane! my hope – my love – my life!' This is the despairing cry of Mr Rochester when Jane bids him farewell for ever, having discovered that he is already married.

Horror This occurs alone in *The Country Girls*, by Edna O'Brien, where it is a covert endearment rather than an insult. It would normally be heard as 'you little horror', addressed to a child who is misbehaving. Spoken by one of the parents of the child concerned, it would probably be said in an affectionate tone. Adults who address someone else's child as 'you little horror' are likely to say it with more feeling. 'You little terror', 'you little shocker' are very similar expressions.

Horse-thief, you old In Britain there are many speakers who would consider this is a typically American term of address, a point rather laboured by Pamela Hansford Johnson. In *A Summer to Decide* she writes: 'Good to see you, Cran, you old horse thief. Isn't that the correct transatlantic style of greeting?' In *An Error of Judgement* she has: ' "Well, Ted, you old horse thief," he said, "which is, I believe, the way Americans greet one another." ' In this instance Miss Johnson continues: 'Ted told him that was the exception rather than the rule,' which accurately describes the situation. The British view of American usage comes from their reading of such novels as *Babbitt*, by Sinclair Lewis, where the following occurs:

Paul and he shook hands solemnly; they smiled as shyly as though they had been parted three years, not three days – and they said:
'How's the old horse-thief?'
'All right, I guess. How're you, you poor shrimp?'
'I'm first rate, you second-hand hunk o' cheese.'
Reassured thus of their high fondness, Babbitt grunted, 'You're a fine guy, you are! Ten minutes late!'

This passage indicates clearly that 'you old horse-thief' is one of those friendly insults that can be used between intimates, especially when softened by 'old'. It has been more generally used than the 'second-hand hunk o' cheese' example quoted above, and is more striking to British eyes and ears than 'you poor shrimp', which British speakers might also use. 'You old horse-thief' is occasionally heard in Britain, used jokingly and normally with a specific reference to the USA.

Hoss, old 'I tell thee what, Hal,' says Falstaff to Prince Henry, in *Henry the Fourth Part One* (2:iv), 'if I tell thee a lie, spit in my face, call me horse.' This seems to imply that 'horse' as a term of address to a man in the seventeenth century would have been contemptuous, but as the *Oxford English Dictionary* points out, the word had also been applied playfully to men since the sixteenth century. The same source quotes T. H. Gladstone, author of *An Englishman in Kansas* (1857): 'Step up this way, old hoss, and liquor,' where horse has taken on a typical American pronunciation and is clearly being used in a friendly way. Confirmation of this comes in *Babbitt*, by Sinclair Lewis (1922): 'Lyte came to the conference exultantly. He was fond of Babbitt this morning,

and called him "old hoss." ' Later in the novel, as proof of a rapidly developing friendship, we are told of Babbitt himself that 'he was at Sam Doppelbrau's at nine. By ten he was calling Mr Doppelbrau "Sam, old hoss." ' In *The Adventures of Huckleberry Finn*, by Mark Twain, a boy of about Huck's own age, who has only been acquainted with him for a very short time, says to him: 'All right – come along, old hoss.' This novel was first published in 1884.

Hostess In former times usually addressed to the hostess of a public tavern. There are many examples in the Shakespeare plays. In *Macbeth* (1:vi) 'hostess' is used vocatively to Lady Macbeth by her guest Duncan. The word occurs rarely in modern times, but *Pray for the Wanderer*, by Kate O'Brien, has a man who is staying with his sister-in-law say to her: 'Oh, my dear hostess, am I a nuisance? Am I eating too much?'

Hound This has been contemptuously applied to a man since the eleventh century. It is similar to 'cur' or 'dog', but used less frequently. Shakespeare has it in *Coriolanus* (5:vi), when Coriolanus is seething with rage at being called boy by Aufidius. Coriolanus refers to Aufidius as a 'cur', and soon afterwards calls him 'false hound'. More modern instances of 'hound' occur in, e.g., *Promotion of the Admiral*, by Morley Roberts, which has 'you damned lazy hound' used by one man to another, and *Doctor at Sea*, by Richard Gordon, where 'you young hound' is used insultingly.

House The *Oxford English Dictionary* describes this as an exclamation that was once used on entering an inn to summon a waiter or the landlord. With that one may compare 'Shop!', still used by customers who enter a shop and find no-one behind the counter. In both instances the exclamation draws attention to someone who needs attention. However, there is some evidence that 'house' was occasionally used as a synonym for landlord. There are examples of such usage in George Borrow's *Lavengro*. 'Can I have dinner, house?' is addressed to the landlord after he has made his appearance. This may never have been general usage, and is certainly obsolete now. The exclamatory use of 'house' has also changed, being an indication now of a 'full house' when playing bingo.

Howler See **Cry-baby**.

Hub, hubby Diminutive forms of husband, in use since at least the seventeenth century. The *Oxford English Dictionary* records E. Ravenscroft, *London Cuckolds* (1688): 'Oh my hubby, dear, dear, dear hubby.' The present author's aunt addressed her husband as 'hub', to the exclusion of every other term including his first name, for fifty years.

Humbug   A word that appeared in the middle of the eighteenth century, from no obvious source. Applied to a person it has the meaning of 'fraud' or 'impostor'. It could be used as a serious accusation, but in *Babbitt*, by Sinclair Lewis, a husband says to his wife: 'Why, you old humbug! Fishing for compliments when I ought to be packing your bag.' The word is not frequently used, either in this affectionate way or as a more contemptuous term. It does occur insultingly, however, as 'you bloody humbug', spoken by Dotty to George, in Tom Stoppard's play *Jumpers*.

Hungry guts   *See* **Greedy**.

Hunk o' cheese, you second-hand   A mild insult, not in general use, used to signal an intimate friendship when it occurs in *Babbitt*, by Sinclair Lewis. *See also* **Horse-thief**.

Hunters, you   Addressed to a group of boys who have been designated hunters in *Lord of the Flies*, by William Golding.

Husband   Wives appear to have regularly addressed their marital partners as 'husband' in the seventeenth century. Shakespeare has many instances of the word being used vocatively on its own, or in phrases like 'good husband', 'gentle husband', 'good sweet husband', 'my husband', and so on. In *Henry the Fifth* Pistol is addressed by his wife as 'honey-sweet husband', and seems to think it no more than his due. In *The Taming of The Shrew* the tinker Christopher Sly awakens from a drunken stupor and is told that he is a lord. His 'wife', a pageboy in disguise, enters the room and addresses him as 'noble lord'. 'Are you my wife, and will not call me husband?' says Sly, and adds that only his men should call him lord. Whether modern husbands are less good, sweet, and gentle than their seventeenth-century counterparts is difficult to say, but they are certainly less often addressed in such terms by their wives. 'Sleepy fat husband' occurs in *The Philanderer*, by Stanley Kauffmann, used by an affectionate wife, but more usual today would be 'hub' or 'hubby'.

Hussy, huzzy, hussie, huzzie   This started out as the word 'housewife' and suffered phonetic mutilation. By the seventeenth century it was already felt to be a separate word, with a meaning that had also lost its respectability. Male speakers seem mostly to have used it to mean a mischievous girl, a jade, or minx. Women using it to other women usually have

sexual looseness or immorality in mind, and use it more forcefully. In Fielding's *Tom Jones* it is equated by one speaker with 'saucy trollop'. In the same author's *Joseph Andrews* it is the word which springs to Mrs Tow-wouse's mind when she finds her maid in bed with her husband. Eighteenth-century novels, in fact, are well-sprinkled with references to hussies, which may partly account for their being so pleasant to read.

In Thackeray's *Vanity Fair* Becky Sharp writes to Amelia and mentions that Sir Pitt Crawley has called her 'you pretty little hussey'. One imagines that she was not too offended by the description. In Oliver Goldsmith's *The Good-Natured Man* Olivia says to Croaker: 'I'm sensible how little I deserve this partiality. Yet, Heaven knows, there is nothing I would not do to gain it.' Croaker replies: 'And you have but succeeded too well, you little hussy, you! With those endearing ways of yours, on my conscience, I could be brought to forgive anything.' One would expect 'hussy' to be used only jokingly in modern times, but it is a serious insult, used by one black American woman to another, in *The Choirboys*, by Joseph Wambaugh. It is equated there with 'bitch'.

Hypocrite, you   An accusation of pretending to be what one is not, specifically, of pretending to have higher moral standards than one really has. The hero of Saul Bellow's *The Victim* twice uses this vocative to another character, supporting it with 'you dirty phoney' and you 'ugly bastard counterfeit' to make sure that the message gets across. 'Hypocrite' has long been used in English, though it was normally spelt without the initial 'h-' until the sixteenth century. Shakespeare uses the word several times, and as a vocative in *Henry the Sixth Part One* (1:iv), Gloucester telling Henry Beaufort, cardinal of Winchester, 'Out, scarlet hypocrite!'

Modern use of the term is well demonstrated in *Pray for the Wanderer*, by Kate O'Brien: ' "They're nice country folks where the respectable conduct their illicit love-affairs at week-ends – " "God forgive them!" "You hypocrite." "Do you mean that I have illicit love-affairs?" "Hardly. But you're not shocked." ' Similarly, *Gone With The Wind*, by Margaret Mitchell, has: ' "Even if you think such things, why do you say them?" she scolded. "If you'd just think what you please but keep your mouth shut, everything would be so much nicer." "That's your system, isn't it, my green-eyed hypocrite?" ' The hypocrite in this case is Scarlett O'Hara, the speaker Rhett Butler. In *The Newcomes*, by William Thackeray, Arthur Pendennis affectionately refers to his wife as 'you little arch-hypocrite' and 'you false girl', and is kissed by her for doing so. By contrast, 'you fucking hypocrite', spoken by one man to another in *Oliver's Story*, by Erich Segal, causes the man so accused to say: 'I don't have to take abuse.' *The Face-Maker*, by Richard Gordon, has a man say to his brother 'you bloody hypocrite' and continue: 'You and your claptrap about faith and the beautiful life hereafter!' 'Hypocrite' is turned into a nonce name in Sheridan's *The School for Scandal*. Lady Teazle tells Joseph Surface: 'Good Mr Hypocrite, by your leave, I'll speak for myself.'

Idiot The word is sometimes used alone in a semi-exclamatory way, especially when someone has just said something foolish. It is also frequent as 'you idiot' and in expanded forms. Thus, an uncle addresses his nephew in *Mariana*, by Monica Dickens, as 'you silly young idiot', though this is more in sorrow than in anger. One cannot imagine the term being used to someone who was really an idiot, someone permanently deficient in mental and intellectual terms. In the novels of Edna O'Brien about life in Ireland, 'you eejit', 'blithering eejit', etc., occur regularly. Connected with such dialectal pronunciation of the word is 'nidget' (nigit, nigid, niget, nigget, etc), found in literature in the sixteenth and seventeenth centuries. 'Nidget' had the same meaning as 'idiot' and arose by transfer of the *n* from the indefinite article – 'an idget' becoming 'a nidget'.

In modern times 'idiot' is usually used lightly, with a meaning similar to clown. It can be an endearment rather than an insult when said by lovers. 'You bloody idiot' is undoubtedly more offensive, and it can be used with venom in other forms, as shown by 'you creeping idiot' in *Scenes of Clerical Life*, by George Eliot. In that instance it is used with contempt by a woman who despises the slow movement of her husband. Its affectionate use is shown in, e.g., *The Business of Loving*, by Godfrey Smith: ' "What do you think of my *Tropical Sin*?" "Your *what*?" "The scent you gave me, you idiot." '

Ignoramus This has had the meaning of an ignorant person since the early seventeenth century, when a play by Ruggles, written to expose the ignorance and arrogance of lawyers, was first performed. *Ignoramus*, the title of the play, was also the name of one of its characters, a lawyer. In modern times 'ignoramus' occurs only seldom as a vocative, and is usually only a mild insult. Rhett Butler, in *Gone With The Wind*, converts it into an endearment when he calls Scarlett O'Hara 'my charming ignoramus'. She has just asked him the meaning of his professed motto, *nihil desperandum*.

Imbecile A variant on the 'idiot/fool' theme, less often used than those common words and perhaps favoured by educated speakers. *The Bell*, by Iris Murdoch, has 'you perfect imbecile' used as an insult. Perhaps this means weak both physically and mentally. 'Imbecile'

could mean either of these when it was first used in English in the sixteenth century, though it has long been taken to refer exclusively to mental deficiency.

Imp Used most commonly in modern times of a child who is 'a little devil', or very mischievous. This term would normally be said with a mixture of affection and irritation after some childish outrage. In *Seven Little Australians*, by Ethel Turner, a young mother calls her children 'you scamps, you bad wicked imps', but laughs as she does so. In *The Dream of Fair Women*, by Henry Williamson, 'you imp' has the meaning of 'you wicked man' when used by a woman to a man. He has just told her a long story as if it were true, then admitted that he made it up. According to the Opies, in *The Lore and Language of Schoolchildren*, 'imp' is also a traditional generic nickname in British schools for a very small child. *See also* **Tich.**

Imperence This was at one time a vulgar corruption of 'impudence', influenced by 'impertinence'. It was used at the end of the eighteenth and beginning of the nineteenth centuries, occurring as a vocative in *The Pickwick Papers*, by Charles Dickens. A young lady admonishes a man with: 'Let me alone, imperence.' In a similar situation, a woman dealing with a flirtatious young man, the term is used again later in the novel to Sam Weller: ' "It's natur; ain't it, cook?" "Don't ask me, imperence," replied the cook, in a high state of delight.'

Impudence The word used as a term for an impudent person. John Dryden, in *An Evening's Love* (1671), has: 'Peace, impudence, and see my face no more.' Mrs Jennings, in Jane Austen's *Sense and Sensibility*, converts the word into a nonce name: ' "Did you not know," said Willoughby, "that we had been out in my curricle?" "Yes, yes, Mr Impudence, I know that very well." ' 'Impudence' was well enough used as a vocative in the nineteenth century to take on another form, 'Imperence', used by uneducated speakers. *See also* **Imperence.**

INANIMATE OBJECTS *See* **PERSONIFICATIONS.**

Infant Occasionally used as a variant of child, baby, etc. It occurs twice in a friendly way in *Absolute Beginners*, by Colin MacInnes, used by a young man to a slightly younger male. There is a very similar usage in *The Late Risers*, by Bernard Wolfe, where 'you goddamned infant' occurs. *Opening Night*, by Ngaio Marsh, has: 'Define, define, well educated infant,' quoted by an actor to a policeman. The quotation is from *Love's Labour's Lost*, where Don Armado, the fantastical Spaniard, says this to his diminutive page, Moth. In Miss Marsh's novel a man in his sixties also addresses a young girl as 'my infant', which causes another man present to refer to her almost immediately as 'the Infant Phenomenon'. This is again a quotation, this time from Dickens and *Nicholas Nickleby* or *The Pickwick Papers*. In the latter novel Sam Weller addresses Master Bardell as 'my infant fernomenon'. Friendly use of 'infant' by a sister to her brother occurs in *The Taste of Too Much*, by Clifford Hanley. In *The Battle of the Villa Fiorita*, by Rumer Godden, it is a young English boy who calls his younger sister 'my poor infant'. Monica Dickens, in *Thursday Afternoons*, has a mother calling her adolescent daughter 'infant'.

Initial of last name, Mr A form of address which is infrequently used in modern times, though when husbands were often addressed by their wives as 'Mr' + last name, 'Mr' + initial of last name was a step towards intimacy. Thus Mr Pott, editor of the *Eatanswill Gazette* in Charles Dickens's *The Pickwick Papers*, is 'Mr P.' to his wife. Similarly, Mr Elton in Jane Austen's *Emma* is 'my dear Mr E.' to Mrs Elton. In Truman Capote's short story *Children on their Birthdays* a woman who is thought to be decidedly eccentric addresses a neighbour as 'Mr C.'

Initial of last name, Mrs In George Eliot's *The Mill on the Floss*, Mrs Glegg is addressed as 'Mrs G.' by her husband. In *The Pickwick Papers*, by Charles Dickens, Mr Weller Senior also uses this form of address to his wife on at least one occasion. The peculiarity of his pronunciation means that it emerges as 'Mrs We'. *The Business of Loving*, by Godfrey Smith, has five examples of 'Mrs D.' used in a friendly way to a housekeeper. 'Mrs B.' is used in exactly the same way to a char/home-help in *The Limits of Love*, by Frederic Raphael. In *A Cack-Handed War*, by Edward Blishen, it is the proprietress of a well-used café who is 'Mrs B.' to her customers. In all these cases a move away from the polite formality of 'Mrs' + last name is achieved, without going as far as the possible condescension of first name usage. In *The Pumpkin Eater*, by Penelope Mortimer, the use of 'Mrs A.' to a woman who would certainly expect to be called Mrs Armitage by the speaker is sneeringly offensive. One's friendliness or otherwise can be emphasized by qualifying this form of expression. Thus in Charlotte Brontë's *Villette*, Ginevra calls Mrs Cholmondeley 'my darling Mrs C.' A comment on this form of address occurs in *Every Day is Mother's Day*, by Hilary Mantel. When a middle-aged woman neighbour remarks 'Nasty weather, Mrs A.' this is followed by: 'Mrs A? As if she were the subject of an experiment.'

INITIALS People are quite often addressed in English-speaking countries by a set of initials, or by a single initial letter. The set of initials is associated by many with American business practice. In Graham Greene's short story *Men at Work* occurs: ' "It's H.G.", she explained to Skate. All the junior staff called people by initials: it was a sort of social compromise, between a Christian name and a Mr.' This may well have been a reason for such usage, helped along no doubt by the business practice of signing memos and other documents with one's initials. However, the initials used in direct address are often those of a person's first name and middle name, not his last name. *Carole*, by Charles Frank, has: 'I asked for silence and addressed J.J. Carpa, not with the usual J.J. but the formal "Mr Carpa".' In *The Business of Loving*, by Godfrey Smith, the central character P.J. Benedict is addressed by an employee as P.J. This business usage can be transferred to other environments. 'We have a little domestic joke, Cornelia and I,' says the narrator in *The Tunnel of Love*, by Peter de Vries. 'I call her C.B. Like a vice-president.' In *Teresa*, by Frank Baker, a wife occasionally uses her husband's initials when speaking to him. The author says that she does so 'quite deliberately, when she means business'. In *The House with the Green Shutters*, by George Douglas, which is set in Scotland, there is a character called James Wilson who puts up a poster to advertise his business. After the opening sentence he refers to himself as 'J.W.' 'He was known as "J.W." ever after. To be known by your initials is sometimes a mark of affection, and sometimes a mark of disrespect. It was not a mark of affection in the case of our "J.W." '

In *The Affair*, by C. P. Snow, a character called G. S. Clark is addressed by everyone, including his wife, as 'G.S.' No explanation of this usage is offered, and the man concerned is certainly not a businessman, but the initials are used as if they constituted his first name. *Blanche*, by Nicolas de Crosta, has the central character addressing her father, as she has done 'from her earliest youth', as 'old J.J.' His name is James Johnson.

C. Northcote Parkinson had commented on the use of initials within an institution other than a business house:

The Royal Naval College, Dartmouth, remained Edwardian to a surprisingly late period of its history. One of many unwritten rules in its earlier days was that masters, blessed (naturally) with private means, should also have double-barrelled names, preferably conveying a hint of naval ancestry. They were known to each other by their initials, but these were strictly those of the double-barrel, Parker-Foley being P.F., his G. (for George) being silent. For all sorts of official and social purposes P.F. was indication enough.

Some sets of initials, of course, are especially meaningful. In *A Temporary Life*, by David Storey, there is a man called R. N. Wilcox. The initials cause him to be known to everyone as 'Skipper', as if the 'R.N.' were letters written after his name, indicating a Royal Navy background. No doubt many real-life nicknames are inspired by sets of initials in this way.

It can sometimes happen that initial letters are given as names in their own right. There was the famous example of Harry S. Truman, where 'S.' was a name, in that his parents never expanded it to reveal what it stood for. Carson McCullers, in *Reflections in a Golden Eye*, writes:

The name he used in the army was not his own. On his enlistment a tough old sergeant had glared down at his signature – L. G. Williams – and then bawled out at him: 'Write your name, you snotty little hayseed, your full name!' The soldier had waited a long time before revealing the fact that those initials were his name, and the only name he had. 'Well, you can't go into the U.S. Army with a goddamn name like that,' the sergeant said. 'I'll change it to E-l-l-g-e-e. OK?'

There have been many real-life examples similar to this.

By contrast, there are many people who bear normal first names but are addressed as if they bear only initials. The diminutive form of Euphemia is Eph. In *Arthur*, by Gordon McGill, the writer says that as a child he was convinced that his aunt Euphemia was called 'F.' There are those whose name is Beatrice who became 'Bee' in direct address, Emily may become 'Em', and so on. But in *Thomas*, by H. B. Creswell, the central character is 'poor old T.' to one speaker, and in Ngaio Marsh's *A Surfeit of Lampreys*, a nobleman addresses a woman called Violet as 'V.' The initial used may be that of the last name. Mr René Quinault, for example, for many years a BBC official, has always been known as 'Q.' to his friends and

colleagues. Perhaps not everyone would appreciate being addressed by an initial or initials. Oscar Wilde, for example, would have been most upset. Hesketh Pearson, in *The Life of Oscar Wilde*, relates that an American once entered his name as O. Wilde in a club visitors' book. Wilde protested: 'Who is O. Wilde? Nobody knows O. Wilde. But Oscar Wilde is a household word.'

Innocent In occasional use as a vocative, with various meanings. It appears to mean 'one who is free of guilt' when Edgar, in Shakespeare's *King Lear* (3:vi), says: 'Pray, innocent, and beware the foul fiend.' It often means 'one of child-like simplicity', and in Scotland, especially, it can mean 'a simpleton, fool'. When Rhett Butler calls Scarlett O'Hara 'my poor innocent', in *Gone With The Wind*, he is implying that her lack of worldly knowledge is both touching and reprehensible. Later, when they are married, the following occurs: ' "Fortunately the world is full of beds – and most of the beds are full of women." "You mean you'd actually be so -?" "My dear innocent! But of course. It's a wonder I haven't strayed long ere this." ' *The Battle of the Villa Fiorita*, by Rumer Godden, has the following conversation between two women friends of mature years:

'It still did not occur to me he was Rob Quillet,' she told Margot.
'With the whole village buzzing about the film for weeks? Didn't you look at his clothes?'
'No,' said Fanny. 'What about them?'
'My dear innocent. Don't you know a suit like that and handmade shoes when you see them?'

A Travelling Woman, by John Wain, has 'you poor little innocent' used in an unfriendly way. *See also* **Ninny**.

Insect Used to refer to a mean and contemptible person since the late seventeenth century, though none of the citations given by the *Oxford English Dictionary* shows the term being used in direct address. 'Presumptuous insect' is said to Eliza Doolittle by Professor Higgins in G. B. Shaw's *Pygmalion*.

Inspector A police rank in both Britain and the USA, immediately below that of superintendent. It also describes the officers of certain humane societies, such as the National Society for the Prevention of Cruelty to Children. The term is used vocatively in almost any detective story. *Dover One*, by Joyce Porter, has forty-three examples of its use, together with six more of 'Chief-Inspector'. Either form could be used as prefixes, followed by the last name of the man or woman concerned. In *Fares Please*, by Edith Courtney, a passenger on a bus says: 'I am sorry, Inspector, I seem to have lost my ticket.' Ticket-inspectors on trains might also be so addressed. The title, to a police inspector, becomes a nonce name in *Wisteria Lodge*, by Arthur Conan Doyle, when 'Mr Inspector' is used.

Intellectual types, you   *See* You + category of person.

INVOCATIONS   *See* RELIGIOUS VOCATIVES.

'Ippo, old Used affectionately to a love-partner who is on the large side in *Love in Quiet Places*, by Bernard Thompson. 'Ippo' is clearly meant for hippopotamus, which literally means 'horse of the water'.

Irishmen, you   *See* You + category of person.

Jack This was at one time a far more commonly used first name than it is at the present time. The frequency of its occurrence caused it to be used as a generic term for any man. It is still often used as a transferred name when addressing a stranger. 'I don't know anyone by that name, Jack,' says a woman rather aggressively to a young man who has telephoned her late at night, in *The Catcher in the Rye*, by J. D. Salinger. There is a friendly use of the term to a stranger in *Daughters of Mulberry*, by Roger Longrigg, three more friendly examples in *The Hiding Place*, by Robert Shaw, an unfriendly instance in *Lucky Jim*, by Kingsley Amis, sixteen friendly examples in *The Liberty Man*, by Gillian Freeman, the high number being caused by the fact that they are addressed to a seaman wearing his uniform. By tradition seamen are particularly likely to be addressed by this name.

The two uses of 'Jack' to a stranger in *Saturday Night and Sunday Morning*, by Alan Sillitoe, are neither friendly or unfriendly, but warily neutral. In certain situations 'Jack' becomes a transferred name because a speaker quotes 'I'm all right, Jack'. The allusion is to a saying: 'Pull the ladder up, Jack, I'm all right,' the general meaning being that 'I don't care what happens to you or anyone else now that I'm safe'.

Jackass A word for a male donkey, applied to stupid people as an insult only since the beginning of the nineteenth century. 'Ass' was used much earlier. In modern American usage 'jackass' has the merit of distinguishing between the animal and 'ass' meaning the buttocks (British 'arse'). R. L. Stevenson, in *St Ives*, has ' "Jackass!" I said, and I think the greatest stickler for manners will admit the epithet to have been justified.' 'Shut up, you jackass' is said by Ravenal, in Edna Ferber's *Showboat*. 'You jackass' is also used by a black man to a white in *An American Dream*, by Norman Mailer. He continues: 'Up your ass, Mother Fuck,' where 'ass' has its buttocks meaning.

Jack Daniels *See* Satan.

Jade This is a separate word from the jade which is a precious mineral, and after which some modern young ladies are named at birth. It is connected instead with an Icelandic word which means 'mare', and which was applied from the fourteenth century onwards to a worn-out horse. By the sixteenth century it was also being applied to a woman, sometimes as a serious insult but more often, especially as time passed, as a playful term equivalent to 'hussy' or 'minx'. It is unlikely that a girl or woman of today would recognize the allusion if addressed as 'you jade'. 'Ah, Grace, you little jade, come here,' says a character to his young niece, in Boucicault's *London Assurance*, a nineteenth-century comedy. The speaker clearly means something like 'you saucy little thing', though interpreted literally, 'you jade' would mean 'you worn out, jaded-looking person'.

Jailer This professional title is used in Oliver Goldsmith's *The Vicar of Wakefield*. Dr Primrose uses 'good jailer'; another speaker creates the nonce name 'Mr Jailer' to address the same person.

Jelly-belly, Crystal Jelly-bottom, Jelly-wobble *See* Fatty.

Jerk Mainly an American term for someone who is thought to be anything from silly to totally obnoxious. As with other insults it is easily converted into a friendly term of address. This happens in *The Philanderer*, by Stanley Kauffmann, where one man uses it to another. 'You jerk' is also friendly in *Daughters of Mulberry*, by Roger Longrigg. It becomes a mild insult in *The Late Risers*, by Bernard Wolfe, and is slightly unusual in being addressed to a woman in *Looking for Mr Goodbar*, by Judith Rossner. 'Of course I'm serious, jerk,' says a man in some irritation to the woman concerned. Chapman, in his *Dictionary of American Slang*, dates the use of the term from the 1930s and says that it derives from another slang expression, 'jerking off', a reference to masturbation. The fuller form of the vocative does in fact occur in *Rabbit is Rich*, by John Updike: 'Ya still got scum on your hands, ya jerkoff.'

Jew 'Jew', used as a term of address, now tends to be aggressive but was not always so. In literature it occurs from time to time, especially in plays or books like *The Merchant of Venice* where a Jewish character is important to the plot. Shylock is at first addressed as 'gentle Jew' by Antonio, but is 'Jew' to Gratiano in the judgement scene. Launcelot addresses Jessica as 'most sweet Jew', and there is a similarly friendly use in *Love's Labour's Lost*, where Costard calls Moth 'my sweet ounce of man's flesh, my incony [fine] Jew'. In Mordecai Richler's *Joshua Now and Then* occurs:

> Greenhorns, you know, new arrivals from the old country, would get off the train with their bundles, scared shitless, and my father would come up to them with this pad in his hand and bark, 'What's your name, Jew?' 'Bishinsky,' they'd say, teeth chattering, or 'Pfeffershnit.' And he'd holler, 'You crazy Jews, this is the British fucking Empire and you can't call yourself by such horseshit names here.'

'Jewboy' is sometimes used of or to a Jewish man or boy in modern times, but this could only be used between intimates who were on friendly-insult terms without giving offence. Richler himself has an example of 'you filthy Jew' used as a covert endearment in another of his novels, *Cocksure*. A wife uses it to her husband, adding 'Ikey hooky-nose' for good measure, as he pretends to drag her into their bedroom, but when she accidentally rolls onto him, making him breathless, she immediately switches to 'darling'. 'You Jewbastard' is used by a black American speaker to a Jewish acquaintance in *The Tenants*, by Bernard Malamud, but without real aggression. The person addressed has just used the word 'shmuck', which leads to a discussion of Jewishness.

Jewel, my This would normally be an endearment, on a par with 'my precious'. In *Settlement with Shanghai Smith*, a short story by Morley Roberts, one man says to another 'We wouldn't part with you, my jewel, not for a thousand', but this is actually a concealed threat. In Shakespeare's *Merry Wives of Windsor* (3:iii), Falstaff woos Mistress Ford with: 'Have I caught thee, my heavenly jewel?'

Jezebel A substitute name used fairly frequently as a vocative in former times. Most people today would probably still know that to call a woman 'Jezebel' would be to accuse her of wickedness and abandonment, though they might not have read her story in the Old Testament Book of Kings I and II. A popular song sung by Frankie Laine made her name known to many in the late 1950s. Samuel Richardson makes much of the use of the name in *Pamela* (1740), when the heroine says to Mrs Jewkes: ' "Why, Jezebel, would you ruin me by force?" ' Upon this she gave me a deadly slap on the shoulder: "Take that," she said; "whom do you call Jezebel?" ' Later she adds: 'I'll Jezebel you, I will!' *The Storyteller*, by Harold Robbins, has an older woman saying to a younger: 'Out of

my house, you whore, you Jezebel!' Shakespeare uses the name only once, and then not vocatively, but his use of the name is extraordinary in that he – or rather, his character Sir Andrew Aguecheek – applies it to a man: 'Fie on him, Jezebel!' (*Twelfth Night*, 2:v).

Jimmy Used by working-class speakers in Glasgow to address a stranger. Correspondents say that this transferred name can be addressed to a woman as well as a man. Mr Kel Hunter writes: 'Though used generically of any stranger, it is always interrogative: 'Ahr yew lookin' for a fecht, Jimmah?' or 'Got the time, Jimmah?' The most obvious and popular explanation for the usage is the frequency of 'James' as a male name in Glasgow. However, it has been suggested that 'Jimmy' or 'Jimmah' is a colloquialized 'Do you mind?' i.e. 'D'ya min'?' In this instance the popular view is probably the correct one, since James has long been a much-used first name in Scotland.

Jitterbug This term was used in the 1930s of a devotee of swing music, especially one who liked to dance to it. The word occurs unusually as a vocative in *The Choirboys*, by Joseph Wambaugh, where an American prostitute says to a prospective client: 'Don't be in such a hurry, you cute little blue eyed jitterbug.'

Jock In Britain, especially, this is often a generic nickname for a Scotsman. The word represents a Scottish and northern English pronunciation of 'Jack', the once-common man's name, though there is no evidence that it was ever especially common in Scotland. Typical friendly use of 'Jock' in this sense occurs in *Doctor at Sea*, by Richard Gordon. When a woman calls a professional American football player 'you stupid jock' in *Only a Game*, by Robert Daley, the meaning is quite different. Earlier in the novel is the comment:

> There was also a third type of girl on campus who, because of a kind of reverse snobbery, refused to date any student with an athletic scholarship. They called the athletes 'jocks', which is not a pleasant word to know some girl has called you.

This slang meaning of jock is now extended to female athletes and sportswomen, though it derives from 'jockstrap'. That word derives in turn from an earlier slang meaning of 'jock', an abbreviation of 'jockum' or 'jockam', 'penis'.

Jockey Before the word 'jockey' became associated with the rider of a horse in a racing context it had the more general sense of a lad or fellow. The word is a diminutive of 'Jock', a variant of 'Jack', once a very common name for a man. The earlier sense of 'jockey' survives to some extent in dialectal usage. In *Saturday*

Night and Sunday Morning, by Alan Sillitoe, which is set in the Nottingham area, a man calls a young boy 'you little bogger, you young jockey'. He may be influenced, however, by the fact that the boy's name is Jacky. 'Jockey' may also be a diminutive of 'Jock', applied to a Scotsman. Its use as such in *The Fortunes of Nigel*, by Sir Walter Scott, brings the rebuke: ' "I am no more Jockey, sir, than you are John," said the stranger, as if offended at being addressed by a name which at that time was used, as Sawney now is, for a general appellation of the Scottish nation.' (Sawney, from Sandy, ultimately from Alexander, was used in the nineteenth century as a generic name for a Scotsman, but has since faded.)

Joe This pet form of 'Joseph' was used during the Second World War to address any American soldier, a 'GI Joe'. 'Joe' is still used colloquially in the sense of 'man', as in J. P. Donleavy's story *The Romantic Life of Alphonse A:* 'They all said: "You're a good Joe".' In Henry Miller's *Tropic of Cancer* there is a comment about vocative usage within a particular group of friends: 'I call him Joe because he calls me Joe. When Carl is with us he is Joe too. Everybody is Joe because it's easier that way. It's also a pleasant reminder not to take yourself too seriously.'

Jonah Used as a transferred name to someone who brings bad luck to others. The allusion is to the story in the Old Testament Book of Jonah, where Jonah tries 'to flee from the presence of the Lord' by taking a ship to Tarshish. The ship is caught up in a terrible storm which abates only when Jonah is thrown overboard. The name is used by a woman to her lover in *Georgy Girl*, by Margaret Forster.

Joy, my *See* Soul's delight, my.

Judge *Brothers in Law*, by Henry Cecil, has a useful passage which runs:

'How would you address Mr Justice Blank if you ran into him in the Strand?'
   'Well, I'd obviously be wrong. How should I?'
   'Judge. "So sorry, Judge," or "Do look where you're going, Judge." If he's in the Court of Appeal, call him Lord Justice.'

'Judge' is the normal term of address in the USA for a man or woman holding such an office. The term can be followed by the last name of the person concerned.

Judy This is now thought of as an especially Australian term for a girl, used in third person reference or as a transferred name in direct address. In the nineteenth century it was commonly used in Britain, especially by sailors, to refer to a girl of loose morals. Judith was not a common first name in Britain in the nineteenth century, so usage was probably inspired by Punch's partner, in the puppet show. Later Australian usage was directly inspired by the number of girls called Judy, later Jody. In G. B. Shaw's *Pygmalion* a taxi-driver addresses Eliza Doolittle as 'Judy'.

Juggins, you 'You juggins' is used by a schoolmaster to a boy in *The Sandcastle*, by Iris Murdoch. The word has been in use in Britain since the end of the nineteenth century and means a fool. Eric Partridge thinks that it is a variant of 'muggins', according to his entry in *A Dictionary of Historical Slang*.

Juicehead Used in American slang of a heavy drinker, a lush. *Waterfront*, by Budd Schulberg, has a man approach another in the street and say: 'A dime – a dime for a cuppa coffee?' 'Don't give me that coffee, you juicehead,' is the reply.

Jumbo Originally the name of a large African elephant at London Zoo on which children used to ride. It was sold to Barnum's circus in 1882. The name is now associated with almost anything of exceptionally large size, and is used as a taunt by children to a fat person. *See also* **Fatty**.

Junior When the eldest son in an American family bears the same first name as his father, he is likely to add 'Junior' after his full name while his father is alive to distinguish himself from his parent. He is also likely to be addressed as 'Junior' by his parents. Another possibility is shown in *Face to Face*, by Edward A. Rogers, where a mother addresses her son as 'Charlie Junior.' 'Junior' is occasionally converted into a first name, and can then take on a diminutive form 'June'. This type of naming, which makes the son a copy of the father, is no longer as fashionable as it once was, the psychiatrists having had much to say about its possible disadvantages to the son.
   'Junior' is still used, however, as a friendly vocative to a strange man or boy, usually but not always when that person is younger than the speaker. 'Hey, junior' is addressed to an unknown boy by an American man in *The Philanderer*, by Stanley Kauffmann. It is similarly used by a British speaker in *Absolute Beginners*, by Colin MacInnes. In *The Choirboys*, by Joseph Wambaugh, an American woman says 'Thanks, Junior' to a man with whom she is irritated, the 'thanks' being sarcastic and the 'Junior' not all that friendly. 'Junior' is also sometimes used as a generic nickname for a very small person. *See also* **Tich**.

Juvenal, my tender Used by Don Adriano

de Armado, the 'fantastical Spaniard' in Shakespeare's *Love's Labour's Lost*, to his page, Moth. Armado at first calls Moth 'boy', then 'dear imp', then 'my tender juvenal', where the last word is a form of 'juvenile'. Moth normally uses 'sir' to his master, but counters 'my tender juvenal' with 'my tough signior'. 'Why tough signior?' asks Armado. 'Why tender juvenal?' says Moth. Armado replies: 'I spoke it, tender juvenal, as a congruent epitheton appertaining to thy young days, which we may nominate tender.' 'And I, tough signior,' replies Moth, 'as an appertinent title to your old time, which we may name tough.' 'My tender juvenal' is a fairly well-known Shakespearean vocative, and is sometimes quoted by one speaker to another.

Kapitän, mein This German form of 'Captain' is quoted in *Absolute Beginners*, by Colin MacInnes. At one time, from 1952–60 especially, most British people would have recognized the phrase as an allusion to the Goon Show, which ran on BBC radio during that eight-year period. It was much used by one of the crazy characters in the show, with names like Eccles, Major Bloodnok, Neddie Seagoon, and Bluebottle, voiced by Harry Secombe, Peter Sellers, and Michael Bentine.

Kate A young lady whose name is Martyn is addressed as 'Kate' by an actor in *Opening Night*, by Ngaio Marsh. He is asked by another member of the cast why he is calling her Kate, and replies: 'I suspect her of being a shrew.' The reference is to Shakespeare's Katharina in *The Taming of the Shrew*. This is a nonce usage; 'Kate' is not normally used vocatively as a transferred name.

Keep, Keeper Used to address a goal-keeper during a game of football or similar game by, e.g., the referee. 'Goalie' is also used.

Kid This word was originally used of the young of a goat, then of other animals. It has been applied to human children since the beginning of the seventeenth century, and is in some respects a synonym of 'child'. The two words would not be interchangeable vocatively, however. 'Kid' could be used to address a young boy, as in *The Contenders*, by John Wain, where the speaker is an older boy, or a girl. Its main use nevertheless appears to be between adults in a friendly way. It is so used in *An American Dream*, by Norman Mailer, where the speaker is a man, and again in *The Philanderer*, by Stanley Kauffmann. An American man uses it to a woman who is only slightly younger than himself in *The Late Risers*, by Bernard Wolfe. In *The Diviners*, by the Canadian author Margaret Laurence, occurs: ' "Look , kid, why don't you come and stay with us for a while?" *Kid*. The word they called each other, way back when. Meaning friend.'

A member of the Names Society, Mr. R. N. G. Rowland, suggests that in Britain 'kid' is used especially frequently by Liverpudlians, though such a statement is difficult to prove. Also difficult to prove is Professor Ernest Weekley's theory that the existence of German

Kind, 'child' helped to make it possible to use 'kid' for a child. The word is certainly used throughout the English-speaking world, as the New Zealand author Anton Vogt shows in his story *The Accident*. There is a motherly woman who is talking to a younger man who has just cut off his toes with a bushman's axe. She says cheerfully: 'How did you do it, kid? Meat short-age isn't as bad as all that.' In J. D. Salinger's *The Catcher in the Rye* occurs:

> How 'bout sitting down or something, Ackley kid?' He didn't like it when you called him 'Ackley kid.' He was always telling me I was a goddam kid, because I was sixteen and he was eighteen. It drove him mad when I called him 'Ackley kid.'

'Kid' may be annoying to an eighteen-year-old, especially when the speaker is sixteen, but for much older people it is probably complimen-tary. 'I thought I'd die,' says a woman to a friend of her own age (about forty), in *Breaking Up*, by Norma Klein, 'if I didn't get into Radcliffe, and here I am, alive and kicking.' 'True,' says her friend. 'The wisdom of middle age.' 'Slow down, kid,' says the forty-year old, 'I'm not ready for middle age yet.' 'Who is?' says her friend. The best-known use of 'kid' by any speaker is probably that of Humphrey Bogart in *Casablanca*, where as Rick Blaine he utters the words: 'Here's looking at you, kid.' The film was released in 1943 but is frequently re-shown. In the Newcastle area of England a speaker might well address a brother, per-haps less often a sister, as 'our kid'.

Kiddie Used by an elderly speaker to a child aged seven in Saul Bellow's *The Victim*. 'Kid-dies' is sometimes used to a group of very young children, becoming 'kiddie-widdies' in baby talk. *Babbitt*, by Sinclair Lewis, has 'Why, you poor kiddy, what have you been worrying about?' addressed to a wife by her husband. This reflects his rather fatherly, protective atti-tude to her. 'Kiddies' is also used to adults in *Rabbit is Rich*, by John Updike: 'Webb Mur-kett's gravelly voice growls, "Well, kiddies, as the oldest person here, I claim the privilege of announcing that I'm tired and want to go to bed." '

Kiddo This is kid with the diminutive ' –o' ending (*see* **O**) which has the effect of creating a true vocative, i.e. a word which it is difficult to imagine being used in third person reference. Its use is much the same as that of 'kid', and the two terms are usually interchangeable. In *Cocksure*, by Mordecai Richler, the speaker who says to a young boy 'Remember your Uncle Ziggy, kiddo?', uses 'kid' to him a moment later: 'You're a swinger, kid.' In *The Late Risers*, by Bernard Wolfe, a husband calls his wife 'kiddo'. The speaker who uses 'kiddo' in *A World of Difference*, by Stanley Price, associates it with the American underworld: 'He put on his phoney American gangster accent and leant towards her. "I jest wanna be fresh with you, kiddo."' The 'kidder' that is used between two men in *When the Boat Comes In*, by James Mitchell, appears to be 'kiddo' in a dialectal disguise, showing its unstressed pronunciation. For another example of 'kiddo' being used to a woman, *see also* the quotation from *The Kennedys* under **Sweetie**.

Kidlet 'I have to run now, kidlet,' says an American wife to her husband in *The Philanderer*, by Stanley Kauffmann. 'Kidlet' is not a usual term, but '-let' is a standard diminutive ending.

Kidress A private nickname, or love name, used to the heroine of *Trixie*, by Wallace Graves. It differs from both normal nickname and normal vocative in being used to one person only by one speaker, and only when they are alone. It is also an invented term, of course, supposedly converting 'kid' into a feminine form.

Kike An extremely offensive way of referring to or addressing a Jew. The term is used far more in the USA than Britain, and is of obscure origin. Leo Rosten, in *The Joys of Yiddish*, derives it from Yiddish *kikel*, 'circle', because illiterate Jewish immigrants signed their name with a circle instead of a cross. Any kind of cross would have been abhorrent to them because of its associations with the crucifixion. In *Portnoy's Complaint*, by Philip Roth, a girl tells a Jewish boy that he is a son of a 'bitch kike'. 'Don't you say kike to me, you,' he tells her. 'You are a kike, Kike,' is the reply. In *Moviola*, by Garson Kanin, 'you fatheaded kike' is addressed to a Jewish man, but it is an insult between friends and no offence is taken.

kind Formerly a well used vocative element, now mainly used in 'kind sir,' which often occurs in 'Thank you, kind sir,' uttered with mock coyness and humility by a woman to a man. 'Kind' usually has its modern meaning of 'benevolent' in Shakespeare. Vocatives such as 'kind' + first name, 'most kind maid,' 'kind master', 'kind gentlemen', 'kind cousin', etc., are found throughout the plays. A modern instance of 'kind sir' occurs in *Georgy Girl*, by Margaret Forster; another is in *A Travelling Woman*, by John Wain.

King, Sir A mock title used as an intimacy in *Georgy Girl*, by Margaret Forster. The many kings in the Shakespearean plays are sometimes addressed as 'great king', 'mighty king', 'silent king', etc.

-kins, -kin Suffixes added to names or words to form a diminutive. There is an etymological relationship with the *-chen* in German words such as *Liebchen*, 'sweetheart'. In *The Word Child*, by Iris Murdoch, a girl whose name is Thomasina is addressed affectionately as 'Tomkins'. Nina Bawden, in *George Beneath a Paper Moon*, has a man say: 'Don't be daft, Sally-kins.' 'Sally *darling*,' says the girl concerned. The man then calls her 'Sally darling' and 'darling Sally', but adds: 'Nice women don't ask for endearments.' *Martin Arrowsmith*, by Sinclair Lewis, has a woman address a man as 'Martykins' and 'Mart', his first name being Martin. In *Howard's End*, by E. M. Forster, a girl extends her brother's pet name, which is usually Tibby, to 'Tibbikins'. *The Half Hunter*, by John Sherwood, has a wife calling her husband 'Teddykins'. As can be seen, '–kins' appears to be the usual form of the suffix, though *Opening Night*, by Ngaio Marsh, has a man whose last name is Fox addressed as 'Foxkin' by a male colleague. In most cases the diminutive form with '–kins' or '–kin' represents *ad hoc* usage, expressing the intimate attitude of the speaker at the moment of utterance. It frequently forms a double diminutive, as the examples above demonstrate, and indeed that appears to be one of its main functions. The suffix can be attached to other terms, not just personal names. *See also* for example **Babykins, Popkins, Lambkin, Motherkins**.

Kinsman This word is rarely used in modern English. It refers to a male relative, properly a blood relation but often used in the seventeenth century of a man related by marriage. There are several vocative examples of the word in the Shakespearean plays. The word occurs most frequently in *Romeo and Juliet*, though usually in third person reference. At one point, however, Capulet addresses his nephew Tybalt as 'kinsman'. The word seems to have been used almost as a synonym of 'cousin', a word which had a wider meaning in the seventeenth century than today.

Kitling This word was used in the seventeenth and eighteenth centuries of a small cat, and occasionally crept into vocative use. Mirabel, in Beaumont and Fletcher's *The Wild-Goose Chase*, says to Rosalura and Lillia, 'Out, kitlings! What caterwauling's here!' Caterwauling refers to the noise made by cats at rutting time.

Kitten *See* **Pet**.

Knave A popular vocative in the seventeenth century, but one which went out of fashion soon afterwards. The word had long been in use, at first meaning a boy, then a young male servant, and finally a rogue. Shakespeare used 'knave' vocatively in the latter two senses. In *King Lear*, for example, the king asks 'where's my knave, my fool?' and then addresses him as 'my friendly knave', 'my pretty knave'. In the same play Cornwall addresses the earl of Kent as 'you stubborn ancient knave, you reverend braggart'. 'Knave' would only be used in modern times as a conscious archaism.

Knight A knight in modern times would normally be addressed as 'Sir' + first name. Shakespearean knights are often addressed as 'knight', 'my dear knight', 'sweet knight', etc. There are thirteen instances of such usage in *Twelfth Night*, for example. Shakespeare, incidentally, would not have punned on the 'night' of his title and a 'knight' such as Sir Toby Belch. English words beginning with 'kn-' were mostly pronounced with the *k* sounded until the middle of the seventeenth century.

Know-all *See* **Clever**.

Know-nothing, Mr This nonce name is used by a woman to a man in *Like Any Other Man*, by Patrick Boyle. He pretends not to know what she is talking about when she asks him a question, though she knows perfectly well that he has understood her meaning.

Lad A lad was originally a serving man or attendant, a sense which had faded by 1700. By the fifteenth century lad had come to mean 'boy', though as with boy, the word could be applied to a man of any age. This was particularly so when used as a term of address in the form 'my lad'. Special senses included the Scottish 'lover', a meaning which was current in the eighteenth century, and the implication of special vigour and spirit which became associated with the word in the sixteenth century. This is still found in statements like 'He's quite a lad,' where 'He's quite a boy' would not have the same meaning, nor would 'He's quite a man'. In modern times the vocative use of 'lad' is especially associated with the north of England, and it can still be applied to a man of any age if the speaker is of the same age or older than the person addressed. 'You're very welcome, lad, I'm sure,' says the mother of a girl to a visiting boy-friend in *When the Boat Comes In*, by James Mitchell. In *The Business of Loving*, by Godfrey Smith, 'good lad' is used to a boy in his early teens, avoiding the condescension of 'good boy'.

Lad, old A variant of 'old boy', normally used by one man to another in a friendly way. There are examples of its use in the Shakespearean plays, e.g. *The Taming of the Shrew* (4:i), where Nathaniel greets Grumio with 'How now, old lad!' and *Titus Andronicus* (4:ii), where Aaron says 'Look how the black slave smiles upon the father, As who would say "Old lad, I am thine own."' 'Lad' is also frequently used as a vocative in the plays on its own in the singular or plural form, and in collocations such as 'my honest lads', 'dear lad', 'young lad', 'good lads'. 'Old lad' continues to be reasonably well used in modern times. Kingsley Amis, in *Girl, 20*, makes it the term regularly used by Sir Roy Vandervane to address a male friend. There are two further examples of its use in *Doctor in the House*, by Richard Gordon; one in *Funeral in Berlin*, by Len Deighton; two in *A Kind of Loving*, by Stan Barstow.

Laddie This diminutive form of lad is especially likely to be used when there is an age difference between the speaker (older) and the person addressed. It is used unusually, and sarcastically, in *Gone With The Wind*, by Margaret Mitchell, when Scarlett asks Rhett Butler: 'why all these lies, my gallant soldier laddie?' In Arthur Hailey's *Hotel* 'laddie' is used by a chief engineer of Scottish origin to his assistant.

Ladies Used to address two or more adult women politely, whether strangers, e.g. at a public meeting, friends or family. 'Well, ladies,' says St Clare to his wife and cousin, in *Uncle Tom's Cabin*, by Harriet Beecher Stowe, 'and what was the bill of fare at church today?' In modern times 'ladies' usually stands alone, though an elderly speaker in polite society might be heard to say 'dear ladies'. In the plays of Shakespeare 'fair ladies' is often used, and 'good ladies' occurs in *Coriolanus* (2:i). Ophelia, in *Hamlet* (4:v), exits with 'Good night, ladies; good night, sweet ladies, good night, good night'.

Ladies and gentlemen The normal formula used to address a mixed gathering. It is occasionally varied, as in *Gideon Planish*, by Sinclair Lewis, where a professor addresses his students as 'young ladies and gentlemen'. In another of Lewis's novels, *Main Street*, Sam Clark introduces the heroine to her new neighbours with: 'Ladies and worser halves, the bride!' The allusion, of course, is to 'better half', which has been used to describe a wife, according to Eric Partridge in his *Dictionary of Historical Slang*, since the late sixteenth century, though the phrase is not used vocatively. Sam Clark could just have easily said 'Folks' or 'Friends', much as Mr Pickwick does at one point, having begun a speech more formally (see *also* quotation under **Friend**). Another semi-formal usage occurs in *Main Street*, when Dr Gould says 'Ladies and gents'. In *Deborah*, by Marian Castle, occurs: 'Ladeez and gentlemun – if any!'

Lady Used to address a woman whose name is unknown in both Britain and the USA, though such usage is not considered to be correct. The term is marginally less polite than the American 'ma'am', and considerably more polite than 'Missis' and such-like terms. In *War Brides*, by Lois Battle, a young American soldier, talking to a young married woman who is a fellow passenger on a train, says: 'This is the heart of America, lady.' In *The Magic Army*, by Leslie Thomas, an American army officer says to an English doctor's wife, whom he knows reasonably well: 'You look like the spirit of spring today, lady.' 'Lady' would be used by e.g. London children addressing a strange woman if she was reasonably well dressed, and if they needed to create a good impression. They are not implying that the woman concerned is a lady of considerable social rank, entitled to be addressed as 'my lady', but they know that lady is a polite synonym for woman. Its use as such is reflected in expressions like 'char-lady' rather than 'charwoman', used of the daily help.

'Lady' is frequently qualified by other words to form vocative expressions of differing value. 'My pretty lady' is the kind of flattering expression used by, e.g., a gypsy fortune teller to a prospective client. Examples of its use, by such a speaker, are in George Eliot's *The Mill on the Floss* and *The Dream of Fair Women*, by Henry Williamson. The gypsies in these two books also use 'my good lady' and 'my little lady', the latter to a young girl. 'Little lady' is used by an older man to an adult woman in a friendly way in *Rebecca*, by Daphne du Maurier, though there is a comment about the forced heartiness of the speaker. 'Young lady' is never used by a young man to his young lady, the girl he is courting, but is commonly used by parents when admonishing a daughter: 'Just what do you think you are doing, young lady?' It is also used by older men to address in a flattering way a woman who is younger than themselves. In *The Stone Angel*, by Margaret Laurence, a doctor uses it to address a patient who is a very old lady indeed: 'Doctor Corby turns to me, smiles falsely, as though he practised it diligently every morning before a mirror. "Well, how are you, young lady?" '

'Dear lady' (with 'dear boy' as the masculine equivalent) appear to be favoured forms of address by older actors in Britain. This also occurs in *The Dream of Fair Women*, by Henry Williamson, where the woman to whom it is addressed says: 'What a conceited bore that man is! How I hate being called "dear lady".' It is probably not the term itself which is offensive, more the over-theatrical way in which this expression tends to be uttered. Nevertheless, it is meant to be friendly when said in *Casanova's Chinese Restaurant*, by Anthony Powell, and *The Fox in the Attic*, by Richard Hughes, where the speakers are both very middle-class. There are further examples of its use in *The Half Hunter*, by John Sherwood, again by a middle-class speaker. Such would almost certainly be the case with the user of any vocative expression beginning with 'dear'. 'Old lady' also occurs vocatively, with 'old' having its usual friendly intention. In *A Cack-Handed War*, by Edward Blishen, it is used by a brash working-class man to a woman serving tea in a café. In *Main Street*, by Sinclair Lewis, it is used in private, as a genuine term of

endearment, by an American husband to his wife. 'Lady' occurs as a vocative in Shakespeare, either alone or as part of a longer expression, but it is not especially frequent. Typical uses include: most dear lady, mine honoured lady, noble lady, poor lady, etc. The word may also be used to qualify another head-word, as in 'dear lady daughter'.

Lady, my This expression would be used by a servant to address the wife of a peer or a peeress in her own right. Other speakers would use 'Lady' + last name, or a polite term such as 'Madam', or if their relationship with the woman in question justified it, her first name. There are probably many people today, however, who worry as much about what to call a titled lady as the ladies of *Cranford*, in Mrs Gaskell's novel. The widow of a Scottish peer is about to visit the town, and the ladies consult:

By the way, you'll think me strangely ignorant; but, do you know, I am puzzled how we ought to address Lady Glenmire. Do you say, 'Your Ladyship' where you would say 'you' to a common person? I have been puzzling all morning; and are we to say 'My Lady' instead of 'Ma'am'? Miss Matty, to whom this is addressed, becomes very flustered. ' "My lady" – "your ladyship". It sounds very strange, and as if it was not natural.'

A more recent puzzle was set in Britain when barristers wondered how to address a lady judge in the high court, a man in that role being addressed as 'my lord'. Mrs G. A. Guthrie, writing to *The Times* newspaper in June, 1988, said:

I note that Lord Justice Woolf has set his seal on 'My Lady Lord Justice Butler-Sloss' as the correct mode of address for that lady. May we take it that the first lady Speaker of the House of Commons will be addressed as 'Mrs Mr Speaker, Madam Sir?'

As with Madam, 'my lady' is sometimes used sarcastically to a girl or woman who is acting in a way thought to be typical of an aristocratic woman. An example of such usage occurs in *The Country Girls*, by Edna O'Brien. In *Hard Times*, by Charles Dickens, the young bank clerk Bitzer answers a query from Mrs Sparsit, who is Mr Bounderby's housekeeper, about whether it has been a busy day, with: 'Not a very busy day, my lady.' Dickens explains: 'He now and then slid into my lady, instead of ma'am, as an involuntary acknowledgement of Mrs Sparsit's personal dignity and claims to reverence.' Thackeray likewise makes fun of a housekeeper who is addressed as 'my lady' by a maid in *Vanity Fair*. *See also* the quote under **Mum**.

Lady-killer Used as a compliment by one young man to another in *Absolute Beginners*, by Colin MacInnes. 'Killer' itself is sometimes used to a person who is considered to be very attractive to the opposite sex.

Ladyship, your A highly respectful expression used to a woman who would otherwise be addressed as Lady Smith or Jones, the wife of a peer or a peeress in her own right. The speaker is likely to be a servant. It is the vocative used by Mellors, the gamekeeper, to his mistress in *Lady Chatterley's Lover* before their relationship develops. In Fanny Burney's *Evelina* Mrs Selwyn congratulates the young heroine on her coming marriage to Lord Orville:

> The moment she had shut the door, 'Your Ladyship,' said she. 'Ma'am!' cried I, staring. 'Oh, the sweet innocent! So you don't know what I mean? – but, my dear, my sole view is to accustom you a little to your dignity elect, lest, when you are addressed by your title, you should look another way, from an apprehension of listening to a discourse not meant for you to hear.'

'Your ladyship' could by used less seriously to a woman, especially a young one, who was acting like a little madam, simply to comment on her high-handedness.

Lamb This word has been used as an endearment since the sixteenth century. It is still in regular use to children or love-partners. In *Jennifer*, by Janet Whitney, a woman uses it to a young girl. A nurse employs it in a similar way in *Mariana*, by Monica Dickens. A father calls his eighteen-year-old daughter 'my lamb', 'my treasure' in *Villette*, by Charlotte Brontë. Women use it to lovers in *Comfort me with Apples*, by Peter de Vries and *An American Dream*, by Norman Mailer. In *Rebecca*, by Daphne du Maurier, 'poor lamb' is addressed to his wife by one of the characters. To these mainly modern examples could easily be added those from earlier times. The Nurse, for instance, in *Romeo and Juliet* twice addresses the thirteen-year-old Juliet as 'lamb'.

Lambie A diminutive form of 'lamb', used exclusively as a term of address. 'Oh, lambie, I'll never again make any organizational or occupational affiliation without your advice,' says a husband to his wife, in *Gideon Planish*, by Sinclair Lewis. The spelling 'lamby' sometimes occurs.

Lambkin This is used by Mrs Jewkes to Pamela, in Samuel Richardson's novel *Pamela*. It inspires the young lady, who had learnt to distrust every sign of affection that Mrs Jewkes shows her, to respond: 'Was this in your instructions, wolfkin?' 'Lambkin' has been in regular use as an endearment since the seventeenth century, used especially to a child. In Reade's *Cloister and the Hearth* occurs: 'We will pray for her, won't we, my lambkin; when we are old enough?'

Lamp-post, walking lamp-post Instant nicknames bestowed by children on tall, thin people. *See also* **Spindleshanks**.

Landlady For the sense development of this word, see **Landlord**. 'Landlady' is rarely used in modern times, though it was common in the eighteenth and nineteenth centuries, addressed to the hostess of an inn. The polite lieutenant who explains to the landlady of an inn that Tom Jones is really a gentleman (in Fielding's *Tom Jones*) calls her 'madam' or 'landlady' indiscriminately.

Landlord As the novels of the eighteenth and nineteenth centuries make clear, the usual way of calling for mine host's attention when arriving at an inn was to shout 'Landlord!' Modern publicans still accept this term as one of their professional titles, and may occasionally be addressed by it. It is unlikely that it is used to the other type of landlord, the one who owns property which he lets to tenants. The use of 'landlord' to describe an innkeeper stretches the original meaning of the word considerably. A landlord was once a land lord, i.e. a lordly owner of land who let it to others. There were likely to be buildings on the land, so the meaning was extended to include those who owned any kind of residential property which they let to others. That meaning has remained in force, but by another extension 'landlord' was used to describe someone who allowed his property to be used overnight for a fee, one who had temporary tenants. Most early innkeepers were landlords in that sense; the coaching inns functioned as hotels. Once the association was established between landlord and innkeeper, it became possible for the modern landlord to be known as such, even though he could no longer offer his customers a bed for the night. The vocative is heard on all sides every Christmas, if at no other time, as carollers sing: 'Come, landlord, fill the flowing bowl/Until it doth run over ... /For tonight we'll merry be,/Tomorrow we'll be sober.'

Land-lubber A seaman's term for someone who does not go to sea, and is ignorant of life on board ship. The term would not normally be used vocatively, though it is used in a friendly way in *Absolute Beginners*, by Colin MacInnes. The speaker is one whose idiolect is marked by a great range of unusual terms of address. Seamen would refer to a clumsy seaman as a lubber. In early use the word also referred to idleness. Monks were therefore known as 'abbey-lubbers', since they appeared to do no work. In Devonshire dialect, 'lubber' became 'lubby'.

Lanky, Lanky Liz, Lanky Panky Instant nicknames bestowed by children on tall, thin people. *See also* **Spindleshanks**.

Lard-ass *See* **Fat-ass**.

Larrikin This is a particularly Australian term, referring to a street rowdy, a young hooligan. The word is thought to derive from Larry, pet form of Laurence, at one time a common Irish first name. The term was in use in Australia by the 1870s. Its use a hundred years later is shown in *A Salute to the Great McCarthy*, by Barry Oakley, an Australian novel first published in 1970. ' "Out!" says Evans, showing the hairy pits of his nostrils as he looks up. "Hooligan! Larrikin! Out!" ' Later in the novel 'larrikin' is used again, equated with 'hoodlum'.

Lass This would be the normal word for 'girl' in the north of England, extending down to the northern Midlands. It is the Scottish term as well, together with its diminutive form, 'lassie'. When Mellors, the gamekeeper in *Lady Chatterley's Lover*, by D. H. Lawrence, lapses into dialect to address his lover he calls her 'ma lass – ma little lass'. In *The House with the Green Shutters*, by George Douglas, which is set in a Scottish town, a husband calls his wife 'lass', alternating it with her first name, 'woman', etc.

Lassie boy *See* **Cry-baby**.

Last name In the eighteenth and nineteenth centuries, a man's last name was probably the term by which he was most often addressed. Such usage has largely given way in modern times to use of his first name. It was always much rarer for a woman to be addressed by her last name, but it could happen. In *Barnaby Rudge*, by Charles Dickens, Miss Miggs is domestic servant to the Vardens before she becomes female turnkey at the Bridewell. While still a servant Dickens says of her: 'Miss Miggs: or as she was called, in conformity with those prejudices of Society which lop and top from poor handmaidens all such genteel excrescences – Miggs.' Servants of an even lower rank were addressed by their first names, or by suitable replacements for their first names if their own were considered to be too fanciful. This situation changed as the twentieth century wore on. In *Memento Mori*, by Muriel Spark, occurs: ' "Did you have a nice evening at the pictures, Taylor?" said Charmian. "I am not Taylor," said Dame Lettie, "and

in any case, you always called Taylor 'Jean' during her last twenty or so years in your service." ' In *Jane Eyre*, Charlotte Brontë says of Lowood Institution: 'the girls here were all called by their surnames, as boys are elsewhere.' This vocative usage emphasized the unsentimental atmosphere that prevailed there.

In certain professional situations, however, women might choose to adopt the same vocative habit as their male colleagues. Thus in Tennessee Williams's *Eight Mortal Ladies Possessed* we have:

'I've heard nothing but Horne out of you for ten years running. Doesn't this Horne have a Christian name to be called by you? What's it *mean?* I don't know what to imagine.' 'Oh, mama, there's nothing for you to imagine,' said Elphinstone. 'We are two unmarried professional women and unmarried professional women address each other by surnames. It's a professional woman's practice in Manhattan, that's all there is to it, mama.'

Professional use to a woman is also found in *Dover One*, by Joyce Porter, where a woman police-sergeant addresses a woman police constable by her last name. *Nurse is a Neighbour*, by Joanna Jones, has the central character using her last name to herself in an inner dialogue, while *The Taste of Too Much*, by Clifford Hanley, has a young man who adopts a tough attitude generally to his girl-friend addressing her as 'Jackson' instead of Alice.

Women sometimes use a man's last name when addressing him. In George Eliot's *Adam Bede* a wife does so to her husband, as does a wife in Edna Ferber's *Showboat*. Another wife who does this to her husband is in *Casanova's Chinese Restaurant*, by Anthony Powell, but this couple have a curious relationship that ends in a separation by the end of the novel. *Unconditional Surrender*, by Evelyn Waugh, has a titled lady addressing the owner of a restaurant by his last name. Waugh comments that 'there was also an odd dilution of odd-looking men who called the proprietor "Mr Ruben". . . .' These are clearly social upstarts who are not familiar with correct vocative usage. *The Liberty Man*, by Gillian Freeman, has a headmistress addressing an ex-pupil by his last name, but this would be strange in modern times. The ex-pupil today would expect his first name to be used, even if the teacher was obliged to be reminded of it. *The Jewel in the Crown*, by Paul Scott, has a woman who is careful to call the soldiers she invites to her home for tea 'Mr' + last name, since 'she knew that private soldiers hated to be called by their surnames alone if the person talking to them was a woman'. This remark would still hold true, but a woman today in a similar situation would probably use first names rather than the formal 'mister'.

At a time when long-standing male friends called one another by their last names, the wives of such friends usually went to the more polite 'Mr' form. There is some evidence, in novels such as *The Limits of Love*, by Frederic Raphael and *Casanova's Chinese Restaurant*, mentioned above, that if the men concerned were in the artistic world, painters, writers, musicians, then the wives might address their husbands' friends by last name only. On the change from last name to first name usage amongst male equals, *see also* the quote from *The Affair*, by C. P. Snow under **First name**. Professional colleagues at one time signalled their membership of the same profession by the use of last names, and were very exact about it. In *The Affair*, for example, a Cambridge don is the subject of an enquiry. The barristers present address him as 'Dr Howard', but we are told that 'Crawford had been punctilious throughout in calling Howard by his surname alone, as though he were still a colleague.' As for barristers themselves, Henry Cecil has this in *Brothers in Law*: ' "D'you think Mr Grimes would mind?" asked Roger. "Grimes, not Mr Grimes," said Henry. "I meant to tell you about that before. Once you're called you call everyone at the Bar by his surname." ' Such last name usage could be friendly in itself, though friendliness could be emphasized by adding a phrase like 'my dear fellow' after the last name.

Many novels have male pupils being addressed by last name, both by fellow male students and by male teachers. Public schoolboys, especially, would at one time have been horrified to hear their first names being used (*see also* quotes under **First name**). In *The Old Boys*, by William Trevor, men who adopted last name usage fifty years previously continue to address one another in that way. In military and quasi-military environments such as the police force, a superior officer, then as now, would usually address a man of lower rank by his last name. Male servants were similarly addressed by their employers. It would have been unthinkable for Bertie Wooster to address his man as anything but Jeeves. Jeeves had probably almost forgotten that his parents, or his creator P. G. Wodehouse at least, actually gave him the first name Reginald.

But for that matter, how often is Sherlock Holmes addressed as Sherlock in all the stories about his adventures? He and his old friend Dr Watson were always Holmes and Watson to each other, and few casual readers would know that the doctor was named John. At one point, Holmes comments on vocative usage, though not to Watson. In *The Mazarin Stone* the villainous Count Syvius says to him: 'Two can play at that game, Holmes.' 'It is a small point, Count Syvius,' says the great man, to whom it is obviously not a small point, 'but perhaps you would kindly give me my prefix when you address me.'

In nearly all situations where a strict hierarchy does not exist, and where a boy or man does not formally acknowledge that some men who speak to him are his superiors, the use of a last name on its own tends to be felt as aggressive or insulting. Two men who are beginning to quarrel in *The Limits of Love*, by Frederic Raphael, say: ' "You think too much about yourself, Halloran, that's your trouble." "Halloran," Stan said. "Back to that, are we?" ' *Lucky Jim*, by Kingsley Amis, has: 'Look here, Dickinson, or whatever your name is,' Bertrand began. Equally aggressive is the 'Look here, Starfield' which begins a speech in *Under the Net*, by Iris Murdoch. *A Kind of Loving*, by Stan Barstow, has: 'You say much more, Lewis, an' I'll wrap a bunch o' fives round your bloody neck.' Later in the same novel occurs: ' "How long have you known my daughter?" she says now, like a duchess asking a gardener for his references. I nearly expect her to say "Brown", but she doesn't call me by name all evening.' *Room at the Top*, by John Braine, has an office boss, who usually addresses his employees by their first names, say: 'Well, Lampton, we'll get our money's worth out of you before you go. . . .' Braine comments: 'The tone was supposed to be one of mock severity, but it came out vicious.'

Use of one another's last names by working-class boys and men, who normally use first names, can either be aggressive or joking. In normal social intercourse, however, last name usage to women is now very rare indeed, while its use amongst males has lessened to a dramatic extent on all sides. Telephone enquiries made in the late 1980s to staff common rooms of several English public schools, for instance, reveal that first names are commonly used amongst the students, while staff addressing them are likely to switch to first names as the students progress through the school. Members of the legal profession also use first names in modern times when they meet socially. The general change to first name usage has at least solved the problem of addressing men whose last name happens to be Love, Dear, Darling and the like, though such names may still, no doubt, sometimes be heard being yelled across the parade ground.

Last name, Brother Used to address a fellow-member of a trade union or guild, or a fellow Christian by evangelical preachers. Examples of the latter usage occur in e.g. *The Heart is a Lonely Hunter*, by Carson McCullers and *The Moonflower Vine*, by Jetta Carleton. In *The Pickwick Papers*, by Charles Dickens, Mr Humm, who is President of the Ebenezer

Temperance Association, addresses his fellow-member as Brother Tadger. He also uses this form to Brother Stiggins, who has come to address the meeting, though Brother Stiggins, thanks to Mr Weller, is in no fit state to speak about temperance, being decidedly drunk at the time. Also in this novel are examples of a legal use of 'Brother' + last name, when a judge addresses Brother Buzfuz and Brother Snubbin. The men addressed are both Sergeants, members of a superior order of barristers (abolished in 1880) from which Common Law judges were chosen. The judge himself would therefore have been a former Sergeant. The main modern usage of 'Brother' + last name is probably amongst trade unionists during formal meetings.

Last name, Lady Used to address the wife of a peer or a peeress in her own right. Lady Chatterley, one of the better-known if not better-understood literary bearers of such a title, is asked in *Lady Chatterley's Lover*, by D. H. Lawrence: 'And how would you like to be Mrs Oliver Mellors, instead of Lady Chatterley.' 'I'd love it,' replies Connie. Immediately prior to this Connie has remarked about her lover that 'I've never called him by name, which is curious when you come to think of it.'

Last name, little Not a standard mode of address, but made well-known in a literary context by Charles Dickens, in *Little Dorrit*. Amy Dorrit is about twenty-two years old when she meets Arthur Clennam and falls in love with him, but she looks much younger. She tells him that she should like to be called Little Dorrit 'better than any name'. Soon afterwards occurs: ' "Little Dorrit", said Clennam; and the phrase had already begun, between these two, to stand for a hundred gentle phrases, according to the varying tone and connexion in which it was used.' Another character in the novel, Flora, nevertheless thinks that 'Little Dorrit' is the 'strangest of denominations'. To Maggy, Amy is 'little mother'; to the turnkey's son, John Chivery, who is also in love with her, she is Miss Amy. In *Anglo-Saxon Attitudes*, by Angus Wilson, the central character Gerald Middleton is at one stage addressed as 'little Middleton': ' "What does it matter to you, little Middleton?" he said. Gerald, hearing the schoolboy form of address, thought, "He's drunker than I realized." '

Last name, Lord The polite form of address to a marquess, earl, viscount, baron, and life peer.

Last name, Master Formerly a manner of addressing men of high social rank or learning, especially those who held the academic title of Master of Arts. In Shakespeare's plays,

those men addressed in this way are also called 'Sir', and we have contemporary evidence that the term was a serious indication of respect. In *The Witch of Edmonton*, by Rowley, Dekker, and Ford, Thorney says: 'You offer, Master Carter, like a gentleman; I cannot find fault with it, 'tis so fair.' Carter replies: 'No gentleman I, Master Thorney. Spare the mastership; call me by my name, John Carter. "Master" is a title my father nor his before him were acquainted with. Such an one am I.' Shakespeare often has characters addressed as 'Master' + last name, though he is also fond of using 'Master' as a prefixed title before the name of a profession, to give: Master Schoolmaster, Master Constable, Master Steward, Master Tapster, Master Doctor, etc. Some of these terms show 'Master' beginning to become less seriously respectful and perhaps instead merely conventional. This process was to continue with 'Mister', which replaced 'Master' in the uses so far quoted by the eighteenth century. Meanwhile the use of 'young master', 'little master' to the sons of gentlemen led eventually to 'Master' becoming associated with youths, while 'Mister' became the adult term.

Until recently 'Master' + first name was usual for boys of good families when being addressed by those lower down the social scale. 'Master' + last name was also used. In Charlotte Brontë's *Jane Eyre*, for instance, the ten-year-old Jane asks John Reed, aged fourteen: 'What do you want?' 'Say "What do you want, Master Reed" ' he instructs her, reminding her that she is a family dependent. A better known literary youth is Charley Bates, in Dickens's *Oliver Twist*, whom the author unfortunately refers to constantly as Master Bates. Dickens clearly did not see the pun, though he created a merry character who would no doubt have enjoyed the joke.

Last name, Miss The polite social title of a young woman who is not married and is not entitled to be addressed by some other social or professional title, such as 'Lady' or 'Doctor'. Now often written as 'Ms', as is 'Mrs', so that the distinction between married and unmarried status is not clear. *The Philanderer*, by Stanley Kauffmann, has:

'Good morning, Russell,' she said. 'Morning, Rose.' This interchange of names was his caste mark. There were three grades of male employees at Tappan Publications: those men without secretaries; those men with secretaries who addressed them by their first names; and the highest group, whose secretaries addressed them as 'Mister' and were addressed as 'Miss'.

This would mean 'Miss' + last name, of course. Eliza Doolittle, in G. B. Shaw's *Pygmalion*, tells

Pickering: ' "Do you know what began my real education?" "What?" "Your calling me Miss Doolittle that day when I first came to Wimpole Street. That was the beginning of self-respect for me." Soon afterwards she says: 'I should like you to call me Eliza, now, if you would.' 'Thank you, Eliza, of course,' says Pickering. 'And I should like Professor Higgins,' adds Eliza, 'to call me Miss Doolittle.' 'I'll see you damned first,' is Higgins's rather ungallant reply.

Last name, Mr The 'Mr' was formerly an abbreviation of 'Master'. Between the late sixteenth century and the beginning of the eighteenth century the pronunciation of 'Master' when used before a family name slowly changed to 'Mister', and a new word was created, used as a prefixed social title for any man not entitled to be addressed by a superior social or professional title. There is a comment in Fowler's *Modern English Usage* to the effect that:

In Victorian days as soon as a girl put her hair up and wore long skirts and a boy went into tails they became *Miss Jones* and *Mr Smith;* and quite a long apprenticeship, perhaps even formal permission, was needed before they were *Mary* and *John* to each other.

This was equally true of the eighteenth century. Sophia Western, in Fielding's *Tom Jones,* may be in love with Tom, but she still addresses him as Mr Jones. Such usage may have continued after their marriage. In Laurence Sterne's *Tristram Shandy,* Mr and Mrs Shandy address each other by those terms. In Oliver Goldsmith's *She Stoops to Conquer,* Mrs Hardcastle resolutely addresses her husband as Mr Hardcastle, though he uses Dorothy to her. She quite clearly considers the more formal manner to be socially correct and fashionable, but there is also the point that when one has become used to addressing a person in a certain way, it can be difficult to change to something else. Mr Knightley and Emma, in Jane Austen's *Emma,* discuss the subject after they have declared their love for one another:

'You always called me "Mr Knightley", and, from habit, it has not so very formal a sound. And yet it is formal. I want you to call me something else, but I do not know what.'
'I remember once calling you "George", in one of my amiable fits, about ten years ago. I did it because I thought it would offend you; but, as you made no objection, I never did it again.'
'And cannot you call me "George" now?'
'Impossible! I can never call you anything but "Mr Knightley". I will not promise even

to equal the elegant terseness of Mrs Elton, by calling you Mr K. But I will promise,' she added presently, laughing and blushing, 'I will promise to call you once by your Christian name.'

Emma is thinking of the moment when she will say: 'I, Emma, take thee, George, etc.'

Men do seem to have found it easier to use a woman's first name. In *The Pickwick Papers,* by Charles Dickens, Mr Tupman draws his lady-love into a corner and begins: 'Miss Wardle! you are an angel.' After further declarations of this kind he says: 'Oh, Rachael! say you love me.' 'Mr Tupman,' says Rachael, 'I can hardly speak the words: but – but – you are not wholly indifferent to me.'

All the above examples concern middle-class speakers. These manners would have been imitated by upward-looking working-class families, anxious to be thought higher in the social scale than perhaps they were, but other families would have used first names freely, both to their own sex and between the sexes. When Fagin tries to address Bill Sikes as Mr Sikes, in Dickens's *Oliver Twist,* the latter is highly suspicious. 'None of your mistering,' he tells Fagin. 'You always mean mischief when you come that. You know my name: out with it.'

In the present century there has been a steady decrease in the use of 'Mr' + last name as a form of address. In *Our Man in Havana,* Graham Greene says: 'It was typical of Dr Hasselbacher that after fifteen years of friendship, he still used the prefix Mr – friendship proceeded with the slowness and assurance of a careful diagnosis.' This is, in fact, unusual, since male friends would more normally have used one another's last names without the prefix before first names began to be generally used. The latter were used socially in the USA before the habit spread to Britain. James Purdy, in *Eustace Chisholm and the Works,* has: ' "Well, do you want me to move out, Mr Haws?" Amos Ratcliffe said. "*Mr Haws,* chicken shit!" he roared at the boy. "Don't you talk up smart to me, you little snot. You'll Daniel me or you'll call me nothing." ' This is an extreme reaction, similar to that of Bill Sikes. An invitation to use the first name would normally be couched in gentler terms, or a speaker who wished to use a first name might check that it was all right to do so. 'Do you mind that I call you Aaron?' asks a man in *Aaron's Rod,* by D. H. Lawrence. 'Not at all,' replies Aaron, 'I hate Misters, always.' 'Yes, so do I. I like one name only.'

In business circles the situation could be rather different. Until very recent times the form of address used by the director of a company to his male employees might indicate with some precision their position in the hierarchy. In *Oneupmanship*, Stephen Potter suggested that Michael Yates would be Mike if he were a fellow-director, Michael if assistant director, Mr Yates if sectional manager, Yates if sectional assistant, Michael if an apprentice and Mike if night-watchman. Though meant humorously, Potter was making a serious point. Those in the middle of a professional hierarchy valued the politeness of the 'Mr'. Iris Murdoch makes the same point in *The Word Child:*

> Skinker, the messenger, came in. He was the only person in the office who called me 'Mr Burde'. The downstairs porters despised me and called me nothing. I was 'Burde' (or sometimes 'Hilary') for ordinary purposes. Skinker's 'Mr' was a tender attention which I appreciated.

Distinctions of this kind may still be made in some very traditional professional circles, but there has, on the whole, been a move towards the universal use of first names at all levels, except in sensitive circumstances.

Such circumstances might involve, for example, a white man addressing a black American. In the days of slavery the latter would never have been dignified as 'Mr' + last name: he was 'boy', or 'uncle' when old. He was obliged to do the mistering to white males, even when the latter were very young. In *The Web and the Rock*, Thomas Wolfe has a Negro addressing some twelve-year-old white boys as Mr Crane, Mr Potterham, Mr Webber, etc. This, says Wolfe, 'pleased them immensely, gave them a feeling of mature importance and authority'. This might be true, though the 'Mr' was being used, of course, because of the speaker's circumstances. It is a different matter in Arnold Bennett's *Clayhanger*, where a boy who has just left school is addressed as 'Mr' instead of 'Master' for the first time, to mark his adult status. The situation for American blacks has changed, as a passage in *Chesapeake*, by James A. Michener, illustrates very well:

> 'Mr Cater, we'd really like to have you . . .'
> 'Name's Absalom.'
> 'Goddamnit!' Steed snapped. 'I spent thirty years in Oklahoma disciplining myself to call you sons-of-bitches Mister. What do you want to be called? Negro, black, coloured – you name it.'
> Absalom laughed. 'My problem is to discipline myself to stop callin' you white-asses Mister. Now what in hell do you want, Steed?'

Steed here is doing what any reasonably sensitive speaker would do – using a polite form to a hearer who might interpret a too-ready use of a first name as condescension. In all such situations in real life it is probably better to admit the problem and ask the hearer how he wishes to be addressed.

There is a special professional use of 'Mr' + last name in British medical circles, discussed under **Doctor**. In *Whisky Galore*, by Compton Mackenzie, there is mention of a special reason for a speaker's reverting to 'Mr' + last name when he normally uses a first name: 'Extreme formality was always a sign that Alec Mackinnon was carrying a good load.' Perhaps this is akin to the cautious movements made by someone who has drunk too much.

In modern times, 'caution' rather sums up the rule for using the 'Mr' + last name form of address to a man encountered socially or professionally. If the hearer does not want or need such formality, he can say so without embarrassment, suggesting a friendlier form. Demanding a politer form of address is far more difficult. The man concerned may not do so, but if the form of address causes an underlying resentment, it will do the relationship little good.

Last name, Mrs It is normally a married woman who is addressed in this way, the last name being that of her husband. This adoption of the husband's last name is a social convention rather than a legal requirement, and in modern times an increasing number of women prefer to continue with their maiden names. Novelists rarely comment on the use of this ordinary social title, though Daphne du Maurier, in *Rebecca*, makes several points. She first has the young heroine of the book becoming excited at the prospect of changing her name: 'I would be Mrs de Winter. I considered my name, and the signature on cheques, to tradesmen, and in letters asking people to dinner.' The sentence 'I would be Mrs de Winter' is repeated many times. The heroine duly becomes Mrs de Winter, and indeed, is only known to the reader by that name, her first name and maiden name are not mentioned, but she is the second wife of Maxim de Winter. The fact that there was a highly successful first wife who bore the same name causes practical and psychological difficulties.

Many married women are exposed to name-sharing of another kind, since their mother-in-law will normally have the same social title as themselves. Married women who are known professionally before they marry by one name may continue to use that name for professional purposes, while using 'Mrs' with their husband's last name socially. This applies not only to actresses and writers, but to teachers and the like. In some cases a woman who has a professional title such as 'Doctor' will use that with her maiden name, though she may also prefix it to her married name. There are minor problems associated with the latter usage: a couple introduced at a medical convention as Mr and Dr Smith would lead other members of the medical profession to assume that the husband was a surgeon, though he might well be a layman.

The polite formality of 'Mrs' + last name may at times by insisted upon by either the speaker or the person being addressed. In *Memento Mori*, by Muriel Spark, a woman invites her housekeeper to address her in future by her first name. The woman concerned chooses to continue with 'Mrs' + last name to keep the relationship on a formal footing. In *The Earnshaw Neighbourhood*, by Erskine Caldwell, a black woman who is working as a home-help insists that her employer call her Mrs White, her married name. 'I never heard of such a thing before from a coloured woman,' is the comment that follows this from the white employer. Black Americans, however, are entitled, most people would say, to be sensitive about this issue. As Frank Yerby points out in *A Woman Called Fancy*, blacks were never normally addressed by polite social titles. 'The women are Mary Jane while they're young, and after that they're "Mammy" or "Auntie." '

In Britain, even unmarried female employees were usually addressed as 'Mrs', followed by their own maiden name, when they reached a certain age. In *Desperate Remedies*, by Thomas Hardy, Cytherea Graye becomes a lady's maid. Someone says to her: 'Mrs Graye, I believe?' 'I am not,' she replies, then corrects herself. 'Oh yes, yes, we are all mistresses.' Her employer nevertheless has the following conversation with her: ' "Now then Graye – By-the-bye, what do they call you downstairs?" "Mrs Graye," said the handmaid. "Then tell them not to do any such absurd thing – not but that it is quite according to usage; but you are too young yet." ' In *Below Stairs*, by Margaret Powell, there is a real-life account of such usage.

> Later on, after I had got to know her better, I said "Mrs McIlroy". The Mrs was just a courtesy title; most cooks, if they had not married and if they were a miss and they were getting on in years, were called Mrs not only by the people they worked for, but by the other servants as well.

When Margaret Powell herself became a cook to a Lady Gibbons, her employer decided that 'I was too young to be called Mrs. She called the other servants by their surnames, but I didn't like that, so we settled for "cook".'

A custom amongst the middle-classes of the eighteenth and nineteenth centuries was for husbands to call their own wives 'Mrs' + last name. The novels of the time make it clear that such usage was widespread; in modern times it might be done jokingly, or by a newly married husband playfully reminding his bride of her new status. In Edna Ferber's *Showboat* it occurs when the husband is especially angry with his wife: 'No more scum than your own

husband, Mrs Hanks, ma'am.' Normal polite use of 'Mrs' + last name by strangers occurs frequently: *The Limits of Love*, by Frederic Raphael, to take just one example, has fifty-one instances of such usage. When the rare authorial comment occurs, it is normally in circumstances where the woman concerned is being addressed as 'Mrs' for the first time, soon after her marriage. In *Up the City Road*, by John Stroud, there is the additional factor that the married woman is only sixteen years old. ' "Ah, well, that's that, then. You're Mrs Parsons now." *Mrs* Parsons? Oh, no! It sounded so *old*. And she hadn't hardly sort of – well, lived, really.'

Last name, Ms   In modern times 'Ms' is often written before a woman's last name. It avoids distinguishing her more precisely as either 'Mrs' or 'Miss', a distinction that many women feel is irrelevant. 'Ms' usually has the spoken form *Miz*, a pronunciation long heard in the southern states of the USA. Thus we find in *Gone With The Wind*, by Margaret Mitchell, Belle Watling saying: 'Please come in here and set with me a minute, Miz Wilkes.' This is to Melanie, wife of Ashley Wilkes. *War Brides*, by Lois Battle, has: 'Then an old Negro man in livery stepped up to her and doffed his cap. "Miz Cunningham?" he enquired politely. "Yes, I'm Mrs Cunningham." ' An article in *Psychology of Women Quarterly*, 11, by Kenneth L. Dion reported in 1987 that women who insist on the use of 'Ms' appear to be more achievement-oriented, socially assertive, and dynamic, but lack interpersonal warmth.

Last name + major   In the nineteenth century, when large families were more common than they are now, it sometimes happened that up to four brothers were in attendance at the same school at the same time. At public schools, such as Eton, where the boys were addressed by their last names, it became customary to distinguish such brothers by adding 'maximus', 'major', 'minor', and 'minimus' to their names. Pedantic schoolmasters were then likely to address them as Smith major, Peacock minimus, etc. Examples of such usage occur in *Dandelion Days*, by Henry Williamson, set not at Eton but in one of the many schools which imitated this practice. Amongst themselves boys often used an abbreviated form of the suffix. 'I say, Templeton mi, your brother's fallen for a skirt' is addressed to a Templeton minimus in *Tamahine*, by Thelma Niklaus. An alternative system used in some schools involved the use of 'primus', 'secundus', 'tertius', etc., after the last name (Latin 'first', 'second', 'third'). There were also schools which mixed these two systems, using a set such as 'major', 'minor', 'tertius'. In modern times it is unusual for there to be more than two brothers at school together – major and minor – and first names have tended to replace last names in many quarters.

Last name (part) 'You will be present on Friday, Boyns?' says one man to another in *The Old Boys*, by William Trevor. 'Yes, of course I shall,' is the reply, which continues: 'Incidentally, I must remind you that my name is Swabey-Boyns. I do not address you as Jar.' (He is speaking to a man whose last name is Jaraby.) In this case Jaraby is well aware that he is using only part of Swabey-Boyns's name. A genuine difficulty could arise if the modern equivalent of Swabey-Boyns was encountered, since he might well write his name as Swabey Boyns, without the hyphen. In *The Ginger Man*, by J. P. Donleavy, there is another example of a man addressed by part of his last name, in this case Danger instead of Dangerfield. This might be classed, however, as a nickname formed from the last name. *Like Any Other Man*, by Patrick Boyle, has a man named McCann addressed as 'Mac', a fate which probably befalls many men whose last names begin with 'Mac' or 'Mc'. The same man is addressed by another speaker in the novel as 'Mr Mac'.

Lawyer Lawyer is not normally used as a professional title in standard English, but the city attorney in *The Liberation of Lord Byron Jones*, by Jesse Hill Ford, is always referred to by the townspeople as 'Lawyer Hedgepath', and addressed in that way by many of them. This creation of a title is understandable for a man who clearly occupies an important professional position in the community, but has no accepted form of address which can be used in the same way as 'Doctor' or 'Reverend'. Another lawyer in the book mentioned above is also addressed as 'Lawyer' + last name, and one speaker says: 'Could you find out about the man they caught, Lawyer?' In *The Middle Man*, by David Chandler, a prostitute says: 'This is my career they're tearing apart, Mr Lawyer,' showing a nonce-name alternative where no true title exists.

Lazybones This term has been applied to a lazy person of either sex and of any age since the end of the sixteenth century. By that time 'bones' was occasionally being used for body in an expression like 'he ran as fast as his old bones could carry him'. 'Lazybones' is a mild expression: if the speaker wanted to emphasize someone's laziness he would probably employ an expression beginning 'you lazy . . .'.

Leader This was once used as a term of address to the driver of a horse-drawn vehicle. 'Keep the box for me, leader,' Sir Pitt Crawley tells the coachman, in *Vanity Fair*, by William Thackeray. The word might also be used to the player of the leading hand in a game of cards, or to the person acting as leader of any group of people. In Sophie Tucker's autobiographical account *Some of These Days*, for example, 'Go ahead, leader' is said by the singer to the leader of the orchestra.

Leaker *See* **Cry-baby**.

Leatherkicker A synonym of football-player, used by a wife to her husband in *A Salute to the Great McCarthy*, by Barry Oakley. During an argument she calls him 'creep', 'leatherkicker', 'peasant'. The man concerned is from a small town in the bush, now living in the city and working as a professional footballer. *See also* **Football-player**.

Lecher This term is used disapprovingly of a man who is constantly thinking about his sexual gratification. The word came into English from French, and is connected etymologically with modern French *lécher*, 'to lick'. In *Hotel*, by Arthur Hailey, the Duke of Croydon makes overtly sexual remarks to his wife. She becomes very angry and calls him 'you lecher'. *The Half Hunter*, by John Sherwood, has a man saying jokingly to a younger man: 'Fie upon you, you odious lecher.'

Leech 'You dirty leech' is said by an American woman to a man who is trying to collect money from her in *The Late Risers*, by Bernard Wolfe. The allusion is to the blood-sucking worm.

Legree, Massa A transferred name in *The Middle Man*, by David Chandler. A man says to a woman: 'Don't ever try to see my wife again.' We are told that the woman to whom this was addressed 'pretended to cower'. She then replies: 'Yassuh, Massa Legree, Ah sho won't.' Use of the name is an allusion to Simon Legree, the brutal owner of a cotton plantation in *Uncle Tom's Cabin*, by Harriet Beecher Stowe. He purchases Uncle Tom and allows his men to bestow a fatal whipping on him.

Liar Used on its own, or qualified by other words in vocative use. On its own it is used insultingly on two occasions in *The Country Girls*, by Edna O'Brien. 'You bloody liar' occurs in *Doctor at Sea*, by Richard Gordon, and this is expanded to 'you bloody little liar' in *Anglo-Saxon Attitudes*, by Angus Wilson. *Rebecca*, by Daphne du Maurier, has 'you damned half-witted liar'. A milder form of this particular accusation, often used by children, is 'you fibber'. When children do resort to 'you liar' they are likely to accompany the vocative with a chant. One such is quoted, rather surprisingly, in *Last Tango in Paris*, by Robert Alley:

'Liar, liar, pants on fire, nose as long as a telephone wire!'

Lickspittle A little used word referring to someone who is so sycophantic that he would lick someone's spittle from the ground. In occasional use since the seventeenth century, and alluded to by Howard Jacobson in *Redback*: 'someone had even hissed lickspittle at me'.

Liege, my Much used by Shakespeare as a term of address to a liege lord, the superior to whom one owes allegiance and service under the feudal system. Sometimes expanded by Shakespearean characters to: good my liege, my royal liege, my gracious liege, dear my liege, my sovereign liege, my most royal liege, etc. Shakespeare seems to use 'liege' simply as a synonym of 'lord'. 'My liege' might be used jokingly in modern times, by a woman pretending to be a vassal to her husband or lover.

Lieutenant Historically, a lieutenant is one who takes the place of another, especially a military officer who acts on behalf of a superior. The French words *lieu tenant* literally mean 'place-holding', and are the equivalent of the Latin *locum tenens*. 'Lieutenant' is much used vocatively in Shakespeare, notably in *Othello*, where Cassio is described in the First Folio as 'an Honourable Lieutenant'. He is addressed either as 'lieutenant' or 'good lieutenant' throughout the play.

In modern military usage, lieutenant as a naval rank for a commissioned officer is immediately below a commander. In the British army a lieutenant ranks immediately below a captain, as does a first lieutenant in the US army. 'Lieutenant' also occurs as a prefix to other military titles, as in 'lieutenant-colonel', where it indicates the rank immediately below the rank which is named afterwards.

In the American police force and fire department, a lieutenant ranks immediately below a captain. Examples of usage abound in military and American crime novels. In *The Magic Army*, Leslie Thomas comments on the reaction of American soldiers when hearing a British officer announce his rank, pronouncing the word in the normal British way as 'lefftenant'. American speakers would use 'lootenant', which is much closer to the French original. Scholars are unable to explain satisfactorily how the curious British pronunciation came about. *War Brides*, by Lois Battle, has a slightly unusual use of the title to an American army officer. He is certainly entitled to be addressed as 'Lieutenant', but the speaker is a very old friend, a former lover, who would normally use his first name. He tells her: 'You've been the best part of the whole trip.'

Her reply, 'Likewise I'm sure, Lieutenant' is presumably a light-hearted attempt to avoid over-seriousness creeping into the conversation, or reflects the common embarrassment at responding to a compliment.

Life, my Judging by the frequency with which this expression occurs in literature, it was once a common vocative used between lovers. The thought behind it seems to be 'that which gives me cause for living'. The *Oxford English Dictionary* quotes a thirteenth century use of it in a religious context, addressed to Jesus Christ. In Shakespeare's *Cymbeline* (5:v) occurs: 'O Imogen! My Queen, my life, my wife!' *The Vicar of Wakefield*, by Oliver Goldsmith, has Dr Primrose saying to his wife: 'Let us have one bottle more, Deborah, my life.' *David Copperfield* has the hero telling his loved one: 'Dora, my own life, I am your ruined David.' These passionate declarations may still be made in private, but they do not often find their way into modern literature.

Light, my Used as an endearment by a man to his wife in Arthur Miller's *All my Sons*. He addresses her as 'my love, my light'. The thought behind this, presumably, is that she is the light of his eye, as the old expression has it.

L'il Abner Used as a transferred name to a hayseed type in *A Salute to the Great McCarthy*, by Barry Oakley. The allusion is to the cartoon character from Dogpatch created in 1934 by Al Capp. In the novel mentioned above the vocative is used insultingly, though the original L'il Abner is handsome and in some ways admirable.

Limb, young In some English dialects, in former times, mischievous or wicked people were referred to as the devil's limbs. By the seventeenth century it was therefore possible to refer to a mischievous child as a limb. The term is applied to Oliver Twist in Dickens's novel of that name: 'Now listen, you young limb.' In *Dandelion Days*, by Henry Williamson, occurs: 'Young limb, what do ee think he did now?' This is addressed to a young boy by a Devonshire woman. The expression appears to have crossed the Atlantic, since Miss Ophelia, in *Uncle Tom's Cabin*, says to Topsy: 'What are you doing there, you limb?' The term is not used in modern times other than by elderly speakers.

Limey Originally applied to a British sailor or ship, later to any British person, the speaker usually being Australian, or American. The original expression was lime-juicer, a reference to the lime-juice which was served on British ships to combat scurvy.

Linesman An official in a football match and similar games who makes decisions about when a ball has crossed the line. He is addressed by his title, or as 'line'. If players or spectators are feeling especially friendly towards him they may address him as 'lino'.

Lingerer A decidedly literary vocative, unlikely to occur in normal speech. *Jane Eyre*, by Charlotte Brontë, has: ' "Jane!" called a voice, and I hastened down. I was received at the foot of the stairs by Mr Rochester. "Lingerer," he said, "my brain is on fire with impatience; and you tarry so long." ' In *The Monastery*, by Sir Walter Scott, 'ye lingerers' is addressed to a knot of beech trees which still bear their withered leaves rather late in the year.

Listeners Formerly used by presenters of radio programmes, but now usually avoided. Other radio vocatives include 'folks', 'fans'. 'Look who's just wandered in, listeners!' occurs in *The Sophomore*, by Barry Spacks.

little A frequent vocative element which can be either an endearment or an insult. It is an endearment, normally, when it is the first word of the vocative group, as in: little boy, little girl, little man, little lady, little one, little dear. Expressions like 'my little darling', 'my poor little child' are also affectionate. When 'you' is the first word of the vocative group the meaning of 'little' can change according to the other words used. Compare the following: you funny little girl, you little goose, you little nitwit, you poor little pigeon, you little rogue, etc., with you bloody little liar, you little squirt, you little cow, you little rat, you little whore, you little upstart, you snotty little beast, you stinking little foul mouth. In the latter examples 'little' is clearly meant to be offensive. Apart from the words that surround it, the tone of voice in which 'little' is uttered can change its meaning. 'Little man', used by one man to another, can be made to sound like a very unpleasant insult indeed. *The Diviners*, by Margaret Laurence, has:

'I think you're getting all worked up over nothing, little one.'
Morag withdraws.
'For God's sake, what is it *now*?' he asks, or states.
'Listen, Brooke – I wish you wouldn't call me that.'
'Call you what, for heaven's sake?'
'*Little one*. Brooke, I am twenty-eight years old, and I am five feet eight inches tall.'

This is a conversation between a husband and wife whose relationship is decidedly rocky. It is noticeable that in all the examples quoted above, 'little' is not replaceable by a synonym

such as 'small'. 'My small woman' does actually occur vocatively in Charlotte Yonge's *Heir of Redclyffe*, where a young man uses it to his sister: ' "Well, Amy, I give you joy, my small woman," said he, talking the more nonsense because of the fulness in his throat.' This looks very odd, and one cannot imagine its being said in modern times.

Loafer 'Get up, you lazy loafer,' says a woman to a man in *Like Any Other Man*, by Patrick Boyle. A loafer is one who loafs about, something which obviously has no connection with a loaf of bread. In Swedish *lofdag* means a leave-day or holiday: Dutch *verlofdag* has the same meaning. A loafer is therefore perhaps etymologically connected with someone who is on leave. The word seems to be popular with Irish writers. Patrick Boyle is Irish, and James Joyce, in his *Portrait of the Artist as a Young Man*, has a priest who calls a boy 'lazy idle little loafer'.

Lobster One man calls another 'you old lobster' in a friendly way in *Gideon Planish*, by Sinclair Lewis. It arouses no comment from the man so addressed or from the author and appears to be a nonce usage. 'Lobster' has no special meaning in American slang.

Logic, Mr A nonce name which occurs in Sheridan's *The School for Scandal*. 'Now, Mr Logic,' says Lady Teazle to Joseph Surface. She is asking by inference: 'what are you going to do about the fact that my husband is coming up the stairs?' A moment before, after a conversation in which Surface has tried to persuade her that she should be unfaithful to her husband because it would improve her relationship with him, she has said: 'if I could be persuaded to do wrong, it would be by Sir Peter's ill-usage sooner than your *honourable logic*, after all.'

Loobey *See* **Dawbake**.

Loon 'You old loon' occurs as a friendly vocative in *The Business of Loving*, by Godfrey Smith. Macbeth, on the other hand, is being insulting when he greets a servant as 'thou cream-fac'd loon'. For Shakespeare the word meant a worthless rogue, an idler, especially one of low birth. Later the word came to mean a clown or lout, though it could also be used of a man or boy without particular meaning. It was fitting that Shakespeare made Macbeth use the word, since it is thought to be of Scottish origin. It was in use by the mid-fifteenth century, having possibly come from Old Norse. In modern American slang there is the expression 'as crazy as a loon', which the editor of the *New Dictionary of American Slang* connects with the bird called the loon. The earlier name of the bird, however, was 'loom', and although its clumsiness and loud cry may have given rise to the American expression, it could have had nothing to do with the Shakespearean meaning of loon. To both British and American speakers, loon is strengthened in its association with craziness because it recalls words like 'lunacy', 'lunatic'.

Loony A shortened phonetic form of 'lunatic' used to mean a foolish person. 'Loony' could also be considered as a diminutive of 'loon', making that term more friendly. 'You old loony' is used by a young man to his friend in *At Arms with Morpheus*, by O. Henry.

Lord, my In modern times this form of address would be heard most frequently in a supreme court in Britain, addressed to a judge. It also remains the formal way of addressing a nobleman below the rank of duke, and a Roman Catholic bishop. There is an affected pronunciation of 'my lord', still occasionally used by some members of the legal profession although it has been mocked by writers such as Dickens. It is often written as 'm'lud' or 'me lud', and is pronounced, as someone once said, 'as near to *mud* as possible'. This courtroom usage underpins a scene in *The Mackerel Plaza*, by Peter de Vries, where the narrator finds himself being interrogated by some acquaintances, including a lawyer. When the questioning comes close to being a cross-examination he begins to use 'my lord' to the questioner. 'Everything in order there, eh, my lord?' He continues:

I spoke, despite the witticism, with my head somewhat atilt and with that high assurance that distinguishes the true martyr from the sullen scapegoat. The vocative was a kind of arm offered to help them up a step on to this higher plane, too, while also supplying a dash of irony we all needed, a bit of the garlic of parody rubbed on the strong meat of these proceedings.

A simpler version of all this is found in *Festival*, by N. J. Crisp:

'When I came on with the suitcase, I could hardly lift it. Some joker had put a couple of stage weights in it. I nearly ruptured myself.' His eyes lingered on Ben Stamford. 'Not guilty, my lord,' Ben Stamford said promptly.

The far more normal use of 'my lord' in a British courtroom context is found in, e.g., *Brothers in Law*, by Henry Cecil. In that particular novel, which has 217 pages in one paperback edition, ninety-five instances of 'my lord' occur, a great deal of the action taking place in court.

In *Bless me, Father*, by Neil Boyd, a Roman Catholic bishop is addressed as 'my lord'. Penelope Gilliatt, in *Splendid Lives*, has the

following: ' "What do you like to be called?" Ridgeway asked [the bishop]. "Well, you could try 'My lord', but I don't really care for it much in conversation, do you? It's a bit of a boulder. That leaves 'Dr Hurlingham' or 'Bishop'." ' Some noblemen who are entitled to be addressed as 'my lord' may share the bishop's feelings about its being a bit of a boulder, but they are likely to meet people who delight in using the vocative.

In *Vanity Fair*, by William Thackeray, occurs:

The old gentleman [Osborne] pronounced these aristocratic names with the greatest gusto. Whenever he met a great man he grovelled before him, and my-lorded him as only a free-born Briton can do. He came home and looked out his history in the Peerage; he introduced his name into his daily conversation, he bragged about his Lordship to his daughters.

The same novel has a comment on the use of the title to those who are not entitled to it: 'a swarthy little Belgian servant who could speak no language at all, but who . . . by invariably addressing Mr Smedley as "My lord", speedily acquired that gentleman's favour.' According to report, a lavatory attendant at a well-known London store follows a similar practice of addressing all his clients as 'my lord'.

Literary examples of 'my lord' addressed to noblemen occur in countless novels. In Shakespeare's plays there is usually someone who is so addressed. 'My lord–' begins the Earl of Northumberland, in *Richard the Second* (4:i), but Richard interrupts him: 'No lord of thine, thou haught insulting man,/Nor no man's lord; I have no name, no title -/No, not that name was given me at the font -/But 'tis usurp'd.' Often in Shakespeare the vocative expression is expanded to 'my dear lord', 'my good lord', 'my gracious lord', 'my noble lord', etc. It is frequently used by a wife to her husband, for – as Katherina says in *The Taming of the Shrew* (5:ii), 'Thy husband is thy lord, thy life, thy keeper,/Thy head, thy sovereign.'

In modern times 'my lord' is still sometimes used by a wife to a husband, either when the wife is in an especially submissive mood or is being playful. Examples of such usage occur in *Main Street*, by Sinclair Lewis and *The Business of Loving*, by Godfrey Smith (seven instances). Shakespeare joked about such usage, however, when used at the wrong social level. When Christopher Sly wakes up from his drunken stupor, and finds that he is being treated like a nobleman (Induction, *The Taming of the Shrew*), his supposed wife says to him: 'How fares my noble lord?' 'Are you my wife,' says Sly, 'and will not call me husband? My men should call me "lord"; I am your good-man.' 'My husband and my lord, my lord and husband,' says the page, acting the part of his wife. Wives have been referring to their 'lords and masters' with as much sincerity ever since.

Lordship, your An alternative form of my lord, used to British noblemen other than dukes, and to high court judges. There are examples of its use to noblemen scattered throughout the Shakespearean plays and the novels of the eighteenth and nineteenth centuries, especially those where a young heroine is finally claimed as his lordship's bride. There is an interesting example of 'your lordship' being addressed to a woman, the speaker's wife, in Mordecai Richler's *St Urbain's Horseman*. The wife is interrogating the husband about his activities, in such a way that he feels he is being subjected to a court-room examination by a judge: ' "Were you with her on this bed?" "I am not answering any more questions. I'm sick of answering questions." "Did she take you in her mouth?" "Yes, your lordship. No, your lordship." ' *See also* **Lord, my** for a similar usage outside a courtroom.

Lot, you A rather unflattering term addressed to a group of people and meaning 'all of you'. 'Come on, you lot! Hurry up,' says a schoolmaster to a group of boys in *Kes*, by Barry Hines. A speaker who was obliged to be polite to the group would certainly have had to use an alternative expression. Angus Wilson jokes pleasantly in *Anglo-Saxon Attitudes*, describing how Mrs Salad deals with her neighbours. 'They starts making' h'objections. I didn't lose my dignity. I just said, "You filthy trollopy lot." ' In *The Magic Army*, by Leslie Thomas, 'Come on, you lot' is said by an army sergeant to a group of men. In *Lanark*, by Alasdair Gray, a man says 'Hullo, you lot' to a group of children in a reasonably friendly way.

Lotus blossom 'My lotus blossom' is addressed by a man to a woman in *The Half Hunter*, by John Sherwood. He also calls her 'my flower', and perhaps 'lotus blossom' should be considered as merely a fanciful variant of that term. The lotus in ancient Greek stories was a fruit which caused its eater to become dreamy, but as a flower it normally refers to the Egyptian water-lily.

Louse The louse is a parasitic insect which infests human hair and skin. The word has been applied to human beings who are considered to be obnoxious since at least the seventeenth century. 'You unfaithful louse' is used as an insult in *The Half Hunter*, by John Sherwood. In *The Day of the Lotus*, by Nathanael West, the word forms part of a longer vocative group: 'you louse in a fright-wig, you'. The adjective 'lousy' also occurs in insulting voca-

tives. 'You lousy swine' is in *A Kind of Loving*, by Stan Barstow; *The Spy Who Came in From the Cold*, by John le Carré, has 'you lousy bastard'. The example of 'you lousy slut' which occurs in *The Business of Loving*, by Godfrey Smith, is an intimacy between lovers.

Lout 'Most sweet lout' is a term of address used by the Bastard in Shakespeare's *King John*. The word 'lout' may have been in use in the twelfth century, during King John's reign, but the *Oxford English Dictionary* is only able to date it from written sources in the sixteenth century. The word has the general meaning of 'country bumpkin', an awkward, clownish fellow, and the Shakespearean vocative use is unusual. 'You lout' is more normal, and is expressive of contempt. 'Liar! Lout! Thick-skulled farmer's boy!' says one boy to another in Henry Williamson's *Dandelion Days*.

Love Literary references, beginning with Chaucer, show that this term has been in use as an endearment since at least the fourteenth century. Originally it was used to a beloved person; in modern times, in Britain, it has become watered down into a friendly term used by men and women mainly to women and children, though in Yorkshire and across the Pennines a male bus-conductor, for instance, might easily address a male passenger as 'love'. Further north, 'hinny' and 'pet' replace 'love'.

Shakespeare's use of the vocative is always in its 'strong' sense, and addressed to a wife or other loved one. In *The Taming of the Shrew*, for instance, there are examples of: love, gentle love, my honey love; elsewhere in the plays one finds: sweet love, my dearest love, my love, etc. Lysander uses the last of these to Helena, in *A Midsummer Night's Dream*: 'My love, my life, my soul, fair Helena!' 'O excellent!' says Helena, convinced that he is making fun of her. This particular play, with its complicated twists and turns of relationships, contains a full catalogue of Elizabethan endearments, as well as genteel insults. Elsewhere, another Shakespearean lover says: 'Call me but love, and I'll be new baptiz'd;/ Henceforth I never will be Romeo.' Love is often used vocatively in the same play.

In *John Halifax, Gentleman*, by Mrs Craik, we find:

'Love' – John usually called her 'love' – putting it at the beginning of a sentence, as if it had been her natural Christian name – which, as in all infant households, had been gradually dropped or merged into the universal title of 'Mother'.

Mrs Craik's sentimentality is not attractive to the modern reader, but it is interesting that she recognized the role of vocatives in substituting for normal names.

There is a comment of a different kind in *Travelling People*, by B. S. Johnson:

It will have been noted that the word *love* has not been used in the narration of the relationship between Kim and Henry, save as a vocative endearment. Some explanation of this is desirable. Neither Kim nor Henry thought of themselves as 'in love' with the other, and if either of them had said 'I love you,' then the other would have immediately suspected insincerity. Yet there was love between them.

There follows an essay on the nature of love, but the interesting point here is the use of 'love' as a vocative to indicate a half-way stage between friendship and love in its full romantic sense.

The following letter, which appeared in the woman's magazine *My Weekly* some years ago, comments on the purely friendly use of love and similar terms: 'For some time now I've been taken to and from hospital twice a week by ambulance. This is a selection of names I've been given by the ambulance men: love, dear, dearest, pet, petal, sunshine, flower, bonnie flower, rosie, bonnie lassie.' The correspondent remarked that she was 91 years old, and thought that the use of such terms 'do more good than the doctor's medicine'.

It is pleasant to know that such vocative usage can be interpreted in the spirit in which it is meant; many women today seem to object to such terms being used to them. The issue was discussed in the pages of the *Guardian* newspaper in November 1987, when it was reported that a London borough council had compiled an inventory of terms 'which can be used offensively'. A columnist, Martin Wainwright, argued that 'love' was merely friendly, especially in the northern counties. In an angry reply, Marilyn Martin-Jones, a lecturer in the department of Linguistics at Lancaster University, said that

A term of endearment like luv can be used by both women and men to express intimacy or solidarity, or it can be used as a putdown. Most women can remember occasions when they have been attempting to make a serious point in conversation or in a meeting at work, and their contribution has been dismissed by a man in terms such as: 'Oh, come on, luv', or 'Don't worry, sunshine.' These practices are often below the level of consciousness. The writing of codes of practice represents an attempt to bring these practices above the level of awareness.

The attitudes referred to by the correspondent would of course remain, conveyed by tone of voice, facial gesture, and the like, even if the

vocatives were not used. Banning the use of vocatives (and *all* would have to be banned, since any one of them *can* be used as a putdown if said in the wrong way) would not change underlying attitudes.

The spelling 'luv', incidentally, has become commonplace in British English. It began as an attempt to indicate pronunciation by working-class speakers, but serves a useful function in distinguishing the term of address from the normal word. As we have seen, in some parts of Britain, 'love' is used by males to males. This usage also occurs in the theatrical profession. N. J. Crisp, in *Festival*, has a theatre director who uses 'loves' to address the entire cast, men and women. This would not be normal social usage in the south of England, where most people would assume that a speaker using 'love' to men was homosexual. *Jake's Thing*, by Kingsley Amis, has two male university colleagues talking to one another. One says: 'You've never fancied them [i.e. women] for an instant and you like them.' 'As you say,' replies the other, 'but Jake, love, you're depressing yourself.'

Lovebirds 'Come up for air, you lovebirds,' says someone to an amorous couple in *Mariana*, by Monica Dickens. In *Diamonds are Forever*, by Ian Fleming, James Bond and Tiffany Case are collectively addressed by the same term. The West African lovebird is a tiny member of the parrot tribe, but lovebird has been applied to various other species where a mating pair of birds show great affection. The vocative is one of a very small group of terms which applies to two people only, though 'two' may be included in the vocative group. 'Hey you two lovebirds' occurs in *Rabbit is Rich*, by John Updike. There is an unusual use of the singular 'lovebird' in *The Dream Team*, by Joe McGinnis. A couple have just been exchanging endearments and acting like lovebirds. A male friend interrupts them and says to the man: 'Let's go to the paddock, lovebird. It's time to look at our horse.'

Love-bucket A playful variant of 'lover' and similar words. An example occurs in *An American Dream*, addressed to a woman friend by a man. Some of the other vocative expressions used by Norman Mailer in this novel and elsewhere are rather idiosyncratic.

Love-dove An American mother uses this to her young son in *Letting Go*, by Philip Roth. It adapts lovey-dovey.

Lovely, my An extended form of 'my love', though making a comment on the appearance of the person addressed rather than the feelings of the speaker. Normally spoken to a child or young woman by a male speaker, with friendly intent. *Anglo-Saxon Attitudes*, by Angus Wilson, has: ' "The top of the morning to you, Johnnie. And to you, my lovely," he said to Elvira, who again did not answer. "Isn't she gorgeous?" he called to John, and left the office.' *The Limits of Love*, by Frederic Raphael, has: ' "The point is, let's go out and celebrate." "Lovely." "All right, lovely, it's a date." ' The vocative 'lovely' is addressed to a woman by a man.

Lovepie A variant of 'sweetie-pie' and 'cutie-pie', used between intimates. It is used by a man to a woman in *Travelling People*, by B. S. Johnson, but is less commonly found than the other ' –pie' examples, such as 'sweety-pie', 'honey-pie'.

Lover Normally used to an intimate partner, as in *Gideon Planish*, by Sinclair Lewis, where a wife uses it to her husband. It is used in exactly the same way in *The Storyteller*, by Harold Robbins. Variant usage is displayed in *The Philanderer*, by Stanley Kauffmann. A man addresses a male friend as 'lover', meaning that he is a successful ladies' man. Mrs Everna Zobell writes from Gosport, Hampshire, to say that locally 'lover' is used as a friendly term of address to a woman, along with 'my love'.

Lover, my An intimacy between lovers, but a friendly term of address in certain English regions, especially the south-west. Correspondents report on common use of the expression to a woman, especially, in e.g., Bristol and Cornwall, where the speaker is likely to be, as Mrs Judy Williams specified in a letter to the *Guardian* newspaper in November, 1987, a shopkeeper, dustman, or meter-reader.

Lover boy Used to a man or a boy who is thought to be particularly successful in attracting women. In *The Taste of Too Much*, by Clifford Hanley, a youth starts to call a classmate 'lover boy' because a girl has begun to show interest in him. 'Finally Peter said, in the manner of an indulgent parent wearied by a nuisance child: "You know, Sidney, if you loverboy just once more I'll bash your teeth back round your tonsils." ' *Like Any Other Man*, by Patrick Boyle, has a woman saying to her lover: 'Come on, lover-boy, what's keeping you?' A young black American prostitute, in *One Hundred Dollar Misunderstanding*, by Robert Gover, says to her client: 'I likes t'see you happy, Loverboy.' The term is used insultingly in *The Front Runner*, by Patricia Nell Warren, where a man yells at a homosexual male athlete: 'Hey, loverboy, whose girlfriend are you?'

Lover-man 'I've got a class, lover-man,' says a young teacher to her lover in *The Middle Man*, by David Chandler. 'Lover-boy' is the more usual term.

Lovey This is 'love' with a diminutive ending. It has been in regular use as an endearment or as a friendly vocative since the eighteenth century. A typical use, by a woman to a young boy, occurs in *The Pickwick Papers*, when Mrs Cluppins addresses Master Bardell. Eric Partridge, in his *Dictionary of Historical Slang*, says that the reduplicated form 'lovey-dovey' was used as an endearment in the eighteenth century. Examples of such usage are difficult to find. The word more normally occurs in third person reference to lovey-dovey couples. *See also* however **dovey**. In *War Brides*, an Australian addresses a young girl as 'lovey-ducks', combining two vocative elements.

lucky A fairly frequent vocative element, expressing the speaker's opinion of the listener's good luck. 'Rotten lucky pig' is used in a friendly way in *The Taste of Too Much*, by Clifford Hanley; 'lucky man' occurs in *Anglo-Saxon Attitudes*, by Angus Wilson; 'lucky dog' is in *A Kind of Loving*, by Stan Barstow; *The Limits of Love*, by Frederic Raphael has an example of 'lucky chap'; *Saturday Night and Sunday Morning*, by Alan Sillitoe, has 'lucky bastard'. All such expressions could equally well be preceded by 'you-'.

Lumpy *See* **Fatty**.

Lunatic An equivalent of 'you idiot', used to a person who is acting foolishly. The word derives from Latin *luna*, 'moon' and reflects the ancient belief that insane behaviour was dependent on changes in the moon. It is a word used by laymen, but strenuously avoided by anyone professionally connected with the mentally ill. 'You bloody lunatic' is used insultingly in *The Limits of Love*, by Frederic Raphael. Such an expression also occurs on public highways, as motorists express their opinion of other people's driving. 'Depraved lunatic', used by a schoolmaster, occurs in *Dandelion Days*, by Henry Williamson. 'You lunatic', spoken in the right tone of voice, can easily become a covert endearment, tacitly expressing approval of someone's foolish behaviour. In *Girls in their Married Bliss*, by Edna O'Brien, where one woman says to another who is on her knees, praying: 'Get up, you lunatic,' it is a term of friendly exasperation.

Lunkhead A colloquial American term for a blockhead. 'You lunkheads' is addressed to a group of soldiers by an NCO in the Laurel and Hardy film *Pack up your Troubles*. *The Middle Man*, by David Chandler, has one American saying to another: 'Don't you see, I loveya, lunk-head!' The origin of the term is obscure, but it may derive from 'lump-head'.

Luv *See* **Love**.

Lynx Used as a term of address by a man to his lover in *The Executive*, by Michael Fisher. Before the vocative is used we hear that 'she was like a suspicious and rather ferocious animal, I thought. "You look like a lynx," I told her.' In the course of their love-play the woman concerned bites the man. 'Damn you, lynx, that hurt,' he tells her. Later, at Christmas, he gives her a present. 'At last she got the wrapping off, lifted the lid and unfolded the wrapping paper. Inside was a lynx fur coat, which was smart and fashionable this season.' In case we have missed the point the author writes: 'I used to say you were a lynx. Now you really are one.' Few vocatives used by novelists get such heavy-handed treatment.

'm A reduction of 'madam' or 'ma'am' in an expression like 'Yes 'm,' used by servants to their mistress in the eighteenth and nineteenth centuries.

Ma A short form of 'Mama' or 'Mamma', normally addressed to the speaker's · mother. Usage began in the early nineteenth century, but the *Oxford English Dictionary* is able to cite evidence that it was considered a vulgarity and laughed at by the educated. In *The Newcomes*, by William Thackeray, Julia Sherrick addresses her mother as 'Ma', while remonstrating with her for addressing Mr Honeyman as 'Mr H.' Both of these vocative usages would have accurately placed the family for nineteenth-century readers. 'Ma' continues to be used in individual families. There are eleven examples in *Absolute Beginners*, by Colin MacInnes, and a further seven in William Golding's *Free Fall*, all addressed to the speaker's mother. In *A Fairy Tale of New York*, by J. P. Donleavy, there is a non-family use by a cab-driver to a woman who lets rooms. He introduces a young man to her by saying: 'He's all right, Ma, just back from college over in Europe.' When a similar thing happens in *South Riding*, by Winifred Holtby, the hearer takes it as an insult: 'He called her "Ma". She felt the insult to her wasted youth, her faded prettiness. Well – she was a Ma, wasn't she?' The most interesting comment on the normal family use of the word comes in *The Diviners*, by the Canadian writer Margaret Laurence. Miss Laurence has much to say on the vocative usage of her characters, and is clearly keenly aware of subtleties of usage.

'Hi, Ma,' Pique says. This *Ma* bit is new. It is as though Pique, at fifteen, has now decided that *Mum* sounds too childish and *Mother*, possibly, too formal. The word in some way is a proclamation of independence, a statement of the fact that the distance between them, in terms of equality, is diminishing, and the relationship must soon become that of two adults.

Ma'am A spelling which indicates a colloquial pronunciation of 'madam'. John Dryden makes it clear that such pronunciation was in early use: 'Madam me no madam, but learn to retrench your words; and say mam; as yes mam, and no mam, as other ladies' women do.

Madam! 'tis a year in pronouncing' (*Evening's Love*, 1668). M. Mare and A.C. Percival, discussing an eighteenth-century family in *Victorian Best-Seller*, remark: 'Her children stood in wholesome awe of her, and never thought of addressing her otherwise than as Ma'am to the end of her long life.' This was Charlotte Yonge's grandmother, wife of a vicar.

The *Daily Chronicle* reported in 1901 that 'the street-car conductors of Boston are compelled to address all their women passengers as "madam".' They are unlikely to have used that pronunciation. Their modern equivalents, and a great many American men, would use 'ma'am', pronounced 'mam', to women unknown to them, especially those women likely to be married. This is a particularly American habit, not used in Britain. The custom of addressing one's mother as 'ma'am' has also been retained in the USA amongst certain middle-class families. Whether it reflects 'wholesome awe', as in the case of Charlotte Yonge's grandmother, has a damaging effect on a vital relationship between mother and child, reflects social pretentiousness or is merely an almost unthinking social custom, are matters for psychiatrists and sociologists to think about.

The special use of 'Ma'am' in British court circles is discussed under **Marm**. There is a comment on the flattering use of 'ma'am' in John Steinbeck's *The Wayward Bus*, where a bus-driver is trying to get a young woman passenger to show interest in him: 'Carefully he made his smile a little respectful. "Man says you're going south on my bus, ma'am," he said. He almost laughed at that "ma'am", but it usually worked. It worked with this girl. She smiled a little.' *William*, by Irene Hunt, has a young boy address an adolescent girl who has just moved in next door as 'ma'am'. 'You don't have to say "ma'am" to me,' she tells him. 'My name's Sarah.' He replies: 'I was raised to say "ma'am" to older ladies.'

Mac, Mack Etymologically 'mac' means 'son' at the beginning of a name like 'MacInnes'. In vocative use to a stranger it is roughly the equivalent of 'man', though it is often more hostile than 'man' would be. 'There's such a thing as being a lady,' says a character in *The Wayward Bus*, by John Steinbeck. The passage continues: 'An edge came into her voice. "Look, Mac," she said, "I can play rough too." '

In J.D. Salinger's *The Catcher in the Rye* 'Mac' is used by a taxi-driver to his young male client, whom he also addresses as 'bud' and 'buddy'. In *Chuck*, by Carl Sterland, an American policeman says to two men in a car: 'Okay, buddy, out. Right now, out. You too, Mac.' In *A Salute to the Great McCarthy*, a novel by Barry Oakley which is set in Australia, a cinema attendant addresses a young male customer as 'Mac'.

Madam In the Middle Ages this was a title of great respect for a woman of the highest social rank, the equivalent of 'my lady'. The expression was borrowed from French, where *madame* had that precise meaning, 'my lady'. In the early seventeenth century the term was still highly valued. Hostess Quickly, of the Boar's Head, reminds Sir John Falstaff in *Henry the Fourth Part Two*, that he had offered to marry her, raising her in the social scale:

Did not goodwife Keech, the butcher's wife, come in then and call me gossip Quickly? . . . And didst thou not, when she had gone downstairs, desire me to be no more so familiar with such poor people, saying that ere long they should call me madam?

By the end of the seventeenth century a writer was complaining that use of this term had 'grown a little too common of late'.

During the eighteenth century it was much used by the middle classes amongst themselves, and by their servants. Women were capable of turning 'madam' into an expression of extreme contempt when using the term to one another, but expected to be given the title by their inferiors, especially once they had married. Samuel Richardson, writing in the 1740s, uses the expression 'to madam up', with special reference to young women who hear the title used to them for the first time. During the nineteenth century the social value of 'madam' continued to deteriorate and there was an increase in the derisive use of the term. An affected lady, a prostitute, or bold young woman could be referred to as 'a madam'. In direct address 'madam', in modern times, could still be used to a young girl who acts in an autocratic way, like 'a proper little madam'. By the end of the nineteenth century madam had also acquired a number of different pronunciations, some specifically connected with certain circumstances. For comments on the variants *see also* the articles on **Ma'am, Mam, Mum, Marm, Mem, Mim, 'm.**

The spelling pronunciation 'madam' has been retained for present-day usage in, e.g., hairdressers, restaurants, and certain shops, where it is used to almost any woman client. It is also used as a prefix to a number of titles, such as 'Madam Chairman', 'Madam Mayor'. The latter use, in semi-professional titles, is a matter of practicality, providing a useful indication of the sex of the title-holder where in former times it would always have been a man. The shop usage is also as much a matter of convenience as politeness. The greeting 'Good morning, madam' is a useful way of saying 'I work here and it's my job to serve you'. The vocative usage is a verbal signal that replaces the uniform that was perhaps formerly worn. Nevertheless, there are those who find it difficult to use a term like 'madam' to any woman, under any circumstances, because it appears to concede that the speaker is on a much lower social level than the person addressed. For Margaret Powell, who was in domestic service in Britain throughout her working life, not using 'madam' was like an emancipation.

One of the ladies I worked for was a Mrs Rutherford-Smith. One day she said to me, 'Margaret, you're a very good worker, and I like you, but you've got one failing and I hope you won't be offended when I tell you what that failing is. You never call me "Madam." ' And then she added, 'You know, Margaret, if I was talking to the Queen I should say 'Madam' to her.' I wanted to reply, 'Well, there's only one Queen but there's thousands of Mrs Smiths.' (*Below Stairs*)

By contrast, those who feel quite confident about their own social standing or professional level may use 'madam' with almost mock politeness. The woman so addressed, however, is no longer being put on a social pedestal. The office-colleague, friend or husband may be hinting that she is rather bossy. An example of such usage occurs in *The Middle Man*, by David Chandler: ' "Really kiss me," she demanded, and arched her neck. "Yes, madam." '

Madame In French this is the ordinary social title of a married woman, or an unmarried woman who has reached a certain maturity. In literature it sometimes represents a use of 'Madam', especially when the speaker has pronounced the word in the French style, with the stress on the second syllable. English-speakers are likely to use it as part of the social title of any foreign woman, not just a Frenchwoman. Thus a member of a visiting Chinese delegation might be addressed as *Madame* Chang, or more simply as *Madame*. Such usage presumably reflects the long-standing status of French as a diplomatic language.

Madcap Originally applied, in the late sixteenth century, to a mad person, a maniac, but the meaning softened until, by the nineteenth century, the word referred to someone who was impulsive and lively, especially a girl. 'You madcap' is said by a girl to her sister in *Lost on Dress Parade*, a short story by O. Henry.

Madman 'You bloody madman' occurs in *The Hiding Place*, by Robert Shaw, but the expression is used almost admiringly. Compare 'you lunatic' and 'you idiot'.

Madonna This was formerly a way of addressing an Italian lady, though the word is now used to describe, or address in prayer, the Virgin Mary. It is used by the fool in Shakespeare's *Twelfth Night* to address his mistress, Olivia, on several occasions. Inasmuch as it is only ever used by one character to address a particular person, it resembles 'Nuncle', used by the fool in *King Lear* to his master.

Madre This Italian word for 'mother' would not normally be used in English as a term of address, but its use is suggested in *The Actor*, by Horace Annesley Vachell. A former governess has become the step-mother of children who then discuss that to call her. 'Of course, we can't call you "Mummy", can we?' 'No, no. "Mummy" and "Mother" are such sacred words. Perhaps, darling, you might call me "Madre" . . . It would be such a nice affectionate name for me.'

Maestro The Italian word for 'master', used mainly in the musical world to address an eminent conductor, composer or musician, especially one who teaches others. The word has been used both in third person reference and vocatively in English since the end of the eighteenth century. A rare use outside the world of music occurs in *Pygmalion*, by G.B. Shaw. Nepommuck greets his former teacher Professor Higgins with this term.

Maggot In the late seventeenth or early eighteenth centuries, a maggot or maggot-pate described a whimsical or capricious person. A modern speaker would think only of the small worm-like creature, the grub of a fly. The man who calls another 'you mean little maggot' in *Like Any Other Man*, by Patrick Boyle, clearly means it contemptuously, though the term is not in general use.

Maid In modern English maid refers to a female servant, but 'maid' would not normally be used as a professional title. In Shakespeare's time 'maid' was far more often used in its general sense of a young, unmarried girl, a virgin. Girls in the Shakespeare plays are thus frequently addressed as: maid, fair maid, good maid, dear maid, kind maid, sweet maid. Occasionally 'maiden', the fuller form of the word, occurs. Thus in *All's Well That Ends Well* (2:i) the King says to Helena: 'We thank you, maiden!' A few lines later he says: 'Fare thee well, kind maid.' This general use of maid survived in some English dialects. 'My good maid' is addressed to a girl in Thomas Hardy's *The Mayor of Casterbridge*, for example. In *The Dream of Fair Women*, by Henry Williamson, a Devonshire man says to his wife: 'Now, don't 'ee fret 'eeself, my maid.' The novel was published in 1919, but the expression might still be heard in the West Country. *Seven Little Australians*, by Ethel Turner, a children's story published in 1894, has a male visitor calling a ten-year-old girl 'my little maid'.

Maidy The diminutive of 'maid', which appears to have been used as a prefix in vocative groups. *The Trumpet Major*, by Thomas Hardy, has Benjamin Derriman calling a young woman 'maidy Anne'. Another speaker later says to her: 'Have ye heard about the King coming, Miss Maidy Anne?'

Majesty, your An honorific title used when addressing a king, queen, emperor, or empress. Used in England since the seventeenth century. Henry VIII and Elizabeth I were addressed as 'your Grace' and 'your Highness'. In the dedication to the Bible of 1611, James I is both 'your Highness' and 'your Majesty'. In modern Britain it is customary to address the Queen as 'your Majesty' at the beginning of the conversation, then continue with 'ma'am'. In ordinary life, 'your Majesty' is used to a man or woman who is behaving in what is thought to be a regal way, usually with sarcastic intentions on the part of the speaker. Special circumstances can also bring about its use. In *A Salute to the Great McCarthy*, by Barry Oakley, a conversation runs:

'You look as if you've been in that bed all your life.'
'I pricked my finger with a needle, you see.'
'I am no prince, your majesty, but a common huntsman.'
'Perhaps your quarry is near. I told you to sit down.'

The speakers are of course alluding to The Sleeping Beauty fairy tale. In *Pinktoes*, by Chester Hines, we have: 'And now, Mrs Mamie Mason, or rather I should say, Your Majesty (toothy smile) . . .'. The woman to whom this is addressed has been elected queen of a masked ball.

Major In Britain the title of an army officer of middle rank. In the USA also an air force and marine corps title. In original military use it was a suffix, part of the rank indicated by 'sergeant-major', previously a much higher rank than now. It had the general meaning of 'senior', as it does in certain British boys' schools where two brothers who are in attendance simultaneously may be distinguished as Smith major and Smith minor. 'Major' should only be claimed as a title by someone who holds, or previously held, the military rank, but at one time it was appropriated by many who were not entitled to it. As a writer in the *Southern Literary Messenger* (1852) put it: 'Every man who comes from Georgia is a *major*.' Sinclair Lewis commented on this phenomenon in *Babbitt*:

> Your Father was taking us to church and a man stopped us and said "Major" – so many of the neighbours used to call your Father "Major"; of course he was only a private in The War, but everybody knew that was because of the jealousy of his captain and he ought to have been a high-ranking officer.'

Lewis continues:

> 'Well, the man – Captain Smith they used to call him, and heaven only knows why, because he hadn't the shadow or vestige of a right to be called "Captain" or any other title – this Captain Smith said, "We'll make it hot for you if you don't stick by your friends, Major." '

See also **Colonel**, yet another military title that was formerly misused. Lewis gives another indication of the common use of Major in his *Main Street*, where he remarks that 'everybody called him Major, but that was presently shortened to Maje . . .'

Mam Either a regional variation of 'Mum', used to the speaker's mother, or a variant of 'ma'am', from 'madam'. There are four examples of the former usage in *Saturday Night and Sunday Morning*, by Alan Sillitoe, along with vocative expressions such as 'good owd Mam' and 'our Mam'. As a form of 'madam', 'Mam' occurs in *The Country Girls* and *Girl with Green Eyes*, both by Edna O'Brien and *Daughters of Mulberry*, by Roger Longrigg.

Mamma, Mama These terms have been used by English speakers since the sixteenth century to address their mothers. In Britain it tended to be in middle and upper-class families where a child used 'Mamma' or 'Mama', stressing the second syllable. It was this pronunciation, presumably, which led to the short form 'Ma'. In the USA these words were usually stressed on the first syllable, leading to 'Momma' as a variant spelling, and 'Mom' as a short form. Both 'Mamma' and 'Mama' still appear to be used: they occur in relatively modern literary texts, but they are much less common now than they were. 'Mamma' occurs three times in *Daughters of Mulberry*, by Roger Longrigg, spoken by an English woman. There are a further six examples of 'Mamma'

in the novel where the speaker is French. Nine examples of 'Mama' are in *The Limits of Love*, by Frederic Raphael, though others in the same novel use 'Mum', 'Mummy', and 'Mother'. Three more examples of 'Mama' occur in *Within and Without*, by John Harvey, though 'Mother' is used vocatively more frequently. Like all the 'mother' words, 'Mamma' and 'Mama' are sometimes used by a husband to his wife if they have children. 'Mamma' is used in this way in the presence of the children in Charlotte Yonge's *Heir of Redclyffe*. In a more recent novel, *The Storyteller*, by Harold Robbins, a husband uses 'Mama' to his wife.

A particular use of 'Mamma' occurs in Charlotte Brontë's *Shirley*, where a daughter says: 'Mamma, I have slept so well.' This is said to a woman who has only just revealed to her daughter their true relationship. Until now she has always been addressed by her daughter as 'Mrs Pryor', 'ma'am', etc. On being addressed as 'Mamma' for the first time 'Mrs Pryor rose with a start, that her daughter might not see the joyful tears called into her eyes by that affectionate word.' 'Mamma' is also one of those words which can, or cannot, be used to a step-mother. *Wives and Daughters*, by Mrs Gaskell, has:

> The question of the name by which Molly was to call her new relation had never occurred to her before. The colour flushed into Molly's face. Was she to call her 'mamma'? – the name long appropriated in her mind to someone else – to her own dead mother. The rebellious heart rose against it. 'Oh, papa! must I call her "mamma"?' 'I should like it,' replied he. 'Why shouldn't you call her "mamma"? I'm sure she means to do the duty of a mother to you.'

Mammy This is sometimes a variant of 'Mamma' or 'Mummy', used to the speaker's mother. There are many examples of such usage in *The Country Girls*, by Edna O'Brien; also in *When the Boat Comes In*, by James Mitchell. One of Al Jolson's best-known songs began: 'Mammy, how I love yah, how I love yah, my dear old Mammy.' 'Mammy' was also formerly used, especially in the southern American states, to a nanny. *Gone With The Wind*, by Margaret Mitchell, contains a loving portrait of Scarlett O'Hara's mammy, who is always addressed by Scarlett in that way:

> Mammy emerged from the hall, a huge old woman with the small shrewd eyes of an elephant. She was shining black, pure African, devoted to her last drop of blood to the O'Haras, Ellen's mainstay, the despair of her three daughters, the terror of the other house-servants.

'Dear Mammy' is also found in George Eliot's *Scenes of Clerical Life*, addressed to a nanny.

Man A commonly used vocative by mainly working-class speakers, usually addressed to an adult male but in many varieties of English addressed also to women. The latter usage shows that the semantic content of the word can be entirely forgotten, the word being used unthinkingly as a kind of oral punctuation. American speakers use the term more than British speakers of English, which may reflect interference from Spanish, where *hombre* is commonly used.

Black Americans and British speakers of Caribbean origins appear to use the word vocatively more than other groups, though it is also very frequent in, e.g., Wales, and English regions such as Tyneside. Welsh pronunciation of man often leads to its being written as 'mun'. *Fares Please*, by Edith Courtney, has: 'Penny tossed her head. "They gave you a black eye." He touched the great purple and yellow bruise gently, then winced. "It hurts, mun." ' 'Mun' is used like this to women as well as men throughout the novel. A correspondent writes from Newcastle to say: 'It is very common to address all and sundry (including women and children) as "man". Sometimes the Christian name is added, with occasional bizarre effect, e.g. one tiny girl yelling to another: "Come on, man Gloria!" ' *Bhowani Junction*, by John Masters, has an Anglo-Indian speaker saying: 'Mavis, what are you doing here, man?' Other women in the book are addressed in a similar way. Used by middle-class speakers, 'man' is often used by a socially or professionally superior to a junior, especially if the speaker is irritated with the hearer. 'Wake your ideas up, man!' might be an army officer addressing a soldier.

Vocative usage can sometimes become very close to being purely exclamatory. In *Travels with Charley*, John Steinbeck reports a conversation in which a speaker says to him: 'Man, oh man, you going to see something. Man, oh man, you never heard nothing like it when they get going.'

As the head-word in a vocative group, 'man' reverts to its generic role and is neutral, the overall sense of the vocative expression being conveyed by preceding elements. 'You coarse man' is used jokingly by a woman to a man in *A World of Difference*, by Stanley Price. 'You terrible man' and 'you silly man' are used in a friendly way by a nurse to a hospital visitor in *Resolve This Day*, by Geoffrey Bainbridge. *Thirteen Days*, by Ian Jefferies, has a typical expression used by an NCO to a soldier: 'you idle, dozy, lazy, dirty man'. This of course would normally be followed by the enquiry: 'What are you?' and the reply: 'An idle, dozy, lazy, dirty man, sergeant.' 'You naughty man' is

used by Miss Wardle to Mr Tupman in *The Pickwick Papers*, by Charles Dickens, and we can be sure that Mr Tupman was delighted to be so called. Expressions like 'good man', 'lucky man', 'you poor man', etc., are common.

'Little man' is sometimes used flatteringly to a young boy, as in the once popular sentimental song: 'Little man, you've had a busy day.' It is used to a child in James Joyce's *Dubliners*: 'My little man! My little mannie! Was 'ou frightened, love? There now, love. There now, Lambabaun! Mamma's little lamb of the world!' 'Little man', however, can be used insultingly to a man who is either physically little, or is of little importance or significance. *See also* **Man, my** and **Man, old**.

-man Added by some speakers to professional descriptions in order to form a vocative. It is sometimes redundant, as in 'sailorman', 'soldierman', where 'sailor', 'soldier' would serve equally well. It is also added to words which would not normally be used as vocatives, e.g. 'reporterman'. Such words are also converted into nonce names, of the 'Mr Reporterman' type.

Man, my In this expression 'my' is used condescendingly rather than in its usual friendly way. There is a tacit assumption that the speaker is of a higher social rank than the person addressed, or in a position to give that man orders. In *Our Mutual Friend*, by Charles Dickens, the landlady of the Six Jolly Fellowship Porters tells Riderhood: 'I am the law here, my man, and I'll soon convince you of that, if you doubt it at all.' In Compton Mackenzie's *Whisky Galore* we have: ' "Look here, my man, don't try to be funny with me," Major Quiblick snapped.' In *Diamonds are Forever*, by Ian Fleming, James Bond deliberately uses the expression to someone who is temporarily acting as a chauffeur, but who certainly does not consider himself a menial: ' "Thank you, my man," said Bond cheerfully, and had the satisfaction of seeing the smile vanish as the driver turned and walked quickly away.' The vocative is sometimes expanded to 'my good man', but this remains both condescending and rather old-fashioned.

Man, old Normally used in a friendly way by middle-class men, especially British men of that type, to other men. In frequent use from 1920–1950, but now less often heard. In fifty representative British novels dealing with life from 1920 onwards, eighty-two examples of old man occurred where the speaker's intention was clearly friendly. There was also one instance of 'old man' used insultingly.

The expression becomes insulting when 'old' switches from its meaning of 'familiar' and is used to refer to age. 'Oh, yeah, you're gonna whip me, old man?' says a Los Angeles police-man to an old man, in *The Choirboys*, by Joseph Wambaugh. 'What gives you that idea, you old man?' says one man to another in *Moviola*, by Garson Kanin. This is during a conversation which began with friendly intentions, but which becomes steadily more aggressive. The speaker who uses 'you old man' is soon using 'you old fart'. Evelyn Waugh, in *Vile Bodies*, has a woman saying to a waiter: 'What's the name of the Prime Minister, you stupid old man?' Such usage is exceptional rather than the rule.

In *The Watch that Ends the Night*, by Hugh MacLennan, a father regularly uses 'old man' to address his student son in a friendly way. Between friends the expression is used in, e.g., *Room at the Top*, by John Braine (nine instances); *The Spy Who Came in From the Cold*, by John le Carré (four instances); *The Heart of the Matter*, by Graham Greene (thirty instances). Perhaps a more important statistic is that 'old man' occurred at least once in twenty of the fifty novels mentioned above. The fullest comment on its use comes in J. B. Priestley's *Bright Day*:

'Any particular reason, old man?' (And this 'old man' of his had a peculiar light glancing tone of its own. It didn't suggest, wasn't meant to suggest, that he was fond of you, that you were old friends, but hinted at a smooth and easy and metropolitan comradeship, turning you into a man-about-town too).

Manager Not normally used as a vocative to one who manages a business, sports team, etc., but it is used to a bank manager by one of his staff throughout *Like Any Other Man*, by Patrick Boyle. The bank manager concerned is not like other bank managers, as it happens, being known for his ability to drink great amounts of alcohol, for his physical strength, and for his attraction to women. The novel is set in Ireland.

Maniac This is often used in modern times of someone who does things in an erratic, uncontrolled way, as in 'He drives like a maniac.' The word is used vocatively by people who are affected by such behaviour, though there must be countless cases where bad drivers do not actually hear the 'you maniac' addressed to them by those they have just offended. In *The Hiding Place*, by Robert Shaw, 'little maniac' is twice used as an endearment, following the usual process whereby an insult can be 'converted'. 'Maniac' is a curious word to use in such circumstances, since it implies irrational behaviour that is decidedly dangerous to others.

Mannie A diminutive of 'man' occasionally

found in dialectal use. Often addressed to a young boy, as in R. L. Stevenson's *Kidnapped*: 'What'll like be your business, mannie?' 'My little mannie' occurs in James Joyce's *Dubliners*. In *The House with the Green Shutters*, by George Douglas, a father says to his son: 'It'll keep, my mannie, it'll keep.' Yet another Scottish example of the vocative is in Lillian Beckwith's *The Hills is Lonely*, set in the Hebrides. An artist tells a local man that he would like to paint him. The Hebridean says: 'Wee mannie, if you dare to lay a brush on me I'll kick the pants off you.'

Marine In *The Front Runner*, by Patricia Nell Warren, 'you big, stupid Marine' is addressed by a young homosexual man to an older homosexual man who has just struck him. The man addressed is a former marine; the speaker seems to consider that the display of physical violence is marine-like behaviour.

Marm A spelling which represents a special pronunciation of 'Madam', via the colloquial form 'Ma'am'. The *Oxford English Dictionary* quotes Lord Lytton, *circa* 1850: ' "Well, Marm–" Mr. Cotton preserved that broad pronunciation of the ellipsis *Ma'am*, from *Madame*, which was formerly considered high bred, and is still the court mode.' This usage was imitated to some extent in the USA, as occasional instances of the 'marm' spelling indicate, especially in nineteenth-century sources. The expression 'schoolmarm', occasionally 'schoolma'am' in early use, appears to indicate that this pronunciation was favoured by certain school-teachers, especially those of a pedantic or priggish nature if one is to judge by the later associations with 'schoolmarm'.

'Marm' might still be used in modern times to address a woman who was acting in a schoolmarmish way, attempting to treat other adults like children. In some American dialects, 'Marm' has for at least a century represented a pronunciation of 'Mama' or 'Mamma'. This may partly have arisen because children in some middle-class families addressed their mothers as 'Ma'am', leading to a certain amount of confusion between the two terms. On the question of addressing the Queen, old-fashioned speakers might still use the pronunciation 'Marm' referred to by Lord Lytton, but recent manuals, such as the *Longman Guide to English Usage* by Sidney Greenbaum and Janet Whitcut, recommend 'Mam'.

Marmee A phonetic spelling of 'Mammy' which is used in *Little Women*, by Louisa M. Alcott.

Marrow A word meaning 'fellow-worker', 'mate' which survives in some north-eastern English dialects, especially in the Tyneside area. It is usually pronounced as if written 'marrer' or 'marra'. The word is first recorded in English in the fifteenth century, and is thought to be of Scandinavian origin, though the original word has not been traced. In Scotland the word can also mean 'one's equal in a contest' and 'a husband or wife'. Some would say, of course, that these two definitions refer to the same person. W. Hamilton, in *Braes of Yarrow* (1724) has: 'Busk ye, busk ye, my bony, bony bride, Busk ye, busk ye, my winsome marrow.'

Marshal In modern times this title is most used to American law officers, either of a judicial district or a city, whose duties are similar to those of sheriffs. The head of a city police force or fire department may also be a marshal in the USA. Historically, the Lord Marshal was a high officer of state, in charge of a king's military forces. Today a Lord Marshal spends more time arranging ceremonies, such as coronations. In military circles the marshal has become the field marshal, a general officer of the highest rank. All this obscures the original meaning of 'marshal', which was 'mare-servant'. He was a man who had control of the royal stables and horses. He then became the man in charge of mounted soldiers, the cavalry, and from there took command of all military forces.

The modern meanings of 'marshal' mostly reflect the idea of a watered down 'state official', watered down in the sense that a marshal today is not quite the key figure he was in medieval England. In Shakespeare's *Richard the Second* (I:iii) 'marshal' is used vocatively to a Lord Marshal. 'Lord Marshal' itself occurs in *Henry the Fourth Part Two* (I:iii). In *The Middle Man*, by David Chandler, 'marshal' is used to a modern American official, one who speaks to a lawyer 'with the calm assurance of a high court justice'.

Martyr This word does not normally occur vocatively, but in *Mountain of Winter*, by Shirley Schoonover, a man who is recovering from a bad hangover is being made to take a sauna bath. 'Put me on the cross, why don't you? Finish me once and for all,' he says to the woman who is forcing him to stay in the steam room. 'And here's your crown of thorns, martyr,' the woman replies, beating him with a bath whisk. A martyr normally would be one who suffers death because of religious beliefs, but the word is used more loosely of those who undergo any kind of severe suffering.

Mary Charles Dickens has an example of this being used as a transferred name to a girl whose name is unknown in one of his *Sketches by Boz*, 'Gin shops':

'Gin for you, Sir?' says the young lady when she has drawn it . . .

'For me, Mary, my dear,' replies the gentleman in brown.

'My name an't Mary as it happens,' says the young girl . . .

'Well, if it an't, it ought to be,' responds the irresistible one; 'all the Mary's as ever I see, was handsome girls.'

In his book *The Cockney* (1953), Julian Franklyn remarks that small girls are still addressed as 'Mary'.

Massa A spelling of 'Master', used to indicate the sub-standard pronunciation of that word by, e.g., Negro slaves, black African servants. There are examples of its use in *The Heart of the Matter*, by Graham Greene.

Master Used as both a social and professional title, though the social use is now rare. It survives in Scotland, where the heir apparent of a Scottish peer is addressed as 'Master'. Formerly, especially in rural dialects, 'Master' was used as a term of respect to a stranger if he appeared to be a gentleman. Henry Williamson gives examples of such usage in Devonshire in the early part of the twentieth century in *The Dream of Fair Women*. 'Turrible hot weather, measter' is spoken by a local man to a visitor in a pub, the 'measter' spelling indicating dialectal pronunciation. Thomas Hardy's *The Mayor of Casterbridge* has 'maister' being used by yokels to farmers and their sons, the latter sometimes becoming 'young maister'. Slaves usually addressed their owners as 'Master', but once again authors use variant spellings, such as 'Marster' in Mark Twain's *Pudd'nhead Wilson*, to indicate sub-standard pronunciation. *Resolve This Day*, by Geoffrey Bainbridge, has a black African servant girl addressing her white employer as 'Master'. This kind of usage is sometimes mockingly copied by women addressing their lovers or wives addressing their husbands, especially if the latter begin to act as if they are slave owners rather than equal partners. As it happens, 'Master' was at one time regularly used by wives to husbands as a perfectly normal term of address in certain parts of England, such as the north east. This practice continued at least until the beginning of the nineteenth century.

In *Room at the Top*, by John Braine, a man uses 'Master' to his office boss with sarcasm. There is very similar usage by an American newspaper man in *The Late Risers*, by Bernard Wolfe. As a professional title, 'Master' might be used to the captain of a merchant vessel, as in the opening scene of Shakespeare's *The Tempest*. *Brothers in Law*, by Henry Cecil, has fourteen examples of 'Master' being used in a legal context, there being several legal functionaries, such as the Master of the Rolls, Master of the King's Bench, etc., who bear the title.

'Master' is also the title of the elected head of certain colleges and institutions. C. P. Snow has forty-five instances of 'Master' being used to the head of a Cambridge college in *The Affair*, though in his novel *The Masters*, which is about the contest between two men for the mastership of a college, he uses this vocative only once. Early in the novel we are told that one of the candidates 'would love to hear himself being called Master'. On the final page of the novel, with the result of the election known, we have:

'Will you dine with us tomorrow–' Jago paused, and then brought out the word – 'Master?' He had got through it. He scarcely listened to Crawford's reply. He raised his glass as Gay proposed the health 'of our new Master'. Jago did not speak again.

This is an outstandingly dramatic, and successful, literary use of a particular vocative.

It is difficult to decide whether it is a social or professional title, but in *The Devil on Lammas Night*, by Susan Howatch, a modern witch uses 'Master' to address a man who is supposed to be the incarnation of the devil. When it was much used as the equivalent of 'sir', 'Master' had a plural form which was roughly equivalent to 'gentlemen', namely 'my masters'. The latter is usually heard in modern times as part of the quotation from Nicholas Breton: 'A mad world, my masters.'

Matchstick *See* **Spindleshanks.**

Mate The original meaning of this word was 'one with whom one shared meat', but it has long had the more general sense of 'companion', 'friend'. It is a very commonly used vocative in British English amongst working-class speakers. It is often used to address a stranger in a friendly way, and indeed, is probably more used to strangers than it is to genuine mates, or friends, of the speaker. 'Mate' is occasionally used by a woman to a man, and perhaps a wife to a husband. In the latter case there may be an intentional reference to mates in the sense of a male-female pair, though 'mates' in this context usually refers to animals rather than to people. 'Mate' is also the professional title of a ship's officer, and there is little doubt that the general use of 'mate' began with sailors.

The true vocative that derives from 'mate' is the diminutive 'matey', which is normally friendly but upsets the hero of Alan Sillitoe's *Saturday Night and Sunday Morning*. ' "I hear you drink a lot, matey." Arthur didn't like being called "matey," it put his back up straight

away.' It is normally used to men, though in Ngaio Marsh's *Opening Night* the encouraging message 'Keep your pecker up matey' is written to a young girl. 'You'll do, mateys,' is said by a farmer to a group of men in *A Cack-Handed War*, by Edmund Blishen. 'Mates' could have been used equally well in this instance.

'Mate' itself, used in a friendly way, occurs fairly commonly in British novels. There are examples in *Within and Without*, by John Harvey; *Under the Volcano*, by Malcolm Lowry; *Thirteen Days*, by Ian Jefferies, where 'matey' is also used; *The Liberty Man*, by Gillian Freeman; *The Limits of Love*, by Frederic Raphael, which includes 'matey' used in a friendly way, but at least one example of 'mate' which is unfriendly. *Up the City Road*, by John Stroud, has a young London girl saying to a male friend: 'Buy us a drink, mate, I'm skint.' She also uses his first name, but the switch to 'mate' is perhaps deliberately designed to remind him of their friendship. In *War Brides*, by Lois Battle, it is a young Australian woman who calls her father 'mate'. She also calls him 'old chap', and addresses him by his first name. In the same novel, another young Australian woman says to her husband: 'We'll be all right, matey.'

Mater The Latin word for 'mother', which public schoolboys began to use in direct address to their mothers in the mid-nineteenth century in Britain. Possibly the term was a useful compromise, as Margaret Laurence says of Ma (*see also* **Ma**). 'You shall have a copy the moment it is published, mater, and read the thing,' says a son in *Cynthia*, by Leonard Merrick. 'I do wish he'd call me "mamma",' says the mother concerned. 'He makes me feel a hundred years old.' This is slightly puzzling; it is difficult to see how 'mater' is more aging than 'mamma'. There is a discussion of the use of 'Mater' in *The Last and the First*, by Ivy Compton-Burnett, the speakers being as precise as Miss Burnett's characters always are:

'You all call me Mater now,' said Eliza with a frown. 'The name was chosen for Hermia and Madeline, because they remembered their own mother. There is no point in it for anyone else.'

'But it is better not to have two names,' said Madeline. 'And Mater has the maternal implication, and yet seems to avoid the deeper one.'

This is yet another suggestion for dealing with the step-mother problem.

Matey *See* **Mate.**

Matron The professional title of the person in charge of nurses and other hospital staff, apart from the doctors, though in Britain this official is now called a 'senior nursing officer'. 'No nonsense, please matron,' says a doctor in *My Brother Jonathan*, by Francis Brett Young, when that lady tells him that she has no free beds. In a boarding school a matron normally has charge of both medical matters and other domestic affairs, such as the care and maintenance of clothes. She is a kind of surrogate mother, and indeed, 'matron' means precisely that, adapting Spanish and Italian *matrona*. An example of this non-hospital use of 'Matron' occurs in *Kate and Emma*, by Monica Dickens. The same author uses the medical vocative in *Thursday Afternoons*.

Mavourneen From the Irish *mo mhurnin*, 'my darling'. It is used by an Englishman to an Irish woman in *The Sleepers of Erin*, by Jonathan Gash. Her response is to tell him: 'And you can stop that.' One would normally expect this vocative to be used by an Irish speaker.

Maw A spelling of 'Ma', indicating a dialectal or sub-standard pronunciation of that word. *St Urbain's Horseman*, by Mordecai Richler, has: 'Things have improved, Maw. I mean these days you can actually plead not guilty.' The speaker is Jewish Canadian in this case. In *A Woman Called Fancy*, by Frank Yerby, a girl from the hill country of Carolina uses 'Maw' to address her mother. *The Taste of Too Much*, by Clifford Hanley, has seven examples of its use in a Glasgow family.

Mawther 'Cheer up, my pretty mawther!' says Mr Peggotty to Mrs Gummidge, in *David Copperfield*. *Chambers Dictionary* gives 'mauther', 'mawther', 'mawr', and 'mor' as forms of the same word, used of a girl, especially a great awkward girl, in East Anglian dialect.

Mayor, Mr In Britain and America a mayor is the nominal head of a city or borough. When the official is a man the normal polite form of address is 'Mr Mayor'. A British example of this usage occurs in *Bless me, Father*, by Neil Boyd. In Garson Kanin's *Moviola* the vocative is spelled out as 'Mister Mayor'. A female mayor would correctly be addressed as 'Madam Mayor'. In certain British cities, such as London, the chief official has the title of 'Lord Mayor', and would be addressed in that way. A woman holding the position would be 'Lady Mayoress' in formal address. This term is also used to address the wife of a Lord Mayor. Husbands of women who are lady mayoresses or mayors in their own right have no particular title.

Historically, 'mayor' is a variant of 'major', but the two titles have been distinct since at least the sixteenth century. Like 'major', 'mayor' is sometimes used on its own, especially in infor-

mal circumstances. In *The Liberation of Lord Byron Jones*, by Jesse Hill Ford, a townsman outside a courtroom says: 'I heard it was a nigger done it. Ain't that right, Mayor?'

Mazidawk A Devonshire dialect term used by Henry Williamson in *A Dream of Fair Women*, where a boy says it to his drunken father. 'Mazi-' is a form of 'mazy', meaning giddy, confused. The ' –dawk' is a short form of 'dawkin', a diminutive of 'daw', 'fool, simpleton'.

me A form of 'my' used in sub-standard or dialectal speech. *Kate and Emma*, by Monica Dickens, has 'me old cock'; *Dover One*, by Joyce Porter, has 'me old beauty' and 'me old dear'; *An Error of Judgement*, by Pamela Hansford Johnson, has 'me duck'; *A Kind of Loving*, by Stan Barstow, has 'me boy' and 'me old sweat'; *The Limits of Love*, by Frederic Raphael, has 'me boy'. *Brothers in Law*, by Henry Cecil, has many examples of the professional affectation 'me Lud', used by barristers in a British courtroom. *See also **my**.*

Meat-face In *The Wayward Bus*, by John Steinbeck, occurs: 'Louie was big, a little on the stout side, but a dresser. His party friends called him "meat-face".' 'Meat-ball' and 'meat-head' are slightly more usual American slang terms. Both refer to a stupid person, which is perhaps not the intention behind 'meat-face'. Steinbeck's comment is an interesting aside on the friendly insult that occurs regularly between friends and intimates.

Medic In American military use, one who is engaged in medical work, a corpsman, trained to give first aid and minor medical treatment. 'I went over with a thud, a wave from the wound carrying me back, forcing my head to the ground with some desire of its own. "Medics," I heard a man yell' (*An American Dream*, Norman Mailer). *The Magic Army*, by Leslie Thomas, has: ' "Medic!" he bellowed over the loudhailer. "Medics to the bridge." ' The speaker is an American army officer on board a ship.

Mem This spelling of 'Ma'am' or 'Madam' is used occasionally in eighteenth- and nineteenth-century literature to represent an uneducated pronunciation of that word. Mincing uses it to her mistress, Mrs Millamant, in Congreve's *Way of the World* (1700).

Members of the jury A collective vocative used in a court of law by barristers and judges. There are three examples of its use in *Brothers in Law*, by Henry Cecil.

Messenger A professional description which can be used vocatively. *The Limits of*

Love, by Frederic Raphael, has a government minister saying: 'Tell me, messenger, what entitles me to park my car outside the door but forbids Sir Samuel here to do so?' The vocative occurs again in *The Word Child*, by Iris Murdoch, but on this occasion is a verbal incident term of address. One person says: 'Of course I don't know, I'm only the messenger.' 'Well, messenger,' says the other, 'you'd better go then. You've done your job. Go.'

Metal of India, my   Sir Toby Belch uses this term to Olivia's chambermaid, Maria, in *Twelfth Night* (2:v), though the Second Folio prints it as 'nettle of India'. The metal reference would be to gold, which was associated with India in the seventeenth century. In modern times Sir Toby might have said 'my golden girl'.

Microbe   *See* Tich.

Midear   A spelling of 'my dear' which indicates the pronunciation by a Devonshire speaker in *The Dream of Fair Women*, by Henry Williamson. Used as a friendly term of address to a stranger, along with 'midears' to a man and woman. In the same author's *Dandelion Days* a Devonshire man uses 'midears' to address two young boys.

Midge   Used as a generic nickname for a small person, alluding to the small insect of this name. *See also* Tich.

Midget   The French master in Henry Williamson's novel of school life, *Dandelion Days*, habitually addresses boys as 'miserable midget'. The word is not in general use as a vocative, but this expression is typical of the personal vocative collocations which some speakers create for their own regular use. Williamson tells us of other favourite expressions used by the same man. They include 'stupid fool', 'idiot', 'depraved lunatic', 'abandoned wretch', and, since he teaches French, *sans culottes* and *gamin*. It is interesting that the group of vocatives he uses paint in themselves a portrait of his rather nasty character.

Milady, Milord   Forms of 'My lady' and 'My lord' which are meant to show the unstressed pronunciation of 'my', especially by foreign speakers. In the nineteenth century both 'milady' and 'milord' became words that could be used in third person reference to designate an English lady or lord, especially one travelling in Europe. 'Milady' is used vocatively in *Lady Chatterley's Lover*, by D. H. Lawrence.

Milkman   Used in Britain to address the man who delivers the milk to individual houses

every morning, a familiar figure in the English suburbs.

Milksop   Recorded since the thirteenth century as a term of abuse for a man lacking courage, and still to be heard in school playgrounds, according to the Opies in *The Lore and Language of Schoolchildren*. The original reference was probably to bread sopped in milk and fed to young infants. *Tom Sawyer*, by Mark Twain, has Injun Joe calling his companion 'Milksop!' when the latter says that a suggested project is dangerous.

Miller   Used as a professional title in former times. Miller Loveday in Thomas Hardy's *The Trumpet Major*, is either addressed in full, with his surname, or as 'miller'.

Milord   *See* Milady.

Mim   A spelling which represents an uneducated pronunciation of 'Ma'am' or 'Madam'. Miss Miggs, the shrewish domestic servant of the Vardens in Dickens's *Barnaby Rudge* uses it to her mistress.

Mims   Used by a young woman to her mother-in-law in *Howard's End*, by E. M. Forster, after some discussion with her husband about what to call her.

Minion   In *The Dream of Fair Women*, by Henry Williamson, a young man addresses a woman as *Mignon*. 'Surely you know,' says the woman so addressed to someone who overhears the expression, 'it is a French word, meaning darling?' The English equivalent of *mignon* in the seventeenth century was 'minion'. This was briefly used in a positive sense, both in third person reference and as a vocative, but it quickly became contemptuous. It referred especially to the favourite of a prince or other person of high rank, owing everything to the favour of his patron.

In vocative use, 'minion' implied a contemptible, servile creature if said to a man. Addressed to a woman the term was the equivalent of 'jade' or 'hussy'. 'Do you hear, you minion?' says Antipholus to Luce, his servant girl, in *The Comedy of Errors* (3:i), 'You'll let us in, I hope?' 'Thou baggage, let me in,' he continues. Juliet is addressed as 'Mistress Minion' by her father, in *Romeo and Juliet* (3:v) when the latter is angry with her.

Minister   Used to address a government minister, who is head of a particular department, and a minister of religion, who is the equivalent of a priest in the non-conformist and presbyterian churches. 'What's the processional order, Minister?' asks a speaker in Maurice Edelman's *The Minister*, a novel about British political life. The term was also much heard in the BBC television series *Yes, Minister*. In *Gone to Earth*, by Mary Webb, the spokesman of a group of parishioners says to a clergyman: 'We bring you the Lord's message, minister.'

Miscreant A miscreant is literally one who does not believe in God, but by the end of the sixteenth century the word had already taken on the more general sense of 'wretch, villain'. When Vernon and Basset quarrel, in Shakespeare's *Henry the Sixth Part One* (3:iv), Basset calls Vernon 'Villain' and says: 'I'll unto his Majesty and crave I may have liberty to avenge this wrong.' Vernon replies: 'Well, miscreant, I'll be there as soon as you.' Later in the same play (5:iii) the Duke of York tells Joan of Arc: 'Curse, miscreant, when thou comest to the stake.' In *King Lear* (1:i) the king calls the Earl of Kent 'Vassal! Miscreant!' By the nineteenth century the word was becoming rare, and was perhaps no longer taken seriously. *The Newcomes*, by William Thackeray, has one military man say to another: 'So will you, too, Butts, you old miscreant, repent of your sins, pay your debts, and do something handsome for that poor deluded milliner in Albany Street.'

Misery A vocative which comments on the miserable demeanour of a person at a given moment, or perhaps on his general disposition. *Georgy Girl*, by Margaret Forster, has 'Misery' used as an intimacy between lovers. In *St Urbain's Horseman*, by Mordecai Richler, occurs: 'Harry, you misery, don't you care about the Jewish children?' This is said by a man who thinks that the person he is talking to is expressing a negative viewpoint. A man says to a young woman; 'What's up, Misery?' in Ngaio Marsh's *Opening Night*. She is in fact upset because of his insensitive reference to someone who has just died.

Miss The conventionally polite way of addressing a young woman who appears to be unmarried but is of marriageable age. Some speakers would use the term to a younger girl. It is used to an older woman in special situations, e.g. to a waitress in a restaurant as a professional title, by British schoolchildren to a female teacher, where again it is a professional, not a social, title. In the past 'Miss' appears to have been used to one's social superiors, not one's equals. Thomas Hardy, in *Desperate Remedies*, has a character of good birth who is obliged to become a lady's maid. The coachman who collects her says 'No, m – '. Hardy explains: 'The coachman was continually checking himself thus, being about to style her miss involuntarily, and then recollecting that he was only speaking to the new lady's maid.'

'Miss' can become the head-word in a vocative group, as in *The Vicar of Wakefield*, by Oliver Goldsmith, where Mrs Primrose at one point addresses her daughter as 'my sweetest miss'. In *The House with the Green Shutters*, by George Douglas, a young man greets two nineteen-year-old girls with 'Ho, my pretty misses'. In *Vanity Fair*, by William Thackeray, Mr Osborne in the course of a single speech addresses the heiress Rhoda Swartz as 'my dear Miss', 'my dear Miss Rhoda', and then 'Rhoda': 'Rhoda, let me say, for my heart warms to you, it does really.' Osborne is interested in having his daughters become friendly with a young woman of wealth. 'Miss' was originally an abbreviation of 'Mistress'.

Missed This highly individual vocative is made the subject of a joke in Lillian Beckwith's *The Hills is Lonely*, which is set in the Hebrides. The characters are mostly Gaelic speakers who use English when they must. The following passage occurs:

'What do you feed them on?' I enquired. 'Duck eggs, Missed,' the reply came with prompt servility. (Euan had never made up his mind whether to address me as 'Miss' or 'Mistress', but his compromise of 'Missed' was, I suppose, as apt a designation as any other for a middle-aged spinster.

Missie See **Missy**.

Missis, Missus These spellings represent the spoken form of 'Mrs', as it is always written when prefixed to the last name of a married woman. 'Missis' could be described as an incorrect form of 'madam', used by uneducated, or unsophisticated speakers, normally to address a woman who looks old enough to be married but is unknown to the speaker. Examples of such usage occur in, e.g., *The Country Girls*, by Edna O'Brien, *Doctor in the House*, by Richard Gordon, *The Fox in the Attic*, by Richard Hughes, and *Saturday Night and Sunday Morning*, by Alan Sillitoe. In the latter novel alone there are eight examples of 'missis' used in a fairly neutral way to a strange woman. A special use occurs in *A Kind of Loving*, by Stan Barstow. A young couple are departing on their honeymoon, having been married a few hours earlier: 'Well, missis,' says the young husband to his bride, once they are alone. 'Aye, mister,' she replies. This reflects working-class usage of 'the missis', to mean one's wife. Novelists are not always consistent with the spelling of 'missis/missus'. Both forms are likely to occur in the same book; in *Ship-Master*, by Gwyn Griffin, they are to be found on the same page.

Missy A diminutive of 'Miss' which has the

effect of converting that word into a true vocative. 'You keep your mouth out of this, missy,'
says an aunt to her young, but nevertheless
married, niece in Truman Capote's short story
My Side of the Matter. In *The Sandcastle*, by
Iris Murdoch, an elderly man who is having
his portrait painted by a much younger woman
says: 'It's time you stopped that now, missie.'
'Missy' is used in a friendly way to a teenage
girl in *Girl with Green Eyes*, by Edna O'Brien.
The term is also much used by the father of
Scarlett O'Hara, in Margaret Mitchell's *Gone
With The Wind*, to address his daughter. He
equates it with 'Puss', 'Daughter', and the like.
War Brides, by Lois Battle, has an Australian
mother saying to her daughter: 'All right,
missy, five minutes.'

Mister The commonest use of 'mister' on its
own, not followed by a name, is by children
who address a passing stranger. In early
November, for example, children displaying
their effigies of Guy Fawkes in the streets of
British cities will accost a man with 'Penny for
the guy, mister!' Adult beggars are also likely
to use the term. In *The Day of the Locust*, by
Nathanael West, occurs: ' "Hey, you, mister." It
was a beggar who had spotted him from the
shadow of a doorway. "A nickel, mister." ' In
An American Dream, by Norman Mailer, a
policeman uses 'Mister' to another man in a
decidedly unfriendly way. Such usage also
occurs in American military circles when an
NCO or officer addresses a man of inferior
rank. There is a decidedly aggressive use of
the term in *North Dallas Forty*, by Peter Gent,
when the coach of a professional American
football team says to a player: 'It's not up to
you to judge what's good and bad here,
mister.' Clearly the speaker could have used
the player's name had he wished.

A rare use of 'Mister' as an endearment is
in *A Kind of Loving*, by Stan Barstow. A newly
married man calls his wife 'Missis' to remind
her of her married status, and is answered by
'Mister'. Also very rare is the occurrence of
'Misters' in the eighteenth-century novel *Cecilia*, by Fanny Burney: 'Mrs Belfield . . . running
into the passage . . . angrily called out-[to the
chairmen] "What do you do here, Misters?" '

The *Oxford English Dictionary* suggests that
'Mister' used alone is only slightly less respectful than 'sir', even though it adds that the use
of 'Mister' is vulgar. One could argue that in
children's language 'Mister' usefully distinguishes those men who are not teachers or
family members, while in adult language it
often stands apart from 'sir', having little to do
with politeness.

A special use of 'Mister' occurs with a question intonation. 'Good morning, Mister –?' is
really a request for the hearer to announce his
last name. The normal use of 'Mister', written

'Mr', as a social title is discussed under **Last
name, Mr**. This prefix is also used in several
professional titles, such as: Mr President, Mr
Chairman, Mr Secretary, Mr Speaker, etc. See
the entries under the word that follows 'Mr'.
'Mr' is also frequently used to form nonce
names, such as 'Mr Policeman'. These are also
discussed under the words that follow 'Mr'.

Mistkäfer *Aaron's Rod*, by D. H. Lawrence,
has: 'Come up, you little mistkafer – what the
Americans call a bug. Come up and be
damned.' Lawrence would have been more
accurate to say that *Mistkäfer* is German for
dung-beetle. *See also* **Cockchafer**, ' –chafer'
and *käfer* being etymologically related.

Misto A spelling of 'Mister' which indicates
uneducated and regional pronunciation, rather
than a use of the vocative ' –o' which occurs in
'boyo', 'lino', etc. The hero of Mark Twain's
Pudd'nhead Wilson is addressed as 'Misto
Wilson' by a black servant girl.

Mistress The earliest meaning of 'mistress'
was a female master, a master-ess. In its sense
of 'mistress of a household' the word
developed into modern 'Mrs', or 'missis' as it
is pronounced. A short form of the word also
gave rise to 'Miss'. The earlier usage where
'Mistress' was used as a term of address in its
own right, or as a prefixed title followed by a
last name, as an address form to any woman
or unmarried girl, is retained in Scotland.
Examples of such usage occur in *Geordie*, by
David Storey and *Whisky Galore*, by Compton
Mackenzie. In the latter novel a Cockney
woman who is addressed by a Scotsman as
'Mistress Odd' makes a point of saying that she
likes that form of address.

The term survived more generally until the
nineteenth century. 'Did you speak, Mis'ess
Anne?' says Festus Derriman to Anne Garland,
in Thomas Hardy's *The Trumpet Major*. 'Mistress' on its own occurs vocatively in *Shirley*,
by Charlotte Brontë. In the Shakespeare plays
'Mistress' is well used, normally on its own, but
also in expressions such as 'noble mistress',
'proud mistress', 'gentle mistress', etc. Shakespeare uses the word as a normal social title
to married and unmarried women, and also
has characters address those who are mistress
of their hearts. The 'illicit wife' sense of 'mistress' has been in use since the fifteenth century. This looms larger in the modern consciousness thanks to the splitting away of 'Mrs'
and 'Miss' as separate words.

Mite The basic sense of 'mite' is something
very small; the word is therefore applied to a
child or to a diminutive person. 'Come here,
you poor wee mite' would typically be said to
a child for whom one feels sorry, but Laurie

Lee, in *Cider with Rosie*, shows that it can be used less sympathetically. Some boys steal an old woman's snuff, but it causes them to sneeze violently when they sniff it. 'That'll learn you, I reckon; you thieving mites,' she tells them.

Miz *See* **Last name, Ms**.

Mom One of the 'mother' group of vocatives, a short form of 'momma', itself a variant of 'mama'. 'Mom' is especially frequent in novels written by American authors, reflecting working-class life. The normal equivalent in British-based novels would be Mum. As with the other 'mother' terms, 'Mom' is used to the speaker's mother and occasionally, to the speaker's mother-in-law. In *War Brides*, by Lois Battle, 'How're the kids, Mom?' is addressed by a young American husband to his wife.

Momma A variant of 'Mamma', used especially in the USA, the word being stressed on the first syllable. It is used by a boy to his mother in an American Jewish family throughout *The Sophomore*, by Barry Spacks.

Mom-mom Used by a young American man to his grandmother in *Rabbit is Rich*, by John Updike. The same speaker uses 'Mom' to his mother.

Monitor A monitor is a student who is appointed to assist a teacher. In former times the monitor was a senior student whose assistance might extend to teaching junior pupils. In junior schools the monitor carries out fairly menial tasks, such as collecting or giving out books, and is rewarded with an enhanced sense of self-importance. 'Monitors, collect the lesson-books and put them away,' says a teacher in *Jane Eyre*, by Charlotte Brontë. The same novel has: 'Monitor of the first class, fetch the globes!'

Etymologically, a monitor is one who admonishes. The term was probably used in a school context because one of the monitor's early duties was to keep discipline, admonishing other students as necessary. In some British public schools monitors are, or were, known as 'praeposters', or 'prepostors'. School prefects are also monitors, though at a more senior level.

Monkey 'God help thee, poor monkey,' says Lady Macbeth to her son, demonstrating a typical use of 'monkey' to a child or young person. Charlotte Brontë has 'What do you want, you little monkey?' addressed to a girl aged six in *Villette*. In *Scenes of Clerical Life*, by George Elliot, 'little monkey' is used by a man to his adopted daughter. There can be few modern children who have not been

addressed in similar terms by an adult at some time in their lives. They know that the term is used playfully, referring perhaps to their energy and continuous movement. 'Go to sleep, you monkeys,' says a tired adult in Edna Lyall's *How Children Raised Wind*. There is an interesting usage by Jonathan Swift, in his *Journal to Stella*: 'Well, little monkeys mine, I must go write; and so good-night.' Apart from Swift's little language, however, 'monkey' does not generally seem to be used as a term of endearment. It is even decidedly aggressive in Garson Kanin's *Moviola*, where a floor manager in a film studio says: 'Listen, you monkeys, when I say "Quiet" I don't just mean a little less noise – I mean QUIET!'

Monkey-face A self-explanatory term of abuse which occurs vocatively in *Girl, 20*, by Kingsley Amis. A young boy says to his father: 'Shut your trap, you fucking monkey-face.'

Monsieur The normal social title of a Frenchman, used with his last name as the equivalent of 'Mr', or as a term on its own, the equivalent of 'sir'. It is used by some speakers to a Frenchman, even when the conversation is being conducted in English, almost as if 'Monsieur' were the man's first name instead of a title which is easy to translate. Novelists also use it at times to show that a conversation given in English actually occurred in French. Arthur Hailey, in *Hotel*, has a French chef who speaks English, but addresses the assistant manager as 'Monsieur McDermott' instead of 'McDermott'. He also uses the French plural form 'Messieurs' when addressing several men, instead of 'gentlemen': 'Messieurs, you will excuse me. Monsieur McDermott, when you 'ave finished, perhaps we could talk together, yes?' *Georgy Girl*, by Margaret Forster, has a girl assistant saying to a male English haidresser: 'She hasn't turned up, Monsieur Herbert,' where Herbert is the first name of the man concerned. This style, 'Monsieur' + first name, might at one time have been classed as a professional title for a hairdresser, but it became associated with effeminacy rather than Frenchness and seems to have faded, though genuine Frenchmen who happen to be hairdressers working in an English-speaking country may continue its use. Historically, 'Monsieur' is *mon sieur*, 'my lord'.

Monsignor A title bestowed on certain high-ranking Roman Catholic priests, usually by the pope. It derives from Italian *Monsignore*, 'my lord', which sometimes causes the Italian plural *Monsignori* to be used rather than Monsignors. It is used as a title on its own, or followed by the last name of the man concerned. In *North Dallas Forty*, by Peter Gent, occurs: ' "Let's kill those cocksuckers!" Tony Douglas screamed.

He caught himself and glanced sideways at the Monsignor, who was standing near him. "Sorry, Monsignor." "That's all right, Tony," the Monsignor replied. "I know how you feel." '

Monster One would expect this vocative to be used only in great contempt, expressing the speaker's views on someone's inhuman behaviour. A multiple murderer might well be referred to as a monster, but in normal life such people rarely have to be addressed by ordinary citizens. 'Monster' has certainly been used vocatively since at least the sixteenth century, and in Shakespeare it can have its full force. Addressed to Caliban, the savage and deformed slave in *The Tempest*, its use is rather special, but in *Timon of Athens*, when Timandra says 'Hang thee, monster!' to Timon, she means it to indicate her view of his wickedness.

Laurie Lee, in *Cider with Rosie*, recounts how, as a young child, he experimentally hit a girl in the playground on her wiry black hair 'without spite or passion'. He was amazed when those around said 'Horrid boy! Little monster!' But 'monster' is used fairly frequently in modern times as a covert endearment. Parents can be heard asking of their children: 'What are you doing now, you little monsters?' In *Absolute Beginners*, by Colin MacInnes, 'you poor old prehistoric monster' is merely an expression of friendship. With this one may compare 'you droll monster' addressed to Festus Derriman, in Thomas Hardy's *The Trumpet Major*, which is said with a smile and is not really disapproving. Dawn Powell has a short story, *Every Day is Ladies' Day*, in which an American woman playfully calls a man 'you monster'.

Used of children, then, the term often means little more than 'mischievous scamps'. Used of adult men – never, it seems, of women – 'monster' is often the equivalent of 'you wicked man', said in such a way as to show that the wickedness is not unattractive. That it *can* be more forceful is shown in *Blue Dreams*, by William Hanley, where 'Fuck off, monster!' is several times addressed to an American television director by an actress.

Moon-calf Mainly a seventeenth-century expression, applied most famously to Caliban, in Shakespeare's *The Tempest*. The word originally referred to a person misshapen at birth, a monstrosity, the influence of the moon being blamed for such accidents of nature. By the nineteenth century novelists such as Sir Walter Scott and R.L. Stevenson were using the word, vocatively or otherwise, in a watered-down sense to refer to a foolish person. Dickens and Disraeli seem to have interpreted the word as 'one who moons about, an absent-minded person'. The term would probably only be used in modern times by speakers with a strong literary background. *See also* **Calf**, which was used in the seventeenth century as a vaguely affectionate insult.

Mope, Madam A nonce name which occurs in *Jane Eyre*, by Charlotte Brontë, addressed by a boy to a young girl who is thought to be moping.

Moppet A term of endearment used especially to a young girl. It derives from 'mop', which was a playful term used to a baby in the fifteenth century. It appears to have meant something like 'you silly thing' at that time. The diminutive form 'moppet' has been in use since the beginning of the seventeenth century. Mr Peggotty uses it to his beloved Little Em'ly in *David Copperfield*, along with other endearments such as 'pretty', 'my pretty', 'my dear'.

Mor *See* **Mawther**.

Moron This has a technical definition in medical circles, describing someone whose IQ is between 50–69, or whose mental age is fixed between eight to twelve. The word is occasionally used as a synonym for 'imbecile' or 'fool'. 'You moron' could be very insulting as a vocative, but like most insults it can be turned almost into an endearment if said in a particular tone to a close friend. The woman who says it to a man in *The Business of Loving*, by Godfrey Smith, does so affectionately. The same cannot be said of the Los Angeles policeman in *The Choirboys*, by Joseph Wambaugh, who addresses his colleague as 'you stupid goofy simple minded idiotic fuckin moron!'

Mother Used by mainly middle- and upper-class speakers to address their mothers. The word is most often used alone, but it can become 'mother darling', 'mother dear', 'my dear mother', etc., is especially if the speaker is a woman. 'Mother' is usually an adult term; young children might well use 'Mummy', 'Momma', or similar terms, then switch to 'Mother' in late adolescence or early adulthood. Working-class speakers are more likely to continue with 'Mum' or 'Mom'. In *Fear of Flying* Erica Jong writes:

I always mutter 'Mother' when I'm scared. The funny thing is I don't even call my mother 'Mother' and I never have. She named me Isadora Zelda, but I try never to use the Zelda. In return for this lifetime liability, I call her Jude. Her real name is Judith. Nobody but my youngest sister ever calls her Mommy.

Some mothers encourage their children to address them by their first names from the beginning; others suggest that this change be made when the children become adults. 'I crept over to the cot to stare at this strange child who called its mother by her Christian name,' writes Gordon McGill, in *Arthur*. It is hardly the child who is strange in such circumstances; it is the mother who is clearly rejecting the verbal acknowledgement of parenthood.

In many families a problem is created when it is necessary to address a mother-in-law or step-mother. In *The Group*, by Mary McCarthy, a son writes to his father: 'Would mother mind asking Kay [the letter-writer's wife] to call her Judith when she writes? Like all modern girls, she has a horror of calling a mother-in-law "Mother", and "Mrs Petersen" sounds so formal.' In *War Brides*, by Lois Battle, an Australian daughter-in-law who has strong reasons for wishing to ingratiate herself with her husband's family uses 'Mother' in a calculated way: ' "Thank you, Mother," she said softly, consciously using the word for the first time and watching its effect on Etna. "But you mustn't say thank you, Daughter. You're part of the family, after all." ' In one family known to the author, a son-in-law uses 'Mother' + first name to address his mother-in-law, though this has the effect of making the woman concerned sound like a nun. Modern step-mothers may be known as 'mother', or one of the 'mother' variants, or by their first names. It depends largely on how old the step-children are when the new marital situation arises, on whether the real mother is still alive and how well the children remember her. See under **Stepmother.**

In *A Lovely Bit of Wood*, by Penelope Gilliatt, an English husband addresses his wife as 'Mother'. This was at one time common practice amongst older couples whose children had become adults, and may still continue. Margaret Laurence comments on the practice amusingly in *The Stone Angel*. A husband who admits that he has many faults points out that he could have been much worse. ' "You know something, Hagar? There's men in Manawaka call their wives 'Mother' all the time. That's one thing I have never done." It was true. He never did, not once. I was Hagar to him.'

From the fourteenth century onwards 'Mother' was sometimes used to address an elderly working-class woman who was in no way related to the speaker. In *The Wind in the Willows*, by Kenneth Grahame, when Toad dresses as a washerwoman, he is addressed as 'mother' by an engine-driver. In *Elmer Gantry*, by Sinclair Lewis, an Englishman uses 'mother' to address an old lady. She remarks to her husband: 'Isn't there a law that permits one to kill people who call you "Mother"? The next time this animal stops, he'll call you "Father"!' 'Only once, my dear,' says the hus-

band. However, in rural areas, especially, it was not unusual for 'Mother' to be prefixed to an old woman's name and used as a social title instead of 'Mrs', as in Old Mother Hubbard.

'Mother' is almost a professional title when used to the superior of a convent or other religious establishment, if the speaker is not one of the nuns who look upon the mother superior as their spiritual parent. In this role the word is of course invariable, whereas the mother of a normal family can be addressed by any of the mother terms, such as: Mum, Mom, Ma, Mam, Mummy, Momma. 'Mother' is also invariable when used by e.g. a judge or magistrate in a juvenile court to the mother of an offender, or by a midwife addressing a woman in labour.

'Mother' remains a word of very special significance. One can understand why many people think it strange when a woman who is entitled to be so addressed rejects the term, and why step-children feel reluctant to use it to someone who is not their real mother. William Thackeray, in *Vanity Fair*, chose to express the thought with full Victorian sentimentality: 'Mother is the name of God in the lips and hearts of little children.'

Motherfucker 'Get the fuck away from my wife, you fucking motherfucker,' says one man to another in *Any Minute I Can Split*, by Judith Rossner. The term is used in low colloquial American speech to a man who is detested. The speaker is probably not thinking of the literal meaning of the expression when using it, the attitude expressed is more meaningful. The *New Dictionary of American Slang*, by Robert L. Chapman, points out that 'mother' in this expression is sometimes replaced by 'mammy', 'mama', 'mommo', while the second element can be replaced by 'eater', 'kisser', 'lover', etc. There is another example of 'you motherfucker', used aggressively by a black male to a white, in Norman Mailer's *An American Dream*. In *The River*, by Steven Bauer, occurs: 'A group of strikers watched him, ready to lunge. "Come on, motherfuckers," Truck growled.' The same novel has an example of 'you selfish motherfucker', used by one man to another.

In environments where obscenities are used frequently, 'motherfucker' can lose almost all meaning and become simply the equivalent of 'man'. Such is the case, for instance, in *North Dallas Forty*, by Peter Gent, which is concerned with professional football players in the USA. 'You muthahfuckah' also occurs in the novel, attempting to show its pronunciation by a black American speaker. 'Motherfucker' can occur elsewhere in the vocative phrase. 'I will fix you for this, you motherfucker bastard,' says a woman to a man in *St Urbain's Horseman*, by Mordecai Richler.

Mother-in-law This term is rarely used, perhaps because of its unwieldy length. Mothers-in-law are accorded different terms of address according to individual family circumstances and wishes. A considerable age difference may make the use of a first name slightly embarrassing for the daughter or son-in-law. There is often a reluctance on the part of the latter to use one of the 'mother' terms. 'Mrs' + last name may sound too formal; 'Mrs' + initial of last name may sound rather common. Many speakers would try to side-step the problem of what to call a mother-in-law by avoiding terms of address altogether and using 'you'. Others wait until a grandchild is born and then use grandmother terms.

New Society carried out a small survey in 1970 asking middle-class families how they addressed a mother-in-law. Ninety husbands and wives were interviewed. Of these, 47 wives used a 'mother' term, though only 21 husbands did so. More husbands than wives used first names to their mother-in-law. The solution for 12 wives and 15 husbands was to use some kind of nickname. The general conclusion of the survey was that women were more willing than men to slip into another child/parent relationship. The men preferred to aim at friendship, not kinship.

In *The Pickwick Papers*, by Charles Dickens, occurs: ' "Mother-in-law," said Sam, politely saluting the lady, "wery much obliged to you for this here wisit." ' The lady in question is actually Sam Weller's step-mother, but 'mother-in-law' was used to describe such a person until the end of the nineteenth century. Sam also uses 'mum' to this lady, but it is his form of 'ma'am', not 'Mum' used to a mother.

If it is sometimes difficult to know how to address a mother-in-law in modern times, it can also be difficult for that lady to know how to address her son or daughter-in-law. In *Hard Times*, by Charles Dickens, Mrs Gradgrind is worried when she learns that her daughter is to marry Josiah Bounderby.

I shall be worrying myself morning, noon and night, to know what I am to call him. I must call him something. It's impossible to be constantly addressing him, and never giving him a name. I cannot call him Josiah, for the name is insupportable to me. You yourself wouldn't hear of Joe, you very well know. Am I to call my own son-in-law Mister? Not, I believe, unless the time has arrived when, as an invalid, I am to be trampled upon by my relations. Then what am I to call him?

In *Colour Blind*, by Catherine Cookson, we are told that 'Kathie couldn't bring herself to call her son-in-law James. To his face she addressed him as "Mr Paterson" and time and again she wondered at the ordinariness of such a name for such an extraordinary man.'

In this case the son-in-law is extraordinary because he is black and has married into a white family.

Motherkins, Motherkin, Motherling The *Oxford English Dictionary* records vocative usage of these various 'mother' diminutives.

Moujik A word meaning a Russian peasant, and not in frequent use as a vocative. 'You clumsy moujik' is used by one man to another in *The Half Hunter*, by John Sherwood, though no explanation is offered as to why the speaker chooses this term. Slightly unusual vocatives, however, are part of his individual speech-pattern. Elsewhere in the novel he uses 'you poor boiling fowl' and 'you bright-eyed overgrown saucebox'.

Mouse A playful term of endearment, mainly addressed to women, as the *Oxford English Dictionary* puts it. It was in use from the early sixteenth century until the end of the eighteenth century. A citizen in *The Knight of the Burning Pestle*, by Beaumont and Fletcher, uses it to his wife, whom he also calls: sweetheart, cony, duck, bird, wench, honeysuckle, chicken, wife, lamb, mine own dear heart, love, honey, and Nell. In *Love's Labour's Lost* it is used by Rosaline to Katharine: 'What's your dark meaning, mouse, of this light word?' Hamlet says sneeringly to his mother: 'Let the bloat King tempt you again to bed;/Pinch wanton on your cheek; call you his mouse.'

Ms *See* **Last name, Ms**.

Muck, Lady This mock name is used to someone who, in the speaker's opinion, is trying to act like a lady – pretend that she is refined and cultivated, though she is in reality 'as common as muck'. An example of its use occurs in *The Amberstone Exit*, by Elaine Feinstein. When a young woman comments on the wild behaviour of some young football supporters, she is addressed by one of them in this way. In *Fares Please*, by Edith Courtney, a man says to a woman: 'What the hell's the matter with you, Lady Muck?' when she shows that she disapproves of his behaviour.

There is an island called Muck in the Hebrides, subject of an onomastic anecdote in James Boswell's *Journal of a Tour to the Hebrides*. Boswell remarks that it is the custom for Scottish lairds to be known by the name of their lands, and continues:

It was somewhat droll to hear this Laird called by his title. *Muck* would have sounded ill; so he was called *Isle of Muck*, which went off with great readiness. The name, as now written, is unseemly, but is not so bad in the original Erse, which is Monach, signifying the Sows' Island... Some call it the Isle of Monk. The Laird insists that this is the proper name.

Mucker Kipling mentioned this term in *Captains Courageous* (1897), implying that it meant a coarse, unrefined person. It has had various other slang meanings, including 'hypocrite', and it is possible that individual speakers redefine it when they use it. In *The Magic Army*, by Leslie Thomas, one British soldier uses it to another: 'She's going to sing for you, then?' 'That's right, mucker.' In context this appears to be the equivalent of 'mate', 'someone who mucks in with you'. It is similarly used in *A World of Difference*, by Stanley Price, where one man says to another, in an artificial Cockney accent: 'Off to Americker, old mucker. Don't yer like it 'ere?'

Muff This is said to or shouted at someone who is playing a sport badly, dropping a ball which should be caught, etc. Dickens was one of the first writers to record the word in *The Pickwick Papers*, where Mr Jingle equates it with 'Butterfingers' while criticizing some cricket players. In modern times the verb 'to muff' is used far more frequently than the noun. The *Oxford English Dictionary* ingeniously suggests that the sporting sense of 'muff' may have been a comment, originally, on someone playing a ball game as if his hands were contained within a muff. There is an extended form of this vocative, 'muffin', which is used as a synonym for 'fool'. It came into use in the early nineteenth century and appears to be still in use. 'You muffin' occurred in the BBC television series *First of the Summer Wine*, which is set in Northern England, used by one girl to another, supposedly in the 1940s.

Mug, you 'What do you mean, you mug?' says a male American speaker to another man, in Mae West's *The Pleasure Man*. In the Laurel and Hardy film *Pack up your Troubles* a sergeant addresses a group of soldiers as 'you mugs'. *A Salute to the Great McCarthy*, by Barry Oakley, has an Australian football setting. The narrator hears the crowd jeering at him: 'Wake up McCarthy! You mug!' The word is roughly the equivalent of 'fool' or 'dupe', the idea behind it being that a mug is something into which you can pour almost anything. A simpleton can likewise be persuaded to believe almost anything. The existence of 'mug' in this slang sense led to the use of the last name 'Muggins' for similar purposes. 'You Muggins' is therefore still occasionally heard as a mild insult.

Mule A mule is the offspring of a male ass and a mare, though the word is loosely applied to the offspring of a female ass and a stallion (properly a hinny). Mules have long had a reputation for stubbornness and stupidity, but 'you mule' does not seem to be used vocatively to people who are thought to be mule-like in either of those senses. *Gone With The Wind*, by Margaret Mitchell, has the following, spoken by Rhett Butler to Scarlett, his wife: 'Their money won't do them any good. Any more than my money has done you any good. It certainly hasn't made a horse out of you yet, has it, my pretty mule?' The novelist adds that 'the quarrel which sprang from this last remark lasted for days'.

Mum Used in Britain to address the speaker's mother, usually when the speaker is a child. Many adults continue to use the term, especially if they are members of a working or lower middle-class family. The normal American equivalent is 'Mom'. In individual families the use of 'Mum' may be extended to a mother-in-law or a step-mother. It is thought that both 'Mum' and 'Mom' ultimately derive from a sound naturally made by infants as they begin to speak, a sound which could equally well be written as 'Mam'. The words for 'mother' in many different languages seem to have been based on this sound. The written form 'Mum' is only recorded from the beginning of the nineteenth century, but it was probably in dialectal use, at least, long before that. In the nineteenth century some confusion was caused by the fact that 'mum' represented a vulgar pronunciation of 'madam'. Thus in *Vanity Fair*, by William Thackeray, we find:

> Miss Horrocks was installed as housekeeper at Queen's Crawley, and ruled all the domestics there with great majesty and rigour. All the servants were instructed to address her as 'Mum' or 'Madam'; and there was one little maid, on her promotion, who persisted in calling her 'My Lady' without any rebuke on the part of the housekeeper.

Tom Sharpe, in *Ancestral Vices*, has: ' "And don't call me mum, girl," said Emmelia. "I am not your mum." "No, mum." ' In Compton Mackenzie's *Whisky Galore* a London railway porter asks a middle-class woman: 'Where do you want to go, mum?' The novel is set in the 1940s. Such usage would rarely be heard in modern times, though the family use of 'Mum' continues. Its association with childhood can mean that there comes a point where a speaker wishes to change to the more adult 'Mother'. In *Arthur*, Gordon McGill indicates one way of doing it:

> 'Dear Mother' was quite a breakthrough. I wrote 'Dear Mother' the first time when I was twenty-one, after years of 'Dear Mum'. I suppose it was a bit cowardly to make the

change in writing, but I couldn't have said 'Mother' to her face one day out of the blue. She wouldn't let me call her 'Ma' or 'Maw' like all the other kids in the street did. I think she really wanted it to be 'Mummy', but I wasn't going to stand for that. I vaguely remember, at four, putting my small foot down at 'Mummy'.

Mumma A variant of 'Momma' which occurs, e.g., in *The Diviners*, by Margaret Laurence. In *Elizabeth*, by Frank Swinnerton, the unusual 'Mummer' is used.

Mummy A word used by young children to their mother. Boys usually stop using this form by the age of twelve or so, though usage varies with each family. Girls, especially middle-class girls, are likely to continue using it much longer. Examples of usage occur, e.g., in *Anglo-Saxon Attitudes*, by Angus Wilson; *The Half Hunter*, by John Sherwood; *The Limits of Love*, by Frederic Raphael; *The Liberty Man*, by Gillian Freeman; *Unconditional Surrender*, by Evelyn Waugh; *Under the Volcano*, by Malcolm Lowry. The word is sometimes extended to 'Mummykins', 'Mummy dear', 'Mummy pet', etc. Rudyard Kipling's story *The Gardener* is about a boy being brought up by a woman he calls Auntie. He asks why he can't call her Mummy. She says he might do so 'at bed-time, for a pet-name between themselves'. The end of the story reveals that she is his true mother anyway.

The Actor, by Horace Annesley Vachell, has a woman saying to a man: 'You are such a baby.' This causes him to make fun of her by calling her Mummy Mirabel (her name). 'Rummy mummy I am,' she comments. There is another instance of this assumed maternal role in *Georgy Girl*, by Margaret Forster. Two young women friends have just come in from the rain. 'I've made a mess,' one of them says. 'You have that,' says the other, 'go and take your mac off at once, do you hear?' 'Yes, mummy,' says her friend, obediently. The variant spelling 'Mumee' occurs in *Thursday Afternoons*, by Monica Dickens, indicating the exasperated pronunciation of the word by an adolescent girl.

Mums A variant of 'Mum' used by Coker to her mother in Joyce Cary's *The Horse's Mouth*. The final '–s' occurs in other vocatives, such as 'sweets', 'Fats'. 'Mums' is found again in *Persephone*, by L. M. Boston, spoken by an English girl to her mother.

Mumsy, Mumsie Variants of 'Mummy' used by some children, especially girls, who may continue to use the term into adulthood. 'Mumsie' and 'Popkins' are used to her mother and father by Alison, the youngest daughter

in Thelma Niklaus's *Tamahine*. 'Mumsey' and 'Mumsey dear' are used by an American girl to her mother in *Sandra*, by Pearl Bell.

Mun *See* Man.

Munchkin In *The Wizard of Oz* the dwarfish helpers were called Munchkins. The term subsequently (after release of the film in 1939) came into American slang to mean a menial, a low-ranking staff-member, especially in the phrase 'low-level Munchkin'. It appears to be used also with reference to a person's small size. In *The Choirboys*, by Joseph Wambaugh, a Los Angeles policeman says to his colleague: 'Hey, munchkin, you're the littlest guy around here. Settle this argument. Do you think there's anything immoral about screwing a midget?'

Muscles An instant nickname which would normally be bestowed on a man who was physically strong but intellectually weak. In *Waterfront*, by Budd Schulberg, it is playfully addressed to a girl by a young man. She has been trying to snatch a ticket from his hand while he circles around her. Finally he says: 'Here ya go, muscles, it was nice wrastlin' with ya.'

Muss A term of endearment used at the end of the sixteenth century, the equivalent of 'sweetheart'. Examples occur in Ben Jonson's *Every Man in his Humour*: 'What ails you, sweet-heart? are you not well? speak, good muss.' The term could be used either to men or women. The *Oxford English Dictionary* tentatively suggests a link with 'muss', a playful word for 'mouth'. It seems far more likely to be a form of 'mouse', though this term was normally addressed only to women.

Mutt, you A reasonably friendly insult, applied mainly to American males. It is a short form of 'mutton-head', and was used for people before being transferred to mongrel dogs. It is roughly equivalent to 'you fool', especially when it becomes 'you dumb mutt', as in *Rabbit Redux*, by John Updike. *A Salute to the Great McCarthy*, by Barry Oakley, has one Australian man saying to another: 'You look like a Dickens character, you silly mutt.'

Mutton-head, you An American rather than a British term, though British sheep are as stupid as their American counterparts. As a term of mild abuse for someone who is thought to be unintelligent, 'mutton-head' has been in regular use since the beginning of the nineteenth century. It has given rise to the short form 'mutt'.

my This is frequently used as the opening word of an intimate or friendly vocative expression. When used as part of a true endearment to someone with whom the speaker is emotionally involved, 'my' appears to have its full possessive meaning. The lover is not simply claiming possession of the loved one: the underlying thought is that the lovers belong to one another, that together they form a complete entity. The 'you are mine' statement is balanced by an equally fervent 'I am yours'.

In the watered-down endearments that are expressions of friendship, 'my' indicates that the speaker includes the hearer in his personal sphere of interest. 'My dear chap', or whatever, signals the acceptance of the hearer by the speaker. The word begins to indicate an assumption of some kind of superiority on the part of the speaker over the hearer in expressions like 'my good woman', 'my lad', 'my girl', etc., especially when such terms are used admonishingly. The implication is that the speaker has rights similar to those of an employer over the hearer. 'My' here is saying: 'you are subject to my wishes.' If the hearer in any of the situations mentioned above accepts the underlying premiss of the speaker, the use of 'my' will either pass unnoticed or will be welcomed. If the hearer does not wish to be part of the speaker's intimate circle of friends, or does not accept that he is in a subordinate position to the speaker, the use of 'my' may well be resented, and this resentment voiced.

It would be over-simplistic to say that 'my' contrasts directly with 'you' in vocative expressions that begin with one of those two words. It is true that a vocative beginning with 'my', especially when followed by a normally endearing word such as 'little', sets up the expectation of an endearment. John Cleese, as Basil Fawlty, makes comic mileage out of this expectation by using vocative expressions such as 'my little piranha-fish' to his wife, Sybil. It is also true that a vocative beginning with 'you' sets up an expectation of an insult, other things being equal. But lovers frequently use exclamatory terms to one another, of the 'you beautiful brute', 'you funny little girl', 'you poor little pigeon' type. And even when the whole vocative expression is very insulting in form, as in 'you silly bitch', 'you swine', etc., the tone of voice used can easily achieve a conversion into a covert endearment. 'My' can, in general terms, be described as an 'accepting' word: the word which acknowledges a distance between speaker and hearer is, as one might expect, 'your': your Honour, your Majesty, etc. 'You' is not so much a distancing word as a declarative one. It makes no claims, merely expresses an opinion. *See also* **our**.

N

NAMES, COLLECTIVE Collective names embrace place names when the latter are used to designate e.g. sports teams. 'Come on, Chelsea!' is an exhortation to the players who at that moment form the Chelsea Football Club team. A collective nickname might also be used: 'Get stuck in, Bees!' to the Brentford side. Many sports teams have names other than place names, so Raiders, Dolphins, or whatever serve the same purpose, identifying individuals beneath an umbrella term. Any group of people who are clearly representing a named entity, whether it be a country or a small club, a town or a business, may be addressed by a group vocative which includes them all, though none of them would be addressed individually by that name. In the case of sports teams, simple colour names may be substituted for the official names: 'Well done, blues!'

Nana, Nanna Used by children in some families to address their grandmother, the word representing an infant attempt at pronouncing that word. 'You nana', however, used in colloquial slang, means 'you idiot'. 'Nana' in this case derives from 'banana' and implies that the person concerned has 'gone bananas', or is crazy.

Nanny A woman employed by a family to take care of young children, and addressed by them – often by her employers as well – by her professional title. This derives ultimately from 'Ann', via its pet form 'Nan', though there may be a link with 'Nana', 'Nanna', childish corruptions of 'grandmother' which are used to address that person. The nanny in *A Surfeit of Lampreys* by Ngaio Marsh is addressed by title by all members of the family for whom she works. Miss Marsh describes the woman concerned as 'the quintessence of all nannies, opinionated, faithful, illogical, exasperating and admirable'. *A Use of Riches*, by J. I. M. Stewart has the vocative spelt as 'Nannie'. An individual nanny may of course be known to the family by her own first name, or a nickname, especially in modern times.

Napoleon In *Pray for the Wanderer*, by Kate O'Brien, this name is transferred to a male friend by a woman speaker because his appearance reminds her of the French emperor: 'One hand fell to his head where he knelt and she took his heavy forelock, twisting it about her fingers. "Napoleon," she said.'

Naughty Used as a vocative element in Shakespeare, this word has the force of 'a thing of naught', something totally worthless. 'Thou naughty varlet', in *Much Ado About Nothing* (4:ii) or 'thou naughty knave', in *Julius Caesar* (1:i) is thus a serious insult. In modern times 'naughty' used alone or in an expression like 'naughty boy', 'naughty girl', is far milder. Addressed to children such terms imply bad behaviour, or behaviour, at least, which goes against the instructions issued by elders. Used to adults, expressions like 'naughty boy' or 'naughty girl' are likely to become covert endearments, especially when referring to sexual behaviour that some might consider to be improper. Friendly use of 'naughty' to an adult occurs in *Free Fall*, by William Golding.

Needle legs *See* **Spindleshanks**.

Neighbour Formerly in common use to a person of either sex who lived in close proximity, often followed by a surname, 'neighbour' is no longer used vocatively. Shakespearean characters regularly call one another 'neighbour': honest neighbour, good neighbour, kind neighbours, gentle neighbours, neighbour Baptista, neighbour Quickly, etc. By the nineteenth century such usage lived on in certain dialects only. In Thomas Hardy's Wessex novels it occurs commonly: 'Dinner is over, neighbour Loveday; please come in' (*The Trumpet Major*).

Neither of you This occurs as a vocative in *The Masters*, by C. P. Snow. A man who is addressing two women says: 'You pretend to like books. But you can't get away from your sex, neither of you.' Most speakers would have used 'either of you' to express this thought.

Nelly A derisive term for a homosexual man, in use since the 1940s. (Nelly is normally a girl's name, a derivative of Helen or Eleanor.) 'You two nellies' is used as a mild general insult to two men in *The Sleepers of Erin*, by Jonathan Gash.

Neophyte This word is now normally used of one who has recently been converted to a church or religious body. It has the more general meaning of someone who is new to any particular activity, and therefore lacking in experience. Ben Jonson uses the word vocatively in this general sense in *Every Man Out of Humour*: 'Away, neophyte, do as I bid thee.' In *The Poetaster* he has: 'He tells thee true, my noble neophyte.' Charlotte Brontë, in *Jane Eyre*, has Mr Rochester say to Jane: 'You have no right to preach to me, you neophyte, that have not passed the porch of life, and are absolutely unacquainted with its mysteries.'

Nephew There may be some uncles and aunts who address nephews by this term in modern times, but such vocative usage is mostly obsolete. It occurs regularly in the literature of the eighteenth and nineteenth centuries, however. Upper middle-class British families were fond of recalling family relationships by means of vocative expressions, though it is doubtful that this extended down through society. In Fielding's *Tom Jones* the hero is called 'nephew' by his aunt. In Thomas Hardy's *The Trumpet Major*, Benjamin Derriman addresses his nephew Festus, whom he fears and dislikes, as both 'nephew' and 'nephy'. When 'nephew' was first used in English it could mean either 'grandson', or 'nephew' in the modern sense. In seventeenth-century literature it frequently means the former, not surprisingly when one remembers that the word is connected with Latin *nepos*, the prime meaning of which is 'grandson'. Shakespeare uses the word, vocatively or otherwise, to mean nephew, grandson, and cousin.

NICKNAME People are often addressed by a nickname in English-speaking countries, a nickname being an extra, unofficial name, not formally given by the parents or legally adopted by the person who bears it. In fifty sample novels, for example, where a full vocative count was made, some kind of nickname was used to address a person on 763 occasions, compared with 5499 instances of a first name being used. It is necessary to say 'some kind of nickname', for there are various sub-categories. Parents may themselves bestow a nickname on a child, not a diminutive form of its first name but a word converted to name status or a name transferred from elsewhere.

A Derbyshire teacher a few years ago reported that his ten-year-old pupils were variously known at home as Crunchy, Boo, Squitface, Popsy Dinkums, Woo, Moonbeam, Muff, Dilly, Dump, Hug, Longlegs, Luscious Legs, Bigpants. Such names arise in a number of ways, varying from verbal incidents to private associations, but the main point is that the resultant names remain in highly restricted use. They are used as intimacies within the family circle and have private meanings for only two or three people. These are 'baby names', in a sense, and as such would be embarrassing to those who bear them if they became known outside the family circle.

Robertson Davies, in *Fifth Business*, is commenting on the diminutive form of a name rather than a true nickname when he says of a boy known to his mother as Pidgy Boy-Boy (an infant corruption of his real name Percy Boyd): 'I knew that I had but once to call him Pidgy Boy-Boy in the schoolyard and his goose would be cooked.'

Other private nicknames are used between lovers. The modern habit of publishing Valentine Day messages in newspapers has revealed something of the naming that goes on in the bedroom: Bogfrog, Boofs, Chonk, Cubbles, Fruitstack, Honeypot, Looby-Loo, Moggo, Oodle, Pokey, Smackeroo, Tablespoon, Widgie, and Zuppy are just a few of those to whom messages have been lovingly addressed in recent years. One imagines that such names are only used when the speaker and listener are alone; that only one speaker uses the name to the person concerned; that the names are not used in third person reference ('I'm meeting Smackeroo at seven'), and that other restrictions apply which would not apply to more public nicknames.

The latter may be group nicknames, used by a child's peer group at school, by fellow-workers in an office or factory, by companions in an army barracks, and so on. Such nicknames take on a referential function; they become meaningful as identification tags to a number of others. Use of such nicknames may be a marker of group membership for both the speaker and the listener.

This ceases to be the case when a nickname becomes totally public and virtually replaces a person's first name, as with Bing Crosby, Buster Keaton, and the like. Mention of these two famous entertainers points to another way in which nicknames differ. Crosby happened to resemble a cartoon character called Bingo, so he ended up with a rather personal nickname. Keaton had a generic nickname bestowed on him because he was a sturdy child. It happened to stick, in his case, but generic nicknames are also used fleetingly. They are of various kinds: Mac, Jock, Taffy, Paddy, and the like being given for reasons of nationality, Scouse, Geordie, and so on for reasons of more local origin.

Other category nicknames include the hundreds used by children to those who are fat or thin; tall or short; learned or stupid; brave or cowardly; spoilsports, nosey parkers, sneaks, or crawlers. A bald man, an old man with a beard, a be-spectacled person – all are likely to have a generic nickname applied to them in a fleeting way. There is also a group of traditional 'clan' nicknames, waiting to be transferred to those who bear a particular surname. Thus, in the armed services, a Miller becomes 'Dusty', a Smith 'Smudger', a Murphy 'Spud', and so on.

'Nickname' in English, apart from not distinguishing between these various types of private and public names, does not indicate whether the name is used with affection or malice. On the affectionate use of such names, Charles Dickens says, in *The Haunted Man*: 'Better be called ever so far out of your name, if it's done in real liking, than have it made ever so much of, and not cared about.' There are limits, however. In *The Wayward Bus*, by John Steinbeck, Chicoy calls a youth 'Pimples' in a friendly way, simply because that is his nickname, but the boy says:

'Mr Chicoy, could we fix it – I mean, could you fix it so you don't call me Pimples any more?' 'What's your name?' he asked roughly. 'Ed,' said Pimples. 'Ed Carson, distant relative of Kit Carson. Before I got these in grammar school, why, they used to call me Kit.'

One problem with nicknames, though, is that they are rarely controlled by the persons who bear them. They are decided upon by others, and gain currency if they seem to be appropriate to a number of others. If they are particularly insulting, or undignified, they may never be used in direct address to the person to whom they refer, which again suggests that we need words to describe those nicknames which are used vocatively, and those which are not.

'Vocative nickname' and 'third-person', or 'referential nickname' are clumsy phrases, but they make an important distinction. What most people would like, if they must have a nickname, is one which is tailor-made rather than off-the-peg, vaguely flattering rather than derogatory, and widely used in an affectionate way rather than viciously used by a small group. William Hazlitt appears to have suffered from the latter type of name, since he says in his essay *On Nicknames*:

Brevity is the soul of wit; and of all eloquence a nickname is the most concise, of all arguments the most unanswerable. It is a word and a blow. A nickname is the heaviest stone that the devil can throw at a man.

It is hard to reconcile that statement with the many innocent uses of nicknames that occur in literature and life. 'Hello, Blitz Baby,' says a mother to her son, in *Absolute Beginners*, by Colin MacInnes. The narrator adds: 'Which is what she calls me, because she had me in one, in a tube shelter with an air raid warden acting as midwife.' *Doctor in the House*, by Richard Gordon, reports on the publican who is known to all medical students as the Padre, while his

pub is the Chapel, since this makes exchanges such as 'I'm popping out to Chapel at six this evening' possible in front of patients. *The Liberty Man*, by Gillian Freeman, has a passing remark about someone who 'had been to public school so they called him Fauntleroy', an allusion to Cedric Errol, the American boy who discovers that he is heir to an earldom, in *Little Lord Fauntleroy*, by Frances Hodgson Burnett.

Sometimes, as Hazlitt says, nicknames are indeed the soul of wit. One thinks of the nurse known as Tonsils 'because all the doctors want to take her out', and of a character like George Chance, in *The Mackerel Plaza*, by Peter de Vries: 'He was a portly number who had all through his schooldays been nicknamed, inevitably, Fat Chance.'

In addition to the various kinds of personal nickname mentioned above, there are collective nicknames which are used vocatively. The obvious example is a sports team, such as an English football club. West Ham United are 'the Hammers' to their fans, and are exhorted to do better each week under that name. 'Get stuck in, Gunners,' would be a suggestion that those playing for the Arsenal football team should make an effort. Many of the individuals playing will have their own nicknames, of course, and will be addressed by them.

Some would say, taking an entirely different view from that of Hazlitt, that the fact that a nickname has been bestowed, and that it is used, is far from being a blow: it is a sign that one has gained acceptance amongst a particular set of people and that they have recognized one's individuality.

Nidget *See* **Idiot**.

Niece This occurs in the literature of the seventeenth, eighteenth and nineteenth centuries, used to the speaker's niece, but modern examples are very difficult to find. Usage seems to have died away as with many other terms of family relationship.

'Niece' is used vocatively in several of the Shakespearean plays, sometimes as a single word, sometimes as part of a longer vocative expression. An example of the latter occurs in, e.g., *The Heir of Redclyffe*, by Charlotte M. Yonge, which has 'My dear, dear little niece' used by an aunt.

Nigger This would now normally be considered an insulting term to use to a black person, though one black speaker might use it to another as a kind of ironic reminder of their shared past.

In *The Liberation of Lord Byron Jones*, by Jesse Hill Ford, a black lawyer objects to use of the word in a southern American courtroom because it 'connotes unhappy conditions under slavery'. The District Attorney argues that it is merely an old pronunciation of 'negro', adding that 'knee-grow reminds me of certain Scandinavian sociologists and others who have assumed an authority and published inaccuracies concerning racial matters which I find not only distasteful but provocative as well.' On the word's origin, the District Attorney may have a point.

H. L. Mencken points out, in *The American Language*, that Southern pronunciation of 'negro' was *nigrah*. The word was undoubtedly much used, and does not seem to have been thought offensive when used by blacks to blacks. There are many examples of such usage in Harriet Beecher Stowe's *Uncle Tom's Cabin* and more in *Gone With The Wind*, by Margaret Mitchell. The latter novel has a white woman from the North refer to a former slave as an 'old nigger', which greatly offends the man concerned. 'He had never had the term "nigger" applied to him by a white person in all his life. By other negroes, yes. But never by a white person.'

In modern times both 'nigger' and 'negro' would be avoided by white speakers, and 'nigger' used vocatively would be offensive in almost any conceivable circumstances. Sammy Davis Junior, in his autobiography *Yes I Can!*, recalls that he was addressed as 'you stinking coon nigger' by a fellow soldier, soon after his arrival at a military base. The same speaker added 'you yellow-livered black bastard' to make sure that his meaning was clear.

In *The Heart is a Lonely Hunter*, by Carson McCullers, a white woman who is arguing with a black girl calls her 'you black nigger'. The word may occur elsewhere in the vocative group, as in Arthur Hailey's *Hotel*. This has a white hotel-guest say to a black employee: 'All right, nigger boy, you asked for it.' *See also* the quotation from *The Choirboys*, by Joseph Wambaugh, under **Asshole**.

In February 1989, when Doug Williams became the first black quarterback to play in a Super Bowl football game, the words of the player's father, used to him as a youngster, were much quoted. 'When people call you nigger, be so good at what you're doing they'll have to call you Mr Nigger.'

Ninny In use since the beginning of the seventeenth century as a term for a simpleton. The word probably derives from 'innocent'.

In *Kipps*, by H. G. Wells, 'blundering ninny' is used by Kipps's uncle to address the hero. *Mariana*, by Monica Dickens, has a mother saying to her daughter, 'Don't cry, you ninny.'

Nip Addressed to a person of Japanese ancestry, though not in polite conversation. The word is an abbreviation of 'Nipponese', which means Japanese. 'Ya cute little fuckin

Nip, ya' is addressed to an American policeman named Tanaguchi in *The Choirboys*, by Joseph Wambaugh. He is described as 'a third-generation Japanese', and in his youth was known as 'Chino' or 'Chink' by those 'who lumped all Orientals together'.

Nipper A mainly British slang term for a small child, usually a boy. Probably derived from the idea of nipping about rapidly. Children themselves may apply the term to another child who is smaller than average. *See also* **Tich**.

Nipple-biter In *St Urbain's Horseman*, by Mordecai Richler, a wife says to her husband: 'Nipple-biter, so there you are.' This is almost an example of a love-name, rather than a normal vocative. A love-name is a nickname regularly used by one partner to another, but only when they are alone. It is only used as a vocative: the user of such a name does not say to a third person that Pooh-bear, or whoever, will be calling for her at six. There is no evidence in this novel, however, that 'nipple-biter' is regularly used by this wife to her husband. It appears to be an *ad hoc* vocative of the love-name type, subject to many restrictions in its use.

Nit 'Thou flea, thou nit, thou winter-cricket thou,' says Petruchio to a tailor, in Shakespeare's *The Taming of the Shrew*. A nit is technically the egg of a louse or other parasitic insect, and our first record of its application to a person in jest or contempt is in *Love's Labour's Lost*. It may, therefore, be a truly Shakespearean insult, one that has survived to the present day.

'You stupid British nits' is addressed to an audience by an African speaker in *Cocksure*, by Mordecai Richler. He equates the expression with 'You Anglo-Saxon pigs'. In another of Richler's novels, *St Urbain's Horseman*, 'you nit' is addressed by a boy to a girl aged four. *Up the City Road*, by John Stroud, has a young London man calling his friend 'nit' as an obviously friendly insult.

Nitwit 'You little nitwit' is a disguised endearment in *The Fox in the Attic*, by Richard Hughes. 'Nitwit' – someone with the wit of a louse's egg, i.e. no wit at all – is too obviously a joke to be used as a serious insult. It seems to be a modern invention, first occurring in the 1920s. *See also* **Nit**. It was possibly 'nitwit' which gave rise to 'twit', which also came into use in the 1920s.

noble A frequently used element in Shakespearean vocatives, referring to high social position, genteel birth, admirable characteristics, and so on. The word is so over-worked that one suspects it must have been very often little more than a conventional noise.

'Noble' + first name is frequent throughout the plays, and amongst a wide range of vocative expressions one finds: noble mistress, noble lord, noble friend, noble sir, noble prince, noble fool, noble captain, noble boy, my noble uncle, noble peer, noble earl, noble lady, noble madam, noble father-in-law.

One would be justified in saying that the word was common currency, since it named an English coin for many centuries.

Nobody Used to a person who is thought to be of no importance socially or professionally. 'You contemptible little nobody' is spoken by an actor to his director in N. J. Crisp's *Festival*.

No-hoper Used to a person who is thought to have no hope of advancing socially or professionally. 'You failed no-hoper' is used by an actor to his director in N. J. Crisp's *Festival*: 'What makes you think, you failed no-hoper, that you can come in here and patronise me?'

Noodle This word appeared in the mid-eighteenth century and was much used to describe a foolish person. One of the earliest authors to use it was Laurence Sterne in *Tristram Shandy*. Mrs Shandy has just given birth to a son but he is not expected to live. Mr Shandy tells the servant girl to run to the curate and have the child christened 'Trismegistus'. She remembers only that it begins with 'Tris', whereupon the curate, who happens to be called Tristram, assumes that his own name is to be used. 'There is no *gistus* to it, noodle!' he tells the servant girl.

This tortured explanation is offered in the book to explain how the hero came to bear the name which his father hated most in the world.

The vocative occurs again in another well-known passage in *Hard Times*, by Charles Dickens. Mr Bounderby's house-keeper, Mrs Sparsit, addresses her employer touchingly as 'my benefactor' to his face, 'yet it is an indubitable fact . . . that five minutes after he had left the house . . . [she] shook her right-hand mitten at his portrait, made a contemptuous grimace at that work of art, and said, "Serve you right, you noodle."' When she is eventually dismissed, Mrs Sparsit pauses to tell her benefactor:

If that portrait could speak, sir – but it has the advantage over the original of not possessing the power of committing itself and disgusting others – it would testify, that a long period has elapsed since I first habitually addressed it as the picture of a noodle. Nothing that a noodle does can awaken surprise or indignation; the proceedings of a noodle can only inspire contempt.

'Noodle' in this sense is of obscure origin. It came into existence some time before the word that describes the pasta.

Novelist Not normally used vocatively, but 'you novelist, you' is addressed to a writer in *Pray for the Wanderer*, by Kate O'Brien.

NUMBER NAME Number names can be heard on any Saturday afternoon in Britain during the football season, as the referee of a match talks to the players. It is accepted in such a situation that the referee cannot be expected to remember the names of twenty-two players with whom he will have contact for a very short time. If he wishes to call a player to him he will call him by the number that player has temporarily assumed.

The practice no doubt extends to other team games. One might argue that it helps the referee to remain impartial if he uses numbers; he is not influenced by any previous acquaintanceship he may have with the person concerned. There is a comment from the player's point of view in *A Salute to the Great McCarthy*, by Barry Oakley, which has an Australian football setting: 'The number on my back, 16. That's me, that's all you are now, a numeral.'

Other temporary situations no doubt arise where a number is the most useful means of identification. Examination candidates are sometimes summoned into a room by number, parachutists or gymnasts in a line may be instructed when to move by this means.

There are occasions when a number replaces a person's name in a more permanent way. James Bond responds to '007', for example, and is well-known under that numbernym. Slightly less permanent was the number that Lawrence of Arabia was given when he became an airman – 338171 – but this at least gave rise to a famous witticism of Noël Coward's. Coward wrote Lawrence a letter which began 'Dear 338171, or may I call you 338 . . . ?'

Charles Dickens furnishes us with examples of both kinds of number names. In *Hard Times* we have: 'Girl number twenty,' said Mr Gradgrind, squarely pointing with his square forefinger, 'I don't know that girl. Who is that girl?' Girl number twenty explains that she is Sissy Jupe, only to be told that she has no right to call herself Sissy, she must be Cecilia.

In *David Copperfield* Mr Creakle, the magistrate, visits a prison and asks: 'Well, Twenty-Seven, how do you find yourself today?' Twenty-Seven says that he is 'very 'umble', a remark which reveals him immediately to be Uriah Heep. The incident is a reminder of Dr Manette, in *A Tale of Two Cities*: 'Did you ask me for my name?' 'Assuredly I did.' 'One Hundred and Five, North Tower,' replies Dr Manette, who had been a prisoner in the Bastille for eighteen years.

Two more Dickensian number names are to be found in *The Pickwick Papers*. Mr Jingle says to a cabman: 'Here, No. 924, take your fare, and take yourself off.' Much later in the novel there is a prisoner in the Fleet Prison who is addressed as 'Twenty', or 'Tventy' as Sam Weller pronounces it. This is because he carries in his pocket a piece of card which he presents to new acquaintances. It bears no name, simply his 'address' within the prison, No. 20, Coffeeroom Flight.

Number names are less used now than in former times, when policemen might be addressed by their superiors as PC 49, or whatever. In short-lived, specialized situations, however, such as those described above, they continue to serve a useful purpose. *See also* the O. Henry quote at **Waiter**.

Number One Used to address the first Lieutenant in a Royal Navy ship. An example of its use occurs in *Mariana*, by Monica Dickens.

Numskull The earlier form of this term was 'numbskull', which shows the thought behind it, a person whose skull, or head, is numb.

'You numbskulls' occurs as a vocative in Goldsmith's *She Stoops to Conquer*. Tom Sawyer is called 'you numskull' by his aunt when he explains why he has poured pain-killer down the throat of her cat. 'I done it out of pity for him – because he hadn't any aunt.' 'Hadn't any aunt, you numskull. What has that got to do with it?' Tom's ingenious explanation is that if the cat had had an aunt she would have administered the medicine to it to help it.

'Numskull' is still in occasional use as a vocative, normally used humorously to someone who is thought to be acting stupidly.

Nuncle A vocative form of 'uncle', possibly arising from a false division of 'an uncle'. It was in use by the sixteenth century and therefore available to Shakespeare, who used it in rather a special way. Only one character makes use of the term, the Fool in *King Lear*, and he uses it only to address his royal master.

The word was used by other seventeenth-century playwrights such as Dryden, however, and continued to be used until at least the nineteenth century in rural dialects. It developed a pet-form 'nunky', while in Thomas Hardy's *The Trumpet Major* it appears as 'nunc' when used by Festus Derriman to address his uncle Benjamin.

Nurse The professional title of one trained to assist doctors in looking after the sick, the elderly, etc. Used in this sense to both males and females. 'Nurse' can also be used to a nursemaid, who looks after young children.

This was the original function of a nurse, who was a 'nourrice', or wet-nurse.

The young black nurse-girl, as she is called, is addressed affectionately as 'nursie' in Doris Lessing's *Landlocked*, a novel set in South Africa. 'How is the patient, nurse?' asks someone in *Anglo-Saxon Attitudes*, by Angus Wilson. In this instance it is a joke, addressed to a young girl who is looking after a guest who has twisted his ankle. The incident provides a good example of role-playing, though temporary, being accompanied by a relevant vocative.

Rather similar usage occurs in *Jane Eyre*, by Charlotte Brontë. Bessie, the housemaid, looks after Jane when she is ill and is called 'nurse' by the visiting doctor.

The most famous nurse in literature is Angelica, as she is called on one occasion only, nurse to Juliet in Shakespeare's *Romeo and Juliet*. Normally she is addressed as: nurse, good nurse, my dear nurse, good sweet nurse, honest nurse, gentle nurse, and honey nurse.

Nut This word is used to describe a person who is odd, eccentric, or crazy, but it will often be interpreted as a compliment rather than as an insult. It stems from the slang meaning of 'nut', i.e. the head, which in turn gave rise to expressions like 'he's off his nut', 'he's crazy'.

The word is often extended to 'nutter' in third person reference, 'nutball', 'nutbar', or 'nutcase' in the USA, but these would rarely be used in direct address.

Examples of usage include 'You're talking gibberish, you nut', in *The Stork*, by Denison Hatch, where one American man is talking to another. In *The Business of Loving*, by Godfrey Smith, a man starts to sing a song and is told by his lover: 'Belt up will you, nut? You're not a patch on Peter Sellers.' The whole conversation is interlarded with friendly insults, the singer replying with 'you lousy slut' a few lines later.

'Silly nut' is also used intimately in *Daughters of Mulberry*, by Roger Longrigg, while *Other Men's Wives*, by Alexander Fullerton, has: 'You came for this, didn't you?' 'How could I have, you nut?' 'Oh, *romantic*.' 'You nut' is here addressed to an intimate woman friend of the male speaker.

Nymphomaniac 'You little nymphomaniac' occurs in *The Front Runner*, by Patricia Nell Warren. Nymphomania properly describes an unhealthy and excessive sexual desire in a woman, and should therefore only be addressed to a woman. The instance cited is spoken by one homosexual man to another, the man addressed being described as 'cheerfully promiscuous'.

O Used as a vocative element in the exalted language of poetry, prayers, and the like, almost as if it were a formal marker of a non-existent vocative case in English.

Impassioned lovers also make use of it: 'O Romeo, Romeo, wherefore art thou Romeo?' Used at the beginning of a sentence it is difficult to distinguish this vocative 'O' from the exclamatory sound that can express a number of different emotions.

In earlier literature, however, it sometimes occurs in a tag vocative where its case-marking quality is clearer. 'Winking away a tear, O Amy,' says a character in Charlotte M. Young's *The Heir of Redclyffe*.

Vocative 'O' is recorded from the thirteenth century, which suggests that it arose naturally, though even then it may have been an importation by learned writers who felt that vocatives needed to be formally distinguished.

A possible support for the 'natural' theory comes in the modern use of suffix '-o', which forms many vocative diminutives, or terms which are more nearly pure vocatives than the words or names which are modified in this way. 'Boyo', for example, is used vocatively, whereas 'boy' is more frequently used in third person reference, while being available for vocative use. 'Kiddo' is a vocative form of 'kid', 'lino' is a vocative diminutive of 'line', itself a short form of 'linesman'.

The suffix '-o' can also be added to proper names to form a diminutive, which is then nearly always used vocatively, rather than in third person reference. *Anglo-Saxon Attitudes*, by Angus Wilson, has a speaker who converts 'John' to 'Johno' on several occasions. 'Daddy-o' is now a standard vocative form, but some would say that it conveniently distinguishes the friendly from the family use of 'Daddy'. 'Three-o' is used as a friendly term of address to a third officer in *Doctor at Sea*, by Richard Gordon, but the '-o' here may derive from 'officer'. 'Dumbo' and 'Fatso' are further examples of vocative conversions which feature final '-o'. *See also* the Wilfrid Sheed quotation under **Sage**.

Oaf 'You great oaf' is now typically a playful insult used by a woman to a man, referring to his clumsiness and hinting at his stupidity. That phrase is used in such a way in Edna Ferber's *Showboat*, for instance. In *Henry's War*, by Jeremy Brooks, 'you oaf' is similarly friendly.

The expression becomes more genuinely contemptuous in *The Ginger Man*, by J. P. Donleavy, when a man calls another 'you stupid intolerable oaf', though he says this silently to himself.

The word came into use in the seventeenth century and is probably a form of 'elf', since its original meaning was an elf's child, a changeling, a misbegotten half-wit. Its pronunciation and written form seem to have gone through many changes, and it is likely that its meaning varies from speaker to speaker.

Office boys, you *See* You + category of person.

Officer 'Take him to prison, officer' sounds like a phrase that could occur in a modern detective story. In fact it is a quotation from Shakespeare's *Measure for Measure* (3:i), though it could have occurred even earlier than the seventeenth century. An officer then, as now, was one who holds an office, though the term has for centuries been used mostly of military officers and those who in some way uphold the law.

'Officer' is still a polite way of addressing a policeman in any English-speaking country, and the term certainly is found in detective stories. 'What do you have here, officer?' occurs in *The Case of the Spurious Spinster*, by Erle Stanley Gardner. *Brothers in Law*, by Henry Cecil, has five examples.

In the USA 'Officer' is also used as a prefix, followed by a last name. Thus a judge might address a policeman who is known to him as 'Officer Smith'. The plural form can be used as necessary. 'Hey, what is the trouble, officers?' is said to two policemen by a man they have stopped in Ed McBain's short story *Hot Cars*.

old A frequently used vocative element, meant to indicate affectionate familiarity in most cases, and usually addressed to a man.

'Old boy' has in recent times been one of the most popular combinations, followed by 'old man' and 'old chap'. Variants include: old bean, old chum, old cock, old fellow, old + first name, old friend, old fruit, old lad, old scout, old son, old thing.

Individual novelists may extend the range. Stanley Kauffmann, for example, in *The Philanderer*, has 'old foop', 'old pineapple', 'old sweet', 'old walrus', all used affectionately.

Love in Quiet Places, by Bernard Thompson, has 'old 'ippo' used by a man to his sleeping partner, a woman who is on the large side if not of hippopotamus proportions.

'Old girl' and 'old woman' occur fairly regularly; Sinclair Lewis uses 'old socks' in *Martin Arrowsmith*; O. Henry has 'old sport' in *Sisters of the Golden Circle*, and so it continues. To all such expressions may be added the 'you old...' type of vocative, which is normally admiring, even though in form it may appear to be insulting.

'You old bastard' is frequently a covert endearment, and further examples met with include: you old basket; you old dark horse, you; you old loon; you old python; you old rascal; you old slob; you old so-and-so.

'Old' is often combined with 'poor' to express sympathy, the resultant expressions being of the 'poor old chap', 'poor old' + first name type, or 'you poor old bastard', 'you poor old thing' type.

In dialectal usage 'old' is used with 'my', as in 'my old duck', 'my old bird', 'my old cock', 'my old sweat'. Dialectal pronunciation of such friendly, working-class expressions is often indicated by variant spellings. 'My' becomes 'me', perhaps, or 'old' is 'owd'.

Occasionally 'old' is used in its aged sense, and can then be insulting, especially in an expression like 'you stupid old man'. Otherwise it indicates that a person is old in the sense of being thoroughly familiar to the speaker, accepted by him as part of the established order.

It is used almost as a synonym of 'dear', especially when addressed to someone who is patently very young. Thus, in *The House of the Seven Gables*, by Nathaniel Hawthorne, a man says to a very young boy: 'What's the trouble, old gentleman?' *Seven Little Australians*, by Ethel Turner, has a step-mother saying to her young daughter: 'Dear little Judy! Be brave, little old woman!'

Old timer An American expression, used to an elderly man, especially one who was once a soldier. In *The Color of Money*, by Walter Tevis, an old pool-player is congratulated with: 'Nice shooting last night, old-timer.' The vocative occurs fairly frequently in western movies.

One A synonym for 'person' in expressions like 'my dear one', 'my own one', though these now have rather an archaic sound to them.

In standard collocations like 'young one', 'old one', 'little one', where 'one' is unstressed, it is usually written 'un' and is often attached to the preceding word.

'My dear one' is used by a man to his lover in *The Sandcastle*, by Iris Murdoch. 'My own one' occurs in a friendly, rather than an inti-mate way, in *The Limits of Love*, by Frederic Raphael.

In *Gideon Planish*, by Sinclair Lewis, a wife who constantly changes the vocatives that she uses to her husband includes 'big one' and 'great one' amongst them. 'Little one' appears in that form in George Eliot's *Scenes of Clerical Life*, used by a man to his eighteen-year-old adopted daughter.

One of you See **Somebody**.

Operator As a term of address 'operator' refers exclusively to the person who operates a telephone switchboard. In other contexts, e.g. in phrases like 'a smooth operator', the word now hints at a successful but unscrupulous person.

Ostler 'What, ostler!' calls a carrier, arriving at an inn in Shakespeare's *Henry the Fourth Part One* (2:i). 'Ostler, bring round my gig,' says a man in *Vanity Fair*, by William Thackeray. For several centuries an ostler would thus have been summoned by customers who needed their horses to be attended to. The ostler was a stableman or groom, an essential servant at wayside inns. The name of his trade derived from 'hosteler', but the initial 'h' – was probably never pronounced.

our 'Our' is used in some English dialects to mean 'belonging to our family'. *Cider with Rosie*, by Laurie Lee, has examples of 'our' + first name: our Mother, our lad. *Saturday Night and Sunday Morning*, by Alan Sillitoe, has 'our' + first name addressed to brothers, sisters, and cousins of either sex, together with 'our Mam'.

Those who use this dialectal form would also when speaking to someone about their family, refer to 'your Mam', etc.

Non-family use of 'our' occurs in *An Indecent Obsession*, by Coleen McCullough. 'There's something in you, our Michael, isn't there?' says one man to another. Both speaker and listener are patients in a small ward, temporarily part of a small, close-knit community vaguely resembling a family. The speaker is Australian, not one who would normally use 'our' expressions to members of his family.

The advantage of the latter usage, as the distinguished British journalist Katharine Whitehorn once pointed out in an *Observer* article, is that it avoids the tendency parents in the south of England have of using 'my' when speaking of the children, something which can infuriate the partner.

The article was a discussion in general terms about the use of 'my', 'our', 'his', 'her' within marriage, but said in passing: 'How very sensible are those areas of the country where "our" is a built-in part of the name, as in "Our

Jane wouldn't do that" or "Come here, our Billy." '

Overcoat, my dear   An intimacy used in *Room at the Top*, by John Braine. The usage is unusual, but the thought behind it is easy to understand, in that an overcoat provides warmth and comfort.

Owctioner   *See* **Auctioneer**.

Own, my   'What delight the words gave her,' says Charlotte Yonge of her heroine, in *The Heir of Redclyffe*, when she is addressed by the man she loves as 'my own'.

'Own' has long been used as an element in affectionate terms of address, emphasizing the feeling of possessiveness that lovers adopt towards their partners, or simply the tender feelings of the speaker. 'Tell me, mine own,' says Hermione to her daughter, in *The Winter's Tale* (5:iii) 'where has thou been preserv'd?'

In Tennyson's *Maud* occurs the rather excessive: 'My own heart's heart and ownest own, farewell.' Oscar Wilde may well have been laughing at such excess in *The Import-ance of Being Earnest*, where Jack Worthing is fond of calling Gwendolen 'my own darling', 'my own one'.

No doubt such endearments are still whispered in appropriate circumstances, but they would sound strange if overheard. Even in private a modern miss so addressed might protest that she is her own woman, not someone else's.

Ox   The vocative meaning of 'ox' has changed through the centuries. In the seventeenth century it meant a fool, as Shakespeare indicates in *The Merry Wives of Windsor* (5:v), where Falstaff says: 'I do begin to perceive that I am made an ass.' 'Ay,' says Ford, 'and an ox too.' At the end of the century we find a character in William Congreve's *The Double Dealer* (1694) calling another man 'fool, sot, insensible ox'.

Modern use of 'ox', applied to a person, implies both stupidity and sluggishness of movement, usually of a large person. The word usually collocates with 'dumb', as in Frank Yerby's *A Woman Called Fancy*, where a woman says to a man: 'She's not lying! Can't you see that, you big, dumb ox?'

Pa A short form of 'papa', used by children in some families to address their father. The habit may be continued into adulthood. The term occurs fairly frequently in nineteenth-century literature, less so in more recent novels. It can be qualified, as in 'pa darling', used by a daughter to her father in *George Beneath a Paper Moon*, by Nina Bawden.

Paddy An instant nickname which can be bestowed on an Irishman in a friendly way if his name is not known. Underlying the usage is the assumption that his name may well be Padraig, or Patrick, since that first name has been a special favourite in Ireland over a long period. St Patrick is the patron saint of Ireland. In *Saturday Night and Sunday Morning* occurs: 'Bert said he was a Mick, and called him Paddy, asking what part of Ireland he came from.'

Padre This is the word in Spanish, Italian, and Portuguese for 'Father'. It is used by members of the armed services to address a chaplain. Some speakers would use it to address any Christian priest. 'I confess I like being called "Padre",' says the Rev. John Gillett, in Rudyard Kipling's *Stalky and Co.*, who is addressed in that fashion by the boys in the school. In *The Choirboys*, by Joseph Wambaugh, a Los Angeles policeman who is a devout Jehovah's Witness is addressed as 'Padre' or 'Father Willie' by his colleagues.

Pagan Someone who does not believe in one of the world's main religions is a pagan. 'Pagans' is used insultingly on two occasions in *Girl with Green Eyes*, by Edna O'Brien.

Etymologically the word refers to someone who lived in a village as opposed to a town, a rustic, though that has never been the meaning in English.

Pain in the ass, you ' "I know what I'm going to give *you*, you pain in the ass," said David to his brother. "A bust in the mouth." ' This passage in *Moviola*, by Garson Kanin, illustrates the use of this insulting expression, which occurs rather more frequently in the USA than in Britain.

The same novel has another example of its use, where its force is softened by the addition of mock insults: 'He turned to the soundman. "And what about you, you pain in the ass, you pest, you useless appendage, you scourge of my life?" '

A milder form of this expression is 'pain in the neck', but although people might say to one another: 'You're a pain in the neck,' 'you pain in the neck' does not seem to be used.

Pal George Borrow, in *Lavengro*, uses many gypsy words which he explains in a glossary. One of them is 'pal', which is glossed as 'brother, friend, mate'. 'Pal' has been generally used in English since the seventeenth century in the latter two senses. It is normally friendly, and used between men.

Like most terms which appear to express friendship, 'pal' can be decidedly aggressive if uttered in a certain way. ' "Listen, pal," I snarled,' writes Garrison Keillor in *Happy to be Here*.

The term is used throughout the English-speaking world, and is often used as a substitute for 'man' in the 'old man' group. In *The Sophomore*, by Barry Spacks, 'old pal' is interchanged with 'old buddy' in a friendly conversation between two American men. The diminutive 'pally' also occurs. It is used by one man to another in *The Late Risers*, by Bernard Wolfe.

The following interesting passage occurs in *A Salute to the Great McCarthy*, by Barry Oakley, which is set in Australia. A man talking to his son says:

'When you're a little bit older, yes, maybe you'll understand.' 'I am a little bit older and I do understand. You're in no position to point the bone'. He takes a step towards me, his arms hanging loose and heavy with menace. 'What's that, pal?' Pal! That was his man-to-man word. Grown up at last!

A correspondent, Mr Kel Hunter, comments on the use of 'pal' in Glasgow: 'Its use usually implies disbelief rather than endearment, e.g. "Oh, course ah beleeve yeh, pal – ah've got rocks in mah heed." ' Mr Hunter says that it is also used when announcing one's intention to punch someone's head in.

Paleface It was James Fenimore Cooper (1789–1851) who convinced us that North American Indians address white men as 'paleface'. The word occurs in *The Spy* (1821) and subsequent novels such as *The Last of the Mohicans*.

H. L. Mencken, in *The American Language*, says that the term is also used by black Americans to address whites, but the Indian associations remain strongest.

Many will link the word with Bob Hope, who was a cowardly dentist in *The Paleface*, a film released in 1948. In *Rabbit Redux*, by John Updike, the term is used by one white American to another. They have been discussing the Vietnam war and comparing it to a Cherokee uprising. The speaker who uses 'Paleface' is taking the part of the Indians and Vietnamese.

Use of the term in children's games occurs in Joyce Cary's short story *Growing Up*: 'The two girls, staggering with laughter, threw themselves upon their father. "Paleface – Paleface Robbie. Kill him – scalp him." '

Palooka Used in American slang, especially, to a large but rather stupid man, often in expressions like 'you big palooka'. A woman might turn it into a disguised endearment.

The word was originally applied to a clumsy boxer or wrestler. H. L. Mencken, in *The American Language*, says that it was introduced in 1925 by Jack Conway, a former baseball player who later wrote for *Variety*. Conway is also credited with the introduction of slang expressions such as 'S.A.' (sex-appeal), 'to click' (to succeed), 'belly laugh' and 'to scram'. 'Palooka' was possibly suggested by Spanish *peluca*, literally 'wig', but used insultingly.

Palsy-walsy 'Whoa there, palsy-walsy,' says a young woman to a man in *The Day of the Locust*, by Nathanael West. In *The Philanderer*, by Stanley Kauffmann, occurs: 'Well, palsy, they're likely to ream you yet.' 'Palsy-walsy' is typical of the reduplication indulged in by children as they experiment with words. This particular expression has been taken over by adults, but is mainly used in third person reference, describing people who are 'palsy-walsy' with one another.

In vocative use 'palsy' or 'palsy-walsy' softens down 'pal', which can occasionally sound aggressive. It recalls 'friendy-wendy', a term by which the playwright J. M. Barrie was addressed by a child. It suggested to him the name 'Wendy', which he used in *Peter Pan* and made famous.

Pander This word should properly be 'Pandar', since it derives from the name 'Pandarus'. This was the name given by Boccaccio and Chaucer to the man who acted as go-between for Troilus and Criseyde, though by the time Shakespeare came to write his version of the story, as *Troilus and Cressida*, a pander already had the meaning of male procurer, or pimp.

Shakespeare himself did not express it in those words. His Pandarus says to the young lovers: 'If ever you prove false one to another, since I have taken such pains to bring you together, let all pitiful goers-between be call'd to the world's end after my name – call them all Pandars.' Elsewhere in his plays he makes it clear that to call someone a pander is insulting.

In *King Lear* (2:ii) 'pander' is equated with beggar and coward as Kent abuses Oswald. *Cymberline* (3:v) has 'you precious pander, villain!'

The word is almost never used in modern English as a noun or vocative, though we talk freely about pandering to someone's wishes, which derives from the same source. The modern insult would be 'you pimp'.

Pap An abbreviation of 'pappy', itself a nursery form of 'papa'. It occurs in *A Woman Called Fancy*, by Frank Yerby, addressed to her father by a girl who lives in the hill country of Carolina. She calls her mother 'Maw'.

Papa A word for father which was introduced into English from French in the seventeenth century and used by polite society. The word was considered genteel, though adults left the word more and more to children as time passed.

It still suggests usage by middle-class rather than working-class families, but is by no means as frequently used as it was until the nineteenth century. Dickens was at his comic best in *Little Dorrit* when he described the advice given to Amy by the aristocratic widow, Mrs General: 'I think, father, I require a little time.'

'Papa is a preferable mode of address,' observed Mrs General. 'Father is rather vulgar, my dear. The word Papa, besides, gives a pretty form to the lips. Papa, potatoes, poultry, prunes and prism, are all very good words for the lips, especially prunes and prism.'

As a result of this, Dickens tells us, Amy 'very nearly' addresses her father 'as poultry, if not prunes and prism too, in her desire to submit herself to Mrs General and please him'.

In *The Moonflower Vine*, by Jetta Carleton, a wife uses 'Papa' to her husband. The couple have many children who use this form of address. The term is also used in the USA in a similar way to 'Daddy', addressed to a man who is unrelated to the speaker. Men would use it to an older man; women might use it to a lover.

The word is most frequently used alone, though expressions like 'my dear Papa' occur. In William Thackeray's *The Newcomes* a child uses the exclamatory 'you dear kind Papa' to his father. 'Papa' + last name and 'Mama' + last name occur in *Little Dorrit*, used by Mrs

Gowan to the Meagles. The latter couple are the parents of her daughter-in-law.

Parade A military term of address, used to men who are on parade, assembled on the parade ground. 'Parade, attention!' would be a command to all men to come to attention. An example of such usage occurs in *The Magic Army*, by Leslie Thomas.

Parasite, you lucky *See* Drone.

Pard A short form of 'Pardner', itself a variant of 'Partner'. 'Nearly time for us to be moving, pard,' says Injun Joe to his companion, in *Tom Sawyer*, by Mark Twain. The fuller form of the word occurs in *North Dallas Forty*, by Peter Gent, where a professional American football-player says to a colleague: 'Now you're talkin', pardner.'

Parent 'My poor parent' is addressed to her father by a woman in *The Dream of Fair Women*, by Henry Williamson. She is an educated speaker, and it is doubtful whether her father hears the comment, as he is very old and deaf.

Parrot The *Oxford English Dictionary* is able to quote a sixteenth century example of 'parrot' used as a vocative. It occurs when a person is thought to be imitating someone else in word or deed. A typical example of the term's use occurs in *Gone to Earth*, by Mary Webb. Two women are talking, one of them asking if the other sees any likeness between her children and Mr Reddin. ' "They favour you," she said. "Not Mr Reddin?" "Mr Reddin?" "Ah. They'd ought to. They'm his'n." "His'n?" "Yes, parrot." '

Parson A parson is technically a priest in charge of a parish, but the word is loosely used of any clergyman. As a term of address, 'parson' is found in, e.g., eighteenth-century novels such as Fielding's *Tom Jones*, and in later dialectal use. 'Is there any fiddler in your parish, parson?' asks a man in *Gone to Earth*, by Mary Webb.

Partner This is used both specifically and more generally as a term of address. Specifically it is used while playing certain card games, such as bridge or whist, where two players partner one another to form a team. Such teams are sometimes formed in sports such as tennis and badminton, and once again 'partner' could be used by the players concerned.

An example of the sporting use of partner occurs in *My Brother Jonathan*, by Francis Brett Young. A young man is playing tennis with a girl he admires. She is more interested in the game than in him, which he finds disconcert-

ing. 'She was quite impersonal; he was not Jonathan or Dr Dakers, he was just "partner." It seemed a pity. Instinctively he diminished his violence in serving to Sheila. "Whatever are you doing, partner?" Edie whispered anxiously.'

A couple dancing together are also partners. When Henry VIII dances for the first time with Anne Bullen he tells her: 'Sweet partner, I must not yet forsake you' (*Henry the Eighth*, 1:iv).

In a business context, partners are those who share the ownership of a company. When Uriah Heep has successfully cheated Mr Wickfield, in *David Copperfield*, he is able to address him as 'fellow partner', which he does with his usual oiliness.

In a more general sense, people who are joined together in a common undertaking of some kind, or are in a similar situation, may loosely consider themselves to be partners. Dogberry, in *Much Ado About Nothing* (3:iv), tells Verges: 'Go, good partner, go, get you to Francis Seacoal.' Dogberry, of course, is a constable, and he and Verges are concerned with lawful business.

Their modern equivalents would be the teams of American policemen who habitually patrol together. 'Give em a few licks for me, partner,' says one policeman to another in *The Choirboys*, by Joseph Wambaugh, a novel in which many examples of 'partner' occur, used between police team-mates. Such teams give a new meaning to the old phrase 'partners in crime'.

In *Promotion of the Admiral*, by Morley Roberts, a man addresses a new companion as 'partner'. They will be working together in future. In some instances, 'partner' is used as a synonym of 'friend', 'mate', etc., either to someone already known or to a stranger. It is not unusual for its pronunciation to be changed to 'pardner' in such circumstances, and incorporated in a phrase such as: 'Howdy, pardner!' This is in imitation of the cowboy talk established in many a western film.

Party Used vocatively in military circles to address a party of servicemen or women. They may be more specifically designated as 'firing party', 'demolition party', etc., since a party is usually selected to perform a specific duty. The term occurs vocatively in *The Magic Army*, by Leslie Thomas.

Party, old This is used by one man to another in the O. Henry short story *The Day we Celebrate*. It is not in regular use, but is justified in that 'party', in many contexts, can refer to an individual person.

In colloquial speech a reference to a 'coquettish little party' would be understood as referring to a girl, and a query such as: 'Who was the party who was here just now?' would refer to a man. 'Old party' as a vocative is therefore the equivalent of 'old person'.

Passion-flower The passion-flower gets its name because of a supposed resemblance to the crown of thorns and other emblems of Christ's Passion. It is a climbing plant with egg-shaped fruit. 'Passion-flower' is sometimes used as a vocative variant of flower, usually by a man to a woman, and usually with reference to sexual passion. Thus a man in *The Half Hunter*, by John Sherwood, addresses 'Dagmar, my little passion-flower,' and equates it a moment later with 'Honeythighs'.

Pat A pet form of Patrick, used as a nickname for an Irishman because of the frequency of Patrick as a male first name in Ireland. St Patrick is also the Irish national saint. *Pray for the Wanderer*, by Kate O'Brien, has: ' "Are they afraid of you in London?" "Not so very, mind you! But they sometimes put on Irish accents to placate me. And the really matey ones call me Pat." ' Paddy is used in a similar way.

Pater The Latin word for 'father', used (along with mater, 'mother') by some public-school educated children to their parents in the early part of the century. When a woman uses 'pater' to her father, a professor, in Angus Wilson's *Anglo-Saxon Attitudes*, the novelist comments that 'in 1936 she still preserved with no self-consciousness much of the vocabulary of her youth'.

Peabrain *See* Dunce.

Peach-blossom A friendly term of address to a woman, especially one whose skin reminds the speaker of the colour of peach-blossom, a delicate purplish pink. There is an example in *Funeral in Berlin*, by Len Deighton, and an embellished one in Katherine Mansfield's short story, *At the Bay*. There a man greets his sister as 'my Celestial Peach Blossom!', but this is closely followed by a comment on 'his absurd manner of speaking'.

A pretty girl, in slang, is quite likely to be described as 'a peach', so this vocative is doubly complimentary.

Peacock Occasionally used in former times to a person of either sex acting in an ostentatiously vain way, strutting about in a manner similar to that of the bird itself. 'Thou wagtail, peacock, puppy' says Belleur to Rosalure, in Ben Jonson's *The Wild-Goose Chase*.

Peanut Frequently applied in the USA to a small or insignificant person, a child, as an affectionate nickname. It is used thus in Dawn Powell's story *The Comeback*, where a man

uses it to his young niece. It is also used in a friendly way in *Daughters of Mulberry*, by Roger Longrigg.

Pearl 'Ho, ho, my dainty, my little pearl! No lady loves her hound, monkey, or parakeet as I do thee.' Thus speaks a mother to her child in *The Witch of Edmonton*, by Rowley, Dekker, and Ford.

'Pearl' has been applied to a person considered precious by the speaker since at least the fourteenth century, as a famous anonymous poem of that period makes clear. In *Pearl* the poet laments the loss of his daughter, who died when she was two years old, but he sees her in a vision and is comforted.

In *The Scarlet Letter*, by Nathaniel Hawthorne, Hester Prynne names her illegitimate daughter Pearl 'as being of great price – purchased with all she had – her mother's only treasure.'

It is not only children who are considered to be pearls. In Shakespeare's *Troilus and Cressida* Troilus exclaims of his loved one: 'There she lies – a pearl.' The term is not used vocatively in Shakespeare, however, and is not frequently found in modern literature.

Peasant Used as a term of abuse to a person, usually a man, to imply that he is without education or manners. The term is certainly not obsolete, as the *Oxford English Dictionary* states, though it is less used now than in earlier times.

The Shakespearean plays furnish several examples: 'prating peasant' (*Comedy of Errors*, 2:i), 'peasant' (*Henry the Fifth*, 4:iv), 'base peasants' (*Henry the Sixth Part two*, 4:viii), 'bold peasant' (*Lear*, 4:vi), all used vocatively.

In *A Salute to the Great McCarthy*, by Barry Oakley, it is used in a modern context, equated with 'creep', spoken by a girl and addressed to a young man.

Peckerhead An insulting term for a man, normally used by other men. An American term, though 'pecker' in its slang sense of 'penis' is known in Britain. 'Lookit, peckerhead, whoever he is, I betcha he never pissed in a hotel sink,' says a character in *Joshua Then, and Now*, by Mordecai Richler. The expression would not be used in polite social circles.

People 'On the stage, people. Come along.' Thus speaks a character in *Mariana*, by Monica Dickens. At first glance 'people' here appears to be a neutral word, a simile for everyone, but it hints at inclusion in a special group, rather as when a public schoolboy talks of 'his people' – the members of his family – attending an open day.

There is the same underlying sense of membership of a community in 'good people', used to address those assembled at a religious or political meeting, though this now has an old-fashioned ring to it.

While being less neutral than it seems, 'people' manages to avoid the vaguely suspicious friendliness of 'you good folk', or 'folks'. 'You people' occurs vocatively; in *The Watch that Ends the Night*, by Hugh MacLennan, it becomes more specific as 'you Montreal people'. This is a different type of vocative, however. *See also* **You + category of person**.

Perce Used as a transferred name to address a man whose name is not known in *Thirteen Days*, by Ian Jefferies. The present author has noted similar usage in London, the speaker being West Indian.

Perry Mason Used as a transferred name to someone who is thought to be acting like the fictional character created by Erle Stanley Gardner for a long series of crime novels, in *St Urbain's Horseman*, by Mordecai Richler. Mason is an investigating lawyer, and much of the action of the novels takes place in courtrooms.

Person, young The *Oxford English Dictionary* says that this expression is used of young women, especially, 'when the speaker does not wish to specify her position as "girl", "woman" or "lady".'

The examples of usage quoted all refer to third person reference rather than to direct address, but in *Lavengro*, by George Borrow, the narrator addresses a girl by this term. In this case the speaker's vocatives are highly unusual: in the same conversation he also calls the girl 'pretty damsel sitting in the farm porch', and 'O daughter of the dairy'.

'Person' rarely occurs as a vocative element, but *The Newcomes*, by William Thackeray, has Arthur Pendennis addressing his wife as 'you reckless little person', the context making it clear that an endearment is meant.

PERSONIFICATIONS It is a fairly common human practice to endow an inanimate object with a human personality and address it directly. We mutter to a machine that suddenly refuses to function: 'What's the matter with you, you stupid thing?' A golfer selects a favourite club and says silently: 'Come on, Calamity Jane, get me out of this.'

It has also become fairly common for people to address things which, while not inanimate, are nevertheless unable to hear what is said, as far as we know, and are certainly unable to reply. Thus the owner of a house-plant who asks it how it is doing today and says: 'I'm sure you're thirsty, here's some water for you,'

perhaps adding a personal name to this statement.

No-one would think Jane Austen's Marianne strange when, in *Sense and Sensibility*, she bids farewell to Norland, the house she loves:

'Dear, dear Norland,' said Marianne, as she wandered alone before the house, on the last evening of their being there, 'when shall I cease to regret you, when learn to feel a home elsewhere? Oh, happy house, could you know what I suffer in now viewing you from this spot, from whence, perhaps, I may view you no more! And you, ye well-known trees – but you will continue the same! No leaf will decay because we are removed, nor any branch become motionless although we can observe you no longer!'

Countless people must have said 'Goodbye, house!' when on the point of moving to a new home. Countless people must also have murmured 'Goodbye, London!' or whatever city they are leaving as their aircraft took off. Vocatives which occurred as a result of personification have not been dealt with separately in this book.

Perverse and obstinate In Sheridan's *The School for Scandal* Sir Peter Teazle says to a young girl: 'Go, perverse and obstinate.' He adds: 'but take care, madam.' An expression such as this when used vocatively is normally followed by a head-word, such as 'girl', 'one', or a first name.

Pet Applied at first to an animal that was treated with special fondness, 'pet' was being used of a person who was a favourite by the eighteenth century. It can roughly be equated with 'darling' when used as a vocative.

In Britain, 'Pet' is mainly associated in modern times with the north-east. James Mitchell remarks, in *When the Boat Comes In*: ' "Yes, pet." "No, pet." Perhaps the strongest terms of endearment they knew, although Tyneside was rich in endearing words – pet, hinnie, bonnie lass.' Mrs Cecily Dynes writes from Australia to say that 'pet' is commonly used there to address children. 'The time got away from us, didn't it, pet?' says an Australian mother to her child in *War Brides*, by Lois Battle.

'Pet' is also used in the USA. Sinclair Lewis comments on its use in *Bethel Merriday*. ' "My pet!" "Pet" was Zed's standard word of endearment, as "darling" and "kitten" were Andy's and "child" was Doc Keezer's.'

An even better-known literary use occurs in *Little Dorrit*, where Minnie Meagles is always addressed as 'Pet' by her parents, so that the word virtually replaces her first name. *See also* **Teacher's pet**.

Peter Pan 'I'm glad you enjoyed yourself, Peter Pan,' says one of the characters in *Sandra*, by Pearl Bell, to a fully grown man who has just been indulging in 'boyish' activities, such as ice-skating. This transferred name alludes to the boy who never grows up, invented by J. M. Barrie in his novel *The Little White Bird* (1902) and made famous by a later stage play. The popularity of the play had much to do with the increased use of Peter as a boy's first name in Britain.

Petkin 'Good night, petkin,' says a man to a woman friend, in Iris Murdoch's *The Word Child*. For the use of the diminutive ending *see also* -kins.

Phoney, you 'You dirty phoney' is equated with 'you hypocrite' in Saul Bellow's *The Victim*. 'Phoney', sometimes 'phony', is well-used in modern times, and certainly refers to fake rather than real qualities.

An ingenious explanation of the word, quoted at the beginning of the twentieth century, was that a 'phoney' was something that had no more substance than a telephone conversation with a non-existent person.

Other etymologists have pointed to the previous existence of 'fawney', probably derived from Irish *fáinne*, 'ring', and referring to a practice whereby a gilt ring was sold to a dupe as if it were gold. The full slang phrase was 'fawney-dropping', since the fake ring was normally dropped 'accidentally' in front of the victim and then made the subject of a conversation.

Pig Used as an offensive term of address in various meanings. It is commonly used by children of someone who eats more than his fair share or who eats in a bestial manner. It is then extended to someone who behaves in a generally selfish way. 'You selfish pig' is used by a young girl to her brother in G. B. Shaw's *Pygmalion*. 'Selfish' again suggests 'pig' to a man in *The Sleepers of Erin*, by Jonathan Gash, who calls another man 'you selfish fucking pig'.

In *A Kind of Loving*, by Stan Barstow, a woman calls her son-in-law 'you filthy pig' when he vomits because he has drunk too much. She then expands the term to 'you filthy disgusting pig'.

In *Room at the Top*, by John Braine, the term becomes an intimacy in 'you slant-eyed Mongolian pig'. 'Pig' itself is an intimacy in *Saturday Night and Sunday Morning*, by Alan Sillitoe, but these examples merely demonstrate the general rule that almost any insult can be turned into a covert endearment.

Since the 1960s 'pig' has again become a derogatory slang term in both Britain and the USA for a policeman. The *Oxford English Dictionary* has an 1812 example of such usage, but marked this as 'obsolete' when the dictionary was published at the turn of the century.

'Pig' addressed to a policeman would be intended as an insult, but American policemen appear to have taken the sting out of the term by accepting it themselves. Thus the football game played in Miami in January 1989 between the Los Angeles Police Department Centurions and the Miami and Metro-Dade County Magnum Force was known to everyone, including those who took part, as the Pig Bowl.

In modern times a man who expresses views associated with male chauvinism is likely to be called 'male chauvinist pig', or simply 'pig'. In *The Front Runner*, by Patricia Nell Warren, male chauvinism is slightly reinterpreted as meaning an unreasonable belief that males should always be heterosexual. Thus the insulting 'you whore', addressed by a heterosexual man to a homosexual colleague is answered with 'you straight pig'.

Pigeon Regularly used of a young girl, a sweetheart, in the sixteenth and seventeenth centuries, and still occasionally found. *Girl with Green Eyes*, by Edna O'Brien, has 'you poor little pigeon' used as an intimacy. In later slang use a pigeon was a man who allowed himself to be swindled easily, especially in gaming.

Pig-fucker Used in American slang of a person one despises. One might expect this term to be addressed to males only, but 'you pig-fucker' is spoken to a woman in *Last Tango in Paris*, by Robert Alley. The same speaker uses 'you goddamn fucking pig-fucking liar' a moment later.

Piggy A taunting name for a fat child used by English children. It becomes the unwelcome nickname of a central character in William Golding's *Lord of the Flies*. *See also* **Fatty**. The term is also used to a greedy child, along with 'pig-hog' and 'pig-bin'. *See also* **Greedy**.

Piker, you 'You piker' is addressed to one man by another in *Redback*, by Howard Jacobson. The term has been in slang use since the 1870s to refer to a timid gambler who is thought to be over-cautious. It can also be used of a mean person.

Pilgrim In the Christian world pilgrims were commonly-met travellers in medieval times. In modern times it is Roman Catholics, especially, who make pilgrimages to holy places such as Lourdes, though they are not thereafter addressed as pilgrim. The latter happens in the Moslem world, where a person who is known to have undertaken the pilgrimage to Mecca is entitled to be addressed by the Arabic word for pilgrim.

The term is used vocatively by Shakespeare in *All's Well That Ends Well* (3:v), when Helena, in the dress of a pilgrim, is greeted with 'God save you, pilgrim!' and is subsequently called 'holy pilgrim'. It occurs again in *Romeo and Juliet* (1:v), in the love-talk between the two young people. Romeo says: 'If I profane with my unworthiest hand/This holy shrine, the gentle fine is this:/My lips, two blushing pilgrims, ready stand/To smooth that rough touch with a tender kiss.' 'Good pilgrim,' says Juliet, 'you do wrong your hand too much.'

Pilot The professional title of a steersman at sea, or one who controls an aircraft. Rarely used as a vocative, but there are several examples in *Goldfinger*, by Ian Fleming, of its use to the pilot of an aircraft.

Pimp The origin of this word, which refers to a man who controls and lives off the earnings of prostitutes, is unknown. 'You low rotten pimp' is used as an insult in *Room at the Top*, by John Braine.

Pimpernel The flower name, used as an endearment to her daughter by the hero's wife in *Gideon Planish*, by Sinclair Lewis. The woman concerned uses a wide range of vocatives. The use of a flower name may have been suggested by her own first name, Peony.

Pinhead A pinhead is something very small and of no importance. Those qualities, plus stupidity, are transferred to a person – usually a man – when he is addressed in this way. The expression is mainly an American one. 'Butt out, pinhead,' says an aggressive man to a stranger in *Happy to Be Here*, by Garrison Keiller. In *Moviola*, by Garson Kanin, a police sergeant corrects a junior colleague: 'Go ahead, folks, do your demonstration.' '*Celebration*, you pinhead,' says the sergeant.

Pinktoe Defined by Chester Hines in his novel *Pinktoes* as 'a term of indulgent affection applied to white women by Negro men, and sometimes conversely by Negro women to white men, but never adversely by either'.

Pinocchio Known to most people from the Walt Disney version of Carlo Collodi's classic children's work *The Adventures of Pinocchio*. The original Italian story was published in 1883. Pinocchio is a wooden puppet who eventually becomes a real boy. The name is transferred in *The Magic Army*, by Leslie Thomas, where a soldier says to another: 'Okay, Pinocchio, we all know you'll be clattering around the dance floor on those little wooden legs.'

Pint-size *See* Tich.

Pipe cleaner *See* Spindleshanks.

Pip-squeak A contemptuous name for a person considered to be of no importance. The word was applied in the 1920s by owners of large motor-cycles to smaller two-stroke machines, and the word may originally have referred to some kind of squeaky mechanical device. Vocative use appears to be confined to Britain, and is not frequent. 'You dirty little pip-squeak' is addressed by a man to a younger man in *The Half Hunter*, by John Sherwood.

Pizza face Not a usual vocative expression, but it is used by a Los Angeles policeman in *The Choirboys*, by Joseph Wambaugh: '"Blow it out your ass, pizza face!" Roscoe shouted to a sputtering acned man in a white Cadillac who was honking his horn.'

PLACE NAME James Boswell, in his *Journal of a Tour to the Hebrides*, says:

There is a beautiful little island in the Loch of Dunvegan, called Isa. M'Leod said, he would give it to Dr Johnson... M'Leod encouraged the fancy of Dr Johnson's becoming owner of an island; told him, that it was the practice in this country to name every man by his lands; and begged leave to drink to him in that mode: 'Island Isa, your health!'

Sir Walter Scott also comments on this custom in *Waverley*:

The Lowlanders call him, like other gentlemen, by the name of his estate, Glennaquoich; and the Highlanders call him Vich Ian Vohr, that is, the son of John the Great; and we upon the braes here call him by both names indifferently.

This explanation is given to an ignorant Englishman. Another such needs to be put right in *The East Wind of Love*, by Compton Mackenzie:

'Don't call me Mr Macleod, young man. I'm not my own factor.' John could not believe that he was meant to address this genially fierce old gentleman as 'Macleod' and went back to the 'sir' he had been using. 'I didn't mean that,' he was told. 'You should call me Ardvore.'

The speaker here is laird of Ardvore. *See also* the quotation from Boswell at **Muck**.

Telephone operators dealing with international calls sometimes address callers by the town from which they are calling: 'Go ahead, London.'

Playmates The catch-phrase 'Hello, playmates' was made famous in Britain by the wartime broadcasts of the comedian Arthur Askey. 'Playmates' was a clever choice of vocative: the word had been used in English since the seventeenth century, but only rarely. Askey was able to link the word with himself in the minds of a whole generation, especially as a term of address. In third person reference 'playmates' is normally used of children who regularly play together.

Another entertainer who managed to individualize a vocative was W. C. Fields, with his 'my little chickadee'.

Pledge This occurs several times as a vocative in *A Fraternal Fraud*, a short story by J. P. Donleavy. The narrator of the story says that he once created a fraternity, a club of male students. It is in this context that 'pledge' can occur vocatively, since one meaning of the noun is 'a person who has pledged himself to be a member of a fraternity or secret society'. Typical utterances in the story are 'Give me your demerit book, pledge, that's two demerits.' 'Say, pledge, I don't like the way you wear your face when you look at me.'

Plonker Applied in English dialectal use to anything large or substantial since the 1860s.

By the 1960s, in working-class London vernacular, the word referred to a man's private part, with no special reference to size. The word by then was also being used as a term of abuse, especially for a man, and some speakers may have seen it as a synonym of 'prick'.

In the 1980s, thanks to the use of the word in popular television series such as *Only Fools and Horses* and *Minder*, the term is far more widely known and used. Many who now use it have probably taken it to mean little more than 'stupid person', and the anatomical reference is not widely enough known to cause general offence to television audiences, as the use of 'you prick' almost certainly would.

There is an American term 'plonk' which can be applied to an obnoxious person, according to Chapman's *Dictionary of American Slang*, but it does not often appear in literary sources.

The Australians have 'plonko', but this is used of a person addicted to plonk, cheap inferior wine. 'Plonk' in that sense is derived from French *vin blanc*.

Many native-speakers, hearing 'plonker' used as an apparently mild insult, must assume that the word refers to someone who plonks things down in a clumsy way, an ungainly oaf.

Plumber Used by other tradesmen and their labourers on a British building site to address a plumber. Occasionally shortened to 'Plum(b)'.

Plumber's mate, you lousy little bastard This particular vocative expression is unlikely to be heard very often, but it is interesting in that the fact of a man's doing a fairly humble job is used against him as an insult.

The example above occurs in Monica Dickens's *Thursday Afternoons*, and we are told that the man to whom the vocative is addressed is incensed. 'He took all epithets literally. That the accusation of being verminous, illegitimate and not even a plumber in his own right should have been heard by Miss Parkinson was too much.' One may compare the carpenter in *The God-Seeker*, by Sinclair Lewis, who is 'you psalm-singing chisel-pusher' to a girl who also calls him 'you Bible-pounding hypocrite'. *See also* **Clerk**.

Podge *See* **Fatty**.

Poem, my little auburn Used by a male speaker to a young woman in *Girl with Green Eyes*, by Edna O'Brien. 'Poem' has been used in a figurative sense, of something as near perfect of its kind as possible, since the seventeenth century.

Polecat, you In Britain 'polecat' is applied to ferret-like mammals. In the USA it refers to the skunk, and like skunk, is applied to a person who is offensive.

In the seventeenth century 'polecat' was normally used to a woman and often had the meaning of 'courtesan'. It occurs only once as a vocative in Shakespeare, in *The Merry Wives of Windsor* (4:ii). On that occasion it is applied to Sir John Falstaff, but only because he is at the time dressed as a woman.

American usage is seen in *A Woman Called Fancy*, by Frank Yerby, where one man calls another 'you stinking, ornery, woman-stealing little pole-cat'.

Policeman, Mr A nonce name used to a policeman in *Dover One*, by Joyce Porter. *The Choirboys*, by Joseph Wambaugh, has 'Mr Police' used to a Los Angeles policeman by 'a black child about five years old'.

Polonius *See* **Rat**.

Ponce A synonym of 'pimp', and like that word, of obscure origin. Both 'you murdering little ponce' and 'you low rotten pimp' occur as insults in *Room at the Top*, by John Braine. In Joyce Cary's short story *The Sheep* 'you ponce' is used by one man to another as a general insult, with no seriously meant accusation that he lives off the earnings of prostitutes.

Poof, poofter *See* **Pouff**.

Poopsie Used by an American man to another male in *The Philanderer*, by Stanley Kauffmann, in a friendly way. The term appears to be a diminutive of 'poop', which can mean a contemptible person in American slang, but is often used as a covert endearment.

poor A word which is frequently used in vocative expressions that express sympathy for the listener, or regret for something that has befallen him. The sympathy may be genuine, but it is often ironic.

Absolute Beginners, by Colin MacInnes, has friendly use of 'you poor old bastard' and 'you poor old prehistoric monster'. *The Bell*, by Iris Murdoch, has 'poor child', 'poor thing', and 'poor' + first name used genuinely. *Brothers in Law*, by Henry Cecil, has a friendly use of 'poor fellow'. *The Business of Loving*, by Godfrey Smith, uses 'poor old' + nickname. *The Country Girls*, by Edna O'Brien, has 'poor you' and 'poor' + first name. *Dover One*, by Joyce Porter, has 'you poor things'; *An Error of Judgement*, by Pamela Hansford Johnson, has 'my poor baby priest' and 'my poor dear', as well as 'poor old' + first name. *Girl with Green Eyes*, by Edna O'Brien, has 'you poor little lonely bud' and 'you poor little pigeon' used as intimacies, together with 'you poor man' used in a friendly way.

Georgy Girl, by Margaret Forster, has a decidedly unfriendly instance of 'poor little boy' being used to a man. *The Hiding Place*, by Robert Shaw, has 'you poor German idiots' used insultingly. *Lord of the Flies*, by William Golding, has unfriendly use of 'my poor misguided boy' and 'my poor misguided child'. 'You poor bastard' in *The Spy Who Came in From the Cold*, by John le Carré, is friendly in spite of its form. 'You poor little innocent' in *A Travelling Woman*, by John Wain, is unfriendly.

'Poor, poor' + first name occurs in *The Pumpkin Eater*, by Penelope Mortimer. *Kate and Emma*, by Monica Dickens, has a similar 'my poor, poor' + first name. The old joke has it that when the wife is 'dear Mary', the husband often ends up as 'poor John'.

Poot This word has various unpleasant meanings in American slang. It is used vocatively to a contemptible person, and is roughly the equivalent of 'you shit'. Peter Gent has it being used by one man to another in a friendly way in *North Dallas Forty*, a novel about professional football in the USA. The men in the novel use insulting terms to one another as a matter of course, 'motherfucker' being almost as common as 'man'.

Pop 'Pop, I have got you a husband,' is a quotation given by the *Oxford English Dictionary*. It is taken from an eighteenth-century novel and is supported by many similar examples to show that 'pop' was once used as a term of endearment for a girl or woman.

In its full form it would have been 'poppet' or 'poplet'. Such usage continued until the end of the nineteenth century, though well before then 'pop' was being used in the USA as an abbreviation for 'poppa', itself a variant of 'papa'.

The main modern use would be by children to their father, especially in America. The word is also occasionally used on both sides of the Atlantic to address a considerably older man whose social standing does not inspire more respect.

In at least one family known to the author, 'pop' is used for the grandfather where 'dad' is used to the father. An Australian correspondent remarks that the word is used there 'by cheeky boys to strange men'. Examples of usage to a father occur in e.g. *Rabbit Redux*, by John Updike, and *The Business of Loving*, by Godfrey Smith.

Popkins An affectionate variant of 'pop', used in *Tamahine*, by Thelma Niklaus, by a middle-class British girl to her father. *See also* **-kins**.

Poppa A variant spelling of 'papa', especially when the latter is stressed on the first syllable. Usually abbreviated to 'Pop', but it occurs as 'poppa', in both cases by a boy to his father, in *Comfort me with Apples*, by Peter de Vries and *The Philanderer*, by Stanley Kauffmann. De Vries spells it idiosyncratically as 'Popper'. In *The Late Risers*, by Bernard Wolfe, 'Poppa' is used by a black American man to another. He is addressed as 'Daddy-o' in return.

Poppet Etymologically, this is an earlier form of the word 'puppet', which has taken over many of its senses. The spelling 'poppet' has been retained, however, since the fourteenth century, for the word applied to a small, dainty person who is highly pleasing. Flora Thompson, in *Lark Rise to Candleford*, relates rather ruefully that neighbouring women were likely to say to her, as a child: 'Never you mind, my poppet. Good looks ain't everything, and you can't help it if you did happen to be behind the door when they were being given out.' In *The Half Hunter*, by John Sherwood, a woman addresses her husband as 'Hugh, my poppet'.

Pops Normally a variant of 'Pop', especially in the USA, addressed to the speaker's father or to an older man. In *The Philanderer*, by Stanley Kauffmann, a wife uses this term to address her husband. 'Thanks, Pops' is said by a son to his father in *Rabbit is Rich*, by John Updike.

Porker, Porky *See* **Fatty**.

Porter While this word immediately suggests a luggage porter at an airport or railway station, it can also be used as a vocative to a porter of a different kind, the doorkeeper or janitor of an institution such as a college or school.

Porter in the 'carrying' sense has to do with Latin *portare*, 'to carry'. In the doorkeeper sense it derives from Latin *porta*, 'door'.

The porters who appear in the Shakespeare plays are mostly doorkeepers and are addressed as 'good porter', 'good master porter'. Gloucester, in *King Lear*, when accused of conducting the king to Dover, tells Regan: 'Thou shouldst have said "Good porter, turn the key." ' The title of 'porter' for a school or college official lives on in Britain.

In *Dandelion Days*, by Henry Williamson, 'the little liveried porter of Colham Grammar School', known as Soapy Sam behind his back, is addressed as 'porter' by both staff and boys.

In many British universities, however, the head porter would always be addressed as 'Mr' + last name. *The Times* newspaper stressed that point when it reported in 1988 on the retirement of Mr George Hales as head porter of Trinity College Cambridge. Mr Hales became nationally known when he ordered Prince Charles, then a student at the college, to get off his bike.

At one time Marie Lloyd regularly sang a song she made well-known: 'Oh, Mr Porter, what shall I do?' Railway porters continued to be addressed as 'porter', however, rather than by this mock name.

Possum The Australian entertainer Barry Humphries, in his role as Dame Edna, is tending to make this term his trademark in the late 1980s, using it to address the guests who appear on his television shows. Asked to explain it by Zsa Zsa Gabor he said that it was 'Australian for darling'. It is in fact a short form of 'opossum', which in turn is applied to several marsupial mammals found in Australia. They can vary in size, the smallest being mouse-like, the largest similar to cats. Opossums are also found in the USA, especially in the eastern states, and once again 'possum' is the normal colloquial form of the word.

'Possum' is occasionally used as an endearment, an example occurring in *The Critic*, by Wilfrid Sheed: 'It's all in your head, possum.' The speaker is a man, and the remark is addressed to the woman with whom he is living.

Postman The man who collects and delivers mail is a postman in Britain, a mailman in the USA. In Somerset Maugham's short story *Episode* a girl runs to catch a postman who has just emptied a box. ' "Postman," she cried, "take this letter, will you." ' In the story she eventually marries the man concerned.

A postman originally carried mail from post to post, from one post-stage to another, along the so-called post-roads. In former times, especially in rural districts, the postman could become a well-known individual. In *Lark Rise*, Flora Thompson writes:

> There was one postal delivery a day, and towards ten o'clock the heads of the women beating their mats would be turned towards the allotment path to watch for 'Old Postie.' 'No, I ain't got nothin' for you, Mrs Parish,' he would call. 'Your young Annie wrote to you only last week. She's got summat else to do beside sittin' down on her arse writing home all the time.'

In *The House with the Green Shutters*, by George Douglas, which is set in a Scottish town, the postman is referred to in the third person as 'Postie', or 'the Post'. At one time he is addressed directly as 'Post', a few moments after he discovers the bodies of three suicides: 'Oh, my God, Post, what have you seen, to bring that look to your eyes? What have you seen, man?'

Pot, you Robert L. Chapman's *Dictionary of American Slang* defines 'pot' in one of its meanings as an obnoxious person, especially an unattractive woman. It is clearly meant in that sense in *Moviola*, by Garson Kanin, where it is supposedly Tallulah Bankhead who calls Paulette Goddard 'you pot'.

'Pot' on its own seldom occurs in British usage (applied to a person), but 'fuss-pot', 'swank-pot', 'big-pot' remain in use. Of these, 'fuss-pot' was earlier 'fuss-box', so it would seem that 'pot' is thought of in the general sense of container. A 'big pot' was possibly one who had or spent a pot of money, a lot of it.

In *Vanity Fair*, by William Thackeray, there is an indication that 'Pots' was used to summon a potman or potboy, whose job was to serve liquor and take it to customers who were outside the premises.

Potbelly, Miss A self-explanatory nonce name used as an intimacy in *Girl with Green Eyes*, by Edna O'Brien. 'Miss Potts' is also used, obviously derived from 'Miss Potbelly'.

Pouff, poof, poofter 'You pampered pouff' is said by one man to another in *Daniel*, by David Thomson. It causes the man so addressed to hit the speaker and become involved in a fight with him. He later discusses the incident with a friend. ' "You're a pouff," she said to try it out. "You're a curtain rail, a towel horse – what a marvellous language. You shouldn't have hit him." "If that's what he meant, I wouldn't have."

"What did he mean?" "A homosexual." ' This writer appears to associate the slang word with a pouf or pouffe, the item of furniture on which one rests the feet. Others connect it with 'puff', as in 'powder-puff', but its actual origin is not known.

PRAYERS See RELIGIOUS VOCATIVES.

Preacher This is not a normal term of address to a member of the clergy, one of whose functions is usually to preach sermons, but it is used by a white lawyer to a black minister in *The Liberation of Lord Byron Jones*, by Jesse Hill Ford. It may be influenced by the minister's use of 'Lawyer' as a vocative, one fairly neutral professional description being returned with another.

Precious This has been in use as an endearment since at least the early eighteenth century, often as 'my precious'. Before that the word occurred as a vocative element, either in its sense of valuable or as an intensive of something bad.

Shakespeare has Ferdinand, in *The Tempest* (3:i) addressing Miranda as 'precious creature', and Anthony calling Cleopatra 'my precious queen', equating that phrase with 'my dearest queen', 'most sweet queen', and the like (*Antony and Cleopatra*, 3:i). On the other hand, in *Cymbeline* (3:v), we have Cloten addressing Pisanio as 'you precious pander and villain', while later (4:ii) he calls Guiderius 'thou precious varlet' and 'thou injurious thief'.

As an endearment 'precious' would often be addressed to a child. Its use between lovers occurs in *Babbitt*, by Sinclair Lewis: ' "George, I wonder if you really like me at all?" "Course I do, silly." "Do you really, precious?" ' In *Gone With The Wind*, by Margaret Mitchell, 'You're mighty pretty, precious' is the last thing Rhett Butler says to Bonnie, the child he adores, before she is killed in a riding accident.

Preserver In *All's Well That Ends Well* (2:iii), the King of France says to Helena: 'Sit, my preserver, by thy patient's side.' She has managed to cure the king of a disease thought to be incurable, and thus saved his life. In *The Tempest* (5:i), Prospero calls Gonzalo 'my true preserver', referring to the many provisions and books which Gonzalo provided him with on his banishment.

Jane Eyre, by Charlotte Brontë, has Mr Rochester saying to Jane: 'My cherished preserver, good night!' She has just woken him and saved him from death by burning.

All these circumstances are rather exceptional, and the vocative is probably not one which would be used in modern times, even to someone who has saved the speaker's life.

It should be noted that modern speakers are likely to say 'You're a life-saver' to someone who has metaphorically saved their lives, e.g., by providing them with a drink when they feel especially thirsty.

President, Mr This term is used to address the president of a country whose chief elected representative is styled President, as in the USA. At a humbler level it is used to the person chosen to preside over a meeting of a society, conference, etc.

The head of certain colleges, universities, and other institutions may be called a president. He or she might well be addressed as 'President', without the prefix, or as 'President' + last name. This is also an alternative form of address for the president of a country. Several examples of 'Mr President' used to the president of a meeting occur in *The Affair*, by C. P. Snow.

Pretty, my A mother addresses her six-year-old daughter by this term in *Gideon Planish*, by Sinclair Lewis. In *Opening Night*, by Ngaio Marsh, a fairly elderly man uses it to a nineteen-year-old girl. The *Oxford English Dictionary* mentions that 'pretty' has been used in a coaxing or soothing way, especially to children, since the fifteenth century.

Countless mothers probably still address their babies as 'my pretty one', continuing this long oral tradition. 'My pretty' is simply a shortened form of such a phrase, or of the 'my pretty maid' of the ballad. The plural 'my pretties' also occurs, and can be used to men as well as women. 'Back to work, my pretties,' says a character in Goldsmith's *She Stoops to Conquer*. Such usage may survive in certain dialects, but is certainly not common.

Prick, you 'Prick' has been a slang word for the penis since the sixteenth century. The word is not in polite use, and this expression is as vulgar as the American 'you shmuck'. As with that Yiddish term, 'you prick' does not make specific reference to the penis, it simply indicates feelings of detestation on the part of the speaker.

In *Portnoy's Complaint*, by Philip Roth, the hero berates himself as 'you little prick' as he considers the unhappiness he has caused his father. He is later called 'you cold-hearted prick' by one of his girl-friends. The same girl makes a more specific reference to his penis when she calls him 'you mean, miserable hard-on, you'.

In *Moviola*, by Garson Kanin, a woman calls a man 'you fat, four-eyed, no good, lying, filthy prick'. 'Four-eyed' is a reference to his wearing of spectacles. 'Stupid prick' is an insult hurled at one man by another in Mordecai Richler's *St Urbain's Horseman*, the speaker being Jewish.

The latter point may be relevant, since both 'putz' and 'shmuck' are commonly used Yiddish insults, both of which could be translated by 'prick'. 'It's easy for you to joke about it, you prick,' says one man to another in *Blue Dreams*, by William Hanley, but we are told that he says it 'fondly', showing the common conversion of an insult into a friendly term of address.

Priest Not normally a vocative in modern times, though the Shakespeare plays have plenty of examples of 'priest', 'brother priest', 'my priest', 'saucy priest', 'churlish priest' used as terms of address. In *Bless me, Father*, by Neil Boyd, there is a joking use of 'me darlin' priestling' by a parish priest to his young assistant.

Prig Used of someone who is thought to be over-precise in speech and manners. It has had this meaning since the late seventeenth century. 'You horrible prig, you' is an intimacy in *An Error of Judgement*, by Pamela Hansford Johnson. R. F. Delderfield, in *Theirs was the Kingdom*, has: ' "I'm not calling you a prig," Avery said, "just a good old British Puritan, and there's a difference. Prigs have secret doubts about themselves, but Puritans don't, not even when the world falls about them." '

Prime Minister Since the middle of the nineteenth century this has been the usual way of describing, and formally addressing the leader of the British and similar governments. It has not always been a complimentary title, and was disowned by Walpole and Lord North. Its first use in *The Minister*, by Maurice Edelman, is dramatic, recalling a similarly dramatic use of 'Master' for the first time near the end of C. P. Snow's novel, *The Master*. A popular television series in the 1980s was *Yes, Prime Minister*, the last words in each of the programmes.

Prince, sweet A girl in *Oliver's Story*, by Erich Segal, quotes 'Good night, sweet prince' from Shakespeare's *Hamlet* (5:ii) as she says good night to a friend. In context the words are uttered by Horatio to Hamlet, who has just died: 'Good night, sweet prince, and flights of angels sing thee to thy rest!'

Princess This would not be used as a vocative to a member of the British royal family who was a princess by title ('your royal highness' or 'Ma'am' would be usual), but it might be used to a foreign princess. Examples of such usage occur in *Daughters of Mulberry*, by Roger Longrigg, 'Principessa' and 'Madame la princesse' occurring in the same novel.

In modern use, 'princess' would be used by, e.g., a father to his daughter as a term of affection similar to 'sweetheart'. It is used by American men to women in *Eustace Chisholm and his Works*, by James Purdie and *The Late Risers*, by Bernard Wolfe. In the latter book the speaker is a policeman who also addresses the woman concerned as 'lady'.

'Princess' has long been used as a flattering term of address to a woman who is not strictly entitled to the title. 'Cesario is your servant's name, fair princess' says Viola (disguised as a young man) to Olivia, in *Twelfth Night*. Olivia questions his use of the word 'servant', but accepts 'princess' as her right, though she is normally described as a countess.

Perhaps a better-known literary princess, though a more specialized example of one, occurs in *The Silent Woman*, by Ben Jonson. Captain Otter in that play invariably calls his wife 'good princess', 'sweet princess', 'dear princess', and the like to her face, though behind her back he tells his friends that he has no wife: 'I confess, gentlemen, I have a cook, a laundress, a house-drudge, that serves my necessary turns.' Mrs Otter, who actually rules the roost, explains at one point why she is entitled to be addressed by her husband as 'princess', having agreed, 'when I married you . . . I would be princess, and reign in my own house; and you would be my subject, and obey me.'

In *The Diviners*, by Margaret Laurence, 'Prin' occurs as a vocative. It is a short form of 'Princess', the first name of one of the characters.

Principal The professional title of the head of some universities, colleges, and schools, used vocatively on formal occasions or on informal occasions by formal speakers.

Prisoner Used to a prisoner in Shakespeare's *Measure for Measure* and possibly in modern times to those held in custody. *Nurse is a Neighbour*, by Joanna Jones, quotes 'Prisoner at the bar', a phrase associated with old-fashioned court-room dramas. In *The Word Child*, by Iris Murdoch, a man who is hanging on to a girl tells her 'You're my prisoner', and soon afterwards says: 'Come along, prisoner.'

Priss, Miss A nonce name that occurs in *War Brides*, by Lois Battle. It is addressed to his sixteen-year-old daughter by an Australian father. She has just made a critical remark about him, and he is presumably implying that she is prissy, primly censorious.

'Prissy' itself may be a blend of 'prim' and 'sissy', or a short form of Priscilla, thought to be the kind of name borne by a prim and prudish sissy.

Private Used to address a private soldier, one who holds no special rank. In use since the sixteenth century, following the earlier use of 'private person' to denote someone who held no civil office.

'Private' can be used on its own, or as a prefix followed by a family name. 'Any pud's better than none, Private,' says a nurse to a soldier-orderly in *An Indecent Obsession*, by Colleen McCullough. Later in the novel a colonel says: 'Private Jones, you're sitting there very quietly.'

When the Boat Comes In, by James Mitchell, has a sergeant saying: 'Say that again, Private Scrimgour, and I will have you shot.' Another sergeant, in Thomas Hardy's *The Trumpet Major*, says: 'Well, what have you to say, Private Tremlett?'

Proddies *See* **Swaddler**.

Professor In Britain it is only a teacher of the highest rank in a university department who is addressed as 'Professor'; in the USA the title is extended, normally, to other teachers at a university or college, and in some cases, to school teachers.

In *Deborah*, by Marian Castle, which is set in Dakota at the beginning of the twentieth century, occurs the following:

'I hope the change will be good for you, Professor.' He was mighty young, she thought, to be a professor, the title by which the local teacher – if male – was always known.

'Don't call me "Professor",' he snapped.

'Why not?'

'Because I'm nothing but an instructor, an underpaid, unnoticed, unimportant instructor at the new University of Chicago. Maybe, after another twenty years and a couple more degrees and a book or so, I might really have become a full professor.'

Against this one can put the comment by Peter de Vries in his novel *Let me Count the Ways*:

'It's good to have you back, Professor Waltz,' she said. I had given up trying to make her understand that I was only an instructor, realizing that the dignity of the house, as well as her own ego, were nourished by use of the more prestigious title.

In *Lucky Jim*, by Kingsley Amis, we find: ' "Thought you'd gone without me. Professor," he added, nearly too late.' Amis has already told us that 'no other professor in Great Britain set such store on being called Professor'. Dixon, the hero of the novel, thinks it expedient to do as his head of department wishes, though later in the novel we are told how he would like to address the professor if he had a free choice in the matter:

he'd just say, quite quietly and very slowly and distinctly, to give Welch a good chance

of catching his general drift: Look here, you old cockchafer, what makes you think you can run a history department, even at a place like this, eh, you old cockchafer?

In the nineteenth century 'Professor' was often adopted as a grandiose title by teachers of dancing, phrenology, and a variety of other subjects.

In 1864 a social commentator was moved to say: 'The word Professor – now so desecrated in its use that we are most familiar with it in connection with dancing-schools, juggler's booths, and veterinary surgeries.' This 'desecration' of the title had happened rather quickly, since it seems to have been only at the beginning of the nineteenth century that the university title began to be used vocatively.

In modern times 'Professor' may still be given as a nickname to anyone who shows signs of intelligence above the average. In the navy, as Wilfred Granville expresses it in his *Dictionary of Naval Slang*, it is lower-deck slang for 'one who is more of a B.A. than an AB'.

A black American speaker in *An American Dream*, by Norman Mailer, uses the term to a white man who is obviously educated: 'I know this Mafia bitch, she's made it with hoodlums, black men, some of the class, now she picks you, Professor, looking to square out. . . .'

Ad hoc usage of the term to someone who passes on information with an air of authority, occurs in *The River*, by Steven Bauer. ' "They're striking," Lewis said. "They want more money, better conditions. They say their labor is the most valuable thing they have." "Where'd you hear that, professor?" Roy asked. "Talking to some of the strikers." '

Rather similar is an exchange between two Los Angeles policemen in *The Choirboys*, by Joseph Wambaugh: 'Suddenly Baxter said: "You know what I think is the best a cop can hope for?" "Tell me, professor." ' *The Critic*, by Wilfrid Sheed, has: 'You don't tell a tennis player to improve his character, you tell him to improve his game.' This is spoken by a man to his wife. She replies: 'Yes, professor.' This is not his professional title, merely an ironic comment on his didactic manner.

Chapman's *Dictionary of American Slang* says that 'Professor' can refer to an orchestra leader or to a piano-player in a saloon or brothel, but he does not make it clear whether the word is used as a term of address to such people.

Provost A title applied to various officials, corresponding variously to 'prior', 'dean', or in secular circumstances, to 'chief official', 'mayor', 'chief magistrate'. The provost could also be a kind of police officer, and in Shakespeare's *Measure for Measure* appears to be the keeper of the prison. 'Hail to you, Provost! so I think you are,' says the Duke, when he visits the prison.

At the universities of Oxford and Cambridge 'provost' is the title given to the heads of certain colleges. There may also be a pro-provost. Philip Leech holds this position in J. I. M. Stewart's novel *The Last Tresilians* and is addressed during formal meetings by that term.

In *The House with the Green Shutters*, by George Douglas, the Provost who is addressed by his title is the chief magistrate of a Scottish burgh.

Prune Applied both in Britain and the USA to a person who is easily taken in, someone who is foolish. In air force slang, specifically, the word was applied to a bad pilot, a 'Pilot Officer Prune'. 'You poor prune' is therefore not an uncommon expression in the Biggles stories of Captain W. E. Johns, which feature the aviator James Bigglesworth, DSO, DFC, MC. The stories began to appear in the 1930s. In *The Business of Loving*, by Godfrey Smith, 'you moonstruck old prune' is uttered in a friendly way.

Puddinghead An American term for an amiably stupid person. Its best-known use in literature is in Mark Twain's *Pudd'nhead Wilson*, where it is the permanent nickname of the lawyer, David Wilson. 'Pudding' itself is affectionately used in *The Limits of Love*, by Frederic Raphael. The speaker is a woman addressing her husband of a few hours.

Pukefish 'You make me sick, you pukefish!' says one American man to another in *The God-Seeker*, by Sinclair Lewis. 'Fish' by itself is used in an expression like 'you poor fish,' where it means a stupid person. The 'puke-' in this example was no doubt suggested by the previous reference to making the speaker sick, since it refers to vomit.

Pumpkin In recent American use, an affectionate term used to a young child by, e.g., its parents. Such usage may be influenced by the '–kin' ending, which is normally associated with diminutive forms of names.

The pumpkin also has a special place in American family life, thanks to its Thanksgiving associations. The example that occurs in *Portnoy's Complaint*, by Philip Roth, is addressed in imagination to a former girlfriend of the hero's.

The term appears to have crossed the Atlantic, since it was used as an endearment in a British television programme broadcast in November, 1988. The speaker was a British army officer, portrayed as rather an idiot.

Punk This term is used by an American male to another in *The Day of the Locust*, by Nathanael West, which was first published in 1939. The same speaker also uses 'you punkola', which he equates with vocatives such as 'you pee-hole bandit' and 'you louse'.

The word is generally expressive of contempt, with perhaps some reference to the slang meaning of a male homosexual's young companion.

In Britain the word would now suggest a young person who dresses in a strikingly unconventional way and likes punk rock music, but this meaning has only been current since the 1970s.

Further American use of 'punk' occurs in Ed McBain's short story *First Offence*, where a man sharing a prison cell with a younger man tells him: 'Don't get smart, punk, or I'll break your arm.'

Puppy, you young In modern use an expression that would typically be used by an older man of a certain social or professional standing to a younger man who was behaving impertinently. Applied to such young men, 'puppy' has been used contemptuously since the end of the sixteenth century. The use of 'young' merely strengthens the insult, though it can be replaced by other words. 'You blasted puppy' occurs, for instance, in *Love in Quiet Places*, by Bernard Thompson.

'Puppy' derives from French *poupée* and was at first used in English to refer to a toy dog rather than a young one. That sense is now, of course, obsolete. Use of 'puppy' may suggest other dog-like insults to the speaker. 'Get off, you puppy,' says Croaker to Leontine, in Goldsmith's *The Good-Natured Man*. He adds: 'Stupid whelp!'

The short form 'pup' occurs in *Pudd'nhead Wilson*, by Mark Twain. A black woman says to a young man: 'Set down, you pup! Does you think you kin skyer me?'

Purser The professional title of the chief steward on a passenger liner, in general charge of the passengers' welfare. He also keeps the accounts and at one time, in the navy, was paymaster, hence the connection with 'purse'. Examples of the vocative occur in, e.g., *Shipmaster*, by Gwyn Griffin.

Puss Normally used to call a cat, but this word has been applied to girls and women since the seventeenth century. In third person reference or in direct address it is often coupled with words that imply slyness.

In *The Heir of Redclyffe*, by Charlotte Yonge, a young man calls his sister 'impertinent little puss'. Her father also calls her 'puss'. There is a similar usage in *Gone With The Wind*, by Margaret Mitchell, where Scarlett

O'Hara is often called 'Puss' by her father. 'You little puss' is used by a father to his daughter in George Eliot's *The Mill on the Floss*. In Boucicault's *London Assurance* a man calls out to a woman visitor: 'Come in, you mischievous puss.'

The diminutive 'pussy' is also found. Dickens makes fun of such usage in *Edwin Drood*. ' "I know that Pussy was looking for me." "Do you keep a cat down there?" asked Mr Grewgious. Edwin coloured a little as he explained: "I call Rosa [his fiancée] Pussy . . . A pet name, sir," he explained again.' There is a further comment when 'Pussy's birthday' is mentioned: 'I'd Pussy you, young man, if I was Pussy, as you call her.'

The modern slang meaning of 'pussy' would make vocative usage, other than in private, rather difficult. A reference to 'pussy' in vulgar speech is to the vulva or vagina, to sexual intercourse or to a woman considered purely as a sexual object. In *The Sophomore*, by Barry Spacks, there is an unusual example of a girl calling her boyfriend 'poor Puss'. She equates it with 'poor baby'.

Pussy-cat This term can be used as a compliment to a pleasant person, usually a woman. The reference is to the cuddlesome, harmless qualities of a cat. The Welsh entertainer Tom Jones had a considerable success with a song called 'Pussy-cat' some years ago.

Put, putt In seventeenth-century slang this word meant a blockhead, or stupid person, though how it came to have such a meaning puzzles etymologists. It continued in use until the nineteenth century and seems to have become especially associated with older men, old duffers. In *Vanity Fair* Thackeray writes: 'The Captain has a hearty contempt for his father, I can see, and calls him an old *put*, an old *snob*, an old *chaw-bacon*, and numberless other pretty names.'

Putty brain *See* Dunce.

Putz, you Used especially by American Jewish speakers as a term of contempt. 'Putz' is vulgar slang for 'penis', but 'schmuck' is more frequently used in that sense. 'Putz' would not be used in polite society, especially before women or children. 'You stinking putz' is addressed by the hero of *Portnoy's Complaint* to himself. It is one of many similar terms which Philip Roth demonstrates in that novel. Another Jewish writer, Mordecai Richler, uses the term several times in *St Urbain's Horseman*.

Quartermaster The title of a petty officer in the navy who attends to the helm, signals, and the like, or an army officer whose task is to supply clothing, subsistence, and accommodation for the troops. 'Quartermaster,' says an American officer in *The Magic Army*, by Leslie Thomas, 'let me have a loudhailer.' There are two naval examples of 'quartermaster' used vocatively in *Doctor at Sea*, by Richard Gordon. In *Thirteen Days*, by Ian Jefferies, a quartermaster in the army is addressed in a friendly way as 'Q'.

Queen, my This expression is still in local use, e.g., in the Bristol area of England, as an endearment to a woman. In modern times it can be addressed to a stranger in a friendly way, much as words like 'love' and 'darling' can be used.

In Shakespeare's *Merchant of Venice* the Prince of Morocco, one of Portia's suitors, calls her 'my gentle queen'. Ferdinand, in *Love's Labour's Lost*, addresses the Princess of France in the poem he writes to her as 'queen of queens'.

A modern variant of this is in *Room at the Top*, by John Braine, where a man addresses a woman as 'queen of my heart'. This is done in a friendly way, not as an intimacy.

The normal use of 'you queen' in modern times is quite different. It would be used to a man in an abusive way, implying that he was homosexual, especially that he played the part of the female partner in a homosexual relationship.

Queer Used to describe a homosexual from the 1920s onwards. 'You cringing little queer' is used by a woman to a male homosexual in *Getting it Right*, by Elizabeth Jane Howard. In *The Stork*, by Denison Hatch, one man says to another: 'You're not going to get away with this, you punk queer.'

North Dallas Forty, by Peter Gent, has an American professional footballer address a team-mate as 'fuckin' queer', but it is not an insinuation that the man addressed is homosexual, merely that he is different from the usual footballer, less manly than they are. 'Filthy queers' is said by a woman to two men known to be homosexual in *The Front Runner*, by Patricia Nell Warren.

Quiz, you 'Oh, you quiz – I know what you are going to say,' says Miss Wardle to Mr Tracy Tupman, in *The Pickwick Papers*, by Charles Dickens. The same speaker has a moment before called Mr Tupman 'you naughty man'; 'you quiz' could be roughly translated in this context as 'you who are quizzing me, making fun of me'.

In an age of television quiz games it is difficult to remember that the earliest meaning of 'quiz', when the word appeared at the end of the eighteenth century, was an odd or eccentric person. It had a variant form 'quoz'. The origins of both forms are a mystery, though a connection with 'queer' has been suggested.

Since 'quixotic' roughly fits the original meaning of 'quiz', in that quixotism is a type of eccentricity, that word may also have played its part. The sense development of 'quiz' into a verb meaning to question someone may have come about by association of the word with other words such as 'question' and 'inquisitive'.

A modern quiz is certainly a kind of inquisition, albeit an enjoyable one. This modern meaning of 'quiz' has of course caused the former meanings, including that which Miss Wardle had in mind, to become obsolete.

QUOTATION VOCATIVES A distinction has been made in this study between quotation vocatives which arise incidentally and those which are applied to specific hearers as transferred names.

A person who sings the Christmas carol which begins, 'Oh, come, all ye faithful' is not consciously applying the term 'all ye faithful' to a specific audience. A speaker who quotes 'Where are you going to, my pretty maid?' to a young woman who is obviously on her way somewhere is applying the vocative expression to her as a transfer.

Transferred vocatives are usually names. A person who expresses surprise at someone's deductive powers is told that it is 'Elementary, my dear Watson'. A meeting in certain circumstances inspires the use of 'Dr Livingstone, I presume'.

The frequency of use of such transferred names almost has the effect of turning them, together with their accompanying words, into normal free-floating vocatives, selected because of the situation in which speaker and hearer find themselves rather than more individual reasons.

They may also arise because of a speech incident, and have an effect on other vocatives used in close context. Thus, the use of 'Watson' may be brought about by a speaker saying: 'Well done, Holmes' to someone who has solved a puzzle.

The use of 'my fair maid' may well lead to 'Sir' being used in return, as it is in the nursery rhyme. Certain names are well enough known in their own right to be used allusively as transfers. Holmes and Watson certainly fall into that category, and Watson does not need its attendant words in order to be used in conversation.

A name like Horatio would probably not be very meaningful if used alone. A speaker would probably quote at least 'There are more things in heaven and earth, Horatio', though he might not think it necessary to add 'than are dreamt of in your philosophy'. However, it is clear that such a quotation, said to someone else, means that Horatio becomes a nonce transfer.

A quotation like 'It's a mad world, my masters', could also turn 'my masters' into a transferred vocative if there were hearers present who could be looked upon momentarily as 'my masters'. As it happens, when that quotation partly occurs in *An Error of Judgement*, by Pamela Hansford Johnson, the speaker says it to himself 'in a silly sort of mumble', and is obviously thinking about the main content of the quotation, not applying the vocative to himself or anyone else.

When transferred names or vocative expressions *are* used, whether inside quotations or not, they can break normal rules. Watson or Horatio, in the instances quoted above, could be applied for example to female hearers.

Quotation vocatives applied as transferred names have been dealt with in separate entries in this book. Those which merely occur in quotations have been ignored.

Rabbi A title of respect accorded to a trained religious leader and teacher of Jewish law. 'Rabbi' has been in use since the first century and represents the Hebrew 'my master'. The word is used alone or as a prefix to a last name. Examples of its use occur in many novels which feature Jewish family life, such as *St Urbain's Horseman*, by Mordecai Richler.

For a full discussion of how a rabbi compares with a Catholic priest or Protestant minister, together with the usual selection of relevant jokes, Leo Rosten's *Joys of Yiddish* should be consulted.

Rabbit Used contemptuously in Shakespeare's *Henry the Fourth Part Two* (2:ii), where Bardolph says to a page: 'Away, you whoreson upright rabbit, away.' The reason for 'rabbit' in this context is not clear: the word was not in general seventeenth century use as a term of abuse.

It occurs rarely vocatively, but is found again in David Storey's *Radcliffe*. A father speaking to his young children says affectionately: 'Here you are, you little rabbits. What did I say I'd give you if you behaved like I said?' One might have expected this to represent normal modern usage of 'rabbit', when it occurs at all, but *The Critic*, by Wilfred Sheed, has one man saying to another, in an internal dialogue: 'Is that understood, you smirking little rabbit?'

Radar Used to address a radar officer in the Royal Navy in *Sylvester*, by Edward Hyams. The term would now suggest to a wide audience the nickname of Radar O'Reilly, the character in the long-running television series *M.A.S.H.* starring Alan Alda as Hawkeye Pierce. Gary Burghoff played the part of Radar, so-named for his uncanny ability to know before anyone else what was going to happen next, to 'hear' things before anyone else heard them.

Ragamuffin Used of a dirty, ragged man or boy as a term of contempt in former times; now applied less vehemently to an untidy child, if used vocatively at all. In *Peregrine Pickle*, by Tobias Smollett, a man tells a coachman: 'Drive, you ragamuffin, you rascallion, you hellhound!'

Rake, Raky One of the instant nicknames which children bestow on a tall thin person. *See also* **Spindleshanks**. The phrase 'as thin as a rake' has been in use since the fourteenth century. In older texts 'rake' may occur vocatively in the sense of 'immoral scoundrel', a short form of 'rake-hell'.

Rascal Formerly a word of much stronger meaning than it has today, when it is normally applied to a naughty child, especially a boy. It originally meant a man who was one of the common herd, a rogue, and a knave. 'You whoreson cowardly rascal,' used to a man in Ben Jonson's *Every Man in his Humour*, is a serious insult indeed.

In *A Trick to Catch the Old One*, by Thomas Middleton, Lucre says to the host: 'How now, you treacherous rascal?' He is answered with: 'That's none of my name, sir.' 'You little rascal' is used by a husband to his wife in *Captains and the Kings*, by Taylor Caldwell. This would be the normal form of the expression used to a child, said perhaps with irritation, but not a serious insult.

'Rascal' was sometimes fancifully extended to 'rascallion' in past times. Thus, in Smollett's *Peregrine Pickle*, a man tells a coachman: 'Drive, you ragamuffin, you rascallion, you hellhound!'

Rat In modern times this is nearly always a term of contempt, though 'you rat', like most insults, can be turned into a covert endearment in the right circumstances. When a woman calls her lover 'Rat!' in *The Philanderer*, by Stanley Kauffmann, it is intimacy that is revealed rather than a contemptuous relationship.

Surprisingly, 'old rat' could once be used as a friendly term between men, if the instance in Stevenson's *Black Arrow* reflects general usage in the nineteenth century. There is some evidence that it does, since Hood refers to a 'poor rat', a man, in a sympathetic way.

Earlier still, in the seventeenth century, human rats were either clergymen or pirates, thanks to punning allusions to curates (*kewrats*) and *pie-rats*. As Shylock says, in *The Merchant of Venice*, 'there be land-rats and waterrats – I mean pirates.'

Shakespeare also used the word in its more general opprobrious meaning, as for instance when Hamlet, hearing a voice behind the arras, says 'How now! a rat?' and stabs Polonius.

In *Jane Eyre*, by Charlotte Brontë, John Reed, a fourteen-year-old boy strikes the ten-year-old heroine and says 'That is for your impudence . . . you rat'. The narrator goes on to say that she is accustomed to John's abuse.

Clearly 'you rat' *could* be used in the nineteenth century as it is in modern times. 'You little rat' is an insult, for instance, in *Absolute Beginners*, by Colin MacInnes. In *Rebecca*, by Daphne du Maurier, we have 'you crazy little rat', which is then expanded to 'you bloody crazy little rat'. In *The Heart is a Lonely Hunter*, by Carson McCullers, occurs 'you pasty-faced, shrunk-gutted, rickets-ridden little rats', addressed by a man to two others.

It is just possible that 'Ratty' could be used affectionately in modern times, since the British middle-classes, if one is to judge by the Valentine Day announcements in national newspapers, seem to be fond of giving loved-ones names taken from nursery tales.

Ratty, in Kenneth Grahame's *The Wind in the Willows*, is one of Toad's friends. There is also a character called Ratty by his friends in Samuel Lover's novel, *Handy Andy*. In that case it is an affectionate diminutive of Horatio, his real name. In *The Sophomore*, by Barry Spacks, there is an illusion to the Hamlet quotation mentioned above. A man tells another, passing on a message from a girl: 'She says to tell you your name is Polonius. What does that mean?' 'It means I'm a rat,' says the man concerned.

Rat-bag 'You skinny, half-sized little rat-bag' is said by a woman to a man in *Shipmaster*, by Gwyn Griffin. It is equated by the speaker with 'you filthy-minded, dirty little beast'. 'Rat-bag' is not a usual term, and is presumably to be interpreted as 'bag of rats'.

Rat-face A term which is occasionally used both in the USA and Britain to someone who is considered to be cunning or treacherous. ' "You shut yer bleedin' rattle, Rat Face," he said contemptuously,' occurs in *Saturday Night and Sunday Morning*, by Alan Sillitoe, addressed by a young man to a woman in the street.

Rat fink 'If you don't like it, rat fink, take it out on the street,' says a policeman to a man in *An American Dream*, by Norman Mailer, inviting him to go outside and have a fight. 'Rat fink' combines two words expressing contempt. 'Fink' has many different meanings in modern American slang, including police-informer and strike-breaker. The origin of the word is unknown.

Razor blade *See* **Spindleshanks**.

Reader Used by eighteenth- and nineteenth-century novelists to address the reader of their works. Henry Fielding, for example, used it eleven times in *Joseph Andrews*, adding instances of 'O reader', '(O) my good reader'. One of the best-known literary quotes is from Charlotte Brontë's *Jane Eyre:* 'Reader, I married him.'

It is no longer fashionable to address the reader of a book in this way, though modern novelists might not go as far as Zoë Fairbanks, who says in her novel *Down*: 'I'm not going to call you "Dear Reader." You aren't "dear" to me. Strangely enough, I feel rather hostile to you. You are prying into my affairs and arriving at conclusions about me, and I don't like that.'

Eighteenth-century novelists, knowing full well that their readers were mainly women, sometimes acknowledged that fact. Thus Sterne, in *Tristram Shandy*, spends a lot of time carrying on a conversation with 'Madam', his reader. Fielding, in *Joseph Andrews*, at one point pauses to address directly 'my fair countrywomen'. Sterne plays safe by using 'sir' as well to his readers, and on the first page of his novel calls them 'good folks'. When offering to dedicate his book to a suitable applicant he resorts to 'My lord'.

The modern fashion, if there is one, is perhaps shown by Philip Roth in *Portnoy's Complaint*. He uses 'Doctor' throughout, as if the whole of his text is being said while he lies on the psychiatrist's couch, though at one point he says: 'And, Doctor, Your Honor, whatever your name is. . . .'

William Thackeray, in an essay-like passage of *The Newcomes*, has:

And as for women – O my dear friends and brethren in this vale of tears – did you ever see anything so curious, monstrous and amazing as the way in which women court Princekin when he is marriageable, and pursue him with their daughters?

Recreant A literary rather than a modern colloquial term. Shakespeare is rather fond of it, using it as a vocative on several occasions to mean either a coward or a deserter. 'Most recreant coward' occurs in *Henry the Fourth Part Two*, but 'recreant' occurs on its own in *King Lear* (twice), *Henry the Sixth Part One*, and *A Midsummer Night's Dream*. Beaumont and Fletcher also have in *The Wild-Goose Chase*: 'You shall be hang'd, you recreant!'

Rector In the Church of England a rector is a parish priest who receives his income from the parish itself (as opposed to a vicar, who receives a yearly stipend). A rector may also be the head of a college or school, especially in Scotland (and more especially of a school which is called an academy).

Examples of professional use to a Church of

England priest occur in, e.g., *The Business of Loving*, by Godfrey Smith and *My Brother Jonathan*, by Francis Brett Young.

Reddy, Red mop, Red thatch *See* **Ginger**.

Rednose Used as an instant nickname for a drunken man by a speaker in *The Natural*, by Bernard Malamud. 'Mind your business, rednose.' The term does not seem to be in general use, though it may be heard more frequently in the future now that Red Nose Day seems to have become a fixture. This is officially Comic Relief Day, but is marked by the donning of red noses on all sides. The second Red Nose Day was celebrated in Britain on 11 March 1989.

Reds, you; Reds, the *See* **COLOURS**.

RELIGIOUS VOCATIVES The vocatives that are used in Christian prayers and invocations would merit a special study. In this book the use of words like 'Father' and 'Queen', addressed in prayers to God and the Virgin Mary, has not been discussed in the articles on those terms.

There follows a list of the vocative expressions which occurred in fifty representative novels, with the number of occurrences indicated: Angel of God, my Guardian dear (1); Christ (2); Christ Jesus (1); dear God (2); *Domine* ('Lord') (8); Father (3); God (41); Heart of Jesus (1); Holy Mary (1); Jesus Meek and Mild (1); Lamb of God (1); Lord (9); Lord Jesus Christ (1); Lord of the seedtime and the harvest (1); Mary Mother (2); Most Merciful Father (1); my God (2).

In novels by Roman Catholic writers more of the many titles of the Virgin Mary are likely to occur. *The Stone Angel*, for example, by Margaret Laurence, has: Holy mother of God; Queen of Apostles; Queen of Martyrs; Health of the weak; Refuge of sinners. *Pray for the Wanderer*, by Kate O'Brien, has: Bright Queen; Star of the Sea.

In Catholic countries some of these vocative titles have become names in their own right, e.g. Dolores, Mercedes, Pilar.

Reporterman 'So, reporterman, what's your story?' is addressed to a newspaper reporter in *The Island*, by Peter Benchley. This form shows an alternative way of creating a professional vocative, other than using 'Mr Reporter'. 'Sailorman', 'soldierman', etc., also occur.

Reprobate, you 'Reprobate' is far too literary and archaic a word to be used frequently in ordinary speech. One can imagine its being used humorously between educated speakers,

in contexts where the accusation of moral depravity would not be taken too seriously.

In *Kes*, by Barry Hines, it is used with a certain grim humour by a headmaster to boys who have broken the school rules and are about to be punished. There is a hint in context that the expression is part of the speaker's idiolect, a favourite phrase which almost serves to identify him: 'He left the door open, and a moment later issued his usual invitation to enter: "Come in, you reprobates!" ' The force of 'reprobate', which in the sixteenth century could mean one rejected by God, has considerably weakened since then.

Reptile People who are considered to be repulsive have regularly been described as reptiles since at least the eighteenth century. Fielding refers in *Tom Jones* to a 'reptile of a critic', for instance. 'Avoid my sight, thou reptile,' is said by Dr Primrose to Mr Thornhill in Oliver Goldsmith's *The Vicar of Wakefield*, and he means it as a serious insult.

The word occurs vocatively, either as a covert endearment, as in *Absolute Beginners*, by Colin MacInnes, or as a true insult. An example of the latter is in *Getting it Right*, by Elizabeth Jane Howard, where one man calls another 'you fucking little reptile'. Reptilia, of course, are animals that move by creeping or crawling.

Reverence, Your Used by Irish speakers to address a priest in, e.g., *The Tinker's Wedding*, by J. M. Synge. This is the main modern use of this expression, though it was sometimes used in former times as a general title of respect for someone of high social standing. It is probably only working-class Irish speakers who would address a priest in this way; 'Father' would be used by all social levels.

In *Bless Me, Father*, by Neil Boyd, a priest's housekeeper addresses him when they are alone on one occasion as 'your irreverence', because he has just said something irreverent. She would probably not have used this term had others been present.

Reverend Since the fifteenth century this word has been associated with members of the clergy. In modern times a minister to whom one was writing would expect to receive an envelope addressed to 'The Reverend John Smith', with a letter inside beginning Dear Mr Smith.

'Reverend' is not technically a title, on a par with 'Doctor', say, though it has certainly become so in the popular mind. A black American minister would now expect to be addressed as 'Reverend' by members of his congregation, and by others if they were being polite. A white speaker in *The Liberation of Lord Byron Jones*, by Jesse Hill Ford, is quoted as saying: 'Reverend, you can ride down to City Hall in the car with me. No need for you to ride in the police cars with the others.' A little later the same speaker says: 'No, Mr Reverend, sir, Your Holiness,' which indicates just how sincere his politeness is.

'Reverend' is used as a title far more often in the USA than in Britain, though James Mitchell, in *When the Boat Comes In*, a novel set in the north-east of England, has: 'Glad you could come, reverend.'

For the purists, 'reverend' would be more correctly used as an element in a vocative group, where it would have its true meaning of 'worthy of reverence'. 'Reverend sir' might therefore be used to a minister, but one could equally well address others as 'reverend father', 'reverend doctor,' etc.

There is an example of the latter term of address in Shakespeare's *The Merchant of Venice*, when Portia says to Shylock 'I pray you, let me look upon the bond' and he replies, 'Here 'tis, most reverend doctor.' Shylock knows full well that Portia is not an ordained minister, but uses the word in its general meaning. To do this in modern times would be misleading, so closely has the word become associated with the clergy.

If 'Reverend' is falsely seen as a professional title, at least it is one which carries prestige. The lay-preacher in *South Riding*, by Winifred Holtby, thus ruefully tells himself after giving a sermon that 'he did it well, much better than the minister, he thought, a little bitterly, aware that he lacked the prestige of a "Reverend".'

An opposing point of view is put in *The Mackerel Plaza*, by Peter de Vries. The hero there dislikes specific terms of address for the clergy:

It was not merely the wish to elude prototype that lay at the bottom of this, though that wish did exist in Mackerel to an exquisite degree; it was, more cardinally, a fear of quarantine, a desire to belong to his species – in which even the deferential 'Reverend' tended to blur one's membership – that made him want ever so much to be known simply as Mister Mackerel.

In *Waterfront*, by Budd Schulberg, a man who is described as 'an occasional Baptist' uses 'Reverent' (the variant spelling indicating substandard pronunciation) to a Catholic priest who is being addressed as 'Father' by the other men in his group.

Rib skin Used of one whose ribs can be seen through his skin, a very thin person. *See also* **Spindleshanks**.

Road hog A term in use since the very end of the nineteenth century to describe a selfish user of the highway, especially a driver who

appears to think the road is for his personal use alone.

'You road hog' is addressed to the driver of a taxi in *The Dream of Fair Women*, by Henry Williamson. In *The Daughters of Mulberry*, by Roger Longrigg, the driver of an old breakdown van is overtaken by a girl on a bicycle. He shows his annoyance by shouting: 'Bloody road-hog'. *The Wind in the Willows*, by Kenneth Grahame, has Ratty shouting at the driver and passengers of a car which has passed him: 'You villains! You scoundrels, you highwaymen, you – you – roadhogs!'

Rodney In various English dialects of the nineteenth century, a rodney referred to an idler, a disreputable man. Its origin is obscure, but it is unlikely to be connected with the first name Rodney, or with the family name.

An example of vocative usage occurs in *My Brother Jonathan*, by Francis Brett Young: 'Yo' mischieful rodneys, gereway out o' this!' This is addressed to children and could probably be glossed as you 'good-for-nothings'.

Rogue This appears to have been insulting when applied to a man, and an endearment when applied to a woman in former times, especially in the seventeenth century.

When the word is used in modern times it is often describing someone whose behaviour merits strong disapproval, but whose charm makes reproof difficult.

The basic meaning of 'rogue' in Shakespearean times was 'beggar' or 'vagabond', and since it was taken for granted that such men were dishonest, the word took on that meaning as well.

Girls who were 'rogues' were merely mischievous, in a pleasant, flirtatious way.

The *Oxford English Dictionary* notes that 'rogue' was applied with especial frequency to servants. This was no doubt because male servants were considered automatically to be rascals, while female servants, if they were young, were there to be flirted with.

'Rogue' occurs vocatively throughout the Shakespeare plays, used alone, as 'you rogue', or in a vocative expression such as 'you mouldy rogue' (to a man), 'you sweet little rogue' (to a woman).

In modern times it occurs only rarely, but there is a friendly use of 'you little rogue' to a woman in *Casanova's Chinese Restaurant*, by Anthony Powell, and friendly use of 'you old rogue' by one man to another in *World So Wide*, by Sinclair Lewis.

Romeo Used as a substitute name for any man who is acting like a lover, a kind of apprentice Don Juan. The allusion is obviously to Shakespeare's character in *Romeo and Juliet*. 'I've had enough of your carrying on,

Romeo,' says a woman to a man who is flirting with one of her employees, in *The Ginger Man*, by J. P. Donleavy. In *Laura*, by Vera Caspary, one man addresses another as Romeo when he sees him embracing his fiancée. *War Brides*, by Lois Battle, has an Australian woman saying to an American: 'Back off, Romeo' when he tries to undress her.

Ronyon, runnion An obscure term used by Shakespeare in *The Merry Wives of Windsor* and *Macbeth*, in the former as a vocative. It appears to mean a fat, bulky woman. *See also* quotation under **Witch**.

Rookie A slang word which originated in the British army but is now widely used in, e.g., American sporting circles, referring to a newcomer. The word is a corruption of 'recruit'. *Only a Game*, by Robert Daley, which is a novel about professional American football, has 'Hey, rookie, don't forget your brains'. 'Brains' refers to his playbook.

Rooster This is a mainly American term for a cock, one that has sometimes been applied to a man who is cocky, or vain.

The occasional instances of vocative use that come to light, however, appear to be reasonably flattering. In George Meredith's *Henry Richmond* an older man calls a younger 'you young rooster', while Sinclair Lewis, in *Babbitt*, has his hero say to a friend: 'Say, W. A., old rooster, it comes over me that I could stand it if we didn't go back to the lovin' wives, this handsome *Abend*.' *See also* **Cock**.

Rosie A variant of 'rosy'. Not in general use as a term of address, but *see also* the letter quoted in the article on **Love**. 'Rosie/rosy' makes a highly acceptable vocative, suggesting that the person to whom it is addressed looks in blooming health and attractive.

Rotter, you In *The Ginger Man*, by J. P. Donleavy, a wife is made to call her husband 'you damnable rotter'. 'Rotter' is more frequently found in stories about public school life in Britain, from the beginning of the twentieth century until the 1930s.

The term seems to have remained British, but used today it would probably evoke a smile rather than give offence. 'Bounder' is rather a similar word, one which would mainly be used as a conscious archaism.

The thought behind 'rotter' is that the person concerned is rotten, in the sense of being morally corrupt, but rotten itself, in that meaning, is now rarely used. *The Observer*, in one of its 'Sayings of the Week' columns (February 1989) reported that the Duchess of York uttered the words 'Oh you rotter' to a weighing machine.

Rudesby An archaic word for a rude, disorderly man. It was well used in the seventeenth century, but faded, revived only by writers such as Sir Walter Scott who had a conscious policy of restoring old words. Shakespeare uses the word twice, the vocative example occurring in *Twelfth Night* (4:i), where Olivia tells Sir Toby Belch: 'Rudesby, be gone!'

Ruffian A dated word for a brutish man, one who engages in criminal activities. Used once by Shakespeare, in *King John* (3:i), and never frequent as a vocative, though James Joyce, in *Dubliners*, has a man addressing another, of lower social class, as 'you impertinent ruffian'.

Rufus *See* **Ginger**.

Rummy An American slang term for a heavy drinker, a lush, or juicehead. Presumably used originally of a rum-drinker. 'Beat it, ya rummy' is said to a man in *Waterfront*, by Budd Schulberg. The same character is addressed as 'you juicehead' elsewhere in the novel.

Runt Applied to a person, this word now usually refers to a person's small size. In the seventeenth century it could also be applied to an ignorant person, and indeed, was first used in that way. It was later an insulting term for an ugly old woman, a hag, a meaning that survived longer in Scotland than anywhere else.

A runt is a term for the smallest pig in a litter, though the word was earlier applied to a kind of sturdy but small ox or cow. It was also the correct term for the stump of a tree. All the senses contain the idea of smallness or under-development, which is the thought that lies behind the vocative.

'You little runt' would normally be an insult, but Sinclair Lewis gives a good example of conversion into a friendly term of address in *Dodsworth*: 'Well, you fat little runt!' said Sam, which meant 'My dear old friend, I am enchanted to see you.' The friend in question replies in kind with 'you big stiff, you big bum'. 'Where the hell have you been, you runt?' says an American wife to her (small) husband in *The Pleasure Man*, by Mae West. The couple exchange insults on a regular basis. In the television series *M.A.S.H.* Frank Burns was also inclined to address Radar as 'you little runt' instead of 'Corporal'.

Russell, Bertrand In *The Occupation*, by David Caute, a wife says sarcastically to her husband: 'It's a wonderful feeling to be married to Jean-Paul Sartre and Bertrand Russell.' She is implying that he is as distinguished a philosopher and writer as those two famous philosopher/writers combined. A moment later she says to him: 'Don't shout at me, Bertrand Russell.' Lord Russell's name would perhaps not usually be transferred in this way, but the speaker knows in this case that the person addressed will understand exactly what she means.

S

Saboteur 'You bloody saboteur you' occurs not in the expected wartime adventure story but in a novel about business, *Other Men's Wives*, by Alexander Fullerton. The man addressed has been successfully engaged in industrial espionage; the speaker is another businessman.

Sadist This is a covert endearment rather than an insult when it occurs in *Absolute Beginners*, by Colin MacInnes. The word now seems to mean one who enjoys inflicting pain on others, without necessarily gaining sexual pleasure from the act.

Sage One of the over-literary vocatives used by Charlotte Brontë in *Jane Eyre* is 'sententious sage', addressed by Mr Rochester to Jane. She has just said to him, in the middle of a philosophical discussion, 'That sounds a dangerous maxim, sir; because one can see at once that it is liable to abuse.' 'Sententious sage!' replied Rochester, 'so it is: but I swear by my household gods not to abuse it.' He is making fun of her moralizing wisdom.

The speaker who uses the vocative in *The Critic*, by Wilfrid Sheed, is well aware that the term is not in common use as a term of address. She is talking to a man who has just confidently expressed an opinion: 'He'll never feel better till he gets rid of that stuff.' 'You think so, O sage?' she comments. The use of the vocative 'O', taken over from Latin into artificial literary prose and poetry, clearly indicates her conscious move out of ordinary colloquial speech. 'Sage' is of course used in its general sense of 'wise man'.

Sah A spelling of 'sir' which indicates a military-style pronunciation of the word. It occurs sixty times in *The Heart of the Matter*, by Graham Greene.

Sailor Used typically to a uniformed sailor by, e.g., a waitress in a café. 'Soldier' would be similarly used. The jokey message 'Hello, sailor' was at one time a regular sight in British sea-side towns, displayed on funny hats worn by girls on the spree. 'What think you, sailors?' is said by Viola to those who have survived the ship-wreck in *Twelfth Night* (1:ii). As it happens, there is an instance of 'my young soldier' used vocatively in the same play (4:i).

In *The Trumpet Major*, by Thomas Hardy,

Jim Cornick innocently says in Anne Garland's hearing that Robert Loveday, the man she loves, is courting another girl. Someone tries to prevent him from continuing, but Anne says: 'Tell it all, sailor.'

In ordinary colloquial use, civilians might address a sailor as 'sailor-boy' or 'sailorman'. The latter occurs in *Shipmaster*, by Gwyn Griffin, where one officer in a submarine says to another, jokingly, 'Oh, you vile old sailorman!'

Sam Normally a transferred name, occurring in 'Play it again, Sam,' said to someone as a suggestion that he repeat an action. These words, as everyone now knows, were *not* actually spoken by Humphrey Bogart in the film *Casablanca*, though that is where the quotation is supposed to come from. One may compare 'Elementary, my dear Watson,' another famous 'quotation' which does not actually occur in any of the Sherlock Holmes stories.

Kingsley Amis makes a joke of 'you sam' in *Lucky Jim*. Amis explains:

'Sam' is a version of 'see', Bertrand's own coinage. It arose as follows: the vowel sound became distorted into a short 'a', as if he were going to say 'sat.' This brought the lips some way apart, and the effect of their rapid closure was to end the syllable with a light but audible 'm'.

There comes a time in the novel when Bertrand says to Dixon: 'I don't happen to be that type, you sam.' Dixon chooses to interpret 'you sam' as a vocative: ' "I'm not Sam, you fool," Dixon shrieked; this was the worst taunt of all.'

Sambo In the eighteenth century, in South America, this word described a mulatto of mixed negro and Indian or negro and European blood. By the mid-nineteenth century 'Sambo' was being used as an automatic nickname for a black male.

The two uses of the word may not be connected. A Spanish origin would suggest itself for the South American usage: it has been suggested that a word in an African language meaning 'uncle' may account for the later nickname, but *see also* the discussion under *-bo* for an alternative suggestion. 'Sambo' is used in *Vanity Fair*, by William Thackeray, to a black servant.

In *An American Dream*, by Norman Mailer, a white man addresses a black man by saying:

'Listen, Sambo, you look like a coonass blackass nigger jackaboo to me.' Sammy Davis Junior says in his autobiography *Yes I Can!* that he was called 'Sambo' by fellow American soldiers, who meant the term to be insulting. It would certainly be avoided by speakers who wished to avoid giving offence.

That was not the view taken by a British judge in 1974, however. A West Indian factory worker who was addressed as 'Sambo' by a white colleague responded by resorting to fisticuffs. The white worker needed treatment in hospital, and subsequently charged the West Indian with assault. The judge's comment was that 'Sambo' was no more than a playful name of the type frequently used by one workman to another, and that it did not justify the assault. One wonders how much account was taken of the way the word was said, which could have made it friendly or insulting.

Sanctimonious, old Madame A nonce name and title used to someone who is making a show of having religious faith in *Anglo-Saxon Attitudes*, by Angus Wilson. The woman has just said: 'You and I, we are different, Mr Middleton; we are willing to be old, we are ready to go.' The man concerned says to himself: 'You speak for yourself, old Madame Sanctimonious.'

Sap An abbreviated form of earlier terms such as 'saphead', 'sapskull', or 'sap pate', all of which meant having a head made of sapwood. The term is therefore similar to 'blockhead', and means a fool, or simpleton. 'You sap' is used by an American man to another in *Tropic of Cancer*, by Henry Miller. An Englishwoman uses it to a man in *Julia*, by H. C. Harwood.

In English schoolboy slang of the nineteenth century, a sap was a swot, one who conscientiously prepared his schoolwork. This meaning probably derived from Latin *sapiens*, 'wise'. 'Swot', 'swotter', or 'swotpot' are the usual modern terms for this rare phenomenon.

Saracen's Head, you old 'You hold your tongue, you old Saracen's Head,' says a military man to a colleague, in Thackeray's *The Newcomes*. The man concerned presumably resembles the typical Turk shown on the innsign of a Saracen's Head public house. 'Saracen' has the vague meaning of 'Moslem', and refers to the time of the Crusades. The vocative is unusual, but might well have been meaningful amongst a group of young men who regularly patronized public houses.

Sarge A colloquial form of 'Sergeant', mainly used by colleagues of the person concerned. *See also* **Sergeant**. Examples of 'Sarge' occur throughout, e.g., *The Magic Army*, by Leslie Thomas, and *Thirteen Days*, by Ian Jefferies.

Satan In modern times 'Satan' is likely to be applied jokingly to a person who is tempting another not to do what he or she should do. In such a situation the well-known quotation from the New Testament, made known to us by Matthew and Mark, is likely to be heard: 'Get thee behind me, Satan.' (In the New English Bible this has become 'Get behind me, Satan.') The words were said by Jesus to Peter when the disciple tried to stop his master from going to Jerusalem.

While Satan is the proper name of the devil, its literal meaning is 'adversary', 'accuser'. Bernard Wolfe, in *The Late Risers*, plays with the quotation and makes a speaker say: 'Get thee behind me, Jack Daniels,' substituting the name of a brand of whisky.

'Satan' has sometimes been used as a substitute name for someone who is thought to be devilish. Shakespeare, for example, describes Falstaff as 'that old white-bearded Satan', but no-one actually addresses him in that way. 'Satan' does occur vocatively in Shakespeare, in *The Comedy of Errors*. When Pinch is trying to exorcize Antipholus of Ephesus he says: 'I charge thee, Satan, housed within this man,/To yield possession to my holy prayers.'

Saucebox Used since the late sixteenth century of a person who is habitually saucy, or impertinent. Such a person was also addressed as 'sir sauce', or 'sauce'. In the USA impertinence is often described as 'sass', which derives from 'sauce', but although a child might be told to stop being sassy, 'sass' is not used vocatively.

'Saucebox' might still be used in modern Britain as it is in the eighteenth-century novel *Joseph Andrews*, by Henry Fielding. A young boy says: 'Yes, papa, I love her better than my sisters; for she is handsomer than any of them.' 'Is she so, saucebox?' one of the sisters replies. She emphasizes the comment by 'giving him a box on the ear'. *The Half Hunter*, by John Sherwood, has one man calling another 'you bright-eyed overgrown saucebox' in a friendly way. He equates it with 'chum'.

Saucy 'You get on with yer tea, saucy!' says a woman to a man in *Love in Quiet Places*, by Bernard Thompson. This is the modern version of 'saucebox', or 'impudence', 'imperence'.

Sausage Used as an endearment in modern Britain, though not with great frequency. 'You stupid old sausage' occurs in *End of a Summer's Day*, addressed by an Englishman to his father. The term is clearly an endearment, not an insult, its form suggesting that 'sausage' might here be a euphemism for 'sod'. But 'sausage' is often used alone to a woman or child, where that derivation would not apply.

Addressed to a child it might be inspired by the sausage-like limbs of a baby, or by the high status the word 'sausage' has for most children, who are generally fond of them. They themselves use the affectionate term 'sausage-dog' for the Dachshund.

If 'sausage' began as a piece of nonsense language to children, its extension to women parallels the use of other child-like words, such as 'baby'. It is used to an adult woman by a man in a friendly way in *Daughters of Mulberry*, by Roger Longrigg.

Savage In occasional use as a vocative, 'savage' can refer either to an uncivilized person or one who is cruelly fierce in behaviour. In the latter sense the word might be jokingly used between lovers. A white lawyer calls his black servant 'you God-damned old savage', adding 'All he lacked was a spear, a drum and a chicken bone', in *The Liberation of Lord Byron Jones*, by Jesse Hill Ford. In Shakespeare's *Troilus and Cressida*, Hector says 'Fie, savage, fie!' to Troilus, chiding him for his fierce disposition.

Sawbones This was a slang expression unknown to Mr Pickwick, according to Charles Dickens. When Sam Weller told him that there were 'a couple of sawbones downstairs' he was obliged to ask: 'What's a sawbones?' Dickens adds that he was 'not quite certain whether it was a live animal, or something to eat'. Weller tells him that a sawbones is a surgeon. In *Tom Sawyer*, Mark Twain has Muff Potter tell a young doctor: 'Now the cussed thing's ready, Sawbones.' As for Sam Weller, when an old lady faints he says to a boy 'Now depitty sawbones, bring out the wollatilly!' By this he is to understand that he has been appointed deputy doctor and should produce some volatile salts, or smelling salts.

Sawney *See* Jockey.

Scab There are many examples of scab used as a vocative in *When the Boat Comes In*, by James Mitchell. Union members use the term to those who are crossing a picket line and breaking a strike. This is the normal modern use of the word in both Britain and the USA, and has been so since the beginning of the nineteenth century.

The word had long existed, however, as a general term of abuse for a man who was disliked. The reference was to a skin disease such as scabies, or to the crust which forms over an open skin-wound.

Shakespeare puns in *Much Ado About Nothing* (3:iii): 'Here, man, I am at thy elbow.' 'Mass, and my elbow itch'd; I thought there

would be a scab follow.' He also uses 'scab' vocatively in *Twelfth Night* (2:v), when Sir Toby Belch says to Malvolio: 'Out, scab!' This general sense of 'scab' continued until at least the end of the nineteenth century. In Kipling's *Stalky and Co.* (1899) there is a reference to 'beastly scabs', referring to unpopular boys.

Modern American use of the term occurs in *The River*, by Steven Bauer: 'Somehow the trucks kept moving, though the union men flung themselves on the truck's hood and were crawling to cover the windshield, block the driver's view. They were screaming now – scabs, scabs, scabs – and hurling obscenities with the bricks.' 'Scab sonofabitch' also occurs in this novel.

Scallawag, you damned This is applied to Rhett Butler in *Gone With The Wind*, by Margaret Mitchell. The word is also spelt 'scalawag' in the USA. The normal British spelling is 'scallywag', and in modern times the word is applied to a child with the meaning 'rascal'.

In the nineteenth century it had the stronger meaning of 'scoundrel', or in Trade Union circles, a loafer, a man who would not work.

The word also had a special meaning after the American Civil War, referring to a white Southerner who willingly accepted the reforms proposed by the Republicans. It was this accusation that was levelled at Rhett Butler.

Scamp 'You little scamp' would be addressed to a child in modern times, implying that he or she had been misbehaving, but that such misbehaviour was only to be expected from a young person. Parents who use the term may well be pleased that the child concerned is showing signs of liveliness.

In the eighteenth century, when the word came into being, it was applied specifically to a highway robber. The latter was one who scampered away after committing his crimes. The word was quickly applied to any worthless person, then playfully applied to children.

In *The Pickwick Papers* Tom is not alarmed when Bob Sawyer calls him 'you idle young scamp', adding 'you vagabond' and 'you groveller' for good measure. 'Go to school, you little scamp' says a man to a child in *The House of the Seven Gables*, by Nathaniel Hawthorne. The Australian children's classic, *Seven Little Australians*, by Ethel Turner, has a young stepmother addressing her children as 'you scamps, you bad wicked imps!'

Scarecrow *See* Spindleshanks.

Scaredy cat A taunt used by children to a child who will not accept a dare. In *The Stone Angel*, by Margaret Laurence, a child touches the face of a dead baby, then dares her friends to do the same. When they refuse to do so she calls them scaredy-cats. Margaret Laurence is a Canadian author, but 'scaredy-cat' could be heard in an English playground, along with: cowardy, cowardy custard; yellow-belly; eggy (i.e. 'yellow'); yolky; scare-baby; windy; funk; funk-pot; feardy gowk. The last of these is a Scottish term; the others are regional and are part of playground tradition. They are dealt with by the Opies in *The Lore and Language of Schoolchildren.*

Scatterbrain Used since the eighteenth century of a person who seems to be incapable of connected thought, a likeable but careless, forgetful person. 'Go on, you scatterbrain' says a girl to her sister, in O. Henry's short story *Lost on Dress Parade.* The same speaker calls her sister 'madcap', a comment on her lively and impulsive nature. 'You scatterbrain, you' occurs in *The River Road,* by Francis Parkinson Keyes.

Sceptic This word is rarely used in its technical philosophical sense, referring to Pyrrho and his followers in Greek antiquity who doubted the possibility of real knowledge of any kind. It is more usually used in the general sense of one who is unwilling readily to believe what he hears, especially the claims of others about their achievements.

It occurs rarely as a vocative, but *Jane Eyre,* by Charlotte Brontë, has: ' "Am I a liar in your eyes?" he asked passionately. "Little sceptic, you *shall* be convinced." ' If this word occurred in an American novel it would be spelt 'skeptic', which is closer to the Greek original.

Schemer A priest in James Joyce's *Portrait of the Artist as a Young Man* calls a boy 'lazy little schemer'. It is likely that any agent noun of the 'schemer' type could be used as the headword in a vocative group.

Schmuck *See* Shmuck.

Schnook *See* Shnook.

School A collective term for all those attending a school, the body of students, and used by, e.g., a headmaster addressing a morning assembly. Examples of its use occur in *The Business of Loving,* by Godfrey Smith.

Schoolmaster This would not normally be used as a professional title in direct address, but there is a fine passage in *Our Mutual Friend,* by Charles Dickens, which demonstrates how it can be converted to that use. Bradley Headstone is talking to Eugene Wrayburn, addressing him by his full name and social title. Eugene says:

'You have my name very correctly. Pray what is yours?'

'It cannot concern you much to know, but–'

'True,' interposed Eugene, striking sharply and cutting him short at his mistake, 'it does not concern me at all to know. I can say Schoolmaster, which is a most respectable title. You are right, Schoolmaster.'

Dickens continues: 'It was not the dullest part of this goad in its galling of Bradley Headstone, that he had made it himself in a moment of incautious anger.'

Eugene continues to use 'Schoolmaster' throughout the ensuing conversation, even after Headstone insists on telling him his name, and contrives to make the word an insult. This is clearly not because of the word itself, which in many countries would indeed be, as Eugene said, a respectable title. It is more the dismissive impact of admitting that a person's name is not worth bothering about, clearly implying that the person who bears the name is of no consequence. Shakespeare has 'Master Schoolmaster' as a term of address in *Love's Labour's Lost* (4:ii).

Scoffer Mrs Weller calls her husband 'scoffer' in *The Pickwick Papers,* by Charles Dickens, when he makes a sly remark after listening to 'an edifying discourse' of Mr Stiggins. She suspects that he is scoffing at what he has just heard, as indeed he is. The slang meaning of 'scoff' would allow this term to be used of someone who was eating too much or too quickly.

Scoundrel, you An insult much used in the eighteenth and nineteenth centuries, addressed to men who were considered to be contemptible.

The word was in use by the end of the sixteenth century, describing a mean fellow at that time, but Shakespearean heroes do not use the word in their taunting of other men. Its origin is something of a mystery, though Professor Weekley draws attention in his *Etymological Dictionary of Modern English* to Old French *escondre,* itself from Latin *ex condere,* suggesting a man who is evasive or has something to hide.

In Fielding's *Tom Jones* a woman tells a man that he is a 'saucy scoundrel', while in Smollett's *Peregrine Pickle* a man tells another that he is an 'impertinent scoundrel'. The latter exclamation earns the speaker a punch on the nose. 'You twopenny scoundrel' occurs in George Eliot''s *Scenes of Clerical Life,* and Mr Snodgrass, in *The Pickwick Papers,* greets the representatives of the law with: 'What do you want here, scoundrels?'

In a passage of general interest to those who use insulting terms to others, scoundrel occurs in Boucicault's comedy *London Assurance*. Cool, a valet, asks Paul Meddle, an attorney-at-law, for advice: 'A fellow has insulted me. I want to abuse him – what terms are actionable?' *Meddle*: 'You may call him anything you please, providing there are no witnesses.' *Cool*: 'Oh, may I? (*Looks round*) – then you rascally, pettifogging scoundrel!' In *The Importance of Being Earnest*, by Oscar Wilde, Jack calls Algernon 'you young scoundrel' when he has presented himself as Jack's brother.

Kes, by Barry Hines, shows the term being used in more modern times. A headmaster says to a schoolboy: 'Fast asleep during the Lord's Prayer! I'll thrash you, you irreverent scoundrel!'

Scouse Used as a friendly term by one man to another in *Thirteen Days*, by Ian Jefferies. *See also* **Geordie**.

Scout In Scottish literature this word appears in various spellings, often as 'scoot', and is a term of contempt for a man or woman. Its origin is obscure, whereas the friendly 'old scout', which occurs between men in novels such as *The Hiding Place*, by Robert Shaw, presumably refers to one who was formerly a Boy Scout. *Vile Bodies*, by Evelyn Waugh, has one man saying to another: 'Cheer up, old scout.' The speaker, as in the Shaw novel, is British.

Scraggy *See* **Spindleshanks**.

Scrote A character in *The Choirboys*, by Joseph Wambaugh, invents this term for his personal usage. The man concerned is a Los Angeles policeman and something of a misanthropist. We are told that he wished there was 'a word as dirty as "nigger" to apply to all mankind'. He rejects 'asshole' as being too common, and asks his colleagues for suggestions. Words such as 'fartsuckers', 'slimeballs', 'scumbags', and 'cum-buckets' are rejected for various reasons, and then someone suggests 'Scrotums?' This is thought to be 'Not bad, but too long.' 'Scrotes, then.' 'That's it! Scrotes! That's what all people are: ignorant filthy disgusting ugly worthless scrotes.' 'A man's philosophy expressed in a word,' comments one of his friends.

Subsequently in the novel the man uses 'scrote' vocatively: 'I heard that faggy remark, Slate, you scrote!' It is also taken up by a colleague. 'I wish Roscoe Rules was here, you lousy scrotes. Roscoe'd fix you.' Roscoe is the man who needed the word in the first place.

'Scrote' is not likely to come into general use, most speakers probably feeling that enough abusive terms already exist – and indeed, a wide range of them are displayed in this novel.

If a new term were needed, 'scrote' has the right kind of unpleasant sound, but is etymologically not very satisfying. To refer to 'all mankind' as bags of flesh which contain testicles is hardly biologically accurate or particularly meaningful.

Scrub Formerly used of a mean and insignificant man, the allusion being to 'scrub' in its sense of a stunted tree. Smollett's *Peregrine Pickle* has a girl calling a man 'you old flinty-faced, flea-bitten scrub'.

Scrubber Used mainly by British speakers of or to a woman whose morals are lax sexually, and who acts like a prostitute. *An Indecent Obsession*, by Colleen McCullough, has a man saying to a woman: 'I was enjoying Miss Woop-Woop in more ways that you'll ever know, you dried-up scrubber,' but Miss McCullough is Australian and is presumably using 'scrubber' in the Australian sense – a person who lives in the scrub.

Scum Applied to a person one despises since at least the seventeenth century, implying that the person concerned resembles, or is as valueless, as the filthy film that forms on stagnant water. The latter is one kind of froth or foam – the original meaning of scum. 'Froth and scum, thou liest,' says Pistol to Evans, in *The Merry Wives of Windsor* (1:i).

In *The River*, by Steven Bauer, a strike-breaker is confronted by the wife of one of the strikers.' "You scum," the woman said, to Tom, directly, and the words got through.' One might expect this insult to 'get through' to anyone, but as always with vocatives, everything depends upon the real attitude of the speaker.

In *Mariana* by Monica Dickens, a man greets a woman friend with: 'Hello, scum.' He is answered with: 'Hello, louse.' The context makes it quite clear that this is merely friendly banter.

'Scum' is clearly a more serious insult in *Pudd'nhead Wilson*, by Mark Twain, where a man calls a nephew who has disgraced the family name 'you cur! you scum! you vermin!'

Scutter, you bald-headed This mysterious term occurs in *The Country Girls*, by Edna O'Brien. 'Scut', a slang word for a person, is probably meant, the change to 'scutter' in context being caused by the rhyming game the speaker is playing: 'You bald-headed scutter, will you pass me the butter?'

'Scut' originally referred to the short, erect tail of a hare, rabbit or deer. It was later applied to pubic hair, and thence to a person.

Shakespeare uses the word only once, and then with what appears to be bawdy intent: 'Sir John! Art thou there, my deer, my male deer?' Falstaff replies to this question of Mistress Ford's with: 'My doe with the black scut!' (*The Merry Wives of Windsor*, 5:v).

The Philanderer, by Stanley Kauffmann, has an American man who calls a woman 'you scut, you slut'.

Second Used at sea to a second mate by other members of the crew. There is an example of its use in *Doctor at Sea*, by Richard Gordon.

Second string A reference to a football or other team player who is a substitute rather than a regular first-team player.

The term derives from archery, and the reserve bow-string carried by an archer. 'Second string' occurs as a vocative in *North Dallas Forty*, by Peter Gent.

The term could be used figuratively, of anyone who is considered to be second-rate, but in this instance the speaker is a professional football player addressing a teammate: 'Fuck you, second string. It'll be a cold day when I signal to you from the bench.'

Senator A title which is used in the USA and Australia to address a member of the Senate, which is the more important of the two councils which form the law-making part of the government. 'Senate' literally means a 'council of elders'.

Longman's *Guide to English Usage* gives the correct form of address as 'Mr Senator', but this does not seem to occur. 'Senator' is used alone, or followed by the last name of the person concerned. 'Why not take us up a little, Joe?' says a senator to a helicopter pilot, in *The River*, by Steven Bauer. 'Certainly, Senator,' is the reply. 'Drop the *Senator*, Joe, I can do without the sarcasm,' says the senator. The two men concerned have known each other since student days, and normally use first names.

Senior Fellow Used as a professional title four times in *The Masters*, by C. P. Snow. The man concerned is a senior fellow of a Cambridge College.

Senior Tutor A professional university title, used in the formal circumstances of an official meeting or by speakers who are habitually very formal. There are nine examples of its use in *The Affair*, by C. P. Snow, all of them by university colleagues. 'My dear Senior Tutor' also occurs. A tutor now tends to be thought of as a teacher, though historically his duties towards his young charges were those of a general guardian.

Señor Used before a personal name, *señor* is the Spanish equivalent of 'Mr', but *señor* is frequently used alone as a term of address, where its meaning is closer to 'sir'. The word derives from Latin *seniorem*, 'older person'. It is found frequently in novels which include Spanish speakers, such as the Mexicans in Steinbeck's *To a God Unknown*. The plural *señores* also occurs.

Señora The feminine version of Spanish *señor*, used before a personal name as the equivalent of 'Mrs' or on its own as roughly the equivalent of 'madam'. Like *señor*, *señora* is frequently left untranslated when a Spaniard or Mexican speaker is using English. It is also used by English-speakers who address a Spanish or Mexican woman.

Señorita A Spanish diminutive of *señora* used to address a young woman or girl, the equivalent of 'Miss'.

Sergeant In modern times this professional title is used mainly to those holding the rank of sergeant in the army, air force, marine corps, or police force. The army rank is that of a non-commissioned officer, ranking immediately above a corporal. The air force rank is equivalent to this, though there are minor differences between British and American usage.

In the British police force a sergeant holds the rank immediately below an inspector. His American equivalent ranks below a captain. Colleagues of both military and police sergeants are likely to address them as 'Sarge'.

In Joyce Cary's short story *Bush River*, a young British officer uses 'Sargy', but this is unusual. A schoolmaster in P. G. Wodehouse's story of public school life, *Mike*, addresses the school sergeant by his former military title, a practice which was at one time common.

In earlier literature references occur to, e.g., the superior order of barristers who are now normally distinguished as serjeants. Mr Pickwick has much to do with Sergeant Buzfuz, who accuses him of systematic villainy in his relations with Mrs Bardell.

Seventeenth-century references to sergeants are often to the officer whose duty was to enforce the judgement of a tribunal, or to arrest offenders and bring them before the court. There is the famous allusion by Hamlet to 'this fell sergeant, death, is strict in his arrest'.

Shakespeare also introduces a sergeant-at-arms into *Henry the Eighth*. This was a man, one of twenty-four specially appointed, of knightly rank, who attended on the king and arrested traitors and similar offenders. 'Your office, sergeant: execute it,' says Brandon (1:i). The sergeant then delivers his one and only speech: 'Sir, My lord the Duke of Buckingham, and Earl of Hereford, Stafford and Northampton, I arrest thee of high treason, in the name of our most sovereign King.' According to Holinshed's *Chronicles* it was Sir Henry Marney who made the arrest in real life.

Apart from its use on its own, 'Sergeant' is often used as a title preceding the family name of the person concerned. The pet form 'Sarge' is not used in this way.

Novelists sometimes indicate sub-standard pronunciation of 'sergeant' with spellings such as 'Sarn't'. 'Sargint' occurs in *Shipmaster*, by Gwyn Griffin. In *Tom Jones*, by Henry Fielding, a nonce name is created by Tom when he addresses a military man as 'Mr Sergeant'.

Sergeant-major In the sixteenth and seventeenth centuries, this was a rank in the British army applied to officers of various levels, but usually superior to captain.

Since the beginning of the nineteenth century it has described a non-commissioned officer of the highest grade, or more strictly speaking, a warrant officer who is intermediate in rank between commissioned and non-commissioned officers.

In the USA a sergeant-major can also be an air force or marine corps rank, immediately above sergeant. Leslie Thomas, in *The Magic Army*, quotes a popular British army song which begins: 'Kiss me good-night, sergeant-major,/Tuck me in my little wooden bed. . . .'

Serpent Used occasionally of or to a person who is treacherous, alluding to the biblical story of the devil disguised as a serpent tempting Eve in the Garden of Eden.

In *A Midsummer Night's Dream* (3:ii), Shakespeare has Hermia say to Demetrius, thinking that he has killed Lysander: 'And hast thou kill'd him sleeping? O brave touch!/Could not a worm, an adder do so much?/An adder did it; for with doubler tongue/Than thine, thou serpent, never adder stung.'

There is a serpent scene in *The Pickwick Papers*, however, which shows Dickens at his comic best. Mr Pott, believing that his wife has been unfaithful with his house-guest, Mr Winkle, descends to the breakfast-room:

'Serpent!'

'Sir!' exclaimed Mr Winkle, starting from his chair.

'Serpent, sir,' repeated Mr Pott, raising his voice, and then suddenly depressing it; 'I said, serpent, sir – make the most of it.'

When you have parted with a man at two o'clock in the morning, on terms of the utmost fellowship, and he meets you again, at half-past nine, and greets you as a serpent, it is not unreasonable to conclude that something of an unpleasant nature has occurred meanwhile. So Mr Winkle thought. He returned Mr Pott's gaze of stone, and in compliance with that gentleman's request, proceeded to make the most he could of the 'serpent'. The

most, however, was nothing at all; so, after a profound silence of some minutes' duration, he said – 'Serpent, sir! Serpent, Mr Pott! What can you mean, sir? – this is pleasantry.'

'Pleasantry, sir!' exclaimed Pott, with a motion of his hand, indicative of a strong desire to hurl the Britannia Metal teapot at the head of his visitor. 'Pleasantry, sir! – But no, I will be calm; I will be calm, sir;' in proof of his calmness, Mr Pott flung himself into a chair and foamed at the mouth.

'My dear sir,' interposed Mr Winkle.

'*Dear* sir!' replied Pott. 'How dare you address me as dear sir, sir? How dare you look me in the face and do it, sir?'

'Well, sir, if you come to that,' responded Mr Winkle, 'how dare you look *me* in the face, and call me a serpent, sir?'

'Because you are one,' replied Mr Pott.

'Prove it, sir,' said Mr Winkle warmly. 'Prove it!'

Serry *See* **Sorry.**

Sewer This is not in regular use as a vocative, but it is used by one man to another in *St Urbain's Horseman*, by Mordecai Richler. The same speaker uses 'you filthy thing' a moment later, which accurately expresses what he had in mind when saying 'sewer'.

Shakespeare comes close to using 'sewer' as a vocative in *Troilus and Cressida* (5:i). When Hector says 'Good night, sweet Lord Menelaus,' Thersites says: 'Sweet draught! "Sweet" quoth 'a? Sweet sink, sweet sewer!'

Shamus An American slang term for a policeman or private detective. 'Shamus' is a phonetic spelling of Seamus, the Irish form of James, a name which would have been common amongst the predominantly Irish police force in the USA in former times. Examples of its vocative use to a policeman or detective occur in the Philip Marlowe stories, by Raymond Chandler. There are also two instances in *Goldfinger*, by Ian Fleming.

Sharp ears Ironically used by one man to another in *Eustace Chisholm and the Works*, by James Purdy. 'I could hear you talking out loud to yourself all down the length of the hall,' says one man. 'Guess again, sharp ears,' says the other, and indicates that his wife is in the adjoining bedroom. He was talking to her, not himself.

Shaver, you young 'Hurry up, you young shavers, you'll be late,' says a man in *Border Country*, by Raymond Williams. 'Ain't shaving quite yet, Mr Price,' replies one of the boys to whom 'shaver' was applied.

'Shaver' could at one time be applied to a man of any age, but in modern use, which is becoming rare, it is nearly always combined with 'young' or 'little' and spoken to a boy who is probably too young to be a shaver in the normal sense.

An early meaning of 'shave' was to fleece someone of his money, or even to steal. Professor Weekley, in his *Etymological Dictionary of Modern English*, draws attention to the parallel use of 'nipper' for a young boy, though originally the term applied only to a young pickpocket who nipped, or stole, things.

'Shave' no longer suggests stealing, and modern use of this vocative would probably evoke a response similar to that of the boy in *Border Country*. It did not worry anyone in the nineteenth century. 'You young shaver' occurs in Dickens's *Oliver Twist*, for instance, and in George Eliot's *Scenes of Clerical Life* we are told that Mr Gilfil called all male children 'young shavers' and all girls 'two-shoes'.

Sheeny An offensive name for a Jew, in slang use since the nineteenth century. It has other slang meanings, such as 'pawnbroker', 'tramp', and 'a mean person'. The origin of the word is obscure, but it is highly unlikely, as Eric Partridge suggests in his *Dictionary of Historical Slang*, that it has anything to do with the sheen of a Jew's hair.

The word is used in the USA rather than Britain in modern times. *Portnoy's Complaint*, by Philip Roth, has a young girl calling a Jewish boy 'sheeny', 'kike', 'hebe', and 'cheap bastard fairy Jew' in the space of a moment or two, all of these being expressions of contempt.

In Garson Kanin's *Moviola* it is supposedly Mack Sennett who addresses a colleague as 'you dumb sheeny', but this is interpreted by the man concerned as a friendly term. Soon afterwards 'you fatheaded kike' is used in a similar way.

Sheep-head An insult addressed to Ishmael, the narrator of *Moby Dick*, by Herman Melville. Captain Peleg is the speaker who says 'thou sheep-head', emphasizing his opinion of Ishmael by kicking him in the rear.

Shepherd Used as a simple professional title to a country shepherd in novels describing rural life in former times, such as *Far from the Madding Crowd*, by Thomas Hardy. The novel contains many examples of its use.

In *The Pickwick Papers*, by Charles Dickens, Sam Weller addresses the hypocritical Mr Stiggins as 'shepherd'. Sam has been told by his father about this spiritual leader of fourteen women, one of whom is Sam's stepmother. Mr Weller Senior is induced to go to one of Mr Stiggins's meetings. 'Here's the shepherd a-coming to wisit his faithful flock; and in comes a fat chap in black, vith a great white face, a-smilin' away like clockwork.'

After eating and drinking a great deal, the shepherd begins to preach, then makes the mistake of calling Mr Weller a miserable sinner. 'I wish you could ha' heard how the women screamed, Sammy, ven they picked the shepherd up from underneath the table.' Sam is more polite to Stiggins than his father was, but his vocative use of 'shepherd' is ironic, being used as if it were a synonym of 'vicar' or 'reverend'.

Sheriff A term which conjures up countless western movies in which lean and hardened heroes confront the badmen.

The American sheriffs are the chief executive officers of the counties, whose duties are to maintain peace, guard prisoners, serve processes, and the like. *Showboat*, by Edna Ferber, has: 'Andy did the honours. "My wife, sheriff." ' In *To Kill a Mockingbird*, by Harper Lee, Atticus questions the official in the courtroom: 'Did you call a doctor, Sheriff?'

Britain also has its sheriffs, and indeed they originated in England as shire-reeves, representing the monarch in a shire. The English sheriffs now have mainly ceremonial duties. Scottish sheriffs are the chief judges in a county or district.

Sheriffs, as officers of the law, are either referred to or appear in several Shakespearean plays. In *Henry the Fourth Part One* (2:iv) a Sheriff comes looking for Falstaff. Prince Hal greets him with: 'Now, master sheriff, what is your will with me?' Falstaff in the meantime hides behind the curtain and is soon asleep.

Shipmate One of the more interesting uses of this vocative in literature occurs in Herman Melville's *Moby Dick*. Ishmael attends the Whalemen's Chapel in New Bedford and hears the sermon delivered by Father Mapple, a former sailor and harpooneer turned minister. He addresses his congregation as 'shipmates', or 'beloved shipmates', and bases his sermon, naturally enough, on the story of Jonah and the whale. For Father Mapple the chapel is a ship, the aisles being gangways.

The *Oxford English Dictionary* cites a nineteenth-century novel which uses 'old ship' as a term of address to a fellow sailor, though it calls the usage 'jocular'. Wilfred Granville, in *A Dictionary of Sailor's Slang*, more precisely limits this expression to the Royal Navy, fishermen, and others using 'shippie/shippy', and says that it abbreviates 'shipmate'. He thinks that the 'old' refers to a former messmate, as it may well do in third person reference.

In direct address, however, 'old' would have its usual friendly meaning.

Shit This much used word – still considered to be taboo in polite society – indicates general feelings of contempt when applied to a person as a vocative. It is especially frequent in American English.

In *Boulevard Nights*, by Dewey Gram, 'you shit' is spoken by a young man to his brother, while 'you shits' in *Portnoy's Complaint*, by Philip Roth, is addressed to two friends of the speaker with whom he is temporarily displeased.

Elizabeth Jane Howard, in *Getting it Right*, has a male character address another as 'you fucking little fly-blown piece of shit', giving vent to very real anger. *Redback*, by Howard Jacobson, has the following:

'You stay where you are,' said Venie. 'You little shit.' Only because she had just come back from New Zealand and had picked up the accent, she pronounced it 'shut.' Every man should know what it is like, just once in his life, to be called 'a little shut.'

Rabbit is Rich, by John Updike, has another example of 'you shit' used by a woman to a man, one who has not realized that she has been in love with him for a long time. In *The Choirboys*, by Joseph Wambaugh, a policewoman in Los Angeles calls a male colleague 'you dumb shit' because he has just challenged a prisoner to a fight and been knocked to the floor for doing so.

Shit-ass, you Used mainly by American speakers to express contempt for an insignificant person, a jerk. An example occurs in Norman Mailer's *An American Dream*, used by a black male speaker to a white man.

Shit-eater A despicable person. Howard Jacobson, in *Redback*, says: 'I'd been called a reactionary and a revisionist and a fascist and a shit-eater for as long as I could remember.'

Shit-face A variant of 'shithead' used by mainly American speakers. While it is obviously insulting in tone it is often used without real rancour. *An American Dream*, by Norman Mailer, has the hero calling the television producer with whom he works 'you shit-face'.

Shithead 'Maxwell, you shithead, get your ass outta my face,' is said by a professional football player to a team-mate in *North Dallas Forty*, by Peter Gent. The man addressed takes no notice of the instruction or the vocative, which he certainly does not think insulting. As the novel makes abundantly clear, normal conversational interchange between professional American footballers is aggressive by normal standards, with obscenities taken for granted. 'You shithead' is also used fairly mildly in *I'll Take Manhattan*, by Judith Krantz, where it is said by an American girl to her brother.

Shitkicker A mainly American term of abuse for a rural person, a hick. It is used by an Australian speaker in *A Salute to the Great McCarthy*, by Barry Oakley, where 'you suburban shitkicker' is addressed to a man who has come from the bush to live in the city.

Shmuck, schmuck Regarded as a taboo word in polite Jewish society. It derives from German *Schmuck*, 'ornament, jewellery' or *schmuck*, 'neat, smart' but in slang refers specifically to the penis or, vocatively, to a person for whom one feels contempt, a jerk, dope, boob, etc. It has the euphemistic form 'shmo'.

In *Portnoy's Complaint*, by Philip Roth, one Jewish boy says to another: 'Schmuck, what'd you go home for?' *Oliver's Story*, by Erich Segal, has an American woman saying to her lover: 'You big romantic schmuck.' She also says: 'Schmuck, I am in a meeting.' There is no mention of this speaker being Jewish. Mordecai Richler, in *St Urbain's Horseman*, prefers the spelling 'shmock' for this vocative.

Shnook, Schnook An American Yiddish term for a meek and ineffectual person, a patsy. In John Updike's *Rabbit is Rich* a father calls his adult son 'you poor little shnook', though the family is certainly not Yiddish-speaking.

'Schnooky boy' is used in a friendly way in *The Limits of Love*, by Frederic Raphael, though there is an edge to it. A man who refuses to acknowledge his own Jewishness says: 'It's a perfectly plausible line to say that one intends to integrate oneself with the country one lives in. Other so called racial groups have done it, I don't see why we shouldn't.' The reply to this, spoken by another Jewish man, is: 'The German Jews did it, schnooky boy, and look what happened to them.'

Shocker, you little *See* Horror.

Short-and-fat, old An *ad hoc* vocative used by a gatekeeper to a stranger who has just called him an idiot, in *The Pickwick Papers*, by Charles Dickens. 'Old' here has its literal meaning, and is part of the insult.

Shorty An instant nickname which can be bestowed on a person who is smaller than average, or humorously upon a person who is taller than average. In *Waterfront*, by Budd Schulberg, a young American addresses a policeman who is shorter than himself as 'Shorty'. *See also* Tich.

Shrew Shakespeare's *The Taming of the Shrew* has probably helped to keep this word alive, and to associate it almost exclusively with women.

In Shakespeare's own time it could equally

well be applied to a man, one who was felt to be malignant, but by the end of the seventeenth century it referred to a scold.

The word does not often occur vocatively in literature, though presumably it may do so in a back-street slanging-match. Shakespeare uses it only once in direct address, when Sir Andrew Aguecheek meets Olivia's chambermaid Maria for the first time and calls her 'fair shrew'. She does not seem to object to the word, but his 'Bless you, fair shrew' is clearly not insulting.

The shrew mouse was reputed in former times to have evil powers, hence the use of the word for a malignant person. 'Shrewd' derives from the same source. This now means 'astute', but originally meant 'hurtful'.

Shrimp, you 'Shrimp' has been applied contemptuously to small people since at least the fourteenth century. Chaucer uses the word in this way in his Monk's Prologue, while Shakespeare has, in *Henry the Sixth Part One* (2:iii):

I thought I should have seen some Hercules.
A second Hector, for his grim aspect
And large proportion of his strong-knit limbs.
Alas, this is a child, a silly dwarf!
It cannot be this weak and writhled shrimp
Should strike such terror to his enemies.

A less contemptuous comparison is made in *Love's Labour's Lost* (5:ii): 'when he [Hercules] was a babe, a child, a shrimp,/Thus did he strangle serpents in his manus.'

Robert Chapman, in his *Dictionary of American Slang*, lists 'shrimp' as the equivalent of 'peanut', used to describe colloquially a very small person. In *Babbitt*, by Sinclair Lewis, a man greets his friend with 'How're you, you poor shrimp?' but this is merely a mild insult which signals their intimacy. 'You shrimp' used by one boy to another in *Rabbit Redux*, by John Updike, is accompanied by a blow, and is meant as a serious insult. *See also* **Tich**.

Shyster, you In *The Middle Man*, by David Chandler, a speaker says to an American lawyer: '*You* help *me*? You shyster! You mouthpiece for crooks and hoodlums!' The second vocative expression here aptly glosses the first, since 'shyster' is used of a dishonest or otherwise contemptible lawyer in American slang.

Amongst the origins suggested for the word, the most likely is a derivation from German *Scheisser*, 'shitter'. Some have tried to blame a Mr Scheuster, who practised law in New York in the nineteenth century, for the subsequent use of the word. Others have said that prisoners were advised to 'fight shy of', avoid, lawyers.

Perhaps the combination of all three pos-

sible sources made the term seem particularly suitable, since it is well-established. The word is also used in Britain.

Signalman Formerly an important member of a ship's crew in the days when communication between ships at sea was largely a matter of using visual signals. 'Well, all right, Signalman?' asks a character in *Border Country*, by Raymond Williams. The person addressed is a railway signalman.

Use of such professional terms is no longer as common as it was. At one time it was something of a tradition in railway circles for men who were working together to use terms such as 'driver' and 'fireman', as well as friendly terms such as 'mate'.

Silkenhair, my This occurs in *The Dream of Fair Women*, by Henry Williamson, and is a good example of how a particular vocative can arise in special circumstances. A mother talking to her five-year-old daughter says: 'Kiss Mummie, my silkenhair. How Mummie wishes her own hair was soft like Quillie's.'

Silly In modern use 'silly' normally means foolish, lacking in common sense. In earlier times it meant deserving of pity, or defenceless. Shakespeare's reference to silly women in *Two Gentlemen of Verona* is to be interpreted in the latter sense.

'Silly' could also mean physically or mentally weak until the nineteenth century, but it is now a mild word to apply to a person. 'It's you I want to marry,' says a man to a woman, in Somerset Maugham's short story *Episode*. 'Well, what's to prevent you, silly?' she replies. In *The Dream of Fair Women*, by Henry Williamson, a wife in her twenties calls her older husband 'you silly' with genuine affection. *Vile Bodies*, by Evelyn Waugh, has a woman saying to a man: 'No one wants to keep you from your wife, you old silly.'

'Silly' is probably used more often elsewhere in the vocative group than as a head-word. 'Silly boy', 'silly girl', 'silly nut', 'you silly bugger', 'silly ass', and the like occur fairly frequently and are usually friendly or intimate rather than insulting.

Sillybilly A gentle term of address, usually far more intimate than insulting, spoken to a child or to a love-partner. It is used to a child in *Room at the Top*, by John Braine. Partridge says in his *Dictionary of Historical Slang* that a sillybilly was originally, in the mid-nineteenth century, the juvenile butt of a circus clown. The second element was no doubt used for rhyming convenience.

Simpleton, you 'Is that poetry, you poor simpleton?' asks a man of his friend, in *Magnus*

Merriman, by Eric Linklater. Simpleton first appears in the mid-seventeenth century, apparently a fanciful formation based on simple and inspired by last names such as Newton. There was at one time a similar 'idleton', which did not survive.

'Simpleton' itself has not survived especially well, though it was given a new lease of life when American college students shortened it to 'simp'. 'You simp' would have been heard in the early part of the twentieth century being bandied about on campuses, and may still be used by those who were students at the time. It occurs, for example, in one of the Isaac Asimov short stories.

Sinners Used by evangelical orators when addressing their congregations, in the sure knowledge that the description accurately describes most of those listening.

'Sinners and brothers, let us pray,' says such a speaker in *Brothers' Keepers*, by Frank Smith. 'You miserable sinners' is used by a religious fanatic in *Moby Dick*, by Herman Melville.

'My friends and fellow-sinners' is used to begin a sermon in *George Silverman's Explanation*, by Charles Dickens. This same author has a rather more unusual example of 'you wenerable [venerable] sinner', addressed to a man who is supposedly looking at the young women who are nearby. The incident occurs in *The Pickwick Papers*, by Charles Dickens.

In the same novel the hypocritical Mr Stiggins, otherwise known as the Shepherd, calls Mr Weller Senior 'a miserable sinner'. Mr Weller responds by knocking him to the floor, not appreciating the term.

In *Saturday Night and Sunday Morning*, by Alan Sillitoe, 'you dirty sinner' is addressed by the hero to himself as he thinks about his adulterous acts with a married woman. He is talking to the woman's husband at the time.

Sir From a historical point of view, 'sir' is a shortened form of 'sire', arising from the unstressed pronunciation of that word when placed before a man's name to indicate that he was a baronet or a knight. Modern holders of those ranks are still addressed as 'Sir John', 'Sir Thomas', etc.

In former times 'sir' was used fairly frequently to form nonce names of the 'Sir Prudence', 'Sir Smug' type. 'Mr' is normally used for this purpose in modern times.

In the fifteenth and sixteenth centuries, especially, a priest could have been addressed as 'Sir' + first name, a usage long obsolete. Also obsolete is the custom in the sixteenth and seventeenth centuries, at some universities, of addressing a Bachelor of Arts as 'Sir' + last name.

These various vocative usages led to 'sir'

becoming a common prefix in expressions like: sir knight, sir clerk, sir page, sir monk, etc. Some of these instances must have been ironic, and some appear to be examples of inverse address, discussed under **Sirrah**.

By the fourteenth century it was already possible to address any man who was socially superior to the speaker as 'sir'. By the eighteenth century it had become the normal term of address between male equals if they were middle or upper-class speakers. Edna Ferber, in *Showboat*, remarks in passing that the gentlemen gamblers on board always 'addressed each other as "sir"'.

It is not clear when 'Dear Sir' became the purely conventional opening for a letter to an unknown man, but there was presumably the thought in the minds of early writers that no offence would be caused by using 'sir' to someone not strictly entitled to be so addressed, though its omission might cause offence. In modern times letters addressed to strangers about whom nothing is known save that they are academic are frequently headed 'Dear Doctor' + last name for similar reasons.

In general terms, then, 'sir' has long been perceived as a term of respect, used by a speaker who acknowledges the seniority of social or professional rank of the person being addressed. It is also long-established as a conventional term which is to be used in a number of situations. One such is in a school, where in Britain, at least, the use of 'sir' to any schoolmaster by a pupil is often enforced, especially when the pupil is aged less than sixteen.

In *Goodbye to All That*, Robert Graves says: 'A preparatory schoolboy, when caught off his guard, will call his mother "Please, matron," and always address any male relative or friend of the family as "Sir", like a master.' This is a reference to a boarding school environment of middle-class children, and refers also to school life in the early part of the present century, but Graves was certainly reporting on personal experience.

The reaction of the 'male relatives and friends of the family' to being called 'sir' would presumably have varied. Some fathers, especially, would have accepted it as their due, as is still the case in some present-day families. A young American informant in 1988 told the author that she normally addressed her parents as 'sir' and 'ma'am', but added hastily that she lived in the Mid-west, and that her family was perhaps a little old-fashioned.

In Harper Lee's *To Kill a Mockingbird* occurs: ' "What are you doing with those scissors, then?" "Nothing." "Nothing what?" said Atticus. "Nothing, sir." ' This is a conversation between an American boy and his lawyer father in fairly recent times. E. M. Forster, in *Howard's End*, says of Mr Wilcox that 'he liked being called sir' by his son. The son in this case also uses 'Pater' on occasion. An adult girl in Jane Austen's *Northanger Abbey* addresses her father as 'sir'.

The justification for all this is to be found in the old use of 'sire' for a parent. We now speak only of male animals siring young, but in former use people talked of their 'sire', meaning their father, and their 'grandsire', their grandfather.

Justified or not, some fathers would seem to dislike being called 'sir'. In *Dodsworth*, by Sinclair Lewis, a father who is so addressed by his son says: 'Don't call me "sir" – I'm still under age for it – I hope!' The man concerned is aged fifty. This objection to 'sir' because of its age implication is shared by other men. *Tamahine*, by Thelma Niklaus, has: ' "How do you do, sir?" Gerald repressed a flicker of distress at a mode of address that put him among the elderly and respectable.'

Henry's War, by Jeremy Brooks, has: ' "Sorry, sir!" cried a spindle-legged urchin.... So, he was "sir" now: one of *them*.' In *The Business of Loving*, by Godfrey Smith, a man says: 'For heaven's sake don't call me sir, it makes me feel so old.' Graham Greene, in *The Heart of the Matter*, has: 'Why do you always call me sir, Wilson? You are not in the police force. It makes me feel very old.' In *Theirs was the Kingdom*, by R. F. Delderfield, a young man says to a boy of thirteen, who is being polite: 'Why do you address me as "sir"?' 'I suppose because you're older,' says the boy. 'Isn't it the polite thing to do to someone a lot older?' 'Not where I come from,' says the young man, grimly. He is a Welshman.

Another reason for objecting to the term is offered by a speaker in *Thanksgiving*, by Robert Jordan, when a young man says

'I understand, sir.' 'Stop that! Don't mind "sir" from an older man. Can't stand it from you youngsters. Always sounds patronizing even if you don't intend it to. I'm "Rollie" to my intimates, "Thorny" to my friends, "Mr Thornton" to others and "sir" to the help.'

This kind of comment seems rather unfair to polite young English schoolboys and young American men who are acting as they have been taught to do, and an educated person should be able to distinguish between polite motivation and sneering patronage, or possibly cringing flattery.

Different views are expressed on the subject by novelists and a sociologist, the first of whom, Zoe Fairbairns, says in *Down*: ' "Excuse me, sir, you couldn't spare me a cigarette, I suppose, could you?" That "sir" did the trick. I had seen tramps go up to ordinary people with "Gottafagmate?" and it usually got them exactly nowhere.' Alan Sillitoe, in *A Tree on Fire*, presents a contrary view:

An attendant pointed to his washed and fuelled car. It disgusted him the way they lavished so many 'sirs'. Such treatment turned him sour – which seemed to increase their deference. He once told an attendant not to call him sir, but from then on he ceased to be helpful, and actually disliked him for reminding him of his civility.

Richard Hoggart, in *The Uses of Literacy*, also puts the view of a more cynical male, referring to

the peculiarly mean form of trickery which goes with some forms of working-class deference, the kind of obvious 'fiddling' of someone from another class which accompanies an over-readiness to say 'sir', but assumes, in the very obviousness with which it is practised, that it is all a contemptuous game, that one can rely on the middle-class distaste for a scene to allow one to cheat easily.

Many men, then, do not appreciate being called 'sir'. They are embarrassed by the implied deference and insulted by the implication that they are of great age.

This only applies, normally, outside those environments within which the use of 'sir' is a matter of convention, or rule. A shop assistant using 'sir' to a customer, for example, is simply signalling verbally that he is an employee, and that it is his job to help. So is a steward on board a passenger liner, yet someone from a rural area, of humble origins, may find the usage strange. 'Geordie laughed and laughed. He had an infectious laugh, so Rawlins began too. "What's up?" he asked. "It's that wee chap calling me sir," said Geordie. "Who does he think I am, Andrew Carnegie?" ' (*Geordie*, David Walker).

In military circles, the use of 'sir' is required by military law to maintain a hierarchy which must always be clear to those who are part of it. There is no question in such circumstances of the speaker being able to choose from a range of possible vocatives and decide whether or not to use 'sir'. The term *is* to be used because of the respective ranks of speaker and hearer, or it isn't.

Having said that, service personnel who are friendly may privately decide to dispense with the formality when they are alone, in which case the senior officer will say something to that effect. In the Biggles books of Captain W. E. Johns, the hero at one point says: 'Never mind the "sir" when you're on the tarmac.' This is to some newcomers who have just joined the squadron. 'My name is Rupert. For God's sake call me that and drop this sir crap,' says an English army officer to his junior in *The Business of Loving*, by Godfrey Smith. By contrast, in *Days of Hope*, by Jim Allen, a conscientious objector who has been forced to join the army is told by an officer: 'You're in the army now whether you like it or not, and you'll address all officers as sir!' In *Bhowani Junction*, by John Masters, another junior officer is told: 'In this regiment subalterns address field officers as "Sir", not "Major", or "Colonel", or even "Chief". You are not in the Royal Army Pay Corps, unfortunately.'

It is sometimes said that women dislike being obliged to call a man 'sir', though they obviously accept the convention if they join one of the armed services or a quasi-military service such as the police force. In the latter organization they would be obliged to use 'sir' both to superiors within the force and to members of the public who looked as if they were reasonably respectable men.

Those women who do object to using the term should take a leaf out of Mrs Sparsit's book. In *Hard Times*, by Charles Dickens, she acts as a domestic servant to Mr Bounderby and addresses him as 'sir', but we are told that 'Mrs Sparsit's "sir" in addressing Mr Bounderby was a word of ceremony, rather extracting consideration for herself in the use, than honouring him.'

Another noticeable use of 'sir' by a woman speaker in literature is in *Vanity Fair*, by William Thackeray. Becky Sharp is determined to ingratiate herself with the Sedley family when she goes to stay with them, not only with the family but their servants. She flatters the housekeeper by showing deep interest in the raspberry jam she is making, and 'persisted in calling Sambo "Sir" and "Mr Sambo", to the delight of that attendant.' She does this in private, of course, being far too astute to do so in front of the family or other servants. Becky Sharp is not quite in the same category as one of the 'poor relations', described by Charles Lamb in his essay on that topic. A poor relation embarrasses everyone, says Lamb, by calling the servant 'sir'.

We can sum up the main uses of 'sir' in modern times by saying that it is used professionally by convention or rule, or as a freely chosen term of politeness, usually by a younger man to an older, especially if the speaker is an American of good education or family.

British speakers do not address a strange man in the street, from whom they are going to ask directions, as 'sir'. Americans are likely to do so if the man being addressed is of a certain age and apparently middle class. Hence the passage in *The Magic Army*, by Leslie Thomas, when an American addresses an English army officer as 'sir'. 'Bryant did not know whether the man had recognized him as an officer or whether it was merely the general American usage.'

In modern times sir is addressed to males only, with 'gentlemen' acting as its normal plural. 'Sirs' would be used in a vocative expression where 'sirs' was the head-word, as in 'young sirs'.

In the seventeenth and eighteenth centuries, 'sir' was regularly, if infrequently, used to women in certain English dialects, as the quotations in the *Oxford English Dictionary* reveal. Today it seems to be Marcie, in Charles M. Schulz's *Peanuts* cartoon strip, who uniquely addresses 'sir' to a girl.

Finally, as an indication of how frequently 'sir' is used as a vocative in modern times, it occurred 1362 times in fifty British novels chosen at random. Several of these had a military setting, it is true, and other professional uses – e.g. 74 instances in *Doctor at Sea*, by Richard Gordon, mainly by stewards to passengers and crew, helped to expand the numbers. 'Sir' was the second most frequently used vocative in that particular corpus, only first names being more frequently used.

Nearly all occurrences of 'sir', incidentally, *are* vocative, though it can occur non-vocatively in a sentence like 'Sir's henchman invited me for a drink', which is in *Festival*, by N. J. Crisp. English schoolchildren regularly say things like 'Sir said I could do that'.

See also **Sirrah, Sire**. 'Sir' also occurs in variant spellings such as 'sair', 'sah', 'sorr', indicating dialectal and sub-standard pronunciations.

Sire The early form of 'sir', originally placed before a man's name to indicate that he was a knight. The word basically means 'senior'. The knightly prefix developed into 'sir': 'sire' became a special term from the thirteenth century which was used to address a king, the equivalent of 'your Majesty'. This usage seems to have lasted until the sixteenth century, when it faded.

In modern times 'sire' would probably only be used in jest, e.g. by a wife responding to a husband who was issuing regal orders.

Siree, sirree An emphatic form of 'sir', used mainly in North America, usually following the words 'yes' and 'no'.

Although the 'sir' in expressions like 'Yessirree', as it is sometimes written, or 'No sirree', was clearly of a vocative nature to begin with, it appears to have lost this sense for many speakers. The 'siree/sirree' element has become an emphatic suffix converting a simple 'yes' into 'Yes indeed!' and a 'No' into something like 'Certainly not!'

In *Face to Face*, by Edward A. Rogers, a woman says: 'I can't say I'm undulating with happiness myself right now. No sir-ee!' This is spoken to her husband, but one has the strong feeling that she would have used the same expression had she been talking to a woman friend.

Sirrah An extended form of 'sir' which began to be used in the sixteenth century and is still to be found in nineteenth-century literature.

Joseph Sedley, for example, in Thackeray's *Vanity Fair*, addresses his servant as 'fellow' and 'sir', and then says emphatically: 'Silence, sirrah!' This perfectly illustrates the use of 'sirrah', which is a use of 'sir' in inverted address, as it is sometimes called. This simply means that the speaker uses to the hearer the term of address which would normally be used by the hearer to the speaker.

Inverted address is not by any means a common phenomenon in English, though in many languages a mother might address her daughter by a term which means 'mother', an aunt use a term meaning 'aunt' when addressing her niece, and so on.

The inverted use of 'sir', which is still used in modern English, occurs when a speaker who is higher in the social or professional hierarchy than the hearer reprimands or expresses controlled contempt to the latter. 'Now then, sir,' says a father to his young son in *Seven Little Australians*, by Ethel Turner, 'was it you lamed Mazeppa?'

This special use of 'sir' seems to have led naturally to a special form of the word, just as 'siree' developed in American English as a specifically emphatic form. The distinction between 'sir' and 'sirrah' was a useful one, and it is odd that 'sirrah' has dropped out of use. If it lives on in the dialectal 'sorry', then its meaning has changed, since 'sorry' is normally friendly. That 'sirrah' was not so is shown by Ben Jonson, for instance, in *Every Man in His Humour*.

'Sirrah' is there equated in close context with 'you knave', 'you slave', 'you rogue', all of which are addressed to the man who is then called 'sirrah'. In *The Alchemist*, also by Jonson, Face calls Subtle 'sirrah'. Dol Common immediately says to Face: 'Nay, general, I thought you were civil.' A century later, in Fielding's *Tom Jones*, 'sirrah' was still being equated with 'scoundrel'.

In spite of all this evidence, a possible alternative explanation for 'sorry' is that 'sirrah' *also* had a friendly use, though few would agree with V. Salmon who, in an article on Elizabethan Colloquial English in *A Reader in the Language of Shakespearean Drama*, concludes from his readings of the plays that 'sirrah' 'seems to have answered the need for a respectful form of address to a youth not yet old enough to be called *master*.' That statement relates to Elizabethan English, it must be remembered, where 'master' was the equivalent of present-day 'mister'. The term which Salmon describes later became 'master' itself.

While 'sirrah' may never have been a respectful form of address (in spite of Salmon's conclusion), it almost certainly had a 'softer' meaning than the one used for serious reprimand. This is best evidenced by its occasional use to women and girls.

Jonathan Swift playfully admonishes Stella in the *Journal* as 'sirrah' and 'sirrah Stella'. Dekker, Fletcher, and Etheredge are seventeenth-century writers who have similar use of 'sirrah' to a woman. Swift appears to equate the word with 'hussy', also used playfully, but it is more likely that 'sirrah' was regularly used to children in mock admonition, so that Stella and other female addressees were receiving a 'naughty child' term of address.

'Sirrah' also occurs in Shakespeare and later writers as a prefixed title followed by a proper name, or by the name of a trade or profession: sirrah Costard, sirrah collier, etc. 'Sirrah' in such cases is merely a mock title, imitating the former practice of dignifying a priest, for example, as 'sir priest', or simply aping the baronet's 'Sir John'.

'Sirrah' is nearly always spoken by a man, though it may have come to be considered as a word of reprimand which could be used by a speaker of either sex to a social inferior.

Used to a social equal or superior, the word would normally have been seen as an insult. If the kindlier uses of the word to women and children are simply the normal mock harshness, converting almost any term into a kind of endearment, then the inverted address theory holds good for the original sense development of 'sirrah' and its later extensions.

In normal modern English usage the word is now obsolete.

Sis A short form of 'sister' used by brothers or sisters of the person addressed. Working-class speakers, usually men, might also use it to a woman unrelated to them. *See also* **Sister**.

'Sis' is used rather unconvincingly in Arthur Hailey's *Hotel*. A conversation takes place between 'Lord Selwyn' and 'the Duchess of Croydon', his sister, both supposedly members of the British aristocracy. Lord Selwyn uses 'sis' during the conversation, though the abbreviated form does not accord with the formality of their speech and their social class.

An Indecent Obsession, by Colleen McCullough, has a patient in a hospital saying to a nurse: 'I beg your pardon, Sister.' She replies: 'You'd better start calling me Sis the way the rest of them do. Sooner or later you will anyway.' 'All right, Sis, I will,' says the man.

This is a special situation, where a nursing sister has charge of a very small ward in which there are only six fairly permanent patients. Her relationship with them is more friendly than one would normally expect; indeed she and one of the patients become lovers. He continues to call her 'Sis' even then, causing her to say: 'Can't you remember to call me Honour?' A similar situation arises in *The Sleepers of Erin*, by Jonathan Gash: ' "Which part of Ireland are you from, Sister?" "Sinead." "Where's that?" She fell about laughing. "Stupid man. It's my name. I mean stop calling me Sister. You're not in hospital any more." '

Sissy A term of abuse for an effeminate man, deriving from 'sister'. In *The Heart is a Lonely Hunter*, by Carson McCullers, it is said by one boy to another because the latter has expressed a wish to have a fancy costume. In *Diamonds are Forever* McGonigle ill-advisedly says to James Bond: 'Come on, sissy.' A similar challenge occurs in *The Choirboys*, by Joseph Wambaugh, where a man says to a policeman: 'C'mon and fight, you big sissy.' Later in the same novel a policeman says to a man: 'You fag! You insolent fucking sissy!' The man concerned has made homosexual advances to him. 'Sissy' is also used as a playground taunt to boys who cry too easily. *See also* **Cry-baby**.

Sister 'You had some kind of oomph, sister,' says a young actor to an actress in *Bethel Merriday*, by Sinclair Lewis. 'Whadya mean "sister"? I never saw you before,' is the reply. This friendly use of 'sister', however, was established in the USA by the middle of the nineteenth century and continues today.

British use of the term was at one time slightly different, if we are to believe Oscar Wilde. In *The Importance of Being Earnest* Jack tells Algernon: 'Cecily and Gwendolen are perfectly certain to be extremely great friends. I'll bet you anything you like that half an hour after they have met, they will be calling each other sister.' Algernon replies: 'Women only do that when they have called each other a lot of other things first.' Later in the play, after a few misunderstandings have been cleared away, Gwendolen does indeed say to Cecily: 'You will call me sister, will you not?'

In modern times girls still have friends who are like sisters to them, but they are less likely to address them as such. As for the male use to an unknown girl, this remains mainly an American habit. Used in Britain it probably reflects conscious imitation of American ways.

'Sister' was formerly used within middle-class families, along with other terms of relationship such as 'husband', 'wife', 'brother'. In the opening scene of Thackeray's *Vanity Fair* the Misses Pinkerton address one another as 'sister'.

In Shakespeare it is frequently used, sometimes as 'sweet sister', 'young sister', 'fair sister', 'good sister', 'my dearest sister', etc. The Weird Sisters, in *Macbeth*, use 'sister' to one another. The word could also be followed by the first name. In *The Taming of the Shrew* Bianca, much abused by Katherina, constantly reminds her of their sisterly relationship by the vocatives she uses, including 'sister Kate'.

Family use of 'sister' from the seventeenth to the nineteenth centuries would have extended to sisters-in-law, step-sisters, and half-sisters. The *Oxford English Dictionary* even provides some evidence that it could have been used to the mother-in-law of one's daughter.

In modern use the short form 'sis' is far more likely to be used to a sister than the full form, though the latter may be used ironically. 'Don't forget you're my younger brother,' says a character in *Mariana*, by Monica Dickens. 'Well, I feel old today, sister,' is the reply.

In professional use, 'sister' has been a title for a nurse in charge of a ward since the late nineteenth century. Use of the term may well have derived from the nuns who were usually the nurses in former times. The religious use of 'sister' goes back to at least the tenth century. By the fifteenth century 'sister', or 'sister' + first name, was being used to address not only nuns, but any female member of a Christian congregation.

In modern times 'sister' has come to be seen as a term suitable for use to any woman who has a clearly identified common interest with the speaker. It is thus used in trade union circles at formal meetings. It is likely to be used by feminists, or by black American girls addressing one another in certain circumstances. In *The Liberation of Lord Byron Jones*, by Jesse Hill Ford, occurs the following:

His widow, Miss Emma, she promised me last night that she would henceforth be a witness for Islam. She asks now to be known as Emma X. She tells me that she has no wish for anything that is the white man's, but prefers to be a witness for the Muslim cause and a black woman of the nation of Islam. Call her Sister Emma X.

Sub-standard pronunciation of sister is occasionally indicated in variant spellings. Truman Capote, in his short story *The Headless Hawk*, has: 'A cab driver hollered: "Fa crissake, sistuh, get the lead outa yuh pants!" '

Sister-in-law This relationship term is rarely used vocatively, especially in modern times, though in the formal drawing-room conversations of the eighteenth and nineteenth centuries it was perhaps more common. A special situation can bring about its use, however. In *A Woman Called Fancy*, by Frank Yerby, a man who wishes to remind his sister-in-law of that relationship addresses her by both her full married title – Mrs Tyler Brantley – and as 'my dear sister-in-law'.

Six-and-eightpence This curious term was applied in British slang of the late eighteenth century onwards to a solicitor or attorney. Six shillings and eight pence, a third of a pound, was for a long time a typical legal fee. Amongst other things it was the amount paid by the relations of an executed criminal to recover the body and give it a Christian burial. In Boucicault's nineteenth-century comedy *London Assurance* Mrs Pert calls Mark Meddle, an attorney-at-law, 'you miserable specimen of a bad six-and-eightpence'.

Skeleton, you avaricious old This is Bill Sikes, talking to Fagin in Charles Dickens's *Oliver Twist*, though the expression smacks more of a highly educated writer with a genius for drawing thumb-nail sketches in a few words than the murderous thug who is supposed to utter it in the book.

Skellum 'Who did you think it was, you skellum?' says a South African woman to her brother, in *Resolve This Day*, by Geoffrey Bainbridge. The word means 'a villain or rascal' and derives from Dutch.

Skin and bones, Skinny, Skinny guts, Skinny Dick Names used by children to taunt thin people. *See also* **Spindleshanks**.

Skinflint Used since the eighteenth century to describe a miserly person, one who would attempt to skin a flint in order to save money. The Opies, however, report in *The Lore and Language of Schoolchildren*, that 'skinflint' is frequently used by children to taunt a thin person, perhaps because of a mistaken link with 'skinny'.

Skinhead In Britain in the early 1970s skinheads were youths who shaved their heads and behaved in an anti-social way.

In the USA the term is used of those who are naturally bald. In *Rabbit is Rich*, by John Updike, 'you twerpy skinhead' is said by one man to another in a friendly way. A few pages earlier the speaker has been saying to himself about the man concerned: 'It's fascinating to Rabbit how long those strands of hair are Ronnie is combing over his bald spot these days.'

Skipper An adaptation of the Dutch word for the captain of a ship, but normally used to the captain of a smaller vessel, such as a trading, merchant, or fishing boat. Examples of such usage occur in *Stella*, by Jan de Hartog.

'Skipper' is also used of the captain of a sports team, though in sports such as bowls and curling the abbreviated form 'skip' has now become the official form. This short form is likely to occur in other contexts where 'skipper' is being used if the speaker is on very friendly terms with the person addressed. Such other contexts include a civilian aircraft, where the chief pilot is either the captain or skipper.

The term is also used by some policemen as a synonym for 'captain'. *The Choirboys*, by Joseph Wambaugh, has: 'Lieutenant Finque blushed and sat back down. He blinked and said "Hi Skipper" to Captain Drobeck.' The men concerned are in the Los Angeles police force. In *Like Any Other Man*, by Patrick Boyle, the man addressed as Skipper is a bank manager, the speaker being his chief assistant. 'Skipper' is used as a variant of the usual 'manager' or 'sir' which the speaker uses.

There is a special use of Skipper in Shakespeare's *The Taming of the Shrew* (2:i), where it is used by an old man to a young man in the sense of 'one who skips', a child.

Skunk, you Used as a playful or serious insult to someone who is acting in an obnoxious way. American speakers are perhaps more likely to use this expression than British speakers, since they are probably more familiar with the animal itself. The latter is a black and white mammal native to North America. When attacked it gives off a powerful and highly unpleasant smell. In *The Wayward Bus*, by John Steinbeck, a young man attempts to assault a girl. 'She was spitting at him like a cat. "You skunk!" she said. "Oh, you dirty little skunk." '

Sky-pilot A playful American slang term for a clergyman, or specifically, a chaplain. It occurs as a vocative, addressed to an American 'reverend gentleman', in *Sandra*, by Pearl Bell, a romantic novel published in the 1920s. A man calls another 'earnest sky-pilot', having sneered at him a moment previously.

Slave Frequently used as a term of contempt in the seventeenth century, but used jokingly in modern times, e.g. when a wife orders a husband to do something in the tone of a slave-driver. There is an example of such usage in *Life at the Top*, by John Braine.

'Slave' is used vocatively throughout the Shakespeare plays, either alone or in expressions like 'abhorr'd slave', 'you transgressing slave', 'thou drunken slave', 'base slave', etc. It is equated with words like 'wretch', 'coward', 'villain'.

Sleepyhead One would expect this term to be used to a child who was showing signs of being ready for bed by a parent. In *Stacy*, by Roberta Leigh, it is used affectionately by a wife to her husband when he shows that he is tired.

Slicker Robert Chapman, in his *Dictionary of American Slang*, defines 'slicker' as either a confidence trickster or 'a socially smooth and superficially attractive person'. He does not make the link with 'city-slicker', used of a smart urbanite, especially when compared with a provincial or hillbilly. That link is clearly present in the following pasage from *War Brides*, by Lois Battle:

'Will you be okay going barefoot?' 'Now aren't you jest the city mouse! Why, the soles of my feet are as tough as nails. And would you believe I'd never heard of hillbillies 'til I came here. Get a move on, slicker. And watch out for yer pants, there's a lot of brambles.'

Slob This word is said to have an Irish origin, referring to soft mud on the sea-shore, and specifically, to a large soft worm used in angling. From the latter it seems to have been applied, affectionately, to a fat and untidy child, then to any lazy, careless person.

In modern times it collocates most frequently with the word 'fat', as in Garson Kanin's *Moviola*, where 'Put me down, you fat slob' is supposedly addressed to the American film actor Roscoe 'Fatty' Arbuckle.

In *The Business of Loving*, by Godfrey Smith, 'sweet slob' is used as an intimate endearment. 'You old slob' occurs in the same novel, used in a friendly way. It is said that Truman Capote remarked that he liked Marilyn Monroe because she was such a 'nice slob'. The word offended her, causing her to slap his face and pour a bottle of champagne over his head, but before her death the actress was indeed living in an untidy manner. 'Oh, get away you – you *slob!*' says an American girl to a man described as the 'neighbourhood derelict' in *Waterfront*, by Budd Schulberg.

Slobber-baby *See* **Cry-baby**.

Sloppy-boppy Used to a man whom the speaker describes as 'a slob' in *The Day of the Locust*, by Nathanael West. The same speaker is given to reduplicative expressions, since she uses 'palsy-walsy' elsewhere in the book. 'Sloppy-boppy' is not a standard slang expression but does manage to suggest a slovenly person.

Slow-coach Used in informal British speech to someone who seems to be moving too slowly. The American equivalent is 'slow-poke'. Dickens seems to have been the first to use the slow-coach metaphor, applying it to Mr Pickwick. Later, in *Martin Chuzzlewit*, he has Mr Pecksniff remark: 'What are we but coaches? Some of us are slow coaches; some of us are fast coaches. We start from The Mother's Arms, and we run to The Dust Shovel.' In *The Battle of the Villa Fiorita*, by Rumer Godden, a young English boy says to his sister:

'Hurry up, slow coach. I have bagged two seats.'

Slow-poke, you An American variant of 'slow-coach', used of a person who is moving too slowly, according to the speaker. The 'poke' is difficult to explain, but may refer to the slow movement of a poke-horse, where 'poke' refers to the packs, or bags, being carried. The 'bag' sense of 'poke' links with French *poche*, 'pocket.' In *Gone With The Wind*, by Margaret Mitchell, occurs: 'Prissy sauntered down the walk at a snail's gait. "Hurry, you slow-poke." '

Slug Used insultingly to a person, this appears to be a transferred use of the word for a creature related to the snail, but with no shell. In fact, the word was originally applied to a sluggard, a slow, lazy person and was transferred to the garden creature several centuries later. When Luciana says to Dromio, in Shakespeare's *The Comedy of Errors* (2:ii) 'thou drone, thou snail, thou slug, thou sot,' it is 'drone' and 'snail' which are being transferred to human application. 'You fat slug' is used insultingly to Piggy in *The Lord of the Flies*, by William Golding.

Slugger A kind of instant nickname that can be used to a man known either for his hard-hitting as a boxer or a baseball player. In *Waterfront*, by Budd Schulberg, it is used affectionately by one brother to another, the latter having been at one time a boxer of some ability.

Slummock Also 'slammock', which appears to have been the original form of the word in English dialect. A slummock is a slut, and the term is 'frequently used as a disrespectful term of address', according to the *Supplement* to the *Oxford English Dictionary*, though it quotes no vocative examples. *Up the City Road*, by John Stroud, has a man saying to a young woman: 'you bloody horrible little slummock'. '*Will* you mind your language, please?' she replies.

Slut This term has been applied to women since the fifteenth century and is still in use. It can mean either that a woman or girl is thought to be dirty and untidy, or that she is a loose woman, a prostitute.

In *The Minister*, by Maurice Edelman, a husband who has just discovered that his wife was unfaithful to him calls her 'you slut', and then expands it to 'you filthy slut'. In *The Late Risers*, by Bernard Wolfe, 'you slut' is used aggressively by a man to a prostitute.

In *The Business of Loving*, by Godfrey Smith, 'you lousy slut' is used admiringly to a woman and is almost as endearment. In former times 'slut' could be used almost as a synonym for 'girl', with no particular imputation of bad qualities, but it was usually qualified with a word like 'sweet', 'dear', 'admirable', etc. It was also used to kitchen maids, as in *Joseph Andrews*, by Henry Fielding, where Mrs Tow-wouse refers to her maid Betty as 'you slut' in fairly ordinary circumstances.

In modern times a house maid would probably greatly object to such a term, which is invariably insulting between strangers, or a recognition of sexual intimacy between man and woman. 'Black nigger slut!' says a white girl in *The Heart is a Lonely Hunter*, by Carson McCullers. In *Bhowani Junction*, by John Masters, 'you little slut' used to a woman by a man is a prelude to their more intimate relationship.

Sly-boots Applied to a cunning or sly person since the eighteenth century. It may originally have been insulting but in modern use is almost complimentary. *Webster's Dictionary* interestingly explains it as a person 'who is sly in an engaging way'. There was at one time a parallel 'smooth-boots', used for what in modern times would be called a smoothie. *Like Any Other Man*, by Patrick Boyle, has a woman saying to a man: 'That'll do now, sly-boots. You're fooling nobody.'

Small fry An instant nickname that can be transferred to any very small person, such as a child. Used either humorously or insultingly. Used to a person of normal size it implies insignificance. Small fry are literally small immature fish. *See also* **Tich**.

Smart aleck A person who tries to give the impression that he knows everything or annoys others by trying to sound clever. *William*, by Irene Hunt, has: 'Amy would have said "Not funny, smart aleck," but Mama didn't.' 'Aleck' is a pet form of Alexander, a name which has always been well used in Scotland. The original smart aleck may have been Scottish, but it is not known who he was. The expression came into use in the 1870s and is known on both sides of the Atlantic.

Smartass Used mainly by American speakers to a know-all, a wise guy, someone who offers an opinion while giving the impression that he considers himself to be of superior intelligence. The term can be used with some viciousness or more playfully, as in *Blue Dreams*, by William Hanley: ' "Smartass," she said, grinning shyly.'

Smart guy A watered-down version of the American 'smartass'. It is converted into a nonce name in *Portnoy's Complaint*, by Philip Roth, when the hero's father tells his young son that 'a doughnut is right, Mr Smart Guy'. There is a similar use of 'smart dick' in *A Salute to the Great McCarthy*, by Barry Oakley, used by an Australian father to his son.

Smarty Used mainly in the USA to someone who is ostentatiously displaying smartness, especially if he is doing so by contradicting the speaker. 'Smarty' is a relatively mild term. An American who is more irate is likely to use: smart aleck, smartass, smart guy, smarty pants, wise-ass, wise guy. A typical use of 'smarty' occurs in *Babbitt*, by Sinclair Lewis:

'Honest, George, what do you think of that rag Louetta went and bought? Don't you think it's the limit?' 'What's eating you, Eddie? I call it a swell little dress.' 'There now, do you see, smarty! You're such an authority on clothes!' Louetta raged.

Later in the same novel Babbitt is having a manicure, and is establishing a friendly relationship with the girl attending to him. She tells him: ' "There was a gentleman in here one day, he was kind of a count or something – " "Kind of no-account, I guess you mean!" "Who's telling this, smarty?" ' The girl concerned clearly feels that this term will not offend her customer. In this instance it even carries a hint of flattery.

Tom Sawyer, by Mark Twain, has Tom tell another boy: 'You think you're mighty smart, don't you?' A moment later he paraphrases this by saying: 'Smarty! you think you're *some* now, don't you?'

Smooth-boots Used mainly in the seventeenth century of a smooth talker, a flatterer. 'Smoothie' would be used in modern times. As a vocative 'smoothie' would probably be a semi-exclamatory response to a flattering speech, though it could also be used ironically to someone who made no attempt to flatter. *See also* **Boots**.

Snail *See* **Slug**.

Snake 'You snake' is probably a short form of 'you snake in the grass', used of a false friend, though the speaker might use 'snake' as a synonym for serpent. In *St Urbain's Horseman*, by Mordecai Richler, the hero makes fun of his brother-in-law at one point by pretending to be homosexual. 'You snake! Sewer!' says the brother-in-law, feeling betrayed.

Sneerer 'You young sneerer. You are laughing at me – that's who you are laughing at,' says Festus Derriman to Anne Garland, in Thomas Hardy's *The Trumpet Major*.

The vocative is a good example of one which is suggested by the immediate circumstances, not one which is part of a stock of available vocative terms which can be used in a variety of situations, such as 'sweetheart', 'darling', 'Miss', 'Sir'. Lord Byron, in *The Deformed Transformed*, has: 'Oh, thou everlasting sneerer! Be silent!'

Snitch, Snitcher, Snitchy Used as instant nicknames by British children for a child unable to keep a secret, or one who relates things to a teacher or parent which are meant to be kept private. Also used, according to the Opies, for a small child. *See also* **Tattle-tale** and **Tich**.

Sniveller *See* **Cry-baby**.

Snob This is a word of obscure origin which began by being a term in slang for a shoemaker. In the early part of the nineteenth century, chiefly due to William Thackeray, the word began to acquire something like its modern meaning of one who looks down on, or snubs, those whom he considers to be socially his inferiors.

More recently a breed of intellectual snobs have made their presence felt, glorying in their own highbrow artistic tastes and sneering at more popular works.

Although snubbing is now associated with snobs, the words are in no way etymologically related. Professor Weekley, in his *Etymological Dictionary of Modern English*, was no doubt right, however, to suggest that the established meaning of 'snub' may have influenced the sense development of 'snob'.

'Snob' occurs from time to time as a vocative: 'you poor bloody little snob' is said by one man to another in Daphne du Maurier's *Rebecca*. *Oliver's Story*, by Erich Segal, has one American man say to another 'you goddamn Harvard snob!' *Unconditional Surrender*, by Evelyn Waugh, has: ' "Will you have a drink?" "What is it?" "Half South African sherry and half something called 'Olde Falstaffe Gin'." "I don't think I will, thank you," said Ludovic. "Snob," said Lady Perdita.'

Snookums A nonsense word used in American slang to address a baby or pet animal. It is used as an endearment but has no precise meaning. There is a reference in Henry Williamson's *The Dream of Fair Women* to a song that was popular in the nineteen twenties: 'All day long he called her snooky-ookums.'

Snoopy A reference not to the remarkable canine character in Charles M. Schulz's *Peanuts* strip, the daydreaming beagle of worldwide fame, but to an American detective, a 'snoop' in slang. 'Turn it off, snoopy,' says a prostitute to a policeman in *The Late Risers*, by Bernard Wolfe.

Snowy This occurs as a transferred name in *Georgy Girl*, by Margaret Forster. The allusion is to a character in a radio series of the 1940s which featured a detective called Dick Barton and his assistant, Snowy. Australian speakers are likely to use 'Snowy' as a generic nickname for anyone with flaxen or bleached hair. They might also use the term jokingly to an Aboriginal.

So-and-so, you Normally a euphemism for a word like 'bastard' when used as a friendly insult. *Black Saturday*, by Alexander McKee, has: 'There was a delighted shout of "Oh, it's you, you fat old so-and-so." ' In *The Catcher in the Rye*, by J. D. Salinger, a woman calls the younger brother of a friend 'you little so-and-so'. Her jokey tone is shown by her remark: 'Tell your big brother I hate him, when you see him,' since she means just the opposite. 'You dirty young so-and-so' is addressed to a young Australian football player in *A Salute to the Great McCarthy*, by Barry Oakley. *A Kind of Loving*, by Stan Barstow, has: 'I won him over.' 'Like you've been winning him over all your life, you old so and so.' 'You dirty minded old so-and-so' is insulting when used in *The Liberty Man*, by Gillian Freeman.

S.o.b. 'Hey, Oliver, you s.o.b.!' says a character in *Oliver's Story*, by Erich Segal. The letters are usually pronounced individually in this euphemistic form of 'son-of-a-bitch'.

The full form of the vocative is occasionally used in Britain; the initial form of it remains American. According to Segal it can be used in the plural. Later in the novel occurs: 'Goddamn hell, you s.o.b.s.' The speaker equates this with 'you lousy bastards'. In *A World of Difference*, by Stanley Price, an American man says to an Englishman: 'You've made a conquest, you lucky s.o.b.'

Socks, old One middle-class young man addresses another by this term in *Martin Arrowsmith*, by Sinclair Lewis. The *Oxford English Dictionary* mentions that Latin *socius* has occasionally been used by educated speakers to refer to an ally or colleague.

Eric Partridge also gives the word as public school slang for a chum. It is tempting to make the link, though most students of Latin would presumably pronounce the 'c' in *socius* as in the word 'social', which derives from it, rather than as the 'ck' in 'sock'.

As it happens a special meaning of 'sock' developed in the nineteenth century, making it possible to refer to a favourite child by that term. This probably came about because of the expression 'sock-lamb', referring to a lamb raised by hand and kept as a pet. It seems most unlikely that this would have led to 'old socks' as a term of address, one which has wider currency than the single literary example given above would suggest. Schoolboy wit may well have made the connection between *socius* and 'sock'.

Sod, you 'Sod' is a taboo word in British English, but commonly occurs as a vocative. Those who use it know that they are expressing contempt for the person addressed, but are probably unaware that 'sod' is a short form of 'sodomist'. The use of 'bugger' as a general term of contempt is comparable. 'Silly sod' is especially frequent in low colloquial speech, presumably because of the alliteration.

'You old sod' occurs in *Girl with Green Eyes*, by Edna O'Brien, but is in that instance an insulting intimacy. 'You clumsy sod' occurs in *Henry's War*, by Jeremy Brooks, but is said without too much rancour by one man to another. 'You young sod' is insulting in *A Kind of Loving*, by Stan Barstow, as is 'you stupid old sod' in *Lucky Jim*, by Kingsley Amis.

'You cheeky sod' is insulting in *Saturday Night and Sunday Morning*, by Alan Sillitoe, but the same novel has examples of 'you sod' and 'you daft sod' used in a reasonably friendly way between men. 'Get up, you lazy sod' is also said in a friendly way by one man to another in *Like Any Other Man*, by Patrick Boyle.

Sodom, child of Used by a religious fanatic to a man whom he also addresses as 'sinner', 'child of adversity', 'Babylonian', etc., in *The Heart is a Lonely Hunter*, by Carson McCullers.

Sodom is the city mentioned in the Old Testament Book of Genesis, a place of wickedness, specifically associated with anal intercourse practised by men. Both Sodom and Gomorrah, another city of great evil, were destroyed by God according to the Old Testament account.

Softie, softy Used of a person who is easily persuaded, a sense it has had since the middle of the nineteenth century. It can also be applied to a person who is over-sentimental, e.g., about animals.

The term is now a mild one in normal circumstances, but it appears to have been more insulting in early use. 'You believed that lie? You little softie!' says a woman to another in *Gone to Earth*, by Mary Webb, and there is no doubt that she means it as an insult. *See also* **Cry-baby**.

Soft skin, little An intimate endearment in *Girl with Green Eyes*, by Edna O'Brien. The vocative is interesting in being based on the sense of touch instead of the more usual visual stimulus. The girl concerned is also addressed in the novel as 'you soft, daft, wanton thing'.

Soldier Addressed usually to a soldier in uniform who does not have a special rank. 'Come, my young soldier, put up your iron,' says Sir Toby Belch to Sebastian, in Shakespeare's *Twelfth Night* (4:ii). The term is used elsewhere in the plays, alone or qualified as 'brave soldier', 'my good soldier', 'worthy soldier', etc. It is especially frequent in the plural form. In *Antony and Cleopatra* (5:ii), Charmian's last words as she dies are 'Ah, soldier!'

The term is used in modern times. *Thirteen Days*, by Ian Jefferies, has a military policeman who uses it, but then goes on to say: 'I didn't see your rank, Sarn't. Otherwise I would have addressed you by your rank.' In *Julia*, by H. C. Harwood, a civilian addressing a soldier says: 'You keep out of this, soldier-boy.'

Somebody, someone These are interchangeable indefinite terms of address, used by a speaker who wishes one of the persons to whom he is speaking to identify himself with it. Examples will make that statement clearer.

In *Saturday Night and Sunday Morning*, by Alan Sillitoe, we find: ' "What did I say?" he pleaded. "Tell me, somebody, what did I say?" ' In *Within and Without*, by John Harvey, someone says: 'I'm going to tell her what my mother thinks of her.' 'Stop him, somebody,' says another person present. In the same book occurs: ' "Am I drunk?" I asked suddenly. "I fear I am. Pray pay no attention to what I am saying." "Go and dance with him, someone, and sober him up," said Jim.'

In this last example the context enables the males who are present to know that they are not included in the 'someone', though the word itself carries no sexual marker. The exclusion of certain hearers can be achieved in other ways.

In the following example the use of 'else' excludes Chadwick: ' "Come on, shove these on – you, Chadwick." Kong threw a pair of boxing gloves at Big Joe, who started pulling them on with a savage, gloating light in his eye. "Here, somebody else – " ' (*The Taste of Too Much*, Clifford Hanley).

'One of you' could normally be substituted for 'somebody' or 'someone' when used alone, though not in this example of 'somebody', used in *Oliver Twist*, by Charles Dickens:

'The door must be opened. Do you hear, somebody?' Mr Giles, as he spoke, looked at Brittles, but that young man, being naturally modest, probably considered himself nobody, and so held that the inquiry could not have any application to him.

Something, you something A written euphemism which occurs in *Brothers in Law*, by Henry Cecil, indicating that the speaker used both an adjective and noun which the author considers to be taboo words. Most modern authors are now prepared to print any words, whether or not they are tolerated by polite society.

Son This is used by parents to their son, and sometimes, preserving a practice that was common in Shakespeare's time, to their son-in-law. In *The Merry Wives of Windsor* Page says: 'Come, son Slender' to Abraham Slender, his prospective son-in-law, but this may not have been general seventeenth-century usage.

'Son' is frequently used by a person old enough to be a parent to a boy or young man who has no family connection. It is also used by religious, especially as 'my son', when addressing younger men.

In modern times it is also frequently used between friendly males of almost equal age. In Britain on any Saturday afternoon footballers can be heard congratulating team-members with 'Well done, my son.' A popular variant for friendly use is 'old son'.

In certain circumstances, when used to an adult, there may be a hint of condescension connected with 'son'. In David Ballantyne's short story *And the Glory*, a shop assistant, who is obliged to address the floor-walker as Mr Myers, is addressed in return by his surname and by 'son'. There is the comment: 'Annoyed at the way Myers spoke, especially at being called son, Larry attended to the customers.'

As an element in vocative expressions beginning with 'you', 'son' can be made insulting by referring to the parents. 'You son of a bitch' is probably the most frequently used example, but in *The Trumpet Major*, by Thomas Hardy, Festus Derriman calls John Loveday, son of Miller Loveday, 'you dirty miller's son', adding for good measure, 'you flour-worm, you smut in the corn'. *Pudd'nhead Wilson*, by Mark Twain, has 'you base son of a most noble father' used as an insult by the uncle of the young man to whom it is addressed.

'Son' on its own is objected to by the young American to whom it is addressed in *War Brides*, by Lois Battle. The speaker is his father, but his reaction on hearing himself called 'son' is to think: 'Don't call me "son." I'm not your son anymore.'

Sonny In use since the late nineteenth century as a term of address for a boy, either the son of the speaker or one unrelated to him. Such usage normally indicates a friendly attitude on the part of the speaker.

The term can become condescending, and perhaps insulting, when used to a man. *Lydia*, by E. V. Cunningham, has an elderly New York cab-driver say to his fare, a man of thirty-five,

'Now just sit back, sonny, and enjoy this ride.' In *The Magic Army*, by Leslie Thomas, an American soldier says to a colleague: 'We got you here to climb, so climb, sonny.' In *The Late Risers*, by Bernard Wolfe, an American policeman uses 'sonny' to a newspaper reporter in a decidedly unfriendly way.

'Sonny' is occasionally used as a first name in English-speaking countries, though its use in that role must create problems at times for its bearer. *Under the Greenwood Tree*, by Thomas Hardy, has the very curious: 'Look here, my sonnies,' he argued to his wife, whom he often addressed in the plural masculine for economy of epithet merely. . . .'

Sonny boy A variant of 'sonny', presumably inspired by the 1929 Al Jolson song 'Sonny Boy'. It can be used, like 'sonny', to a young boy, though it is also sometimes used to an adult. 'What's the matter, sonny boy?' says a character in *Lucky Jim*, by Kingsley Amis, addressing a colleague of his own age, but it is noticeable that the only other use of the term in the novel is by the same speaker, Atkinson, to the same man, Johns. This suggests that the expression in this instance is idiolectal, or a kind of personal nickname. *A Salute to the Great McCarthy*, by Barry Oakley, has a man saying to one who is slightly younger: 'Make way, sonny boy, and let me get to that lovely lady.'

Son of a bitch, you 'You're a ham, you son of a bitch, and you know it,' says an American man to another in *The Philanderer*, by Stanley Kauffmann. This comes in the middle of a friendly conversation, and the man addressed takes no offence.

The term is similar in many ways to 'bastard' in that can be used as both a serious insult or almost as a compliment, according to who says it to whom, and in what tone of voice. Some speakers might say it as 'son of a b'. *See also* **S.o.b.**

All of these variants can be softened down by including the word 'old' and made more abusive by the inclusion of other words, as in 'Well, well, you old son of a bitch, where the hell have you been?' and 'You stupid son of a bitch. You nearly ran me down.' The plural form 'you couple of lazy sons of bitches' is used insultingly in *Doctor at Sea*, by Richard Gordon.

In modern times 'son of a bitch' and its variants are thought of as American terms of contempt rather than British. They were certainly used in Britain in former times. 'You son of a b-' occurs in *Joseph Andrews*, by Henry Fielding (*see also* **Bitch** for the novelist's comments on that word).

As for Shakespeare, he comes very close to using it in *King Lear* (2:i), when Kent embarks on a long string of insults to Oswald. 'What dost thou know me for?' asks Oswald, and is told in reply that Kent knows him for a 'knave, rascal, whoreson rogue, beggar, coward, pander' *and* 'the son and heir of a mongrel bitch'.

Son of a gun, you An approving expression used mainly by men to men, though Carson McCullers, in *The Heart is a Lonely Hunter*, has 'you old son of a gun' used by a girl to her brother.

The term is said to derive from a child born to a serving soldier, normally illegitimate, according to Eric Partridge, *A Dictionary of Historical Slang*. Brewer's *Dictionary of Phrase and Fable* prefers to link it with sailors, at a time when women were allowed to live on board Royal Navy ships. If the paternity of a child born on board was uncertain, it was entered in the log as 'son of a gun'. The Partridge explanation is the more likely: either way it is clear that this expression once meant 'bastard'.

That original meaning has long been forgotten. 'Bastard' is itself often used approvingly by intimates, as are expressions like 'you son of a bitch', so the change from insult to compliment ('son of a gun' now meaning something like 'you amazing fellow') is understandable.

Sopranos *See* **Choir.**

Sor, Sorr Spellings of 'sir' used by some writers to indicate dialectal pronunciation, usually Irish. Examples of 'sor' occur throughout *The Sleepers of Erin*, by Jonathan Gash.

Sorceress A synonym of witch, used of one who is able to bewitch a man, or practise magic. The former use occurs in *Jane Eyre*, by Charlotte Brontë, where Mr Rochester says to Jane: 'What have you done with me, witch, sorceress?' The latter meaning is in George Eliot's *Adam Bede:* 'Ah! you witch-mother, you sorceress! How is a Christian man to win a game off you?'

Sorry This word is used in English dialects in various forms, including: serry, surra, surry, sirree, surree, sorree, sorrah. These are mostly phonetic renderings, used in letters to the author about the use of the term in such counties as Nottinghamshire, Derbyshire, Shropshire, Lancashire.

D. H. Lawrence, in *Sons and Lovers*, has a Nottingham man addressing his work-mate with 'Shall ter finish, Sorry?' The word appears to be similar to 'butty', and is used to a friend, inevitably male, by a man.

All the evidence points to the word's being an extension of 'sir', similar to 'sirrah', but the sense development is mysterious.

An alternative explanation – that the word

derives from the expression 'So how are ye?' – is not worth serious consideration.

Sot This word at first had the general meaning of a stupid person. By the sixteenth century it was closely associated with drunkenness, and its modern meaning is a drunkard. Modern speakers, addressing such a person, would probably reinforce it by saying something like 'you drunken sot', expressing strong disapproval of the person concerned.

In earlier times the word was often used alone. It occurs three times in Shakespeare's *Twelfth Night*, for instance, and is used again vocatively in *A Comedy of Errors* (2:ii).

Soul 'Stay, gentle Helena,' says Lysander in Shakespeare's *A Midsummer Night's Dream*, 'hear my excuse;/My love, my life, my soul, fair Helena!' 'My soul' in such a context is clearly a passionate endearment.

There is a similar usage in *Cymbeline*, when Imogen hangs around her husband's neck, embracing him. He says to her: 'Hang there like fruit, my soul,/Till the tree die!' With this it is interesting to compare the dialectal usage of later times in *Gone to Earth*, by Mary Webb:

'Tell us more, Hazel!' pleaded Edward. 'What for do you want to hear, my soul?' Edward flushed at the caressing phrase, and Mrs Marston looked as indignant as was possible to her physiognomy, until she realized that it was a mere form of speech.

'Mere form of speech' is perhaps going too far, but the force of 'my soul', 'good soul', or 'souls' used to a number of people, had certainly weakened considerably by the nineteenth century, as the novels of Thomas Hardy make clear. 'Come in, souls, and have something to eat and drink,' occurs in *Far from the Madding Crowd*, where 'souls' could be replaced by 'friends'.

In modern English 'soul' is little used vocatively, and in third person reference may mean little more than person in an utterance like 'She's been very ill lately, poor soul.' In *Uncle Tom's Cabin* Eva is 'you sweet, little obliging soul' to her father, the vocative being perhaps inspired by the Christian sentiments she has just uttered.

Soul's delight, my One of the extravagant terms used to his wife by Mr Mantalini, in Charles Dickens's *Nicholas Nickleby*. She is also: my heart's joy; my sense's idol; my joy; my life and soul; my essential juice of pineapple; my cup of happiness's sweetener; my existence's jewel; my sense's joy; my soul; my gentle, captivating, bewitching and most demnebly chick-a-biddy, amongst other things.

Mr Mantalini's expressions are as false as

his name, which was originally Muntle. We are left in no doubt about his hypocrisy, though some of the terms he uses would not sound amiss in the mouths of genuine lovers, such as Romeo and Juliet. They, for example, address one another by such expressions as: dear saint, love, my soul, my love, sweet dear love, sweet. Mantalini lives off his wife's earnings until she is made bankrupt, whereupon he separates from her.

Sow The *Oxford English Dictionary* has a number of quotations showing 'sow' being used vocatively as a term of abuse for a fat, lazy woman. In *Kes*, by Barry Hines, it is used by a young boy to his brother, who is in a drunken sleep at the time: 'Get back to sleep... you pig... hog... sow... you drunken bastard.' The boy then uses those words in a kind of incantation: 'Pig hog sow drunken bastard.' This is chanted as the speaker circles around the bed where his brother is lying.

Spark, my The word 'spark' meant quite different things in the seventeenth and eighteenth centuries according to whether the word was applied to a woman or a man. It was a compliment when applied to a woman, having much the same meaning that 'bright spark' still has in British English. The woman who was a spark was probably both beautiful, cheerful and intelligent.

A male young spark was someone who dressed elegantly, perhaps foppishly, and was vain of his appearance.

In direct address 'my spark' was the usual formula, and it was not particularly admiring. 'Hark'ee, my spark, none of your grinning!' says Captain Mirvan to Mr Lovel, in Fanny Burney's *Evelina*, and adds that if the grinning continues, Mr Lovel will have his ears boxed.

Sparks This would be addressed to the wireless officer in a merchant ship, according to Wilfred Granville, in *A Dictionary of Naval Slang*. It has the alternative purely vocative form 'Sparko'. Amongst British building workers, Sparks is the nickname automatically granted to an electrician.

Sparrer In *Cider with Rosie*, by Laurie Lee, one man says to another: 'Hey, Bert! 'Ow's Bert? 'Ow you doin', ole sparrer?' This is presumably a form of 'sparrow', as it is when a London Cockney greets a friend as 'me old cock-sparrer'.

The *Oxford English Dictionary* cites cock-sparrow in this sense in Farquhar's *Love and a Bottle* (1698): 'Would you debauch my maid, you little cock-sparrow?' However, the full form is normal, not 'sparrow' used on its own, and the Laurie Lee example is ambiguous. It could

be 'sparrer', one who spars in a boxing ring, and therefore mean 'sparring-partner'.

A Kind of Loving, by Stan Barstow, is set in Yorkshire, and has the following exchange between two young men: 'Howdo, Willy.' 'Ah, Vic, me old cock sparrer.' The novel also has several examples of 'cock' and 'old cock' used as friendly vocatives between men.

Speaker, Mr The Speaker of the British House of Commons is chosen by the House itself from amongst its elected members. He acts as chairman of debates in the House and is normally addressed as 'Mr Speaker'. If someone is temporarily deputizing for him, that person may well be addressed as 'Mr Deputy-Speaker'. The office of Speaker was established in the fourteenth century and has subsequently been imitated in many other parliamentary systems. In *The Minister*, by Maurice Edelman, an author with considerable personal experience of the British Parliament, members are shown using 'sir' as an alternative to 'Mr Speaker', or adding 'sir' after that expression: 'But Mr Speaker, sir....'

Spindleshanks Applied to a person with long, thin legs since the sixteenth century, and still in playground use, according to the Opies in *The Lore and Language of Schoolchildren*. They list the synonymous: Spindle Dick, Spindle legs, and Spindle sticks. These terms are always disparaging, as Colleen McCullough indicates in *An Indecent Obsession*. The man who says: 'Don't you preach at me, spindleshanks!' to another man snarls the words.

Other words which may be used as taunting terms of address to very thin people include: Bag o' bones, Bean pole, Broomstick, Fusewire, Hairpin, Lamp-post, Lanky Liz, Lanky Panky, Matchstick, Needle legs, Pipe Cleaner, Rake or Raky, Razor blade, Rib skin, Scarecrow, Scraggy, Skin and bones, Skinny, Skinflint, Skinny guts, Skinny Dick, Taper, Thinima, Tin ribs.

Spitfire This word was applied to a cannon in the early seventeenth century. By the end of that century it was being used of a person with a fierce temper, in much the same way as a modern person might be described as 'a little spitfire'. King Lear, in the midst of a storm, says 'Spit, fire; spout, rain,' and Shakespeare no doubt had the cannon image in mind as he thought of the lightning.

Typical vocative usage is shown in *Gone to Earth*, by Mary Webb, when a young woman strikes a man across the mouth and he says: 'All right, spitfire! Mum's the word.' It also occurs in George Eliot's *The Mill on the Floss*, spoken by a boy to his sister. Later he addresses her by the nonce name 'Miss Spitfire'. Since the Second World War 'spitfire' has been associated especially with the British fighter-plane which was given this name.

Splitter A term of abuse used by children, especially, to one of their number who has turned informer to a teacher or parent. In criminal slang to split on someone is to inform the police about his activities. 'Splitter' would be an accusation of a fairly serious offence in the eyes of the speaker. The mere inability to keep a secret would cause one of the 'tell-tale-tit' terms to be used. *See also* **Tattle-tale**.

Spoil-it-all, Mr A nonce name used in *Rabbit Redux*, by John Updike. A young man has just explained what happens in a film. 'Thank you, Mr Spoil-it-all. I feel I've seen it now,' says his mother.

Spoilsport Used in an exclamatory way to someone who is thought to be spoiling the sport, or pleasure, of others. The term has been in use since the beginning of the nineteenth century.

Spooney, spoon Used in the early nineteenth century with the meaning 'fool, simpleton'. This is said to be because the household utensil is both open and shallow. 'You little spooney' is used by a boy to his young sister, who is crying, in George Eliot's *The Mill on the Floss*. 'Spooney' later came to mean someone who was foolishly in love, and later still, an effeminate man. The vocative uses seem to have disappeared in modern English, though the verb 'to spoon', meaning to court in a sentimental way, has survived.

Sport This word was applied to young men in general, regardless of their sporting interests, at the beginning of the twentieth century, especially in the USA. It then became possible to use the term to address a man, either one well-known to the speaker or a stranger. 'Sport' occurs in some of the O. Henry short stories, and in Nathanael West's *The Day of the Locust* an American woman says to a man: 'Come on, sport – bottoms up' as she attempts to make him drink. In *Babbitt*, by Sinclair Lewis, the hero is in his late forties and at one point has 'to endure the patronage of the young soda-clerks'. We are told that 'they called him "Old Georgie" and shouted, "Come on, now, sport; shake a leg." '

In modern times the use of 'sport' is especially associated with Australia, where the vocative is frequently used, but 'sport' or 'old sport' may still be heard in other parts of the English-speaking world.

Its continued use in the USA, for instance, is demonstrated in *Rabbit Redux*, by John Updike, where it is used by a man to a male acquaintance. In *The River*, by Steven Bauer,

it is used by an American man to a young girl, the daughter of an old friend. In O. Henry's short story *Sisters of the Golden Circle*, a detective says to a suspected criminal: 'Come on, old sport,' but he says this 'pleasantly'.

Spouse A wife or husband can refer to 'my spouse', meaning 'my married partner', my wife or husband as the case may be. The word would therefore seem to be a convenient marital term of address, but it has never been commonly used, other than briefly in the eighteenth century. It was then mainly used by husbands to wives. In *The Way of the World*, by Congreve, we find Mrs Millamant declaring: 'I won't be called names after I'm married; positively I won't be called names.' She goes on to specify that the names she objects to are 'wife, spouse, my dear, joy, jewel, love, sweetheart, and the rest of that nauseous cant, in which men and their wives are so fulsomely familiar'.

Spread In the British building industry a plasterer is addressed as 'spread' by other tradesmen and their labourers.

Squad Used in military circles to address a small number of men who have been formed into a sub-division of a company for some special purpose, such as drill. An example of vocative use occurs in *The Magic Army*, by Leslie Thomas. *Goldfinger*, by Ian Fleming, has 'bomb squad' used in a similar way.

Squall-ass *See* **Cry-baby**.

Squealer Used as a term of abuse to someone who informs the authorities – the police in the case of adults, teachers or parents in the case of children – of activities they are not supposed to know about. *See also* **Tattle-tale**.

Squib In the sixteenth and seventeenth centuries, applied to a man considered to be insignificant. In modern use, used by some British children as an instant nickname for a very small child. In the latter sense it probably derives from the dialectal meaning of 'squib', a synonym of a squirt or syringe, used by children to squirt water. *See also* **Tich**.

Squire From the seventeenth century until the late nineteenth century 'squire' was used to address country gentlemen who were considerable land-owners. The word was used alone, or with a family name.

Earlier meanings of squire, such as 'young man of noble birth attendant on a knight', had become historical by the time the above-mentioned vocative usage began.

In modern times 'squire' is used much more rarely in third person reference, and would sound old-fashioned if used in direct address, if used, that is, to a person who really could be described as a country squire.

The word is regularly used today in a vaguely humorous way, by, e.g., market traders addressing male customers. It avoids in such a situation the cold politeness of 'sir' and the perhaps over-familiarity of 'mate'.

In *Hard Times*, by Charles Dickens, Mr Sleary addresses Mr Gradgrind as 'squire', or attempts to, at least: ' "Thquire!" said Mr Sleary, who was troubled with asthma, and whose breath came far too thick and heavy for the letter s, "your thervant!" ' In *Judgement Day*, by Penelope Lively, a young electrician says to a vicar: 'O.K., squire, not to worry.'

Some commentators consider this modern British use of 'squire' to be friendly. There is reason to suspect, however, that it is a little contemptuous. The speaker will often be using it to a man whom he considers to be middle-class, perhaps because of the person's speech or clothes. The deliberate misuse of the vocative system shows that the speaker is not prepared to be genuinely deferential.

In *Jake's Thing*, by Kingsley Amis, a barely polite shop assistant eventually asks a customer who has queried the price of chocolates: 'You want them, do you, squire?' The whole tone of the conversation makes it clear that he cares very little whether the customer wants them or not. *Up the City Road*, by John Stroud, has a young Londoner addressing his landlord as 'squire', and again his tone is not friendly. 'Look, squire, I'm paying the hell of a lot for not very much.'

Squirt, you little 'Get away, you little squirt, before I spit on thi an' drown thi,' says a boy from the north of England to another in *Kes*, by Barry Hines. 'Squirt' is now thought of as a fairly mild insult, usually addressed to children, especially if they are smaller than average. It would once have been far more insulting, since 'squirt' formerly referred to the thin excrement associated with diarrhoea, or to diarrhoea itself.

By the nineteenth century 'squirts' was used in that sense, though only in the dialects of south-west England. British dictionaries tend to say that 'squirt' in its slang sense of a paltry person originated in the USA.

Robert Chapman's *Dictionary of American Slang* says that this meaning was imported into America from Britain. It is used by the Australian author Nevil Shute in *No Highway*, where 'you bloody little squirt' is a covert endearment.

Stager, old 'Why, you chicken-hearted old stager,' says Festus Derriman to an actress, in *The Trumpet Major*, by Thomas Hardy. The lady concerned claims to be twenty-two, and

although she is older than that, she hardly qualifies for the description 'old stager' in any sense. Hardy seems to be using it to mean one experienced in the world of the theatre. The phrase 'old stager' has a far more general sense of one who has long experience of life.

The earliest uses of the expression appear to owe nothing to the theatrical stage, but to suggest a connection with Old French *estagier*, or perhaps Latin *stagiarius*. Such terms were used to describe monks who had spent their lives within the confines of the monastery.

The phrase continues in use, though it is rare as a vocative.

Star 'Hey, star!' says a girl to a boy in *The Blinder*, by Barry Hines. He has just achieved some fame locally as a football player. This sense of 'star', which began in the theatre and was applied to someone of exceptional talent or audience pulling-power, began in the late eighteenth century.

Steam-roller *See* **Fatty**.

Step-mother The *Oxford English Dictionary* mentions that the term 'step-devil' was once used as a synonym of 'step-mother'. Certainly the latter term is a difficult one to live with, thanks to the wicked step-mothers of many a children's tale.

Speakers usually try to find some other term to use as a vocative, but it can be difficult. In *Love for Love*, by William Congreve, Miss Prue uses 'Mother' to her step-mother, and is not thanked for it:

'Mother, Mother, Mother, look you here.' 'Fie, fie, Miss, how you bawl – Besides, I have told you, you must not call me Mother.' 'What must I call you, then? Are you not my father's wife?' 'Madam; you must say Madam. By my soul, I shall fancy myself old indeed, to have this great girl call me Mother.'

This is an eighteenth-century view, and most modern step-mothers, one suspects, would be only too glad to be addressed as 'Mother'. *Border Country*, by Raymond Williams, has the following exchange:

'Why do you call her your Mam?' Will asked. 'She's not, so why call her it?' 'But she's been my Mam, since they got married.' 'It's still wrong. What they do doesn't make it different.' 'What should I call her? Stepmother sounds nasty.' 'If it's nasty, say it.' 'But it isn't nasty, it only sounds it.' 'If it sounds it, it is.'

The term used by a step-child will of course depend on how old it was when its father remarried, and on whether its real mother is still alive. It might also make a difference if the step-mother has children by a former marriage, or the present marriage, who address her by one of the 'mother' terms. With step-parenthood becoming ever more common, those concerned would probably be glad to turn to a standard term of address that would avoid embarrassment and acknowledge the relationship in a fairly neutral way. No such term exists. Rumer Godden, in *The Battle of the Villa Fiorita*, describes a couple who both have children by former marriages, but intend to marry.

'Mr Quillet.' Hugh and Caddie had punctiliously called Rob that until Fanny stopped them, 'Call him Rob,' but neither of them did except when they talked of him to one another. The awkwardness of what Pia was to call Fanny was worse. 'I hope one day she will say "mother" like the others,' said Rob but Fanny shook her head. 'We can only hope for that.' Pia's manners shrank from saying 'Fanny'. She said 'You' and to Hugh and Caddie 'Your mother'.

Steppie Captain D. Bromley-Martin RN, writing to *The Times* in July 1984, reported that his children 'arrived with a ready-made grandmother in office, i.e. a step-grandmother. At a family conference it was decided that she should be known as 'Steppie', 'and so it was'.

Steward The professional title of a club or college official, in charge of food and drink supplies, and of a man who serves passengers on a ship, plane, or train. There are also stewards who control crowds at public gatherings, and more specialized stewards who manage estates. Any of them could be addressed as 'steward' while performing their duties.

Literary examples tend to be concerned with ships' stewards, such as Dough-Boy in *Moby Dick*, by Herman Melville. *Doctor at Sea*, by Richard Gordon, has several instances of this vocative.

Stewardess The professional title of a woman who waits on passengers, especially other women, on board ship. The term was also transferred to airlines when they began operations, and an air-stewardess could be addressed in this way. It would only be used by rather formal speakers, however. 'I wonder if you'd mind, stewardess, laying down my umbrella,' says Mrs Crane, in Katherine Mansfield's story *The Voyage*.

Stiff, you big In *Tender is the Night*, by F. Scott Fitzgerald, Dick addresses himself as 'you big stiff'. The term might more usually be used by a woman to a man, complimenting him on his physical size while implying that he was rather stupid at the same time.

'Stiff' remains an American rather than a British word in its slang senses. British speakers would not use it to refer to a labourer, for instance, nor would they have used it in its earlier slang sense of a hobo. If they described a corpse as a stiff they would consciously be using an Americanism. The possible implication of 'you big stiff' is that the person addressed has as much intelligence as a corpse.

Stinker Used in modern times as a fairly mild insult, though it seems to have been much more forceful at the turn of the century. *Webster's Dictionary* defined it in 1911 as 'one who is disgustingly contemptible, a stinkard'. 'Stinkard' is now obsolete, but 'stink-pot' might occasionally be used as a variant of 'stinker', usually in a light-hearted way. In *Jake's Thing*, by Kingsley Amis, occurs: 'Jake! You stinker. This is good old Marge. Remember me?' The speaker is an American woman, telephoning to renew an acquaintanceship. *Brothers in Law*, by Henry Cecil, has 'you filthy stinker' and 'you old stinker' used as insults.

Stink-pot, you Used by one student to another, both of them males, in James Joyce's *Portrait of the Artist As a Young Man*. 'Go away, you stinkpot. And you are a stinkpot.'

Stranger In rural areas, both in Britain and the USA, this term was formerly the normal way of addressing a person who was a stranger to the district and whose name was unknown. Examples of such usage occur in Thomas Hardy's *The Mayor of Casterbridge*, and in *The Shadow of the Glen*, by J.M. Synge.

American usage is displayed in the novels of James Fenimore Cooper, depicting life in the early nineteenth century.

Later, in a thousand western movies, 'stranger' was to become closely associated with cowboys, who were thought to accost every city slicker who walked into a saloon with: 'Howdy, stranger.' Nathanael West, in *The Day of the Locust*, writes: 'Tod found his Western accent amusing. The first time he had heard it, he had replied, "Lo, thar, stranger," and had been surprised to discover that Earle didn't know he was being kidded.'

The main use of 'stranger' as a vocative in modern times is to one's friends and acquaintances who haven't been seen for a while. The word is especially likely to be used to someone one used to see regularly, and who has now reappeared after a lengthy absence. It is used at the moment of meeting, by speakers of either sex to a man or woman.

In the British Houses of Parliament 'stranger' has the sense of one who is not a member of the House or an official. In *The Minister*, by Maurice Edelman, a policeman calls out 'Hats off, strangers,' as the Speaker's Procession passes by on its way to the Chamber. The policeman, being a stranger in this sense himself, removes his own helmet.

Strings *See* **Violins**.

Stripling A word in use by the thirteenth century, referring to a slender young man, one passing from boyhood to manhood. The word is not in frequent use, but is found occasionally as a vocative in earlier literature, e.g. 'pretty stripling', addressed to the young tapster in Ben Jonson's *Bartholomew Fair*.

Strumpet To Shakespeare, who uses this word vocatively in, e.g. *Hamlet, The Winter's Tale, Othello*, 'strumpet' meant a prostitute. It is doubtful if a modern woman would understand it in that sense. She would think it a very old-fashioned word, one which was expressing disapproval, but might not interpret it specifically as prostitute. 'You audacious strumpet' is used to Jenny Jones in Fielding's *Tom Jones. Love in Quiet Places*, by Bernard Thompson, has one girl calling another 'you cheap strumpet'. This novel was published in 1961, but the word is very rare in twentieth-century literature.

Stubby A generic nickname for a short person, especially one who is thick-set. *See also* **Tich**.

Stud Used in modern slang of a sexually prodigious man, the allusion being to a studhorse, a stallion kept for breeding. 'Stud' is twice used as a friendly term of address to a man in *Absolute Beginners*, by Colin MacInnes. The same novel also has 'you horrid little studlet' used as an intimacy. In Norman Mailer's *An American Dream* a woman calls a man 'you angel ape of a stud'.

Stuffy Used in a friendly way to someone who is being stuffy, old-fashioned and formal that is, in *A Travelling Woman*, by John Wain.

Stumps, Stumpy A generic nickname for a short and a stumpy person. *See also* **Tich**.

Stupid This word is a frequent element in a vocative group of the type 'you stupid fool', but it is also used alone. 'Don't do that, stupid,' is a fairly mild utterance, used especially by children to each other, and likely to produce the retort 'Stupid yourself!'

The right tone of voice can easily convert 'stupid' into a covert endearment or a term of friendliness. *Judgement Day*, by Penelope Lively, has a young girl saying to a boy: 'It's not playing, you stupid. It's acting.' In Richard Hughes's *A High Wind in Jamaica* occurs: ' "I didn't know England would be like this," said Rachel: "it's very like Jamaica." "This isn't England," said John, "you stupid!" ' John, in this case, is about twelve years old; Rachel, his sister, is several years younger.

Addressed to an adult, 'stupid' is likely to cause great offence. Thus, in Benjamin Disraeli's novel *Sybil* a man who is marshalling men says to one of them: 'Come, stupid, what are you staring about? Get your men in order, or I'll be among you.' 'Stupid!' says the man so addressed, 'And who are you who says "Stupid"? A white-livered Handloom as I dare say, or a son-of-a-gun of a factory slave. Stupid indeed! What next, when a Hell-cat is to be called stupid by such a thing as you?'

Stupid-head A variant of blockhead. 'Think it's the same boy, Stupid-head?' says Blathers, the Bow Street officer to a young man in Dickens's *Oliver Twist*.

Submarine A nonce nickname used by Eddie to Rodolpho in Arthur Miller's *A View from the Bridge*. Rodolpho is an Italian illegal immigrant to the USA. Eddie's comment is: 'Watch your step, submarine. By rights they oughta throw you back in the water.'

Sucker A sucker is someone who is easily fooled, a rather innocent person, like a baby which is still at its mother's breast. A typical situation in which it would be used is described in *Cocksure*, by Mordecai Richler:

> 'I'll flatten him. *Like this*,' he said, his right hand suddenly flashing upwards towards Diana's chin. It was a feint. But Diana, taken by surprise, stupidly raised her guard, presenting Hy with a splendid opportunity to bury a right hook in her belly. 'Ooof,' went Diana, staggering backwards. 'Sucker,' Hy hissed.

The term is used in a fairly friendly way between American males in *The Philanderer*, by Stanley Kauffmann and *I'll take Manhattan*, by Judith Krantz. In *Boulevard Nights*, by Dewey Gram, 'Hey, sucker!' is used by a boy to another in a decidedly aggressive way.

The word is probably used more often in the USA than in Britain, though British speakers would certainly understand the use of the term. It may occasionally be a euphemism for the obscene 'cocksucker'. The latter term is used frequently, for instance, in *North Dallas Forty*, by Peter Gent, where one of the football players concerned also uses 'sucker' to a teammate.

Sugar Used as an endearment, with obvious reference to the sweetness of the person addressed. Frank Kennedy calls Scarlett O'Hara 'sugar' after their marriage, in *Gone With The Wind*, by Margaret Mitchell, but modern American authors usually make the speaker a black man rather than white. Such is the case in *An American Dream*, by Norman Mailer and *The Tenants*, by Bernard Malamud.

Sugarboy In *The Liberation of Lord Byron Jones*, by Jesse Hill Ford, this term of address is used by a black American woman to the white man who is her regular sexual partner. The latter is not old enough to be described by the more usual term, 'sugar-daddy'.

Sugar-plum An American husband uses this term to address his wife affectionately in *The Philanderer*, by Stanley Kauffmann. The reference is to a sweet or candy made of boiled sugar.

Sugar-plum is little used as a vocative, though the term was formerly often used metaphorically to refer to anything pleasing, especially to something that was used as a bribe.

Sugarpuss Used by an older American woman to a younger in a friendly way in *War Brides*, by Lois Battle: 'Okay, sugarpuss, see y' tomorra.' The term combines two standard endearments.

Suh A spelling sometimes used to indicate the pronunciation of 'sir' by certain speakers, usually those with a pronounced regional or sub-standard accent. *The Storyteller*, by Harold Robbins, has: ' "Where to, suh?" the redcap asked. "Have yo' ticket handy?" ' In *The Middle Man*, by David Chandler, a white American woman playfully responds to her lover's compliments about her love-making by saying: 'Why, kind suh, all mah men tell me that.' *The Choirboys*, by Joseph Wambaugh, has a woman from Texas asking a Los Angeles policeman: 'Suh, kin you tell us where the Gen'ral Hospital is?'

Sunny Jim This is used in the same way as 'sonny' or 'sonny boy', usually to a young boy, occasionally to an adult male. It recalls a cartoon character who advertised a breakfast cereal *circa* 1903.

In Britain the term is also specifically associated with James Callaghan, Labour Prime Minister (1976–79), well known for his ready smile and apparently sunny disposition.

Sunshine Used in modern colloquial English as a friendly endearment to address a child or woman, especially. In American slang 'sunshine' refers to a kind of LSD, the drug which induced hallucinations.

Superintendent The title of a British police officer of middle rank, and used on its own or followed by the last name of the person concerned. It occurs alone in *Goldfinger*, by

Ian Fleming, *The Limits of Love*, by Frederic Raphael, and *Watcher in the Shadows*, by Geoffrey Household. In *Jane Eyre*, by Charlotte Brontë, it is used to the superintendent of a charity school by the visiting patron: 'Teachers, superintendent, I beg of you not to allow the waters to stagnate round her.'

Superman A transferred name, referring to the refugee, from the planet Krypton, of superhuman powers, created by Jerome Siegel and Joe Schuster in the 1930s. One of the most famous American comic-book characters, whose biography, as with most modern fictional characters, can be read in David Pringle's excellent book, *Imaginary People*.

The name is typically transferred to anyone who is claiming to be better than average, or thought to be so by the speaker. *Festival*, by N.J. Crisp, has:

'Like everyone else, I was born with a brain, a body, and my own talents,' Cramer said. 'The only difference between me and the rest is I know that's all I need, or ever will.'
'Well, good luck, Superman,' Valerie said.

In *The Taste of Too Much*, by Clifford Hanley, one boy says to another: 'Take it easy, Superman,' with nothing having been said previously to inspire the friendly use of the term.

In Truman Capote's short story *The Headless Hawk*, a man is annoyed by two girls sitting at the table in a diner where he is eating with a friend. 'Vincent said if they didn't shut up ... "Oh, yeah, who do you think you are?" "Superman. Jerk thinks he's superman." ' This is an interesting indirect vocative, since the speaker is both answering her friend's rhetorical question while addressing the man in front of her.

Surgeon, Mr *See* Barber, Mr.

SURNAME *See* Last name.

Surra, Surree, surry *See* Sorry.

Swabber In *A Dictionary of Sailors' Slang*, Wilfred Granville lists 'swab' as 'a term of opprobrium for a useless seaman'. He adds the explanation 'because he is as wet as one', i.e. as wet as the mop which is used by a swabber to clean the decks. It was sailors of very low rank who were normally given this task, and the behaviour of such men when ashore led to 'swabber' becoming a term for any contemptible man.

It had this meaning in Shakespeare's time, and is thus very curiously used in *Twelfth Night* (1:v). Maria says to Viola, who is disguised as a young man: 'Will you hoist sail, sir? here lies your way.' There is no particular reason for this lapse into sea-faring metaphor, but it inspires Viola to reply: 'No, good swabber; I am to hull here a little longer.' The reference to hulling is to drifting in the wind with the sails furled, which is correct enough, but the 'swabber' seems out the place.

Shakespeare may be alluding to the literal meaning of 'swabber', one who clears the decks, and not to its slang meaning. Maria appears to be trying to remove him from the scene, as a swabber might try to remove something from the deck.

Swaddler This word is said to have been applied originally to a Methodist minister in Ireland because he often referred to the Christ child in His swaddling clothes. From being a personal nickname it became a general term for Methodists, then was still further extended to all Protestants. James Joyce, in *Dubliners*, has: 'the ragged troop screaming after us "Swaddlers! Swaddlers!" thinking that we were Protestants.' 'Proddies' is another commonly used term in Ireland for Protestants, used both vocatively and in third person reference.

Swain The earliest meaning of this word in English was 'boy' or 'servant'. Traces of this survive in compounds like 'boatswain', 'coxswain'. By the seventeenth century the meaning had shifted across to 'peasant labourer', or 'shepherd'.

Petruchio, in Shakespeare's *The Taming of the Shrew*, calls his servant Grumio 'you peasant swain', but he means it insultingly, following it immediately with 'you whore-son malt-horse drudge!' 'Swain' was clearly not a normal term for a manservant by this time. In *The Winter's Tale*, Polixenes in disguise addresses the prince, his son, as 'swain', but we are told by Perdita that Florizel has obscured his rank 'with a swain's wearing'.

The word 'swain' was romanticized from the seventeenth century onwards by the pastoral poets, and turned into a country lover. A girl might jokingly refer to her 'swain' in modern times, but the word has mainly survived in name form, as the last name 'Swain' or the Scandinavian first name 'Sven'.

Sweat, old Normally used of a former regular soldier, one who sweated many a time on the parade ground or in battle. It can be extended to any man and used as a friendly term of address, as in *A Kind of Loving*, by Stan Barstow, where one young man greets another with: 'Well, how's life, me old sweat?'

Sweet Used vocatively as an endearment in its own right, as the head word in a longer vocative expression such as 'old sweet' (used by a man to his mistress in *The Philanderer*, by Stanley Kauffman) or 'dear sweet' (used in

An American Dream, by Norman Mailer), or as an element in expressions like 'my sweet baby', 'my sweet darling girl'. *Absolute Beginners*, by Colin MacInnes, has an example of 'sweet' used in a friendly rather than intimate way to a girl.

The more usual 'my sweet' is found in *Henry's War*, by Jeremy Brooks; *Lucky Jim*, by Kingsley Amis; *The Limits of Love*, by Frederick Raphael; *The Pumpkin Eater*, by Penelope Mortimer; *Room at the Top*, by John Braine. *A Travelling Woman*, by John Wain and *Within and Without*, by John Harvey, both have examples of 'my poor sweet'. The latter novel also has 'my sweet girl', 'my sweet darling girl' used as intimacies.

Shakespeare often uses 'sweet' + first name vocatively, as well as: sweet lord, sweet lady, sweet youth, sweet love, sweet coz, good sweet husband, sweet sister, sweet one, sweet prince, sweet playfellow, sweet friend, and many more. 'Sweet', for Shakespeare, was clearly one of those conventional vocative elements, along with 'good', 'noble', 'gentle', and the like.

Sweetheart A term of endearment, the equivalent of 'darling', since the end of the thirteenth century. The expression was at first two separate words, but their constant use together caused their fusion.

Shakespeare uses 'sweetheart' vocatively in six of his plays. In *King Lear* it is the name of a dog. The term is used between lovers, between parents and children (usually to daughters), between good women friends (e.g. *The Merry Wives of Windsor*).

In *Cass Timberlane*, by Sinclair Lewis, we are told that 'he had always, since the age of three, called his mother "Sweetheart", so that it had become her pet name among the choice little set of the fastidious matrons of Grand Republic.' Lewis would have been justified in saying that it had become her nickname rather than pet name, but one sees what he means. 'Sweetheart' is occasionally used between men. *The Wild-Goose Chase*, by Beaumont and Fletcher, has Belleur saying: 'I beseech you, good sweet Mirabel, sweet-heart'.

A modern instance of use between men, where the threatening tone makes it clearly a sarcasm, occurs in *Fletch*, by Gregory McDonald. A newspaper librarian says to a reporter: 'Anytime I can do you a favor. . . .' 'You can. Fuck off.' 'Return this file before you go home, sweetheart, or I'll report you.'

Normal use of 'sweetheart' as an endearment occurs in such novels as *Brothers in Law*, by Henry Cecil; *The Country Girls*, by Edna O'Brien; *Goldfinger*, by Ian Fleming; *The Heart of the Matter*, by Graham Greene; *Room at the Top*, by John Braine; *Saturday Night and Sunday Morning*, by Alan Sillitoe; *A Travelling*

Woman, by John Wain; *Under the Volcano*, by Malcolm Lowry; *Within and Without*, by John Harvey.

Sweetie   Often used alone as an endearment, though 'you poor sweetie' occurs in *Rabbit is Rich*, by John Updike, addressed by one woman to another.

The term is not always appreciated by those to whom it is addressed. 'Don't worry about it, sweetie,' says a man to a young woman, in *The Stork*, by Denison Hatch. 'Don't you call me "sweetie" again, you son of a bitch,' is the reply. During the same conversation the man also uses 'toots' to the woman – another term to which the hearer is likely to object.

In *Thanksgiving*, by Robert Jordan, occurs: ' "Do you want a drink, sweety?" Mrs Channing asked. "Don't call me sweety," Eric snapped. "I'm sorry, dear boy." "I'm not your boy, either," Eric said.' Peter Collier and David Horowitz, in *The Kennedys*, tell us: 'with Jack it was airline stewardesses and secretaries. They appeared almost nightly at the Georgetown house, in such numbers that Jack often didn't bother to learn their names, calling them "sweetie" or "kiddo" the next morning.'

It is significant that at least two novelists link the use of 'sweetie' with homosexual speakers. Homosexual men use the term to women friends in *The Exhibitionist*, by Henry Sutton and *The Middle Ground*, by Margaret Drabble.

Sweetie pie   A variant of 'sweetheart', used by American speakers rather more than by British speakers. 'Sweetie pie, how long is it since you've touched the piano?' a husband asks in *Gideon Planish*, by Sinclair Lewis. It is used by a wife to her husband in *The Philanderer*, by Stanley Kauffman, and in *Eustace Chisholm and the Works*, by James Purdy, it is a woman who says to her lover: 'All you got to do, sweety pie, is hold my little hand on the way there.' 'My sweetie pie' occurs in *Opening Night*, by Ngaio Marsh, addressed to an actress by a playwright.

Sweeting   'How fares my Kate?' says Petruchio, in Shakespeare's *The Taming of the Shrew*. 'What, sweeting, all amort [nearly dead]?' Othello also says to Desdemona: 'All's well now, sweeting; Come away to bed.'

This term of endearment had been in use for two or three centuries before Shakespeare's time, and it was to continue for at least a century more. 'That's not the thing, my little sweeting,' says Croaker to Miss Richland, in Goldsmith's *The Good-Natured Man*. The word does not seem to be used in modern times, though various other 'sweet' expressions survive.

Sweetling   A variant of 'sweeting', in use since the seventeenth century. It is used as an intimacy in *The Country Girls* and *Girl with Green Eyes*, both by Edna O'Brien.

Sweetness   An occasional variant of 'sweetheart', 'sweetie', etc. Used by a young American male to his sister in a television film shown in 1988. It occurs also in *World So Wide*, by Sinclair Lewis, used by a man to a female friend.

Sweets   A variant of 'sweet', 'sweetheart', etc., commonly used as an endearment. It is used by a man to a woman in *The Mackerel Plaza*, by Peter de Vries, the two being on intimate terms. A husband says it to his wife in *The Philanderer*, by Stanley Kauffmann. In another novel by Peter de Vries, *The Tunnel of Love*, a woman asks a man: 'Are you O.K., sweets?' There are six further examples of 'sweets' used as an intimacy in *The Limits of Love*, by Frederic Raphaël, all by the same woman to her husband.

Sweet Tooth, Mr   This nonce name occurs twice in *Brothers in Law*, by Henry Cecil. The expression 'sweet tooth', used of one who has a special liking for sweet things, dates from the fourteenth century.

Swine, you   'Swine' is now used far more often as an insulting vocative than as a normal word. In normal usage it has been replaced by 'pig' (occasionally by 'hog'), both of which are themselves used as terms of address, and both probably less forceful than 'swine'.

It is usually men who are called 'swine', by women or other men, and use of this particular term has been common since the fourteenth century. It is a convenient shorthand way of telling someone that you think him dirty, greedy, and ugly. Those features are sometimes emphasized by repetition, or further unpleasant characteristics are mentioned: 'you lousy swine' occurs in *A Kind of Loving*, by Stan Barstow; 'you dirty little swine' is in *No Highway*, by Nevil Shute; 'you bloody swine' (as well as examples of 'you swine') in *The River of Diamonds*, by Geoffrey Jenkins; 'you fornicating swine' is in *Bhowani Junction*, by John Masters, and so it goes on.

Between intimates, insults can of course be merely friendly or a kind of covert endearment. 'You mean old swine' is used in that way in *Room at the Top*, by John Braine, the 'old' having a softening effect.

Swot, Swotter, Swotpot   *See* **Sap**.

Taffy, Taff A generic nickname for a Welshman. It derives from the Welsh pronunciation of 'Dafydd', Welsh 'David'. Examples of its use occur in *Henry's War*, by Jeremy Brooks.

Tail-chaser A man who is interested in women purely as sexual objects. 'Tail' has long been used in slang expressions related to sexual activity, to the buttocks, and to the penis. Kingsley Amis, in *Lucky Jim*, has: 'I can take Christine away from you without that, you Byronic tail-chaser.'

Tailor The word is used vocatively in Shakespeare's *The Taming of the Shrew* (4:iii). The man concerned also has a heap of insults addressed to him by Petruchio: thou thread, thou thimble; thou yard; three-quarters; half-yard; quarter; nail; thou flea; thou nit; thou winter-cricket, thou; thou rag; thou quantity; thou remnant. 'Quantity' is used in the sense of indefinite amount or small amount, and is the equivalent in this context of 'rag'.

Tallow-catch This is thought by some editors of Shakespeare's *Henry the Fourth Part One* to be what Prince Hal calls Falstaff, the full expression being 'thou whoreson, obscene, greasy tallow-catch'. Tallow is a kind of animal fat used to make candles. Other editors have taken the word to be 'tallow-ketch' and interpreted it to mean 'tub of tallow'. *See also* **Fatty**.

Tank *See* **Fatty**.

Tap *See* **Cry-baby**.

Taper *See* **Spindleshanks**.

Tart Originally applied to a girl who was pleasing in appearance as a compliment, but since the end of the nineteenth century used to describe a vulgar, immoral woman. It is used as a friendly insult in *Festival*, by N.J. Crisp, when a director calls an actress 'you daft tart'.

Tarzan The name of an English foundling, reared in an African jungle by apes, created by Edgar Rice Burroughs in 1912 and used by him as the hero of twenty-four books. 'Tarzan' is otherwise John Clayton, Lord Greystoke, but it is as Tarzan that he is known around the world, thanks to the many films which have supplemented the books and made his exploits known. He is a natural superman, of great physical strength but also very intelligent, able to commune fluently with animals and haltingly with other humans. His 'Me Tarzan, you Jane' remark is humorously quoted by many a young man jokingly acting as a he-man before his girl-friend. 'Tarzan', a name which Burroughs does not seem to have explained, is frequently used as a substitute name to anyone who appears to be making an ostentatious display of physical strength, rescuing damsels in distress, etc. Examples of such usage occur in *Geordie*, by David Walker and *Absolute Beginners*, by Colin MacInnes.

Tateleh A diminutive form of *tata*, the Yiddish word for 'Dad' or 'papa', often used to address a small boy. It is so used in *The Storyteller*, by Harold Robbins, where a Jewish father says to his son: 'I'll see you tonight, *tateleh*.' Calling a child 'little father' may derive from name-magic beliefs. Attributing age to a young boy was meant to fool the child-hating demons. Leo Rosten, offering this explanation in *The Joys of Yiddish*, compares the use of *bubeleh*, used to both sexes, and *mameleh*, used to little girls. Such usage, however, suggests the inverse address which is common in many languages, discussed under **Sirrah**. Yiddish endearments are often retained in an English conversation by those acquainted with that language.

Tattle-tale Used of a person who cannot keep a secret. The term is used by an American speaker in *Except for Me and Thee*, by Jessamyn West. The variant 'Tell-tale-tattle' is used by one girl to another in *Girl with Green Eyes*, by Edna O'Brien.

Other variants include: Blabber-mouth, Tell-tale-tit, Snitcher, Splitter, Squealer, Wide-mouth. A great many English dialect variants for a tell-tale are listed in *The Lore and Language of Schoolchildren*, by Iona and Peter Opie.

Tawny-coats A Shakespearean vocative which identifies those referred to by the colour of the coats they are wearing. It is Gloucester, in *Henry the Sixth Part One* (1:iv) who cries 'Out, tawny-coats!' to the retainers of Henry Beaufort, bishop of Winchester. His own men, wearing blue coats, force the others to leave.

For a similar *ad hoc* vocative *see also* **Chap with the red whiskers, thou**.

Shakespeare has other vocatives which include 'tawny'. Lysander, in *A Midsummer Night's Dream* (3:ii) tells Hermione: 'Out, tawny Tartar, out! Out, loathed medicine! O hated potion, hence!' *Titus Andronicus* (5:i) has 'tawny slave' addressed to a child, that of Aaron the Moor and the empress Tamora.

Taxi There is considerable doubt about the vocative status of 'Taxi', used as a call to attract a taxi-driver's attention. Once the driver is near enough to be spoken to he is addressed as 'driver', or 'cabbie', never as 'taxi'. Many would therefore argue that 'Taxi!' is simply a conventional cry similar to 'Shop!', the latter meaning 'There is someone in the shop who needs attention'. 'Taxi!' could likewise be interpreted as 'I need a taxi'.

'Taxi' seems to move nearer to vocative status in the following passage from *Thursday Afternoons*, by Monica Dickens: 'Oh, look, there's a taxi. Do yell for him. Taxi!' Here the summons is clearly perceived as being a call to the taxi-driver. Compare the use of 'House'. Perhaps taxi only becomes a true vocative in the familiar joking exchange: 'Call me a taxi, please.' 'Okay, taxi.'

Teacher Addressed to a teacher, or to a person who is temporarily acting like a teacher. The scene described by Laurie Lee in *Cider with Rosie* is concerned with village school life in the early 1920s:

> Each morning was war without declaration; no one knew who would catch it next. We stood to attention, half-crippled in our desks, till Miss B walked in, whacked the walls with a ruler, and fixed us with her squinting eye. 'Good a-morning, children!' 'Good morning, Teacher!'

Most modern teachers probably prefer to be addressed by name in such a situation, and few try to rule by fear these days.

In *The Liberty Man*, by Gillian Freeman, 'teacher' becomes a friendly vocative when used by a young man to his former teacher. They are no longer in a teacher-student relationship, something the young man finds difficult to adjust to.

Looking for Mr Goodbar, by Judith Rossner, has a man who addresses his lover, who happens to be a teacher, as 'Teach'. Once again there is novelty in the fact that his relationship with a teacher is so different from those he knew as a child.

In *Georgy Girl*, by Margaret Forster, a girl is asking a man questions about himself and his career. 'Why did you work there in the first place?' she asks. 'Please teacher,' he says, 'because I had to earn my living.' An interrog-

ation situation such as this often causes a vocative such as 'my lord', 'your lordship', 'Mr District Attorney', or some other court-room term to be used. 'Teacher' is more unusual in such a context, but reflects the man's feelings about being put into, a subordinate position by the questioning.

A character in *Pygmalion*, by George Bernard Shaw, says to Higgins: 'You come from 'Anwell. Go back there.' Higgins, meaning to be helpful, points out that the place-name is '*H*anwell'. 'Thank you, teacher,' says the man who has been corrected, with a great deal of sarcasm.

In some instances 'sir' or 'miss', the normal terms by which teachers are addressed, may be used in these teacher-like situations, but only if the speaker is pretending to adopt pupil status. Simple professional use of 'teacher' by someone other than a student occurs in *Jane Eyre*, by Charlotte Brontë. The patron of a charity school is paying a visit and tells the assembled staff: 'Teachers, you must watch her [i.e. Jane].'

Teacher's pet An accusation levelled at certain children by their peers, if the latter consider that undue favouritism is being shown by the teacher to the child concerned. An example occurs in *Deborah*, by Marian Castle, a novel set in Dakota. The Opies, in *The Lore and Language of Schoolchildren*, remark that such a child may also be called: Pet or Petty, Teacher's good boy, holy angel, little innocent.

A child who has become the teacher's pet by making up to the teacher comes in for abuse by being called: toad or toady, worms, crawler, grease boy, grease rat, goody-goody, namby-pamby, according to the district in which the school is situated. Such terms tend to be passed from one generation of schoolchildren to another in playground exchanges, but each area, and sometimes each school in an area, has its own traditions.

Tearful Tilly *See* **Cry-baby**.

Tell-tale-tattle, Tell-tale-tit *See* **Tattle-tale**.

Temple, Shirley Used as a transferred name in a friendly way in *The Country Girls*. Miss Temple became famous overnight as a child star in the early 1930s, causing a great many little girls born at that time to be given her first name.

Tenors *See* **Altos**.

Ten-ton *See* **Fatty**.

Terror, you little *See* **Horror**.

Tessie, Two-ton Used as a transferred name

by English children to any fat girl or woman. Tessie O'Shea was, as her nickname indicates, fairly large in build. She was a popular singer in the music-halls whose career continued into the early 1970s in films.

The lot of you, the pair of you, the pack of you, the two of you, the three of you, etc. This construction shows at best a neutral way of addressing a group of people, but more normally a fairly aggressive way of doing so. Typically the speaker would be a schoolmaster addressing pupils, for example, or an officer addressing his men. 'The rest of you' is said in a fairly kindly tone in *Casanova's Chinese Restaurant*, by Anthony Powell; *Doctor at Sea* has unfriendly examples of 'the lot of you' and 'the pair of you'; *The Taste of Too Much*, by Clifford Hanley, has unfriendly use of 'the lot of you' and 'the two of you'; *A Travelling Woman*, by John Wain, has a fairly neutral use of 'the two of you'.

Irish dialectal use is shown in J.M. Synge's *The Tinker's Wedding*, where 'the two of yous' occurs. An American-Irish speaker in *Waterfront*, by Budd Schulberg, uses 'the rest of yuz' in an aggressive way: 'The rest of yuz. Outa the way. Trucks comin' through.'

Thief Normally an insulting accusation, the seriousness of which depends on what is alleged to have been stolen. 'You thief' said by one child to another because of a stolen chocolate biscuit, for instance, would be thought of as part of childhood's ongoing war of words.

Examples of its use by youngsters occur in *Girl with Green Eyes*, by Edna O'Brien and *Lord of the Flies*, by William Golding. 'Thief' is often used alone – sometimes as 'horse-thief' – but in *Babbitt*, by Sinclair Lewis, an employee who is being dismissed by someone he thinks has underpaid him, says: 'you keeping us flat broke all the time, you damned old thief, so you can put money away for your saphead of a son. . . .'

The traditional cry of 'Stop, thief' presumably asks other people to stop the thief. The thief himself is unlikely to stop in his tracks simply because he is asked to do so.

In Shakespeare, 'thief' is usually a powerful insult and is fairly well used as a vocative. Thus Cloten, in *Cymbeline* (4:ii) tells Guiderius: 'Thou art a robber,/A law-breaker, a villain. Yield thee, thief.' Later he says: 'Thou injurious thief,/Hear but my name, and tremble.' In *Twelfth Night* occurs 'Notable pirate, thou saltwater-thief.' In *Othello* (1:ii) Brabantio faces Othello with: 'O thou foul thief, where hast thou stow'd my daughter?'

Thing 'O thou thing!' says Leontes to his wife Hermione, in Shakespeare's *The Winter's Tale*.

He means that she is not worthy to be called a person since he believes, mistakenly, that she has been unfaithful to him. This contemptuous use of 'thing', applied to a person, seems logical but is by no means typical in modern times.

The word is usually qualified in some way, and is likely to show pity or affection. 'Poor thing' is frequently said to someone in a sympathetic way. This can become 'you poor thing', and occur in the plural form as 'you poor things'.

In George Eliot's *The Mill on the Floss* a boy calls his sister 'you greedy thing', in mild reproach. *Gideon Planish*, by Sinclair Lewis, has a woman addressing her lover playfully as 'you bad thing'. *Doctor at Sea*, by Richard Gordon, has a homosexual male making use of 'you mean thing'. In *Girl with Green Eyes*, by Edna O'Brien, 'you soft, daft, wanton thing' is used as a verbal caress. 'Sweet thing' is similarly used by a boy to a girl in *Boulevard Nights*, by Dewey Gram.

Monica Dickens comments on an idiolectal usage in *Mariana*: 'another boy who had played in the match, who was a baronet, called everyone "my dear old thing." ' Perhaps the ultimate proof that 'thing' can be used affectionately comes in *Anglo-Saxon Attitudes*, by Angus Wilson. 'Thing' is converted into a diminutive form, 'Thingy', and used by the children in a family as a nickname for their mother.

'You great bragging thing', addressed to Festus Derriman by Anne Garland in Hardy's *The Trumpet Major* is irritated rather than contemptuous, and has additional interest because of Derriman's reply, which is a request to be called names. 'I give you free liberty to say what you will to me. Say I am not a bit of a soldier, or anything! Abuse me – do now, there's a dear. I'm scum, I'm froth, I'm dirt before the besom – yes!' Anne refuses to abuse Derriman, whose odd behaviour is perhaps to be explained as a feeling that he needs to be punished for having offended her.

'Old thing' occurs from time to time, and is always friendly or affectionate. Examples are found in *Georgy Girl*, by Margaret Forster; *No Highway*, by Nevil Shute; *The Pumpkin Eater*, by Penelope Mortimer; *A Season In Love*, by Peter Draper and *War Brides*, by Lois Battle. In the last of these the speaker is a young Australian woman consoling her mother. For a journalistic comment an 'old thing', *see also* **Boy, dear**.

Thingummy Grose's *Dictionary of the Vulgar Tongue* (1785) described this term as 'a vulgar address or nomination to any person whose name is unknown'. It is the word 'thing' with a meaningless suffix, though some early writers preferred to write 'thing o' me'. Perhaps it is slightly less vulgar when prefixed by a social title, as when the surgeon, in Dickens's *Oliver Twist*, says to the mid-wife: 'It's all over, Mrs Thingummy!' *See also* **What's-your-name**.

Thinker, deep Used ironically to a man who has questioned orders given to him by the speaker in *Waterfront*, by Budd Schulberg. The man concerned is certainly not a thinker, but he is confused on this occasion by being Told to kill his brother.

Thinima A child's joking name for a thin person, punning on 'Fatima'. *See also* **Spindleshanks**.

Third Addressed by seamen to a third mate in *Doctor at Sea*, by Richard Gordon. The same officer is also addressed in a friendly way as 'Three-o'.

Thou See Introduction, page 18.

Thug 'You vulgar thug' is used by a male American speaker to a taxi-driver in *The Ginger Man*, by J.P. Donleavy, but 'thug' is not in general use as a vocative. In third person reference it describes a vicious criminal, having originally referred to a member of an Indian criminal gang, infamous for strangling their victims.

Thumb, Tom Used as a generic nickname for a very small person, especially a child. The name is transferred from *The History of Tom Thumb*, by Richard Johnson, published in 1621, or from one of the later literary or filmed versions of the story. *See also* **Tich**.

Tich A commonly used generic nickname in Britain for a very small person. An uncle applies it to his niece in *Mariana*, by Monica Dickens, though she is in fact quite tall. The term is most used in the school playground, where it is used insultingly.

The children who use it in modern times are unaware that they commemorate a British music-hall artist, known as 'Little Tich' although he was born Harry Ralph. As a child Ralph resembled the claimant in the famous Tichborne Case, in which Arthur Orton, a butcher's son, claimed to be Roger Charles Tichborne, heir to a baronetcy.

Other names which can be used as instant nicknames for a small person include: Squirt or little squirt, ankle-biter, flea, half-pint, imp, junior, microbe, midge, nipper, pint-size, shorty, shrimp, small fry, snitch or snitchy, squib, stubby, stumpy or stumps, tiddler, Tiny Tim, Tom Thumb, weed. Words meaning a tall person can also be used sarcastically to a small person.

Tiddler A word used by British children for the stickleback, a very small fish found in both fresh and salt water, a favourite objective in the fishing expeditions of young children. The term is applied by adults to a small child, and by children to a child who is especially small. 'Tiddler' probably represents a childish attempt to say 'stickleback', through forms such as 'tiddlebat'. *See also* **Tich**.

Tiger Typically used by a woman to a man who is a virile lover, as in *The Exhibitionist*, by Henry Sutton, where 'Here I am, tiger' is said by a woman lying on a bed, waiting for her partner to join her. A man uses it to a woman in John Updike's *Rabbit Redux*, again with reference to energetic love-making. The term can also be used in a complimentary way to a child, implying that the child concerned has lots of energy. It is used in this way in *Ordinary People*, by Judith Guest, where it is addressed to a young boy by an adult, but it could easily be used to a girl. There is, of course, no sexual innuendo present when used in this way.

Tim, Tiny A name transferred to a very small child by other children. It comes from *A Christmas Carol*, by Charles Dickens, where Tiny Tim is the crippled son of Bob Cratchit. *See also* **Tich**.

Time, Father A reference to the conventional personification of time as an old man carrying a scythe and an hour-glass. Used as a transferred name in *A Kind of Loving*, by Stan Barstow. A young man says to a girl: 'You're only a kid. You won't be leaving your mother for a while.' She replies: 'Well you've got to think about the future, haven't you? Many a girl's married and started a family at eighteen. Anyway, how old are you, Father Time, if it isn't too personal a question?'

Tin ribs *See also* **Spindleshanks**.

Tiny 'He's only a little man,' says an Australian speaker in *A Salute to the Great McCarthy*, by Barry Oakley, 'but you want to watch him because he can crucify you if he wants. That right, tiny?' The man addressed here replies 'Cut it out,' not appreciating the term.

Most of the expressions drawing attention to someone's relatively small size, such as 'tich', 'nipper', 'pip', 'shorty', 'shrimp', 'weed', and the like are insulting, although 'tiny' appears to fit in well with the vocative system. Its ' -y' ending gives it the appearance and sound of a friendly diminutive. The rather odd 'big tiny' is used by a wife to address her husband in a friendly way in *Gideon Planish*, by Sinclair Lewis. The woman concerned uses a wide range of vocatives as endearments.

Tit *See* **Tuppence**.

Toad The toad has been considered rather loathsome since at least the sixteenth century. Modern children might still call an unpleasant person 'old toad', but they would probably ensure that they were out of range of that person's hands before doing so.

A Trick to Catch the Old One, by Thomas Middleton, has a slanging match which begins: 'Toad!' 'Aspic!' 'Serpent!' 'Viper!'

Shakespeare uses the vocative in *Richard the Third* (4:iv), where the Duchess of York says to Richard: 'Thou toad, thou toad, where is thy brother Clarence?' In *Timon of Athens* (4:iii), Apemantus and Timon insult each other at length, and it is Apemantus who finally resorts to 'Toad!' He is answered with 'Rogue, rogue, rogue'. *As You Like It* (2:i) has a passing reference to the 'ugly and venemous' toad; that phrase sums up what a speaker has in mind when he uses this insulting vocative.

As a footnote, Kenneth Grahame, in *The Wind in the Willows*, says that the term of address which most offends Toad of Toad Hall is 'my good woman', addressed to him when he is disguised as a washerwoman.

Toe-rag This term has been applied to a tramp or vagrant since the 1870s, but has recently been made almost fashionable as a term of abuse, thanks to its use in popular British television series such as *Minder* and *Only Fools and Horses*. The reference is to a rag wrapped round a foot in place of a sock.

In modern use, when used as a fairly mild insult, the word implies that the person being addressed is of as little value as such a piece of cloth.

Tommy Ernest Weekley, in *The Romance of Names*, writes: 'Many people, in addressing a small boy with whom they are unacquainted, are in the habit of using Tommy as a name to which any small boy should naturally answer.' This was written in 1914. In his book *The Cockney*, published in 1953, Julian Franklyn says: 'Small boys are still addressed as Tommy and son or sonnie, small girls as Mary.' After Tommy Atkins was used as a specimen signature on a form 'Tommy' became the generic name for a British private soldier in the 1890s. There is an example of its friendly use in *Thirteen Days*, by Ian Jefferies.

Toots, tootsie, tootsy These remain mainly American expressions, though made famous by e.g. Al Jolson's song 'Toot, toot, tootsie, goodbye' and a more recent Dustin Hoffmann film *Tootsie*.

The speakers are almost invariably male, addressing women who are increasingly likely to object to being labelled with one of these forms. It was noticeable that Dustin Hoffmann, supposedly a woman called Dorothy in the film, made a speech in which (s)he emphasized that 'tootsie' was not acceptable as a mode of address. Jolson was presumably not being disparaging to his loved one in the song, but times have changed.

The 'toots' form is readily found in fiction. In *Bethel Merriday*, by Sinclair Lewis, a brother uses it to his young sister. In *The Stork*, by Denison Hatch, a man uses it to his secretary. Neither sister nor secretary appears to object.

The origin of 'toots/tootsie' is presumably connected with the earlier use of 'tootsie-wootsie' for a child's or woman's foot.

'Tootsie-wootsie' for foot in baby language is analogous to 'Georgy-Porgy', 'friendy-wendy' and other similar expressions which arise from linguistic playfulness on the one hand, and the lisping pronunciation of young children on the other.

It has also been suggested that 'toots' may be a euphemistic form of tush or tushie (buttocks). The origin here is a Yiddish word, used in an expression like *zees tushele*, 'sweet bottom'. Babies are affectionately addressed in that way.

American women know that, when considered as purely sexual objects by some men, they are likely to be referred to as a 'nice piece of ass'. If they associate 'toots/tootsie' with that kind of attitude, one can understand their objection to the term.

Topsy Used as a transferred name to a black African girl by a white man in Joyce Cary's short story *A Touch of Genius*: ' " 'Ere," Robbins called. "You with the pot – 'ere, yaller girl, 'ere, arf a minute, Topsy." ' The girl concerned is described as coffee-coloured, coming from the south of Nigeria. The allusion is to the character created by Harriet Beecher Stowe in *Uncle Tom's Cabin*. Topsy in that book is a little orphan slave-girl, famous for her announcement that she was never born, never had no father, nor mother, nor nothin'. 'I 'spect I just growed,' she says.

Tosh Eric Partridge records many meanings of 'tosh' in *A Dictionary of Historical Slang*, but none explains the friendly use of this term between men as an equivalent of 'mate', 'chum', etc. It was heard reasonably frequently in Britain in the 1950s, but seems to have faded. *A Kind of Loving*, by Stan Barstow, which is set in Yorkshire, has two examples of its use. 'Well, just as you like, tosh,' says one young man to another, 'I'll be seein' ye, then.' 'Ay, be seein' ye, Willie,' says the other. The same speaker uses the term again elsewhere. A correspondent reports on the use of 'Tosh' in the Bristol/Gloucester area of England.

Tourist Not normally used as a vocative. It occurs in *Looking for Mr Goodbar*, by Judith

Rossner, because a man visits the area where a woman lives and is said by her to be 'taking it all in like a tourist'. She therefore says to him: 'So what do you think, tourist?'

Towzer A transferred use of what is taken to be a typical dog's name when it occurs in *A Salute to the Great McCarthy*, by Barry Oakley. A young wife says to her husband: 'You look like a bewildered little dog. C'mon Towzer, yap, yap. bow wow!'

Toy-man Used by a wife to her husband in *Gideon Planish*, by Sinclair Lewis. The wife is one who uses a very wide range of vocatives to her husband, such as 'lover', 'hero', 'big one', 'Toy-man' is interesting in that it recalls the modern term 'toy-boy', used of a male lover who is younger by a considerable margin than his female partner.

Traitor Used of a person who betrays anyone who trusts him or, more specifically, of a person who betrays his allegiance to his king or country.

The term occurs vocatively in ten of the Shakespearean plays in both of these senses.

More modern instances occur in, e.g., *A Cack-Handed War*, by Edward Blishen, where a farmer calls a group of conscientious objectors 'traitors'. They have refused to fight for their country on religious grounds. A more personal application lies behind 'you damned traitor', addressed to Professor Middleton, hero of Angus Wilson's *Anglo-Saxon Attitudes*.

Trash Applied to worthless people since the seventeenth century. *The Country Girls*, by Edna O'Brien, has two examples of the word being used insultingly to a girl. In *Absolute Beginners*, by Colin MacInnes, 'white trash' is used insultingly.

Treacle A variant of 'honey', 'sweetie', etc., being used in London in the late 1980s. The speakers are usually men, those addressed young girls. In one of his letters Lord Byron referred to his 'treacle-moon' (i.e. honeymoon) being over.

Treasure In *Awakening*, by John Galsworthy, a mother who is trying to comfort a child who has just awakened from a nightmare calls him both 'treasure' and 'my precious', the terms being synonymous in such circumstances. Oliver Goldsmith, in his play *The Good-Natured Man*, has Leontine call Olivia 'my life's treasure', but the phrase is not emphasized in any way: 'Don't, my life's treasure, don't let us make imaginary evils, when you know we have so many real ones to encounter.'

'Treasure' is sometimes used as a nickname for a girl who is well built, a pun on treasure-chest. It can also be a given name. A caller on a radio phone-in once told the present author that she was named 'Treasure Ireland'.

Treasurer Used on its own, or as 'Mr Treasurer', 'Madam Treasurer', to the official in a club or society who looks after the association's money, but only in the context of a formal meeting.

Tribe Used in joking reference to a family, especially a large one, 'tribe' can also be used as a collective vocative to family members. In *Saturday Night and Sunday Morning*, by Alan Sillitoe, a woman at a family Christmas party comes into a room and says: 'Come on, Tribe, get summat to eat.' Another speaker in the same novel says: 'She's got too many kids to look after. I've never seen such a tribe.'

Tripod Inspired by the 'third leg' of the man addressed when it occurs in *North Dallas Forty*, by Peter Gent. A conversation is taking place between professional football players as they take a shower: ' "Hey, tripod." O. W. Meadows pointed out the obvious endowment of a black rookie named Sledge. "If that thing gets hard, there ain't gonna be room in here for the rest of us." ' This is an *ad hoc* usage; 'tripod' is not listed in Chapman's *Dictionary of American Slang* as a term for a man with a large penis.

Trollop A word used to describe a woman who is either slovenly or sexually loose. Modern women are perhaps less likely to be called trollops than were their sisters in the eighteenth century.

Thomas Wolfe may have been right to illustrate contemporary usage as that of a concealed endearment, used by a speaker who is being consciously archaic.

In *The Web and the Rock* occurs: 'O you damned, delectable, little plum-skinned trollop! I will eat you like honey, you sweet little hussy!' 'How have you got the heart to call me names like that?' says the woman concerned. 'Because I love you so! That's why! It's love, pure love, nothing on earth but love!' *Like Any Other Man*, by Patrick Boyle, has an Irishman saying to his lover: 'Why don't you mind your own bloody business, you meddling trollop?'

Troops This would theoretically be addressed to a troop of soldiers, but in *War Brides*, by Lois Battle, a father uses it to his family. The man concerned is in military uniform as he speaks, though he is in the navy rather than the army:

'Have you got everything, Dawn?' he asked, the authoritarian tone returning to his voice. 'Okay, troops, let's move out. In order now. Faye, you take your sister's hand and lead the way. Your mother and I will bring up the rear. Ready, march.'

Truant The original meaning of truant was 'idle vagabond', 'rogue'. Since the sixteenth century the word has had the particular meaning of one who absents himself from school without permission. Shakespeare has a reference to playing truant, in this sense, in *The Merry Wives of Windsor* (5:i), but does not use the word vocatively. Mr Rochester, however, addresses it to Jane in Charlotte Brontë's *Jane Eyre*: 'Truant! truant! Absent from me a whole month: and forgetting me quite, I'll be sworn!'

Truepenny In the sixteenth and seventeenth centuries, 'truepenny' was used to describe an honest fellow, a man of genuine metal. Hamlet uses the word vocatively to the ghost of his father in *Hamlet* (1:v): 'Art thou there, truepenny?'

Trumpery An obsolete term that was formerly applied to women as a vocative, in the sense of 'trash, rubbish'. Goldsmith's *The Vicar of Wakefield* has: 'Out, I say . . . tramp, thou infamous strumpet. . . . What! you trumpery, to come and take up an honest house without cross or coin to bless yourself with.' In *Uncle Tom's Cabin*, by Harriet Beecher Stowe, Aunt Dinah says to two black girls: 'Get out wid ye, ye trumpery; I won't have ye round.'

The word is connected with French *tromper*, 'to cheat', and appears to have meant originally something which was of less value than it appeared.

Tub, Blood, Grub Tub, Tubs, Tubby *See* Fatty.

Tubbelina *See* Fatty.

Tub of puke An insult addressed to a prisoner by a Los Angeles policeman in *The Choirboys*, by Joseph Wambaugh. 'You stinking tub a puke' is the full expression, 'puke' referring to 'vomit'.

Tube-rose, you poor forced In *Main Street*, by Sinclair Lewis, a young wife tries to improve her husband's literary taste by reading poetry to him. He is politely interested, but it is clear to her that he will not change his ways or reading habits. 'She read with an eye cocked on him, and when she saw how much he was suffering she ran to him, kissed his forehead, cried "You poor forced tube-rose that wants to be a decent turnip!" '

The tube-rose is a flower, but not, as it happens, a rose. 'Tube-rose' simply means tuberous, the plant being of the amaryllis family, cultivated for its fragrant white flowers.

More to the point, 'tube-rose' is certainly not a usual vocative. This example merely demonstrates how a specific situation can cause a particular speaker to use a particular expression to a particular person, in a way that no rule of vocative usage could possibly anticipate.

Tuppence A variant spelling of 'two pence', representing the normal pronunciation of those words when they describe a sum of money. British speakers still talk about 'not caring tuppence' whether something happens or not, using tuppence to mean 'very little'. The word has roughly that meaning when used as an affectionate nickname, usually to a child. *Mariana*, by Monica Dickens, has: 'She began to grow. Bus-conductors no longer addressed her as "Tuppence".' *Thirteen Days*, by Ian Jefferies, has 'you tuppeny tit' used as an insult between men. 'Tit' normally refers in slang to the female breast. Here it is probably meant to suggest something soft, while the 'tuppeny' reference means 'of little value'.

Turd This word, meaning a lump of excrement, is not used in polite circles, but it has a fine oral history as an insulting term of address. There is documentary evidence of its use from the fifteenth century, and it is still in use on both sides of the Atlantic and beyond. 'Come on, stand up, you dirty little bar-fly, you nasty little jumped-up turd,' says Bertrand to Jim Dixon, in *Lucky Jim*, by Kingsley Amis. 'You old turd' is used in a friendly way between male intimates in *Redback*, by Howard Jacobson. The speaker is Australian.

Turkey Used in American slang to mean 'a jerk, a stupid person'. *The Choirboys*, by Joseph Wambaugh, has a Los Angeles policeman saying to a colleague: 'Not behind them, turkey! Pull up *next* to them.' A black policeman, later in the novel, says to another colleague: 'Take that, you jive turkey.'

Turnip It is possibly the vague resemblance between this root vegetable and the human head which causes turnip to be applied to people. Sam Weller hints at its meaning when he writes a Valentine card in *The Pickwick Papers* and says: 'Afore I see you, I thought all women was alike, but now I find what a reg'lar soft-headed, inkred'lous turnip I must ha' been; for there ain't nobody like you.'

In *Echoes*, by Maeve Binchey, a novel which is set in Ireland, a girl says to her younger sister, 'you thick turnip, you'. In *The Occupation*, by David Caute, one man calls another 'old turnip' in a friendly way. In Thomas Hardy's *The Mayor of Casterbridge* the dialectal form 'turmit head' is used as a mild term of abuse.

Tutor A professional title used mainly in university circles on formal occasions. Two examples of 'Tutor', plus four of 'my dear Tutor', occur in *The Affair*, by C.P. Snow. *See also* **Senior Tutor**. Non-university examples of 'tutor' used as a vocative are found in *The Wild-Goose Chase*, by Beaumont and Fletcher, where Lugier is tutor to Rosalura and Lillia-Bianca.

Twat A character in Edward Blishen's novel *A Cack-Handed War* addresses most of the men he works with as 'y'bloody twat', possibly thinking that it means no more than 'you silly fool'.

In the USA especially, there is far more awareness of the fact that 'twat' refers to the vulva, and is therefore equivalent to 'cunt'.

This seems to have been the original meaning in the seventeenth-century, when the word appeared in low forms of literature. That it is possible to misinterpret the word was most famously shown by Robert Browning, in his poetic drama *Pippa Passes*. Browning had apparently seen a reference to 'an old nun's twat' in a seventeenth-century source. Not knowing the word, he took it to refer to part of a nun's attire and used it accordingly, to be followed by writers as innocent as himself.

The use of 'twat' by a husband to his wife in *Cocksure*, by Mordecai Richler, is decidedly not innocent. In *Surfacing*, by Margaret Atwood, a husband calls his wife 'twatface'. This does not seem to be a standard expression, but Eric Partridge, in his *Dictionary of Historical Slang*, mentions that 'cuntface' is used to an ugly person.

Twerp A word expressing general contempt, implying that the person so called is stupid. Used both in Britain and the USA, e.g. by Frank Burns to Radar O'Riley in *M.A.S.H.* It has interestingly been suggested that a certain T. W. Earp, who was once President of the Oxford University union, inspired the formation of the word.

Twinkletoes This would be addressed to someone who shows skill at dancing. In the 1920s there was a dance step known as the twinkle, but it did not survive. It is difficult to know whether the dance step was named before the expression 'twinkletoes' came into being, or *vice versa*. A girl at her first dance is addressed as 'Mademoiselle Twinkletoes' in *Her First Ball*, by Katherine Mansfield, a story which was published in 1922.

Twins This occurs as a vocative in *The Devil on Lammas Night*, by Susan Howatch, addressed to a brother and sister: 'Twins, did you see a letter which Uncle Matt left on the living-room table last night?' It is probably only children who would be addressed in this way. There is another example of 'twins' used to address twin-brothers in *A Surfeit of Lampreys*, by Ngaio Marsh.

Twister, you In modern British slang, a twister is a cheat, a slippery person. It is used by one man to another in *Pray for the Wanderer*, by Kate O'Brien. The speaker thinks that the man so addressed is not giving him a straight answer. 'Dirty little twister' is used in *Saturday Night and Sunday Morning*, by Alan Sillitoe, to someone who has just won a card game. This could be a serious allegation of cheating, but in context the insult is merely friendly.

Twit This word seems to have come into use at about the same time as 'nitwit', and looks as if it is derived from it. It has a similar meaning and area of usage, being a rather mild, usually affectionate insult. 'Lucy, wake up, you stupid silly twit,' says a boy to his sister in *The Devil on Lammas Night*, by Susan Howatch.

Tyrant Used historically of someone who seizes sovereign power in a state and becomes an absolute ruler, often enforcing that rule with acts of cruelty.

The word is used more loosely of anyone who exercises power, and it could once be applied to anyone who acted in a cruel way.

The term occurs vocatively in several Shakespearean plays. *The Winter's Tale* (3:ii) has Paulina saying to King Leontes: 'What studied torments, tyrant, hast thou for me?/What wheels, racks, fires? what flaying, boiling/In leads or oils?' Later she says: 'But, O thou tyrant! Do not repent these things.' *Macbeth* (5:vii) has young Siward saying to Macbeth: 'Thou liest, abhorred tyrant.' A moment later Macduff enters and says: 'Tyrant, show thy face.' A figurative use of 'tyrant' occurs between lovers. Thus Romeo is for Juliet her 'beautiful tyrant, fiend angelical', because he has slain Tybalt.

In *Jane Eyre*, by Charlotte Brontë, Rochester says to Jane: 'But listen – whisper – it is your time now, little tyrant, but it will be mine presently.' In such cases the listener is a tyrant in having total power over the speaker, though willing submission to his or her rule is implied.

U

-ums A diminutive ending which appears to derive from baby-talk, in words like 'diddums'. 'Snookums' is found as a nonsensical endearment. In Sinclair Lewis's *Gideon Planish*, the hero's wife sometimes calls him 'Gidjums'.

'Un An unstressed form of 'one', frequently attached to a preceding adjective in vocative expressions such as 'old'un', 'young'un'. 'You daft'un' is addressed by a woman to her brother in *When the Boat Comes In*, by James Mitchell. *Lord of the Flies*, by William Golding, has 'all you littluns' addressed to a group of small boys.

Uncle Used by a speaker to address the brother of his father or mother, or the husband of an aunt, an uncle-in-law.

The term is used alone, or followed by the first name of the man concerned, especially if the speaker is a child.

Usage varies in individual families, but a young nephew or niece who uses 'Uncle' + first name is likely to switch to first name usage in adolescence. In *Consenting Adults*, by Peter de Vries, there is the comment: 'A milestone in our personal relations almost slipped by unnoticed. She had dropped the Uncle business.'

Like Any Other Man, by Patrick Boyle, has a young woman who says to a family friend: 'And what'll I call you? The last time I stayed here you were Uncle Jim.' 'Augh, that was in Brian Boru's time. When the pigs were running bare-footed. You would be entitled to drop the Uncle by this time.' The young woman was 'a slip of a schoolgirl' on her previous visit, but is now an adult. Her use of 'Uncle' to address a male friend of the family continues today in British working-class families, though the change to first name only probably comes at a younger age than previously.

In *An American Tragedy*, by Thomas Dreiser, a young woman deliberately tries to capitalize on the relationship implied by the use of 'Uncle'. She is addressing the father of her girl-friend: ' "I can't, Uncle Samuel!" called Sondra, familiarly and showily and yet somehow sweetly, seeking to ingratiate herself by this affected relationship.'

A writer in the *Gentleman's Magazine*, December 1793, says: 'It is common in Cornwall to call all elderly persons Aunt or Uncle, prefixed to their names.' 'Names' in this context probably means last names.

Such usage was probably meant to be friendly, as perhaps was the use of 'Aunt' and 'Uncle' to elderly slaves in the southern states of America. But Harriet Beecher Stowe's Uncle Tom was only that. He was never addressed as 'Mr' + last name, nor does the reader of *Uncle Tom's Cabin* ever learn the last name of Tom and his wife Chloë.

The use of 'Uncle' to address a black American in modern times would offend the hearer, reminding him of a time when either 'Boy' or 'Uncle' was considered to be sufficient identification for any black man. In *An American Dream*, by Norman Mailer, a black American is able to make 'Uncle' an insult by using the term to a white man.

'Uncle' is well used in the Shakespearean plays, often qualified, as are all such terms, to make expressions like: dear uncle, worthy uncle, my noble uncle. The latter term is used by Bolingbroke to York, in *Richard the Second* (2:iii), but York is not impressed when Bolingbroke kneels to him. 'Show me thy humble heart, and not thy knee, Whose duty is deceivable and false.' 'My gracious uncle!' 'Tut, tut! Grace me no grace, nor uncle me no uncle. I am no traitor's uncle.'

Monica Dickens, in *Thursday Afternoons*, plays a literary joke when one man addresses another with: 'Nice evening, Uncle.' She explains: 'This was not as familiar as it sounded, for the man's name was Mr Uncle, ironically, as his only nephew or niece was an abortive effort of his wife's sister's, with a deformed palate and a lolling head.' 'Uncle' does actually exist as an English surname, as does 'Eame', which represents Old English *eam*, 'uncle'.

Universe, Mr Used to a man who has just displayed great strength in *Like Any Other Man*, by Patrick Boyle. The allusion is to a title bestowed on the winner of a competition to find the world's most perfectly developed man. The speaker who uses this name in the novel is an admiring woman.

Upstart A term of abuse for a person whose social or professional position has suddenly risen, and who is felt to be making improper use of his new-found power. 'You little upstart' is addressed, in *A Kind of Loving*, by Stan

Barstow, to her son-in-law by a working-class woman. The young man in question has normally been polite to her, but has arrived home drunk and is doing some plain speaking. In this instance her use of the term clearly indicates her own feelings of social superiority.

Urchin This word now suggests a small boy, one who is dirty and untidy and gets into trouble. Its primary meaning, however, is 'hedgehog', though the latter word has replaced it in that sense except in 'sea-urchin'.

As a vocative addressed to a boy, 'urchin' has been used since the sixteenth century. The term was also at one time applied to a girl, especially one who was ill-tempered or roguish. Croaker says to Olivia, in Goldsmith's *The Good-Natured Man*: 'You did indeed dissemble, you urchin, you; but where's the girl that won't dissemble for a husband?'

Such usage is now obsolete. Modern use of the term to a young boy would suggest that he was mischievous, a brat.

Usher In general terms, an usher is a person who shows people to their seats, e.g., in a church. An usher in a court of law keeps order. 'Who is that, who dares address the court?' says the judge who is trying Mr Pickwick's breach of promise case. 'Usher.' 'Yes, my Lord?' 'Bring that person here instantly' (*The Pickwick Papers*, Charles Dickens).

The feminine form of the word is 'usherette', used of the cinema attendant who shows people to their seats, but she would normally be addressed as 'Miss'.

Varlet A variant of the word 'valet', a gentleman's servant. By the beginning of the seventeenth century it had also acquired the special meaning of bailiff, or sergeant-at-mace.

In Ben Jonson's *Every Man in his Humour*, Musco disguises himself as a varlet. 'A kind of little king we are,' he muses, 'bearing the diminutive of a mace.' He is addressed directly as 'varlet' by several characters in the play, also as 'officer'. Jonson was well aware of the fact that by the time his play was performed (1598) 'varlet' also meant a rogue or rascal, and was frequently used as a term of address with that meaning.

The word would now only be used vocatively, or in any other way, by someone who was joking.

Varmint This word derives from vermin, which is itself used as a reproachful form of address, but an expression like 'you young varmint' means little more than 'you bad boy'. It is mostly applied, in fact, to a mischievous child, especially a boy, but is little heard in standard English on either side of the Atlantic.

It is one of the words which writers of children's stories keep alive, putting it into the mouths of colourful country characters. 'Hands off me, ye meddlesome varmint!' says a father to his young son, in *Jennifer*, by Janet Whitney. It is used with more force in *Gone with the Wind*, by Margaret Mitchell. At one point Scarlett says to Rhett Butler: 'You get out of this buggy, you dirty-minded varmint.' Laurie Lee, in *Cider with Rosie*, has an old lady who says to some village girls: 'You baggages! You jumped-up varmints! Be off, or I'll fetch me broom.'

Vassal This is vocatively used by Shakespeare in both its technical sense of one holding lands from a superior in the feudal system and in its debased sense of a person so humble as to be a slave.

The former usage occurs in *Henry the Sixth Part One* (4:i), where Gloucester says to Vernon and Basset: 'Presumptuous vassals, are you not asham'd/With this immodest clamorous outrage/To trouble and disturb the King and us?'

The latter use is in *King Lear* (1:i), where Lear says to Kent: 'O Vassal, miscreant!' Modern use of 'vassal' is rare, and normally joking. In *The Taste of Too Much*, by Clifford Hanley, a young man says to a male friend: 'Silence, vassal,' when the friend has said that he will not have the courage to do something.

Venom, dear This is a purely Shakespearean vocative, occurring in *Twelfth Night* (3:ii). It is addressed by Sir Toby Belch to Sir Andrew Aguecheek, who has just announced: 'No, faith, I'll not stay a jot longer.' Sir Toby says: 'Thy reason, dear venom; give thy reason.' The term is presumably inspired by Sir Andrew's mood at the time. He is feeling venomous, or embittered, because he has just seen Maria being pleasant to a young man in the orchard, though she treats Sir Andrew himself with disdain.

Vermin 'Thou vermin!' says a man to another in *The Alchemist*, by Ben Jonson. This seems to have been something of a fashionable insult at the end of the sixteenth and beginning of the seventeenth century. But as with 'you rat', which is a similar expression, 'you vermin' came to have a milder application as time wore on, and was not necessarily used as a serious insult. This is especially true of the variant 'varmint'. 'Vermin' itself is clearly a serious insult in Mark Twain's *Pudd'nhead Wilson*, where an uncle calls his nephew 'you cur! you scum! you vermin!'

Vermont, my dear This most unusual term of address occurs in *Uncle Tom's Cabin*, by Harriet Beecher Stowe. Augustine St Clair is arguing with his cousin, Ophelia, about slavery during the latter's visit to his Louisiana plantation. St Clair normally addresses her as cousin, but suddenly says: 'My dear Vermont, you natives up by the North Pole set an extravagant value on time.' The vocative has all the appearance of being a useful literary device, reminding the reader that Ophelia is a visitor from the north, rather than being a reflection of real usage. *See also* **PLACE NAME**.

Vicar In the Church of England this title is used of a parish priest. 'Monday I'll start then, Vicar,' says a housekeeper to George Radwell, vicar of St Peter and St Paul, in *Judgement Day*, by Penelope Lively.

In an episode of the BBC soap opera *East Enders*, a male speaker jokingly addressed a young clergyman as 'Vic', much as if his first name was 'Victor'. The abbreviation is consistent with working-class treatment of 'Doctor', 'Sergeant', 'Corporal', and the like, which regularly become 'Doc', 'Serge', 'Corp'.

'Vicar' is not a title in the Roman Catholic Church, though the pope might be referred to as the Vicar of Christ. This uses the word in its etymological sense of one who substitutes for another.

In its use to Church of England vicars, writers seem to be uncertain about the need to capitalize the word or not. Miss Lively, quoted above, uses 'Vicar'. Leslie Thomas, in *The Magic Army*, uses 'vicar' throughout the novel.

Villain This was originally the same word as 'villein', referring to a serf who was attached to a villa, or estate. Such serfs were low-born and of rather primitive habits, and some were naturally disposed to base or criminal behaviour. The latter became the 'villains', or scoundrels and criminals of today.

As a term of address to such persons, 'villain' has been in continuous use since the fourteenth century. From the sixteenth century it has also been used more playfully. In such cases it is often softened by the use of other words, so that the vocative becomes 'you little villain', 'you young villain'.

Shakespeare has many examples of 'villain' used as a serious accusation, but there is also, in *The Winter's Tale*, 'Sweet villain! Most dear'st! my collop!' used by Leontes to his page. 'Sweet villain' also occurs in Prospero's letter to Lorenzo in Jonson's *Every Man in his Humour*.

In *Tom Jones*, by Henry Fielding, Mrs Partridge calls her husband 'villain'. In *The Pickwick Papers* Winkle is 'villain' according to Mr Pott, editor of the *Eatanswill Gazette*. Other Dickensian characters no doubt make use of the term, but it is now more rarely used as a vocative.

In police circles in Britain it is used to refer to criminals in the third person, but policemen do not usually say: 'You're under arrest, you villain'.

The playful use of the term of address continues, influenced by the theatrical use of 'villain' to describe the anti-hero of a play. Serious use of the term may also be possible. D. H. Lawrence, in *Aaron's Rod*, has: ' "You villain," she said, and her face was transfigured with passion as he had never seen it before, horrible. "You villain!" she said thickly'. This is a wife addressing the husband who has left her, but has briefly returned.

Violins Addressed by the conductor of an orchestra to the players of those instruments in *The Beethoven Conspiracy*, by Thomas Hauser. 'Bass clarinet, you must play louder' also occurs, a page or so later. The use of the name of the instrument to identify the person who plays it has been common practice since the seventeenth century.

Examples occur in any novel which features an orchestra in rehearsal, such as *Girl, 20*, by Kingsley Amis, which has: 'First oboe, remember not to take that minim off till the next beat,' and 'Strings, overall, a little more warmth if you can'.

Vixen Female foxes are evidently very bad-tempered and to call a woman a vixen is to say that she is 'a nasty quean, a slut, a scold', as Burton expressed it in *The Anatomy of Melancholy*.

In *A Midsummer Night's Dream* Shakespeare has Helena say of her closest friend, Hermia: 'O, when she is angry, she is keen and shrewd;/She was a vixen when she went to school;/And, though she be but little, she is fierce.' 'Let me come to her,' says Hermia in reply, and has to be restrained from showing just how fierce she can be.

Shakespeare does not use 'vixen' as a vocative, but 'you little vixen' is a typical expression used to a girl or woman who is being aggressive verbally or physically. It is spoken by Reddin to Hazel in *Gone to Earth*, by Mary Webb, when Hazel attacks him for being cruel to an animal. Its use in that particular book could hardly be more poignant, given that Hazel has a pet fox and dies trying to save it from the hunting pack.

In *The Billion Dollar Killing*, by Paul Erdman, a husband says to his wife: 'Martha, you old vixen. And you always tell me that you can't tell the difference between a mark, franc and lira when we go on vacation.' The wife has just revealed that she is more aware of money matters than the husband supposed, and he appears to be thinking of vixen merely as a feminine form of 'fox', in its sense of somebody who foxes you by being cleverer than you anticipated.

World So Wide, by Sinclair Lewis, has: ' "I'm not a round-heel like Livy." Olivia was like a leopard leaping. "You little vixen. And I am not a . . . I don't even know what the vile word means!" "How come it makes you so sore then?" ' 'Round-heel' in American slang refers to a promiscuous woman.

W

Wack, Wacker *See* Wag.

Wag This word now refers to a joker, or a clever and amusing talker. Until the seventeenth century it was a term applied to a mischievous boy as an endearment, especially by his mother. Falstaff calls Prince Hal 'sweet wag' in *Henry the Fourth Part One* (1:ii). In *The Two Gentlemen of Verona* (5:iv) Valentine says to Julia, who is disguised as a boy: 'Why, boy! why, wag! how now! What's the matter?'

R. N. G. Rowland has suggested in private correspondence with the author that 'wag' may have given rise to 'wack', then 'wacker' in dialectal English speech, especially in the Liverpool, Manchester, Sheffield, Hull area.

The latter terms are used as the equivalent of 'mate', 'pal', 'friend'. 'Wacker' is used in a friendly way in *Lucky Jim*, by Kingsley Amis. Another correspondent, however, Sergeant D. C. Summers, who was born in Liverpool in 1943, says that he has never heard 'wack' or 'wacker' used in that city, as is often stated to happen.

Wagtail 'Thou wagtail' was a commonly used vocative in the seventeenth century. Applied to a young man it was usually contemptuous, applied to a woman it was always contemptuous, and was roughly equivalent to calling her a whore.

The term is in no way connected with the small bird which bears this name. It refers to one of the obscene meanings of 'tail', which to a seventeenth-century Englishman was either the male or female sex organs.

The female reference has survived in slang use, where references to a piece of tail are to a woman considered merely as a sex object. Use of 'you wagtail' to a man occurs in *King Lear*. Oswald refers to 'this ancient ruffian, sir, whose life I have spared'. Kent replies: 'Spare my grey beard, you wagtail.' In Beaumont and Fletcher's *The Wild-Goose Chase*, Belleur says to Rosalura: 'Thou wagtail, peacock, puppy, look on me: I am a gentleman.'

Use of this term seems to have died out by the end of the eighteenth century.

Waiter This has been the professional title of the man who waits upon clients in a restaurant since the mid-seventeenth century. It replaced the earlier term 'drawer'.

Mr Narindar Saroop, writing to the *Times* (3 June 1988) about the difficulty of attracting a waiter's attention, was of the opinion that 'shouting "waiter" is no longer acceptable, if it ever was'. He went on to ask: 'why don't restaurants consider following the eminently sensible custom employed in two well-known clubs, where all the excellent staff are called Charles in one, and George in the other?'

In the follow-up correspondence no-one pointed out that such re-naming could be considered patronizing, or suggested that if names were to be used, the waiter's real name might be more appropriate. Not that Charles Dickens would have thought so. In *The Pickwick Papers*, Chapter 30, he describes Mr Bob Sawyer as one who

> had about him that sort of slovenly smartness and swaggering gait, which is peculiar to young gentlemen who smoke in the streets by day, shout and scream in the same by night, call waiters by their Christian names, and do various other acts and deeds of an equally facetious description.

In O. Henry's short story *The Little Rheinschloss* there is a description of a large restaurant where the waiters wear numbers. The narrator of the story, perhaps reflecting normal usage at the time, addresses one of them throughout as 'Eighteen'. One can imagine modern waiters objecting to that practice, but surely Mr Saroop missed the point? Waiters, like the rest of us, dislike being shouted at, but it is difficult to believe that they object to being addressed politely by their professional title.

Waitress De Quincey, in his *Autobiographic Sketches* (1854) remarks that 'social changes in London have introduced a new word – viz. *waitress*, which word, twenty-five years back, would have been simply ludicrous'. The word is certainly no longer ludicrous, but it is less used than 'waiter' as a term of address, 'Miss' being preferred.

Wall The famous literary example of wall used as a vocative occurs in Shakespeare's *A Midsummer Night's Dream*. Pyramus, otherwise Nick Bottom, the weaver, addresses Tom Snout, playing the part of the wall: 'Oh wall, O sweet and lovely wall,/Show me thy chink, to blink through with mine eyne.' The wall obligingly holds up his fingers to represent the chink, a scene which never fails to amuse an audience.

'Wall' can be heard as a vocative on any Saturday afternoon in Britain, in the course of a football match. When a free-kick is to be taken anywhere near the opposing goal, several defenders will normally form a human wall. They will invariably stand nearer than the ten yards specified in the rules of the game, and will be told, collectively, to retreat by the referee. He is unlikely to address them as 'sweet and lovely wall'. 'Get back, wall,' is the more usual instruction.

Walrus Used in American slang since the 1920s, according to Chapman's *Dictionary of American Slang*, to refer to a short, fat person.

British speakers of English would probably associate the word with the walrus moustache, which hangs down both sides of the face like the tusks of the walrus. In *The Philanderer*, by Stanley Kauffmann, an American wife addresses her husband affectionately as 'old walrus'.

Wanker The hero of *Jake's Thing*, by Kingsley Amis, is subjected to this insult and soon afterwards says to a colleague:

'Damon, what's a wanker?'
'These days a waster, a shirker, someone who's fixed himself a soft job or an exalted position by means of an undeserved reputation on which he now coasts.'
'Oh. Nothing to do with tossing off, then?'
'Well, connected with it, yes, but more metaphorical than literal.'

Partridge says in his *Dictionary of Historical Slang* that the 'correct' form of this slang term should be 'whanker', adding that 'to whank', in the sense of masturbate, came into use in the late nineteenth century.

No etymology is offered, but it is tempting to connect the word with 'whanger' (also 'whang', 'wang'), a slang word for the penis.

Wanton Used as both a vocative in its own right, and a vocative element, in *Girl with Green Eyes*, by Edna O'Brien. The longer expression is 'you soft, daft, wanton thing'. 'Wanton' here suggests slightly improper amorousness.

Warden In Britain a warden is likely to be the chief official in an old people's home, a remand home for delinquent children, and similar institutions where the inmates have to be guarded or protected in some way. In a Youth Hostel his function is to see that the rules of the establishment are obeyed by visitors.

In prisons, especially American prisons, the warden is the man or woman in charge, often known in Britain as the prison governor. 'He has a very bad influence on Royston, hasn't he, Warden?' says a character in *On the Loose*, by John Stroud, a novel which describes life in a children's home.

Wart This word is not usually a vocative. It occurs in *Henry the Fourth Part Two* (3:ii) only because it is the name of Thomas Wart, one of Falstaff's recruits. There are of course punning references to the name: 'Is thy name Wart?' 'Yea, sir.' 'Thou art a very ragged wart.' James Pennethorne Hughes later wrote a book called *Is Thy Name Wart?* for the benefit of those who bear unusual family names, one at which others are prone to comment on for their own amusement.

True vocative use of the word is found in *The Choirboys*, by Joseph Wambaugh. A Los Angeles policeman says to a prisoner: 'You think you can whip my ass, you wrinkled wart.' 'Yeah,' says the man, and knocks him out with a left hook.

Watchman In modern times used of a man who guards a building or complex of buildings, especially as a night watchman.

The word was originally used of a military sentry, then was applied to a constable of the watch, a man who before the Police Act of 1839 patrolled the streets at night to protect people and property.

Shakespeare does not use 'watchman' vocatively, but refers to watchmen in both of these earlier senses. *The Pickwick Papers*, by Charles Dickens, was published 1836–7. When Mr Dowler calls 'Watchman, stop him, hold him, keep him tight, shut him in, till I come down,' referring to Mr Winkle, it would have been the constable of the watch he was addressing.

Water-can, water-hog, waterworks, Waterworks Willy *See* Cry-baby.

Watson A transferred name referring to Dr John H. Watson, friend to Sherlock Holmes, and recorder of the great detective's adventures. 'I have my methods, Watson,' is spoken by a man in Len Deighton's *Funeral in Berlin*, the speaker assuming the role of Holmes. The phrase is a near quotation of 'You know my methods, Watson,' which occurs in *The Crooked Man*, by Sir Arthur Conan Doyle.

More usually heard is the phrase 'Elementary, my dear Watson,' which Holmes is supposed to have said to his friend when the latter was congratulating him on solving yet another case. The nearest Arthur Conan Doyle came to writing those words was in *The Dancing Men*, where Watson cries 'Excellent!' Holmes simply says: 'Elementary.' Nevertheless, 'Elementary, my dear Watson' is likely to be used by any speaker who is being congratulated on his logical thinking or solving of a puzzle. The full phrase occurs in *The Limits of Love*, by Frederic Raphael. *Travels With Charley*, by John Steinbeck, has: 'Tell me, please, what made you think I was in the theater?' 'Very simple, Watson. First I saw your poodle, and then I observed your beard.'

Weed A derisive term for a very small or insignificant person, or for a taller person of no physical strength. Used mainly in British English. *See also* **Tich**.

Weeping willow *See* Cry-baby.

Weirdo The adjective 'weird' converted into a noun and used vocatively to an odd or eccentric person. In this case the suffix ' –o' does not indicate frequent vocative use, as is often the case. 'Weirdos' are probably talked about more in the third person than addressed directly as 'weirdo' or 'you weirdo'.

Welcher The use of 'you welcher' has been noted in speech, television plays, and the like. It is addressed to someone who makes a bet of some kind, loses, then refuses to pay. Some American speakers pronounce the word to rhyme with 'squelcher', though the word was originally 'Welsher' and is sometimes found in that spelling.

Welshmen appear to have had a reputation for dishonesty at some stage, leading to the nursery-rhyme: 'Taffy was a Welshman, Taffy was a thief.'

Wench This old-fashioned word for a girl or woman would probably only be used jokingly in modern times, though from the sixteenth century it was commonly used as an endearment to a man's wife, daughter, or sweetheart.

In the Shakespeare plays many young ladies are addressed as 'wench', 'sweet wench', 'good wench', etc. Such usage persisted into the nineteenth century.

In George Eliot's *The Mill on the Floss* a father calls his daughter 'my wench'. Mrs Gaskell, in *Cranford*, has: 'So, Martha, wench, what's the use of crying so?' In *The Exhibitionist*, by Henry Sutton, set in the 1960s, use of the term to his lover by a male character is clearly humorous.

Since the word was at one time especially associated with country girls, milkmaids, and other country wenches, and with serving wenches, or maid servants, it could never be applied to young ladies of high birth. Until the eighteenth century 'wench' was also commonly used of prostitutes.

It is probably the serving-maid connotation which has survived most strongly, so that a man using the term in modern times implies that the woman concerned is there to attend

to him. Few men now dare to do such a thing seriously, hence the joking usage. 'You think last night was enough to quench my burning passion?' says a young American to his bride, in *War Brides*, by Lois Battle. 'Come over here, m'wench,' he adds.

Wet eyes *See* Cry-baby.

Whatsit, Mr An impolite nonce name used to a man whose name is not known or not remembered, a variant of 'What's-your-name'. 'Now, Mr Whatsit – you just stop listenin' to that jabber' is said aggressively by an Englishman to an Italian in *Shipmaster*, by Gwyn Griffin.

What's-your-name 'Here, you sir, what's-your-name, walk in, will you?' This is Mr Perker, attorney to Mr Pickwick, unceremoniously telling a man to come into his room.

Similarly, in *Hard Times*, Mr Bounderby says in his typically blunt way: 'Here, what's-your-name! Your father has absconded – deserted you – and you mustn't expect to see him again as long as you live.'

Often the expression is used by a speaker who feels that he is in a superior position to the person being addressed, and implies, in spite of apparently enquiring about that person's name, that the speaker cannot be bothered to learn it.

Dover One, by Joyce Porter, has it in the marginally more polite form 'Mr What's-your-name', though the speaker who uses it there does so in a very unfriendly way. *Vile Bodies*, by Evelyn Waugh, has: 'Judge What's-your-name, got any money?' addressed to an American judge by a British woman.

Wheezy This occurs as an *ad hoc* nickname, used rather unkindly by a young man to his cousin who is still a schoolboy. The latter is wheezing because he suffers from asthma. The characters concerned meet again when they are both a little older in *The Face-Makers*, by Richard Gordon, and use each other's first names. 'Wheezy' does not appear to be a permanent name; it is used only during one conversation, though several times, when there is no-one else present. The speaker would no doubt have known that its use in the hearing of adults would have brought a severe reprimand.

Whelp This was the normal word for a young dog until largely replaced in that role by 'puppy'. In vocative use 'you young whelp' is sometimes synonymous with 'you young puppy', used to a saucy or impertinent young man, but it can also be a stronger term of abuse, akin to 'son-of-a-bitch'. 'You most notorious whelp' is used by Face to Subtle in *The Alchemist*, by Ben Jonson. 'You little whelp' occurs in James Joyce's *Dubliners*, used by a father to his son as he beats him. 'Stupid whelp' is used by Croaker to a young man in *The Good-Natured Man*, by Oliver Goldsmith.

Whiskers Used in a friendly way by a woman to a bearded man in *Love in Quiet Places*, by Bernard Thompson. English children might well cry out 'Beardie' or 'Fungus Face' to such a person. In the past they would have shouted 'Beaver', which became the name of a children's beard-spotting game in the 1920s.

White boy This was a term of endearment for a man during the seventeenth century. It meant a favourite, pet, and was used in third person reference, occasionally as a vocative.

Its normal modern use is shown in *Rabbit Redux*, by John Updike, where a black American woman uses it to a white American. The same novel has an example of 'white man' used in a similar way. *One Hundred Dollar Misunderstanding*, by Robert Gover, has a young black American prostitute using 'white boy' to her client.

Whiteshit Used by a black American male to a white man in Bernard Malamud's *The Tenants*. It is made a feature of the character's speech that he takes a standard insult such as 'bastard', 'prick', or 'shit' and replaces the 'you' that would normally precede it with a qualifying word such as 'Jew' or 'white'.

Whoosis, Mr The equivalent of 'Mr What's-your-name' when used in *Goldfinger*, by Ian Fleming, though Chapman's *Dictionary of American Slang* says that 'whoozis' is used of unnamed things, 'whoozit' of unnamed persons.

Whore A woman who might be described in the third person as a prostitute is unlikely to be called 'you prostitute' in direct address. 'You whore', making use of the rather more old-fashioned term, would be the more likely expression.

It is used to a woman who has behaved immorally more often than to a woman who has actually practised prostitution, so the vocative could be said to mean something like 'you loose woman'. In Bernard Thompson's *Love in Quiet Places* 'you whore' is used by one woman to another. In *Free Fall*, by William Golding, 'you bloody whore' is used insultingly. In *Absolute Beginners*, by Colin MacInnes, the insult is 'nigger's whore'. 'You filthy black whore' occurs in *Cocksure*, by Mordecai Richler.

'You whore' occurs in Shakespeare, and the word is much used in *Othello* when Desdemona is suspected of infidelity by her husband. Shakespeare cannot resist punning wordplay,

and Desdemona says: 'I cannot say "whore";/It does abhor me now I speak the word.'

The variant spelling 'hoor' is used throughout *Like Any Other Man*, by Patrick Boyle, a novel set in Ireland, mainly in third person reference. Finally a man says to his lover: 'You poxy hoor, you dosed me.'

In all the above examples the person addressed was a woman: in *The Front Runner*, by Patricia Nell Warren, 'you whore' is addressed to a homosexual man by another man who is heterosexual. He is answered with 'you straight pig'.

Whoremaster In occasional use by North American speakers to men who are thought to be lecherous, or to spend a lot of time with prostitutes. 'You fucking anti-semitic whoremaster' is used by a Jewish speaker to a stranger in *Cocksure*, by Mordecai Richler.

Whoreson The son of a whore would inevitably have been illegitimate, so 'whoreson' is a synonym for 'bastard'. It was used as a term of contempt mainly until the seventeenth century, e.g. in Ben Jonson's *Every Man in his Humour*, where Stephano calls a servant 'Whoreson, base fellow'. He is admonished by his cousin for using such 'unseason'd rude comparatives'. But 'whoreson' was sometimes used between intimates in a fairly friendly way, rather as 'bastard' is used in modern times.

In either its abusive sense, or as almost a disguised compliment, it could become an element in a vocative group. 'Ah, you whoreson little valiant villain, you!' occurs in Shakespeare's *Henry the Fourth Part Two*. It is possible to find literary occurrences of 'whoreson' after the seventeenth century, but one suspects that the authors concerned are well steeped in Shakespeare and his contemporaries and are preserving usage that was no longer current. Keats, for example, uses 'whoreson' as an adjective, but that poet's vocabulary, when writing, certainly reflected Shakespeare more than nineteenth-century colloquial speech.

Wide-mouth *See* **Tattle-tale**.

Widow A widow is no longer addressed by this term, though an examination of Shakespeare's plays will show that it was common as a vocative in the seventeenth century. It occurs many times in *Henry the Sixth Part Three* (3:ii), the scene in which Elizabeth Woodville, widow of Sir John Grey, petitions Edward IV for her late husband's lands. 'Widow, we will consider of your suit,' says the king, and repeats this term several times as he tries to persuade her to become his mistress in return for her property. She ultimately marries him. In Benjamin Disraeli's novel *Sybil* Mrs

Carey is addressed as widow. In the dialects of the time (mid-nineteenth century) she might also have been addressed or referred to as 'Widow Carey'.

Wife While wives in earlier times appear to have regularly addressed their partners as 'husband', husbands do not seem to have returned the compliment and used 'wife' as a normal term of address.

There is a useful passage in *The Taming of the Shrew* where Christopher Sly, a tinker who has been told that he is a lord, asks what he should call his supposed wife (actually a page-boy in disguise). He is told that he must call her 'madam'. 'Alice madam, or Joan madam?' asks Sly. It is a pleasant joke, but seems to indicate that while first names were used at the lower end of the social scale, and respectful titles at the upper end, 'wife' was not normal anywhere. On those occasions when it does occur in literature it has rather a cold ring to it, much as if it were 'woman' rather than 'wife' that was being said.

As it happens, the earliest meaning of 'wife' was 'woman' in a general sense, a meaning retained in compounds such as 'ale-wife', 'fish-wife'.

In modern times 'wife' would probably be used jokingly, either in mock severity or as a general pleasantry. ' "Hi, wife," he said cheerfully,' occurs in Judith Rossner's *Looking for Mr Goodbar*.

The term can also be softened down by the addition of a diminutive ending. Recorded diminutives include: wifekin, wifelet, wifeling, wifelkin, and wifie. Mrs Henry Ward, for instance, writes in *Robert Elsmere*: 'I know you have troubles of your own, wifie.'

Petruchio, in *The Taming of the Shrew* (2:i) calls Kate 'wife' once he has agreed with her father that he will marry her. There is a similar anticipatory use of the term in *Jane Eyre*, by Charlotte Brontë. Jane says: 'Sir, I will marry you.' 'Edward – my little wife!' says Mr Rochester, asking her to use his first name instead of 'Sir'.

Willy-walloo This interesting vocative occurs in an O. Henry short story, *Ulysses and the Dogman*. Two old friends meet after an absence of several years. One man says to the other: 'You ding-basted old willy-walloo, give us your hoof.' The same speaker uses 'you dinged old married man' and 'you fat old rascal' as affectionate insults. The 'ding-basted' is probably euphemistic for 'damn and blasted'.

'Willy-walloo' has not found its way into the dictionaries, but is presumably to be equated with 'rascal'. The man addressed in the story is called Jim Berry, so it does not appear to play on a diminutive of 'William'.

Windy A playground taunt hurled at a child who is not courageous, who gets the wind up, as the slang expression has it. *See also* **Scare-dy-cat**.

Wing-commander A Royal Air Force rank corresponding to a naval commander or an army lieutenant-colonel. Used alone or as a prefix followed by the last name of the person concerned. It is used by a ship's purser to a passenger in *Shipmaster*, by Gwyn Griffin.

Wiseacre This is an older form of 'wise guy'. It was used from the end of the sixteenth century until the nineteenth century to refer to a wise person, or one who wished to be thought wise, at least. The word is said to have been a corruption of Dutch *wijsseggher*, a wise-sayer, or sooth-sayer.

In Fanny Burney's *Evelina* the word is turned into a nonce-name: 'Why pray, Mr Wiseacre, how are you pleased for to regard it yourself? Answer me to that.' 'Mr Wiseacre' is also used vocatively in *Peregrine Pickle*, by Tobias Smollett.

Wise-ass, you A variant of the 'smart-ass', 'wise-guy' group, used by American rather than British speakers, but not in polite society. There is an example of its use in *Moviola*, by Garson Kanin: ' "I'm on the nine-o-clock flight," I said. "You stay where you are, wise-ass." '

Wise guy Used with varying degrees of aggression to someone who is ostentatiously revealing his knowledge, especially if the person addressed has corrected something said by the speaker.

Like the older 'wiseacre', 'wise guy' can be converted into a nonce name. 'But you haven't answered me, Mr Educated Wise Guy,' says a father to his son in *Portnoy's Complaint*, by Philip Roth.

'Wise guy' itself is decidedly unfriendly when it occurs in Len Deighton's *Funeral in Berlin*. *The Middle Man*, by David Chandler, has: ' "Wiseguy," Grizzard hissed contemptuously.' In *Waterfront*, by Budd Schulberg, occurs: 'Listen, we'd like t'talk t'ya a minute.' 'Ye're talking to us right now, ain'tcha?' 'Wise guy.'

Wit Now more commonly used in the form 'half-wit', but 'wit' itself could once be used vocatively. *The Wild Goose Chase*, by Beaumont and Fletcher, has Mirabel greeting two young gentlewomen with: 'Bless ye, sweet beauties, sweet incomparable ladies, sweet wits, sweet humours!'

Witch There is a big difference in modern usage between 'you witch', said to a young woman, and 'you old witch' said to an older woman. The former term is complimentary, meaning that the person concerned is bewitching in appearance. The latter term shows 'old' being used to mean 'elderly', and not as a word expressing affection.

'Witch' in this case is the equivalent of 'hag' or 'ugly woman'. Lord Lytton said that he 'found every woman a witch', an ambiguous statement. He presumably meant that he found every woman bewitching.

This friendly, admiring use of the term occurs in *Laura*, by Vera Caspary: 'Your name, witch, is sizzling on all the wires in the country.' The *Oxford English Dictionary* dates this usage from the eighteenth century only, but the following passage from *The Witch of Edmonton* (1623), by Rowley, Dekker, and Ford, is relevant:

Just: Why laugh you?
Mother Sawyer: At my name,
The brave name this knight gives me: 'witch.'
Just: Is the name of witch so pleasing to thine ear?
Mother Sawyer: A witch? Who is not?
Hold not that universal name in scorn then. What are your painted things in princes' courts.
Upon whose eyelids lust sits, blowing fires
To burn men's souls in sensual, hot desires,
Upon whose naked paps a lecher's thought
Acts sin in fouler shape than can be wrought?
Just: But those work not as you do.
Mother Sawyer: No, but far worse.
These by enchantments can whole lordships change.
To trunks of rich attire . . .
Are not these witches?
Just: Yes, yes, but the law
Casts not an eye on these.
Mother Sawyer: Why, then, on me,
Or any lean old beldam? Reverence once
Had wont to wait on age; now an old woman
Ill favour'd grown with years, if she be poor
Must be call'd bawd or witch.

The vocative uses in the Shakespeare plays of 'witch' are all insulting. Shakespeare usually describes a witch as a hag or quean, describing her as foul and ugly, wrinkled, monstrous. In *The Merry Wives of Windsor* (4:ii) is the famous scene where Falstaff dresses as an old woman in order to escape the attentions of a jealous husband. He is beaten nevertheless as the husband says: 'Out of my door, you witch, you hag, you baggage, you polecat, you ronyon! Out! Out!' 'Witch' is addressed knowingly to a man in Ben Jonson's *The Alchemist*, as it could be in former times.

In Old English 'witch' had both masculine and feminine forms. The application of the word to a man continued in some English dialects until the present century.

Witness Used in a law-court to a person who has been called to give evidence. The witness is not necessarily someone who saw or heard something relevant to a crime, but someone who has useful knowledge to contribute in a more general way.

The original meaning of the word was knowledge, understanding. Thus an expert witness, rather than an eye-witness, may be called to give his or her views.

Woman This is used by a parish priest to his housekeeper throughout *Bless me Father*, by Neil Boyd, but he does it only when no one else is present and she is well aware that he is being mockingly severe with her.

Modern husbands use the term in a similar way, implying that they are lords and masters and their wives are at servant level. They have to make it very clear that they are joking, for the expression is greatly resented, otherwise, by the woman to whom it is addressed.

A typical comment on its use occurs in Charlotte Brontë's *Shirley*, when Mrs Gale offers a loaf to a guest and is told: 'Cut it, woman.' Miss Brontë continues: 'The "woman" cut it accordingly. Had she followed her inclinations, she would have cut the parson also; her Yorkshire soul revolted absolutely from his manner of command.'

In *The Pickwick Papers*, by Charles Dickens, Mrs Raddle also objects to the word being applied to her, even though it is not used vocatively. It is Mr Benjamin Allen who ventures to say to her:

'But you are such an unreasonable woman.'
'I beg your parding, young man,' said Mrs Raddle, in a cold perspiration of anger. 'But will you have the goodness just to call me that again, sir?'
'I didn't make use of the word in any invidious sense, ma'am,' replied Mr Benjamin Allen, growing somewhat uneasy on his own account.
'I beg your parding, young man,' demanded Mrs Raddle in a louder and more imperative tone. 'But who do you call a woman? Do you make that remark to me, sir?'

Soon after this Mrs Raddle is proclaiming loudly that 'everybody knows that they may safely insult me in my own 'ouse while my husband sits sleeping downstairs'.

Sir Clifford Chatterley, in D. H. Lawrence's *Lady Chatterley's Lover*, would have been well aware of the insulting nature of 'woman' used baldly as a vocative. It is a measure of his discomposure when he says to his wife: 'Where have you been, woman?' when she returns to the house having been absent in a storm.

Speakers sometimes try to soften the expression by expanding it to 'my dear woman' or 'my good woman'. In *Memento Mori*, by Muriel Spark, a patient addresses the ward-sister as 'my good woman'. 'The ward felt at once that Granny Duncan was making a great mistake,' Miss Spark tells us. They know that the ward-sister will be greatly offended. One also remembers that when Toad of Toad Hall dresses as a washer-woman in order to effect his escape from prison, he is addressed by an old gentleman as 'my good woman'. Kenneth Grahame remarks of the incident that it 'angered Toad more than anything that had occurred that evening'.

All this offence is caused by 'woman' being virtually synonymous in these contexts with 'serving-woman, woman of the lowest social rank', but it goes beyond that. Use of the term usually sounds at best condescending and at worst contemptuous.

A passage in *An Indecent Obsession*, by Colleen McCullough, is interesting in that woman appears to be used merely to draw attention to the listener's sexual identity. A male speaker says: 'I'm the best there is. I really am – oh, woman, I can make you shiver and yell your head off and beg for more!' The revulsion felt by the woman addressed is due to the overall statement, not the use of the vocative.

In *Howard's End*, by E. M. Forster, a husband addresses his new wife affectionately as 'little woman', but *see also* the entry on **little** for a feminine objection to that term.

Womanizer A disparaging term used of or to a man who spends a lot of time with women, usually for sexual reasons. 'You bladdy (= bloody) womanizer' is addressed by one man to another in *The River of Diamonds*, by Geoffrey Jenkins.

Women, you *See* You + category of person.

Wonderboy 'What's on your mind, Wonderboy?' says one man to another, in *The Executive*, by Michael Fisher. The man so addressed has just won the Executive-of-the-Month Cup, and the speaker is rather jealous.

'Wonderboy' seems to be an adaptation of 'Wonder Woman', the Amazon from Paradise Island, a comic-book heroine who first appeared in 1941. It could also be an *ad hoc* invention, sarcastically applied to someone who can perform wonders.

Wop An insulting term for an Italian, used since the beginning of the twentieth century. It is said to derive from *guappo*, meaning 'dandy, dude, stud', used as a greeting by male Neapolitans to one another. 'You dirty Wop' is used in anger by a woman to an Italian in *Daughters of Mulberry*, by Roger Longrigg.

'You wretched, gutless wop' is used insultingly in *Stop at Nothing*, by John Welcome.

Work'us Addressed to Oliver by Noah Claypole in *Oliver Twist*, by Charles Dickens. The fuller form of this vocative would be 'workhouse boy', Oliver having been born in that institution.

Worms *See* **Teacher's pet**.

Worship, your 'Worship' now carries primarily a religious association, but the word originally referred to someone worthy of respect and honour. 'Worthy-ship' would in fact be a better indication of what the title 'your Worship' implies.

It is used in Britain to a magistrate or mayor in formal circumstances, though the former would often be called 'sir' or 'madam', the latter 'Mr' or 'Madam Mayor'. Dickens has a character in *The Pickwick Papers* whose accent transforms 'your Worship' into 'your Wash-up'.

In *The Limits of Love*, by Frederic Raphael, the term is made insulting by deliberately using it incorrectly to a clergyman. Thomas Hardy, in *The Mayor of Casterbridge*, has a country bumpkin use the incorrect form 'your worshipful'. It is not used vocatively, but the variant 'Your Washout' is suggested in *The Dream of Fair Women*, by Henry Williamson.

worthy A favourite vocative element in former times, used like 'good', 'fair', 'honest', etc. In modern English, speakers do not usually address 'worthy Sebastian', 'worthy lady', 'worthy lord', 'most worthy gentleman', 'most worthy madam', 'worthy brother', 'worthy sir', 'worthy friend', etc., as they do in the Shakespearean plays and other literature of the period.

The words probably became little more than a conventional noise before disappearing from the vocative system, though we still speak about people of some importance as 'worthies'.

Wowser A mainly Australian term for a puritanical prude. The origin of the expression is unclear. It is used as a mild insult to a man by an Australian woman in *Redback*, by Howard Jacobson.

Wretch This word is now rather old-fashioned, but it came easily to speakers in former times who wished to abuse someone. It was in regular use from the fourteenth to the nineteenth century, with the meaning of 'vile person', and was either insulting enough on its own or was strengthened by the addition of 'damned', 'vile', 'inhuman', 'dishonest', or some such word.

Occasionally it is found as 'poor wretch', where the meaning is rather different. The typical poor wretch has suffered deep misfortune and is to be pitied for his unhappiness. Examples of both usages abound in literature before the twentieth century.

In Shakespeare's *King John*, one of many of his plays where the word occurs vocatively, 'thou wretch' is equated with 'thou slave, thou coward'.

In *Dandelion Days*, by Henry Williamson, which deals with school life in the early part of the twentieth century, a schoolmaster uses 'you depraved wretch' to a boy, but the speaker's use of language is rather archaic. Elsewhere the same master uses 'witless wretch'.

Like Any Other Man, by Patrick Boyle, has an Irish woman saying to her lover: 'Good morning, wretch. No need to ask did you sleep well.' In James Joyce's *Portrait of the Artist as a Young Man*, Stephen Dedalus says to another young man: 'That was the first definition I gave you, you sleepy-headed wretch.'

Yank 'That's the way, Yank,' says an attendant in a British cinema to an American soldier, in *The Magic Army*, by Leslie Thomas. The novel contains several other examples of the term, including the plural form 'Yanks'. American soldiers in Britain, regrettably, became used to the slogan 'Yanks, go home' which appeared in public places after the Second World War.

'Yank' is short for 'Yankee', which to a non-American means 'an American'. To Americans it means someone from the northern or northeastern states of the USA, especially New England. The word has been ingeniously, but not necessarily accurately, explained as originating from 'Jan Kees', name of an early Dutch settler.

Yellow-bellies Used by an English farmer in *A Cack-Handed War*, by Edward Blishen, to refer to conscientious objectors, men who refused to join the army during the Second World War. He also calls them 'rats' and 'traitors'. Such men were generally known as 'conchies' and probably became used to being abused for standing up for their principles. *See also* **Scaredy-cat**.

Yellows, you; Yellows, the *See* COLOURS.

Yid A highly offensive word for a Jew, an abbreviation of Yiddish. 'Dirty yid' is spoken by a woman to a man in *Vile Bodies*, by Evelyn Waugh. 'Take that, Yid,' is said by a man in Len Deighton's *Funeral in Berlin* as he knocks him unconscious.

Yokel A contemptuous term for a country bumpkin, in use since the beginning of the nineteenth century. It may derive from the connection of a yoke with a ploughman, though yokel was also a dialect word for a kind of woodpecker. The word is not often used vocatively, but *The Half Hunter*, by John Sherwood, has: 'Keep your trap shut, yokel, and listen.' This is said by one man to a younger man, with no specific reference to the country origin of the latter.

Yolky *See* **Scaredy-cat**.

You In an utterance like: 'Hey, you! What do you think you're doing?' the first 'you' is clearly vocative, while the others are pronominal.

Vocative 'you' is usually stressed more strongly than the pronoun, and often occurs in what might be called a vocative position, so that the word order of the utterance signals the word's changed role.

'You' used vocatively is frequently an insulting or aggressive term, or one which expresses contempt for an inferior. In Galsworthy's *In Chancery* a character calls a waiter by saying 'Hullo, you!' A modern client in a restaurant would be likely to receive a surly response to such a call.

Vocative 'you' can be softened if uttered in a friendly way. In *Eating People Is Wrong*, by Malcolm Bradbury, a man at a party says hello to a young woman. 'Oh, hello, you,' she replies.

There is an exclamatory 'you' that a speaker utters when he or she meets someone unexpectedly, where the tone would normally be one of surprise. Clearly this would not be interpreted as condescension. There is another kind of surprised 'you' where the meaning is 'you of all people', as in an utterance like: 'You swindled me – you!' *See also* **you + appositional name, phrase or clause**.

'You' can become the head-word of a vocative expression and take on whatever value resides in the adjective that is used to qualify it. Common expressions are 'lucky you!' 'poor you!' 'You' also has a neutral, plural function in expressions like 'the rest of you', 'both of you', 'all of you', 'the lot of you'.

You-all This special form of 'you' is a well known feature of colloquial speech in the American South. It appears to date only from the mid-nineteenth century, though attempts have been made to trace it back to Shakespeare and the King James Bible. Other scholars have argued about whether it is ever used in the singular.

The general feeling is that in educated use it is always implicitly, if not explicitly, plural. Thus 'you-all take care now', even when apparently said to one person, really means 'you and your folks take care'. In uneducated use 'you-all' is perhaps mistakenly applied to one person. The new form 'you-alls' is then brought into play to achieve the plural distinction.

You and personal name An expansion of 'you' to emphasize its plurality and to indicate who else is referred to by it. 'You're very busy chauffeurs, you and Una,' says a speaker in

Pray for the Wanderer, by Kate O'Brien. The name used could be preceded by a social or professional title – 'you and Mr Smith', 'you and Dr Jones'.

You and your + nominal group This is an exclamatory type of vocative referring to something which is especially associated with the person being addressed. In *A High Wind in Jamaica*, by Richard Hughes, occurs: ' "I could smell it was an earthquake coming when I got up. Didn't I say so, Emily?" "You and your smells!" said Jimmie Fernandez.'

Mountain of Winter, by Shirley Schoonover, has: 'You and your temper. Running him off like that.' *The Colour of Money*, by Walter Tevis, has one man who says to another: 'You and your exquisite sensibilities!' This is countered by: 'You and your damned insights!' *Saturday Night and Sunday Morning*, by Alan Sillitoe, has the dialectal 'yo an yer bloody grett clod 'oppers', referring to the hearer's large boots.

Lillian Beckwith, in *The Hills is Lonely*, has: ' "Padruig, Padruig," Morag chided the unseen occupants. "You and your ferrets! The smell of them is near knockin' Miss Peckwitt over backwards." '

You + appositional name, phrase, or clause With this kind of vocative expression the speaker typically expresses surprise or regret that what he or she is saying must be said to this particular person, as opposed to someone else. 'You of all people' sums up that thought. One man might say to another: 'You robbed me; you, John!' where the intonation pattern would be the same if the speaker continued 'the friend I trusted most'.

That clause might in fact take the place of the name, as might the phrase 'my best friend'. For that matter, the vocative 'you' in such an utterance could be expanded by any number of appositional components. 'You robbed me; you, the man who is god-father to my children, the man I have always treated as one of the family, the man I thought I could trust completely, who swore to me that I could always rely on him,' etc., etc. It would of course be possible to say: 'You robbed me; the man I trusted most!' omitting the second, vocative 'you'. In this case 'the man I trusted most' retains many vocative qualities, if not all of them.

As such an expression is lengthened, however, getting further away from pronominal 'you', most speakers would be tempted to support it with a vocative 'you' somewhere in the string. There would also be a strong tendency for such expressions to become a third person substitute for 'you' in a kind of echo of the original thought: 'You robbed me: the man I trusted most robbed me!' This is not true of normal vocative expressions, and the kind of vocative phrases and clauses mentioned above clearly belong in a category of their own.

A literary example occurs in *The Portrait of the Artist as a Young Man*, by James Joyce, which has: ' "You should be ashamed of yourself," said Father Arnall. "You, the leader of the class!" '

You + category of person This is an exclamatory kind of vocative used when someone is thought to display the characteristics of a certain category of people.

English people, for example, may be thought by foreigners to behave at times in ways which are noticeably and particularly English, so the vocative 'you English!' will be used.

It occurs, in fact, in *Dover One*, by Joyce Porter; *Funeral in Berlin*, by Len Deighton; *Shipmaster*, by Gwyn Griffin. In each case the speaker is not English. *Funeral in Berlin* has a similar example of 'you French', spoken by someone who is not French, but addressed, as are the examples above, to someone who does belong to the category mentioned.

'You women', which occurs in *Sandra*, by Pearl Bell, is another typical vocative of this kind. The speaker would always be a man, and we are once again dealing with an exclamatory vocative, not a mere exclamation. It is a vocative utterance in that it tells us about the speaker's attitude to the person who is present, which a straightforward exclamation probably would not do.

The attitude is usually light-hearted bewilderment or surprise at the behaviour of the person concerned, which is thought, however, to be typical of a category of people rather than individual.

Occasionally the attitude is more aggressive or unfriendly. This is easily indicated by either the inclusion of other words in the vocative group, or by the category to which the listener is assigned. The following examples may make the point more clearly: 'you young men', used in *The Affair*, by C. P. Snow; 'you bloody historians and your periods', in *Anglo-Saxon Attitudes*, by Angus Wilson; 'you anarchists', in *The Fox in the Attic*, by Richard Hughes; 'you impetuous young people' and 'you office boys', in *A Kind of Loving*, by Stan Barstow; 'you Irishmen' and 'you aristocrats', in *The Limits of Love*, by Frederic Raphael; 'you intellectual types', in *Room at the Top*, by John Braine.

One further point to mention about this type of vocative is that all those who fit the category are not being addressed by the speaker at the time. There is clearly a difference between a sentence like 'Come here, you men', addressed to say, three men, and 'you men!' when uttered by a woman to one or more men in order to express some kind of reaction to their typically masculine behaviour.

You + nominal group The commonest use of 'you' in vocative expressions is as an introductory word, followed by a nominal group. Such vocatives tend to be insulting, or reproachful, or mockingly so.

At their simplest they are two-word expressions such as 'you fool', 'you bitch', 'you pig'. They frequently include an adjective: 'you bloody liar', 'you dirty beast', 'you little upstart'. They can on occasion become as extensive as the vocative in *Lucky Jim*, by Kingsley Amis: 'you bloody old towser-faced boot-faced totem-pole on a crap reservation'. 'You' is sometimes brought into play again to round off such expressions. The *Oxford English Dictionary* states that this is 'often' the case. That may have been true in earlier times.

Shakespeare has vocatives of the 'you puppet, you' type, that one occurring in *A Midsummer Night's Dream*. In David Garrick's *Bon Ton*, first produced in 1774, we have 'you wicked wretch, you'; 'you beast, you'; 'you rascal, you'.

Sometimes this final 'you' appears to be used for emphasis, as in the modern 'you bastard, you', but Kipling's 'ye long, limp, lousy, lazy beggar, you', in *On Greenhow Hill* is clearly not to be taken too seriously by the person to whom it is addressed. As for Becky Sharp's remark to Joseph Sedley, in Thackeray's *Vanity Fair*, her 'Don't be leading our husbands into mischief, Mr Sedley, you wicked, wicked man, you,' leaves that gentleman feeling decidedly pleased and flattered.

It may be that this final 'you' is in modern times becoming a signal to the hearer that a covert endearment is being used, or an expression, at least, that is certainly not to be interpreted at its face value. On the frequency issue, in a vocative count of fifty fairly modern British novels which contained at least a hundred vocative expressions introduced by 'you', only two were rounded off by a final 'you'.

In *The River of Diamonds*, by Geoffrey Jenkins, 'you bastard, you' is friendly when said by one man to another. The same novel has fifteen other examples of vocatives introduced by 'you' where the word is not used at the end. *Saturday Night and Sunday Morning*, by Alan Sillitoe, has an insulting use of 'you bastard, you'. The novel has another twenty-seven 'you' + nominal group vocatives. On this evidence it is no longer true to say that 'you' *often* completes a vocative expression that has been introduced by that word. It can, incidentally, occur at the end of a vocative group without being used at the beginning. *The Liberation of Lord Byron Jones*, by Jesse Hill Ford, has 'low-down Federal bastard, you' used as an insult. What appears to be dialectal

usage is found in *Like Any Other Man*, by Patrick Boyle, where Irish speakers use 'Good, you boy, you' and 'Good, you girl, you'. There is a rather similar usage by a Welsh speaker in *Other Men's Wives*, by Alexander Fullerton: 'You think that's possible do you, you Bland you?' 'Bland' is here the last name of the hearer. These instances would be decidedly unusual in standard English.

You + prepositional phrase In this kind of vocative the speaker qualifies 'you' with an *ad hoc* phrase that will enable the hearer to know who is meant. In Joyce Cary's short story *A Touch of Genius*, for instance, a white man calls to a native girl: ''Ere, you with the pot.'

In *Thursday Afternoons*, by Monica Dickens, a doctor giving a lecture to some nurses says: 'What are the two fundamental classes of anaemia? You at the end.' The nurse concerned is affronted at being identified in this way, since the basic vocative being used is 'you', which is seldom polite.

You two An expression used to address two people which can vary from friendly to unfriendly depending on the way it is said. Examples of usage occur in *Under the Volcano*, by Malcolm Lowry (fairly friendly), *Stop at Nothing*, by John Welcome (both friendly and unfriendly examples), *The Old Boys*, by William Trevor (friendly), *Memento Mori*, by Muriel Spark (friendly), *The Masters*, by C. P. Snow (friendly), *Lucky Jim*, by Kingsley Amis (friendly), *Lord of the Flies*, by William Golding (friendly), *A Kind of Loving*, by Stan Barstow (fairly neutral), *The Half Hunter*, by John Sherwood (unfriendly), *An Error of Judgement*, by Pamela Hansford Johnson (friendly), *The Country Girls*, by Edna O'Brien (friendly), *The Bell*, by Iris Murdoch (friendly).

Other numbers could replace 'two', of course: *A Woman Called Fancy*, by Frank Yerby, has: '"All right, you three," Sheriff Bowen growled; "get moving."' There would be a strong tendency for a speaker to switch to an expression like 'all of you' if he were addressing more than three people. *The Magic Army*, by Leslie Thomas, has an angry speaker who expands 'you two' to the unusual 'you *bloody* two'.

On rare occasions 'you two' is addressed to a single person, the second person being known to both speaker and listener but not actually present. 'You hitting it off, you two?' occurs in *Absolute Beginners*, by Colin MacInnes, and refers to the partner of the person addressed who is not there at the time.

You... you... you There is an old joke which has one man enraged with another, but so angry that he cannot think of what to call him. All he manages to get out is 'you...', which he then repeats as he searches for the right insult. The other man replies: 'Don't you call me a "you-you".'

Novelists quite often indicate this state of near speechlessness by having a speaker begin the vocative sequence with 'you', repeat it once or twice, then give up as the words fail to come to mind. The vocative expression is left dangling for ever.

An example of 'you... you... you...' occurs in *Like Any Other Man*, by Patrick Boyle. A man is trying to tell a woman what he thinks of her but cannot think of anything adequate. He clearly wants something stronger than the 'stupid, horn-mad, careless bitch' which he has used a moment or two previously. Sometimes the speaker gets as far as the adjective which follows 'you...' and then trails off.

North Dallas Forty, by Peter Gent, has: ' "You lousy..." My voice and energy tailed off as I was unable to conceptualize a proper insult.' *Gone With the Wind*, by Margaret Mitchell, has Scarlett O'Hara saying to Ashley Wilkes: ' "You lowdown – lowdown –" What was the word she wanted? She could not think of any word bad enough.'

young By no means as frequently used a vocative element as 'old', and normally applied to hearers who really are young, whereas 'old' can be used to hearers of any age.

The speaker is usually noticeably older than the person addressed, unless the former is deliberately flattering the hearer. That is the case in *The Stone Angel*, by Margaret Laurence, where a doctor addresses a very old lady as 'young lady'.

The same term can sound quite different when used to a girl, as in Edna Ferber's *Showboat*: 'Now then, young lady, want it or not, you'll eat some of this broth.'

'Young man' and 'young woman' are similar expressions that can be either friendly or unfriendly according to the tone in which they are uttered. When Dr Primrose calls his daughter 'young woman' in *The Vicar of Wakefield*, by Oliver Goldsmith, she is most upset. 'Why so cold a name, papa?' she asks him. 'This is the first time you have called me by so cold a name.' The good doctor immediately says: 'I ask pardon, my darling.'

'Young', significantly, is often included as an element in an insulting vocative expression. 'You young hound' occurs in *Doctor at Sea*, by Richard Gordon; 'you cheeky young bleeder' is in *A Kind of Loving*, by Stan Barstow, along with 'you young sod'; *Saturday Night and Sunday Morning*, by Alan Sillitoe, has 'you bloody young fools'; *Stop at Nothing*, by John Welcome has 'you young pup'.

'You young clip' is decidedly unfriendly in *The Taste of Too Much*, by Clifford Hanley.

However, apparent insults which include 'young', when addressed to young boys or girls, are often covert endearments or are actually friendly. Such is the case with 'you young blackguard' in Len Deighton's *Funeral in Berlin*, 'you young rogue' in *The Heart of the Matter*, by Graham Greene, 'you long-legged young bugger' in *The Hiding Place*, by Robert Shaw, and so on.

Even when 'young' is part of a friendly expression, it is tinged with condescension on the part of the speaker; used in an insulting way it is meant to remind the hearer that his or her age entitles the older person who is speaking to some respect.

Young men, you *See* You + category of person.

Young people, you impetuous *See* You + category of person.

Youngster This term is normally used to a boy, though it could theoretically apply to a girl. In the eighteenth century the word was specifically used of boys and junior seamen on board ship. It was sometimes extended to junior officers, in the army as well as the navy.

Earlier still, in the sixteenth and seventeenth centuries, 'youngster' carried a suggestion of liveliness and briskness, though coupled with immaturity.

Normal modern usage of the vocative is shown in *The Island*, by Peter Benchley: 'What did you say your name was, youngster?' 'Justin.' 'Well, Justin, why don't you carry this for me?'

In *Tender is the Night*, by F. Scott Fitzgerald, Rosemary says to Dick: 'I must go, youngster.' This is a joke, referring back to an earlier discussion between them where Dick has pointed out that he is a middle-aged man while she is still almost a child.

Young'un This has become a fairly conventional spelling to indicate the pronunciation of 'young one' when used vocatively or otherwise. 'Young'n' also occurs, as in Jim Allen's *Days of Hope*, where an older man says to one who is considerably younger: 'Take my tip, young'n.' There is some evidence that 'young'un' is more likely to occur in the north of England than elsewhere, and be used to a boy or a young man rather than to a girl.

It occurs in literature since the nineteenth century, e.g., in George Eliot's *Adam Bede*, in the form which shows it to have become a common expression. As 'young one' it is found in Shakespeare, e.g. when Lucius comes across Imogen, who is disguised as a young man, he says: 'Young one,/Inform us of thy fortunes' (*Cymbeline*, 4:ii).

Your Used vocatively as a replacement for

'you' in a number of titles or mock-titles, such as: Your Eminence, Your Grace, Your Majesty, Your royal Highness, Your Honour, Your Worship, Your Reverence, Your Lordship, Your Ladyship, Your High-and-Mightiness. *See under* the final element in each case. Titles making use of 'your' have been in use since the fourteenth century.

yourself Frequently added to a vocative that has just been used, and turned back on the person who used it, usually to express indignation that the expression was applied to the listener in the first place. *Every Day is Ladies' Day*, a short story by Dawn Powell, has: 'I didn't tell you even *half* about it, old dear.' This is said by a man to a woman in her fifties, who immediately snaps: 'Old dear yourself.' *Seven Little Australians*, by Ethel Turner, has: ' "Bunty, you're a pig," sighed Meg. "Pig yourself." '

Youse, yous, yuz These are variant spellings which try to indicate an uneducated pronunciation of 'you', occurring in Irish and other dialects of English. These forms can be used to one person or several.

Youth Used by one man to another in the rural dialects of certain English counties, such as Derbyshire.

Zed This is the British pronunciation of the letter z, usually *zee* in the USA. Shakespeare has Kent call Oswald, in *King Lear* (2:ii), 'Thou whoreson zed! thou unnecessary letter!' The last statement is not strictly true, since z is not actually a redundant letter as is c, which could always be replaced by s or k, and q, which could be k. Nevertheless, only a wordsmith like Shakespeare would have conceived such a linguistic insult. Sinclair Lewis, in *Bethel Merriday*, has a character who is called Zed Wintergeist. Another character speculates that he may really be a Zedekiah.

Zombie Commonly thought of as a person who has died and been brought back to life by voodoo rituals, thanks to a great many horror stories and films. The people so described in the West Indies have almost certainly been drugged and buried while in a state of coma. The word is applied metaphorically to people who act in a weird manner or move as if they are in a trance-like state. In Vera Caspary's novel *Laura* 'you beautiful zombie' is said to a girl who is thought to have been murdered, though the body, which has been discovered was in fact that of another girl.

Zur A spelling of 'Sir' used to indicate dialectal pronunciation. It is used by a working-class Devonshire man to a middle-class man in *The Dream of Fair Women*, by Henry Williamson. Another Devonshire man uses it to an American army officer in *The Magic Army*, by Leslie Thomas.